PRAISE

WILLIE

BY JAMES S. HIRSCH

"[James] Hirsch has given us a book as valuable for the young as it is for the old. The young should know that there was once a time when Willie Mays lived among the people who came to the ballpark."

—Pete Hamill, *The New York Times Book Review*

"Does a better job than any book before of getting at what it means to be Willie Mays."

—*Sports Illustrated*

"James Hirsch has written an enormously entertaining and wide-ranging biography—a fitting tribute to Mays . . . and a thoughtful account of the complex and often misunderstood man. . . . True baseball fans will delight in the author's edge-of-seat game reports and picture-perfect descriptions of Mays's superlative talents. . . . This is a superb baseball book, but it's also a riveting narrative of Mays's life and times."

—*The Seattle Times*

"A terrific new biography . . . [an] always engaging and enlightening book . . . A wonderful introduction to the magical life of one of the finest athletes ever."

—*San Francisco Chronicle*

"James S. Hirsch compellingly recounts Mays's career . . . giving even Mays's iconic moments, such as 'the Catch' in the 1954 World Series, a sense of tension as if they were unfolding anew. . . . Great baseball reading, by an accomplished writer . . . about a wondrous ballplayer and man with gifts beyond the diamond."

—Associated Press

"The book, documenting Mays's rise from the Negro Leagues star to major league icon, also serves as a history lesson."

—*USA Today*

"Tautly written . . . Mr. Hirsch captures Willie's greatness on the field."

—*The Wall Street Journal*

"A strong book that is as much a history of American race relations as it is a sports story."

—*Houston Chronicle*

"It took Hirsch seven years to convince Mays to cooperate with his book. And the story of it is worth the wait."

—*New York Post*

"Remarkable . . . A complete biography of a man who is far more complex than the 'Say Hey Kid' the New York writers portrayed. I recommend it highly."

—*The San Francisco Examiner*

"Willie Mays had everything—except a first-rate biography. That omission has now been addressed by James S. Hirsch, who has produced a piece of artistry worthy of Mays in center field."

—Bloomberg News

"Hirsch has produced a masterful biography that has the same freshness and excitement that Mays generated as a player. All the highlights are there in shining, solid detail. It's a must-read for any baseball fan."

—*Tampa Bay Online*

"James S. Hirsch presents a complex portrait of the Say Hey Kid who made 'the Catch'—perhaps baseball's most spectacular, lasting moment."

—*San Antonio Express-News*

"Hirsch's biography deserves a place alongside the work by top chroniclers Roger Angell, Bill James, Roger Kahn, and Robert Creamer. Highly recommended for all baseball fans."

—*Library Journal*

"Willie Mays is one of the most captivating figures in baseball history. Play after play, year after year, he thrilled us with his unmatched combination of speed and power, skill and daring. Hirsch tells us Willie's compelling story, from his humblest of upbringings in Alabama to his rise, in the face of immense prejudice, to become one of Major League Baseball's early African American players to his becoming an enduring American icon as the 'Say Hey Kid.' I love Willie Mays because he played his game and lives his life with more than talent—he has the mind and heart of a champion."

—President Bill Clinton

"It's really a pleasure to read the true facts about the life and career of the greatest center fielder of all time."

—Kareem Abdul-Jabbar

"You can make a strong case for Willie Mays as the most complete player in baseball history. And now, at long last, here is the complete and definitive biography of the 'Say Hey Kid.'"

—Bob Costas, broadcaster, NBC Sports and
Major League Baseball Network

ALSO BY JAMES S. HIRSCH

Hurricane:
The Miraculous Journey of Rubin Carter

Riot and Remembrance:
The Tulsa Race War and Its Legacy

Two Souls Indivisible:
The Friendship That Saved Two POWs in Vietnam

Cheating Destiny:
Living with Diabetes

WILLIE MAYS

THE LIFE, THE LEGEND

JAMES S. HIRSCH

AUTHORIZED BY WILLIE MAYS

SCRIBNER

NEW YORK LONDON TORONTO SYDNEY

SCRIBNER
A Division of Simon & Schuster, Inc.
1230 Avenue of the Americas
New York, NY 10020

First Scribner paperback edition March 2011

SCRIBNER and design are registered trademarks of The Gale Group, Inc.,
used under license by Simon & Schuster, Inc., the publisher of this work.

For information about special discounts for bulk purchases,
please contact Simon & Schuster Special Sales at 1-866-506-1949
or business@simonandschuster.com.

The Simon & Schuster Speakers Bureau can bring authors to your live event.
For more information or to book an event contact the Simon & Schuster Speakers Bureau
at 1-866-248-3049 or visit our website at www.simonspeakers.com.

Manufactured in the United States of America

3   5   7   9   10   8   6   4   2

Library of Congress Control Number: 2009049214

ISBN 978-1-4165-4790-7
ISBN 978-1-4165-4791-4 (pbk)
ISBN 978-1-4391-7165-3 (ebook)

To the memory of Cat Mays,
who gave his son his greatest gifts,
and to Mae Allen Mays,
whose grace and beauty
touched the soul of a legend.

CONTENTS

WILLIE MAYS

PROLOGUE

On May 24, 1951, a young center fielder who had dazzled crowds in the minor leagues left Sioux City, Iowa, traveling light: a change of clothes and some toiletries, his glove, his spikes, and his two favorite thirty-four-ounce Adirondack bats. The twenty-year-old Alabaman was driven to the airport in Omaha, Nebraska, where he bought a ticket from United Airlines for an all-night journey, landing in New York early the following day. He had been there once before, three years earlier, to play in the Polo Grounds with the Birmingham Black Barons. On that team the veterans had protected him, instructing the youngster on how to dress, act, and play ball; on how to represent his team, his city, and his race. But now, on a sunny morning at La Guardia Airport, Willie Mays slid into the back seat of a taxi and pressed his face against the window, alone. He had never seen so many people walk so fast in his life.

Mays was driven to the midtown offices of his employer, the New York Giants, and promptly escorted inside. At 5-foot-11 and 160 pounds, he did not yet have the sculpted body that would later evoke comparisons to Michelangelo's finest work. He was taut and fluid, but not physically imposing. Only his rippling forearms and massive hands, each one large enough to grip four baseballs, hinted at his crushing strength.

Mays entered the office of Horace C. Stoneham, the Giants' shy but personable owner, who was rarely seen in the clubhouse or interviewed by reporters. He had thinning hair, a ruddy complexion, and thick-framed glasses, and while his counterpart at the Brooklyn Dodgers—Walter O'Malley—had the aura of a corporate chieftain, Stoneham more closely resembled a rumpled bank manager who preferred the intimacy of his office to the bustle of the lobby. Alcohol was his most notorious vice, but undue loyalty wasn't far behind. He liked to hire family members and fellow Irishmen and hated to trade or cut Giants who had lost their usefulness. But give him his due: he cared deeply about his players, about their finances, their family, and their well-being, and he would help them as he would his own children.

1

He also needed good players, and he never needed one more than he needed Willie Mays.

The Giants were a family business, and Stoneham was only thirty-two when he inherited the team after his father's death in 1936. At the time, the Giants were the National League's preeminent franchise, having won eleven pennants and four World Series since the turn of the century. They captured consecutive pennants in Horace's first two years at the helm—clubs essentially assembled by his father—but the team grew stale, fan interest declined, and championships became a memory.

In 1951, after a dismal start, the Giants risked, not just a losing season, but irrelevance or even ruin. The franchise had lost money in each of the last three years and had been eclipsed by New York's other baseball teams. Their blood rival, the Brooklyn Dodgers, had won three pennants in the last decade, with Ebbets Field featuring social history as well as fierce competition. Since 1947, the Dodgers had been led by Jackie Robinson, whose breaking of the color barrier, combined with electrifying play, made for riveting theater. Yankee Stadium, meanwhile, was its own showcase of dominance and glamour: five World Series championships in the past decade, one deity in center field. Joe DiMaggio would turn thirty-seven in 1951, his final season, after which the landscape would be ready for a new hero. But the Yankees had already found their next wunderkind in the zinc mines of Oklahoma. The rookie Mickey Mantle—his brawn and speed exhaustively chronicled in spring training, his alliterative name tripping off the tongues of wide-eyed reporters, his blond crew cut and blue eyes capturing the hearts of young fans—was poised to be Gotham's next baseball god.

Who needed the Giants?

"Glad you could make it so soon," Stoneham told Mays as the rookie entered his office. "But they aren't glad where you came from."

Mays, confused, said nothing.

"The Minneapolis fans," Stoneham said. "They're upset." Mays had begun the season with the Minneapolis Millers, a Giants' farm club. In thirty-five games, he had hit .477; one searing drive, in Milwaukee, punctured a hole in the fence. Stoneham told Mays that the Giants were putting an ad in a Minneapolis newspaper to apologize for taking the local team's prodigy. "We're going to tell them," Stoneham said, "that you're the answer to what the Giants have got to have."

Mays remained silent.

"It's unusual, I know," Stoneham said, "but—is something the matter?"

Mays finally found his voice, high-pitched and earnest: "Mr. Stoneham, I know it's unusual, but what if—"

"What if what?"

"What if I don't make it?"

Stoneham pointed to a folder on his desk, stuffed with papers. Mays saw his name on the cover.

"You think we just picked your name out of a hat?" Stoneham demanded. "You think we brought you up because somebody saw your name in a headline one day in Louisville or Columbus or Milwaukee or Kansas City? You think nobody's been watching you? You think managers haven't been up nights doing progress reports, that our own scouts haven't checked you out time and again? You think all of this is something somebody dreamed up in the middle of the night two days ago?"

Mays stood there, unsettled by the barrage.

The owner pushed a buzzer beneath his desk and spoke into the intercom: "Ask Frank to come in here." He looked at Mays. "Got luggage?"

"No, sir. It's still back in Minneapolis. They're sending it on."

Stoneham nodded and pushed the buzzer again. "Ask Brannick to save out seventy, eighty dollars," he said, referring to the team's dapper traveling secretary, Eddie Brannick. Then to Mays: "Buy yourself a couple things—underwear, shirts, socks—until your stuff gets here."

The door opened, and Frank Forbes, a black fight promoter hired by the Giants to be Mays's chaperone, walked through. "Here he is," Stoneham said. "Take him with you." He extended his hand. "Good luck, Willie."

"Thank you, Mr. Stoneham. I hope I can get into a few games, get a few chances to help. I hope you won't be sorry."

"I won't be sorry." Stoneham turned away, then suddenly turned back. "Get in a few games? Get a few chances to help? Don't you know you're starting tonight?"

Mays's mouth went dry. "Starting? Where?"

Stoneham glared at him, then laughed. "Center field!" he barked. "Where else?" He looked at Forbes. "Get him out of here, Frank."

The Giants were already in Philadelphia, where they would begin a three-game series that night at Shibe Park. Forbes and Mays hustled to Pennsylvania Station, boarded a train, and sat in a Pullman parlor car. Mays had seen the opulent coaches in the movies, the ubiquitous Negro porter fawning over white passengers. But now Mays was the passenger, and the swivel armchairs were layered with meaning. His father, Willie Howard Mays, Sr., had been a Pullman porter, making beds in the sleeping cars chugging out of Birmingham. The train's quiet rhythm lulled the white passengers to sleep, and the elder Mays, wearing a white jacket, would listen to the sound of the whistle at night, signaling which engineer was driving the train. "He'd lay his hand on that rope," he said, "and it was like an autograph."

Now his son sat in a Pullman car, heading south on an eighty-five-mile trip that the young man could not have envisioned even a month earlier, with the clicking of the wheels saying to Willie: *You're a Giant. You're a Giant. You're a Giant. You're a Giant. . . .*

Willie Mays began his major league career poorly—he went 1-for-26—but he slowly found his way. He blasted home runs over the lights at the Polo Grounds, chased down fly balls in the cavernous outfield, unleashed deadly throws to the plate, and ran the bases with daring glee. But what mesmerized his teammates, what captivated the crowds, was his incandescent personality, bringing, his manager said, "a contagious happiness that gets everybody on the club" and moving Branch Rickey to observe that the rookie's greatest attribute "was the frivolity in his bloodstream [that] doubled his strength with laughter."

Newspapers promptly hailed the "Negro slugger" as "the Amazing Mays" and "the Wondrous Willie," a unique blend of speed and power who performed with childlike exuberance. But the most prescient account appeared on June 24 in the *New York Post*—one month after his debut—which chronicled a stunning baserunning feat as "part of the legend" of this new marvel.

Long before his Rookie of the Year Award, long before his two Most Valuable Player awards and his one batting title and his 12 Gold Gloves, long before his 24 All-Star Games and his 3,283 hits and his 660 home runs, and long before "the Catch," Willie Mays was a legend. And by the time he retired, he was an American icon whose athletic brilliance and stylistic bravado contributed to the assimilation of blacks during the turbulent civil rights era, a distinctive figure of ambition, sacrifice, and triumph who became a lasting cultural touchstone for a nation in search of heroes.

Mays represented the quintessential American dream. He was the poor Depression-era black kid from the segregated South who overcame insuperable odds to reach the pinnacle of society, and he succeeded by hewing to the country's most cherished values—hard work, clean living, and perseverance. He also benefited from great timing. Had he been born fifteen or even ten years earlier, he would have played most if not all of his career in the Negro Leagues, probably remembered, along with Josh Gibson, Oscar Charleston, and Cool Papa Bell, as a mythic but ill-defined figure who was victimized by America's racial hypocrisy. Had he been born ten years later, he would never have been part of perhaps the most celebrated era in sports history—New York in the 1950s—when baseball dominated the sports culture, integrated teams stole the march on civil rights, ballparks sponsored miracles, and legends were born.

Mays was the youngest black player to reach the major leagues, and his ascension in 1951 coincided with other powerful social and economic forces. Television, for one, was emerging as a transformative medium in sports. Fans across the country could now watch baseball in real time, the grainy black-and-white images turning an anonymous player into a national hero (Bobby Thomson, following his "Shot Heard 'Round the World," being the most conspicuous example). Several decades would pass before baseball highlights became daily fare, but television still contributed to Mays's popularity by broadening access to his spellbinding performances: the spinning catches followed by laser throws; the churning legs rounding second base, his feet barely brushing the dirt, his cap sailing off like a flimsy derby in a windstorm; the giddy smile that bespoke his love for the game. Mays was a completely new archetype, the first five-tool player before anyone else had even opened the shed.* But he always saw himself as an entertainer first, and television gave him a national stage.

Mays was an unlikely celebrity, but he flourished in an increasingly intense media culture. He appeared on television variety shows, talk shows, sitcoms, and in documentaries—timid, to be sure, but also handsome, respectful, and self-deprecating. Magazines splashed him on their covers while recording artists celebrated him in song, screenwriters immortalized him in films, and cartoonists grandly etched him in print. He was the game's first true international star, playing before huge crowds from Mexico to Venezuela to Japan in winter league games or exhibitions. He was a worthy antidote to Ralph Ellison's lament that the Negro was the "Invisible Man."

Mays's star power made him the most luminous prize in baseball's great migration westward in 1958, when the Giants and Dodgers moved to California. This shift symbolized the broader demographic tilt of the country and turned the national pastime into a transcontinental enterprise. Mays benefited from baseball's entrance into new markets and new stadiums with new corporate sponsors, all of which helped make him the highest paid player in the league, topping the magical $100,000 figure in 1963. He left the game ten years later, just as the system that had restricted players from the open market was about to collapse. A new era of baseball was about to begin.

Mays's career exquisitely overlapped one of the great social movements in American history—the modern civil rights era. One of the most recognized and admired black people of that period, Mays led by example, yet his role in the movement became the most controversial part of his leg-

* A five-tool player can hit for average, hit for power, run, catch, and throw.

acy. In some quarters, he was scorned as a "do-nothing Negro" or an Uncle Tom for refusing to actively support civil rights or even to speak out when he himself was victimized or his hometown of Birmingham was terrorized. But Mays countered racial discrimination on his own terms in ways that he understood—as a role model who never drank or smoked, who avoided scandal, and who gave his time and money to children's causes; as a player who excelled through discipline, preparation, and sacrifice; and as a man who brought Americans together through the force of his personality and his passion for the game. Mays knew his influence, particularly on the bigots. "I changed the hatred to laughter," he said. "That's what I think."

Mays also had his disappointments. His first marriage ended badly, with a painful public divorce and an adopted son with whom he is no longer close. (His second marriage, however, to a beautiful, educated professional has been a source of love and strength for more than thirty-five years.) Financial troubles, caused mostly by overspending, dogged him through his playing days. Bad financial advice cost him as well. He was one of the most durable players in history, but the pressures took an enormous toll, physically and emotionally, causing several hospitalizations during his career. At times gruff and impatient, Mays was not the easiest to approach, and his desire for privacy contributed to flare-ups with reporters, some of whom attacked him in print. The give-and-take of friendships was not his strength. His distrust of others, born of betrayals and affronts, ran deep, and strangers with uncertain motives needed to tread lightly when they entered his space.

Who is Willie Mays? It's a fair question. He has a small circle of loyal friends who love him unconditionally, but even they rarely see his wounds. To his fans, he has long been an enigma who spoons out just enough biographical morsels to nourish their curiosity but not satisfy their appetite.

The pity is that the most appealing parts of Willie Mays have nothing to do with baseball.

But baseball is his rightful legacy, and now, almost sixty years after he nervously asked Horace Stoneham if he was good enough, his accomplishments loom larger than ever. Baseball has never been more popular, but the steroid era—an endless train of congressional hearings, legal maneuverings, and hollow pledges of reform—has tainted records, vindicated cynics, and placed the biggest names under suspicion.

No one ever doubted Willie Mays. He not only played the game as well as anyone who's ever taken the field but he also played it the right way. He is now revered for capturing the joy and innocence of a bygone era, a transcendent figure who is compared to the most important men in American history. In the presidential campaign of 2008, Barack Obama emphasized his biracial appeal by pairing John F. Kennedy with Martin Luther King, Jr.; Abraham Lincoln with Willie Mays.

Heady company indeed, though maybe not a stretch for a man who seemed to embody the impossible. "The first thing to establish about Willie Mays," Jim Murray once wrote, "is that there really is one."

CHAPTER ONE

ALABAMA ROOTS

It was a mineralogical oasis in the land of cotton and corn, a swath of hard, jagged terrain through central Alabama whose riches lay dormant for thousands of years. Jones Valley was bounded on one side by Red Mountain, packed with limestone and iron ore, and on the other by low ridges that covered precious veins of coal. Dolomite lay beneath the valley itself. These raw materials allowed the region's largest city, Birmingham, founded in 1871, to become the industrial heart of the South. Its main product: steel.

The cornfields surrounding Birmingham gave way to a new pyrotechnic vision. Twenty-ton electronic locomotives hauled coal or iron, blasted from their ancient beds, to the sweltering mills, where hundred-foot-high blast furnaces coughed smoke and flame and sprawling open-hearth ovens converted molten iron to steel. By the late 1930s, the valley produced more than 4 million tons of ore and 13 million tons of coal each year. The largest company—Tennessee Coal, Iron & Railroad (TCI), a subsidiary of U.S. Steel Corporation—hailed "the adventure of steel making" for its wholesome conveniences: "the family automobile, the kitchen sink, your lawn mower, the bed springs that make possible a comfortable night's rest."

This great adventure would not have been possible without black miners and millworkers. Many were farmers who came to "the Pittsburgh of the South" believing that heavy industry would deliver them from agrarian poverty. In 1922, the novelist Clement Wood, describing a black family's move from rural Alabama to Birmingham, captured the era's promise in all its volcanic glory: "A spell had been laid over everything—a spell of hot beauty. The sky was washed with a flaming glow, brightest upon the bellies of the low-hovering clouds. A pillar of solid fire shone off to the left; then a long mound of red winking eyes; and in the building directly in front, ruddy gold flame . . . even the car tracks pulsed gold."

Willie Mays grew up in the mill towns outside Birmingham, but for him the sky was not washed with a flaming glow and the car tracks did not pulse gold. He wanted nothing to do with steel, wire, or coal or with

9

the other menial jobs that were then available to black men in the South. "I didn't have any heroes," he later said, "who folded underwear in a laundry." While his success in baseball could be traced to his sublime natural skills, it was also driven by more pragmatic considerations. Willie Mays wanted a better life for himself and his family, and baseball was his ticket to that life. His father made sure of it.

Willie Howard Mays, Sr., was born in Tuscaloosa, Alabama, in 1911, when most southern blacks were Republican, the party of Emancipation. So he was named after William Howard Taft, the Republican in the White House. The corpulent president was an ironic namesake: Willie Mays's nickname was Kitty Cat or just Cat, a reference to his feline grace and explosive quickness. He did everything fast—talked fast, played cards fast, walked fast. But most of all, he was cat-quick on the baseball field. Small and muscular, he did not so much glide after a ball—he pounced. He had a bowlegged, pigeon-toed walk, a gait that his son would inherit. Cat Mays's father, Walter Mays, was a sharecropper and a fine pitcher in his own right, and Cat Mays, describing his father's talent, said, "It went from him to me and to the third generation, my own son."

Exactly when Cat Mays arrived in the Birmingham area or with whom is unclear, but surely he or his family was lured by the mines, mills, and furnaces that produced the valuable metals. But Birmingham had something else—baseball.

Compared with the North, baseball and its precursors came slowly to the South. The game was rarely played there before the Civil War and did not take root until after Reconstruction, when railroads helped create small towns and trading villages. Typically an urban game, baseball gradually found a home in these southern communities, the teams themselves viewed as symbols of progress. Both whites and blacks played, though the sport had special meaning among freed slaves. In the postbellum South, baseball was the most popular event at the annual "Juneteenth" (Emancipation) celebrations; the contests, when combined with food, dancing, and music, were imbued with a holiday spirit that was later evident in the Negro Leagues.

In southern mining communities and steel plants, baseball was also designed to tighten the bonds between labor and management. Industrial jobs moved workers from the seasonal rhythms of farming to the uncompromising dictates of the clock. The "boss men" wanted faithful employees who would adhere to their grinding regimen; they also wanted their workers to shun the labor unions who sought footholds in these new outposts. That loyalty could not be bought by wages alone. The company towns had to provide schools, housing, health care, and recreation, and few activities stirred more passion than baseball. The hotly contested Industrial Leagues, in which each team was sponsored by an individual company, produced some of the game's best early players, notably "Shoeless Joe" Jackson. The leagues were also a godsend for their sponsors—a collective enterprise that did not threaten management's hegemony but did reinforce workers' allegiance to their employers, who bought their uniforms, scheduled their games, and covered their expenses. It was a small price for labor peace.

While the South is often associated with football, it was no accident that both Cat Mays and his son embraced baseball, which was "the most important ritual in the industrial community," according to the scholar Christopher Dean Fullerton.

That ritual was particularly spirited in Birmingham, whose Industrial League was considered the largest and most competitive in the South. It was created in 1905, with virtually every enterprise having its own team. The squads were segregated, the game's appeal crossing racial lines. By 1928, there were thirty white teams and eight black, the latter group with names like ACIPCO (American Cast Iron & Pipe Company), Stockham Valve, and the Pratt City Nine. Some contests drew several thousand fans, many of whom had no place to sit, save an empty hillside. The games were covered by newspapers, presided over by company officials, and highlighted by marching bands and jubilee singers. In some cases, workers were hired strictly for their talents on the diamond and rewarded through higher wages and bonuses as well as lighter work schedules.

The best white players went on to play in organized baseball, and after 1920, the finest black athletes could graduate to the Negro Leagues. But even the professional black players didn't necessarily make more money than their peers in the Industrial Leagues. The black professional teams typically received a percentage of the gate receipts, which were erratic at best, and earnings were also reduced by travel expenses.

The benefits of hitting and catching a baseball were not lost on Cat Mays. Most of the mining and mill jobs were dangerous, but starting as a young man, perhaps even before he was twenty, Mays swept floors in TCI's wire mill in Fairfield, nine miles southwest of Birmingham, and played baseball for the Fairfield Wire Mill team. Sweeping floors was a reward for his athletic prowess, a benign task that allowed him to leave work at 2 P.M. and head for the ball field. The mill paid him $2.60 a day, but the work wasn't steady. The Great Depression throttled Birmingham—the worst-hit city in the country, according to the Roosevelt administration. So Cat Mays scraped by as a kind of baseball free agent, selling himself to the highest bidder (to an Industrial League team or to one that barnstormed through the South). "I made it during the Depression," he later said, by playing "for anybody who'd give you money. Because every time somebody come to get me to play baseball, I'd say, 'I can't go, man—I got something to do.' And he'd say, 'Come on, man, I'll give you $2.50.' Sometimes when things was bad, you'd have to go for ten cent a game. And for that money, you *learned* baseball."

At some point as a teenager, Cat Mays met a slender young woman named Annie Satterwhite. Born in Randolph County in eastern Alabama (corn, wheat, cotton), Annie was one of seven children (one sibling had died young). The family moved to Westfield, an all-black village whose houses were owned by TCI and whose residents worked in the adjacent mills in Fairfield. Annie was an exceptional high school athlete in both track and basketball. The principal, E. J. Oliver, later said that Annie was "the type of young person you like to deal with, because she soon became knowledgeable about what the values were in life."

Little is known of the relationship between Cat Mays and Annie Satterwhite, but on May 6, 1931, their son was born—Willie Howard Mays, Jr. Annie was very light, which gave the baby's skin a cinnamon tint. According to one account, perhaps apocryphal, the doctor who delivered the boy exclaimed, "My God, look at those hands!" They seemed to extend directly from his forearms, with no tapering for his wrists.

Willie's teenage parents—Annie was sixteen, Cat, nineteen—never married each other, so they faced the question of where the baby would live. Grandparents, often enlisted in such circumstances, were not an option. Annie's mother had died several years earlier, and her father had abandoned the family; by one account, he rode out of town on a bicycle. What happened to Cat's parents was also unknown, at least to Willie. In an employment form for the Pullman Company, Cat identified his mother as "Susie Smith," but he never told Willie anything about his paternal grandparents. Like his maternal grandparents, they were presumably the children or grandchildren of freed slaves. Neither of Willie's parents ever shared that particular history.

Willie Mays always recalled his childhood as a joyous, sunlit time surrounded by loving friends and family who encouraged his dreams and sheltered him from hardship. Those cheerful memories have been confirmed, decades later, by those who grew up with him. But it is also true that Willie's childhood had many moving parts, with a large, shifting constellation of relatives, a fractured immediate family, the harrowing death of a loved one, a physical confrontation with his stepfather, and the specter of abandonment. Broken families, particularly during the Depression, were not unusual in the South for white families as well as black. Yet Willie's childhood was in no way typical.

As a baby, he was given to his mother's two younger sisters, thirteen-year-old Sarah and nine-year-old Ernestine, who were his principal caretakers and who called him Junior. They initially lived in Westfield, with Sarah as the most important female figure in the boy's life, a role she played even after Willie left Alabama to play for the Giants. Cat was also a constant presence, providing for his son financially as well as emotionally. But he lived elsewhere, and his jobs—in the mill, on the baseball teams, and later on the railroad—meant long absences from home. The makeshift family expanded to include two more children born out of wedlock, one from Sarah and one from Ernestine. Both women also married. Sarah married Cat's cousin Edgar May, who at some point lost the "s" on his last name. (Or perhaps Cat Mays's family added the "s.") Sarah May ended up raising her sister's son while married to his father's cousin.

The family struggled in the early years. While Cat Mays's economic fortunes later improved, he had little money when Willie was a baby. Westfield was a typical company town, rigidly controlled by TCI, which paid employees in scrip for use at the company store. Willie was raised in a slumping frame house, with three bedrooms and a kitchen, a coal stove, a wood-burning fireplace, and a privy. The family was so desperate that it could not afford a can of milk for three cents. "We didn't know what to do," Ernestine recalled. "But a lady next door, she had a baby the age of Willie. We'd go over . . . and take Junior over and tell Mrs. Josephine, and she would let him nurse her breast. So that way he would get some fresh milk, sweet milk."

Cat Mays claimed he never forced his son to play baseball. Look what happened to Joe Louis. Joe's mother supposedly bought him a banjo, and he ended up in the boxing ring! So Cat did not compel Willie to play the game and did not buy him a glove until he asked for one. But make no mistake: Cat wanted his son to play baseball and to play it better than anyone else. He exposed Willie to the sport as early as possible, and the gravitational pull was irresistible.

Even before Willie could walk, Cat gave him a two-foot-long stick and a rubber ball, and the future home run champion, sitting on his diapered butt, whacked the ball and crawled after it. To get the child walking, Cat leaned him against a chair, rolled a ball across the floor, and yelled, "See the ball! See the ball!" He then turned Willie loose.

Cat later said, "I knew he was gonna be special as soon as he started walking, right around the time he got to be one year old. He's one year old, and I bought him a big round ball. Willie would hold that big round ball and bounce and chase it. If it ever got away from him, he'd start to cry. You couldn't believe how good Willie was, one year old, chasing down that big round ball. Little bit of a thing, but even then his hands were sure and strong. I'm telling you the truth. Right then, when he was one year old, I knew he'd be a great one." He added, "I was pretty good, but my hands are regular size. Willie gets those big hands from his mother."

By the time Willie was five, Cat was throwing the ball to him outside, yelling, "Catch it!" They lived near a cornfield and cow pasture, which was also used as a ball field. They went out in the afternoon, sometimes in the rain, the father taking his son to each position and showing him how to play it, then teaching him about hitting and throwing and baserunning. Cat told him that he had to be good at everything—all positions and all parts of the game. The more things you could do on the field, the more likely you would stay on the team. They used a rock and rags for their baseball and a stick for their bat, and Cat would smack ground balls across the rutted terrain, giving Willie some early lessons in bad hops.

The boy had initiative. As Cat recalled, "By the time Willie was six, I'd come home from work and catch him across the street on the diamond all alone, playing by himself. He'd throw the ball and hit it with the bat and then run and tag all the bases—first, second, and third—and then when he got home, he'd slide. He learned that from watching me."

In time, father and son would play pepper, with real bats and balls, fifteen feet apart, Willie pitching and Cat hitting—liners, bunts, pop-ups—forcing Willie to make quick adjustments, Cat yelling encouragement: "Pick it up! You're dug in like a potato! How can you go to the side? Bend those knees!"

According to Willie's boyhood friend Herman Boykin, "Cat was an indoctrinator. On a daily basis, he kept saying to Willie, 'You can do this!' He wanted Willie to be self-sustaining so he wouldn't have to work in the mills."

Cat took his son to watch the Birmingham Black Barons, exposing him to Negro League players while also having fun in the stands. At one game, when Willie was five or six, Cat announced that he was a magician. "Stand up," he said, and everyone in the crowd stood. "Sit down," and they all sat. Several years passed before Willie learned about the seventh-inning stretch.

Sports at their most basic level—throwing, catching, running—were woven into his daily life. Each morning, on his way to elementary school, he walked to Charles Willis's house, a rubber ball in his hand. As he waited, he bounced the ball against the ground, and when Charles appeared, they walked to school and played catch, which they continued after classes were out, when they walked to a field to play in a pickup game. "When I try to remember events as a kid," Mays later said, "in my memories, somehow a ball always ends up in my hands."

Willie's baseball education intensified when he was ten and allowed to sit on the bench at his father's Industrial League games. Suddenly, he was around hard-muscled men discussing the intricacies of the sport—how to play a right-handed pull hitter who was facing a pitcher with a slow curve, how big a lead to take from first base against a southpaw with a quick delivery. With fans cheering, Willie watched the drama unfold, always paying close attention to his father. The players were all good, but Cat's breakneck speed was combined with a certain flair as well as a mastery of the game. On a close play on the bases, he would deftly slide on the opposite side of the tag. His son tried to copy the moves. Before Cat's games, now on a real ball field, Willie would run to first and slide, then get up and run to second and slide, and then to third and slide, and then to home and slide again.

He soon asked for his own glove.

In 1938, Cat Mays's mill wages and baseball earnings allowed him to move the family to adjacent Fairfield. A step up from Westfield, with better houses, neighborhoods, and schools, it proved to be an ideal setting for Willie. Like Westfield, the town was safely beyond the more racially charged Birmingham, but its origins as a "model industrial city" accounted for its relative stability.

When U.S. Steel bought TCI and its land holdings in 1907, it began developing wire mill and coke plants outside Birmingham. The city's disease-ridden shacks and negligent services diminished the workers' productivity, a concern of mill companies across the South. Seeking an alternative, U.S. Steel enlisted private investors to build a town that was patterned after "the Garden Cities of England," an urban-planning effort at the turn of the century. The goal was a carefully planned community that would soften the harsh edges of industrial life. Ground was broken in 1910. The former president Theodore Roosevelt, visiting the next year, proclaimed the effort "simply extraordinary," and even the social reformer Jane Addams commended the undertaking.

The town was originally named Corey, after W. E. Corey, the president of U.S. Steel. But scandal (an affair with a New York chorus girl) cost him his job, so U.S. Steel's chairman, hoping to give his nascent community a clean start, asked the new president for another name. He didn't have one, though he volunteered that he lived in Fairfield, Connecticut.

Fairfield seemed to be a perfectly fine name, suggesting that northern capitalists were creating a "fair field" for the workers. In 1914, Fairfield, Alabama, opened its first wire mill while it also aspired to set a new example. Across the country, congested cities were rightly seen as breeding grounds for crime, leading reformers to urge the development of pristine physical environments to improve human behavior. Fairfield's town planners wanted to increase the residents' exposure to the salutary benefits of nature: roads were laid gently up and around slopes; ten thousand shrubs and thousands of trees—chinaberry, pine, fig, pecan, walnut—were planted; ball fields provided pastoral recreation.

Like most model towns, however, Fairfield could not meet its lofty goals. It had plenty of greenery, but other plans—a major drainage system, sanitary outlets attached to every lot, the paving of more than twenty miles of streets—all fell short. Most streets remained dirt roads until at least the 1940s. Long two-foot ditches, carrying rainwater, ran down some streets into a larger ditch, where pigs raised in yards or fields would drink. The wind-blown soot from the mills fell on streets and porches. The many houses without plumbing relied on large wagons, driven by mules, to carry away human waste. Even the wisteria next to the tennis courts fell into neglect. According to the Birmingham historian Diane McWhorter, the steel industry's boom-and-bust cycles, combined with U.S. Steel's uneven commitment to its southern operations, turned Fairfield into "a mill town of perpetual promise and insolvency."

But if Fairfield wasn't a social utopia, it was still, for Willie Mays, a very good place to live, a biracial town of predictable rhythms and clear expectations. Unlike the company-owned houses in Westfield, many Fairfield residents owned their dwellings, reflected in freshly painted fences, well-tended yards, and blooming gardens. Some parents taught their children that Fairfield was not a suburb of Birmingham but Birmingham, a suburb of Fairfield. For many years, Fairfield was the home of one of the richest black men in the South, A. G. Gaston, whose businesses included a funeral home, so advertised on hand fans distributed at church.

The physical hazards of the mills and mines, combined with constant economic perils, sustained an ethic of self-help, discipline, and sharing, where the A&P Supermarket sold goods on credit, families shared garden vegetables with hungry neighbors, and everyone sacrificed.

Recalls* one of Willie's peers: "Our parents took us to church on Sunday, sent us to school on Monday through Friday, and then sent us to the movies on Saturday and then to a baseball game after the movies. The men worked in those mills and mines while the ladies washed clothes over a

---

* Present tense is used for quotes from author interviews.

scrub board, heated irons, and cooked over a wood-burning stove so that the men could come home and cut the grass, trim the hedges, water the plants, feed the chickens, and whip my bad backside for the trouble I got into before sitting down to eat a meal that was prepared by their lovely ladies."

While the Depression made subsistence living the norm, the children still had fun. Whether riding their new roller skates down a hill on Christmas morning, fighting a stray turkey like a matador on a main thoroughfare, eating delicious ice cream from Dr. Parham's Drug Store on a warm summer evening, or just playing ball, they were active, busy, and rigorously protected. "We were somewhat sheltered from the harsher realities," says U. W. Clemon, who was born in Fairfield in 1943 and became Alabama's first African American federal judge. "You could own your own house in Fairfield, and you could buy what you needed in private stores."

While Fairfield's racial divide was always clear, it was less dehumanizing than in other southern towns, certainly less so than in Birmingham. Blacks and whites had separate neighborhoods, schools, movie theaters, water fountains, and trolley seats. The northern industrialists who controlled the town had to abide by segregation, but they made some effort to treat blacks fairly; a hospital in Fairfield, for example, did attempt to provide separate but truly equal care.

The disparities were more evident beyond Fairfield. A streetcar ride to Birmingham would pass an amusement park and baseball field for whites only, as well as beautifully tended white neighborhoods of plush lawns, colorful flowers, and green pastures dotted with horses. The streetcar would then reach Birmingham, where city ordinances segregated the steps at the train station and barred blacks and whites from playing checkers with each other. Any downtown clothing store gladly welcomed Negroes, but if they wanted to try on the clothes and shoes, they had to pay for them first and do it at home.

Fairfield lacked the palpable racial tensions of Birmingham, probably because so many residents, black and white, worked together in the mills. The town's superior overall condition—the newer houses, the more attractive neighborhoods—helped defuse hostilities as well. For the children of either race who just wanted to play sports, so much the better.

Willie Mays was happily insulated from racial concerns for much of his youth. He lived in the black Interurban Heights section, where every child knew the rules: you had to sit in the back of the streetcar, you had to address white adults as "Mister" or "Miss," you could patronize only certain theaters or had to sit in the balcony of a racially mixed movie house.

But these restrictions didn't bother Willie—they were part of life as he knew it or he found ways around them. To avoid sitting in the back of the streetcar, Willie and his friends would simply jump on an outer platform and ride for free. He kept a positive view. The balcony seats in the movie house didn't disturb him, he recalls, "because we got the better view."

Willie saw the superior yards in Fairfield's white neighborhoods but never felt envy or anger. And why should he? The white kids were not just his friends but, more important, his teammates. Despite the laws that imposed segregation, black and white youths in Fairfield found one another on the diamond, basketball court, and football field, where Willie's prowess was evident early. The white children—no surprise—wanted Willie on their team, and Willie couldn't be bothered with skin color. Playing in this social bubble, his only concern was winning.

But Willie could not escape the outside world entirely. When adults saw the racially mixed teams, they would call the police, who would break up the games, or sometimes the police acted on their own. Just plain dumb and crazy, Willie thought. The teams would reconvene when the cops left.

Willie never forgot these episodes. As an adult, his generosity toward children was driven by many considerations, but his own experience as a youth was critical: if children were left alone, he believed, they would do the right thing. It was the adults who screwed things up.

CHAPTER TWO

RAISED TO SUCCEED

Though Willie Mays's most important influence was Cat, his father was also an enigma to his son. He never told Willie anything about his own youth in Tuscaloosa or about his parents or any other family members. He once mentioned to Willie that he had fathered a daughter; Willie never met her. Cat's biography was a cipher, his personal life a mystery, an unusual reserve in a community that placed a great emphasis on oral history. But this reticence was not a shield for despair. Cat was also an irrepressible optimist, with a deep faith that truth and goodness would prevail. "I told Willie, 'Just tell the truth and be true to yourself, and you can go on,'" he said late in his life. Disputes of any kind could often be traced to a single cause, he believed. "You know what the problem is?" he would say. "Somebody is not telling the truth."

Despite the economic turmoil and institutional racism, Cat Mays seemed immune to the world's ills. "I never saw Cat negative in any way, I never saw him angry, and I never saw him reprimand," says Loretta Richardson, who is Aunt Sarah's daughter and the only other living member of the household in which Willie was raised. She recalls how the three children in the house—she, Willie, and Aunt Ernestine's son, Arthur (who was called "Arthur B"), all first cousins—would meet Cat after he left the mill and race him home. Cat always won. "Even when he talked about playing baseball and not getting to the level he wanted"—he never made it beyond the Industrial League—"he never said it with anger or regret," Richardson says. "He just said, 'It wasn't my time.'"

Richardson, who is seven years younger than Willie, also fondly remembers how much attention Cat lavished on all three cousins: "He loved Willie, but he loved all of us."

Willie absorbed every side of his father's personality. As an adult, he vigorously guarded his privacy, rarely talking to his friends, let alone the press, about his youth, his family, or his personal feelings. He had nothing to hide, but his own steely diffidence paled in comparison to Cat's. "My father," he says, "was much more private than me."

19

Willie also possessed his father's sanguine temperament: the seeds of the "Say Hey Kid"—the perpetually smiling man-child who electrified the major leagues—were sown long before he reached the Giants. "I felt nothing bothered him," says Richardson. She would tease him that Sarah was her mamma, not his; Willie's own mother had married and was living about five miles away. Richardson grew up as "Loretta May," having taken her stepfather's last name, so she would tweak Willie about the "s" in his name.

"That shows the possessive form!" she'd yell.

"I'm using it!" Willie would shout back.

Provocations aside, Richardson says, "I don't recall him ever complaining." Bill Powell, a teammate of Willie's with the Birmingham Black Barons, said, "I played with him for two years, and I never saw him frown."

The only time Willie appeared sullen was when his team lost. "He was basically a quiet, happy-go-lucky kid, but he was always very competitive," says Otis Tate, a friend from Fairfield whose finger is still sore—sixty years later—from catching a ball that Willie threw to him at third base. "Whatever he did, he tried to win, and he'd get mad if he didn't win. But you would never know it because that's when he'd go into his little shell."

Mays credits his father for his high spirits, which always helped him through adversity—from racial insults to financial setbacks to hitting slumps. "My father gave me that one thing, positive thinking, that allowed me to look past whatever was happening," he says. "If you say to me, well, 'there had to have been some pain,' sure there was some pain. But if you can overcome your pain and do your job, the pain disappears the next day. That's where the positive thinking comes in."

While Cat pushed Willie to succeed, he never yelled at him or embarrassed him. Even when he had to discipline Willie, he never raised his voice, and that approach had a profound effect on Willie's relationships with managers and other authority figures. He responded to encouragement, support, love—everything his father gave him—but recoiled from criticism, ridicule, and sarcasm, the more so if it came from a harsh voice.

Neither threats nor punishment was required to deter Willie from drinking or smoking. They were bad for you, Cat told his son, would slow you down, make you think fuzzy. One day, he found Willie smoking and drinking on a street corner with a friend, so he took him home. "You want to smoke?" he asked. "Okay, smoke it." He handed Willie a White Owl cigar. Willie took several puffs and thought he was going to die.

"You want to drink?" Cat asked. "Drink it." He gave Willie a glass of Old Crow. The boy took several sips of the bourbon whiskey . . . and never drank again.

Cat urged other children to follow these same restrictions. "Cat always told us, 'I'll do anything for you, but you have to go by the rules,' " Herman Boykin says. "We all knew that if you smoked or drank, you wouldn't be as good in sports."

Cat also gave Willie his initial guidance on dealing with whites. And it wasn't complicated. Be respectful. Don't cause trouble. And remember that you will often need white people to help your own people. Cat noted that Fairfield's grocery stores were owned by whites. What if your black neighbor was hungry and you needed to buy him food? You'd have to go to the white grocer, so nothing good comes of racial confrontation. In time, Willie would be told about the repercussions of offending whites, but as a boy the message was clear—don't bother whites, and they won't bother you.

In many ways, Cat spoke the black gospel of the South, a doctrine derived from Booker T. Washington, the former Virginia slave who had died in 1915 but whose ideas still held sway. His response to white supremacy had been cooperation between the races, the encouragement of thrift and business among blacks, and the acquisition of land. Washington founded the Tuskegee Institute, whose mission was to train the "head, heart, and hand" of students who would then elevate the race culturally, socially, and economically. Progress would not come from dissent or confrontation but from self-improvement and accommodation. His most famous words endorsed the doctrine of separate but equal. "In all things that are purely social," he said in Atlanta in 1895, "we can be as separate as the fingers, yet one as the hand in all things essential to mutual progress."

Northern blacks ridiculed his attitude as feckless capitulation to legal racism. But for southern blacks, there were few alternatives. In the first half of the twentieth century, the impoverished, agrarian South, with its history of black servitude and oppression, was no arena in which to demand meaningful civil rights. This status quo would not survive, but Cat Mays's message to his son would not be forgotten. Long after the civil rights movement had roiled the South, Willie Mays continued to embrace those lessons of hard work and self-improvement as well as compliance and accommodation.

Sports weren't Willie's only outlet. He loved practical jokes, comic books, and action movies. He would watch Westerns his entire life, drawn by their moral clarity, physical acrobatics, and the mythic cowboy—the lonely, taciturn bulwark against greed and betrayal. As a teenager, Willie played pool avidly, though the owner of the pool hall—Big Tony—wouldn't open the place until 4 P.M. He told the kids they needed to stay in school and do their homework, then they could shoot pool, which Willie did, expertly, on old, battered tables in the back of the room.

Willie was no stranger to mischief. Conspiring with friends, he'd sneak into peach orchards, pluck the fruit off the trees, and hurl them to his confederates; his job carried the most danger, but he had the best arm. Watermelon patches were also easy targets. Without money, Willie and his friends filched pork rinds on occasion from a general store. "Willie's hands were quicker than your eyes," Otis Tate recalls. When Willie was at Fairfield Industrial High School, he'd sneak out of the building through a "floor crawl." Fearing that his dirty clothes would betray him, he went to the school laundry room, where students were taught cleaning and pressing, and wash his overalls before returning to the classroom. With his friends, Willie rode in an open dump truck and taunted other drivers, instigating sharp turns and near collisions. The hijinks infuriated their own driver, Herman Boykin, who took them to their baseball game, pulled the gear, and dumped them into a mass of adolescent merriment.

"Willie got into minor things, but they never had to put the chastise on him, because he never really crossed the line," Boykin says.

Besides his father, three other adults ensured that Willie stayed on course.

Aunt Sarah was known as "Dute," which, like many nicknames in the South, had uncertain origins; hers may have come about because she was considered cute. A small, compact woman with short hair, she had a deep Christian faith, high ambitions for the children she raised, and an authoritarian resolve that held the family together. Though barely a teenager herself when she began caring for Willie, she was his mother in all but name. She fed him, disciplined him, and signed his report cards. When Willie, in 1952, had to identify his guardian or parent on an agreement with Art Flynn Associates, an advertising firm, he wrote: "Sarah Mays."

She was the perfect complement to Cat. While Cat did not attend church, Sarah "confessed [to] Christ" as a young girl and attended Jones Chapel A.M.E. Church in Fairfield every Sunday. She made sure Willie, properly dressed, went as well. Willie's education was important to Cat, but Sarah emphasized it as part of a larger message of self-improvement and achievement. "My mom talked about it all the time—you have to be better than the rest to even be recognized for being good," Loretta Richardson says. Sarah wanted her daughter as well as Willie and Arthur B to attend college. That would spare them the hard labor endured by most southern blacks—domestic work for women, the trades, farming, or the mills for men. When Richardson brought home her first report card with mediocre grades, her mother said, "You won't bring another C in here." And she didn't.

Though Sarah accepted that Willie would never excel academically, she made sure he attended school and made the effort. In his senior year in high school, according to his report card, he received mostly Bs but got As in Cooperation, Effort, and Sportsmanship.

Sarah also gave Willie his chores and his curfews. "She didn't whip me that much, because I didn't like it, but she made sure I was in by eleven," Willie says. Sarah married Edgar May after the family moved to Fairfield, but Edgar was killed in India in World War II. As a widow, Sarah received monthly Social Security checks, which she supplemented by working as a receptionist in a doctor's office and later as a licensed practical nurse at a hospital. A dedicated gardener, she grew green beans, peas, tomatoes, and squash, and she planted trees and shrubbery in the yard as well. "She ran the family," Willie says. "She would make things happen. If we needed money, she could get it."

Sarah opened her house to all comers. "It was just a happy place to be," Richardson says. "My mother was friendly and warm, and she just seemed to draw people around her. Every weekend we had friends over—it was like the Do-Drop Inn." Adds Herman Boykin: "Sarah fed us every day. Four or five of us were running together, playing ball, and Willie just brought us over, and Sarah would open the table for us. She was that kind of person."

For all of her nurturing, Sarah never displayed physical affection with any of the children. As Richardson notes, "I had to learn to hug people." The same could be said for Willie. His friend Charles Willis describes Sarah as "a good woman who took care of Willie as any mother would for her own child . . . but Willie never had motherly love. Motherly love should have come from Sarah, but she didn't give him that."

Nevertheless, Sarah's devotion was undeniable. Willie liked to watch the football games on Saturday afternoons at Miles College in Fairfield. Without money for tickets, he would climb a tree and watch from a perch twenty-five to thirty feet above the ground, although it was against the rules. One time when he was twelve, he tried taking a nap in the tree, but he got too comfortable and plunged to the earth. Breathless and sore, he made it home, but fearing the wrath of Aunt Sarah, he didn't say a word. That lasted until he tried to pick up a bucket of coal and pain shot through his right arm. He confessed to Aunt Sarah, but instead of reprimanding him, she showed strength and mercy. "She carried me to the hospital," Willie says. "My aunt was kind of a tough lady."

The arm—his throwing arm—was broken. By then Willie had already shown that he might play ball beyond the sandlots of Fairfield, but a damaged arm could change all that. The arm was set in a cast, and all Willie could do was wait. "We were worried to death," Boykin says.

Before the injury, Willie threw the ball sidearm or even with a submarine type of motion. It was peculiar, but it generated sufficient thrust and felt natural. When the cast came off, he started throwing the ball three-quarters overhand. That delivery felt more comfortable, and he started throwing the ball harder. It appeared that a mere flick of the wrist generated enormous power. The healing of the broken bone had either strengthened his throwing arm or forced him to use a more potent delivery.

If Aunt Sarah was Willie's stern matriarch, his aunt Ernestine was the doting older sister. Known as "Steen" but also called "Glamour Girl," she was a bit of a rebel—she smoked Lucky Strikes, wore makeup, and had a sense of style and design. At home, she selected heavy drapes for the fall and winter, white organdy curtains and spreads in the spring and summer, and she accented them with crocheted doilies on end tables. An immaculate housekeeper, she never let a used fork sit long on the table without clearing it. Ernestine also brought in precious dollars, working the nighttime shifts as a waitress or barmaid at various restaurants and clubs, and she would share her earnings with Willie, leaving ten dollars on his dresser so he had plenty of lunch money for school. "She always made sure I had enough food," Willie says.

The last member of the household was Otis Brooks, a good-natured friend of Cat's from Mobile who was called "Uncle Otis," though he wasn't related. He worked with Cat at the mill, but he mainly helped with chores around the house. He also had a special relationship with Willie, like that of an older brother. When Sarah wouldn't let Willie leave until he had completed his chores—cleaning up the yard, washing dishes, chopping wood, bringing in the coal—Otis gently intervened. He gave the boy a wink and did the chores himself so Willie could play ball. Kindness was not his only motive—he saw something special in the boy. He was the first to say, "Willie, you're going to be a ballplayer, and I don't want your hands messed up." Willie never forgot it.

The family pulled together—Cat at the mill, Sarah running the house, Ernestine working at the clubs, Otis helping with the chores, and Willie going to school, playing sports, and babysitting for his younger cousins. The children felt protected by their parents and by the entire community. "I didn't know life could be so cruel," Richardson says, "until I left home."

Nevertheless, tragedies did occur. Because the family always had more bodies than beds, Willie would often share a bed with Otis, who usually woke up first. But one morning the eleven-year-old boy woke up with Otis's arms around him. Otis just lay there. Willie called his name and shook him, but there was no response. Though Otis did not seem to have any medical problems, he had died in his sleep.

"That shook him up because Otis was like a brother," Boykin says. "Willie would follow him around, and Otis would tell him to do all the right things."

Mays claims the death left him more worried than upset. "When you lose a friend like that, someone who's taken care of you, you have concerns," he says. But life in the South, he suggests, was always fragile. He downplays any lasting impact of waking up in the arms of a dead man, but he rarely acknowledges emotional wounds. He went to Otis's funeral but only grudgingly attended funerals thereafter.

By the early 1940s the Depression was over, and with wartime industrial production in full gear, Cat Mays found new opportunities.

Following a fellow ballplayer, he moved to Detroit for a job at the Kelsey-Hayes Wheel Company, which produced machine guns, tank components, and other military parts. After the war, he returned to Fairfield and, in December of 1945, was hired as a porter for the Pullman Company, a job that brought him new esteem.

Celebrated in film, literature, and song, Pullman porters were indispensable servants to white passengers and symbolic figures of black advancement. Cat rarely discussed his experiences with his son, but the job surely reinforced his broader messages to Willie. While the porter's job was the worst on the train, it was still the best in the black community and far better than work in the mines and mills that Cat wanted Willie to avoid. Porters were expected to be deferential, efficient, and dutiful and were instructed to ignore all racial insults. And if they could survive the indignities, they would receive decent tips and see America in all its splendor—a bargain similar to the one made by black baseball players, a bargain that Cat wanted his own son to make.

For a while, Cat juggled two jobs, riding the rails on the weekend and working in the mill during the week. His improved finances, with contributions from other family members, allowed them to "trade up" homes in Fairfield, with Willie ultimately living in three different houses. He first lived in a rented three-room shotgun—a bed in the first room, a twin bed in the second, and a bath in the kitchen. Some nights Cat slept there, other nights in a house he built at 5507 Avenue G, across from Miles College. When Cat moved to Detroit, Sarah and the rest of the family moved into that house, with its two bedrooms, a dining room, and a trendy "Youngstown" kitchen: white metal cabinets and Formica countertops with chrome trim.

But the house could not be considered modern. Willie recalls walking to the outhouse and fending off chickens as he used it. "They would bite you," he says. Three large tubs were aligned on the back porch: the family washed the dishes in one tub, rinsed them in the second, and bathed themselves in the third.

When Cat returned to Fairfield, he built a superior two-bedroom house for his family on top of a steep hill at 216 57th Street. A floor furnace warmed the rooms; a full bathroom featured a tub and a small gas heater; feather mattresses cushioned the nights; a front porch was used for sing-alongs and jacks; pear, peach, and apple trees filled the backyard; and a trapdoor in the wood floor provided access for a black cat that earned his keep by catching mice.

Sarah and Ernestine made sure little was wasted. The garden vegetables were used to make soup with lean beef bones as its base; the rest of the vegetables were canned. They baked their own bread and rolls while raising chickens and hogs, but Willie wanted nothing to do with the bloody slaughter. He once heard a hog squeal before it was killed with an ax. Thereafter he left home before the execution and returned after the animal had been skinned, gutted, and cleaned up. Willie was on more comfortable ground tending a neighbor's cow, whose milk would be used for Aunt Ernestine's sweet butter. Combined with peaches, yeast, malt, potatoes, and raisins, the concoction would ferment into peach brandy.

Compared with those of most of his peers, Willie's family thrived. They hired a laundress, and Willie had enough money to take friends to a grocery store for lunch meat, bread, tomatoes, mayonnaise, and cake. His father not only bought him gloves, bats, balls, spikes, bicycles, and other sports equipment but also purchased several Hickey-Freeman suits when Willie became a teenager. Both father and son had a passion for clothes; Cat wore Petrocelli suits exclusively. Most of Willie's friends had no suits, so he would lend them one of his, with rules. Anyone with a date could borrow a suit, as well as a shirt, tie, and shoes, but he had to return the suit clean. "If you didn't bring it back clean," Willie says, "you couldn't wear it again."

When Willie began earning money from semiprofessional teams or the Birmingham Black Barons, his stature was only enhanced. Other kids had jobs, but none that paid as much as Willie's (he ultimately received $250 a month as a Black Baron). That made Willie valuable. When a fight broke out that required the police, Willie's friends would make sure he had left the scene (by car, if available). "If I got put in jail and they got put in jail, who was going to get them out?" he says. "I could get them out because I had the money, and if I needed money, I could get an advance on my salary."

Athletic and handsome, Willie was popular with girls, his baseball income making him that much more desirable. He had one serious girlfriend, Minnie Hansberry, who was quiet and pretty, with long hair, high self-esteem, and class. Willie's friends thought they would marry, but the relationship didn't survive once Willie left Fairfield.

Willie learned something else in his youth. Successful men not only lived better than others but also were usually more highly respected. The signs of success were hard to miss, and they were personified in Dr. Drake, one of Fairfield's two black physicians. He dressed nicely in a suit and tie, carried cash (credit cards didn't exist), and always drove a new car when he made house calls.

"We'd play in the street," Mays recalled, "and there would be Dr. Drake, driving up in his big white Cadillac. The only ones we knew back home who had Cadillacs were doctors and lawyers. The car that hit my fancy was Dr. Drake's. Right there and then, I started dreaming that someday I would own one like that. I knew I'd never be a doctor or a lawyer. I wasn't that good in school, but I began hoping that maybe I could make my goal through baseball."

Willie's father and aunts set equally high expectations. "They were concerned about the quality of our lives, that we would have a better life than they had—in terms of living well, not being poor, being highly respected," Richardson says. "They wanted us to do something that brought pride to ourselves." She received a master's degree in education from the University of Colorado and was a public school teacher for thirty-four years. "I got to the point where I wanted to do something sloppy, but my instincts wouldn't let me," she says.

The same was true for her cousin. "Willie could have had all of those baseball skills but still not have had all of those accomplishments," she says. "But he wasn't raised to do anything halfway."

CHAPTER THREE

SUPERNATURAL GIFTS

They called him "Buck Duck" or just "Buck," though Willie never knew how he got that nickname. Ernestine later speculated that it came from his "high behind." Several decades after Willie Mays became one of the greatest brand names in baseball history, his childhood friends still call him Buck.

And Buck was different from everyone else. It wasn't just his strength, speed, and agility but also how he did things—he was brashly inventive, visually dramatic, unpredictably daring. Willie hated chores, for example, but not if he could turn them into a game. Mop the floor? Turn the mop into a dance partner and whirl it across the linoleum (he'd seen it in the movies). Dry the dishes? Slide them down the counter or flip them in the air, then dive before they crash (he'd seen it in baseball games). He chopped wood so the pieces fell in precise cuts, ironed jeans with perfect creases, turned his bicycle with grace and balance. "I knew he was not an ordinary person—I could sense that early on," Loretta Richardson says. "Most people do routine things the routine way, but he would do things with more creativity than anyone else."

He rode his bike by standing on the crossbar or even on the handlebars, and sometimes he would carry three friends with him, perched on the handlebars, the crossbar, and Willie himself, the quartet barreling down a hill and holding on for dear life. That was tame compared with Willie's penchant for standing on the back fender of Herman Boykin's truck as it sped at 60 mph from town to town. "It was absolutely crazy," Boykin says.

Willie was later celebrated as a five-tool player, but that neglects his other sensory gifts. His peripheral vision was superb, allowing him to execute perfect no-look passes on the basketball court and avoid collisions in the outfield. His hearing was so sharp that he could pick up soft conversation from the other side of the room. "Someone would make an off-the-cuff statement, and he could hear you," Boykin says. "It was a little uncanny." It helped Willie get quick jumps on balls in center field, the crack of the bat foretelling the ball's flight.

"His ears were a weapon," Boykin says.

Mays concedes that his exceptional talents made him unique as a youth. "I don't like to say this too much, but I was something special, and all the young kids I ran around with, they knew that," he says. "So they all protected me from a lot of things that ordinary people get in trouble with." Adults also looked out for him. His teachers allowed him to leave school early for baseball practice. When he was ill, Dr. Drake made house calls but wouldn't necessarily charge the family. "He was one of the guys who said I was going to be a great, great athlete," Mays says. In fact, everyone— family, friends, teachers, professionals—made it easy for him. "They knew that I had a chance of doing something better than they did, so life wasn't too hard for me."

As a boy, Willie enjoyed listening to cowboy songs on his aunt Sarah's radio, memorizing the words to such favorites as "I'm an Old Cowhand." He fantasized about becoming a cowboy himself, and Sarah suggested he might become a singing cowboy. "We'll call you Bing," she said. But sports took priority, even on the radio. When Willie was ten, he listened to the reports of Joe DiMaggio's fifty-six-game hitting streak, giving him a new idol. "Call me DiMag," he told Charles Willis. He actually followed three players—Stan Musial and Ted Williams as well as DiMaggio—reading stories about them in the Sunday newspaper and watching newsreel footage before movies. But DiMaggio was his favorite. His comprehensive skills, combined with grace and poise, evoked his father's injunction for Willie to become a complete player. He studied how the Yankee center fielder threw, ran, and hit, and patterned his open batting stance after him.

The possibility that he might play in the major leagues never crossed his mind. His dream was to play for the Birmingham Black Barons. But when Jackie Robinson opened the 1947 season at first base for the Brooklyn Dodgers, he had a new hero and greater aspirations. "I had a hope then that I could be one of those guys," he says. "I didn't know how, but that was in my mind. I could do the same things they could do if I got the chance."

Baseball probably wasn't his best sport. "He was always a great athlete," Otis Tate says, "but he was better in basketball and football," which he played in high school.

The football team, called the Baby Hornets, regularly scrimmaged against college squads. Even as an underclassman, Willie could easily break tackles and kick the ball fifty to sixty yards. But he played quarterback, his rippling arm providing uncommon strength, his long fingers allowing him to expertly guide the ball. "He was the greatest passer I've ever seen," says William Richardson, a friend. "He was just unbelievably accurate, and he could throw the ball sixty, seventy, eighty yards on a line." The local newspapers compared him to Harry Gilmer, five years older than Mays, who was starring at the University of Alabama. That a black high school student was being compared to a white college player—they both used the "jump pass"—was itself a breakthrough. Mays's most acclaimed moment in football occurred when his team played against Booker T. Washington High School in Pensacola, Florida. With three minutes left and Fairfield losing, 7–0, Mays "heaved a seventy-yard pass which was caught, then he ran for the extra point and tied the game," according to a school history.

His exploits were equally dramatic in basketball, where he played "quick forward," relying on a picturesque "skyhook" with an unusually high arc. One year, he led Jefferson County in scoring and his team to a state championship. "We had a center," Mays says, "and when he got the rebound, the first thing he would do is look for me, because I was down the court already." He could score thirty or even forty points a game, but he says that he would often stop at twenty because "that was enough."

Mays concurs that baseball was his third sport, but the decision to make it the centerpiece of his life was never in doubt. Practical considerations won out. Football meant excessive risk of injury; basketball required height. But the most important factor was money. For most of Mays's youth, there were no equivalents in football or basketball to baseball's Negro Leagues. By the time he reached high school in 1946, segregation in professional athletics had begun to crumble, with the three major team sports integrating in a five-year period—the National Football League and the All-American Conference in 1946, Major League Baseball in 1947, and the National Basketball Association in 1950. But professional football and basketball players first attended college. Willie received scholarship offers in both sports, but college didn't appeal to him; football was nixed as well because blacks didn't play quarterback in the professional leagues.

Even before the major leagues were integrated, baseball offered the most financial opportunity. Black players in the Industrial Leagues, Negro Leagues, and semiprofessional leagues were all paid, and Willie participated at an early age. When he was fourteen, his father would take him to his Industrial League game as an extra man, and Willie would play if the team was shorthanded or the score was lopsided. The teams would either charge admission or pass the hat, then split the proceeds. Willie would receive a full share, some days ten or twelve dollars.

Around that time, he also began playing for the Fairfield Gray Sox on a sandlot field enclosed by railroad ties. The youngest player on the team, Willie proudly wore his first uniform—a blue cap inscribed with an "F" and GRAY SOX printed across his chest. The players weren't paid, but Willie was able to showcase his skills for leagues that did pay. Shortstop was his initial position, but he threw so hard, the first baseman complained. So the manager, Cle Holmes, had him pitch, but Cat Mays objected because a pitcher's lot was too risky. He had taught his son to hit, run, and field so Willie could play as long as possible. If he was turned into a pitcher by some benighted manager and hurt his arm, his career would be over. Cat's anxiety grew when, after pitching nine innings, Willie came to bat with the game tied. He smashed the ball and sped around the bases with the winning home run, only to become dizzy and collapse on the field. When he opened his eyes, his father was looking at him. "You were bearing down too hard out there," he said. "This is what happens."

Cat told his son that he needed to avoid injury so he could stay on the field. The advice was practical, but it was about more than just baseball. Jon Miller, the longtime announcer for the Giants, has heard Mays describe how his father tried to protect him. "This was about survival," he says. "This was about a young black man who would go out in the white world. If you get hurt and can't play, they'll dump you like some trash on the side of the road."

Cat told Willie's manager that if he wanted the youngster on his team, he would need to find another position for him. And he did: he sent Willie to center field.

Willie had no objection to playing the same position as DiMaggio, and while the move may have been driven by circumstance, center field suited him perfectly. The infield confined him. Now he was free to roam.

Even as a teenager with the Gray Sox, Willie made plays that fans would talk about for the rest of their lives. David Stokes was seven years old, sitting in a red wagon, when he watched Willie track down a ball in deep center field as a runner tried to score. "We thought he was going to throw the ball to the second baseman," Stokes recalls. "Instead, he threw the ball to home plate. No one could believe it. The catcher put up his arms, but the ball went over the catcher and over the fence."

The ball hit a small shop, smashing against a sign—DUCK INN—on the door. "After he hit the sign, most of the kids in Fairfield, including me, started throwing footballs, baseballs, and rocks as far as we could," Stokes says. "Everyone wanted to throw the ball like Willie." When Willie lost a fight to a burly teenager, the defeat devastated Stokes. "To me he was indestructible."

Stokes, now a retired master sergeant from the army, has only briefly met Mays, yet his connection runs deep. When he was eleven, the aunt who raised him died, and as he stood next to the open casket in the crowded church, with the choir singing hymns and the trumpeter playing his mournful tribute, the grieving boy thought of Willie Mays, racing across the outfield, his body and arm whirling with raw, balletic fury. "Willie," he says, "was our hero, our Superman, our role model."

Willie loved sports partly by default. "In the South," he said, "you only had certain things you could do, and if you didn't play a sport, what else could you do?" But his commitment was more layered. While he was drawn to the playing fields by his father and his own natural skill, sports also had rules, structure, and clarity. For a soft-spoken youth who would live in four houses before finishing high school and was indifferent about school and church, sports were his refuge.

"During baseball season, we played till late afternoon," he said. "When baseball season was over, we played basketball till eleven or twelve at night. And football we played—especially in the summer—until nine o'clock. I used to play on the high school football team, and then we'd go play sandlot ball on Sundays, without any shoulder pads. And when we didn't have shoes, I used to kick barefoot."

As a teenager, Willie made one effort to get a real job. Britling's Cafeteria in Birmingham hired him to wash dishes, and he lasted one day, apparently quitting before he was fired. He left early because he didn't want to miss his game. "I ain't going back for the money," he told his father, "because I want to play baseball."

That was fine with Cat, who had already warned him about the coal mines—if he worked there, he would die there. Lung cancer might get him, or the mine itself might collapse on him. The fenced-in mills weren't much better, disabling workers with severed fingers, ripped shoulders, burned arms, and shattered eardrums. Some men walked out so dirty that their wives couldn't recognize them, so hot they could pour sweat out of their shoes, so dazed that they confirmed what Cat said of the mills: they were death traps.

"Okay," Cat told his son upon hearing of his aborted career as a dishwasher. "You play baseball, and I'll make sure you eat."

In the South's strata of black baseball, community teams like the Fairfield Gray Sox were sometimes called semipro, even though compensation wasn't offered. The industrial teams and the minor league circuits were a notch higher, both feeding into the actual Negro Leagues, as they are now known, in which the Birmingham team played.

In 1946, Willie Mays turned fifteen and was attracting attention from beyond Fairfield and Birmingham and even Alabama. Beck Shepherd was a baseball enthusiast in Chattanooga, Tennessee, who owned a minor league team that played in the Negro Southern League, the Chattanooga Choo Choos.

Like a dozen other owners, scouts, and managers, both black and white, Shepherd later claimed that he "discovered" Willie Mays, in this case playing baseball on a "cow pasture diamond" in Alabama. As he told a reporter, "I said to myself right then, 'Get this boy to play on your Choo Choos, and you've got it made.'" He wanted to sign Willie to a contract, but Aunt Sarah told him Willie had to finish school. "Let me have that boy for five years, and he can buy his own school," Shepherd told her. Sarah held firm.

Willie never signed a contract, but he was allowed to go to Chattanooga, where he moved into the Martin Hotel and played for the Choo Choos during the summer. They were hard to miss on the road, what with "Choo Choos" scrawled on the side of the bus, and they played games from Texas to New York. "We learned it was a big world," says Harold Shepherd, Beck's son and a batboy on Willie's team. On the road, when the men found nightclubs and other diversions, Harold and Willie went to the movies or played cards in their hotel room.

Willie was initially assigned to shortstop, but the first baseman had trouble with his throws from deep short—on one play, the ball simply ripped off his glove. Willie returned to the outfield, where his education in baseball continued. "We'd go out there early, look at the field, and see what's wrong," recalls his teammate Frank Evans, who is ten years older than Mays. Some fields had embankments; others, slopes or ditches. "You don't wait until you get in the game to see what's out here," Evans told Mays, "because otherwise you can get yourself killed."

Evans worked with Mays on his baserunning ("tag everything with your left foot") and hitting, but he offered no pointers on throwing. "The Lord blessed him," he says, "with a helluva'n arm."

Mays's youth made him the target of jokes so severe that on one road trip, Beck Shepherd stopped the bus and told his team to ease off the boy or he'd leave them all on the road. "Willie and I would have finished the trip alone," Shepherd later said. "Willie was a better ball club all by himself than all the rest of the players I had put together." The teasing stopped.

Willie had other concerns. The players were paid a percentage of the gate, so if rain canceled the game, they received no money. On one road trip, bad weather postponed four or five games, and Willie was running out of cash. "We'd eat loaves of stale bread and sardines and crackers and RC Cola, and I remember—we were in Dayton, Ohio, at the time—I said to myself, if this ever gets over, I'm quitting," Mays said.

Back in Chattanooga, he called his father and said he was coming home. He told Shepherd he was returning to Birmingham because his mamma was sick, and he asked for $2.50 in bus fare.

"You be back tomorrow?" Shepherd asked.

"Yeah," Willie said.

He never returned. He had been with the team about a month.

The Choo Choos folded several years later, and by the time Mays was playing in the Polo Grounds, Shepherd was running a shoeshine parlor in Chattanooga. But his brush with the future Hall of Famer had a residual value. In 2005, a copy of a Choo Choos team photograph with Mays sold on eBay for $2,750.

The following year, Willie was playing for the TCI wire mill team with a special teammate—his father. Cat was thirty-six, still fit but past his prime. They patrolled the outfield, father in center, son in left. Since Willie was a boy, he had measured his own talent by his father's. *How much faster, stronger, and smarter was he than I?* The gap had been closing until this season, when fly balls that Cat once would have handled—if only to protect his son—were now fair game for either. "My father had always been a symbol of strength to me, strength and ability," Willie said. "But one day you grow up and you surpass your father. I know now that it's a fact of life, even though it made me feel strange at the time."

He remembers the game in which the torch was finally passed. It was the last contest of the season, and Willie knew he was almost ready for the Birmingham Black Barons. A line drive was hit between Cat and Willie, and Cat yelled, "Let me take it!"

Willie knew that Cat had earned the right to catch that ball, then he realized that his father was too far back and the ball was sinking too fast. So he did what his instincts and training had prepared him to do—he raced in front of his father and caught the ball off the top of his shoes. Afterward, no words were spoken on the field or back in the dugout.

"I knew that I'd shown him up," Willie said. "And he knew it. I've never apologized to him for making the play. He's never apologized to me for trying to call me off." They could still share their lives, but they could no longer share the same outfield. "The only thing worse than being shown up by youth is being shown up by your own flesh and blood," Willie said. "Because then you have to pretend that you like it."

CHAPTER FOUR

A MOTHER'S LOVE

Annie Satterwhite didn't raise her first son, but she was still part of his life. While news stories about Willie's childhood usually overlooked his mother or mistook her for Aunt Sarah, she had a significant impact on the player, and the man, that he became.

Cat Mays apparently wanted to marry Annie, but she wasn't interested. If Annie ever felt awkward or guilty about asking her two younger sisters to care for Willie, she never told him. Annie ultimately had plenty of practice in motherhood.

Her marriage to Frank McMorris produced ten children, eight girls and two boys. She had two sets of fraternal twins, a boy and a girl, though in each case the boy was stillborn. The family settled in the Powderly section of Birmingham, about five miles from Fairfield. Cat and Annie remained friends, allowing Willie to visit his mother easily by walking, biking, or catching a ride.

Like Cat, Annie was a talented athlete. In the early 1930s, when Willie was a baby, Annie starred on her high school basketball team, which won three consecutive state championships. But while Cat was carefree and soothing, Annie was fiery and intense. According to her son Charlie McMorris, "Both my mother and my father had tempers, but my mother more so." She was a tough, resourceful country woman, he says. "She could cook most anything, and she would walk outside and say, 'Give me one of those chickens.' And every day was Thanksgiving." She also brooked no dissent from any child. "We had a wood-burning stove," McMorris says, "and she would take that piece of wood and knock your behind with it. Not one of the kids talked back to her."

Her husband was also strong-willed, leading to a combustible relationship. Altercations were not uncommon, and their furies, against each other or strangers, sometimes spilled into the open. Frank was a plumber and Annie a laundress, but they also sold whiskey—"kind of like bootleggers," according to McMorris. On one occasion, at one of Willie's baseball games, Annie had a bottle of moonshine in her apron pocket. A patron

35

wanted to buy it, but an argument ensued over the payment, leading to a brawl. "Daddy jumped in, others jumped him, and my mom took that bottle and hit the man in the head," McMorris recalls.

Willie describes his mother as a "good lady" who, whenever he visited, would feed him and give him money. He played basketball and other games with his half-siblings but was never part of that family. He says he did not feel abandoned or neglected by his mother, and Herman Boykin, who drove him on some of his visits, saw Annie's tenderness toward him. "Willie never felt disconnected to her," he says. "Love overshadowed everything."

Annie was also one of his biggest fans. When Willie reached the Birmingham Black Barons, she would sit behind home plate in a white hat and red blouse and cheer boisterously for her son. When he became a major leaguer in 1951, she pinned a Giants pennant on her wall and followed the games on radio. When a reporter for the *Baltimore Afro-American* wanted to interview Willie Mays's mother, Annie called Sarah and asked if she wanted to present herself as Willie's mother. Sarah said no. The reporter did interview Annie, and the story, published on October 9, 1951, described a mother's love for her now-famous son. Annie said her three biggest days were when Willie signed with the Giants, when he played in his first big league game, and when the Giants won the pennant. "We were lucky to beat the Dodgers," she said, "but I thought we'd win all the time."

Willie knew about the tensions between his mother and stepfather and tried to stay clear of them. But one day when he was a teenager, Annie and Frank visited his house, and an argument broke out between them. "My mom had a mouth, and she didn't back up," Willie says. The hostilities escalated, and Frank raised his fist and started punching his wife. Frank was about the same size as Willie but not nearly as strong. Willie jumped in, grabbed his stepfather, and threw him against the wall.

"If you ever come into this house again, you sit in that chair and don't move," Willie told him, "because if you do, I'll whip your goddamn ass." In retrospect, Willie says, he may have thrown his stepfather too hard, but "from that day on, when they came over, my mother would run around the house, and he would sit in that chair."

On April 15, 1953, Annie gave birth to her eleventh child, Diane, but she hemorrhaged badly and died on the way to a hospital. She was thirty-seven. Her death stunned her children, who had come to believe that giving birth, at least for her, was routine. Mays learned of her death while he was in the army, stationed at Fort Eustis in Virginia, and he was granted a leave to attend her funeral.

Mays almost never talks about his mother—friends of his for more than fifty years say they've never heard him mention her—perhaps because he doesn't like to talk about, or even consider, sad events or unpleasant memories. "It don't pay to dig up the past," he once said. "Let it rest." But there is little doubt that his mother—and her raising of a large family that did not include her firstborn—played an important role in shaping Mays, who many years later would use ANNIE as a computer password. "It contributed to his insecurity and drove him to overcome it," says one close friend. "He thought, 'My mom might have left me, but I am something and I'm going to prove it.' I think that is part of what makes Willie tick. I don't think it's something that a child lives through and is not affected by."

On Mother's Day in 1954, a year after Annie's death, Mays described his feelings in an as-told-to story for the *Chicago Defender*, a black newspaper.* He saluted Annie as someone who supported him unconditionally in his career (preparing chicken tenders, sweet potatoes, and chocolate layer cake for his road trips as a teenage ballplayer) and who contributed generously to her church (which sometimes meant sending her children out to solicit funds). Willie also said that his mother had prepared him for her own death. "One of the things she told me constantly was how uncertain life was and how futile it was to grieve over the loss of someone you love. . . . If she died and I broke down because of it, it would be just as bad as both of us dying."

That steely temperament, forged as a young athlete to overcome any adversity, defined Mays's career as well as his life. He did not let his own pain or suffering deter him from his goals. The essay's most telling section was its conclusion. "Someone once asked me if I carry a picture of her," he said. "I don't. A picture would take me back to the past, might aggravate the hurt of knowing she is gone—physically. I'd rather carry her image in my heart and that's the way she'd want it."

Willie Mays never looked back, on anything, and what he brought with him he rarely shared with others but carried silently in his heart.

---

*He told the story to Alfred Duckett, who would later collaborate with Martin Luther King, Jr., on his "I Have a Dream" speech and would ghostwrite Jackie Robinson's autobiography, *I Never Had It Made*.

CHAPTER FIVE

THE BLACK BARONS

Willie's close relationship with his father made it natural for him to seek out others like Cat—strong but nurturing figures who would push him to succeed while protecting him from unwanted intrusions or outright predators. Leo Durocher would be his most storied mentor, but before reaching the majors, Willie fell under the tutelage of an Alabama hero who prepared him for greatness in the Negro Leagues and beyond.

Lorenzo Davis looked like a Roman Centurion, 6-foot-3 and black as coal; even when relaxed, he seemed to stand at attention. Davis was born in 1917 in the small coal mining town of Piper, Alabama. Its Negro school ended in ninth grade, so his family moved to Fairfield so he could attend high school. After he joined the basketball team, Davis was sitting on the bench when fans began to chant the name of his hometown: "We want Piper! We want Piper!" He was Piper Davis thereafter.

He received a partial scholarship to play basketball at Alabama State College, but during his freshman year his family ran out of money, so he returned to Fairfield, where he initially worked in the coal mines. After two miners were killed in accidents, he found a job as a pipe fitter for $3.26 a day. He played in the Industrial League on the weekends, a line drive hitter with long, smooth strides and a strong arm. The Black Barons noticed, and in 1942 the team signed him for $500 a month. He was an instant star. Described in press accounts as "the best second baseman in the Black leagues," Davis led the team to pennants in his first two full seasons and was named a starter in four consecutive East-West All-Star games. His renown grew further when he played for the Harlem Globetrotters in the off-season.

In 1945, Davis came close to history, drawing the attention of several scouts for Branch Rickey, president of the Brooklyn Dodgers, who was looking for a black player to integrate the major leagues. Rickey chose Jackie Robinson instead. "If [Davis] had a chance when he was young, he'd have been outstanding," the Dodger scout Clyde Sukeforth later said. Davis was thirty years old in 1947, and he still appeared headed for the majors. The St. Louis Browns purchased a thirty-day option on him from the Black Barons, but they never placed him on their roster and let the option expire. Davis spent the year in Birmingham.

Early in the 1948 season, the Black Barons were on a weekend road trip in Chattanooga, and at the hotel Davis bumped into Willie Mays, who was in town playing for one of the industrial teams in the Birmingham area. Davis had played with Cat Mays in the Industrial League before he joined the Black Barons, so when word spread about a gifted young center fielder named Mays, Davis knew who he was. But he was surprised to see him playing for money.

"Boy, what are you doing here?" he asked.

"I'm playing ball," Mays told him.

"If they catch you playing for money, they won't let you play those high school sports," Davis said.

Willie shrugged. "That's okay."

Davis had good reason to be intrigued by any prospect, for he had a new job that year, managing the Black Barons. The team had won two Negro League pennants in the 1940s and three in its history, but never a World Series. If Davis invited Willie for a tryout, he could be criticized for recruiting a callow teenager, but the possibility of a championship was too much to resist.

The next weekend, the Black Barons had a game in Atlanta, and Davis again saw Willie.

"You still interested in playing ball?" Davis asked him.

Willie said he was.

"Then have your daddy call me," Davis said.

Willie had first seen the Black Barons when he was five or six and had dreamed of playing for them ever since. When he got home, he told his father about his conversation with Davis, and Cat promptly called his former teammate.

Davis was still worried about the rules that forbade high school athletes from receiving money for playing on professional teams.

"If he plays with me," Davis told Cat, "he can't play in no high school competition."

"I don't care," Cat said. "If he wants to play, that's up to him." Cat gave Davis one piece of advice: "Don't holler at him. If you want something done, tell him and he'll do it, but if you holler, he's going to back up, and you're not going to get anything out of him."

Davis told Cat to have his son at the ballpark on Sunday at twelve-thirty. The Black Barons had a doubleheader on the Fourth of July.

• • •

Willie Mays's time in the Negro Leagues was relatively short but significant for what he learned both on and off the field. Just as he would play in Major League Baseball's golden age of the 1950s, he participated at the very end of the finest era in the history of the Negro Leagues: skilled teams were still enthusiastically supported by proud communities before integration made them anachronisms. Mays himself was one of the last great products of the Negro Leagues, and he brought with him black baseball's energy, sass, and theatrical flair, which sustained the legacy of those leagues long after they had faded away.

The Black Barons' name was derived from the city's white baseball team, the Birmingham Barons of the Southern Association, a Class AA league. (The Barons' claim to fame occurred when Michael Jordan played for them, in 1994.) While the white Barons had a strong following, the Negro team played in no one's shadow. Called "the jewel of Southern black baseball," the squad was formed in 1920 with players from the Industrial League. With only fifteen or sixteen on the team, their main weakness was overtired pitching, but in all other aspects they were equivalent to AAA baseball or the major leagues—and probably superior defensively.

The Black Barons were at once a source of deep pride for the city's growing Negro population and a defiant rejection of the racist imagery of blacks as simpletons or savages. Though not in huge numbers, white fans attended the Black Barons' games at Rickwood Field (in segregated seating), and they watched the best players in the game: local stars like Mule Suttles and Satchel Paige as well as visiting greats from Josh Gibson to Jackie Robinson.

But it was African Americans who most vigorously supported their team, and the Black Barons were beloved celebrities. On game days, they would walk or ride down Fourth Avenue, the heart of the black community, preening in their freshly laundered uniforms. Local businesses showered the players with gifts. The hitter who slammed the season's first homer would get a diamond-studded watch from a jeweler, two dinners from a restaurant, and $50 from a funeral home. Salons and dress shops would sponsor young women for the annual Miss Birmingham Black Baron Beauty Contest. Some games would feature jitterbug contests, marching bands, and various dignitaries, including "the brown queen of Birmingham."

John W. Goodgame was a perfectly named pitcher for the Black Barons; when his career ended, he became the pastor of the Sixth Avenue Baptist Church South. On Sunday mornings he would end his sermon, "Well, I'm going to the ball game," and encourage his parishioners to follow suit.

The fans' loyalty wasn't blind—they loved their team when they won but denounced them with equal gusto when they lost. "The ragged, list-less, puny performance by the locals against Memphis," said the *Birmingham World*, the city's black newspaper. "Birmingham fans like a hustling, fighting, chatty baseball club. They don't like players too lazy to trot off and on the field, to speed back and tag up and who are too indifferent about the game to pep things up."

The Black Barons survived the Depression and, in 1940, were sold to Tom Hayes, the heavyset son of a Memphis undertaker, who oversaw the team's most successful years. An appealing part of the team was its ballpark, Rickwood Field. Built in 1910 for the white Barons, the concrete and steel structure cost $75,000 and was seen as a monument to baseball's success in the South. Its main entrance featured twin parapets and fanciful masks to evoke a movie house, while a graceful cupola hovered above the grandstand. In the 1930s, steel-frame light towers allowed Rickwood to become the first minor league park with night baseball. The grandstands could hold seven thousand spectators. Connie Mack, the legendary manager of the Philadelphia Athletics, personally laid out the diamond so the sun wouldn't interfere with the outfielders. The field itself favored pitchers, with straightaway center at 470 feet.

By the start of the twenty-first century, Rickwood stood as America's oldest ballpark. It may have been a baseball paradise, but it also reflected the South's racial hierarchy. The segregated stands gave white fans superior seats. In some years, the Black Barons and their opponents couldn't use the clubhouses but had to dress in one of the city's black hotels, either the Palm Leaf or the Rush. At Black Baron games, African Americans could work as concessionaires and gatemen, but the ticket sellers had to be white. The most frustrating disparity was the most obvious: the team didn't own its park but was forced to pay rental fees—a black enterprise enriching white owners—and was subject to the whims of white schedulers.

In the major leagues, Mays was often described as the game's most exciting player, and his style can be traced to his years with the Black Barons. The black game placed greater emphasis on speed, creativity, and daring, for it was designed to explicitly entertain fans at a time when organized entertainment was limited. Negro League games featured a range of performers, such as tap dancers, jugglers, vocalists, and bands, and the players themselves were part of the show. Of course the teams played to win, but victory wasn't the only criterion for success.

At an extreme, the teams relied on showboating and clowning—literally. In the 1930s and 1940s, the Indianapolis Clowns fielded two players as a comic duo, Reese "Goose" Tatum and Richard "King Tut" Martin, the latter wearing a clown outfit and oversized glove, a cigar between his teeth. Goose Tatum blended sports and vaudeville, first as a Clown and later as a rapid-dribbling Harlem Globetrotter, recycling some stunts—such as throwing confetti on the fans—in both acts. Other teams played "shadow ball," in which fielders whipped an imaginary ball around the diamond, recording "outs" with great flair.

Some of these tactics dated from the 1880s, when black barnstorming teams used comedy to draw crowds, but slapstick was also controversial for its perpetuation of negative stereotypes of blacks, as seen in minstrel shows or in Stepin Fetchit roles. As Piper Davis said, "If you was black, you was a clown. Because in the movies, the only time you saw a black man he was a comedian or a butler. But didn't nobody clown in our league but the Indianapolis Clowns. We played baseball."

The Clowns, it should be noted, still fielded some good players, including, in 1952, an eighteen-year-old Alabaman named Hank Aaron.

In the 1920s, Babe Ruth's dominance as a power hitter turned Major League Baseball into a slugger's game, slow and predictable, with less emphasis on base stealing, bunting, and the hit-and-run. The Negro players, still striving for entertainment, refined those skills, which, combined with the loose structure of the leagues, contributed to freewheeling theatrics. The games involved constant movement, dancing off bases, subterfuge, improvisation, and verbal jousting. Players would throw balls behind their back or under their legs, or a shortstop would use his bare hand to tap the ball out of his glove to the second baseman to start a double play.

Just as segregation fostered the spirituals, blues, and jazz—designed to perpetuate black culture—the strict racial divide allowed Negro baseball players to develop their own athletic imprint.

When Willie Mays arrived at Rickwood Field, he had been given no assurances that he would make the team. He was given a faded uniform (number 21) with BIRMINGHAM across the chest and a cap inscribed with three Bs on the front.

"Go shag some flies," Piper Davis told him. His center fielder, Norman Robinson, was a 5-foot-8 speedster with a weak arm, and Davis had heard about Willie's gunshots from the outfield.

His new teammates were skeptical. "I ain't never seen a ballplayer like that in my life," Bill Powell, a right-handed pitching ace, recalled. "When he came out as a little ol' boy, his pants were too big for him, his bat was too heavy."

The doubleheader against the Cleveland Buckeyes began, and Mays, sitting out the first game, was doubtful as well. Now turned seventeen, he was more than ten years younger than most of his teammates. He wasn't nervous about his age—he had always played with older boys or grown men—but these guys were bigger and stronger than anyone he'd played with. And they were good. He didn't appreciate how good until he reached the major leagues; the Black Barons, he believed, were equal to anything he saw there.

He just sat.

"Watch," Davis said. "Watch what's going on."

The Black Barons won the first game, and before the next one began, the players gathered in the clubhouse, cooling off and drinking sodas. Mays felt isolated, alone. Then Davis approached him. "I'm going to let you play the second game," he whispered. "I don't know how you're going to do. Play left field and give it your best shot."

Davis called over the equipment manager, Roosevelt Atkins, and handed him a slip of paper. "Roo, hang this lineup in the dugout." Davis looked at Willie and winked. Listed seventh in the order was "Mays, LF."

The manager was standing near home plate when he heard one of his players say, "That little boy's in left field." Others crowded around the lineup card and were complaining as well.

Davis returned to the dugout and asked, "How's the lineup look to you fellows? If anybody don't like it, there's the clubhouse, and you can go back in there and take off your uniform if you want to. And you can take it with you."

He had no takers.

Mays had to face Chet Brewer, a tall right-hander who entered the Negro Leagues with the Kansas City Monarchs in 1925, six years before Willie was born. In this instance, youth prevailed—Mays rapped two singles. After the game, Davis told Willie that he was hired and the Black Barons would pay him $250 a month, though it would increase to $300 if he hit over .300 in any one month. (He never did in his first season.)

Mays hadn't cleared every hurdle. He was completing his sophomore year of high school, and neither Davis nor Cat would let him travel with the team until classes ended. Moreover, his playing for the Black Barons, even at home games, created an uproar at school. He had received payments from other teams for several years, but the visibility of the Black Barons brought his play to the attention of the school's principal. As Davis predicted, E. J. Oliver called Willie into his office and said that if he was compensated for playing baseball, he would not be able to play high school sports in Alabama. He also threatened to suspend Willie. The youngster wanted to play baseball, but was it worth dropping out of high school? A meeting with Cat Mays, Aunt Sarah, and E. J. Oliver was hastily called.

Oliver was an unforgiving disciplinarian who held his students account-able, including Willie. He lived outside the city to avoid encounters with parents—he believed that could lead him to favor one of their children. To get to school, he rode a streetcar to Birmingham, transferred to the Bes-semer line, got off at the Vinesville Station, and walked a mile through the woods—a total of thirty-two miles a day for forty-three years. His well-pressed suits, shined shoes, and carefully trimmed mustache conveyed pre-cision and control. There were many rules. Students had to handle books and periodicals in the library with clean hands, applaud moderately in the auditorium, and walk purposefully in the halls. Girls had to wear dresses or skirts no higher than an inch above the knee. Any act of mischief or insubordination was grounds for corporal punishment, which was sanc-tioned by one of Oliver's favorite biblical proverbs: "Foolishness is bound in the heart of a child, but the rod of correction shall drive it from him."

Willie Mays felt his wrath, and strap, once. Caught playing in the hall, he was summoned to the principal's office and told to bend over a chair. Oliver's message—obey the rules—was delivered with a half dozen deci-sive whacks.

Oliver, a graduate of Tuskegee, was also a progressive educator. His students were taught Negro history long before it became fashionable. He oversaw a wide range of clubs—math, science, drama, debate—and encouraged his best students to travel to Montgomery for academic meets. He celebrated black ambition, including athletics. He showed his students newsreels of Jackie Robinson playing for the Dodgers. But as its name sug-gested, Fairfield Industrial High also focused on the trades—such as tai-loring and auto mechanics for boys, home economics and cosmetology for girls. Oliver was determined that all his students would be productive citizens once they graduated.

The principal reinforced Mays's values of deference, sacrifice, and disci-pline, but the youth's desire to play for the Black Barons undercut another tenet. In Oliver's view, for blacks, education was the path to economic salvation. He expected all of his students to graduate, and he feared that Willie would now be distracted from his schoolwork. Oliver was also not beyond self-interest. Willie helped Fairfield win in football and basketball, increasing ticket sales and putting money in the school's coffers. All of that would be gone if he played for the Black Barons.

What occurred at the meeting with Cat, Aunt Sarah, and Oliver was never disclosed to Willie. Ultimately, Sarah and Cat got what they wanted: Willie would continue to play for the Black Barons and without any dis-ciplinary action, but he could travel with the team only when the school year was over. Willie did indeed lose his eligibility to play high school sports, except when the team played outside Alabama. (He helped the football team win a game in Florida.) The move outraged his classmates, who believed he was putting his interests above the school's. But Willie was unmoved. He loved football and basketball, but baseball was now his profession.

In 1948, Piper Davis knew that all Willie needed was the opportunity. "He was an infant compared to the folks he was going to be playing with, but you could see the talent in him," he recalled. "He had that something special inside."

His job was to teach Willie on the field and protect him off it. In truth, he tried to protect him on the field as well. Mays was not expected to be an everyday player, but Norman Robinson broke his ankle, leaving center field open. The job was suddenly Willie's, though the corner outfielders tried to take advantage of him. One game, when a ball was hit to right or left, the other outfielders yelled, "Come on, Willie! Come on, Willie!" forcing him to make long runs for the ball.

Davis would have none of it, and between innings, he called over the offending Black Barons. "You're going to have to earn your money," he barked. "We can get anybody to stand out there and yell, 'Come on, Willie!' I don't want you running him foul line to foul line."

While Mays was precocious, he was still unpolished. His arm was as powerful as rumored, but Davis instructed him to charge the ball as fast as possible, especially with a runner on second base. This advice, in hindsight, seems self-evident, but the practice wasn't common at the time. In organized ball, outfielders were instructed to field grounders on one knee to ensure that the ball didn't skip past them. When Mays reached the major leagues, he stunned baserunners when he charged the ball—he played the outfield like the infield.

Davis found other ways to help. Playing second base, he would signal to Mays in center field what pitch was being thrown, and on the bench he would tell him what the pitchers would try to do and who would knock him down. On the bases, he implored Mays to slide more aggressively into fielders who tried to block him from the base. At the plate, Mays struggled with the curveball, but Davis told him to stand straighter, keep his shoulder pointed toward the pitcher, and resist lunging. Ironically, major league pitchers tried to get Mays out with hard stuff, high and tight, because he now killed curveballs.

Davis emphasized forcing the action, speed, and aggression, especially on the bases. "If you think you can make, try it," he'd say. Toughness was equally important. In a game against the Memphis Red Sox, Mays sped toward home plate and barreled into All-Star catcher Clinton "Casey" Jones. Mays and the ball arrived simultaneously, the runner's spikes catching Jones high on the leg and leaving a long, bloody gash. Jones dropped the ball, but Mays felt terrible. When he reached the dugout, he headed straight for Davis.

"Piper, I couldn't help it. I didn't have to hit him like that."

Davis took him aside. "Willie, that's the man to hit. He's got all that equipment on and he beats up on everyone, so he's the one to tear up. He won't block the plate on you no more."

On another occasion, Mays hit a home run off Chet Brewer. His next time up, the veteran pitcher drilled him in the arm with a fastball. No ball had ever hit him so hard. Mays crumbled to the ground and began to cry. When he looked up, Davis was glowering over him and kicked him.

"Skip, they're throwing at me," Mays said. His screechy voice rose even higher when he was excited.

Davis made no effort to help him up. "Boy, you see first base?"

"Yes, sir."

"Point to it."

"It's right down there," Mays said, motioning down the line.

"Then get up and go down there, and the first chance you get, you steal second, and then third."

Davis turned and walked back to the dugout, and Mays trotted down to first. He stole second and then third. He scored on a fly ball.

Back in the dugout, Davis said, "That's how you handle a pitcher."

Willie saw "shadow ball" in his first year with the Black Barons. The game stopped in the seventh inning, and, as he recalls, "they played baseball without the baseball." His teammates were running around the bases and sliding into home just before the tag. "It was fun and entertaining, and people loved it," he says, "but the real value was the mental part. You had to think what you were going to do with the ball even when there was no ball. You had to exercise your mind."

Mays had always competed to win, but now, playing before large crowds, some reaching ten thousand, he realized he could be more than a baseball player. "In the Negro Leagues, we were all entertainers," he says. "And my job was to give the fans something to talk about each game."

In later years, he would contrive plays to incite fan reaction—such as slipping to the ground before making a catch—but at this age his natural ability was enough to generate howls, particularly on the bases and in the outfield. "He was the most exciting young player you've ever seen," outfielder James Zapp recalls. "It was a thrill just to watch him in a rundown because most of the time, he'd get out of that hot box." Adds Bill Powell,

"He did some impossible catches in the outfield, and then people would just stand there and shake their heads."

On one drive to left center, Willie and the left fielder arrived at the ball simultaneously and nearly collided. The left fielder missed the ball, but Willie leaped and caught it barehanded, then threw it to the infield before anyone knew what happened. It was remarkable—a barehanded catch deep in the outfield—except Willie did it twice more. Using his over-sized hand like a glove, he learned to charge and scoop up base hits with his right hand and throw the ball home in one fluid motion. "Nobody," Davis later said, "and I mean nobody, ever saw anybody throw a ball from the outfield like him, or get rid of it so fast."

The Negro League's quintessential showman was Leroy "Satchel" Paige, the ageless right-hander, all legs and arms, whose windmill wind-up, famed hesitation pitch, and memorable quotes fueled his popular-ity. Among his rules for staying young: "Go very light on the vices, such as carrying on in society—the social ramble ain't restful." His unerring control and ability to change speeds also made him, according to some experts, the greatest pitcher of all time—any color, any league.

Mays faced Paige in one game, in the summer of 1948, when Paige, forty-one and playing for the Kansas City Monarchs, had been pitching professionally for more than twenty years. Mays knew little of the legend, and his first time up, he hit a fastball for a double. As he dusted himself off, Paige walked toward him. "That's it," he muttered.

Mays wasn't sure what he meant, but he heard Paige tell his third base-man, "Let me know when that little boy comes back up."

Next time up, the third baseman said, "Satch, here he is."

Paige walked halfway to home plate and said to Mays, "Little boy, I'm not gonna trick you now. I'm gonna throw you three fastballs, and you're gonna sit down."

Paige threw three fastballs, and Mays sat down.

Shortly thereafter, the Cleveland Indians signed Paige, who would pitch for five years in the American League and then, at fifty-eight, would return for one additional game for the Kansas City Athletics. But he never faced Willie Mays again.

The greatest year for baseball in Birmingham's history was 1948. Its white team drew more than 440,000 fans, a Southern Association record, on its way to winning the Dixie Series. Shortstop Artie Wilson of the Black Barons hit .403, winning the batting crown for the second straight year, and the team won the Negro American League Championship, taking the series against the Kansas City Monarchs, 4–3. In the second game, Willie Mays's game-tying single in the bottom of the ninth allowed the Black Barons to win in extra innings.

In the World Series, Birmingham played the Negro National League Champion Homestead Grays, which over the years had produced such stars such as Cool Papa Bell and Josh Gibson and this year featured future Hall of Famer Buck Leonard (known as "the Black Lou Gehrig"). The Grays, who had beaten the Black Barons in the World Series in 1942 and '43, won the first two games of this series.

In game three, Mays made a leaping catch against the center field wall and also threw out Leonard at second base. With the score tied in the bottom of the ninth and two men on and two out, Mays stepped to the plate and singled sharply up the middle, winning the game. But it was the Black Barons' only victory of the series, with Homestead winning, 4–1.

Willie Mays proved he belonged. He struggled at the plate, hitting only .226 for the year, but he still made his mark in the field and on the bases. The *Birmingham World* first mentioned him on September 28: "Willie Howard Mays is the find of the year, if not the rookie of the year. He can hit, field, throw and deliver in the pinch. He lacks experience and has a feeble batting average. But he will break up your ball game and turn hits into putouts with sensational catches."

The season produced one of the most famous photographs in Negro League history. The picture, by Ernest Withers, features the Black Barons in their brick clubhouse after they won the league championship. The jubilant players, many with their shirts off, are pressed together, smiling, cramped in a corner beneath an exposed lightbulb and flimsy hangers, a gritty, victorious image of camaraderie, unity, and love. But in the back row, hidden by arms and shoulders, there is a smooth ebony face without a smile, only wonderment and innocence, a boy among men.

Cross-country bus rides became part of the romantic lore of the Negro Leagues, a celebration of male bonding and roadside adventure that satisfied the wanderlust of any ballplayer. But the rides were also grueling marathons marked by cheap hotels, lousy food, and—particularly in the South—racial indignities. The Black Barons spent more time on the road than most teams: they were one of only two southern teams in the Negro American League, which meant long trips to Kansas City, Chicago, Indianapolis, and Cleveland. Exhibitions, meanwhile, took them from St. Louis to New York.

For Willie Mays, the endless hours on the bus, combined with his sojourns in faraway cities, gave him a view of the country that most of his high school peers could only dream about. These experiences contributed to his sense that baseball was really one big traveling family, quarrelsome at times, but beholden to the greater good of the clan. Willie was still protected, but his time with these older men, intimately familiar with the angry, violent subtext of Jim Crow, broadened his education on how to survive the country's racial codes.

The cross-country experience was full of contradictions. Negro Leaguers might be denied food or gas by the very people who would patronize their games later that day, but that didn't deter the players from performing at their highest level. Their exploits made them heroes in their own community but reminded them of their subordinate position in the country at large.

"It was an arduous existence, which consisted of long rides, low pay, and a game almost every day," said Monte Irvin, who starred with the Newark Eagles in the 1940s before playing with the New York Giants. Players would wash their clothes in the morning and dry them by holding them out the window on their ride to the next town. Barred from hotels in some cities, teams would sometimes sleep on the bus, in rooming houses, or even in jails. "The traveling conditions were almost unbelievable," Irvin said. "That was the tragic part about traveling, particularly in the South, where we couldn't even stay in the third- or fourth-rate hotels."

Negro Leaguers later bristled at this vagabond image—puttering across America, nearly broke, bordering on desperation—as obscuring the dignity of their efforts and their own resourcefulness. Roy Campanella, who began his career in 1937 with the Washington Elite Giants, recalled that the bus combined home, dressing room, dining room, and hotel. "Rarely were we in the same city two days in a row," he said. "Mostly, we played by day and traveled by night; sometimes we played both day and night and usually in two different cities . . . [But] I loved the life despite the killing schedule."

The team's bus would sometimes pick up Willie in Fairfield. "He was just standing there on the highway with his suitcase, a little country boy," recalled James Zapp. Other times, the bus driver would pretend not to see Willie and drive right past him, alarming him until he saw the bus circle back to get him.

The driver, Charlie Rudd, was also the team's navigator, mechanic, and batboy, though he was called "batman" because he was in his fifties. Rudd had more faith in the vehicle than it deserved. Its brakes once went out on a hill outside Asheville, North Carolina, and one of the older players began calling out signals. "If we came to a right turn, everybody leaned left, and vice versa," Piper Davis recalled. "I'm saying to myself, 'Lawd, get me out of this,' and finally the 'batman' used his gears, so we stopped. It's lucky we didn't meet nobody or catch up with nobody."

On another occasion, the bus broke down completely on the way to Montgomery. Davis left on foot and returned a half hour later driving an ice truck. "Got to play a game, fellas," he called out. Mays and his teammates piled into the frigid vehicle and, with the back door open, shivered for the next forty miles.

Rudd picked up the players in front of Bob's Savoy Café, the largest Negro café in Birmingham, and Davis demanded that they be on time. It didn't always happen, but Rudd seemed to know when tardy players were moments away from arriving. He would stall for a few minutes by cleaning the windshield, wiping the headlights, or checking air in the tires.

But on one occasion he couldn't save Willie when the boy arrived early at the Savoy. The owner, a large, light-skinned man, had a table for Willie so he could keep an eye on him, but after his meal Willie put his suitcase on the bus and walked down the street to shoot pool. He lost track of time, and the bus rumbled off. Alerted, he raced outside, found a taxi, and, with the car blaring its horn, caught up with the bus several miles outside Birmingham.

"You can't leave me!" he shouted at Davis in his high voice.

"You don't want to be late," he said, "so get your little chicken butt on your seat and sit down so we can get going to Kansas City." Davis didn't reimburse the taxi fare, and Willie was never late again.

As the youngest Black Baron, Mays sat in the back, over the rear wheel, and watched this traveling ecosystem. There were memorable characters, such as pitcher Nat Pollard, who was called "the prophet" and later became a preacher, and catcher Pepper Bassett, who by reputation never met a hanging curveball or a pretty lady he didn't like. Card games drained a lot of time. Tonk, a kind of knock rummy, was the most popular. Other players sang gospel songs, told jokes, or read newspapers; third baseman John Britton studied the sports pages and told Willie how many hits DiMaggio had. Some players discussed their sexual conquests. But the most popular topic was simply baseball.

Some rides would start at midnight, hurtling past cotton fields and prairies so the team could avoid a hotel bill. A different city every night: Kansas City or Chicago, Little Rock or Memphis. They would eat out of paper bags or stop at grocery stores along the way. At one bus station in New Orleans, black cooks and waitresses would give them special service in the back. One time, a white customer complained about being neglected. The manager walked into the back and yelled at the waitress. Willie always remembered what happened next: "She took off her apron, placed it over her chair, and walked out the door without saying a word."

Willie's teammates were accommodating, to a point. One night, over a long, bumpy road, he was jounced so badly that he moved to the front of the bus to sit with Bassett, who at 6-foot-3 and 225 pounds was one of the biggest players on the team. Willie tried to get him to move, but he wouldn't. So Willie asked Davis, sleeping nearby, for assistance, but Bassett opened his eyes and growled, "You better get away from me." He took a swing, missed, and hit an overhead rack. Willie retreated.

Willie was usually an adept sleeper, on some occasions able to snooze by lying on the duffel bags stuffed in the back. In the major leagues, when he traveled by train, New York Giant announcer Russ Hodges said that Mays "was the greatest sleeper I ever saw." He could be wide awake on an airplane as it began to taxi on the runway and be asleep by takeoff. As a Black Baron, resting was easier after the team bought a modish blue and silver bus called the Blue Goose; it had reclining seats, air-conditioning, and reliable brakes.

Piper Davis had assured Cat that Willie would be protected—the boy couldn't go anywhere without a chaperone. To ensure that he got to bed early, Davis rotated Willie's roommate, always putting him with the next day's starting pitcher. Davis assumed that tomorrow's hurler would prefer sleep to late-night temptations.

While Willie's classmates may have spent their summers reading about other places in America, Willie was visiting them and could report back on his experiences. He talked about New York, where the bus caught fire in the Holland Tunnel and Willie had to rescue his two suitcases before playing at the Polo Grounds. He described St. Louis, where he attended his first major league game at Sportsman's Park and saw Stan Musial hit. He discussed Philadelphia, where he got a close look at the Liberty Bell; he told his classmates about the crack. "It was a history lesson," Mays says. My classmates "got it from books. I got it from life."

The Black Barons demonstrated character and pride in ways beyond winning games. How you looked also made a statement. "We were one of the sharpest dressed teams in the league," Bill Greason says. "We walked off that bus and were well respected. We wanted to represent our city well, our people well, and our team well." Fashion carried other advantages. "Piper and the rest of us told Willie, 'If you're looking good, the girls will look at you. And if you're looking decent, you don't have to talk as much.'" Both appealed to Willie.

If a player didn't have nice clothes, his teammates chipped in and bought him some. Such gestures were common in the Negro Leagues. The teams didn't have trainers, so the players gave one another rubdowns. The ballparks didn't have lights, so the guys strung their own. The owners didn't have money, so the teammates shared what they had. "It was the togetherness," Greason says. "We all dealt with family problems, but we all helped each other out. [The Black Barons] were the best group I've ever been around."

The Black Barons gave Willie more formal tutorials about his own baseball heritage. He learned, for example, that Jackie Robinson wasn't the first black player in the major leagues. As far back as 1872, Negroes played in organized baseball, but they always faced resistance, and by the 1890s, the color line had been firmly established. The Black Barons delighted in telling the story of how Ty Cobb, touring Cuba in 1910, teamed with players of color. The race-baiting Cobb was outraged that three of them had out-hit him. "We would laugh about that on the rides: good ol' Ty—the Georgia Peach—miffed at being outhit," Mays later said.

He received a more pointed education about race in America. In Fairfield, he had been relatively insulated from overt hostility, his carefree personality putting everyone, black and white, at ease, his athletic achievements making him a budding celebrity. The Black Barons cast race relations in a different light. They understood how tenuously they clung to their freedom as well as their lives.

They played for a team in Birmingham, which was different from the rest of the country, even different from many other places in the South. Different—as in more hostile to blacks. Controlled by white supremacists, the city crushed any hint of Negro defiance with swift, violent efficiency. That message was delivered in 1942, when a black man in Birmingham argued with a white bus driver about three cents in change. The man stepped off the bus, and the driver shot him six times. No charges were filed. The violence was organized and systemic. In 1947, a year before Mays joined the Black Barons, a reenergized Ku Klux Klan adopted a new tool to keep black families out of white neighborhoods: dynamite.

On August 18, 1947, six sticks were used to blow up the house of a black man who had successfully sued to end Birmingham's racist zoning laws. Within two years, so many black homes had been detonated in one area that it was known as Dynamite Hill, and the city was nicknamed Bombingham. Its most famous bombing, killing four black girls at the Sixteenth Street Baptist Church in 1963, culminated years of terrorism against the African American community. In the civil rights era, the man most closely associated with using police-state tactics to uphold segregation was Eugene "Bull" Connor, the city's police commissioner. He was elected to office in 1937 and was responsible, in 1963, for turning fire hoses and attack dogs against peaceful demonstrators.

Birmingham's suffocating bigotry stunned the black journalist Carl T. Rowan, who visited the city around 1950 and encountered passive Negroes who "dare not be seen" on any street after sundown. He discovered that blacks in Birmingham lived under a shadow of intimidation and oppression, and he was left "aghast by the obvious fear in the eyes of innocent people."

All blacks in the South were in peril, for southern authorities had long been arbitrarily arresting African Americans on trumped-up charges, such as vagrancy or loitering, and leasing them into corporate slave camps. Douglas A. Blackmon, in *Slavery by Another Name*, documents the pervasive use of this practice in the coal mines surrounding Birmingham; headstones still mark the sunken graves of those who died in collapsed prison mines. Blackmon estimates that in 1930, "the great majority" of African Americans in the Black Belt of the South were almost certainly trapped in some form of coerced labor.

Negro baseball players, in comparison, led a charmed life, so the Black Barons had good reason to bear their resentments quietly. At the 1948 Negro League World Series, several games were played at Pelican Park in New Orleans, and black fans, including the wives of players, were separated by chicken wire, corralled like farm animals. But those affronts could be endured compared to other forms of oppression.

Bill Greason, seven years older than Mays, was the second youngest player on the team. He says the veterans taught all the young players how to survive in an unjust, unforgiving world. "With all the rejection we had to suffer, you had to learn to laugh and keep going," Greason says. "Don't let anybody know they hit your weak spot. Just keep going as if you didn't hear it, and try to make your enemy your friend. If you perform well enough, they'll come to your side."

He recalls the night that a white fan threw beer on him and called him names. He went to the dugout and changed his uniform but never said a word. "If they try to anger you and you smile, sooner or later they let you go," Greason says. After he retired, he used his compassion and forgiveness as the pastor at Bethel Baptist Church in Birmingham.

This conciliatory approach echoed Piper Davis's advice to Willie on getting hit by a pitch: brush yourself off, run down to first, and steal a base. Physical retaliation or verbal sparring serves no purpose.

The Black Barons taught Mays that defiance was self-defeating, or as Mays describes it: "Keep your mouth closed." He credits his father for insisting that he remain positive, but the Black Barons prepared him to overcome racial assaults. "I was programmed," he explains, "to do these things before I got into professional ball. You had to understand that they were going to call you names, you had to understand that whatever you did it was going to be negative because of who you were. I knew that stuff from the Black Barons."

Mays repeatedly uses the word "programmed" in describing his preparation for the outside world, a hardwiring of stoicism and strength that no adversary could reverse.

CHAPTER SIX

THE GIANTS CALL

The *Chicago Defender* was America's most influential black newspaper, a staunch advocate for baseball's integration with more than half its readers outside Chicago. It also recognized the game's broader role in the quest for racial equality. So Mays achieved a certain milestone when the *Defender,* on August 27, 1949, published an article: MOVE OVER, YOU VETS, WILLIE MAYS IS COMING UP LIKE A PRAIRIE FIRE. It said that Mays, "a mild-mannered young chap," was "probably the most promising youngster to come up to a Negro American League team in a long number of years." Some major league scouts were already looking at him. A photograph shows Mays in his baggy uniform with his hands on his knees, a broad smile across his face, an image of confidence and joy.

The *Defender*'s enthusiasm was understandable. Mays had joined the Black Barons as a rough, uncut diamond, but his brilliance soon emerged. In his second year, he raised his average to .311, and in the first nine home games of 1950, he was batting .394. But his hitting was almost secondary; over the years, the Black Barons had many fine hitters. What stood out was Willie's glorious arm. "He is a sensation at throwing long balls that spell OUT for the surprised runner," the *Birmingham World* reported on April 11, 1950. "Mays in a recent game with the Cleveland Buckeyes chocked a 295-foot-fly; threw the ball the entire distance to home and cooled a probable three-run rally." The paper, which nicknamed him "the Arm," published a photograph of Willie on May 9 beneath the headline: DEATH TO BASESTEALERS. The story noted that Mays "is believed to have the best long throwing arm in Negro baseball today."

Mays hit fourth in the lineup, and his teammates called him "Sonny Boy"—or maybe it was "Sunny Boy." Either name fit. At Rickwood Field, white reporters began writing about him and young ladies threw pennies his way on the outfield grass.

Willie was unfazed. "He didn't receive accolades so that he was puffed up and proud," Bill Powell said. "He always had that pleasing personality, always jovial, always laughing. . . . He was clean cut, no drinking,

55

no smoking. All he drank were pops. No matter how many accolades he received, he was still Willie Mays."

But he couldn't save the Black Barons or the Negro Leagues. Once Jackie Robinson stepped onto the field with the Brooklyn Dodgers on April 15, 1947, joined eleven weeks later by Larry Doby with the Cleveland Indians, the attention of black baseball fans switched to new ballparks. The Black Barons may have drawn record crowds in 1948, but elsewhere attendance plummeted. That year, African Americans preferred seeing Robinson and, by then, Roy Campanella in New York, St. Louis, Boston, and other National League cities. Larry Doby and, by July, Satchel Paige were the big attractions in American League towns. In August, for example, Paige drew 51,000 for a game at Comiskey Park in Chicago, which he won, 5–0. Several nights later, the annual East-West Negro League All-Star Game at Comiskey drew 37,099, a 30 percent decline from the previous year. By 1951, the paid attendance was down to 14,161.

Black newspapers, which had once been the Negro League's greatest advocates, were now devoting their coverage to the major league pioneers; they were the battering ram against the country's broader walls of segregation. When the Homestead Grays won the 1948 World Series, its hometown newspaper, the *Pittsburgh Courier,* covered the event in two paragraphs amid stories about black major leaguers. The Grays folded in 1951.

The Negro League owners were trapped in a downward spiral. To reduce their losses, they had to sell their top players, which accelerated their demise. In 1948, the owners of the Newark Eagles sold their top player, Monte Irvin, to the New York Giants for $5,000. The Kansas City Monarchs sold six players, including Paige. The Black Barons' owner, Tom Hayes, facing his own financial crisis, had begun to auction off his superior players.

In 1949 Artie Wilson, the best shortstop in black baseball, was sold to the Oakland Oaks in the Pacific Coast League for a reported $10,000. After the 1949 season, Piper Davis was sold to the Boston Red Sox for $7,500, with the promise of another $7,500 if he made it to the major leagues. Pitcher Alonzo Perry was also dispatched to the Oakland Oaks for $5,000 (though he returned to the Black Barons the following year).

That Willie Mays would end up in the major leagues was inevitable, but the scouting and signing of him is a story of missed opportunities, colossal blunders, and blinkered racism.

Some scouts blew their chance for immortality simply because they couldn't judge talent. In 1949, a Pittsburgh Pirate scout was following the Black Barons, and Piper Davis approached him in a hotel lobby in New Orleans.

"Give us $2,000 and you can have that kid," he said.

"Nah," the scout said. "Even if we got him, we'd make a pitcher out of him."

"Ah, shit," Davis said under his breath. In an interview years later, Davis said: "They could have had Clemente in right and Mays in center."

The team with the inside track on Mays was the Boston Braves, one of whose scouts, Bill Maughn, lived in Cullman, Alabama, about fifty miles north of Birmingham. On a June night in 1949, driving through Birmingham, he decided to catch a Black Barons' game at Rickwood. In the second inning, with runners on first and third for the opposing team, the hitter drove the ball off the left field scoreboard. The left fielder picked it up, and the center fielder raced over, yelling, "Give it to me! Give it to me!" As Maughn recalled, "I'll be dog-gone if the left fielder didn't shovel pass it to him like a football player and the center fielder threw out the runner trying to go from first to third." Four innings later, the center fielder "goes to right-center and he has to turn and throw and he gets another one by eight feet, trying to go from first to third."

Maughn had never seen anything like it. He also didn't know anyone there, so he asked a ticket seller who owned the Black Barons. The ticket seller introduced him to Tom Hayes, who told Maughn the name of the boy in center field. Hayes also said that one of Maughn's colleagues had already been there—he showed the scout the business card of Henry Jenkins, the Boston Braves' farm director. Hayes said that he had spoken on the telephone to the Braves' owner, Lou Perini, as well, and the Braves had offered $7,500 for Willie.

Given Hayes's cash crunch, he probably would have sold Mays right then. But the major leagues prohibited any team from signing a player who was still in high school; in fact, teams weren't supposed to even make contact with those players. The Braves had asked the major league commissioner, Albert "Happy" Chandler, to waive the rule for Mays, given that he was already playing for money, but Chandler decided the rule still applied. Jenkins told Hayes that he would contact him as soon as Willie graduated the following year.

But Maughn was taking no chances. Seeking to gain his trust, the scout introduced himself to Mays, following him the rest of the season and picking up the trail in the spring of 1950. "I'd stand on the roof at Rickwood and watch him, and I knew this guy was mine," Maughn said. On May 1, 1950, Maughn wrote to Jenkins: "In regard to Willie Mayes, well, here is the best standout prospect available in the nation. When I say he could even pitch for my money, I am not fooling, as he is the fastest human being throwing from 60 feet 6 inches that I have ever seen." Of course, Maughn hadn't seen Mays pitch, nor had he learned to spell his last name, but that didn't matter. He continued: Willie "graduates the 15th of the month and I plan on being in Birmingham that date. . . . Harry, this boy is it, believe me."

Jenkins, meanwhile, repeatedly assured his boss, Perini, that the Birmingham boy was going to be a great Brave.

On May 31, Willie dispelled E. J. Oliver's worst fears and, having completed all of his classwork, graduated from Fairfield Industrial High School.* In his senior year, he was not absent or tardy a single day. Baseball commitments, however, did preclude him from graduation practice, so at the ceremony itself he didn't adhere to the precision marching. "He was kind of skipping and dancing around," Loretta Richardson says. "Mr. Oliver was gritting his teeth, getting red, but everybody got through it."

Willie Mays received his degree in cleaning, dyeing, and pressing, which happened to overlap the interests of a baseball player to whom he would later be compared. As a youth at St. Mary's Industrial School for Boys in Baltimore, Babe Ruth excelled in the tailor shop, sewing shirts.

Unknown to Willie, while he was receiving his degree, Maughn was talking to Hayes about his baseball contract. Hayes wanted $7,500 when Willie signed and another $7,500 if Willie was still with the Braves a year later. Willie himself would receive a $4,000 bonus, according to this proposal, and would finish the year with the Black Barons. Maughn countered that the Braves would want Mays to report to one of their farm clubs immediately.

On May 21, a Sunday, the Braves sent down a second scout, Hugh Wise, to watch Willie play a doubleheader, and the youngster struggled, with only one hit in eight at-bats. Wise feared that Mays might not hit big league pitching and concluded that he wasn't worth $7,500. Maughn argued that Wise had seen him play only one day, but Wise said he had seen enough. After a full year of scouting Mays, the Braves never made an offer.

Perini later lamented how myopic financial considerations cost him the greatest center fielder ever. But money wasn't the primary issue when teams, including the Braves, were paying tens of thousands of dollars for prospects. The issue was race. In 1950, the Braves fielded their first black player, Sam Jethroe, who was originally signed by the Brooklyn Dodgers but then sold to the Braves for $150,000. Jethroe, a fleet-footed center fielder, was a

---

*One of his teachers was Angelina Rice, whose daughter, Condoleezza, would be the secretary of state under President George W. Bush. When she first interviewed with President Bush, she impressed him with stories about her mother's experiences with Mays.

very good player—he would be the National League's Rookie of the Year—which might have encouraged the Braves to bring in more blacks, even those with questionable hitting skills. But bringing in two Negroes in one year could be seen as excessive. One at a time was sufficient. As Maughn ruefully noted in a 1965 interview, "They moved slower back then."

Two years later, the Braves did pay the Indianapolis Clowns $10,000 for Hank Aaron, who reached the majors in 1954. (The club had moved to Milwaukee in 1953.) Aaron spent twenty-one years with the team in Milwaukee and Atlanta, and—but for the blunders of his organization—could have been part of the greatest one-two punch in baseball history.

While Maughn had lost his man, he was still eager to help Mays. On June 17, 1950, he bumped into New York Giant scout Eddie Montague at an all-star high school game in Atlanta. Montague said he was going to Birmingham to evaluate Black Baron Alonzo Perry, a strapping 6-foot-3 first baseman. The Giants had already signed two black players, Monte Irvin and Hank Thompson, and were looking for more. "Listen," Maughn said, "you forget about Perry. Willie Mays is the one that you want."

According to Montague, Maughn never referred to the wunderkind by name, just as "a young Negro ballplayer . . . with a great arm." On Sunday, June 19, Montague and a fellow Giant scout, Bill Harris, reached Birmingham for a Black Baron doubleheader. As Montague later recounted, "I had no inkling of Willie Mays, but during batting and fielding practice, my eyes almost popped out of my head when I saw a young colored boy swing the bat with great speed and power, and with hands that had the quickness of a young Joe Louis throwing punches. I also saw his great arm during fielding practice, and during the games his speed and fielding ability showed up. . . . He lined a double off the right field wall, sent the left fielder back to the fence on a whistling drive, and then hammered a double into center. This was the greatest young ballplayer I had ever seen in my life."

During the game, the two scouts moved around the ballpark to watch Mays from different angles but saw most of the game from the roof, where Montague clocked him running to first base. "Four seconds is about the best you can expect from a right-handed batter," he later said. "Yet Willie was doing that and even faster. Only speedy lefties can get down to first under four seconds." Montague also met Tom Hayes and promptly asked him how much he wanted for his center fielder. Hayes said $15,000, half now and half when he reported, though he wanted to keep Mays for the balance of the season. After the game, Montague met Mays in the locker room, and all he saw "was muscles and a magnificent pair of shoulders." But the scout was also impressed by his "likeable attitude." He told Mays he would see him the following night in Tuscaloosa.

Jack Schwarz, the director of the Giants' farm system, was reading the newspaper at his home in Massapequa, New York, when the telephone rang. It was Harris from his hotel in Birmingham. "He told me he had seen enough of Perry to know he was not the man we wanted," Schwarz recalled. "But he thought the Black Barons had one player worth having, a nineteen-year-old kid named Mays—Willie Mays. Harris reported that Mays could hit to either field, that he could run, that he had a real good arm. As I listened, it added up to a routine description of a player who happens to strike a scout favorably. Nothing more, nothing less. Then Montague got on the phone. Now it was different. Montague fairly exploded. 'You've got to get this boy!' he shouted. 'He'll be in the big leagues in two years. Don't ask any questions. Just go get him.' That was the convincer. From then on, we went after Willie."

They had little time to waste. On June 2, the *Birmingham World* reported "persistent talk that scouts of the Boston Braves, Boston Red Sox, the Brooklyn Dodgers and the Cleveland Indians are hot on the trail of center fielder Willie Mays."

On the following night in Tuscaloosa, Montague arrived alone at the ballpark so early that "if it had not been for the groundskeeper, I would have been lonely." When the Black Barons got off their bus, he quietly approached Mays and asked to speak with him in private.

"Would you like to play professional baseball, Willie?"

"Yes, sir," Willie said.

"Would you like to play for the Giants?"

"Yes, sir."

The scout told him he would speak to Tom Hayes about his contract.

"What contract?" Willie asked. "Mr. Hayes doesn't own me." While Willie did sign a contract for his first season, he had not for the remaining two.

Montague said if that was the case, he would deal directly with him, and Willie gave him his phone number and address in Fairfield. Montague assumed he had to move fast, because he saw Brooklyn Dodger scout Ray Blades at the game in Tuscaloosa, in which Mays smoked several line drives and made a fine catch and throw.

The next morning, when Montague called, Willie said he'd have to deal with his aunt Sarah. She came to the phone, and the scout asked how much it would take to sign Willie. Sarah said $5,000. Montague said he had to touch base with his home office, then he'd be at their house that afternoon. He spoke again with Schwarz.

"If he's that good, go and get him," Schwarz said.

At the house, Willie introduced Montague to his aunt and Loretta. At 4 P.M., Cat arrived home from the mill, the contract was drawn up, and the whole crew proceeded to a notary to have the document signed and notarized. Cat signed for his underage son. According to Montague's later account, the bonus was actually for a thousand dollars less than what Sarah had requested—Montague talked her down to $4,000, plus a salary of $250 a month. The Giants also paid Tom Hayes $10,000, mainly to keep the team on good terms with him. That move didn't sit well with Cat. "Why should Mr. Hayes get anything?" he asked Montague. "I ain't signed no contract with Mr. Hayes; Willie ain't signed no contract with Mr. Hayes."

"Well, we don't want no trouble later," Montague responded. "He might come back and try to sue us."

Horace Stoneham, the Giants owner, sent Hayes a telegram on June 21, confirming the transaction though (like Maughn) misspelling the prospect's name: "Willie H. Mayes Jr."

Montague recalled Cat Mays "as a proud man that day when Willie signed his first contract." Loretta remembers that after the scout left, her mother wept. She would give Cat $250 and Willie $3,000, which he used for a new green Mercury and some clothes.

Willie felt gratitude and elation. He knew that organized baseball had accelerated the signings of top Negro players, and now, if he performed well with the Giants' minor league affiliates, he could play in the same league as his heroes—DiMaggio, Musial, Williams, and Jackie Robinson.

On one level, Mays's signing seemed to suggest how alert major league teams were to promising young Negro players. Mays had just turned nineteen and was barely out of high school. But the signing was actually a case study in baseball's halting efforts to integrate. Mays was not a hidden gem—he was the most charismatic star of the very league that was funneling its best young talent to the majors, with 1950 marking the third year out of four in which a black player (Jackie Robinson, Don Newcombe, and Sam Jethroe) had won the Rookie of the Year Award.

By 1950, five years had passed since the Dodgers had signed Jackie Robinson from the Kansas City Monarchs, but only four of sixteen teams in the major leagues had blacks on their rosters (the Dodgers, Indians, Giants, and Braves; the Browns had had three but had released them). Both the Giants and the Braves had approached Mays, but where were the other fourteen teams?

At least two other organizations had reports on Mays—the Dodgers and the Chicago White Sox. In the case of the Dodgers, both Robinson and Roy Campanella recommended Mays after they played against him in 1949 during a barnstorming tour through the South, but a scout named Wid Mathews watched Mays that year and concluded, "The kid can't hit a curveball." Nonetheless, another Brooklyn scout was back on the trail in 1950. The Dodgers certainly knew the immense value, on the field and at the gate, of developing dynamic Negro players. But they apparently passed on Mays because they already had three established African American stars (Robinson, Newcombe, and Campanella), they had two others meriting promotion, and they feared having too many blacks. Sportswriters speculated that "the magic number" for black players on any one team was five; exceeding that threshold increased the risk of a backlash from white fans. By 1955, Dick Young of the *Daily News,* noting the significant financial investment of baseball owners, opined that five blacks were not excessive but eight might be. This informal quota also applied to professional football, where teams restricted the number of black players to seven or fewer.

Bill Maughn, the Braves' scout, acknowledged that his team didn't sign Mays because it had just acquired Sam Jethroe from the Dodgers, and Branch Rickey, in discussing that sale, conceded the unspoken quota: "Ownership thought there was a surfeit of colored boys on the Brooklyn club."

The Boston Red Sox sent its scout, George Digby, to evaluate Mays, and Digby later said, "He was the greatest prospect I ever saw." But the Red Sox had just signed Piper Davis and would not sign a second; the team would be the last in the major leagues to integrate, in 1959.

Mays was a free agent for three weeks, between his graduation from high school and his signing with the Giants, and virtually all of Major League Baseball missed him. Bill Maughn knew why: "It was the color line at the time," he told *Look* magazine in 1955. "That explains how Willie was on the loose for a solid month. . . . The teams which had signed Negro players felt they had enough, for the time being, at least. Those who didn't have any were not interested at the time. Most of the scouts I told about Willie, after the Braves turned him down, were Southerners, who would be inclined to [look the other way]."

That was certainly the case with New York's third baseball team, the Yankees, who were determined to keep the squad white. In 1949, their general manager, George Weiss, heard about a young center fielder with the Birmingham Black Barons; his bosses notwithstanding, Weiss dispatched his part-time scout Bill "Wheels" McCorry to Alabama for a report. Though born in upstate New York, McCorry—according to Roger Kahn—"has the attitudes of a Southern Klansman, which he made little effort to conceal."

He reported that Willie Mays could run and throw but was not worth signing because "the boy can't hit a good curveball." The Yankees did not put a black player on its roster until Elston Howard, in 1955.*

The New York Giants were not deterred by race. They simply needed good players. As Charles "Chub" Feeney, the vice president of the Giants and a nephew of Horace Stoneham's, said, "Of course we knew segregation was wrong. My uncle knew it and I knew it, but pure idealists we were not. Competing in New York, against the Yankees and the Dodgers, the resource we needed most was talent. . . . In 1949, the Negro Leagues were the most logical place in the world to look for talent."

Still, the Giants were guilty of more subtle bigotry. On June 22, Eddie Montague wrote a letter to Jack Schwarz, in part to celebrate his own skills in outmaneuvering their other rivals as well as to offer an evaluation of Willie: "If Mays has any flaws in his ability it is in not knowing how to run and I would like to suggest that we employ a track coach to help him." This could be turned to the Giants' advantage. "If Jesse Owens or some other great negro runner is around the New York area I believe it would be a great publicity angle and worth the time and money to hire him." No track coach was ever needed for Willie Mays.

Montague also spoke highly of his ability to sign Mays for only $4,000 but noted that his true financial worth was higher. "In my opinion, Mays is a definite major league prospect and had he been a white boy I haven't any doubts but that he would have been a bonus ball player."

"Bonus ball players" were those who signed under the so-called bonus rule, which existed in various forms from 1947 to 1965. Its goal was to limit bidding wars that favored the wealthiest franchises. If a team signed a player above a certain threshold ($4,000 to $6,000, depending on the year), that "bonus baby" had to stay on the big league roster for the next two years. But if he wasn't ready for the big leagues, he would be deadweight on the bench and would have his development stymied—possibilities designed to limit outrageous bonuses in the first place.

Under this rule, bonuses were still paid, but the amounts varied significantly. In 1950, the Pirates paid a $100,000 bonus to a forgotten pitcher named Paul Pettit, who won one game in the majors. In 1954, Sandy Koufax's father, Irving, asked for a $14,000 bonus for his son, which he calculated as the cost of a four-year education. The Giants too were in the bonus game, though not profitably. In 1954, they gave $35,000 to infielder Joey Amalfitano, who spent two years on the bench before being sent to the

* Yankee manager Casey Stengel, after seeing Howard play, famously commented, "When I finally get a nigger, I get the only one that can't run."

minors for four years, and the Giants shoveled another $60,000 to pitcher Paul Giel, who after six years retired with a 5.39 ERA and an 11–9 lifetime record.

Black players were largely excluded from these quick-hit riches. The economists Anthony Pascal and Leonard Rapping found that in 1968, one out of five white major leaguers who had signed before 1959 had received bonuses greater than $20,000, but none of the thirty blacks playing in 1968 who had signed in the 1950s had received that inducement.

Mays says that Stoneham quietly gave him an extra $10,000. Stoneham never declared the amount—even his scouts didn't know—which would have triggered the bonus rule. But even $10,000 was a pittance compared to the sums given to other highly touted prospects. The Giants treated Mays no differently from the way any major league team would have treated him, but before he ever stepped on the field in organized baseball, his skin color had cost him tens of thousands of dollars, maybe a hundred thousand dollars (which, in 2010, would be about $895,000).

Mays knew nothing about the slight and remains grateful to an organization that took a chance on a nineteen-year-old kid and soon paid him at the highest levels of his profession. Whatever was denied him long ago doesn't bother him today. "I don't look at race that way," he says. "If I did, how could I have accomplished the things that I did? You can't go back sixty years."

Mays has another reason to feel good about his personal history: he was lucky to have absorbed the ethos of black baseball while still having a full career in the majors. He played in what was the final Negro League World Series in 1948, and he left Birmingham two years before Tom Hayes sold his team. Negro squads continued to play through the 1960s, but they were easily ignored in a decade when 23 percent of major league players were African American.

The Black Barons played until 1963, but most of the players, including Piper Davis, never made it to the majors. Still, their legacy survived. In June of 1950, their finest protégé boarded a train and headed north, taking with him his glove, some sandwiches, the wisdom of his mentors, and the dazzling spirit of the great Negro Leagues.

CHAPTER SEVEN

THE MINORS

Willie Mays was too nervous to eat. On the train ride out of Birmingham, he fumbled with the bag of sandwiches that Aunt Sarah had made, but mostly he stared out the window. It was June 23, 1950, a beautiful spring day, and the lush green countryside looked familiar and comforting. But it was now zipping past him, and he knew he would miss it—he already did. He stood up, walked from car to car, and wondered if he'd be leaving the mill town of his youth for good. His senior prom was that night, but Willie decided to skip it so he could make his first game. He tried to make amends with his girlfriend by lining up another escort— a friend to whom Willie gave clothes, money, and a car for the evening— and now Willie wondered what songs they would be playing. "Till I Waltz Again with You," perhaps, or "On Top of Old Smokey." The kids would be jitterbugging or holding each other close. Willie realized he no longer had time for that. He was now a full-time professional ballplayer.

Many years later, Mays said that his biggest thrill in baseball was signing his first contract with the Giants, but on the train out of Birmingham, he mostly felt fear and disbelief, tinged with amusement. The Giants were paying him good money for a chance to get to the big leagues. He would have played for free.

His new employer wasn't certain where to put him. The Giants' first choice was their Class A team, which was several rungs below the majors. But that squad was part of the Southern Association, which included the Birmingham Barons, and the Giants were not about to send their prize recruit into the heart of the Old Confederacy. Another option was Sioux City, Iowa, where its Class A affiliate played in the Western League, but that too was risky. Racial tensions had been simmering there since an American Indian had been buried in a cemetery for whites, and the Giants feared the arrival of a black baseball player could plunge that town into turmoil.

So Mays was sent to the Trenton Giants in the Class B Interstate League, which he considered mildly insulting—the Black Barons were far better than any team on that circuit. But Trenton was close to New York, so Hor-

ace Stoneham and other Giant executives could watch him, and most of
the teams were in small northeastern towns, such as Wilmington, Dela-
ware, and Lancaster, Pennsylvania.

That environment was presumably less hostile, but Mays would still be
the first black player in the league. His debut would be in Hagerstown,
Maryland, the league's only city south of the Mason-Dixon Line, a hub for
slave traders before the Civil War and a town that still honored its antebel-
lum past. Memorial Stadium, where Mays would play his first game, was
three blocks from Rose Hill Cemetery, where two thousand Confederate
soldiers were interred.

At the Hagerstown train station, Mays was picked up by the team's radio
announcer, who drove him to the stadium, and in the visitor's clubhouse,
he saw his uniform, with TRENTON inscribed across the chest and the
number 12 on the back. The game had already begun, so Mays watched
the rest of it from the dugout. That alone was significant. As the sports
columnist Frank Colley wrote in the *Daily Mail* the following morning:
"History was made last night as far as the color line is concerned when the
Trenton Giants placed a colored player in uniform and he sat out the last
two innings of the ball game on the bench."

Mays himself was unsettled. He had played baseball his entire life, but
never before had he been the only black person in the dugout or on the
field, nor had he been in a stadium populated almost entirely by white
people. That first night, the team's manager, Chick Genovese, greeted
Mays warmly and eased some of his concerns by saying that he would be
the squad's center fielder, but Mays's apprehension quickly returned.

After the game, the team bus drove Mays to the colored section of
Hagerstown and dropped him off at the Harmon Hotel on Jonathan Street.
A fine establishment that served the heavyweight champion Jack Johnson
and the jazz great Ella Fitzgerald, the Harmon still wasn't the Alexander
Hotel, where the rest of the Trenton Giants were staying.

Mays wasn't particular about hotels, but he had never been separated
from his teammates before. He knew about segregation, but his segregation had always been collective—with friends, relatives, or teammates,
who derived strength and pride from their unity. Now he was segregated
and alone.

Some of his teammates noticed his fears. Shortly after midnight, Mays
heard a knock on his window. Three players had climbed the fire escape
and were now entering his room. One of them, Bob Easterbrook, told him
they wanted to check up on him.

"Hey, man, I don't need no help here," Mays said.

Easterbrook said they were going to spend the night.

"I can handle it," Mays insisted.

The three players stayed and slept on the floor. At 6 A.M., they got up, climbed out the window, and returned to their hotel. Mays next saw them when the bus picked him up at 4 P.M. Nothing was said of the visit and, as far as Mays could tell, no one else knew about it. But on his first night in organized baseball, he slept soundly.

The incident made a lasting impression. Throughout his career, Mays often received special treatment because of his talent, but in this case he hadn't played a single inning when his teammates arrived. To ensure his safety, they risked their careers and even their own safety. Mays had learned from the Black Barons that your baseball team was your family, but these Giants had confirmed that the family circle included white players as well. Racial considerations were secondary. The team protected its own.

Mays needed that support for the impending storm. The next day, Genovese put him in the lineup, playing center field and batting sixth. When he walked out of the dugout, he heard someone shout, "Who's that nigger walking on the field!" A ten-year-old boy named Bob Miller later remembered hearing one fan yell, "Crapshooter!" while another one screamed, "Watermelon man!" The catcalls and epithets continued through the game. As Bob left the stadium, his father said, "They sure were tough on that young kid."

Mays ignored the taunts, which probably hurt him less than his performance: he went 0-for-3. He also took the collar in the next day's doubleheader—"I went 0-for-Maryland," he later said—and he worried that his poor showing reinforced the bigots' view that he was unfit for this league. He took some solace when the public address announcer asked the crowd to stop booing him.

The racial insults continued in other towns, and Mays wanted to respond. But Cat Mays kept tabs on his son by calling him on the phone, and he urged restraint. Willie recalls, "He knew I would fight very quickly. So he would always call and say, 'You gotta turn the other cheek.' I would say, 'I'm not gonna turn no other damn cheek.' And he would say, 'Nah, the only way you're gonna get ahead is to make sure you downplay it. We need you to play baseball. We need you to do things the right way, and the right way is to take whatever they have to dish out, and take it strong.'"

Mays's struggles at the plate continued as well. He made outs in his first twenty-two at-bats, but Genovese did not let him become too dispirited. The manager recognized that Mays was pressing, so he urged him to relax, to not overswing, to not worry about home runs; just make contact. The base hits would come.

His teammates rallied to his side even before Mays started hitting. They recognized that his natural gifts seemed to spill out of him like whiskey from a shaky tumbler. He was the team's fastest player, had the best arm, and made plays that no one had ever seen or even imagined. Against a Wilmington power hitter, he raced back to the 405-foot sign in dead center field, jumped, and caught the ball barehanded as it sailed over the fence. Regaining his balance, Mays threw the ball on a fly to home plate. As one Trenton infielder said, "I never knew a peg could come in so fast from the outfield. He could throw a ball 200 feet and make your hand sting."

Mays's skin color was not his only physical distinction. Without weight lifting or physical training, he appeared to have been carved from granite. First baseman Bob Myers told him that he had the largest forearms he'd ever seen. "They look like Popeye's," he said.

His teammates called him Junior, which his aunts had used at home, a name that easily attached to someone whose youth was matched by innocence. The high voice. The big smile. The determination to please. They all made him popular. During one game, Mays was decked by a high fastball. Thrown at many times in the Negro Leagues, he now glared at the pitcher, got to his feet, and resumed his batting stance, making it clear that he could not be intimidated. The next batter, right fielder Eric Rodin, sent a more explicit message. He bunted down the first base line with the intention of bowling over the pitcher when he tried to field the ball. It rolled foul, averting a collision, but both benches still emptied.

On another occasion, Giant catcher Len Matte told Mays that he would take care of any racial incidents on the field and that he, Willie, should not get involved. As the year wore on, the race baiting from fans and opposing players diminished until, according to Mays, "I just didn't hear it anymore."

Off the field, he lived alone in a boardinghouse in Trenton, but on the road, the Giants sent him a Hispanic roommate from the New York Cubans. The arrangement was contrived, and Mays disdained the newcomer as a showboat from the big city while he was just a country boy. When Mays overslept and missed the team bus, Genovese yelled at the roommate, who was gone in a month.

Mays was the first black player with whom most of the Trenton Giants had played, but if any of them had misgivings, his engaging demeanor dispelled them. On the bus, Genovese would nudge his players to sing songs, and Mays would start off with "Clarence the Clocker," and soon everyone would join in. In Mays's eyes, the bus rides were no different than those he had taken with the Black Barons, teeming with goodwill and camaraderie, young men who loved baseball and dreamed about making it to the big leagues. In 1950, white Americans across the country denied blacks equal treatment on buses, but on the Trenton Giant bus, Willie Mays received special treatment. In need of rest, he would pile the duffel bags in the back, lie down, and sleep.

Mays experimented in the field. During batting practice, he saw how close he could play in center while still being able to track deep flies. On ground balls, he realized that if high grass or soft ground slowed the ball, he could still reach hits in the gap while also snaring low line drives that would otherwise go for singles. For years, Mays would walk on the outfield grass before a game and throw a ball down to determine if the surface was fast or slow.

Mays thought he had already mastered baseball strategy, but Genovese, along with Trenton Giant general manager Bill McKechnie, expanded his education. Sitting on the bench before games or riding on the bus, the two men fired questions at Mays.

"One-and-two, hitter's weakness is high inside, where do you pitch him?"

"You're on second, one out, long fly to center, center fielder's arm is average. Do you tag up? If not, how far off do you lead?"

"Last of the ninth, score tied, your pitcher coming up, two out. Do you let him bat or do you pinch-hit for him?

Mays asked why they were asking him things that only a manager would have to worry about. McKechnie told him that someday, he could be a manager.

"Where?" Mays demanded. "Negro League someplace? Ain't gonna be no Negro Leagues anyhow, time you get through raiding 'em."

McKechnie said that even if he didn't become a manager, the more he understood about the game, the better he'd play it.

Still not convinced, Mays wanted to know why he had to answer questions about pitching—he'd certainly never be a pitcher.

"Because," McKechnie said, "the only way to be a smart hitter is to start thinking like a pitcher."

Mays's hitting continued to improve, more for average than home runs, as he drove balls to all parts of these small-town ballparks. His assists began to pile up as well. Each week Genovese sent the New York Giants increasingly glowing reports on Mays. One report said, "He's a major league prospect. Possesses strong arms and wrist, runs good, has good baseball instinct. Wants to learn. Should play AAA ball next year."

Horace Stoneham got the message. After watching the New York Giants play a day game in Philadelphia, he and several associates rented a car and drove to Trenton, where they watched Mays for the first time at Dunn Field. McKechnie tried to temper his expectations, saying, "He might be a little tight because you're here."

As Stoneham recalled, "Well, Willie got about two hits in the first few innings, and in the seventh he came up and hit a ball into a gas station that was across the street beyond the left field fence. That's how tight he was."

He played in eighty-one games for Trenton, a bit more than half a season. He had 306 at-bats and hit .353, which led the league, though he didn't win the batting title because he had too few plate appearances. He had twenty doubles, three triples, four home runs, and fifty-five RBIs. His home run total wasn't as high as he would have liked, but he assumed no one would complain. He also led the league in outfield assists, with seventeen.

He pushed himself every at-bat, fly ball, throw, and stolen base. He crashed into walls, covered the alleys, dove on the outfield grass. Combined with nerves and anxiety, it all wore him down. Near the end of the season, on a humid afternoon in Harrisburg, Pennsylvania, he collapsed from fatigue after a stretch of doubleheaders, requiring an ambulance. Mays was fine, but it was an odd spectacle—this nineteen-year-old kid, a paragon of physical strength, drained of all energy. He didn't know how to pace himself.

But one spell of exhaustion was a tiny cloud on an otherwise brilliant debut. He was leaving Trenton for a bigger stage.

Mays returned to Birmingham, where Piper Davis rounded up some players to compete against major leaguers on a barnstorming tour. The games allowed Mays to meet two black players with the New York Giants, Monte Irvin and Hank Thompson. More important, the major league team was managed by Jackie Robinson, who had watched Mays play with the Black Barons, but Mays had not seen Robinson before. His most significant impression on Mays had nothing to do with baseball. The barnstorming team included three white Dodgers—Ralph Branca, Gil Hodges, and Pee Wee Reese—which, Mays assumed, was the first time an integrated professional baseball team had ever taken the field in the South. That may not have been accurate, but it was certainly true in Birmingham. That Jackie Robinson led that team, in Mays's eyes, was further testament to his character and courage.

Mays's performance in Trenton confirmed the ecstatic scouting reports from Alabama, so the Giants figured he could bypass Class A and AA ball and go directly to the club's AAA team, the Minneapolis Millers in the American Association, just one step from the majors. Mays believed he could reach the big leagues after two seasons in the minors, even though many top prospects required twice that long. Jobs in the majors were tight. In 1950, there were about twenty-seven minor league jobs for every major league position. Thanks to expansion, by 1990 the ratio was six to one.

But Mays understood the challenge in 1950.

"You had to be better than good to make the majors," he said. "You had to be great."

Stoneham also believed that Mays needed a full year in Minneapolis, which seemed minimal seasoning for a player so young. Mays could develop into a brilliant player, but he had been out of high school less than a year when the Millers' spring training began in March 1951 in Sanford, Florida.

The city was segregated, so Mays spent much of his free time in a movie theater with a special entrance for blacks, who sat in a roped-off section in the balcony. Mays didn't care. His only concern was his play on the field, and the theater was no different from those in Birmingham. Finding solace in the darkness, he spent hours watching movies, often double features, preferring the Westerns.

Unlike the Trenton Giants, the Millers had two veteran players from the Negro Leagues, both of whom had joined the Millers the previous year. So Mays had roommates. One was pitcher David Barnhill, a strikeout artist whose wicked curveballs elicited complaints that he doctored or nicked the ball. The other was Ray Dandridge, one of the finest players in the history of black baseball.

Raised in the cornfields of Virginia, Dandridge was twenty when he joined the Detroit Stars in 1933. Short and bow-legged, he was a master glove man at third base who perfected a sidearm toss from his knees, which he used after a diving stop. In his eleven seasons in the Negro Leagues, he hit for what is believed to be a lifetime .355 average. Some baseball experts claim that Josh Gibson was his only superior and that no white third baseman was his equal. Unhappy with his meager pay in the Negro Leagues, he played a number of seasons in Mexico, where his hitting prowess gained him national fame.

In 1949, he returned to the United States and was managing the New York Cubans when the Giants offered him a contract to play for the Minneapolis Millers. With only one goal left—to play in the major leagues—Dandridge accepted. He was thirty-six, and in his rookie season in organized baseball, he hit .362, two points shy of the batting title. The following year he came back even stronger, winning the Most Valuable Player Award and leading his team to the pennant. In his third season, it appeared he might finally receive his call to the varsity when Giant third baseman Hank Thompson was spiked in the toe and had to sit out. But at the time of the injury, July 18, Dandridge himself was in the hospital for the removal of his appendix. So in the summer of 1951, the Giants installed a slumping outfielder named Bobby Thomson at third, where he stayed for the rest of the year. And Ray Dandridge never got his call to the big leagues.

During spring training, Dandridge recognized that Mays would not suffer the same fate. They lived in the same roominghouse, and Dandridge, only two years younger than Cat Mays, formed a paternal bond with the young player.

"You've got a great chance," Dandridge told him. "When I played in the black leagues, we were barnstorming most of the time. Sometimes I played three games in one day. We made about $35 a week and ate hamburger. You're going to eat steak and you're going to make a lot of money. You just keep it clean and be a good boy."

To reach the majors, Mays had to impress Leo Durocher, the combative baseball lifer who had been hired by the Giants three years earlier but had so far failed to bring home a pennant. The previous year, Durocher had seen Mays play in Harrisburg; he noted Mays's "torn shoes and worn spikes" but also remembered the raw ability. He wanted Mays to start with the Giants that spring, but Stoneham said no. The boy was too young and, besides, he would likely be drafted that year by the army. Durocher relented but had the Millers schedule an exhibition game so he could get a good look at the prospect.

The game occurred early in March, a special 9 A.M. contest in Sanford between the Millers and Ottawa, another Giant farm club. Durocher was accompanied by Stoneham and Carl Hubbell, the Hall of Fame screwball pitcher who was responsible for player personnel. (The Giants had moved their spring training to Phoenix in 1947 but held camp in St. Petersburg, Florida, in 1951, then returned to Phoenix.)

"Hey, kid, what are you going to show me today?" Durocher asked Mays before the game. "I've got quite a report on you from Trenton, kid. This guy Chick Genovese thinks you're the greatest he ever saw."

"Oh, really. What'd the report say?"

"It says that your hat keeps flying off." Durocher laughed. He took his seat in the bleachers amid a scattering of fans puzzled by the early start.

Mays didn't know that the game had been called specifically for Durocher to watch him, but he was eager to impress. He began the game in left field but was then moved to center. Durocher wanted to see him run, and he did not disappoint.

As Durocher recounted years later: "I could tell you every move Mays made that day. He made a couple of great catches in the outfield. He threw a guy out trying to go from first to third on a base hit into left center. A shot. Threw another guy out at the plate late in the game. A shot. Hit a bullet into right center for two his first time. Struck out on a sidearm curve. Popped up. The last time he came up, Red Hardy, a good veteran pitcher, tried to get him with the sidearm curve again, and Mays hit it over the clubhouse in left field, about 370 feet away. 'Not ready, huh?' I said. 'I want him.' "

Durocher decided he had seen enough after seven innings, so he, Stoneham, and Hubbell left without acknowledging Mays. The young player was rattled by their abrupt departure. He wondered if he had done something—thrown to a wrong base, missed a cutoff man, failed to take an extra base. "When the game was over, I just sat in front of my locker, so tired I couldn't even shake my head," he later said. "I felt like a raw rookie who had just flunked his only chance."

Mays did not see Durocher again that spring and soon refocused his efforts on making the Millers. They were managed by Tommy Heath, a rotund former catcher who knew he would not have Mays for long. One morning, Heath called him into his office and said, "Willie, we're taking you with us to Minneapolis, but I kind of have the feeling that you're not going to spend the whole summer with us. I think it's only a matter of time before the Giants call you up."

The words lifted Mays's spirits, and he continued to have a terrific spring training, prompting a sportswriter from Minneapolis to write several glowing stories about him. The reporter's editor asked him to tone down the praise, but the writer said, "I have been toning it down." Expectations were high when Mays reached Minneapolis.

He rented a room on Fourth Avenue South, right across the street from Dandridge and Barnhill. Their presence removed the isolation he had experienced in Trenton and eased the transition on the ball field. On Opening Day, he woke up, looked outside, and saw snow. He had only seen it once before and, certain the game would be canceled, went back to sleep until the telephone rang a few hours later.

"Why aren't you here?" Heath demanded.

"It was snowing."

"It's stopped now, and we're about to start the game."

"But I never played in snow before."

Heath explained that a helicopter was used to blow the snow off the field. Mays scrambled to dress and, as he headed toward Nicollet Park, wondered if Piper Davis ever had to play in snow.

The conditions didn't faze him. In the first inning of the first game, Mays, wearing number 28, made a fine running catch near the flagpole in deep center, about four hundred feet away. Batting third, he singled in his first plate appearance and later hit a home run. The next day, the *Minneapolis Tribune* published photographs of him and the snow. He was an instant sensation, fulfilling the preseason hype and making plays that fans would talk about for years.

There was, for example, the game on May 7 against the Louisville Colonels, in which a bruising hitter named Taft Wright drove a ball over Mays's head. But Mays, according to game reports, "literally climbed the right-center field wall to pick off Taft Wright's jet drive." Mays later said it looked as though the ball was going to hit high on the fence, so he had to "improvise" a way to catch it. "I just caught my spikes in the wall, and I sort of walked up the wall. How high, I couldn't estimate, but I caught the ball and threw it back in."

The runner on second base thought the ball was a hit and didn't stop until after he crossed home plate and reached the dugout. Wright, meanwhile, cruised into second base and was wiping his hands, kicking the dirt, and preparing to take his lead when the umpire told him the bad news.

"You're out," he said.

"No, I'm not," Wright said. "He didn't catch that."

When he continued to protest, his manager had to come out and escort him off the field. He refused to believe Mays had caught the ball. Thirty years later, a Minneapolis sportswriter who'd been covering the game bumped into Wright in Orlando, Florida, and reminded him of the play. "That little son of a bitch never did catch the ball," Wright said. "How could he catch that?"

In another game, at Columbus, the opposing team had the bases loaded and no one out in the bottom of the ninth. The Miller outfielders had to play shallow, and the hitter lined the ball over Mays's head. He raced back, jumped, and caught the ball facing slightly away from home plate. He whirled around and fired a bullet to home. The runner barely beat the throw, but after the game the Millers' catcher, Jake Hurley, told Mays, "Willie, you're losing your control. That pitch was on the outside corner. If you had put it on the inside corner, we would have had him."

Mays displayed his power at Borchert Field in Milwaukee. He hit a ball so hard that it blew a hole in the outfield fence; rather than repair it, the grounds crew drew a white circle around it.

After a road trip early in the season, the Millers returned home, and in sixteen games, Mays went 38-for-63 (.603 average). He also celebrated his birthday on May 6. He was now twenty years old. His teammates chided him about his high voice, which was barely audible when he got excited. But at the plate or in the field, his nerves left him and his confidence rose.

Opposing pitchers threw at him, just as they had when he was with Trenton. Mays didn't believe the brushbacks were racially motivated. Rather, he played in an era when intimidating hitters—by moving them off the plate, knocking them down, or drilling them—was a cornerstone of pitching, particularly against a young player racking up hits. He had confronted the same threatening tactics as a Black Baron and, even though batting helmets were not yet worn, insisted that knock-down pitches didn't bother him. He thought he was quick enough to dodge them, and he usually was.

But in Minneapolis, as in Trenton, the tight pitches gave his teammates a chance to show their support. When a tall Louisville pitcher winged a fastball past Mays's head, Heath sprinted out of the dugout, stopped at the foul line, and yelled, "If you come close to him again, I'll meet you right here."

Mays was moved by his manager's response and believed Heath would go to any length to protect him. Heath would have protected any of his players, but he also recognized Mays's unique value to the Giants. "He's as good, at this stage, as any young prospect I ever saw," Heath said. "In fact, I'll go out on a limb and say he's the best I ever had anything to do with. . . . What do you look for in a player? You look for a good eye, speed, a good arm, baseball sense. He has 'em all."

The fans noticed, not just in Minneapolis, but also in St. Paul, which had its own team in the American Association. Before a game at Lexington Park, more than five thousand fans showed up just to watch Mays in fielding drills, and, according to the *Pittsburgh Courier*, "he drew a round of applause seldom accorded to any player in the circuit. . . . When a Minneapolis player, always regarded as a deep-rooted enemy, can draw more cheers than the most popular St. Paul player, then he's pretty good."

The local media swooned as well. One sportswriter wrote: "Many veteran observers feel he may well become the greatest player his race has yet produced." The *Minneapolis Tribune* splashed an outsized tribute to Mays across six columns. The headline was SUCH A ONE IS WILLIE, and the newspaper used drawings from actual photographs that depicted Mays as a modern superhero. A full-body-length drawing showed him swinging a long bat, his massive forearms rippling with muscles. Another drawing depicted him holding a bat with his shirt off, his perfectly cut torso and chiseled biceps defying the human form. Read the caption: "big hands . . . sinewy arms . . . pug nose . . ." A picture was also drawn of Mays climbing the outfield wall, reaching up to catch the ball, saying: "Ah got high aims."

The presentation foreshadowed Mays's coverage in New York. Both his skills and his body were otherworldly, beyond compare with those of mortals, but both his youth and his race led to subtle condescension. Even the use of "Willie" in the headline and the story was telling. Athletes were usually referred to by their last names, and many blacks, then and now, rightfully interpret the inappropriate use of their first name as a sign of disrespect. (White masters did not give slaves last names.) It's unlikely that anyone in Minneapolis would have seen the *Tribune*'s use of "Willie" as disrespectful—Mays certainly didn't—but it reinforced his childlike aura, which bigots could easily stereotype.

With Mays no longer on the East Coast, Stoneham couldn't follow his development directly, so he dispatched a veteran scout, Hank DeBerry, to watch him play. A scout is cautious by nature. If he raves about a player who never pans out, his job could also be on the line, so most evaluations are tempered and qualified. But DeBerry held little in reserve when he filed his report on Mays:

> Sensational. Is the outstanding player on the Minneapolis club and prob-ably in all the minor leagues for that matter. He is now on one of the best hitting streaks imaginable. Hits all pitches and hits to all fields. Hits the ball where it is pitched as good as any player seen in many days. Everything he does is sensational. He has made the most spectacular catches. Runs and throws with the best of them. Naturally, he has some faults, some of which are: charges low-hit balls too much, runs a bit with his head down. There may have been a few times when his manager needed a rope. When he starts somewhere, he means to get there, hell bent for election. Slides hard, plays hard. He is sensational and just about as popular with local fans as he can be—a real favorite. The Louisville pitchers knocked him down plenty, but it seemed to have no effect on him at all. This player is the best prospect in America. It was a banner day for the Giants when this boy was signed!

Sadly, DeBerry never knew how right he was. On September 10, 1951, he died of a heart attack. As Roger Kahn wrote: "I like to think that before he died, when he gazed at Willie Mays, Hank DeBerry saw his promised land."

After thirty-five games, Mays was hitting .477, almost a hundred points higher than anyone in AAA ball. He had eight home runs, thirty RBIs, and eight stolen bases, and he was riding a sixteen-game hitting streak, in which he had a .569 average. Louisville's efforts to intimidate him didn't pay off—he hit .563 against the Colonels in seven games. He believed the Millers had a good shot at the pennant, and he had a girlfriend in Min-neapolis as well. The Giants were struggling, he knew, but the last thing on his mind was getting a call to New York. With or without snow, Minneapolis was just fine.

But his torrid hitting was noticed in New York. As Tom Sheehan, the Giants' chief scout, recalled: "We pick up the papers one week and say, 'Hey, Willie's hitting .300.' Next week, we look and it's .350. Another week, and it's .400. Finally, holy mackerel, Willie's up to .477, which has to mean he's going at something like a .600 clip. . . . So he's got to come to New York."

The Millers traveled to Sioux City, Iowa, for an exhibition game, and on their day off Mays went to the movies. As was his custom, he went alone. Even with friends on the team, he looked forward to time by himself. Perhaps it was all the nervous energy he brought with him to the field, the high expectations he placed on himself, or the pressure to succeed that drove him from his earliest days. He tired easily, but the isolation renewed him, the movies allowing him to escape in a way that cleared his mind and relaxed his body. He always enjoyed films with surprise endings, but on this spring day in 1951, he got one like no other.

Midway through the movie, the projector stopped, the lights came on, and a man appeared onstage to make an announcement: "If Willie Mays is in the audience, would he please report immediately to his manager at the hotel."

Mays's first thought was that something had happened to his father or Aunt Sarah, or maybe to someone else at home. He rushed back to the hotel and headed straight for Heath's room.

Heath had sought out Mays after receiving a call from Durocher, who told him that Stoneham had granted him his wish. The Giants were calling up Mays.

"You just broke my heart," Heath had told Durocher, "but I don't blame you. If this boy isn't as good a ballplayer as there is in the country, we might as well all pack up."

Now Mays knocked on his door and stepped inside. "What's up, Skip?"

"Guess what?" Heath said. "I just got off the phone with New York. Let me be the first to congratulate you."

"What for?"

"The Giants want you right away."

"Who says so?"

"Leo himself."

Mays was dumbstruck. Then petrified. He wasn't ready to go.

"Call him back," he pleaded.

"What for?"

"Tell him I don't want to go to New York. I'm happy here, and we got a good chance to win the pennant."

Now Heath was stunned. He tried to talk sense into him. "You have a chance to go to the big leagues. It's something you always wanted. It's something every kid always wanted."

"I know," Mays said. "It's just something that I'm not ready for."

Heath wasn't about to call Durocher, who had a short fuse in the best of circumstances. "You better talk to Leo yourself," he said, and he placed a call to New York.

"Leo, I got Willie here, and he's got something to tell you."

Mays heard a loud voice on the other end of the phone—"Tell me what!"—as Heath handed him the receiver.

Mays took a deep breath. "I'm not coming," he said.

Mays braced himself for a rebuke, but he could not have anticipated the volcanic eruption that followed. "What the hell do you mean you're not coming!" A minute-long tirade followed, with the most creative use of profanities Mays had ever heard, the gist of which was that the Giants had signed him for this purpose and he was in no position to refuse.

Mays held his ground, admitting that he was scared and insisting that he wasn't ready for the majors. He said he couldn't hit big league pitching.

"What are you hitting now?" Durocher asked.

"Four-seventy-seven," Mays said.

"Well," Durocher said, "do you think you could hit two-fucking-fifty-five for me?"

"Sure," Mays said, "I think so."

"Well," Durocher said, his voice rising again, "I could tell you my troubles with the whole fucking ballclub, but the Giants don't have enough money to pay for how long the goddamn phone call would take if I took the time. So get up here! We're playing in Philadelphia, and I want you there." He hung up.

Mays handed the phone back to Heath, saying, "It looks like I'm going to Philadelphia." He was on a United Airlines flight to New York that night. Heath called Tom Sheehan, the scout, and said, "Tom, you'll think I'm crazy, but this is the only guy I ever saw who can bat .400."

Mays was indeed scared that he couldn't hit major league pitching, but his fears were heightened by the inflated expectations of others. "I didn't want to go because I knew there'd be more pressure on me, joining a team that was going bad," he later said. "The Giants were in a losing streak, and they'd be looking to me."

Mays's departure was a crushing blow to the Minneapolis baseball fans, many of whom had been waiting for the warm weather to see him play. They became members of the I Didn't See Him Club. Mays's loss hurt the entire league. An official with the Milwaukee team estimated that it cost the American Association $250,000 in gate receipts.

Stoneham recognized the disappointment in Minneapolis, so he bought a four-column ad in the Sunday *Minneapolis Tribune*:

> We feel that the Minneapolis baseball fans, who have so enthusiasti-cally supported the Minneapolis club, are entitled to an explanation for the player deal that on Friday transferred Outfielder Willie Mays from the Millers to the New York Giants. We appreciate his worth to the Millers, but in all fairness, Mays himself must be a factor in these considerations. On the record of performance since the American Association season started, Mays is entitled to his promotion and the chance to prove that he can play major league baseball. The New York Giants will continue in our efforts to provide Minneapolis with a winning team.

The announcement was disingenuous. Yes, Mays had had an extraordi-nary six weeks, but he had played in only 116 games in organized baseball, less than a full year of minor league experience. Stoneham believed that a full season in Minneapolis would have served Mays best, but he was des-perate to revive his sagging franchise. The unusual nature of Stoneham's letter—after all, who had ever heard of a baseball owner justifying a per-sonnel move to a minor league city—won him high praise. As the *Tribune* said in an editorial: "That Stoneham letter quite frankly sent our imagina-tions reeling. We have not witnessed such a tender observance of the ame-nities since Alphonse first bowed to Gaston in the comic strips."

Mays's promotion carried some bitter irony. At the time, the Giants had four black players, and to make room for Mays they cut one of the four—Artie Wilson, the former Black Baron shortstop who had been his teammate in Birmingham. Wilson had finally made it to the majors with the Giants in 1951, but he played sparingly and was just 4-for-22 at the plate. Some saw his demotion as enforcing the unofficial quota for blacks on a single baseball team. Others believed that his skills were limited: he couldn't pull the ball to right field, allowing opponents to stack the left side with defenders. Age was also a factor. At thirty-one, Wilson had plenty of baseball left, but his best days were behind him. In later interviews, Wil-son himself said that he urged Durocher to call up Mays and maintained that he would rather play in the Pacific Coast League than sit on the bench in the majors. He played in the PCL for ten more seasons.

Ray Dandridge was not that forgiving. When he entered the Millers' clubhouse in Sioux City, he was told that Mays had left for New York. Later he recalled: "I had to go pack his stuff and send it to him. I felt glad for him. I said, 'Maybe I'll be next.'"

But with Thomson soon to be installed at third, Dandridge was never summoned, despite tearing up the league for his third straight season, hitting .338 for the year. He played in organized baseball for three more seasons.

That some sort of racial quota kept so talented a player from reaching the Giants is clear. If the roles of Dandridge and Mays had been reversed—if Mays had been the established veteran in 1951 and Dandridge the thrilling young phenom—Dandridge would have been promoted. One was lucky, one wasn't. Mays himself was too young to appreciate the disappointments around him, even when they involved men like Dandridge. His mind was teeming with his next challenge. Dandridge, for his part, did not resent Mays's success. In the coming years, he spoke with pride of the boy he briefly tutored in the minors.

Dandridge earned some vindication when he was elected to the Hall of Fame in 1987, and he probably understood that Stoneham was one of the more progressive owners of his era in the signing of black players. But he never forgave him. In the early 1970s, he and Monte Irvin saw Stoneham at an event in San Francisco. Dandridge approached him.

"You know," he said, "I really don't like you, because if I could have played in just one game in the majors, my career would have been complete."

Stoneham looked sheepish. "Yeah," he said. "I made a mistake."

CHAPTER EIGHT

THE SAVIOR ARRIVES

The Giants could have eased Willie Mays into the spotlight, managed the public's expectations, and given the youngest black player ever to reach the major leagues time to adjust. Instead, on May 24, 1951, the Giants held a press conference and distributed a news release announcing the purchase of Mays's contract from Minneapolis. "No minor league player in a generation," the Giants said, "has created so great a stir as Mays has in Minneapolis." Leo Durocher regaled reporters as well as his own players with stories about this young marvel he had seen in spring training. The manager also announced that the team's talented center fielder, Bobby Thomson, would move to left field, which displeased Thomson and surprised reporters. As the *New York Daily Mirror* wrote on May 25, "Amazin' Willie Mays, who apparently does nothing short of amazing, wrote another amazing page into his short amazing career yesterday. . . . Today he is a Giant. Not only that, he's the regular center fielder, shoving Bobby Thomson, the best CF in the National League, to left field for tonight's game in Philadelphia. It's amazin'."

The hype was all the more surprising in light of the Giants' dismal track record with highly touted rookies. In 1940, the team touted Johnny Rucker as "the new Ty Cobb" (both came from Georgia), gave him a hysterical nickname ("the Crabapple Comet," after his hometown), and saw him retire after six mediocre years. More recently there was Clint Hartung. A 6-foot-5, 220-pound greyhound, he was twenty-four years old when he joined the Giants in spring training of 1947. Reportedly, he could hit a ball 700 feet and had a bazooka for an arm, which could be deployed in the outfield or on the mound. His nickname—"the Hondo Hurricane," in honor of his hometown in Texas—evoked a force of nature. Reporters anointed him the second coming of Babe Ruth. But Hartung fizzled, both as a pitcher (29–29 over four years, with a 5.02 ERA) and a position player. By 1951, he hung on as a utility outfielder, retiring the following year with a career batting average of .238.

Now here was Willie Mays, promoted with the same gusto that intensi-

81

fied the pressures on young Hartung. Skepticism was understandable. The
New York Daily Mirror columnist Dan Parker, using the alliterative style
favored by sportswriters of the day, asked, "Will Willie Mays rescue the
Giants from the daze they've been in for days and days? Mays may merely
lead them into the maze, as other Spring phenoms have in bygone days."

The Giants, however, had good reason to herald their new find. The
team, once part of baseball royalty, had been mediocre, or worse, for
more than a decade. In New York's baseball pantheon, they played a dull
third fiddle to the implacable, regal Yankees and the boisterous, pioneering Dodgers. Those teams had flourished over the past decade while the
Giants hadn't won a Series in eighteen years or a pennant in fourteen, the
worst drought in club history. The organization was also being squeezed
financially by an old, poorly located ballpark and a declining fan base. The
Giants needed more than a center fielder. They needed a headliner, a savior, someone who would restore the glory of a dynasty.

Despite their recent woes, the Giants were still the most successful team
in the modern history of the National League. Founded in 1883, the club
was first known as the New Yorks and played their games on a polo field
on the corner of Fifth Avenue and 110th Street. Two years later, their manager Jim Mutrie, known for his ever-present stovepipe hat, leaped to his
feet during a rally and screamed, "My big fellows! My giants!" The club's
nickname was born. In 1902, the Giants hired the man whose temper,
arrogance, and savvy would define them for the next three decades. John
McGraw was a stout, red-faced Irishman who fought umpires, cursed
players (his and anyone else's), and was called "Little Napoleon" for his
authoritarian rule, but his judge of talent and burning desire helped him
win 2,763 games, making him to this day the major league's second winningest manager (behind Connie Mack and ahead of Tony La Russa).
McGraw also cut a distinctive image off the field, his friendships with politicians, judges, and actors raising his own swaggering profile. "McGraw's
Giants," as they were called, had the game's most dazzling idol. Christy
Mathewson was an apollonian figure who never drank or cursed, wore
a cape when he entered the field at the Polo Grounds, and, beginning in
1903, won at least twenty games in twelve consecutive years.

The Giants won six pennants between 1904 and 1917, plus the World
Series in 1905. They were no less powerful in the early 1920s—four consecutive pennants and two World Series championships—while fielding a trio of future Hall of Famers: Bill Terry, the dour, slick-fielding first
baseman whose lifetime batting average was .341; Mel Ott, the gentle, left-
handed slugger whose quirky batting style—lifting his front foot com-

pletely off the ground before swinging—helped him win the National League home run title six times; and Carl Hubbell, the wiry screwball specialist who posted five consecutive twenty-game seasons.

But for all their star power, the Giants in the 1920s and '30s were eclipsed by the Yankees—more specifically, by Babe Ruth, whose prodigious home runs and unrestrained personality brought his team their first championships, redefined the game, and stirred the public's imagination like no athlete in history. By 1932, McGraw had gone eight years without a pennant; exhausted and frustrated, he retired from the game and died two years later. So great was his memory, however, that twenty years after his death, his widow was still receiving requests for his autograph, which she fulfilled by sending his canceled checks.

The Giants' next manager was Terry, who would lead the team to one more stretch of greatness—three pennants in five years and one World Series. But the decline came swiftly. Even when McGraw's Giants didn't win pennants, they were almost always competitive. But no more. They finished fifth in 1939 and would be in the bottom half of the National League in eight out of the next ten years. The team, according to the Giant loyalist Roger Angell, had entered the long "Valley of the Shadow."

The troubles coincided with a change in the club's ownership. The Giants were a family business, acquired for $1 million in 1919 by Charles Stoneham, a freewheeling financial wizard, gambler, and sportsman who had dodged various Wall Street scandals (twice indicted, never convicted) to amass his fortune. But after the stock market crash of 1929, the Giants proved to be his most valuable asset. When he died in 1936, his son, Horace, became the principal owner at the age of thirty-two.

Horace saw his first Giants game when he was six and was fifteen when his father bought the team. "Dad came home one night," he recalled. "Mom and I were sitting there and I remember just what he said. 'Maybe we're gonna have a ballclub.' It was quite a moment." After home games, John McGraw came to their house and talked baseball for hours with the elder Stoneham. His son listened intently. A self-described poor student, Horace dabbled at three prep schools and briefly attended Fordham College, then his father sent him to California to work underground in some copper mines he owned. Horace was interested in engineering but didn't have the grades for admission to the right colleges. So he returned home, doing the one thing he knew he loved—working for the Giants. Toiling in the front office, he had a front-row seat for McGraw's finest teams, and when Charles Stoneham died, Horace not only assumed his father's desk but also his favorite perch to watch the games in the Polo Grounds: from the window in the clubhouse, deep in center field, 505 feet from home plate.

It was the perfect lair for the shy, stocky owner, who was rarely seen in the clubhouse, granted few interviews, and had thin skin. "I always liked it better up there," he said. "I don't like having people give me hell in the stands." Seclusion also allowed him to generously imbibe with friends, relatives, and colleagues, who would sometimes have difficulty leaving the office until the Scotch bottles were empty. Stoneham's drinking buddies included players, such as Giant left fielder Dusty Rhodes, who described himself as "Horace Stoneham's bartender. . . . We used to get loaded all the time." Later, Stoneham's bouts of public intoxication were a source of embarrassment, but in his early years as owner, alcohol was not a problem. What enraged fans was the Giants' miserable play, and many blamed young Stoneham, whose most conspicuous qualification for the job was his last name.

On one point, the owner was rightfully criticized. Stoneham had a weakness for the home run, believing a team of sluggers had the best chance of winning while also creating the most excitement. He was not the only one to hold that view in an era still dominated by Ruth's accomplishments, but Stoneham learned the limits of the long ball in 1947. Featuring mastodons like Johnny Mize, Willard Marshall, and Walker Cooper, the Giants hit a major league record 221 home runs and led the league in runs scored and slugging percentage—and finished fourth. No one stole more than seven bases. They were slow, one-dimensional, and uninspired.

The following year, the desperate Stoneham went to his bitter adversary, the Brooklyn Dodgers, and enlisted the one man whom Giant fans viewed as the antichrist of baseball. His decision shaped, and maybe even saved, Willie Mays's career.

For many years, the rivalry between the Dodgers and the Giants was based more on proximity than parity. While the Giants racked up victories and pennants, the Brooklyn team amassed losses and name changes—from the Trolley Dodgers to the Dodgers to the Robins and back to the Dodgers. They were best known, however, as "dem bums." They would win only two pennants between 1901 and 1940 and would not win a World Series until 1955. In the 1930s, when the Giant manager Bill Terry was asked about the Dodgers, he said, "Are they still in the league?"

Even when the teams weren't competitive, some tensions were inevitable. The only two teams in the same city in the same league, they played each other twenty-two times a year, battling so often that resentments always lingered. Their respective ballparks highlighted their contrasting images. While the Polo Grounds was a quiet, stately cathedral for baseball purists who had been raised on the stratagems of John McGraw, Ebbets

Field was a neighborhood gem that befit the team's underdog image, a raucous carnival whose stands featured musicians blaring their horns, a woman ringing her cowbell, and an organist who once played "Three Blind Mice" when the umpires appeared.

The rivalry did not assume its full venomous zeal until 1939, when the Dodgers appointed Leo Durocher their player-manager. One of the most colorful and polarizing figures of the era, he was a human spear of a man who would rejuvenate the franchise and, more than anyone else, escalate hostilities between the teams.

Durocher certainly knew how to win, having played for two of the most storied teams in baseball history, the Murderers' Row Yankees in the late 1920s and the St. Louis Cardinals' Gashouse Gang in the 1930s. A light-hitting, 5-foot-9 shortstop, he had neither the skill nor strength to survive on ability alone. He was a scrapper who got by on good speed, an excellent glove, and sharp spikes; he claimed he'd trip his mother rounding third base if it would help him win a game. (He allowed that he would pick up poor mom and brush her off.) Durocher's most distinctive asset may have been his brassy voice, which he used mercilessly to berate umpires, heckle opponents, and urge his pitchers to harm opposing hitters: "Stick it in his fucking ear!" he would yell from shortstop. At a time of lyrical nick-names—the Wild Horse of Osage, the Sultan of Swat—Durocher's was simply the Lip, from which obscenities constantly roared.

He famously directed his savage tongue at Mel Ott, the beloved Giant known for his perpetual geniality. After retiring as the National League's all-time home run hitter, Ott was hired as the Giants' manager, and his team once hit five home runs in a game against the Dodgers. The follow-ing day during batting practice, the broadcaster Red Barber approached Durocher.

"Those were real nice home runs," he said.

"Oh, come on!" Durocher yelled. "They were pop flies!"

"Now, Leo, be a nice guy. Be a nice guy and admit they were real nice home runs."

"Nice guy?" Durocher sneered. "Who wants to be a nice guy? Look over there at the Giant bench. Where would you find a nicer guy than Mel Ott? And where is he? In eighth place."

The quip, recast as "Nice guys finish last," entered the lexicon.

Durocher could be an affable rogue and a rough-hewn charmer, but no one would ever mistake him for a nice guy. In high school in West Spring-field, Massachusetts, he whacked his science teacher across the back with the metal pole used to raise the windows, effectively ending his education and costing him a baseball scholarship to Holy Cross. As a Yankee, he feuded bitterly with Babe Ruth, who accused Durocher of stealing his money. As the Dodger manager (he stopped playing in 1945), he instigated beanball wars, triggered fights on the field, launched verbal assaults, and made, according to one writer, "a science out of dirty play." Durocher himself said his first rule was, "Don't clutter your brain with ethics." And: "Good sportsmanship is so much sheep dip. Good sports get that way because they have so much practice losing."

Durocher was despised by many sportswriters, who respected his baseball acumen but loathed his ego and arrogance. Dick Young, the abrasive *Daily News* columnist, prepared a young reporter for his first meeting with Durocher:

"Figure, you and Durocher are shipwrecked and you both end up on this little raft with sharks swimming all around. Leo slips into the water. A shark closes in. You dive in and pull him out. But while you're rescuing him, the shark comes up and takes your right leg. You bleed like hell, but somehow you survive. The next day, you and Durocher start even."

Initially, Stoneham belittled Durocher's appointment to the Dodgers. "If Durocher keeps them hustling," he told the *Brooklyn Eagle,* "I feel they have a great chance for sixth place." But the turnaround came quickly. Before 1939, the Bums had finished in the top half of the league only twice in the previous eight years. But in their third year under Durocher, they won their first pennant in twenty-one years and would finish in the league's top half in eight of nine years. He played aggressive, daring baseball—double steals, squeezing with two strikes, pinch-hitting on a hunch; there was nothing he wouldn't try. And the Giants hated him. During that period, the Dodgers embarrassed the hapless descendants of McGraw and Mathewson, winning 118 out of 187 games, with two ties. The Lip had the last laugh.

Off the field was another story. Durocher's love of pool halls, gambling joints, short skirts, and nightclubs guaranteed controversy. An altar boy who was raised in a neighborhood of poor Catholics, he seemed determined to leave behind his material deprivation and his faith. He favored fast cars, monogrammed shirts, hand-painted ties, and expensive cologne, a true dandy who bragged so readily about his sexual conquests that Roger Kahn said he was practically guilty of "public fornication." He lost the right to receive communion and have his confession heard, but he said he didn't give a damn. At various times, he was accused of assaulting a fan, beating his wife, impregnating a young woman, swindling players, and even throwing games for money. None of the charges stuck, but scarred by intractable debts, bounced checks, and stormy marriages, he ran afoul of creditors, ministers, and judges, leaving Branch Rickey to observe: "Leo has an infinite capacity for going into a bad situation and making it worse."

To which Durocher responded: "Carve it on my gravestone, Branch. I have to admit it's sometimes true."

Durocher's personal life took an improbable turn when he courted the actress Laraine Day, whose devout Mormonism and rectitude on the screen presented a bizarre contrast with her flamboyant suitor. His apartment, to take one example, did not impress her: it included a bar built like a dugout, trimmed with autographed baseballs, the tops of stools made of catchers' mitts, the legs baseball bats, the floor covered with linoleum in the pattern of a baseball diamond. Day despised baseball. "I happened to be one of the heretics who had never seen a regularly scheduled baseball game," she said, "never read a sports page, and had a good hearty disdain for the little men who made such a fuss over it."

Her romance with Durocher had another problem. Inconveniently, she was married, and her husband publicly accused Durocher of seducing his wife. Day's affection for the manager had some rationale. Durocher had a soft spot for kids, and he showed genuine warmth toward Day's two young adopted children. Day divorced her husband in January of 1947 and, one day later, married Durocher in Mexico. As legal authorities tried to determine if they were man and wife, the Catholic Youth Organization censured Durocher for "undermining the moral training of Brooklyn's Roman Catholic youth by his conduct both on and off the baseball diamond."

Ironically, the controversy coincided with Durocher's finest moment in professional baseball. For all his personal faults, he judged players on their merit, not on their backgrounds or reputation or their race. The color he cared about was green: if a player could help his team win and put more money in his pocket, he would embrace him. Durocher's principles were tested during spring training of 1947, when the Dodgers were in Panama for some exhibition games. Jackie Robinson had not yet been named to the team, but the promotion was expected. With the Dodgers billeted at Fort Gulick in the Canal Zone, a number of players, mostly from the South, began circulating a petition that they would not play with Robinson.

A Dodger official woke up Durocher at 1 A.M. and told him the news. Fearing that the team could irreparably splinter, Durocher promptly got his coaches out of bed and told them to bring the players to the kitchen behind an army mess.

"Boys, I hear some of you don't want to play with Robinson," Durocher began, as players leaned against chopping blocks and stoves. "Some of you have drawn up a petition. Well, boys, you know what you can use that petition for. Yeah, you know. You're not that fucking dumb. Take the petition and, you know, wipe your ass."

Durocher told them that he'd play an elephant if it helped him win, and Robinson was no elephant. He was a great player who could run and hit and who was going to win pennants and earn money for all of them. "And there's something else. He's only the first, boys, only the first. There's many more colored ball players coming right behind him, and they're hungry, boys. . . . Unless you wake up, these colored ball players are gonna run you right out of the park."

The petition died.

Unfortunately, Durocher was not able to reap the benefits of his noble stand. Before the season began, Major League Baseball's Commissioner A. B. "Happy" Chandler suspended him for one year, the official reason being for "an accumulation of unpleasant incidents . . . and conduct detrimental to baseball." No specifics were given. Durocher was forced to watch his replacement, the veteran coach Burt Shotton, win the pennant and secure a place in history as Jackie Robinson's first manager. Durocher was reinstated in 1948, but the team, playing poorly, was in sixth place by July. The Dodger owner, Walter O'Malley, had already concluded that Durocher was "poison at the gate," and Branch Rickey, the son of a Methodist preacher who was fond of quoting Scripture, viewed his manager as a superb field general but an unrepentant heathen. Rickey demanded Durocher's resignation.

Across town, the Giants were faring no better. Mel Ott, in his seventh year as manager, had never finished higher than third; twice his teams finished last. Durocher was right. Surrounded by cronies, Ott could neither urge nor bully his players to greatness or even mediocrity. He had been with the team for twenty-two years, and to Stoneham, who valued loyalty above all else, Ott was family—Horace was a boy when he had first met him. But now Stoneham had to fire Ott or watch his club sink further into the abyss. "My daughter," he recalled, "didn't speak to me for a month."

Stoneham didn't have any internal candidates but had been impressed by Burt Shotton's calm stewardship in Durocher's absence. So on July 15 he called a meeting with Branch Rickey and told him that he was firing Ott. He needed a replacement.

"Who did you have in mind?" Rickey asked.

Stoneham drew his breath. "I want your permission to talk to Burt Shotton," he said.

"I have plans for Burt."

"Doing what?"

"Managing the Dodgers."

Stoneham was shocked. "What about Leo?" he asked.

"I'm about to dismiss him," Rickey said. "Why? Do you want to talk to him instead of Shotton?"

Hiring the loathsome, tarnished Durocher, as the Giant fans saw him, would be an act of heresy, but Stoneham saw opportunity. He arranged to meet Durocher at his Manhattan apartment. Arriving first, he asked Laraine Day for a drink and told her that he hoped Leo would be managing the Giants soon. Day needed little convincing. She walked to her console radio, tuned to WHN, which was about to broadcast the Dodger game. "Then why am I listening to this?" She clicked off the radio and asked, "Scotch, Mr. Stoneham, or bourbon?"

Durocher had one final visit with Rickey. He wanted to know his job status in Brooklyn if he didn't take the New York job.

"Your future lies over the river, Leo," Rickey said.

Durocher quickly came to terms with Stoneham, receiving a raise that made him the highest paid manager in baseball. On July 17, the front page of the *Daily News* blared: LIP REPLACES OTT! BURT BACK WITH FLOCK!!

Durocher was satisfied, though Laraine Day begrudged the Dodgers. Responsible for the decor in Leo's office at Ebbets Field, she had everything moved to his new office at the Polo Grounds save an autographed picture of Branch Rickey on the wall. Day had it moved to a nearby bathroom, directly over the toilet. Day herself assumed a higher profile with the Giants. She did a television show before each game from the Polo Grounds, in which she interviewed players or coaches. Her loyalty to the Giants was not appreciated at Ebbets Field, however, where a Dodger fan, during one game, threw his paper-bag lunch at her.

Durocher moved quickly to remake the Giants into his image, a hustling team that could play defense, run, and battle until they bled. He traded the lumberjacks (Mize and Cooper) and acquired the gritty double-play combination of Alvin Dark and Eddie Stanky, both of whom could bunt, hit-and-run, and barrel into catchers. The moves, as Day noted, were risky. "Leo was on the horns of a dilemma," she said. "The home run hitters were great favorites in New York, but he felt they would never bring the Giants a pennant. He could keep them—and get booed, or he could trade them and possibly get murdered."

Durocher brought up the Giants' first three black players, Monte Irvin, Hank Thompson, and Ray Noble (a black Latin), and he improved his pitching through good trades (Jim Hearn from the Cardinals) and good luck (Sal Maglie returned from the Mexican League). Wins still came slowly, leaving the Giant fans to boo Durocher or to forswear the team entirely. But in the second half of the 1950 season, the Giants won thirty-four out of forty-six games in one stretch and finished third, five games out of first. Durocher was certain that he finally had his kind of team. He told reporters, "If we don't win it next year, boys, you can have me. You can write whatever you want about me and you'll get no complaints. Because if we don't win it by at least six games, I don't fucking belong in baseball."

Stoneham was no less eager for a championship, in part to prove himself as an owner but also for more practical reasons. The Giants were suffering financially, having lost $466,503 from 1948 to 1950, while both the Yankees and Dodgers were in the black. The Giants, in fact, were hemorrhaging during a highly profitable era in baseball. But their aging ballpark, combined with its location in Harlem, had become increasingly problematic. White fans were moving to the suburbs, parking was scarce, and night games heightened anxieties. The emergence of television, meanwhile, brought baseball to people's homes. Gate receipts fell as attendance dropped from a record 1.6 million in 1947 to barely 1 million in 1950.

With three teams in New York, the Giants had always had to compete for fan and media interest, but the pressures had intensified. The Yankees and Dodgers continued to win, but they had captured the public's imagination in different ways. The arrival of Jackie Robinson in 1947 galvanized black Americans and riveted whites. His scintillating play meant fans could watch stalwart hitting and brilliant baserunning as well as dramatic social change. Commentators discussed Robinson's political significance. The addition of the young black stars Roy Campanella and Don Newcombe created further excitement. Whatever Branch Rickey's motives—commercial gain or racial progress—he clearly placed the Dodgers in the vanguard of the country's most important social movement in the twentieth century. The Giants' Monte Irvin, Hank Thompson, and Ray Noble were pioneers who withstood racial indignities, but they were not icons. They could not duplicate Robinson's cultural import, his media acclaim, or the devotion from fans, even those in Harlem.

The Yankees were touting a very different drawing card. In spring training of 1951, a nineteen-year-old switch-hitter named Mickey Mantle created an uproar when he began hitting 430-foot home runs and was timed running to first base in just over three seconds. He was to have begun the year on the Yankees' AAA squad in Kansas City, but his .402 batting average in Florida elevated him to the varsity—all the better for reporters, who'd already made him a folk hero: the handsome small-town kid from Oklahoma with short blond hair, blue eyes, and a dramatic combination of power and speed, arriving in the twilight of Joe DiMaggio's career, offering the possibility of yet another pinstriped demigod in the House that Ruth Built. Mantle confirmed the breathless expectations when he blasted a home run over the scoreboard at Ebbets Field in an exhibition game. When the season began, Yankee fans wanted to see him themselves.

The Giants began the 1951 season with a collection of good players but no real stars, no charismatic leader, and no answer to Robinson or Mantle. That was painfully clear in the outfield. Bobby Thomson was a diffident Scotsman who seemed incapable of emotion. With the laconic Don Mueller in right and the bland Whitey Lockman in left, observed one writer, "the Giants' outfield seemed like a trio of morticians."

The Giants won two out of their first three games, but then lost eleven in a row on their way to a 6–13 start. It was inexplicable for a team that had the league's best record in the second half of the previous season, and Durocher directed maniacal rages at his players. After one loss, recalled a Giant, "he was so hot you could've fried eggs on the language coming out of his mouth." Laraine Day said, "I won't say that Leo was suicidal on several occasions, but I give myself credit for saying nothing that might put the idea into his head."

Compounding matters were the Dodgers, who won twenty-eight of their first thirty-six games. Stoneham faced the prospect of a near-empty Polo Grounds by July. On May 1, Arthur Daley wrote in the *New York Times*: "As far as the Giants are concerned, the damage has already been done. It will take a miracle for the Giants to win the championship now."

One ray of hope centered on the organization's young Negro outfielder in the minor leagues. During the losing streak, a Giant scout told reserve infielder Bill Rigney: "Don't let the guys give up, because we're going to bring up a young player from Minneapolis, and he might just be the difference for this club."

The Giants started winning in May, taking eleven of fourteen games, and Durocher began reworking his lineup. Monte Irvin, a natural outfielder, had been at first base, where his mounting errors were impairing his hitting. On a hunch, Durocher switched him and left fielder Whitey Lockman, even though Lockman had never played first. But he held his own, and a grateful Irvin, repatriated to the outfield, found his stroke.

Durocher, however, still didn't believe he had enough speed or punch in the lineup. He was demanding Mays's promotion from the outset of the season, and six weeks later, after three days of phone calls, Stoneham finally relented. By May 25, the Giants were a respectable 17–19, in fifth place, only 4½ games behind the Dodgers. Mays was not joining a sinking ship but a vessel that was picking up steam. Nonetheless, the Giants became a very different team once Willie Mays arrived.

Word of his promotion traveled fast. A wire service reporter found Mays at the airport in Omaha, Nebraska, waiting for his nighttime flight to New York. How many black men in 1951 had ever flown on a commercial flight out of that airport? But there is Mays, photographed wearing a plaid sports coat over a white mesh shirt with a black collar, a black waistband, and pleated pants. A fedora with a stiff brim completes the stylish look. Leaning against the United Airlines counter between a white ticket agent and a white passenger, Mays appears somber, calm, and determined.

He knew nothing of the pressures confronting the Giants, only that they had started the season badly, nor was he fully aware of the hype surrounding his promotion. He figured he would initially be a role player, contributing as a pinch runner, defensive replacement, or spot starter. He landed in New York, and as his taxi moved through Manhattan, he warmly recalled the last time he had traveled there, with the Birmingham Black Barons, when they played at the Polo Grounds after their bus caught fire in the Holland Tunnel. Now he hoped his meeting with Horace Stoneham at the Giants' offices would go quickly, for Durocher had said on the phone that he was supposed to be in Philadelphia that night.

Mays was still carrying his two baseball bats in a golf bag when he reached the midtown offices, and as he rode the elevator, one woman looked at him, looked again, and said, "My God." She turned her head and pretended not to see him.

Though so nervous he initially could barely speak to his boss, Mays appreciated Stoneham's confidence. The owner had no doubts about his talent. What he wasn't sure of was Mays's toughness.

"Willie, they're going to try to find out about you fast up here," he said. "They're going to try you out with pitches at your cap."

Mays shrugged. "That's okay, Mr. Stoneham. When I played in the Negro Leagues, they threw at me too, only it didn't count."

"What do you mean?"

"They couldn't hit me."

"They throw harder up here," Stoneham warned.

"They can throw as hard as they want," Mays said. "I won't be there."

Before Mays left for Philadelphia, he had to take care of one last piece of business. Eddie Brannick, the Giants' traveling secretary, presented him with a new contract, already filled out. Under salary it read $5,000. There was no discussion. Mays read it, signed it, and was gone.

On the train to Philadelphia, he passed through Trenton, and he recalled how Chick Genovese and Bill McKechnie would fire questions at him on the bus, envisioned their staying up late at night to write reports about him for Stoneham, and he was comforted by their concern. The Pullman car rumbled over a bridge, and out the window Mays saw a sign: TRENTON MAKES, THE WORLD TAKES.

Mays opened the door of his hotel room to a familiar black face. "Hi there, roomie," Monte Irvin said. He was twelve years older than Mays, a muscular man with a slope-shouldered, tapered body and a quiet, dignified aura. One writer compared Irvin to a lean, mahogany Buddha; another said he spoke like a Latin professor. Mays had met Irvin, as well as Hank Thompson, the previous year when they came through Birmingham on a barnstorming tour, and he was glad that he knew at least two of his new teammates.

"Does skip know you're here?" Irvin asked.

"I don't think anyone knows I'm here," said Mays, which was fine by him. He just wanted to blend in.

Irvin reached for the phone and dialed another room. "Skip, three guesses who just checked in." Minutes later, Irvin and Mays were in Leo Durocher's plush hotel suite. The manager stood in the center with a deck of cards in his hands (he'd been playing solitaire). He had thinning, dirty blond hair, combed tightly back, and was a whirlwind of moving hands, quick steps, and rapid-fire comments. He was known as "Fifth Avenue" for his extravagant clothes—the custom-made suits and argyle socks and pearl-buttoned shirts, all delivered from Sulka's. Though he was in Philadelphia for only a weekend series, his closet was stuffed with more suits and ties than Mays had ever seen outside a store.

"Glad to see you here, son," Durocher said. "Glad you're hitting .477." He told Mays how he had wanted him to be with the club since spring training, but Stoneham wouldn't let him. "He said you needed more seasoning, but I could see you were a natural and only needed to play." Durocher told him not to worry about anything. His only job was to hit and field.

Durocher's efforts to build his confidence had begun. The manager correctly assumed that the transition would be rocky. How could it not be? In less than one year, Mays had moved from Fairfield Industrial High School to the New York Giants—from the provincial South to the sprawling metropolis, from a regimented lifestyle to endless temptations, from a black canvass to a glaring white tapestry. To survive, he would need unconditional support and an extensive education.

"Why do you have all the suits?" Mays asked.

"Because I'm the only asshole in this organization with an ounce of brains," Durocher said. "Ballplayer buys an expensive suit, then lets the hotel clean it for him. Hotels care about how quick they do a suit, not how good they do it. This way I can change to a new suit and leave the ones I was wearing till I get home, so they can get a decent cleaning and pressing. Remember that."

That night's game against the Phillies was at Shibe Park, built in 1909 as the major leagues' first steel and concrete stadium. When Mays walked into the clubhouse, he noticed how solemn it was, at least compared to the usual banter of the Black Barons. Maybe every fifth-place team is quiet, he thought. There isn't much to talk about. His locker was next to Irvin's, and a jersey with the number 24 hung inside. "Mays, 24" seemed fitting, given that he was called to the majors on May 24. He was still looking at his number when Durocher walked over to him.

"Son, you're batting third and playing center field."

Mays stood in disbelief. Batting third and playing center field? Isn't that what Joe DiMaggio did? Isn't the third hitter supposed to be your best batsman? Isn't your center fielder the one who takes charge, leads the team, makes plays? He tried to mask his fears by giving Durocher a big smile, but his heart was pounding. He sat down and tried to gather his thoughts, focus on his responsibilities. Someone passed him a baseball to autograph. He'd autographed balls before for fans, but now no fans were around. He picked up the ball and wrote, "Willie Mays." Then he added, "#24." It looked so . . . real. He wished his father and aunts could see him now.

Newspapers in New York and Philadelphia whipped up interest in his debut. The *New York Times* published a story and photograph beneath the headline MAYS, NEGRO STAR, JOINS GIANTS TODAY. Just before 6 P.M., on a cool, clear evening, Mays walked onto the spacious field, with the outfield alleys stretching more than 400 feet and the center field wall at 447 feet. The reporters who crowded into the press box noticed an unusual stirring this night. Hundreds of black fans, who normally attended only when Jackie Robinson was in town, had been eagerly waiting for Mays. So too were the players on both the Giants and Phillies. As Mays walked to the batting cage for his pregame cuts, the relaxed atmosphere suddenly gave way to anticipation and excitement. Mays stepped in, felt loose, and began swinging.

Bill Rigney recalled, "He popped it up, hit a weak grounder, fouled one back . . . then all of a sudden he hit a rocket that landed in the middle of the upper deck in left field. Then he hit another rocket that went over the roof. Then he hit one that hit the right field scoreboard. Everything stopped. The Phillies stopped warming up and Ashburn and Hammer and Puddin' Head Jones and all the others stopped to watch him hit. He got everyone's attention. He was amazing."

Phillie pitcher Robin Roberts remembered: "I'm thinking, 'Wow, I've got to face this kid tomorrow night. How will I pitch to him?' He was hitting them over the left field grandstands."

Stoneham had driven to the game with other Giant executives, and after Mays was done hitting, Durocher walked past Stoneham's box. The owner yelled, "Hey, Leo, how do you like him?"

"I'll marry him," Durocher yelled back.

Next, Mays jogged into the outfield and, according to the *New York Times,* "started winging the ball in from deep center to third and home plate without a hop. It was a tremendous exhibition and impressed one and all."

But Mays's nerves showed in the actual game. He took a third strike in his first at-bat against Bubba Church and finished the night 0-for-5. He also misplayed a fly ball in the first inning for a triple and later bumped into Irvin in right field on a ball that fell for a double. His debut could not have gone much worse, and yet it didn't matter, certainly not to reporters. "Inspired by the presence of their flashy rookie, Willie Mays, the Giants rallied for five runs in the eighth inning," the *Times* reported.

The next day was more of the same. Mays went hitless against Roberts, but the Giants' Larry Jansen pitched a shutout for a win that pushed New York to the .500 mark. On Sunday, Mays went 0-for-4 against Russ Meyer, but the Giants notched another victory.

Now 0-for-12, Mays was sulking on the train ride back to New York, wondering if he really could hit this pitching. Irvin tried to relax him. "Listen, man," he said, "we won three in a row without you hitting. Now figure it out. As long as you don't hit, we win. Only trouble'll be if you get a hit."

The Giants returned to the Polo Grounds, and Mays came out early before the series opener against the Boston Braves. He took extra batting practice, he told Durocher, "because I'm not feeling easy up there." He feared his slow start would prompt catcalls from fans. Before the game, he was sitting in the dugout when his name was announced in the batting order. Loud cheers rose from the stands. Mays turned to Irvin. "Is everybody here crazy except me?" he asked.

Pitching for the Boston Braves was Warren Spahn, a lean, cunning veteran who would win more games than any left-hander in major league history. With his huge leg kick, crooked delivery, and long fingers that snapped off curveballs, he was difficult to time. In the first inning, Mays stepped to the plate and assumed his classic stance—legs astraddle, weight equally divided between both legs, the bat held high. In form and movement, he was a clear descendant of DiMaggio's, with one barely noticeable exception: the thumb on Mays's top hand extended off the bat, sticking out like it was sore, except it wasn't. It was simply a quirk. When the pitcher threw the ball, the thumb wrapped back around the handle, a movement that Mays believed gave him more balance and strength.

Spahn threw his first pitch, and Mays took a curve on the outside corner. Mays then swung and missed badly on a fastball. Apparently overmatched, he guessed curve, and guessed right. His bat flashed across the plate—*crack!* For a moment, there was silence, then a gasp, as fans tried to register what they saw. The ball didn't tower or loft. It soared, flying over the left field roof, still rising on one long line as it disappeared into the night. Thunderous cheers rolled across the stands, and Mays jogged purposefully around the bases, head down, unsmiling, seemingly embarrassed by the adulation. Spahn stood with his hands on his hips, looked down, and kicked the dirt behind the rubber. When Mays reached the dugout, he slapped hands with Durocher, who smiled like a proud father.

As Robert Creamer wrote in *Sports Illustrated:* "The crowd . . . roared and cheered as though Willie had just won the World Series. It was a strange, tingly thing to be part of, because all that the crowd was saying really was, 'Welcome, Willie. We've been waiting for you all our lives.' "

The Giant announcer Russ Hodges said, "If it's the only home run he ever hits, they'll still remember him."

Spahn said, "For the first sixty feet, it was a helluva pitch."

Durocher: "I never saw a fucking ball leave a fucking park so fucking fast in my fucking life."

The savior had arrived.

CHAPTER NINE

ROOKIE OF THE YEAR

Willie Mays's rookie year would not be his finest or the year of his greatest celebrity, but it was his sunburst, creating a perception of athleticism, innocence, and joy that would shape the public's view for years. By happenstance and calculation, he had chosen baseball as his livelihood, and it proved to be the perfect stage for a sport that was about to be transformed.

Baseball reigned supreme in 1951, with games generating $55.4 million in ticket sales, more money than all the other sports combined. Professional football, basketball, and hockey remained on the cultural periphery. America was a baseball nation, where millions of kids played in thousands of leagues and where games derived from the national pastime—stickball, kickball, stoopball, wallball—deepened childhood ties to the sport. In November, former president Herbert Hoover said baseball was second only to religion as a positive influence in American life; only boxing and horse racing challenged the major leagues in popularity. Including the Negro Leagues, there were thirty big league baseball teams in 1951, more than all the professional football, basketball, and hockey teams combined.

For all its dominance, the major leagues were concentrated in the northeast quadrant of America, with half of the sixteen teams clustered in Boston, New York, Philadelphia, and Washington. A "western" trip took players no farther than St. Louis and Chicago, and there were no teams south of the Ohio River. Fans around the country could follow their favorite stars on radio and black-and-white newsreels as well as in newspapers, but the game itself was played largely in the Northeast, and it was played more frequently, and with greater competitive fury, in New York than anywhere else.

New York was the only city that claimed more than two teams, with the Dodgers, Giants, and Yankees entrenched in three of the city's five boroughs. Between 1947 and 1957, a stretch bracketed by the arrival of Jackie Robinson and the departure of the Dodgers and Giants, New York was the nation's baseball capital. The city did not hold a monopoly on baseball luminaries. Ted Williams, Stan Musial, Ernie Banks, and Hank Aaron, to name just four, all played outside New York. But the city's own stars inevitably received more attention because New York dominated the country's growing publishing, radio, television, and recording industries, and the teams dominated as well. Between 1947 and 1957, every World Series but one had at least one squad from New York; a New York club won all but two of the championships; and seven times, both teams in the Series represented Gotham.

The ticker-tape parades aren't the only reason the era is celebrated with pride and nostalgia. The New Yorkers who embraced Jackie Robinson, and the black Dodgers and Giants who followed, were on the right side of history. The period was a comforting time when neighborhoods had some semblance of continuity, when baseball owners displayed loyalty to their cities, when the game itself was still a game. The players, raised during the Great Depression and drawn from farms, factories, and coal mines, were not that far removed, economically and socially, from their fans. With one-year contracts, the stars as well as the scrubs understood the tenuous existence of the working class, for they themselves were a bad season or a twisted ankle away from unemployment or at least a significant pay cut. Many lived in urban neighborhoods, perhaps walking distance from the ballpark. They were visible and without pretense, taking jobs in the off-season to make ends meet. They didn't just represent the city for which they played—they were of it.

Those intimate ties would be shattered in the 1950s, a period of growth and upheaval that reshaped the landscape of New York baseball and the country at large. Commercial air travel, with nonstop, transcontinental flights, connected the coasts. National highways linked new suburban developments. Air-conditioning opened markets in the Sun Belt. Long-distance calls could be made without an operator. Credit cards spawned a new consumer culture. There was sugarless chewing gum, power steering, Dacron suits—America was expanding, spending, and innovating.

And in 1951 the NAACP filed a class-action lawsuit against the Board of Education of Topeka, Kansas, demanding that twenty black schoolchildren be admitted to a segregated elementary school. One of the children was Linda Brown, and the trial of *Brown v. Board of Education* began on June 25.

In another breakthrough, Blumstein's Department Store in Harlem featured a group of Negro and white window mannequins in summer frocks and play clothes. Civic leaders gathered to celebrate this bold symbol of integration. "This is only the beginning," Jack Blumstein said.

Change was coming from all directions.

• • •

Few commercial developments were more important, to the country and to baseball, than television. In 1948, Americans had 400,000 sets; by 1950, they had 10 million, and by 1957, 42 million. Baseball had been televised in New York since 1947, but most fans there and around the country still relied on radio for live games, a programming staple at local, regional, and national levels.

But 1951 marked a turning point in what would become the inseparable relationship between this new medium and the national pastime. The networks, still in their infancy, could not broadcast live shows from coast to coast. *Toast of the Town* (after 1955 *The Ed Sullivan Show*), for example, would broadcast live in New York on Saturday night; the tape would then be flown to California the next day and be televised there that night. But by 1951 an underground coaxial cable, combined with radio transmitters and receivers, allowed the networks to televise events live across time zones.

The technology, to be sure, was crude. On most sets, the actual black-and-white images were fuzzy; in some cases, blizzards broke out on the screen when an airplane flew overhead. The first baseball games in color were broadcast in 1951, though, as Red Smith noted, the players all emerged with "magnificently bronzed complexions" and Gil Hodges's arms appeared "encased in a pelt of somewhat lovelier tone—about the shade of medium roast beef—than Gil wears in real life."

But the sport itself, as national televised entertainment, had arrived. In 1953, ABC aired the first national *Game of the Week* on Saturday, with commentary from the inimitable Dizzy Dean, the former star pitcher for the Cardinals' Gashouse Gang. He described how players "slud into third," "swang the bat," and returned to "their respected bases," and he urged his viewers, "Don't fail to miss next week's game." Saturday baseball, shown on various networks over the next half century, became a weekly institution.

However gradual its steps, television showcased players in all corners of the country, forged connections with distant fans, and elevated stars to heroic status. In that sense, the medium paralleled a similar change in communications technology of a previous generation. At the beginning of the century, Americans would gather in town squares or urban arenas and watch pitch-by-pitch recreations of World Series games on large electrical scoreboards. In the 1920s a new medium, commercial radio, expanded baseball's reach and changed the experience itself for its followers.

Radio, however, represented just one new medium in America's "new way of knowing." According to the historian Jules Tygiel, movies, newsreels, tabloid newspapers, magazines, and advertising were all "revolutionizing people's ability to vicariously participate in the world around them." And baseball was a prime beneficiary. Fans who only a few years earlier could never have hoped to see or hear a big league game could now listen to radio broadcasts or watch their heroes in movie houses and in dramatic photo displays.

The new media needed a messenger, and they found one in Babe Ruth. His dominance on the field would have made him famous in any era, but his ascendance in the 1920s made him a highly visible national folk hero who embodied the thrilling, sybaritic jazz age. Newsreels, radio, and even several forgettable movies celebrated the Babe's exploits; he may have been the most photographed American in the decade, his hefty torso and platter-face smile appearing on the cover of major periodicals as well as such arcane journals as *American Boy, Strength,* and *Hardware Age.* In a decade when the modern celebrity was virtually invented, the new media helped to make Ruth both mythic and accessible.

By the 1950s, when the next communications revolution occurred, new heroes were needed, and they would emerge.

The New York Giants weren't the only ones who needed Willie Mays. So too did the major leagues. By 1951 the game had grown stagnant, the league—with the exception of the black and Latin players—seemingly frozen in time. All sixteen teams had been rooted in their respective cities since the turn of the century. The newest park was Cleveland's Municipal Stadium, which had opened in 1932. All the others, except Yankee Stadium, had been built before 1915. The actual game, as the baseball historian Bill James has noted, "was perhaps the most one-dimensional, uniform, predictable version of the [sport] which has ever been offered to the public." Most teams had little use for bunting, hitting behind the runner, or stealing bases, which was so rare that it was considered a "surprise play." Jackie Robinson stood out not only because of his skin color but because of his speed, excitement, and versatility. Defense, meanwhile, was desired but not honored, the Gold Glove Award not introduced until 1957. With few exceptions, baseball strategy consisted of trying to get someone on base and then hitting a home run.

Mays would have made a splash no matter when he entered the major leagues, but 1951 served him unusually well. His skills shined brightly on a sluggish team in a plodding league, in a big-stage city that was about to lead a communications revolution. He was a game-changing catalyst in a storied rivalry about to embark on a historic pennant race, a radiant contributor to an era forever consecrated as the golden age of baseball.

Mays had one more thing going for him: the historic Polo Grounds, whose bizarre configuration was an ideal setting for his talents. The stadium itself, hunched on the eastern shoulder of Manhattan beside the Harlem River, was an acquired taste. Derided by some as a metropolis of steel and concrete whose age and squalor could incubate a communicable disease, it was also celebrated as "an absurd and lovely" sanctum built at the foot of a cliff—Coogan's Bluff—so patrons actually walked downhill to their seats. Roger Angell wrote:

> You came slowly down the John T. Brush stairs in the cool of the evening, looking down at the flags [and] the tiers of brilliant floodlights on the stand and, beyond them, at the softer shimmer of lights on the Harlem River. Sometimes there was even a moon, rising right out of the Bronx. As you came closer and were fingering for your ticket in your pocket, you could hear brave music from the loud-speakers, broken by the crack of a fungo bat, and through a space in the upper deck you caught a glimpse of grass, soft and incredibly green, in the outfield. You walked faster, tasting excitement in your mouth and with it—every single time—the conviction of victory.

One oddity of the Polo Grounds was that no one ever played polo there. The name was derived from a polo field used by a Giants team in the 1880s. When the squad moved uptown, to Eighth Avenue between 155th and 157th streets, the name moved with it. When that structure burned down in 1911, it was replaced by an opulent wonder, wired for telegraphs and telephones, the facade of the upper deck displaying a decorative frieze depicting allegories in bas-relief. The roof was decorated with eight shields on successive panels representing the teams in the National League; the box seats were designed on the lines of the royal boxes of the Coliseum in Rome, while the aisle seats had the Giants' logo, "NY," carved in iron scrollwork. Attendants in white uniforms peddled scorecards. *Baseball Magazine* called the Polo Grounds "the mightiest temple ever erected to the Goddess of sport"—a venue for boxing and football as well as baseball, where Jack Dempsey, Jim Thorpe, and the Four Horsemen of Notre Dame all found glory.

The stadium's most distinctive feature was its elongated shape—from above, it looked like a horseshoe, a footprint, or even a bowling alley. The right field foul pole was 258 feet from home plate, the pole in left 22 feet farther, which allowed many pop fly home runs down the lines. But the stands, instead of curving into a conventional oval, extended straight out until they reached the outfield bleachers. The alleys were about 450 feet away. Dead center was even farther, a staggering 505 feet, where the massive green scoreboard urged patrons to buy Chesterfields and where the clubhouses offered a distant haven for a struggling pitcher sent to the show-ers. "To a batter standing at home plate," Jonathan Eig wrote, "center field at the Polo Grounds looked like it ended somewhere in the Hamptons."

To Willie Mays, the Polo Grounds were magical even before he became a Giant. When he played in the Negro Leagues, several Black Barons had told him about their duels there against Satchel Paige or Josh Gibson, and of course Mays played there as a Black Baron. Compared to the tired parks in black baseball, the Polo Grounds seemed like a pastoral shrine.

With Mays in center field, the stadium joined the most spacious tract in the major leagues with the man uniquely qualified to cover it. Buck O'Neil, the Negro League star who later scouted for the majors, once said: "There were men faster than Willie Mays, but I never saw one faster with a fly ball in the air." The Polo Grounds gave Mays a sprawling pasture for those skills—the quick jumps, the pell-mell running style, the rocket arm—and made possible, in the 1954 World Series, the defining play of his career. He would have been badly miscast in, say, Ebbets Field or Wrigley Field. As Donald Honig wrote, "Putting Mays in a small ballpark would have been like trimming a masterpiece to fit a frame."

Initially, the Polo Grounds didn't bring much luck to Mays; he almost didn't survive his first two weeks.

His home run off Warren Spahn marked his arrival in New York but did not end his slump. The following day, against Boston, he went 0-for-3 in the first game of a doubleheader and made outs in his first two at-bats in the second game. Leg cramps then forced him to the bench. Mays tried to put up a brave front after the game. "It's only a slump," he told reporters. "I've been taking a lot of pitches because I want to see what they throw up here. Now I've found out. They're throwing me the same stuff I was bel-tin' in Minneapolis. Not many curves either. They're giving me the sort of stuff I want."

In truth, he was repeating his experience from a year earlier, when he began 0-for-22 with Trenton. The harder he tried, the worse he performed. Maybe the pitching was too tough; maybe the Polo Grounds, with 54,500 seats, was too daunting. Regardless, the pressure was all self-imposed. Mays had played in only six games, four of which the Giants had won. The press and the fans remained patient; his teammates, sympathetic. "If anything, he seemed even younger than twenty," Alvin Dark recalls. "He just seemed to be a kid, maybe seventeen or eighteen."

The next day, at home against the Pittsburgh Pirates, was even more dis-tressing. Mays came to the plate four times with men on base but didn't register a hit or drive in a run. The Giants won, 8–2, but after the game

Mays retreated to the clubhouse. He was now 1-for-26 (.038), and he feared he would be sent back to Minneapolis. Maybe it was just as well. Smaller parks, easier pitching, fewer fans. He had dreamed of playing in the major leagues, and he had failed. Now, slumped in front of his locker, he wept.

Giant coach Herman Franks saw Mays and went upstairs to Durocher's office. "You better do something about your boy," Franks said.

"What's the matter?"

"Well, Leo, he's in front of his locker, crying."

Durocher raced down the stairs, entered the locker room, and saw his rookie crying uncontrollably. He understood how much pressure Mays had been putting on himself, how unforgiving his own standards were. Some managers would have dismissed the kid right there. Mays was only the seventeenth black player to reach the majors; twelve teams, three quarters of the league, remained white. Baseball's "great experiment" had not reached a definitive conclusion, and the managers who accepted the racism of the day would have seen Mays as evidence that most Negroes were unfit for the majors. But not Leo Durocher.

He sat down next to Willie, put his arm on his shoulder, and asked, "What's the matter, son?"

When Mays became excited or nervous, particularly in his early years as a pro, his voice would run so high that it sounded like a chirping canary. Sometimes Durocher couldn't even hear him.

"Mr. Leo," Mays said, "I can't help you. I can't even get a hit. I know I can't play up here, and you're gonna send me back to Minneapolis. That's where I belong. I don't belong up here. I can't play up here . . ."

Durocher couldn't tell if Mays had stopped talking or if his voice was simply no longer audible. Mays believed that Durocher was angry but wasn't showing it. The manager, however, was more alarmed than anything else, realizing that his prodigy's shattered confidence could quickly derail his season, and given black players' shaky status in the majors, maybe much more was at stake. He patted Mays on the back.

"What do you mean you can't hit? You're going to be a great ballplayer!"

"The pitching is just too fast for me up here. They're going to send me back to Minneapolis."

Durocher's voice was steady and soothing. "Look, son. I brought you up here to do one thing. That's to play center field. You're the best center fielder I've ever looked at. Willie, see what's printed across my jersey?"

Mays nodded.

"It says Giants," Durocher continued. "As long as I'm the manager of the Giants, you're my center fielder. Tomorrow, next week, next month. You're here to stay. With your talent, you're going to get plenty of hits."

Durocher told Mays there were five things a player had to do to be great: hit, hit with power, run, field, and throw. "Willie, you could do all five from the first time I ever saw you. You're the greatest ballplayer I ever saw or hoped to see."

Praise wasn't enough. As Durocher saw it, Mays needed some specific advice in the way that a man in a burning building needed a ladder. Regardless of whether the ladder worked, at least it gave some immediate hope.

"Willie," Durocher cried, "you and your damn pull hitting!"

Durocher had noticed that Mays was turning over his right hand too quickly when swinging, producing soft ground balls to the left side. "I don't know why you don't take the ball to right field. You can hit it into the bleachers here, over the fence, anywhere you want, yet you're still trying to pull the ball all the time. For you to do something wrong is an absolute disgrace. And I know you don't want to disgrace me, do you, Willie?"

Mays wiped his eyes.

"Go home and get some sleep," Durocher said. "Tomorrow's another day."

He walked back to the staircase to his office but suddenly stopped.

"And by the way—who do you think you are? Hubbell?"

Mays stared at him. "Hubbell?"

"The way you wear the legs of your pants down nearly to the ankles," he said. "Pull them up."

"Why?"

"Because you're making the umpires think your strike zone's down where your pants are. They're hurting you on the low pitch."

Mays had worn his trousers long to imitate DiMaggio and Williams, but the next day he pulled them up, and he also concentrated on keeping his top hand back. Durocher dropped Mays from third to eighth in the batting order, telling him someone needed to spark it, and, what the hell, it might as well be him. Mays said he would try. Durocher had reassured him. As long as "Mr. Leo" was his manager, he was safe. Against the Pirates that day, he hit a single and a triple, the latter traveling more than 400 feet to right center, and the Giants won, 14–3. In the next game, against the Cardinals, he hit two doubles and scored the game's only run in a 1–0 victory. His 1-for-26 drought was followed by a 9-for-24 spree, and the Giants were above .500 to stay.

On the surface, Durocher and Mays could not have been more different—the cynical boulevardier and the guileless man-child, but each needed the other, Durocher boosting his yearling's fragile self-esteem, Mays coming through with clutch hits and acrobatic catches. Durocher understood that Mays required both a gentle touch and unconditional support. Piper Davis knew that as well, though he had the benefit of Cat's guidance—"Don't holler at him." Durocher figured it out on his own. "With Willie," he later said, "you have to just keep patting him, keep rubbing him." And so he did, lavishly extolling Mays to anyone who'd listen. Russ Hodges recalled, "Mays was the only player I ever saw who could do no wrong in Durocher's eyes. Everyone else felt the lash of Leo's tongue sooner or later, but Willie never did. Durocher even got a kick out of his errors. One day at the Polo Grounds . . . Willie dropped a fly ball. . . . I looked toward the Giants' dugout, and Leo was laughing."

Durocher believed he could state the same thing to two players but convey very different impressions—the tone and body language spelled the difference. If he thought a veteran made a mistake because of laziness or poor preparation, he played the bully with loud, harsh inflections: "You play like *my* kid. What the *hell's* the matter with you. *Bear down out there.* How the *hell* can *you* make a mistake like that."

With Mays, however, he turned sentences into questions, used a softer voice, and communicated bewilderment, even hurt. "You play like my *kid*. What the hell's the *matter* with you? *Bear* down out there. How the hell can you make a mistake like that?"

Durocher also launched a public campaign for Mays, sparing no adjective to raise the fans' expectations further. He initially compared Mays to Pete Reiser, a switch-hitting rookie sensation who played for Durocher as a Dodger in 1941; Reiser's star-crossed career was curtailed by injury. In June, Durocher told the *New York Post*: "You got to like [Mays]. He's got less experience than anybody I ever had playing for me, but he doesn't seem bigheaded or too eager or too anything." By August, Durocher told the *Sporting News*: "This is the best-looking rookie I've seen in twenty-five years in baseball. I look at Willie and you know who I see? Pete Reiser when he came up. . . . There's nobody in the league got a better arm than this kid. There's nobody got more power. There's nobody can go get them any better than he can. . . . And he's just a baby. In two years, Mays is going to be the greatest ever to lace on a pair of spiked shoes."

Durocher wanted Mays to confirm his high opinion, so the needs of both men meshed perfectly. Pleasing his own father or those, like Piper Davis, who were father figures had always motivated Mays. He played for men who taught and protected him, who loved him, and now Leo Durocher played that role. Mays said at the time, "All those nice things that Leo says about me make me feel like I wanna go out there and do all those things he says I can do."

He was equally intent on satisfying the fans: "I know they expect much from me. I wanna be good more than they want me to. . . . I'm miserable down inside when I mess up a play in the field or when I don't get a hit."

Durocher's paternal touch, his gentle discipline, was evident when Mays didn't show up for the start of the Giants' doubleheader in Pittsburgh on June 17. His roommate, Monte Irvin, was also missing. Durocher seethed.

At the Crosley Hotel across the street, Irvin and Mays were eating in the dining room when their waiter asked, "Aren't you guys playing today?"

Irvin said they were. "Why do you ask?"

"Well, I think they're playing now," the waiter said. "In fact, I know they are, because I've got it on the radio."

The ball game's starting time had been moved up by one hour, but neither Irvin nor Mays had gotten the message. They paid their bill and ran to Forbes Field, and someone told Durocher that his missing players had arrived. The manager walked into the clubhouse and said, "It better be good."

Irvin said no one had told them about the time change.

"All right, get dressed and come on out."

Both players saw action, but it didn't help—the Giants lost, 11–5. They took the second game, but Irvin went hitless for the day and Mays dropped a fly ball. In the clubhouse, Durocher told Irvin and Mays to meet him in his hotel room. Both players were nervous, uncertain of their punishment. The meeting didn't last long.

"I don't know why you guys were late and why you didn't know the game had been moved up an hour," Durocher said. "Monte, you ought to know not to be late. You're old enough to know better." And to Mays: "And you, you little son of a gun, you haven't been here that long, and you ought to have more respect for Monte than to keep him up late."

Mays made no effort to defend himself or deny any wrongdoing. Durocher knew that Mays wasn't responsible—he just wanted to make a point. "I'm going to say this and then I'm finished," he said. "The next time it happens, it'll cost you $500." Irvin and Mays were never late again.

This level of attention given to a twenty-year-old could create problems in the clubhouse, so Durocher appealed to the other players in the same way he appealed to the Dodgers who threatened not to play with Jackie Robinson. "Look, there's something about Willie Mays," he said. "I don't know whether you see it, but I see it. He's a young boy, he's a baby. But he's got more talent in five minutes than the rest of us have in our lifetime. It doesn't mean that I don't like you fellows equally well. But I think it does something for Mays if I keep telling him, 'You're the greatest, no one can carry your glove, nobody can put your shoes on.' I think it makes him a better player, and as long as it does, buddy, he puts money in your pocket and mine."

From the outset, Mays was a willing student, asking Monte Irvin for the tendencies of each hitter and seeking guidance in the outfield on positioning. Years later, computer analyses could create detailed profiles of every hitter, but during Mays's career, the players usually had to get scouting reports on their own. Mays did that and much more. He once asked Irvin how he stole home with a left-handed hitter at the plate, defying conventional wisdom, because the catcher had a clear shot at him. Irvin said that it's sometimes *easier* to steal home with a lefty at the plate. "Did you notice how the third baseman was playing very wide because a pull hitter was at bat? So I could take a bigger lead."

The Giants' double-play combination, two combative Southerners, continued Mays's education. Second baseman Eddie Stanky, from Mobile, Alabama, was described by Durocher as someone who "can't run, can't hit, can't field [but] he just knows how to win." If anything, he was meaner than Durocher: he once said, "I would spike my mother if it meant being safe on a close play." He succeeded with creativity as well as tenacity, which he showed around the second base bag. With runners on first and second, nobody out, and a ground ball hit to the shortstop, Stanky would make the putout at second, but instead of turning the conventional double play, he'd throw to third and catch the runner making a wide turn.

Dark, from Comanche, Oklahoma, was a quarterback at Louisiana State University, and his ruggedness in baseball earned him the captaincy from Durocher. At shortstop, his job was to peer toward the catcher, get the sign, and flash his fingers behind his back so Mays could anticipate where the ball would be hit. On other pitches, Stanky did the same at second. They taught Mays that fastballs are struck differently from curves and changeups. An outfielder's toughest chance is a line drive right at him, and the pitch's speed influences the arc of the ball: fastballs will sail over the fielder's head, a slower pitch will drop faster. On the bases, Dark and Stanky explained how to stay in a hot box so other runners could advance and how to draw throws to protect the trailing runner.

Not all of this was new to Mays, but the repetition and emphasis made a difference. He learned just by observing. He had always assumed, for example, that a runner stole bases on either the catcher or the pitcher, but by watching Whitey Lockman, he realized that the first baseman played a role as well. If the first baseman places his right foot against the inside corner of the bag, the runner can dive back head first. But as Lockman demonstrated, if the first baseman's right leg is directly between the runner and the bag—standing, literally, as a barrier—a headfirst dive can easily be blocked. The runner needs to slide with his foot extended, spiking the first baseman if necessary but also requiring a shorter lead. First basemen who used the conventional stance to hold runners gave Mays a better chance to steal.

Mays rewarded Durocher's faith in him. After his clubhouse pep talk, he began spraying the ball all over the field and soon posted a ten-game hitting streak, culminating on June 14 in a 3-for-5 performance against Cincinnati. He hit .408 during the stretch, collected four homers and sixteen RBIs, and raised his average to .280. He also helped the Giants win ten of twelve games. On June 22, after they had lost two straight, Mays hit a tenth-inning three-run homer in Chicago off knuckleballer Dutch Leonard to give the Giants a 9–6 win. Cub manager Frankie Frisch sought help from his friend Charlie Grimm, who had managed against Mays in Minneapolis:

"How should we pitch to this kid?" Frisch asked.

"How the hell should I know, Frankie," Grimm barked. "He hit .580 against us."

Mays's friends and family in Fairfield tracked his progress through telephone calls, newspapers, and the radio. No one was prouder than Cat. "He was all smiles," Herman Boykin recalls. "He would come around and say, 'That's my son.'"

Mays still had his slumps but never lost his confidence. On July 3, against the Phillies at the Polo Grounds, he was mired in an 0-for-15 spiral when he stroked three hits, including a game-tying homer in the thirteenth inning. The Giants won, 9–8, putting them ten games over .500, their high mark until the middle of August and still within striking distance of the Dodgers. Later in July, Mays had an eight-day stretch in which he had only six hits, but they were all home runs. He was also stealing the occasional base; he had seven for the year, which would increase in later seasons but still wasn't bad for a power hitter. DiMaggio didn't steal seven bases in one season in his entire career.

Mays made his greatest mark in the field. He played the shallowest center field since Tris Speaker, whose proximity to the infield was less risky during the "dead ball" era. After Mays caught Richie Ashburn's sinking line drive in short center, Ashburn quipped, "Goddammit, can't someone tell that guy this isn't the Little Leagues." Mays also charged grounders as no outfielder had ever done in organized ball. Outfielders tended to lay back, which suited the era of lumbering, station-to-station baseball. But Mays tore after base hits with a headlong rush, scoop, and throw. It was a radical concept—an outfielder who played like an infielder, derived from his experience with the Black Barons. He occasionally overcharged balls—a costly blunder in the acreage of the Polo Grounds—turning singles into doubles, triples, or even inside-the-park homers. But the miscues were offset by his gunning down advancing runners—he had twelve assists for the year, or one every ten games. The Dodgers' Carl Furillo had the most assists in the majors, twenty-four, averaging one every seven games. In his first month or two, the baseball writer Arnold Hano concluded, Mays "had revolutionized outfield play: outfielders today must be shortstops in their approach to ground-ball base hits."

Even if other outfielders copied his aggression, none could match his singular exploits. On the evening of July 24, the Giants played the Pirates at Forbes Field, where the center field fence was 457 feet from home. When left-handed Rocky Nelson hit a soaring drive to the deepest part of the park, Mays broke fast, calculated the ball's flight, and sprinted toward the brick wall. But as the ball began to descend, it flared toward left field. Still running at full speed, Mays appeared deep enough, but the ball, sinking fast, remained to his right. He adjusted his route and briefly ran parallel to the wall. He could not get his glove into position, so he reached out with his large, bare hand. The ball smacked the palm. The third out was recorded. When Mays turned toward the infield, a smile creased his face.

Mays had caught balls bare-handed in the minors and with the Black Barons, and he had almost made a leaping, bare-handed catch two nights earlier at the Polo Grounds. But the fans at Forbes Field had never seen anything like it. Mays touched his cap to acknowledge the crowd, ran off the field, and walked three steps down into the dugout. He expected handshakes, but Durocher was looking at the lineup card. Bobby Thomson was cleaning his spikes. Hank Thompson was drinking at the water fountain. Others sat there with their arms folded. No one patted him on the back, said "Nice catch," or even looked him in the eye.

At Durocher's orders, they were giving Mays the silent treatment, a small prank on their eager-to-please outfielder.

Confused, Mays confronted his manager. "Hey, Leo, didn't you see what I did out there?"

Durocher looked at him and shrugged. "No, I didn't see it. You'll have to go out there and do it again before I'll believe it."

Branch Rickey saw it. He was, by then, the general manager of the Pirates, and he sent a note to the visitors' dugout: "That was the finest catch I have ever seen and the finest catch I ever hope to see."

A team photograph was taken of the 1951 Giants at the end of the season. Beneath the clubhouse at the Polo Grounds, three rows of men are presented in their bridal white uniforms, their faces stoic, solemn. Only one player doesn't quite fit in. Not because he's black or his baggy uniform appears to be swallowing him or he looks so young, but because his face has a heartwarming smile—as if no one told the kid he's not supposed to be happy. Willie Mays not only played different—beyond the color of his skin, he *looked* different. He tilted his black woolen hat forward, for example, so the rear band ran precariously high on his crown. The visor's jaunty angle protected his eyes from the glare of the sun or lights, but its teetering repose also ensured that it would fly off when he rounded the bases or chased fly balls, a pulsating flourish turned into pure theater.

In one game his rookie year, Mays raced in for a line drive, and as he dove with arms extended, his hat blew off. He caught the ball with one hand and his hat with the other (called "the double catch" by reporters). He displayed a similar flair when his cap launched as he made a wide turn around first base. He put on the brakes and dove back to the bag, grabbing his hat with one hand while touching the base with the other. His cap could be a stage prop or even a riveting subplot on a given play. In one instance, he tried to go from first to third on a hit and, as recounted in the *New York Journal-American*, "Mays turned back between second and third to get the cap that had, as usual, blown off his head. The throw already was on its way to third [and] it was a run at the moment that could have meant the game and, in retrospect, the pennant for the Giants [but] he rescued his precious cap [because] Willie instinctively had timed the play so accurately that he knew he could retrieve his cap and make it safely into third. Which he did."

Reporters invariably described such plays as "instinctive," but even as a rookie, Mays was a savvy showman who, importing the stylistic brio of the Negro Leagues, wanted to give the fans, the players, and the writers something to talk about. "With the average player, you take for granted what he's doing," Hank Thompson said. "But Willie was different. It isn't often that you watch another guy play ball. But you always watched Willie, because there was always the chance that he was going to do something that you'd never seen before."

The love affair between Mays and the New York baseball fans began at the outset. "I don't think any ballplayer ever related to the fans as quickly as Willie," Red Smith wrote. "Maybe Giant fans were more trusting, but they seemed to believe from the very beginning that he was the real article, that he had bypassed 'promise' and 'potential' and showed up in full arrival." Grantland Rice tagged him as "the kid everybody liked." There was something irresistible about the way Mays, after missing a tough chance in the field, reprimanded his glove. "Shame on you for not catching that ball," he'd say, slapping the mitt. Several weeks after he had joined the Giants, a writer walking through the stands in search of a story was startled to hear parents pointing to the field during batting practice, saying to their children, "There he is. There's Willie."

Mays introduced a new aesthetic, a combination of drama and athleticism that broke fresh ground on the playing field. As the *New York Times*'s Arthur Daley noted at the end of the season, "He was blessed with that rarest intangible, color. He was a colorful player and this had nothing to do with the pigmentation of his skin. His crowd appeal was immense because of the Wonder's flair for the spectacular."

In one of the keenest observations of Mays, Daley wrote: "It just seemed as though he could do nothing unostentatiously."

Reporters dubbed him "Willie the Wonder," "the Amazin' Mays," or "the Minneapolis Marvel," but those tags didn't stick. They were too conventional, too generic, relying on the crutch of alliteration instead of something truly original. A better moniker soon evolved. Mays had a habit of greeting people with "Hey," which was often used instead of "Hello" where he grew up. His "Hey" was a high-spirited chirp, and because he was terrible with names and was constantly being introduced to strangers, he would follow his greeting with a question: "Hey, how you doin'?" or "Hey, where you been?" hoping that he might learn who he was talking to. A reporter for the *New York Journal-American*, Barney Kremenko, noted how frequently Mays used "Hey." Thus was born the nickname, "the Say Hey Kid." It was pithy, unique, and flowed directly from his being. So perfectly attuned was the name to the character that neither age nor injury nor the long, sobering grind of experience ever replaced it.

But the name was also misunderstood. The public and the press thought that Mays liked to call out "Say hey!" He did chant those words for a record that was produced in 1954, but according to Mays, he never used the phrase in any conversation. The confusion reigned for years. As early as 1955, reporters noted that Mays no longer said "Say hey," which was seen as evidence of his waning innocence. In 1970, *Sports Illustrated* mourned: "It has been 15 years, probably, since Mays last actually said, 'Say Hey!'" Mays made no effort to set the record straight. He always enjoyed being "the Say Hey Kid."

Once Mays knew he belonged, he lost his timidity with his teammates. He always enjoyed pranks, and the Giants' sullen clubhouse needed a few laughs. Mays bantered, snapped towels, battled in the showers, and led choruses of "It's Howdy Doody Time" on the train. He let his nails grow, put his index finger in someone's ear, turned his finger—and laughed uproariously. His teammates began covering their ears when they saw him coming. Whitey Lockman said Mays was "the life of the party. . . . It would not be right to call him a clown. He was just bubbling over with excitement and enthusiasm."

Durocher recalled, "He electrified the clubhouse. When he came in, all eyes were on him. The other players would make jokes around him and Willie would laugh in that tenor voice and suddenly everyone would feel good and know that our team had no more worries." Reporters were also smitten. "Willie answers all your questions breathlessly," said Bill Roeder of the *New York World-Telegram Sun*. "He sounds like a guy who has just been told that his house is on fire."

His teammates found Mays an easy target; they sometimes used a coarse hairbrush to scrub him down in the shower. In the locker room after one victory, they walked past him on their way to the shower, patting him on the back, each player with concealed shaving cream in his hand. Mays soon looked like a stick of cotton candy. In mock horror, he cried out in complaint, his voice, according to one sportswriter, sounding like "a ferryboat whistle tooting frantically in a fog."

On one occasion, he was given a handsome clock for a bubble gum endorsement. He was admiring it with cries of exultation when Durocher came in.

"You have to hand that thing over," he said sternly.

"How come?" Mays asked, his eyes getting large.

"First-year players have to hand over all gifts to the manager."

"Is that in the contract?"

"Right there in small print."

Mays complied. "Whatta I want to know the time for?" he said resignedly.

One day, Mays was walking to the clubhouse in center field after batting practice, and Earl Rapp, a journeyman outfielder with little speed, said, "Race you the rest of the way for five dollars."

"Let's go," Mays said. They took off, and Mays easily won.

"Okay," Rapp said. "Let's have the five."

"What do you mean? You owe me five! I beat you."

"Wasn't anything about beating anybody," Rapp said. "I just said I'd race you."

Sal Maglie was standing nearby. "Hey, Maglie!" Mays yelled. "What am I supposed to do?"

Maglie didn't hesitate. "Pay him."

Before Mays could reach into his pocket, another race was arranged, this one legitimate. Mays won by ten yards and squared his bet.

Even warm-ups could be turned into performance art, as Mays showed when he played "pepper" with Monte Irvin and Durocher. The game involves a hitter's rapping ground balls or liners to fielders ten to fifteen feet away, but Durocher had a different approach. As a member of the Gashouse Gang, he, with Pepper Martin and Joe Medwick, played a version that more closely resembled three jugglers in a circus, a game that Durocher's new partners embraced. For example, with Irvin hitting, Durocher seized a line drive and wound up to throw it back, but in a blur of elbows and knees tossed the ball to Mays, who snared it, faked a throw to Irvin, and floated the ball back to his manager. When Durocher lunged for it, Mays slapped him in the gut with his glove. "Ooof!" Durocher grunted. Mays spun away, keeling over in laughter.

Fans showed up early for these lively exchanges: the wily Durocher, with nimble hands and crackling ad libs, versus the amateur Mays, with his captivating pantomime and wailing ripostes. Mays and Durocher would place bets on the pepper games—each error by Willie would cost him a Coke. One morning, Durocher smashed the ball well to Mays's right, and all he could do was knock it down with a full-stretch lunge.

"Coke!" Durocher roared. "That's six you owe me."

"Ain't no Coke for that!" Mays cried in his high, plaintive voice. "That's a base hit."

"Six Cokes you owe me."

"Monte, what you say, roomie?"

"Six Cokes," Irvin deadpanned. Mays pouted while the appreciative fans cheered and hooted and the reporters noted his indelible spirit.

"Willie's exuberance," Roger Kahn says, "was his immortality."

Not everyone immediately embraced Mays, whose arrival forced Bobby Thomson to switch positions. "Naturally, you stay a little laid back when a new kid comes and takes over a key position," Lockman recalled. "We knew a little about Willie but didn't know whether he would be able to do the job, having just turned twenty. But after watching him for a while, we could certainly see he was going to be something special. Later in the season, there were a couple of players who began feeling resentful that Leo paid so much attention to Willie."

The black players in the league were clearly targeted by pitchers for brushbacks and beanballs. Of the four batsmen who were hit most often, three were African American: the Braves' Sam Jethroe (eleven times), Monte Irvin (nine), and Jackie Robinson (nine). As Horace Stoneham predicted, Mays was targeted, but as Mays had known, his quick reflexes allowed him to escape—pitches hit him only twice. One writer noted that Mays hit the dirt "as violently as anybody [and then] he's up in a second and back over the plate, waving his bat ominously and offering no word of complaint. His teammates recognize that as the mark of a real professional."

The Dodgers were particularly aggressive, and their catcher, Roy Campanella, delighted in taunting Mays—he called him "my pigeon." When Mays stepped into the box, Campanella would start the razzing: "What do you say, pup? What do you say? What do you say, Willie? When you going to get married? You getting much?"

Mays would address his tormentor as "Mr. Campanella," urging him to "leave me be," until one day he stepped out of the box and asked Durocher, who was the third base coach, for help.

"He's bothering me," Mays told him.

That could be easily solved, Durocher told him: "Pick up a handful of dirt and throw it in his face." Mays told Campy he would do just that if the catcher kept harassing him.

One time, Dodger pitcher Preacher Roe almost drilled Mays with a pitch at his chin. As Mays stared at him from the ground, Campanella said, "You think he's a good pitcher, Willie? Well, wait till you see Newcombe. He just hates young niggers."* It was a joke designed to rattle, but the hazing came with an edge. Campanella had spent nine years in the Negro Leagues and didn't believe Mays had paid his dues—it all came too easy, too fast. He deserved to be knocked down. This resentment softened over the years, but not in Mays's rookie season. Campanella said, "When I was his age, I couldn't get into the majors. I had to learn the hard way. This kid walks right in, and he's gonna have to learn the hard way too."

The Giants recognized the pressures that uniquely affected their Negro players, so they asked the boxing promoter Frank Forbes to be their guardian. Forbes was a distinguished fifty-eight-year-old Harlemite, a former athlete himself (baseball, football, and boxing) who favored bow ties and erudite phrases. In 1951, his principal responsibility was Willie Mays.

"When I first met Willie," Forbes later said, "I thought he was the most open, decent, down-to-earth guy I'd ever seen—completely unspoiled and completely natural. I was worried to death about the kind of people he might get mixed up with. He'd have to live in Harlem, and believe me, that can be a bad place, full of people just wanting to part an innocent youngster from his money. Somebody had to see to it that Willie wasn't

---

* In the 1980s, Roger Kahn and his daughter, Alissa, were invited to the White House, and President Reagan recounted that knockdown pitch, with Campanella's comment. "My daughter was shocked," Kahn says.

exploited, sift the chalk from the flour, figure out who was in a racket and who was in a legitimate organization."

His first task was finding Mays a suitable place to live. When they met, Mays was living near the Polo Grounds, in a railroad flat with seven rooms, an arrangement made through a family acquaintance in Fairfield. Forbes disapproved. The place was crowded, with two or three sleeping in a room, and far too loud with conversation and "hilarity." It was no place for a ballplayer. Mays needed a "good home environment" with "good home-cooked meals," and Forbes found one: the first floor of a house owned by David and Ann Goosby, on the corner of St. Nicholas Place and 155th Street, a short walk from the ballpark.

"Mrs. Goosby," as Mays called her, reminded him of his aunt Sarah. She was a stout, light-skinned matron who cooked two meals a day for Willie (breakfast: bacon and eggs, hash browns, fruit, and milk; dinner: steaks or chops, vegetables, and potatoes), cleaned for him, washed his clothes, and smothered him with stern affection. As she told *Time* magazine, she spoke to Willie "about taking care of himself . . . not that he needs it often. Willie's a good boy. About all I have to lecture him on besides eating properly is his habit of reading comic books. That boy spends hours, I swear, with those comics." She also became one of his biggest fans, the walls of her living room soon adorned with his photographs above her floral sofas, her tables lined with his trophies. Mays had his own bedroom, which gave him space to stock his expanding wardrobe, and Ann Goosby was impressed by her boarder's fastidiousness: "He's not flashy, but my, is he fussy. He won't wear anything that's the slightest bit wrinkled or spotted."

Mays couldn't go anywhere far without Forbes—a diner, a menswear store—though he discovered that his most persistent challenges were not from hustlers or gamblers but from young women. Of the half a dozen or so ladies who stood outside the clubhouse seeking autographs after games, "maybe four or five would be after Willie," Forbes recalled. "Some would rush up with autograph books and have notes in the books—'My name is so-and-so and you can reach me at such-and-such a number.' When I have seen such notes, I have taken them and torn them up then and there. When Willie saw them, he would look at them but make no comment. He would never say anything about them. Some he just put in his pocket and others he paid no attention to. He probably threw the notes away when he got home."

Mays found dates; Forbes just tried to screen out the undesirables. That Mays didn't drink alcohol made his job easier, but Willie's love of cherry Cokes still left him vulnerable. On one occasion, Forbes was at a bar in Harlem, Bowman's, when someone came in and announced the sighting of a certain woman drinking sodas at a nearby drugstore. The woman's taste for brandy made her foray into carbonation rather odd until Forbes realized this particular drugstore was frequented by Mays. He smelled a trap. He rushed to the emporium and found Mays at the food counter, soft drink in hand, chatting with the woman. She was dressed nicely.

Forbes concluded that quick intervention was required. He sat on the stool next to her and ordered the most muscular drink on the menu, a double chocolate ice cream soda with extra cream. Once it arrived, he reached over for a straw and intentionally knocked it onto the woman's lap. In mock alarm, he jumped back and bumped the would-be seductress off the stool. "When she hit the floor," Forbes said, "she was really a mess, but I had to do it to protect Willie. I apologized most profusely."

Mays remained serenely above the fray, only commenting later to Forbes, "Damn. She sure got messed up."

Forbes was not above self-promotion, and he contributed to the view that Mays was unnecessarily coddled, even patronized, by the Giants. But Mays appreciated that an experienced hand was looking out for him. Many years later, he lamented that teams no longer provided their young players with guardians. Those players now had lawyers, accountants, and agents, but to Mays they were high-priced mercenaries paid to advance their clients' financial interests as well as their own. They were not part of the larger baseball family; they were not there to actually protect young men, to help them find a place to live, to escort them shopping, to divert them from trouble, and, if need be, to knock an ice cream soda into the lap of a fashionable temptress.

Once Mays moved in with the Goosbys, Durocher began to call almost every night, and their relationship deepened as the season progressed. Durocher offered tips on playing pool, buying clothes, negotiating with the owner, dealing with the press, dating, and being a big leaguer. Even Ann Goosby was surprised at their closeness. "Willie takes that man's word for just about everything," she said. "He almost won't make a move unless he's talked to him first."

One evening, Durocher was to pick up Mays in his new black Cadillac and drive him to a father-son fan banquet in Hackensack, New Jersey. By now, Mays was friendly with the kids on the block, so he told them that his chauffeur was coming to pick him up in a limousine. It was hard to fathom—luxury transport for a mere baseball player, in Harlem no less, so by the time Durocher drove up, several dozen people were waiting for him. Mays opened the back door, waved to everyone, and shouted, "Okay, James, let's go!"

Durocher played along, obediently driving off before telling Willie to get his ass in the front seat. Durocher, however, had the next surprise. Once at the banquet, he told Mays he was going to have to say a few words. Mays had never given a speech and wasn't about to now.

"Nothing to it," Durocher said. "Just tell them you're happy to be here. Stuff like that. When I think you've said enough, I'll pull on your coat so you'll know you should sit down."

Mays had no escape, and it was even worse than he'd imagined. He was the first speaker called, and when he stood and looked into the room of upturned faces—more than twelve hundred—he felt more nerves than before a big game. He began hesitantly.

"Mr. Leo is the main speaker," he said, "so I'm not going to say much." While he was stammering for more words, a black boy hollered something from the back. Mays couldn't make out the question and looked at Durocher, who told him to ask the boy to come up front.

Mays did, and the boy stepped forward with awestruck eyes. It was hard to say who was trembling more, Mays or the boy. Finally, the boy asked, "Willie, who's the greatest center fielder in baseball?"

Mays just stared at him and delivered the perfect answer: "You're looking at him."

The crowd went wild. Mays grinned, and Durocher grabbed his coattail and began pulling it. "Sit down," he said, "you got 'em now! You don't have to say anything more!"

Mays was so completely unaffected, so transparent, that he always amused Durocher. On the road, he would approach him in the hotel lobby, pull out his pockets, and ask to borrow twenty dollars. "I'm empty, man."

"Well, what do you want from me?"

"I know you're loaded, man. You're loaded."

Durocher would pull out a twenty-dollar bill, Mays would snatch it, and the next day when Durocher asked for his change, Mays would again plead poverty, claiming he bought ice cream for a group of kids.

But Durocher needed no excuse to spoil him. He would invite Mays into his room and show him a mohair sweater or a handsome sports coat. "How'd you like one of these?" he'd ask. And before Mays could respond, he'd say, "Well, it's yours!" And Mays would beam with appreciation.

If Durocher was Mays's father figure, then Monte Irvin was his surrogate older brother. Their friendship played a decisive role in both their careers and the fate of the '51 Giants.

Understated and respectful, Irvin took remarkable care never to offend. His name, for example, was Monford Merrill Irvin, and he was called

"Monty." But when he reached the big leagues, he changed his name to "Monte" because when he signed baseballs, the *y* ran into the names of other players. He was born in Alabama, one of thirteen children, but in grade school his family moved to Orange, New Jersey, where he lived in a hardscrabble, integrated neighborhood. Monte could have easily found trouble but turned to sports instead.

He almost died as a senior in high school when he contracted hemolytic streptococcus, a potentially fatal infection. The doctors thought they needed to amputate his left arm to save him. "No," his mother said. "He's an athlete. If he wakes up with no left arm, he'll die anyhow." She called on a "higher doctor." Monte survived, leading him to conclude that he had been saved for a special mission on earth. That mission was baseball, played with gratitude and honor.

At nineteen, he joined the Newark Eagles in the Negro Leagues, a fast, right-handed-hitting outfielder who could catch, throw, and drive the ball with power to all fields. So great was his potential that one of his high school teachers called a major league owner, urging him to watch the kid play. The owner sent three different scouts. Their conclusion: "He's the next DiMaggio."

The owner was Horace Stoneham. But it was 1938, and Stoneham was no pioneer. "It was too soon," he later told Irvin. So Irvin stayed with the Eagles and by 1941 may have been the best player in the Negro Leagues, averaging .409 over two full seasons. The following year, he played in the Mexican League, got married, and hit .397 on his honeymoon. He was just reaching his prime when he was drafted by the army and served in a segregated engineering outfit in England, France, and Germany. After the war, he was playing baseball again, and in 1945 the Brooklyn Dodgers approached him about signing with them. But while Irvin was stationed overseas, he developed an inner-ear imbalance, which cost him his timing and even some of his strength. He told the Dodgers he wasn't ready. Jackie Robinson got the call instead. By all rights, Irvin should have broken the color line: he and Robinson were born less than a month apart, but he had more experience than Robinson and, but for the effects of a freak military ailment, he was the better player. He missed his chance at history.

Irvin stayed with the Newark Eagles. Four years later, Stoneham amended his previous oversight and signed him to a contract. When Irvin made his debut for the Giants in July of 1949, he was already thirty years old.

The Giants had pegged him as their Great Black Hope, a counterpoint to Robinson, and he indeed increased the attendance of African Americans at the Polo Grounds. But his performance was erratic. After a disappointing start in thirty-four games in 1949 (.224 average, seven RBIs, and no home runs), he began the 1950 season in the minors. He returned to the Giants in a month and, over 110 games, had a good year: .299 average, with fifteen homers and sixty-six RBIs.

But 1951 began as a disaster. Playing out of position at first base, he made eight errors in thirty-four games—he said he felt like "a bear trying to open a sardine can"—and was hitting .276 with two homers. He was dropped to eighth in the order. He was bitter about his defensive assignment and, his career seemingly stalled, sullen about the glory that had eluded him. His fortunes began to improve when he was returned to the outfield in the middle of May, but the arrival of Willie Mays did far more.

Irvin saw something special in the young man from his own state of Alabama. Irvin saw himself. He had been nineteen when Stoneham concluded "it was too soon" to bring a black player to the majors, but the time was right for Mays. Irvin believed he could be a role model, a credit to their race, someone whose accomplishments on and off the field could far exceed any of his own.

Durocher told Irvin, "Tell him what to do and how to do it." That partly referred to baseball: Irvin positioned him in the outfield and advised him on what pitchers threw, how well they held runners, and which catchers had good arms. Mays helped Irvin as well. After the two bumped into each other on their first night in the outfield in Philadelphia, Durocher ordered that any ball Mays could reach was his to catch. The corner outfielders could cede the gaps and just protect the lines, reducing their burdens. Irvin had a good arm, but on some balls hit over his head, Mays sprinted to medium left field to serve as the cutoff man, shortening the distance for Irvin while giving the Giants a much stronger arm for throws to home plate.

Off the field, Irvin saw Mays for what he was—good-natured, shy, naive, unschooled in city life, untouched by cynicism. Mays all but shouted out his vulnerability. At one point, he signed an exclusive bubble gum testimonial, but then he signed another testimonial, equally exclusive, for the bubble gum's chief competitor. Something had to be done, so he sent the second company a letter that said in full: "Being an infant, and under 21, I could not sign legally with you people. Please forgive me. Willie Mays."

As Irvin recalls: "Coming from the South, he didn't have a lot of the social graces or the sophistication that he should have, but he was a quick learner." In restaurants, Irvin taught him how to order food (for eggs, "just say medium"), what fork to use, how much to tip. Mays bought a car in New York, a Pontiac, because that's what Irvin drove, but it sat in a parking lot. Durocher didn't want him to use it, and Mays wouldn't learn how to drive until the off-season. Irvin told him the places to go and—more important—the places and people to avoid: "sharpies," "numbers runners," "pimps," and "unsavory characters" as well as "bar maids" and women with bad reputations or questionable motives. Mays had already heard some of this advice from the Black Barons as well as from Frank Forbes, such as the warning not to date white women (Mays never did).

"All the women came after him," Irvin says. "He would ask me, 'Irv, do you know this girl?' I'd just say, 'If she's got a good reputation, then good luck.'"

Irvin, like Durocher, recognized how sensitive Mays was to criticism, so he made sure never to embarrass him when he did something wrong. "If it were me," Irvin would say, "I'd do it this way."

Sometimes his advice was taken, sometimes not. Irvin, for example, believed that Mays's reluctance to talk to reporters hurt his endorsement opportunities. As a rookie, Mays allowed Durocher to do most of his talking, and Durocher typically screened interview requests as well. But by 1954 Mays was still uncomfortable around many writers and in some cases wouldn't speak with them, even those eager to praise him. Irvin told Mays to look at Mickey Mantle, who was depicted in the press as a personable fellow ready to share a good joke and an easy laugh.

"I think if you just kid around with reporters a little more, be a little friendlier and be more like Mantle, you'd get more endorsements," Irvin said.

"I have to be me," Mays replied.

Irvin was also mindful that the journalists were using Mays to perpetuate negative stereotypes about Negroes. At the time, blacks were often presented in literature and film as having an "innate gayety of soul"; they lived an "entire lifetime of laughs and thrills [of] excitement and fun" in a society burdened "with unnatural inhibitions." Mays had his first brush with the Stepin Fetchit image—servile and simpleminded—in Minneapolis but would experience it more broadly in New York. One newspaper cartoon in 1951, echoing the cartoon that had appeared in Minneapolis a year earlier, depicted Mays in action, saying, "Ah gives baserunners the heave ho! Ah aims to go up in the world."

While he was constantly described as a great "natural" or "instinctive" player, the cliché was often used to patronize him, to diminish his intelligence, to imply that he was simply following the impulses of his body. As the *New York Journal-American*'s Bill Corum wrote, "He is no mental Giant, Willie. . . . Yet baseball is played by instinct and a fellow with a quick eye, sense of timing and natural instinct for it seldom makes the wrong play. My observation of Mays is that he was born with these things. The born ball player with physical equipment."

Even the favorable representations of Mays depicted him as a poorly educated naif. As the *Sporting News* wrote, "With his wide, white smile gleaming out of a pug-nose, baby face, Willie says, 'If you worry about one thing, pretty soon you start to worry about others. I don't worry about nothin.'" On another occasion, the *Sporting News* published a story about a reporter's asking Mays what it felt like to be the game's most "exciting" player. Mays misunderstood the word, confusing it with "excitable," and he responded, "I don't know why they call me that. I don't ever get excited. I just play my game and let others get excited."

Durocher contributed to the unfavorable perceptions. His protection bordered on condescension. With Mays calling him "Mr. Leo" and Durocher responding with "my boy," with the manager's screening interview requests and the center fielder's allowing Leo to answer for him, at times they projected an uncomfortable image—in Roger Kahn's words—of "straw boss" and "plantation hand." In Durocher's autobiography, he claimed that Mays "could hardly read or write when he came up," which was false. (Mays's postcards from the time demonstrate competent writing skills.) Durocher defended his pampering as a means of restoring Mays's confidence, but the effect was also to infantilize him at a time when blacks were already stereotyped as intellectually inferior.

Monte Irvin knew that some black fans were uncomfortable with the relationship. "It bothered me a little too," he says. "I saw what was going on. I thought the whole situation could have been handled a little better." He also feared that the public did not respect Mays beyond his baseball skills. "All he did was go out there and play great baseball, but I also wanted him to carry himself with a certain amount of dignity," he says. He encouraged Mays to get a tutor and improve his elocution, but Mays was reluctant. "It's never too much trouble," Irvin told him, "if you want to progress the right way."

In truth, with a high school degree, Mays had as much education as most big league players, who were hardly exemplars in diction and grammar. What worked against him was his race and his southern roots. "Black folks had their own language, a comfortable language that we all understood," says Mays's cousin, Loretta Richardson. This separate language made them "bilingual," she says, as they spoke an informal "black dialect" as well as standard English. "When you got into proper places," she notes, "you had to speak proper language"—a language, however, that her cousin had not mastered as a suddenly famous rookie.

Indeed, Mays was self-conscious about his voice, his verbal skills, and his education, so he was grateful to Durocher for rescuing him. "When the newspapermen used to ask me questions," he recalled, "I didn't know how to answer. Leo knew how scared I was, and he told the newspapermen to ask him the questions, and he'd try to answer them for me. I never forgot that."

In years to come, when he had more self-confidence, he committed himself to improving his speaking skills, paying attention to the sounds of words and making connections with audiences—everything, in other words, that Monte Irvin had once urged.

If Irvin's maturity inched Mays into adulthood, Mays had a more catalytic effect on Irvin. They played silly games on the road, such as Captain of the Room—whoever got more base hits that day was Captain for the night, so the other guy had to carry the bags, get the newspaper, and answer the telephone. Mays wouldn't allow Irvin to be discouraged, even when he was slumping. The rookie brought his portable record player on the road, and one night after Irvin had taken the collar, Mays put on some music and started humming. When Irvin demanded that he turn it off, Mays asked if he wanted to play cards. Or go to the movies. Or shop for clothes. Irvin kept shaking his head.

"I know you not hitting, but what good you going to do worrying?" Mays said. "Be like Willie. I don't worry about nothing."

When Irvin started to argue, Mays cut him off. "There's good in every bad," he said.

What meant the most to Irvin was simply Mays's presence. His running gags and pealing laughter seemed to disperse his own gloom and frustration. "Willie gave me a lift," Irvin says. "You always knew when he was around, because the love of life just flowed out of him, and it got to the point where it was a pleasure to come to the ballpark every day."

It showed in Irvin's performance. Despite his bad start in 1951, he led the team in batting average (.312), RBIs (121, which also led the league), and on-base percentage (.415); was tied for first in stolen bases (12); and was second in homers (24) and slugging percentage (.514). By far his finest year in the majors, he finished third as the National League's MVP. But he said he was not the most important player on the team. "The single greatest factor [in our pennant run], beyond a shadow of a doubt, was the presence of Willie Mays. . . . He just made it better for everybody," he said.

At the All-Star break, the Giants were 44–36 and eight games behind the Dodgers. The Giants brought up second baseman Davey Williams from Minneapolis—Stanky was fine, but Durocher wanted to look at Williams for the next year. The move seemed reasonable, for the Giants couldn't close the gap in July, and by early August, the Dodgers appeared to have sealed the race. On August 9, they beat the Giants, 6–5, in a bitter ten-inning contest that concluded a three-game sweep. The Dodgers had now won twelve of fifteen against the Giants and were 12½ games in front. Afterward, in the thinly partitioned locker rooms at Ebbets Field, the Dodgers taunted Durocher: "Leo, Leo, you in there? Eat your heart out, Leo! Yeah, that's your team! Nobody else wants it!" Next they sang, "Roll out the barrel. We've got the Giants on the run." Finally, Jackie Robinson stood outside the locker room. He and Durocher had had an ugly falling out when Durocher returned as the Dodgers' manager in 1948, and these two single-minded, competitive men now hated each other. With the pennant seemingly in hand, Robinson raised a bat, pounded the door, and unleashed a victor's stream of epithets.

There was a pause. Then Eddie Stanky walked over to the door and yelled, "Stick that bat down your throat, you black nigger son-of-a-bitch." Stanky, as well as Bill Rigney and Alvin Dark, turned and suddenly saw Monte Irvin. The three white men stood sheepishly until Irvin, a slight grin forming on his face, said, "That's good enough for me, Eddie."

The next game, on August 11, was another Giant loss to the Phillies, giving them six losses in the last eight games. After the Dodgers won the first game of a doubleheader, the Giants trailed by 13½ games. At some point in July or August (the date is unclear), Dodger manager Charlie Dressen summarized the race: "The Giants is dead."

But the Giants also had Willie Mays, and while no pennant race turns on a single catch or throw, Mays was responsible for one memorable play that convinced his teammates that any game down the stretch, no matter the inning or odds, could be won.

On August 15, the Giants and Dodgers played each other again, this time at the Polo Grounds before 21,007 fans. The Giants had won the first game of the series, giving them four in a row and stirring thoughts of a comeback. The Dodgers still had a comfortable lead but wanted to squash a possible uprising. Mays had cooled off at the plate—he hit just two homers in August—but in less than three months, he had proven he belonged in the big leagues.

With Jim Hearn pitching for the Giants, New York grabbed a one-run lead in the first inning, but the Dodgers' Ralph Branca kept the game close and Brooklyn pushed a run across in the seventh. In the top of the eighth with one out, Billy Cox was on third, and Carl Furillo, a right-handed pull hitter, was at the plate. Mays shaded him to left center. Furillo drove the ball into right center, and Mays took off. At first glance, it appeared a certain run. The ball was either going to fall for a hit or Mays would catch it and Cox would tag up and score. Cox, a defensive specialist, had come to the majors as a shortstop, and he looked like one—slender and fast. As Mays closed in on the ball, Cox stood poised at third in a sprinter's stance. Mays extended his glove and speared the drive—an outstanding catch—but the play was just getting started. Cox bolted for the plate as Mays was barreling toward the right field line, his momentum carrying him away from the play. He was in no position to throw, but when he planted his left foot, he sharply pivoted counterclockwise, his number temporarily facing home plate, his eyes flashing intensely before the bleacher fans. It appeared as if the impact of the ball had given him the additional thrust to pirouette in spikes. Without hesitating or even looking, he whipped his right arm around and fired the ball, then corkscrewed his body into the ground. His hat flew off. He peered under his armpit and tried to follow the drama at home plate.

Despite Mays's impossibly awkward position, the ball, according to one writer, "took off as though it had a will of its own," cutting through the air like a bullet, taking aim at the orange-trimmed black letters across the chest of first baseman Whitey Lockman, who had positioned himself to cut off the ball. The catcher, Wes Westrum, screamed, "Let it go!" Lockman ducked, he later said, "more out of self-preservation than anything else." Westrum, built like a block of granite, hadn't removed his mask because he didn't expect a play, but now both ball and runner came bearing down. He later estimated that when the ball reached him, it was traveling 85 mph, and if the umpire had called it, it would have been a strike. Russ Hodges had the call: "Willie Mays . . . is reaching up with one hand, he's got it, he spins 180 degrees. Cox breaks for home. Wait a minute! Wait a minute! The ball comes into Westrum on the fly. Cox slides, and Westrum cuts him down at the plate! Cox is out! Billy Cox is out!"

Inside the Polo Grounds, there was a momentary silence, similar to the response when Mays hit his first homer, as if the fans couldn't comprehend what they had just seen. Then the stadium erupted while Cox sat staring at the plate in disbelief. The double play complete, Mays trotted off the field, and when his teammates greeted him on the top steps of the dugout, he shrugged his way through, as though uncomfortable with all the fuss. He was already thinking about the bottom of the eighth—he was the first man up.

When he walked to the plate, he received another standing ovation and still another when he lined a single to left. The next hitter, Westrum, launched a home run into the upper deck, and the Giants won, 3–1.

After the game, Jackie Robinson said it was the greatest throw he'd ever seen, but his manager, Charlie Dressen, was less magnanimous. "I'd like to see him do it again. If he does it again, I'll say he's great." Furillo was bitter. "That was the luckiest throw I ever saw in my life," he said. "He can try that fifty times and he won't come close again."

But Eddie Brannick, the Giants' well-groomed traveling secretary known for his lilting Irish brogue and his kindness to reporters, made a rare visit to the clubhouse to compliment Mays. "I have been in baseball for forty-five years," he said. "I have seen Speaker, DiMaggio, Moore, all of them in center, but I've never seen anything like that throw. This kid made the greatest play I ever saw."

Indeed, the play became known as "the Throw," except it wasn't really the throw that made it spectacular. It was Mays's improvisation, the subtlety of his footwork, the ability to redirect his momentum toward home plate. Strictly speaking, it was an "instinctive" play in that he had never mapped it out on a practice field, but while chasing the ball, he envisioned how he would catch it, spin, and throw. The key was to glimpse the cutoff man in his peripheral vision, so he had a target—and hope the cutoff man was positioned correctly. Nevertheless, Bill Corum wrote that Mays only attempted the play because he wasn't very smart: "A thinking ball player probably would have thought . . . that the play was impossible and never have attempted it."

Mays's teammates gave him his due. As Lockman later said, "I was absolutely astounded. I'd had balls thrown to me by Stanky, or whoever was playing second, only a few feet away, really hard—you know how hard it is, you hardly have time to react. Well, this ball was like that, only it was coming from, what, 250, 275 feet away. I remember seeing Willie throw, and the next instant the ball was on top of me."

Because the play was not filmed, it survives only in written accounts and in the fading memories of those few who saw it. But Mays knows it was one of his greatest feats ever on the playing field. As he said at the time, "It was the perfectest throw I ever made."

It also cut the Dodger lead to 10½ games.

The win continued a streak that would reach sixteen games, culminating in a doubleheader sweep against the Cubs on August 27, which cut the Dodger lead to five games. Oddly, with the exception of Mays and Westrum, the Giants were not that good defensively. In August they committed at least one error in twenty-two consecutive games. But they were led by fine pitching, the double-play combination of Dark and Stanky, and the emergence of Irvin as a consistent force at the plate. Irvin credits Durocher for encouraging his team without applying undue pressure. He would not implore, "We have to catch the Dodgers" or "You have to get a hit." Rather, he'd say, "Let's see how close we can come" or "I need another hero today—who's going to step up?"

Mays's inexperience showed at times. On September 3 in the Polo Grounds, Mays hit what appeared to be an inside-the-park homer against Robin Roberts of the Phillies. But he missed third base and was called out, and the Giants lost, 6–3. Another time, he ran from first to third on a drive to the outfield. When the ball was caught, he raced across the diamond, forgetting to touch second, and was doubled off. He made rookie mistakes in the outfield as well. He could be too aggressive, charging past grounders, overthrowing bases, or taking balls that would have been easier caught by teammates. Though Durocher had told him to catch everything in sight, some reporters accused him of "hogging" balls.

Mays's miscues were easily forgiven, however, as his popularity extended beyond the Polo Grounds. At the time, players were occasionally given their own "day," for some special tribute, in their own ballpark. But on August 17 in Philadelphia, Shibe Park was the unlikely site of Willie Mays Day. The residents of nearby Trenton wanted to honor Mays for his previous season in their town. A nine-man citizens committee in Trenton organized the tribute, and with several thousand Trentonians in the stands, a ceremony was held before the game. Mays received, among other things, $250 in cash from the Carver YMCA, a plaque from the city of Trenton, a golf bag and clubs, and an oil painting of himself, in his Giants uniform, leaping for a catch.

The bleacher fans in the Polo Grounds, perhaps discomfited by a rival city's celebrating their hero, pooled their coins together and, on September 1, gave Mays a new wristwatch.

On September 8, the Giants lost to the Dodgers in a blowout at Ebbets Field. With the Dodgers ahead, 7–0, in the eighth inning, Dressen ordered Jackie Robinson to squeeze a run home. After the game, Durocher cheerfully dismissed the suggestion that the Dodgers were rubbing it in. Asked why, he said, "Because now I've got their motherfucking bunt sign, that's why."

After winning the next game, New York was now 5½ games behind, and the schedule had broken against them—they were in the midst of a sixteen-game road trip. On September 11, they split a doubleheader in St. Louis, putting them eight games out on the loss side. Newspapers began printing the Dodgers' magic number: 11. But the Giants kept winning, inching to five games out on September 15, though the fans were losing faith. One week later, with the Giants 4½ games out, fewer than twelve thousand people showed up at the Polo Grounds with the Boston Braves in town. The Giants won while the Dodgers lost a doubleheader, then the Giants reeled off four more straight wins, including two in Philadelphia. On September 27 and 28, as the Giants rested, the Dodgers lost two games, finally tying the teams as they headed into the last two games of the regular season. The race had captivated New York. The *Times* began putting the scores on the front page, and at the featherweight title fight between Sandy Saddler and Willie Pep at the Polo Grounds on September 26, the public address announcer gave the Giants' score between each round.

In the final weekend, the Giants faced the Braves in Boston, with Warren Spahn pitching. Mays was still struggling at the plate, perhaps feeling the pressure of the pennant race, and went hitless for the game—but was still a key offensive player. In the second inning, he drew a walk. At the time, if he wanted to steal, he would nod his head just enough so that the bill of his cap would bob. If Durocher consented, he would show Mays the palm of his hand. Now Durocher, standing in the third base coaching box, looked at Mays and thought he saw his cap bob. Durocher couldn't believe it. As he later said, "Warren Spahn had the best move to first base anybody had ever seen. You didn't steal second base on Spahn. You just tried not to get picked off. But sure enough, the bill on Willie's hat jumps again. He not only wants to run against Spahn, he wants to run right now. . . . I'm sweating, and this rookie, all he wants to do is run? You want to go, son, here's the palm. Go ahead. Boom! He stole second base clean as a whistle, dusted off his pants, and the cap is going up and down again. He stole third just as easily and scored on Don Mueller's single. We scored two more runs before the day was over, but the game was won right there. He took the pressure right off the whole club, especially their dandy little manager."

The Dodgers won their game against the Phillies as well, setting up the final day of the regular season. The Giants, in another low-scoring contest, took a 3–1 lead into the ninth; the Braves rallied for a run, but starter Larry Jansen held on to win. After Irvin caught the final out, the Giants rushed onto the field and engulfed their exhausted pitcher. Mays went 0-for-4 with a strikeout.

The Giants finished the season at 96–58, winning their last seven games and forty out of their last fifty-four. At least for now, they had sole possession of first place for the first time.

When Mays reached the clubhouse, he thought the Giants were going to win the pennant, for the Dodgers had been trailing in Philadelphia. But there was no celebration. Initially down, 6–1, the Dodgers had rallied and were now losing, 8–5, in the fifth. With six cases of unopened champagne at the ready, the Giants gathered around radios in a steamy locker room, expecting to celebrate, and for more than an hour they paced, cheered, and cursed, awaiting their fate. Finally showered and dressed, they left Braves Field by bus, and when they boarded the Merchants Limited, the premier Boston–New York train, the Dodgers were still losing by three. The champagne came with them. Heading toward Grand Central Station, the Giants ate steaks and played cards. "They were having a hell of a time," Herman Franks recalled. "They were cutting each other's ties off."

Giant Vice President Chub Feeney could follow the Dodgers' game on a telephone in the back of the train—he dialed into a radio station in New York—and he relayed the action, play by play. The Giants heard that the Dodgers scored three runs to push the game into extra innings, but when the Phillies loaded the bases with one out in the bottom of the twelfth, Feeney lost his contact at the station.

With two outs, the Phillies' Eddie Waitkus smashed a low line drive to the right of second base. Surely this would end the Dodgers' season. But Jackie Robinson ran to his right, dove, and caught the ball with his glove just off the ground. He fell hard on his shoulder, scraped his face, and stayed on the ground, but he finally rose and walked unsteadily to the dugout. In the top of the fourteenth, in what might have been Robinson's greatest day in the majors, he came up with two outs and crashed a homer off Robin Roberts, giving the Dodgers a 9–8 win. A reporter on the Giants' train was told of the score by phone; word soon spread, and the champagne was never opened.

Five thousand fans met the Giants at Grand Central Terminal at nine-thirty that night, and another throng, not as large but equally boisterous, greeted the Dodgers at Penn Station. The resurrection of the Giants over the last two months had been matched by the Dodgers' improbable comeback in one game. The teams would now face each other in a best-of-three playoff series; the winner would face the Yankees. Little else in New York seemed to matter. As the *New York Times* editorialized the next day: "Now the playoff comes. For the next few days, just as in the past weeks, even the grimmest of world-wide news will have an overshadowing rival for attention in the whirl and clash of the great American game. This is as it should be. It is not thoughtless or careless to turn away from time to time to the drama of fine sport, and what we have witnessed and, one hopes, will be privileged to continue witnessing for at least two more days, is the highest and most inspirational drama we could hope for."

In September, the Giants won twenty out of twenty-five games. What Mays remembered from the race—what all the Giants remembered—was how the team pulled together. "I don't think there's ever been a club in the history of baseball that's been closer than the New York Giants were the last week of that season," Rigney later said. "I mean, guys were help-ing each other out so much, it was unbelievable. . . . We were still making errors, throwing to the wrong base, that kind of thing, but instead of get-ting on the culprit, or giving him the silent treatment, everyone else would sort of swarm around him and shower him with encouragement and love."

The team's racial diversity made its unity even more meaningful. "Back in those days, the race business was still a big problem for baseball," Irvin recalled. "And we had, what, four or five black guys on the club, all from down South somewhere. . . . And then we had all these white guys, and a lot of them were Southerners—Dark, Stanky, Lockman, Hearn, Ken-nedy, at least a dozen others. And yet there was never any anti-feeling on the club. Everybody pulled for everybody, no matter the color. In that respect, it was a very unusual club. Most every other club that had blacks in '51, there were problems. Even the Dodgers had problems. They still had guys on that club who were upset about playing with black men. My guess is that the Dodgers probably lost six or seven games purely on that alone."

To Mays, the Giants' togetherness simply confirmed his notion of base-ball as a family enterprise. Just as the parents, uncles, or older brothers help out the youngest in the clan, the owner, the manager, and the veter-ans help out the inexperienced and the unsure. Mays still marvels at how much support he received from Dark and Stanky as well as Durocher, Irvin, Forbes, and the entire organization. That was the significance of his rookie season. Baseball's familial bond was as powerful in the major leagues as it was in the cornfields of Alabama.

Mays had hit less than .200 down the stretch, which seemed to confirm Durocher's decision in August to drop him in the order. He put Mays in the seventh hole, flipping him with Bobby Thomson, who had had a rocky year himself. Thomson was miffed at Durocher, and perhaps Mays him-self, for removing him from center field. Durocher, for his part, didn't believe Thomson showed enough emotion, and the disgruntled player rode the bench for a while; by the end of June, he was hitting just .220 with nine homers. But he rebounded in the second half, moving to third base in July to replace the injured Hank Thompson, and he proved to be one of the Giants' most productive hitters, finishing the season with a team-best 32 home runs, 101 RBIs, and a .293 average.

The first playoff game, at Ebbets Field on a beautiful afternoon with temperatures in the low seventies, continued the hitting trends of the regular season. Mays went 0-for-3 and struck out twice against Dodger starter Ralph Branca. Overmatched, he didn't want to face Branca again.

But Thomson was one of the stars, hitting a home run, and the Giants won, 3–1, behind Jim Hearn.

In game two, at the Polo Grounds, Durocher could have started his ace, Sal Maglie, but he wanted to give his exhausted veteran one more day of rest. So the ball went to the erratic Sheldon Jones, a spot starter that year with a 6–10 record and a 4.26 ERA. He lost to the Dodgers, 10–0, the lousy weather intensifying the misery. Mays went 1-for-4 and committed an error.

Day baseball was a communal event, and fans followed the games from their offices, factories, taverns, and schools. That was never more true than in the deciding playoff game on Wednesday, October 3. The Dow Jones ticker sprinkled baseball updates among the stock quotes. The New York Telephone Company expanded its time-of-day service so that callers heard the time as well as the inning and the score. Belmont Park announced updates in between races. A Brooklyn prison provided portable radios for its inmates. Libraries set up televisions in conference rooms. Taverns without TVs were empty.

Media interest had soared. The World Series was to be the first sporting event to be televised live. That New York would be the site of all the games was fortunate, because it had the best facilities for transmission. But as the season wound down, a new possibility emerged for television—a playoff and a World Series. This double bonanza, wrote Charles Einstein, "touched off the wildest set-buying spree in all of television's history, before or after. In some cities, the sale of TV sets actually exceeded the sale of radios, even though the latter's totals included the radios in automobiles."

The radio kingpins were also at the final playoff game, including the Liberty Mutual network, which was carried on 520 stations, and powerful KMOX of St. Louis, which dispatched the animated Harry Caray to the Polo Grounds. Eight separate broadcasts aired the contest, but the story was television. By the time the game began beneath gray skies at 1:30 P.M., Americans across the nation were watching 16 million TVs, the first pitch seen, as Joshua Prager wrote, "by more sets of eyes than had ever before beheld a ball's flight."

Ironically, the game's attendance was only 34,320; the previous game's was more than 38,000. Threatening weather may have been a factor or just the nature of an unexpected third game. The crowd did include Jackie Gleason, Frank Sinatra, and Toots Shor, who, with tickets from Durocher, rode to the Polo Grounds in a limousine stocked with booze.

Both teams had their aces on the mound. Don Newcombe, the flame-throwing right-hander, and Sal Maglie, a curveball specialist with a reputation for knocking hitters down, had more than twenty wins apiece, but they each had tired arms. Newcombe had pitched more than fourteen innings over the weekend; Maglie had thrown a complete game on Saturday. Neither figured to be around by the end.

The Dodgers got off to a good start. Taking advantage of two walks by Maglie, they scored a run in the first, and a Thomson baserunning blunder snuffed out a scoring opportunity in the second. Maglie settled down and retired eleven in a row. The Giants appeared ready to rally in the fifth when Thomson stroked a double, but Mays couldn't advance him. By the seventh inning, the score was still 1–0, and as the skies darkened, the Giants finally broke through. With Irvin on third and Lockman on first and nobody out, Thomson hit a fly ball to Duke Snider in center, and Irvin dashed home to tie the game.

Mays came up once again. At that point, he was hitless for the day and 1-for-9 in the playoffs, with three strikeouts. He could give the Giants the lead with one swing or at least advance Lockman into scoring position. With the Dodgers down to their final six outs, Mays could be the hero.

He hit into a double play. *I could have been on the bench,* he thought, *and helped the team just as much.*

In the eighth, the Giants fell apart. With Snider on first and Pee Wee Reese on third, Maglie uncorked a wild pitch, giving the Dodgers their second run. Maglie walked Robinson intentionally and Andy Pafko bounced a hard grounder to third, but Thomson failed to scoop it—the play was generously ruled a hit—and Snider scored as the ball bounced into left. The Dodgers led, 3–1, and with two outs, Billy Cox made it 4–1 with a single past the demoralized Thomson. Durocher replaced Maglie, who in the clubhouse saw Horace Stoneham. "Sal, you had a hell of a year," he said. "Have a beer."

The tension was gone from the Dodgers' bench. Laughing and joking, they were certain of victory, their confidence reinforced by Newcombe's quick retiring of the Giants in the eighth.

The Dodgers went in order in the ninth, leaving the Giants one last try. The number two hitter in the order, Alvin Dark, was leading off, which meant Mays would be sixth up. Newcombe had given up only four hits and showed little signs of weakening. Mays doubted he would get another at-bat and sat quietly at the end of the bench.

Dark quickly fell behind in the count, 0–2, but then reached out for a fastball and slapped a ground ball wide of first for a single. With Don Mueller, a left-handed hitter, up next, the Dodgers inexplicably had first baseman Gil Hodges hold Dark. Down by three, Dark was not going to steal (he had twelve stolen bases for the season), and Mueller was a good pull hitter. Mays noticed the mistake from the dugout. So did many of the other Giants, including Mueller, who said he saw that hole on the right side "sitting there like a deer in the hunting season." He hit the first pitch to the right side, a certain double play if Hodges had been positioned correctly. Instead, the ball went through for a hit, chasing Dark to third. The tying run now came to the plate in Monte Irvin, but the slugger popped out to first. Two outs to go; an announcement was made in the press box: "Attention, press. World Series credentials for Ebbets Field can be picked up at six o'clock tonight at the Biltmore Hotel."

The next batter, Whitey Lockman, came to the plate thinking home run, and he smashed the ball into the left field corner. Dark scored and Mueller made it safely to third, but he didn't slide and, stepping awkwardly on the base, popped a tendon in his right ankle. He collapsed and was soon carried into the clubhouse on a stretcher. Clint Hartung, who had seen little action in recent weeks, ran for him. Durocher later said the selection of the broad-shouldered Hartung had little to do with strategy: as the third base coach, Durocher had been taunting Newcombe throughout the game and feared that after the final out, the bruising pitcher was going to attack him. Hartung was the only Giant big enough to stop him.

With the score 4–2 and runners at second and third, Dressen came to the mound, joined by the entire infield. Newcombe had thrown only 100 pitches, but he was spent, having thrown thirty-two innings in the last eight days. Three hurlers were ready in the bullpen—Ralph Branca, Carl Erskine, and Clem Labine. The next hitter, Bobby Thomson, watched the conference from the on-deck circle, with the next hitter peering out from the dugout. Mays wasn't sure who'd be pitching if he were to bat, but he knew he didn't want to face Branca. He had had one single and one double in nineteen at-bats against him, plus two walks and four strikeouts.

The first choice out of the bullpen might have been Erskine, but Dressen was told that he was bouncing his curveball, so Branca got the nod. A tall, swarthy right-hander, as a twenty-one-year-old in 1947, Branca posted a 21–12 record, won a World Series game, and was considered one of the best young pitchers in the game. He never developed into a star but by now was a dependable veteran. He had pitched eight innings just two days earlier.

Thomson headed for the plate, and Mays grabbed his bat. Just as center field in the Polo Grounds was oversized, so too was the area around home plate. It lay seventy-four feet from the backstop and was in the center of a large circle of dirt. Mays walked to the outer edge of that dirt, stopped, and dropped his right knee to the ground—as if he wanted the closest seat possible. He was usually not religious, but just as there are no atheists in a foxhole, there are none in the on-deck circle with a playoff series on the line. Mays began to pray: *Please don't let it be me. Don't make me come to bat now, God.*

With first base open, the Dodgers could have intentionally walked Thomson, who had smashed a home run off Branca in the first playoff game, to set up the double play, and given Mays's record against Branca and his playoff slump, that seemed like a reasonable move. But it would have violated one of baseball's hoariest axioms: never put the winning run on first base. There was another consideration—the Dodgers' high regard for Mays. As Branca said the following spring, "Willie may not have had a great average last year, but the Dodger pitchers all respected him. You could fool him, but you couldn't make any mistake and get away with it. He was too liable to get a hold of one and ruin you. . . . No, I never gave any thought to walking Thomson, and I don't think Dressen did either."

When Branca reached the mound, Dressen said, "Get [Thomson] out." Durocher, walking up to Thomson along the third base line, had only a few more words: "Boy, if you ever hit one out, hit one now."

The time was just shy of 4 P.M., and the Giant fans were clapping wildly. Branca's first pitch, a fastball, was taken for a strike on the inside part of the plate above the knees, a pitch that a low-ball hitter like Thomson would usually swing at. Some Dodgers believed Branca had gotten away with one. As Thomson recalled, "It's true, that first pitch was a blur, not because it was so fast but because I was so nervous my eyeballs were vibrating."

Durocher thought that Branca had thrown Thomson a slider for his home run the other day and figured he would see fastballs today.

"C'mon!" Durocher yelled to Thomson. "He'll come back with one!"

The catcher, Rube Walker, replacing the injured Campanella, called for another fastball. This one was a bit higher and more inside than the last pitch. Branca thought it was a good pitch—high and tight, tough to hit. But Thomson stepped in the bucket and uppercut the ball, powerfully rotating his broad back. He hit the ball flush, a line drive to left field toward the 315-foot mark. Branca yelled, "Sink! Sink! Sink!" Instead it sailed.

No one had a better view than Mays. When he looked up, he didn't think it would be a home run. The crowd soon knew otherwise, and so did Russ Hodges, who screamed: "There's a long drive. It's gonna be . . . I believe . . . the Giants win the pennant! The Giants win the pennant!"

Recalled announcer Ernie Harwell: "It was the biggest crowd noise I ever heard, a complete eruption, like the sky was being pulled apart."

Left fielder Andy Pafko, at the wall, gazed up plaintively into the stands. Thomson raced around the bases, dancing with joy. Durocher ran with him from third base. The other Giants fled the dugout and amassed at home plate. Photographers circled the gathering mob. Jackie Robinson stayed on the field, hands on hips, unwilling to leave until he saw Thomson touch each base. Ralph Branca picked up the rosin bag, threw it down, and began his long march into history.

In the clubhouse, Sal Maglie hoisted the bulky Horace Stoneham, put him down, then did a jig with the delirious owner.

And Willie Mays froze, paralyzed with excitement and wonder and relief, his knee still on the ground when Thomson touched second base. By the time he moved, he was on the fringe of the celebration, unable to break through the swarming mass, but he jumped like a pogo stick on the mob, leaping higher than anyone else. As one writer observed, "He was acting like a condemned man who had just received the midnight call from the governor."

The players made their way to the clubhouse, and the fans who had stormed the field were mostly respectful, patting the players on the back and urging them to beat the Yankees the next day. Once in the clubhouse, the Giants discovered how much confidence the locker room attendant had; he had put the champagne away. He pulled it out and plunged it into ice, but the Giants ended up drinking warm champagne. For Mays, it was his first sip, and he almost vomited—or, as Irvin described it, "he got excited and fell out."

Durocher said he was surprised that the Dodgers didn't intentionally walk Thomson. "I'm glad they didn't," Mays said. "I didn't want the pennant hanging on my shoulders." Outside the clubhouse, fans were shouting the names of individual players—Thomson, Stanky, Irvin, and of course Willie—and a police officer finally entered the locker room and said the players needed to do something or the crowd would never disperse. Mays was one of several who walked onto the steps and waved. Flash bulbs popped. Pennants waved. Hats were thrown to the sky, and the cheers wouldn't die. Mays couldn't believe the World Series started the very next day.

Several Dodgers, including a tearful Duke Snider, made their way into the Giant clubhouse. Jackie Robinson tapped Bill Rigney on the shoulder. "I want you to know one thing," he said. "We didn't lose it. You won it." He turned around and walked away.

At the time, neither Mays nor anyone else could have envisioned the historical significance of "the Shot Heard 'Round the World." The journalist George W. Hunt wrote, "It was likely the most dramatic and shocking event in American sports and has since taken on the transcendent character of Pearl Harbor and the Kennedy assassination." Decades later, the *Sporting News* declared it the greatest moment in baseball history, and *Sports Illustrated* ranked it the second greatest moment in sports history (after the U.S. hockey team's victory over the Soviet Union in the 1980 Winter Olympics). The U.S. Postal Service honored it with a stamp. It has been the subject of books, documentaries, poems, sermons, and debates. It was the center of *Underworld,* Don DeLillo's epic novel about America in the second half of the century. It inspired some of the best sportswriting in history (Red Smith: "Now it is done. Now the story ends. And there is no way to tell it. The art of fiction is dead. Reality has strangled invention. Only the utterly impossible, the inexpressibly fantastic, can ever be plausible again") and some of the worst ("Bobby Thomson brought New York City, the entire country, indeed many parts of the world, to a limp and traumatized ending. The joy of Giant partisans was orgasmic").

Willie Mays was a witness to history and the answer to a future trivia question—"Who was the on-deck batter when Bobby Thomson hit the Shot Heard 'Round the World?" One can only imagine what would have happened if Mays had faced Branca. Mays thinks that Durocher would have pinch-hit for him, but Durocher later said that Mays would have hit—he didn't pinch-hit for Mays the entire year.

Had Mays driven in the winning run, his emerging cult status would have reached unimaginable heights—he would indeed have been the Giants' savior who could deliver miracles. But at that moment, with him literally shaking, a winning hit seems unlikely, and had he made the final out, some of the luster of his rookie season would have been lost. He would have blamed himself for the team's defeat and carried that burden into the off-season.

In truth, the outcome served Mays well. He was given credit for raising the Giants' play and their spirits, and a new mantra, pushed by Durocher, had begun: with Willie Mays, we can't lose.

For Mays himself, the Miracle of Coogan's Bluff was pivotal beyond the winning of a pennant. He was embarrassed by his timidity, ashamed that he did not want to be the man at the plate with the game on the line. He was determined to change that. As he gained experience, he accepted those decisive challenges, he craved them, he wanted to be in the batter's box, staring at the pitcher, with the contest hanging in the balance. Fear did not best him again.

Thomson's immortal blow lost some of its shine with the disclosure of Durocher's elaborate effort to steal his opponents' pitching signals. Rumors about the scheme had swirled for years but were confirmed by the *Wall Street Journal* reporter Joshua Prager. His story on January 31, 2001, described how a Giant coach or player positioned himself in the center field clubhouse with a Wollensak telescope, which could be used to steal the signals given by the catcher. A bell-and-buzzer system was used to relay the pitch to either the Giants' bullpen or dugout. A player there would use various means to communicate the pitch to the hitter—crossing his legs, for example, or tossing a ball.

In Prager's story, Thomson was equivocal on whether he got the sign before his home run: "I'd have to say more no than yes." Even if he had, it was within the rules, for Major League Baseball didn't ban sign stealing with a "mechanical device" until 1961. Nonetheless, the Dodger fans, not to mention Ralph Branca himself, took solace: a devious tactic had been used to help the Giants win games the last two months of the season, including the clincher against Brooklyn.

Willie Mays is circumspect on the issue. He would never say anything to diminish the achievement of another player, particularly a teammate and friend. He also says that stealing signs was always part of the game— everyone did it. Asked if he got signs through the bell-and-buzzer system, he laughs. "Look how I hit," he says. From August 1 to the end of the regular season, he hit just .266 with three home runs. At the Polo Grounds in the postseason, he was 1-for-7 against the Dodgers; against the New York Yankees, he had two singles in ten at-bats, with one RBI in Game Three; he hit into three double plays. "If I had gotten any signals," he says, "they sure didn't help me."

The World Series, which began less than twenty hours after Thomson's home run, was anticlimactic. Though the Giants hadn't been to the Series since 1937, the euphoria from the pennant championship could not be sustained. And the Giants were tired, especially their pitching staff, having gone the final six weeks with just three starters, Maglie, Jansen, and Hearn. The Yankees didn't have their best team in history—only one regular position player, rookie Gil McDougald, hit over .300, and none drove in a hundred runs or hit thirty home runs—but they had won ninety-eight games to finish five games ahead of Cleveland and featured three excellent starting pitchers: Eddie Lopat, Vic Raschi, and Allie Reynolds, who had a combined 59–27 record. They also had two future Hall of Fame outfielders, one old, one young, which gave the games a whiff of nostalgia and a fleeting glimpse of the future. The Fall Classic had a unique intimacy as well—the Polo Grounds and Yankee Stadium were in sight of each other, separated only by the Harlem River.

The Series broke a racial barrier that may not have affected the outcome but added an intriguing subplot to the games and placed Mays at the center of history.

The Giants began the season with Hank Thompson as their starter at third, but he was injured on July 17. Bobby Thomson, who after Mays arrived became the team's fourth outfielder, was given the third base job, and his hot bat allowed him to stay there after Thompson was healthy again. By the season's end, Hank Thompson was stuck on the bench, but he now found himself in the starting lineup in the World Series. Don Mueller's playoff injury left a vacancy in right field. Logic dictated that Bobby Thomson, an excellent outfielder, would be sent to right field, and that Hank Thompson would regain third base.

But Durocher had other ideas. He kept Bobby Thomson at third and sent Hank Thompson to the outfield, where he had played in only 10 of his 308 major league games. The move made no sense except in one regard: Hank Thompson was black, and in joining Mays and Irvin, the Giants had the first black outfield in big league history—in the World Series, no less. The trio had made history on June 3 in the Polo Grounds, when they were on base at the same time, a breakthrough noted in the press but not welcomed by all the fans. To cover the outfield symbolized something more permanent. Durocher said nothing to either Irvin or Mays about his decision, and neither particularly cared about the racial precedent—they were just hoping Thompson would end his season-long funk (for the year he hit .235, with eight home runs and thirty-three RBIs).

Durocher was sensitive to the country's racial dynamics. In April 1954, the Giants played an exhibition game in Birmingham shortly after the city passed an ordinance to allow interracial competition. On a disputed play at third base, Hank Thompson got into a nose-to-nose argument with the umpire, a shocking example of black defiance. Durocher calmly walked out of the dugout and stood in front of the photographers poised to shoot, then waved them off. Nothing came of the confrontation.

Durocher himself wasn't that interested in social statements. But he was a renegade who liked nothing more than embarrassing the baseball establishment that loathed him.

At the time of the 1951 World Series, only five major league teams had black players,* and Yankee General Manager George Weiss was known for making overtly racist comments. The Yankees did not have a black player on their roster for four more years. Durocher assumed that Bobby Thomson and Hank Thompson would handle their responsibilities on the field,

---

* Ironically, one team, the St. Louis Browns, had two black players in 1947 but cut them after barely a month. One of those players was Hank Thompson.

and the sight of three black men chasing fly balls in Yankee Stadium was too much to resist.

The press noticed. A photograph of the three men, each holding a bat, was published across the country. The bigots also paid heed. While Mays and Thompson struggled in the Series, Irvin lashed out eleven hits in six games and also stole home, prompting an anonymous quatrain to circulate in the press box:

> *Willie Mays is in a daze*
> *And Thompson's lost his vigor,*
> *But Irvin whacks for all the blacks—*
> *It's great to be a nigger.*

Leo Durocher had made his point. In spring training the following year, he sent Bobby Thomson to the outfield and Hank Thompson back to third base.

What made the Series special for Mays was Joe DiMaggio. He saw the thirty-six-year-old for the first time on the field, surrounded by reporters, before the opening game, but he was too shy to introduce himself. A photographer approached him and asked if he would pose with DiMaggio. "Why would he want to take a picture with me?" Mays asked.

The photographer introduced him to DiMaggio and took their picture. The two chatted for a few minutes, a dream come true for Mays. DiMaggio had announced in spring training that this would be his final season, but Mays didn't know that. The only time Mays got to see his hero play was when DiMaggio was trying to beat him.

The Giants split the first two games and in Game Three, at the Polo Grounds, demonstrated their grit. In the fifth inning, they held a slim 1–0 lead, with Stanky on first. Anticipating a hit-and-run, the Yankees pitched out and appeared to have guessed correctly—Stanky was trying to steal. Catcher Yogi Berra made a perfect throw to shortstop Phil Rizzuto, but Stanky kicked the ball out of his glove and reached third. He scored on a single by Dark on the way to the Giants' 6–2 victory.

DiMaggio was a miserable 0-for-12, and to Mays he looked tired. DiMaggio may have gotten a break when rain washed out Game Four, giving him a day off. He did not go out in disgrace. In the next game, against Maglie, DiMaggio finally singled. His next at-bat, in the fifth inning, with one man on and the Yankees leading, 2–1, he lined a low curveball over the left field fence. It was the turning point of the game, and as DiMaggio circled the bases to the cheers of the Yankee fans, the most amazing thing happened.

In center field Mays started to clap, his right hand slapping his glove. He didn't even know he was clapping. It just seemed like the thing to do, to acknowledge the man whose grainy newsreel images were the model for his own batting stance, whose grace in center field and poise under pressure were always his own ideal. Mays stopped once he realized what he was doing, grateful that no one had taken a picture while he cheered the enemy.

The Series marked the only time that Mays, DiMaggio, and Mickey Mantle were all on the field at the same time, though the three would intersect in the Series with heartrending consequences.

Mantle, after a slow start that sent him to the minors, returned to the Yankees and posted fine rookie numbers (.267, thirteen homers, and sixty-five RBIs). His skills, like Mays's, appeared to have justified the hype. Playing right field in the World Series, he was told by his manager, Casey Stengel, that he should take everything he could get toward center because DiMaggio had a sore heel. In the fifth inning of the second game, Mays lifted a fly ball to right center, and he thought Mantle was going to catch it. Mantle thought so too. He sprinted into the gap, and just as he was about to haul it in, DiMaggio called him off. Mantle stopped, and the spikes of his right shoe caught the rubber cover of a sprinkler. He heard a sound like a tire blowing out. His knee collapsed and he lay motionless, a bone sticking out of his right leg. The terrible injury reduced his speed—he had probably been faster than Mays—and plagued him in later years, giving him the aura of a tragic hero whose true greatness was never completely realized. That Willie Mays, Mantle's only real peer in athletic skills, actually hit the ball that limited those skills was a cruel twist of fate.

After tying the Series 2–2, the Yankees crushed the Giants in the next game, 13–1. DiMaggio went 3-for-5, driving in three runs and impressing Mays with his resilience. He showed the rookie who the best center fielder in the Series was. Mays was 0-for-2, striking out once.

In the sixth game, at Yankee Stadium before 61,711 fans, history seemed poised to repeat itself. The Giants' Dave Koslo faced Vic Raschi, whom Irvin described as one of the best pitchers he'd ever seen. The game was tied 1–1, when Hank Bauer's two-out, bases-loaded triple in the sixth inning gave the Yankees a 4–1 lead. In the eighth, DiMaggio smacked a leadoff double and was thrown out at third trying to advance on a ground ball to the pitcher. The crowd, sensing the end, gave him a standing ovation as he trotted off the field.

The Giants entered the ninth trailing, 4–1, the same score that began their ninth inning against the Dodgers exactly one week earlier. Stanky, facing Johnny Sain, led off with a single, and Dark followed with a bunt hit. Lockman then drilled a single to center, loading the bases. With Irvin, a right-handed hitter, up next, Yankee manager Casey Stengel made a seemingly bizarre move: he lifted Sain and called for left-hander Bob Kuzava, a midseason acquisition with no World Series experience. Neither Mays nor anyone else on the Giant bench could figure it out, though in fact Kuzava fared better against righties than lefties. Irvin crushed a long fly to left center, but left fielder Gene Woodling ran it down for the first out. Stanky tagged and scored while the other two runners advanced. Next came Bobby Thomson—once again, hitting with the Giants behind, 4–2, with one out in the ninth.

This time, there would be no Shot Heard 'Round the World or even as far as Harlem. He flied out.

Dark scored, leaving the tying run on second with two outs. What had been the subject of speculation the week before—with the championship at stake, would Mays deliver like a true champion or choke like a petrified rookie—would now play out. Except for one problem: Mays was now batting eighth. In all the other games in the Series, he had hit seventh, but for this game Durocher dropped him one spot in the order.

Ironically, Game Six had been Mays's best of the Series, with two singles and a run scored. But coming into the game he was 2-for-19 (a .105 average), with one RBI, and Durocher demoted him accordingly. Now, with the Giants down to their last out and Mays expected up, he wasn't there—as if Durocher had made one last move to protect his rookie, to ensure that Willie would not be exposed to the potential shame or ridicule of making the final out of the World Series.

The scheduled hitter, Hank Thompson, was replaced by pinch hitter Sal Yvars, who lined out. Once again, the game ended with Willie Mays on deck.

Mays did not begrudge the change in the batting order. He said, "I had played like a twenty-year-old."

He was still proud of his year. He could have given up after his terrible start, but he didn't, and years later he often described his rookie season to children as a lesson in believing in yourself when you're at your lowest and persevering through hardship. Mays did just that. In 121 games, he hit .274, with 20 homers, 68 RBIs, and 7 stolen bases. Those numbers, combined with his outfield play, earned him the Rookie of the Year Award, receiving eighteen out of twenty-four first-place votes. He was the third consecutive black player to win it, the fourth in five years. A black Cuban for the Chicago White Sox, Minnie Minoso, had the best rookie season in the American League (.326, 112 runs scored, 76 RBIs, 31 stolen bases), but he lost the award to the Yankees' McDougald (.306, 72 runs scored, 63 RBIs, 14 stolen bases).

The sportswriters were not ready to vote a black player the Rookie of the Year in both leagues, but such resistance to integration could not hold. The players were simply too good. In the National League, three out of the top six vote-getters for MVP were black—Roy Campanella won the award; Monte Irvin finished third, Jackie Robinson, sixth. In the American League, Minnie Minoso was fourth in MVP voting. The black players' contributions translated into victories: the five teams that were integrated for the entire season finished in the top half of the standings while only three of the eleven all-white teams finished in the top half. And since the color barrier had been broken, four out of five World Series had featured at least one African American.

"Perhaps other clubs," the *Sporting News* wryly noted, "will soon add Negroes as good luck charms."

A new era had begun, and while the black ballplayers had raised the level of the game, Willie Mays would redefine it.

CHAPTER TEN

WAR STORIES

Willie Mays took his World Series paycheck of $5,000, the most ever paid to players of a losing team, and returned to Fairfield, where he bought his second car, a green Mercury convertible. His father didn't know how to drive, so he enlisted his friends, Otis Tate and Herman Boykin. Seeking an open, flat space, Tate took Mays to a ball field and taught him how to steer and shift gears while motoring around the bases. He drove the way he ran, full tilt. "He drove a car faster than anyone I ever knew in my life," Boykin says. Mays was not a reckless driver—he was never involved in any accidents of note—but he loved the speed and status of luxury cars, which remained a lifelong passion.

Mays wasn't home for long. He was soon playing for Roy Campanella's Major League All-Stars, a barnstorming squad that competed against Negro League stalwarts in exhibitions across the South. Campanella's team included the Giants' black outfield, undoubtedly a big draw. But Mays had to be in Birmingham on Saturday, October 27—the city declared it Willie Mays Day. He would be the guest of honor at an afternoon parade, and in the evening, his barnstorming team would play against the Black Barons at Rickwood Field, where Campanella would give him a trophy.

The city's tribute made sense. Birmingham had a rich baseball history, and now its native son was bringing it glory. What's more, the city's powerful police commissioner, Eugene Connor, was an avid sports fan, baseball being his favorite. Before entering politics, he broadcast minor league games from a radio station with information from a ticker tape. Mays himself grew up listening to those games. "He's o-u-u-t-t!" was one of Connor's bellowing phrases. The *Sporting News* described Connor as "one of Dixie's most popular announcers." He was unusually adept at "shooting the bull," filling the time between pitches with amusing chatter, a skill that led in part to his memorable nickname, "Bull" Connor.

Baseball, in short, was Connor's springboard into politics, and in a perfect world, he would have been the master of ceremonies for Willie Mays Day. Instead, he killed it.

The bands and schoolchildren had already gathered for the parade when the authorities broke it up "by decreeing its permit had been canceled," according to the *Birmingham News* columnist Alf Van Hoose, who wrote about the aborted event in 1968. (The local press does not seem to have covered it at the time.) Van Hoose did not spell out why the parade was canceled. He didn't have to. Bull Connor was not about to let his city honor a black man. Van Hoose noted the irony of Birmingham's position: "No official recognition had ever been taken of Birmingham's most famous athlete, a man not without honor in every great city in the land." Van Hoose, who covered sports for more than four decades in the South and was inducted into the Alabama Sports Hall of Fame, called the incident "an embarrassment."

It's unclear whether the city also shut down the scheduled exhibition game. Newspapers published advance articles, but there are no stories about the game itself.

Almost sixty years later, Mays himself says he has no recollection of those events, which suggests the game was not played. He also says he bears no ill will toward Birmingham, and even if he did, he would not say so publicly. (The worst thing he'll say about Bull Connor is that he got overexcited announcing ball games.) Mays, to be sure, loved the adulation, but Birmingham's snub probably didn't bother him if only because he was celebrated everywhere else.

Besides, he wasn't the biggest loser. The man who lost the most—the baseball aficionado who would have stood shoulder to shoulder with America's new idol, who would have exalted the Say Hey Kid's accomplishments, who would have basked in the reflected glory of Willie Mays—that man was Bull Connor, doomed by his own bigotry.

Mays had more important worries than a canceled parade. The day he returned home, he received a letter from the Selective Service, instructing him to report to Draft Board 122 in Fairfield within ten days. America was at war. Mays thought he wouldn't have to serve and applied for a 3-A classification: "registrant deferred by reason of extreme hardship to dependents." With his stepfather struggling to keep a job, Mays was contributing part of his paycheck to his mother and his nine half-siblings; the army would pay him only $75 a month. He thought that constituted hardship. Uncle Sam had other ideas.

The armed forces were ill prepared in June 1950, when the North Korean Army crossed the 38th parallel, triggering the U.S. involvement in the Korean War. The military needed an additional 500,000 recruits, and the Selective Service was soon drafting 80,000 men a month.

The draft itself was a sensitive matter, particularly in the early days of the Cold War. Young men were expected to serve their country, to fulfill their "military obligation," at a time when the line against Communist aggression had to be drawn and when the junior senator from Wisconsin, Joseph McCarthy, claimed to hold the names of American traitors. *Time*'s Man of the Year in 1950 was the American soldier, who fought bravely against Communism.

Baseball stars such as Joe DiMaggio, Stan Musial, and Ted Williams served in World War II, and the game's best athletes were expected to serve in the feverish environment of the early 1950s. Those who didn't, like Mickey Mantle, were ridiculed. Mantle's draft board had classified him as 4-F—physically unfit; his chronic osteomyelitis, or inflammation of the bone, in his left leg disqualified him. The classification was met with scorn and disbelief—how could someone who could hit, throw, and run like Mickey Mantle be physically unfit for anything? He received hate mail and heard cries of "coward," "draft dodger," and "Commie." His draft board in Oklahoma was also vilified. The backlash was so intense that the Yankees asked the draft board to reexamine the case, even if it meant losing Mantle for two years.

Mindful of perceptions, the Selective Service did not exempt baseball players. The Yankees' Whitey Ford and Billy Martin were drafted in 1950. The Phillies that year lost a top starter, Curt Simmons, when his Pennsylvania National Guard unit was mobilized. The army drafted Don Newcombe in 1952. The player who drew the most publicity was Ted Williams, a World War II aviator whose Marine Corps Reserve unit was also activated in 1952. To allay concerns that Mantle received special treatment, his draft board had him examined three more times; he was still deemed 4-F (though strong enough to hit forty-four home runs in 1952 and 1953).

Willie Mays didn't hide his feelings. At a draft physical in Birmingham, where the government tested his coordination, Mays told the *Birmingham News*: "Naturally, I'm not interested in the army, but if I have to go, I'll make the best of it."

Mays passed his physical, but he also had to take an aptitude test. The Armed Forces Qualification Test had a hundred multiple-choice questions that examined verbal and math skills and gauged a candidate's ability to perform certain tasks. The test wasn't difficult—its main purpose was to match recruits with suitable assignments. But failing it was a disqualification for the draft.

As the principal breadwinner in his family, Mays believed he shouldn't have to serve, so he flunked the test on purpose. It was a bad decision. The well-publicized results reinforced the image that Mays was "no Einstein." A reporter for *Sport,* noting that Mays had failed the test, seemed impressed when he watched him autograph a bat "in a series of firm, swift strokes . . . a legible and handsome signature."

More important, Mays's gambit didn't work. His draft board initially said that it would not ask for a second exam, but it changed course and demanded that Mays be retested. No explanation was given, but the draft board officials may have determined that Mays, who graduated in the upper half of his high school class and had traveled more widely than most people in Alabama, was no dummy. When he took the exam again in January, a proctor looked over his shoulder. Mays passed.

The cat-and-mouse game wasn't over. Mays formally requested an exemption because so many family members depended on him, but his appeal was rejected by his draft board as well as Selective Service officials. Exemptions were supposedly given in one of two circumstances— for married men who were fathers and for men who were present in the home of those claimed as dependents.

Mays failed on both counts, but the Selective Service acknowledged that he was drafted because of who he was. Mays "owes perhaps a greater obligation to his country than other boys, because of his promise in the sports world," said Colonel James T. Johnson, the top Selective Service official in Alabama. The rationale was absurd. As Gayle Talbot of the Associated Press said, "Just why does Willie owe a greater debt to his country than the kid on the next block who throws like a sissy? Are boys being penalized because they are promising athletes?"

Truth be told, Mays was an imperfect army recruit for another reason: he didn't like guns.

The news of his conscription did not surprise the Giants. Horace Stoneham didn't want to bring Mays up in 1951, in part because he expected Willie to be drafted. Assuming they would not be so lucky again, the Giants traded Eddie Stanky to the Cardinals for outfielder Chuck Diering before the 1952 season. Mays, however, didn't know when he'd have to report to the army, so he went to his first spring training with the Giants.

For years, the Giants had trained in Miami, but in 1947 they moved their camp to Phoenix; the Cleveland Indians also migrated to Arizona, settling in Tucson for their training. Less rain, drier heat, and lower costs were among the lures of these small desert cities. The Indians' owner, Bill Veeck, also recognized that Arizona's racial climate was better than that of Florida, whose laws prohibited blacks and whites from competing on the same field. Whether Stoneham considered race in moving to Phoenix is unclear, but teams with black players were clearly motivated to leave Florida. By 1953, five of the seven integrated squads trained in either Arizona or California.

While conditions were better in Arizona, Jim Crow was still enforced. In 1948, the Indians' Larry Doby couldn't stay with his teammates at their hotel in Tucson but had to live with a black family two miles from the ballpark. Two years later, the Giants' first black players, Monte Irvin and Hank Thompson, could stay with their teammates at the Adams Hotel in Phoenix but were not allowed to linger in the lobby, use the swimming pool, or eat in the dining rooms (they had their meals in their own rooms). When Irvin complained to the Giants, he was told that those were the laws and there was nothing the organization could do. Irvin didn't press his complaint because he didn't want to jeopardize his chances of making the team.

These conditions hadn't changed when Mays attended his first spring training. The setting was actually an improvement for Mays on the previous year's spring training in Florida, when the black Minneapolis Millers lived apart from their teammates. At least now Mays lived in the same building as everyone else.

As the civil rights movement gained momentum in the second half of the 1950s, spring training's racial hypocrisy became a flash point for activists, black journalists, and the players themselves. Most of the attention remained on Florida. By the early 1950s, most Florida towns, unwilling to forfeit their lucrative fees as training sites, allowed integrated games, but they still imposed strict racial codes for transportation and housing and in the hotels, restaurants, and movie theaters. The most outspoken critic was Jackie Robinson, though other black players, typically those not raised in the Jim Crow South, also demanded an end to the humiliation. In the early 1960s, the St. Louis Cardinals' Curt Flood, Bob Gibson, and Bill White all objected to segregation in St. Petersburg, and some restrictions, such as separate housing, fell.

There was less criticism from the players in Arizona, perhaps because they knew conditions were worse elsewhere. When the Giants and Indians broke camp, they played exhibition games in Los Angeles and San Francisco, then headed east while playing in Salt Lake City, Denver, Oklahoma City, Dallas, and other southern cities, where many fans had not seen integrated teams. Racial slurs were common, but the black players—the Indians and Giants combined had about eight in the early 1950s—had little recourse if they wanted to play in the big leagues. They endured the taunts and found other ways to cope. When the Giants had a game in Dallas, for example, Irvin said he and Durocher could only laugh at the drunk, pathetic fan who kept yelling, "Get up, nigger!" when Luke Easter fell to the ground with a pulled hamstring. "It was really comical and wasn't nearly as bad as it sounded," Irvin said. "But again, we were used to that kind of stuff, so it didn't make any difference." Vic Power, a native of Puerto Rico who spent eleven years in the major leagues, used humor against degradation. With the Indians in the late 1950s on a trip through Little Rock, Arkansas, a waitress told him that the restaurant did not serve Negroes. "That's all right," Power said. "I don't eat them."

Willie Mays said he didn't need any coping mechanisms against racial indignities. As a product of the Deep South, he had been warned. He had been prepared. And he would not be deterred. As he says, "There wasn't much you could do except ignore them and play the games."

Leo Durocher began spring training in good spirits. For the previous season, hailed as the greatest comeback in the history of the National League, he had been named Manager of the Year by the Baseball Writers Association of America. He had received twice as many votes as the runner-up, the Yankees' Casey Stengel. Mays was upbeat as well, eager to play as long as he could until the army called him up, and the fans and the press celebrated his arrival in Arizona. He was still a shiny bauble on a dull, flat landscape.

The *New York Journal-American,* for example, contrasted Mays to Dodger outfielder Carl Furillo, "one of the best players in the game," whose "close mechanical perfection is something of a guarantee that nobody ever would dream of going to the park to watch him perform." Mays's unpredictable brilliance, on the other hand, made it possible for him to "draw more at the box office than a well-nigh perfect but colorless player."

Lengthy stories were published about Mays taking infield practice, snaring ground balls hit so fast that "flames seem to be leaping from the seams," and firing to home plate with such velocity that Durocher had to dive for safety, only to rise and "threaten the player with his fungo bat." The *Sporting News* reported: "Willie Mays, a keen showman, is rapidly becoming the idol of local fans that Mickey Mantle was last year. . . . Willie intrigues them with his antics, his amazing throwing arm and his lively pepper games with Durocher. He makes a perfect straight man for the Giant pilot."

And when Durocher approved of a play, he picked up where he left off the year before: "That's my boy, that Willie!"

During camp, Durocher invited the team to a dinner party at his home in Santa Monica, California, where the athletes could mingle with the manager's celebrity friends, such as Gracie Allen, Ava Gardner, Jack Benny, George Burns, and Kirk Douglas. Thanks in part to Durocher, Mays befriended many movie stars and television personalities over the years, including Rat Pack luminaries Frank Sinatra, Dean Martin, and Sammy Davis, Jr. Mays felt comfortable with fellow entertainers, and they enjoyed the company of an athletic superstar. Mays was always eager to fit in. In 1952, he had brought to Arizona sports coats and slacks, but when he was told that conventional attire at Durocher's party was a suit, he bought one for $150.

The good mood that spring came to a swift end during an exhibition game in Denver on April 2. The Giants were playing the Indians, and Monte Irvin came to bat in the second inning. Irvin believed this was a pivotal year for him. After last season, Horace Stoneham had doubled his salary to $25,000, a good sum in those days. But shortly after signing the new contract, Irvin realized he could have received $10,000 more if he had been more adamant. How many more good years did he have left? He needed a strong season to cash in on his success.

Facing Bob Lemon in the game at Denver, he drew a walk and was on first base when Mays lined a hit into right center. Irvin sprinted around second and tore for third. The outfielder, Pete Reiser, realizing he had no play on Irvin, threw to second to try to cut down Mays. Unaware, Irvin never let up but continued to third, legs churning, dirt flying. The high altitude made it harder to breathe, so he was somewhat winded when he heard the ball hit shortstop Ray Boone's glove. Irvin tried to pull up, but something went terribly wrong. "His spikes caught," Arnold Hano wrote, "and his body's furious momentum, unleashed, pinwheeled over the leg and flipped Irvin on his face."

The noise alone was harrowing. "On the bench," Bill Rigney said, "we could hear the ankle pop like a paper bag." Irvin's fibula in his left ankle had snapped, thrusting through the flesh. He screamed, rolled over, and smothered his face in the crook of his right arm. Third base coach Herman Franks covered his eyes and walked away, later explaining, "I couldn't stand to look at it." Neither could Irvin. When trainer Doc Bowman reached him, he kept saying, "Doc, I don't want to look at it." A cigarette helped calm him as Bowman wrapped his leg with a sock and administered a shot to ease the pain. The ambulance seemed to take forever.

Willie Mays never made it to second base. When he saw and heard the calamity at third, he collapsed to the ground, pounded the dirt, and began to cry. His first thought: the injury was his fault. If he hadn't hit the ball to right center, Monte would be okay. The shortstop tagged out the stricken Mays. A photograph shows a distraught black player on the Indians, Harry Simpson, walking off the field with his arm around Mays, who has tears in his eyes, a grimace on his face, and his left hand below his heart. He looks as if his best friend had just been shot.

Durocher was more practical though no less dour. "They're carrying our pennant chances off the field," he said. Irvin had surgery that day and was out until August.

By the time the season began, Willie knew he'd be reporting to the army at the end of May. The team started hot, as if it knew it had to stockpile wins before it lost its center fielder. During one stretch in April, the Giants won sixteen out of eighteen games. Sal Maglie won his first nine, and Larry Jansen, six out of seven. Though Irvin was disabled, his baserunning advice to Mays from the previous year still paid off.

In the opening game against the Phillies, the score was tied in the bottom of the sixth when Mays led off against Robin Roberts with a single. He advanced to third on Don Mueller's hit. Next to the plate was Whitey Lockman, a left-handed hitter. Mays didn't steal home, as Irvin had done in a similar circumstance, but when the third baseman inched toward the shortstop, Mays could lengthen his lead and force the action. As the *Baltimore Afro-American* wrote: "Mays displayed one of his hitherto unknown talents. . . . He began taking long leads off of third, ala Monte Irvin and Jackie Robinson, thus harassing Roberts to the point that the Phils' ace threw wildly." Mays scored on the bad pitch, and the Giants won, 5–3.

Any notion that Mays's rookie season was a fluke was put to rest in the Giants first game against the Dodgers at Ebbets Field, where he made what might have been the greatest catch of his career.

With the Giants leading, 6–5, the Dodgers had two on and two out in the bottom of the seventh, and Bobby Morgan was the hitter. He pulled the ball into deep left center, so far "that it was doubtful that anyone in the park, even the most optimistic of the Giant rooters, entertained a hope that [Mays] would reach it," wrote one reporter. But Mays fled across the outfield, reached the base of the wall, and dove just to the right of the 351-foot marker. He caught the ball backhanded, then crashed to the ground, bounced on the turf, and smashed into the rubber base of the wall. He lay motionless. Left fielder Hank Thompson, who was replacing Irvin, ran over, lifted Mays's glove and pulled out the ball. Umpire Jocko Conlan, who had hustled into the outfield, threw up his right fist.

The batter was out, the inning was over, but Mays was still down. Durocher and Doc Bowman sprinted out of the dugout. So too did envoys from the Dodgers—Ralph Branca, Roy Campanella, Carl Furillo, Gil Hodges, Pee Wee Reese, and Jackie Robinson. There were anxious moments as Mays, struggling to regain his breath and focus, barely moved for several minutes. The Dodger announcer Vin Scully later said that he wondered if Mays was still alive. Watching on TV in his hospital bed was Monte Irvin, who later said, "My heart was in my mouth." Mays finally got up, and more than thirty-one thousand fans gave him a standing ovation. As he headed off the field, he saw the outline of Jackie Robinson walking away. Mays was touched.

"Jackie was coming out here to see if I was all right?" he asked Durocher.

Robinson had done just that, but Durocher saw an opening. "Are you nuts?" he said. "He only came out here to see if you still had the ball in your glove."

The Dodgers won in extra innings, but after the game the talk was about Mays.

Pee Wee Reese: "The greatest catch I ever saw in my life."

Jackie Robinson: "That was the most amazing catch I ever saw."

Giant coach Fred Fitzsimmons said he'd never seen "a better play in thirty-seven years in this business."

Hank Thompson: "He could have been seriously hurt, maybe with a shoulder separation, because he landed awful hard on the shoulder, but that's the way he is, because he never thinks of protecting himself."

Watching the game from the stands was General Douglas MacArthur, a baseball fan, who said, "It was a wonderful game, but for me the big show was Willie Mays."

Irvin again: "I can't think of another player who would have dogged that kind of catch for fear of getting hurt. It would just be instinctive to protect yourself. Willie didn't. . . . A foot deeper, and the ball, Mays, and the wall would have created some jumble."

Mays himself ranks it as one of his top three catches. Some of his most spectacular grabs are ranked lower because, in his mind, he had them all the way. Others, he was uncertain about, and he was uncertain about Morgan's. What raised that catch to another level was his hanging on after he slammed against the ground and the wall. Mays rarely left his feet to make catches; asked why, he says, "Because I didn't have to." This time, he had to. With his arms outstretched, he absorbed the full impact of the landing, suffering lacerations on his right elbow, thigh, and knee. Though undiagnosed, he probably suffered a slight concussion. Overnight his side stiffened, and the team expected him to miss at least one game. But the next day he arrived at Ebbets Field three hours early for heat treatment. This was no time to rest, he figured; his season would be over in less than six weeks.

Mays's final appeal to the Selective Service for hardship status had been rejected on April 11. He asked that he report to the army in New York, not Fairfield, so he wouldn't lose a day traveling. His reporting date was finally set for May 29, so he was at Ebbets Field on May 28 for his final game in 1952—exactly one year after his New York debut at the Polo Grounds.

Mays had entered the season with questions about his hitting. His power was undeniable, but his rookie batting average of .274 suggested holes in his swing (he still lunged at balls), and his decline at the end of the season indicated that pitchers had found his weak spots.

Those concerns were not allayed during his aborted 1952 season, in which he hit only .236 in thirty-four games. Some reporters speculated that pitchers had indeed caught up with him; others wondered if Irvin's absence had unsettled him or if the unrelenting media scrutiny was wearing on him. All these factors probably contributed to his slow start. Mays, however, dismissed the chatter, noting that ten out of his thirty hits had been for extra bases (including four home runs), and he had twenty-three RBIs; only Bobby Thomson had more. Mays was also a streak hitter, and he believed he was just getting into a groove—he had two doubles and a home run in his penultimate game. All those hits were to right field, a sign that his slump was ending. Durocher, not surprisingly, guaranteed that Mays would have hit at least .275 had he played the entire year.

Most important, at least to Mays, was that he knew he was helping the Giants win. When he went into the army, they had the best record in baseball, 26–8, with a 2½-game lead over the Dodgers.

His final game, before more than fifteen thousand Dodger fans, was a poignant farewell. For all the bitterness between the Dodgers and Giants, Mays was embraced by both sides. When the batting orders were announced before the game, the crowd cheered Willie's name. "This was in Brooklyn, mind you, where 'Giant' is the dirtiest word in the language," Red Smith wrote. "And the Giant they were talking about and cheering is a baby only one year in the major leagues, a child who is only learning to play baseball."

Before the game, Durocher was muttering how he wished the army had taken him and left Willie. His words were rarely taken at face value, but he was believable when he said, "I sure am going to miss him, and I don't mean only on the field."

Mays himself betrayed no nervousness about his impending army stint, placing it in a positive light. "It's undoubtedly for the best," he told reporters. "I'm still young and I might as well do my army duties now. If everything goes well, I'll only be twenty-three when I get out. Many a fellow hasn't even reached the majors by then, so there will be plenty of time for me to play baseball. I'll probably be better off, stronger, more mature in every way."

While he wasn't sure what to expect over the next two years, the army itself didn't intimidate him. "I was raised to say 'yes, sir,' and I always respected authority," he said. He was less scared than sad, for he was leaving the one thing he loved and saying good-bye to Leo, Monte, the Giants, the fans, the umpires, and even the Dodgers. The army would never treat him so well.

The game itself was unremarkable. In his first three at-bats, Mays took a third strike, flied out, and grounded out, while in the field he charged a line drive so hard that, according to Red Smith, "the collision would have been fatal if he'd missed the catch." The crowd was riveted by his every move. "There was a feeling in the stands that, somewhere along the way, he would break loose," the columnist Frank Graham wrote. When Mays came up for his final at-bat in the eighth inning, the Dodger faithful rooted for him, "everybody in the place howling, clapping, yelling for a farewell hit."

On the first pitch, Mays took a mighty swing, topping the ball straight down and flailing so hard that he lost his balance and crashed to the ground. The second pitch he missed on another big cut. He finally met the third pitch head-on, a low fastball, and scorched it to the left side—but Pee Wee Reese grabbed it at shortstop. The loud applause followed Mays to the dugout, where he tipped his cap hurriedly.

The game ended with another Giant victory, their seventh in a row, and the crowd cheered Mays again as he jogged in from center field. Some fans asked him for his autograph, and all four umpires wished him well. In the clubhouse, he received a jeweled tie clasp from his manager and a portable radio from his teammates. Photographers flashed their bulbs, friends slapped him on the back, and Leo hugged him.

Tears fell from Willie's eyes as he said, "Just hold 'em until I come back, fellas," and in Brooklyn's fading light, the organist Gladys Gooding played "I'll See You in My Dreams."

Private Willie Mays was inducted at Camp Kilmer in New Jersey and then sent to Fort Eustis in Virginia, in the coastal town of Newport News. Established in 1918, Fort Eustis was primarily used for physical training and for teaching unarmed combat. Mays, assigned to the Transportation Replacement Training Center, completed eight weeks of basic training, though he never took soldiering seriously. One Monday morning, he came out late for roll call with his hat turned backward, a pant leg pulled up, and his shoes untied. "He was just having fun," says Fred Lovell, who was in Mays's company. "He would come out and sort of put a show on for the other people."

That did not sit well with a new master sergeant, who had just returned from Korea and didn't know Mays was a ballplayer. The sergeant thought he needed to teach the upstart a lesson, so he threw Mays to the ground, held him, and began cursing him. Mays could hold his own in any brawl but knew not to fight a white officer, who, according to Lovell, "was mad as a wet hen." Lovell had become friends with Mays and had also known the sergeant since before they were in the army. Urged by other members of the company, he walked over to the red-faced sergeant, put his hand on his shoulder, and said, "The only friend I got in this company is this man." The sergeant listened, calmed down, and released Mays.

Mays was eventually able to repay Lovell. After Mays became an instructor in physical training, he simply marked Lovell's card every time he was supposed to take his training test. Lovell, who raised chickens in Georgia after leaving the army, said more than fifty-five years later, "Willie Mays was one of the nicest guys I ever met."

Mays qualified for overseas service by December 23, 1952. Photographs were released of Mays in his uniform, creased hat, and shiny black shoes, saluting an officer, doing calisthenics, and marching. But the photos were a ruse. Mays never went overseas and was never close to combat, beyond making a hard slide into second base. Mays's job in the army was to play baseball.

Just as the military had boxing exhibitions, it sponsored baseball teams, and the Fort Eustis Wheels now had the Rookie of the Year wearing their quirky uniform: the letters across the chest, Ft. E ustis, written in an elegant cursive, the E in lonely isolation, while a large, blocky E appeared on the front of the cap. But to Mays the uniform felt good, and the stakes were high. He was told that his company commander bet on games, and his job was to win them.

He was given all the necessary amenities. Halfway through the season, when Mays said he was sore, the commander brought in a black trainer from Richmond to rub him down. Mays was excused from KP, guard duty, and virtually all other responsibilities. This would keep him fresh, though First Lieutenant (Retired) Virgil Saxon says that Mays was excluded for practical reasons as well.

"Those young recruits would have just mobbed him," he recalls. Mays never asked for special treatment—he was just given it. "He didn't play up his fame or anything. He was a very humble guy," Saxon says. Asked what Mays did in the army, he says, "Played baseball and read a lot of comic books."

Mays later said he understood the role that he was assigned: "If you didn't feel like soldiering, they didn't mind, but if you didn't feel like playing that day, they got mad as hell."

He was not the only professional ballplayer in the military to get a pass. He would play with or against Brave pitcher Johnny Antonelli and Red Sox outfielder Karl Olson. There were two Pirates, infielder Dick Groat and pitcher Vernon Law, as well as Don Newcombe and numerous minor leaguers. These players followed in the footsteps of Stan Musial, who in 1945 was drafted by the navy, served on a ship repair unit in Pearl Harbor, and played baseball every afternoon to entertain service personnel.

The military used ballplayers as well as boxers like Joe Louis as entertainers, and Mays was the ultimate drawing card. "There would be four or five thousand people attending those games," recalled Lieutenant Colonel (Retired) Stu Hoskins. "We didn't have a place to put them." Mays played the game with the same abandon that he had used with the Giants. In July, with Fort Eustis winning, 19–0, he stole home. Durocher gasped when he read it in the newspaper and promptly called his wayward prodigy to ask, in no uncertain terms, if he was out of his fucking mind. Fuming and sputtering, he called as well when he heard that Mays had sprained his ankle playing basketball. But he also played the good cop, sending money to Mays to smooth out any hard feelings and cover any needs. Stoneham was generous too, sending Mays a new car each year he was in the army.

It was in the army, as a baseball instructor, that Mays developed his most distinctive fielding trait. On one occasion, his pupil thought the way to catch a fly ball was to hold the glove face up, below the belt, as if he were taking out an old railroad watch and looking at it. "You gotta be crazy," Mays told him.

The soldier suggested that Mays try it. He began throwing him fly balls, and Mays caught them with his glove around his belly button, palms up, thumbs out. At first it felt peculiar, but then he noticed something. When he caught the ball in front of his face, the conventional way, his body and feet would be in unpredictable positions. When he caught the ball at his belt buckle, his body would automatically be in the "rightest, most comfortable stance." He also believed he saved fractions of a second throwing the ball from that position because once he caught it, his arm did not have to whip all the way around. He tried it out in army games and liked it. The "basket catch" was born.

Mays was not the first to use it on a regular basis. One of his own teammates, Bill Rigney, caught infield pops that way, and some baseball writers have questioned whether the basket catch actually helped Mays. Arnold Hano believes that Mays would have dropped fewer balls using the conventional technique—although, given that he set the career record of

7,095 outfield putouts, his approach couldn't have hurt him too much. Nonetheless, the catch was of a piece with a frequent comment by writers that Mays had a "knack for making the easy catches look hard."

Some commentators ascribed a deeper cultural significance to Mays's unusual glovework. Gary M. Pomerantz compared the night that Wilt Chamberlain scored 100 points in the NBA to Mays's basket catch, which he called "an unnecessary and showy display of virtuosity." Pomerantz wrote, "A tradition runs deep in black culture and athletics to respond to the challenge of humiliation with just this kind of gorgeous, awe-inspiring *overkill* as proof of value in a world that would devalue black life and performance." As further examples of such overkill, he cited the young Cassius Clay's "big-mouthed showmanship," Malcolm X's "overheated rhetoric," and James Baldwin's "snaking, furious sentences."

Mays didn't necessarily feel confined by the norms of baseball or society, but he did want to create a new template, to expand the boundaries of the possible. He acknowledges that the basket catch appealed to him in part because of its dramatics and daring. Fans took comfort in balls that were caught at or above the chest. The outfielder never lost sight of it until it smacked in his glove, and if the ball did pop out, he could still recover before it hit the ground. All safeguards were lost with the basket catch. A bobble cannot be saved, and the outfielder will temporarily lose sight of the ball after it passes eye level until it hits the glove below the waist. "That gives it a sense of risk, of danger," Mays says—a frisson of excitement that he loved to create.

He developed another fielding edge in the army. He slipped the glove up on his long, powerful fingers so that the bottom half of his palm stuck out of the mitt, leaving his fingers in its heel. The greater portion of the glove was empty. "The pocket, where the ball hits, doesn't have any of me at all," Mays said. This would have been impossible for most players, but Mays's strong hands allowed him to control the glove, and by sliding it up, he added several inches to his reach. The photograph of his most famous catch, in the 1954 World Series, shows the heel of his hand exposed as the ball settles in his glove.

Mays's laughter and high voice gave the impression of someone who was excitable or immature, but even as a young man he had a smoothness, an unshakable calm, that served him well in tense moments. That was true of his most memorable road trip in the army.

The journey began as just another baseball game, against the Camp Lejeune Marine Corps in North Carolina, which Mays helped to win through his cunning. He came to the plate in the top of the eighth with a man on first, and he lined a single to right; the baserunner rounded second and headed for third when Mays inexplicably took off for second. He had no chance of beating the right fielder's throw at second base. "I couldn't believe my eyes," Bob Akers, who played for Camp Lejeune, later said.

Abruptly, Mays threw up his hands, as if to say, "You got me." And there he stood, defeated, like Lee at Appomattox, prepared to negotiate the terms of his surrender. The shortstop caught the ball and dashed toward him. Then Mays retreated. The shortstop threw the ball, and Mays was now at full speed, in a hot box, a diversion so maddening that the fielders didn't notice his motioning the man on third to scamper across the plate. Fort Eustis won, 1–0. "Willie taught us the art of winning big league style," Akers said.

While most of the Fort Eustis team rode down on a bus, Mays drove his convertible, and after the game, Akers struck up a conversation with one of his passengers. Before long, Mays was driving three marines and an army private to Jacksonville, where they stopped at a bar and began ordering. To Akers's surprise, Mays drank only Coke, and despite his standing, he was without pretense. When they complimented his baserunning, he said, "Aw, it was just something that came up."

When the bar closed after midnight, Mays drove his four passengers along a rutted country road and stopped at a shack, where they were met by a beefy man in overalls, no shirt, and a gun. One of the marines collected some money from his fellow passengers, followed the man inside, and returned with a quart of clear liquid—"a fiery substance that burned lips, tongue, and tummy," Akers said. "The purest white lightning we ever drank." The fruit jar was passed around, each man taking a swig. When it went to Mays, he held it, put it to his lips . . . and gave it back. It was a gesture of solidarity, of camaraderie. His temperance made him an outlier but not an outcast.

The night wasn't over. On a road outside Jacksonville, flashing red lights appeared in the rearview mirror, and a sheriff's car drove toward them. Mays had not been speeding, but the sight of a black man driving a Mercury convertible in the dead of night in the pinewoods of North Carolina was sufficient cause to stop him. One of the marines hid the fruit jar as Mays pulled over.

The sheriff walked to the side of the car, looked at its occupants—four black men and Akers, who was white, all in civilian clothes—and asked, "What's a white boy doing with a bunch of niggers?"

Akers mumbled something and shook his head.

"Y'all been drinking?"

"We had a couple of beers," a marine said.

Turning to Mays, the sheriff said, "Boy, let me see your driver's license."
One marine said, "Say, you know who this is? This here's Willie Mays."
"I don't give a rat's mother who it is. Shut up before I run you all in."

Mays silently handed over his license as well as his military identification card.

If the sheriff took them in, Mays had the most to lose. He was the driver, the baseball star, the celebrity. The publicity could have been devastating, particularly if the moonshine was discovered. But Mays never flinched; he showed no emotion, and he didn't say a word. He gave the sheriff no opportunity to rebuke him. He knew he'd have these kinds of experiences—he'd been programmed. The sheriff returned his documents.

The marines and the army private handed over their military IDs. That they were all servicemen clearly weighed in their favor. Jacksonville was a strong military town, so any effort to railroad them would not have been well received. "Okay, get your black and white asses back to the base," the sheriff said.

Mays started the car and drove off, and nothing more was said of the encounter.

Akers always remembered how Mays's disposition on the baseball field—his standing on the basepaths, unnerved and motionless as all hell broke loose around him—matched his coolness in the car. In both cases, Akers said, "he was in total control."

Mays lived off the base, and like almost everything important in his life, baseball played a central role in his arrangements.

When he arrived at Fort Eustis, Mays agreed to play for a black semi-pro team called the Newport News Royals. A player he knew from the Negro Leagues, Joe Anthony, had recruited him, and Mays juggled the weekend games in the semipro league with the military contests during the week. Anthony had a fourteen-year-old nephew, James "Poo" Johnson, who befriended Mays at the games. "We hit it off right away," he says.

The teenager knew that Mays's baseball schedule often kept him away from Fort Eustis, so he asked his parents if Mays could live with them in Newport News. It wasn't terribly practical: Mays still had to report to the base, and the Johnsons lived an hour away, in a dingy brick apartment building. But all the parties agreed to the arrangement. The benefits to Poo were obvious. "God just put Willie Mays in my life, and I was the hero in the neighborhood," he recalls. Mays gladly sacrificed the convenience and comforts of the military camp for the security and friendship of an extended family—Poo lived with his two sisters and his parents, while his grandmother and uncle were nearby. For the rest of his army tenure, Mays stayed with the Johnsons, sleeping in one of the twin beds in Poo's room.

On the ball field, Mays was almost always the youngest, but in his Harlem neighborhood and now in Newport News, he was often surrounded by youngsters, and he enjoyed his new role. Mays would buy the kids ice cream, give them extra sweaters that menswear stores had sent him, take them for rides, get into snowball fights, and play flag football. Crowds would watch the football games on Sunday mornings, and Johnson swears that Mays could throw a football farther than any quarterback in the NFL.

In some ways, Mays was still a kid himself—he and Poo would have farting contests—but he recognized that he was now a role model and, in Poo's case, a big brother.

"I had a habit of going out late," Johnson recalls, "and he would read me the riot act. He would tell me, 'Don't do anything that would make your mother feel bad.' I was hanging out with guys who were into drinking and smoking, and Willie steered me away from that. He said, 'Take care of your body. If you want to play sports, you have to take care of your body.' "

Mays realized how his celebrity could be a positive force. When a white grocer in Newport News, a friend of the Johnsons, was struggling, Mays started shopping there. He talked it up, and others—black and white—began shopping there as well.

In a low-income community, Mays's own success was writ large, but his generosity tempered most resentment. He would loan his new car to soldiers or friends. He made sure that Poo and his two sisters had lunch money, and he helped with the rent for one of their neighbors. One winter, Mays had just purchased two double-breasted overcoats when he and Johnson saw a homeless man on the street. "Man, you cold," Mays said to him. He took off his blue overcoat and gave it to him.

Johnson recalls, "We saw that guy on the street several times that winter, and he still had the overcoat on."

On a furlough in the summer of 1953, Mays surfaced at the Polo Grounds and walked into the clubhouse for the first time in over a year. Everybody ignored him. Finally someone shouted, "Hey, Willie, where you been?"

"You know where I been—in the army."

"Oh." And everyone turned away.

Mays shrieked with joy at the gag—the silent treatment, again—and had a laugh with his slumping teammates. He told reporters that watching the game was hard because it made him nervous; Durocher speculated that Mays's absence would cost the Giants twenty wins that year.

• • •

Mays never considered himself an agent of social change, but he made history nonetheless. Sometimes he was the first black to integrate a white organization, but as a member of the Newport News Royals, he was responsible for white players integrating a black organization.

At any given game, Mays was allowed to invite three army players onto the black Royals team, and the invitations were attractive—each player was paid for the game. Mays would invite white guys, driving them in his car. His agenda was simple: he wanted to win, and these players were the most talented. Because he had more than three good players to choose from, he would rotate the lineup, allowing more men to get paid. The Royals, with their games in small-town Virginia or rural North Carolina, were typically denied access to restaurants, but black families would invite them for meals. Now things were different. Now white players, accompanied by Willie Mays, walked into black homes, sat down at their table, and ate their food. No one questioned it. Mays broke other taboos. He would take a soda from a white player, put a peanut in it, sip it, and give it back. Everyone would stare, and he would turn and laugh.

"I did it," Mays says, "because I felt that whatever I would do, they would do. Everybody would watch it, and it was no big deal." He recalls having long talks with several white players. "They would ask me questions, 'Why do they call you different names?' I would say, 'I don't know. They're just ignorant. They hear things and try to repeat it.'"

Willie downplays the social importance of his actions, but Poo Johnson, then and now one of Mays's few close friends, says Willie understood the racial barriers he was breaking. "He was aware that he was helping the cause, and this was his way of doing it," Johnson says. "Instead of stepping out and marching, he was changing attitudes one person at a time."

Mays had a furlough in November 1952, so he rejoined Roy Campanella's barnstorming team in the South. One of his teammates was Monte Irvin, recovered from his broken ankle, and Irvin returned to New York with an effusive report on his protégé. "You'd never have thought Willie had ever been away," Irvin told reporters. "He looked as if he'd been playing every day all season." Of course, Mays had been playing almost every day, but the impression was that even while training for war, Mays's baseball skills had not been impaired. Irvin said he saw Mays grab a line drive off his shoetops, straighten up, "and throw one of those patented strikes to double up the runner [at third]. You'd never seen such a surprised guy in your life as that runner."

• • •

In January 1953, Mays once again filed papers asking for an army discharge on the grounds of financial hardship. This time he listed twelve dependents, including two half-brothers, seven half-sisters, his mother, and his two aunts. His mother was pregnant as well. Mays's chances seemed favorable, for other big leaguers had been released from the service after claiming hardship. The Dodgers' Billy Loes and the Indians' Bob Kennedy had been sent home for that reason. So too had the Yankees' Billy Martin, though the army then changed its mind and recalled him to duty.

Mays's appeal was again rejected.

On April 15, Mays's mother died while giving birth to her eleventh child—he called the day he received the news his worst in the service, and he attended her funeral in Fairfield. He was certain the army would let him go now. The baby, Diane, survived, so the financial needs of his family were even greater. But the army again spurned his appeal. Mays later said, "I always have believed that if a lesser-known soldier had gone through that ordeal, he would have been free to leave. I don't know whether the army was concerned because the public thought it would be playing favorites or whether there was just some technicality. All I knew then was that I was very sad. . . . It didn't help my final months in the army."

Certainly the Giants wished he was out, for his value, actual and perceived, had skyrocketed. The Giants had a .765 winning percentage when he left the team. For the remaining 120 games in 1952, it dropped to .550. Given Mays's struggles, his departure couldn't be measured in the loss of, say, hits or runs scored. His contributions were described as intangible, almost mystical. While Mays was on the team, the Giants had stolen fifteen bases in thirty-four games (Mays getting four). But over the next nineteen games, they stole just one base while winning about half their games. According to the *Sporting News,* "Stolen bases in themselves aren't too significant, but in this case they do point up to one of the big reasons why the Giants have been struggling. . . . The going of Mays tipped the balance. Whereas the Giants were once full of running, they've now lost their daring and fire—both on the bases and in the field."

The Giant pitchers were definitely affected. Sal Maglie was knocked out of five straight games after Mays left, in part because of poor outfield play. "He just made such a difference out there," Maglie said after the season. "You didn't have to worry about striking guys out all the time. You just gave the batter a pitch that he'd hit to center and you knew that somehow Willie would get it. That takes a lot of pressure off the pitcher and gives him a chance to save his best stuff for the real tight spots. Maybe it's subconscious, but I've been bearing down too hard ever since Willie left."

Without Mays and Irvin for most of the year, the Giants were still competitive, winning ninety-two games and finishing in second place, 4½ games behind the Dodgers, and earning Durocher a new two-year contract. But the team collapsed in 1953—or, more specifically, the pitching collapsed. The Giants won seventy games and finished thirty-five games behind the Dodgers. They actually hit better in 1953 than in 1952—scoring forty-six more runs and hitting twenty-five more homers, though the numbers are a bit deceiving. It was a hitter's year generally, with a 15 percent increase in runs scored in the National League. The Giants' ERA jumped accordingly, to 4.25 from 3.59, but lousy defense, particularly a slow outfield, contributed to the high total.

Durocher, as he tended to do with bad teams, lost interest; at some point he allowed the players to make out the lineup. He also developed a habit, when a ball fell in the outfield, of saying, "Willie would have had it," and to any reporter who happened by, he waxed nostalgic about his boy Willie.

Mays's baseball career in the army ended on July 25, 1953, when he chipped a bone in his left foot sliding into third base for Fort Eustis. His foot was in a cast for more than six weeks, and he was confined to the base hospital. Mays had faced major league pitchers that season: Joe Landrum and Erv Palica of the Dodgers, Tom Poholsky of the Cardinals, Alex Konikowski of the Giants, as well as Antonelli and Newcombe. And in fifty-seven games he had hit .389, driven in fifty-four runs, and smacked fifteen homers, striking deep blows into the pinewoods of the South that people would talk about for decades.

After the 1953 season, the Giants traded their World Series hero, Bobby Thomson, to the Milwaukee Braves for Johnny Antonelli. Trading the author of the most famous home run in Giant history was difficult, particularly for a loyalist like Horace Stoneham, but the team could not compete without better pitching. Thomson was also expendable because the Giants' center fielder was returning.

Mays's defense alone would be a lift. As the Giant publicist Garry Schumacher said, "Willie catches the triples." (Others, including Vin Scully and the Dodger official Fresco Thompson, were later quoted as saying, "Willie Mays's glove, where triples go to die.") But Mays's greatest contribution would be as an antidote to the "chamber of gloom" that had become the Giants' locker room. As the Sporting News wrote, "He'll give the Giants a happier club house. . . . There'll be laughs and yelps and nobody will get a chance to sit and brood over the hits they didn't get, the bad pitches they made, or the bobbling balls that got away. Willie won't let them."

• • •

The army released Mays on March 1, 1954, but his service did not leave the news entirely. He was one of ten athletes whose military records were investigated by the Armed Services Defense Activities Subcommittee in Congress. The records of Whitey Ford and Billy Martin were also scrutinized. The investigators were charged with determining if these athletes had been "pampered" or "coddled" while in uniform. Congress issued a report on July 22 confirming that they had been. Mays himself was never interviewed or asked to appear before Congress, and his reputation suffered no real harm, but at a congressional hearing in May, he—along with two other African American athletes, retired boxing champion Sugar Ray Robinson and featherweight champion Sandy Saddler—received most of the attention. The subcommittee members said they had investigated Mays because of complaints by "GI's, their parents, and other citizens." Obviously, not all of Mays's peers appreciated his special treatment.

The congressional hearing conveyed the army's corrupt handling of personnel that worked in Mays's favor. One investigator, Lloyd B. Kuhn, testified that two soldiers were "levied" for overseas duty on December 13, 1952, while Mays was passed over. Brigadier General Herbert Powell, deputy chief of staff for personnel, testified that the failure to put Mays in required basic training "was clearly a violation of directives."

Congressman Charles P. Nelson of Maine asked one witness, "When a fellow like Willie Mays is inducted into the army, how does he happen to be assigned to Fort Eustis?"

Lieutenant Colonel Alfred H. Crawford, Jr., who was stationed there, said he wasn't sure, but "we think there was shenanigans pulled." He drew a chuckle when he said, "Our ball team was mediocre, but Willie Mays was one of the finest players I've seen in my life."

Neither the hearing nor the report captured the government's truly farcical treatment of Mays. He had a legitimate financial hardship case. Nonetheless, the Selective Service drafted him in part to demonstrate that it treated everyone equally, yet the army gave him preferred treatment at every step. For baseball's finest outfielder, it was a Catch-22.

Mays never even knew that he was part of a congressional investigation or a government report. Had he known, he wouldn't have cared. He had done nothing wrong, and now his army days were over. But to his credit, he never exaggerated his military service or made himself out to be a false hero. As he said in an autobiography, "I have no pride in my Army career. But I have no apologies for it either. I did what the man said."

CHAPTER ELEVEN

"I'D PLAY FOR FREE"

R oger Kahn was not in good spirits when his newspaper, the *New York Herald Tribune*, sent him to the sun-baked hills of Arizona in February of 1954. Kahn's father had died in October, and he would no longer be covering the team that he loved, the Brooklyn Dodgers. They were the best beat in baseball—a talented roster that served up drama and heartbreak (the Dodgers had lost four out of the last seven World Series, including the last two) and Jackie Robinson, through whom Kahn had written insightfully about bigotry in baseball and society. The twenty-six-year-old reporter had covered the Dodgers for the past two pennant-winning years, and in time he would write his classic, *The Boys of Summer*, about that team. But now he was assigned to the New York Giants—the *fifth-place* Giants—known for their despondent players and despotic manager.

Leo Durocher quickly shook him from his stupor. Kahn described him as "cheap and obscene and devious and suspicious and wholly magnificent [whose] vital exuberance renewed me." Durocher told Kahn that he would tell him stuff that no other reporter knew, threatened to tell his boss that the young writer was a "no-good, lying, cocksucking, motherfucking son of a bitch" if he betrayed him, and assured Kahn that he could get movie stars to sleep with him if he just stuck with Leo. Kahn, having read *Faust*, declined the offer.

Kahn quickly sized up the real story of spring training: the fanatical expectation of Willie Mays's return. A mythology about him had settled in. When Mays joined the Giants in 1951, the team was in fifth place. After he arrived, the team finished in first place. When Mays played with the Giants in 1952, they were in first place. Then he left, and they fell to second, then last year they were back in fifth place. Without Mays, they had no chance. With him, they were winners. And now, with his return, they would win again. That was the assessment of Horace Stoneham and Leo Durocher. So too of Chub Feeney. A graduate of Fordham Law School, he was Stoneham's nephew, so he joined the family business and became the Giants' de facto general manager. Feeney knew what day Mays would be released by the army, so he had a habit, after a drink or two, of singing, to the tune of "Old Black Joe": "In seven more days / We're gonna have Willie Mays." Each day he lowered the number of days until Mays would arrive. "That song, like the sandy wind, became a bane," Kahn lamented.

But the Giants were again forced to hype Mays's return. Their failure in the previous year had driven fans from the Polo Grounds; in two years, attendance had plunged 23 percent, to 811,518 (fewer than 11,000 fans per game), and had fallen 33 percent since 1946. So the Giant officials pumped reporters with stories about Mays, who could revive fan interest. Meanwhile Durocher, who was always an outsider in Stoneham's clubby world, had lost much of his standing in the organization. He needed to win to keep his job.

It was 1951 all over again, and the Giants needed the return of their savior.

While Kahn was nobody's puppet, he fulfilled the Giants' wishes. On February 28, the Sunday before Mays was to report, he wrote a story beneath the headline: SHADES OF PAUL BUNYAN. The article read in part: "It's only human to wonder whether this is a man or superman. . . . Willie is 10 feet 9 inches tall. He can jump fifteen feet straight up. Nobody can hit a ball over his head, of course. . . . Willie's speed is deceptive. The best indication of it is that he's a step faster than any line drive ever hit. . . . Willie can do more for a team's morale than Marilyn Monroe, Zsa Zsa Gabor and Rita Hayworth, plus cash." To push the gag further, the *Herald Tribune* published a doctored photograph of Mays that distorted his legs, making them twice the length of his upper body.

Few players in major league history have entered a season with Superman and Paul Bunyan as their peers. Advance ticket sales rose.

It was unexpectedly cold on the morning that Mays was discharged from Fort Eustis, and the Giants dispatched Frank Forbes to retrieve him. Mays, having gained about ten pounds of muscle, was bigger and more mature than when he'd entered the army, but the Giants were still protecting him. Forbes met him at the gate, gave him his overcoat, and stuffed newspapers in his own shirt to stay warm. He then drove Mays to the Washington airport. That day, four Puerto Rican nationalists had entered the House of Representatives and opened fired from a gallery, wounding five legislators. With tensions high, the authorities at the airport stopped the two dark-skinned travelers and questioned them. Frank Forbes insisted that he and Willie Mays were just trying to get to spring training. Once cleared, they still had to wait five hours but finally boarded an American Airlines flight at midnight.

The next day at Giants camp was "M Day," according to Kahn. At Phoenix Municipal Stadium, where old stands extended partway down each line and a wood fence ringed the outfield, the players were stretching and warming up for an intrasquad game. The clear sky allowed for maximum visibility, and whenever a plane appeared in the distance, someone cried, "Willie's plane!"

"Feeney," Kahn said, "this is ridiculous."

Not to Feeney, who sang, "In no more days, we're going to have Willie Mays."

Mays's plane landed in Phoenix shortly before 11 A.M., and he was met by Garry Schumacher, who picked up Mays's two identical suitcases. One was heavy; the other, so light that he thought it was empty.

"Willie, what the hell you got in these bags?" he asked.

"In the heavy one, I got all my clothes," Mays said. "In the other one, just my glove and my jock strap."

Schumacher interpreted that to mean one thing—he had "come to play" and did not want his clothes tainting his baseball items.

Mays went straight to the clubhouse at the ballpark. On the field, in whispers at first, the players began telling each other, "Willie's here." The first man to greet him was the clubhouse attendant Eddie Logan, followed by a gaggle of reporters and photographers. The first player to see him was Sal Maglie, naked and dripping wet.

"Hey, where you been?" Mays piped.

"In the showers," Maglie replied.

"That's just what I thought," Mays said. "Knocked out again."

Monte Irvin saw him next, pumped his hand, and asked, "How's your game, roomie?"

"What game?" Mays asked.

Irvin smiled and shook his head.

"You mean pool?" Mays asked.

"Your game, roomie," Irvin said. "I mean baseball."

Photographers converged, taking pictures of Mays while he was buttoning his baseball shirt, tying his new spikes, and shaking hands with everyone in sight. He finally emerged on the runway leading to the field. Halfway up, someone yelled, "Hey, Leo, here comes your pennant!" A jubilant Durocher met him and, with his right arm around Mays's neck, almost mauled him in a bear hug. The last time Mays had seen Durocher do that was when Bobby Thomson hit his home run. Seconds later, Mays moved up the runway toward more cameras, a big grin on his face, his teammates pressed around to welcome him. He finally reached the dugout, where reporters could ask him some questions. The light banter had one revealing, and widely reported, exchange when Mays was asked if he had signed a contract yet.

"No, but I'm easy to sign," he said. "I love to play."

"There's a story out of Fort Eustis," a reporter said, "that says you want $20,000."

Mays blinked. "How could I ask for that kind of money?" he said. "That man Stoneham would take a gun and shoot me if I asked for that kind of money. Whew."

By law, Mays could earn no less than what he was making when he entered the army, and that's what he got—$13,000.

The game began with Mays on the bench, stalking and squirming, eyeing Durocher, who let the tension build. The slight ankle fracture Mays had incurred the previous summer had healed, and he had played basketball all winter. Now he was ready for baseball. Finally, in the fifth inning, Mays was sent in to pinch-hit. He ran to the batter's box and, first pitch, swung mightily and missed. Lunging for the ball, he was out of sync and struck out on two more swings. But he was still a sight. Kahn didn't believe he'd ever seen anyone swing so hard.

An inning later, with Mays in center, a sinking line drive was hit toward him, and he charged forward, dove, and made a graceful somersault as he caught the ball. "For Willie, that's absolutely nothing," Barney Kremenko told Kahn. The next time Mays hit, Kahn wondered if a contrarian story might be in order about how rusty Superman had become. He was looking for specific flaws in Mays's form when he hit a fastball 420 feet over the fence.

An inning later, with a runner on first, a batter slammed a long drive to right center. Mays raced to the right center field fence, speared it, spun, and threw a strike to first base, doubling off the runner. There were cheers, howls, and pandemonium ensued. The camp was electric. Last year's walking dead had been revived. Soon, another hitter walloped a ball to dead center. Mays galloped fifty feet straight back and caught the ball over his shoulder.

After the game, Mays deflected questions on how well he'd do this year. "All I know is that I got a lot of work to do," he said. "You gotta work to be a regular."

Roger Kahn was less restrained: "This is not going to be a plausible story, but then no one ever accused Willie Mays of being a plausible ballplayer," he wrote. "This story is only the implausible truth."

Durocher was more succinct: "Willie must have been born under some kind of star."

· · ·

Kahn was aware of Mays's image as "loveable but an American primitive." When he spoke to Mays during long train rides that spring, he found someone who may have been naive but was more thoughtful and serious than the stereotype. In one conversation, Mays told him there were three important things about playing in the major leagues: "First, you got to love the game. If you don't love the game, how are you gonna learn about it? Second, you got to watch your drinking. I seen guys, good players, they liked to drink more than they liked to play ball. I don't see how you can drink a lot and be a great player. Then you got to get your sleep. You don't have to go to bed by eleven, but twelve, twelve-thirty, something like that. You ought to be in bed by then because you have to get eight hours of sleep. You shouldn't get more. A fellow gets to sleeping too much, he gets lazy. You shouldn't sleep too much and you shouldn't sleep too little. Eight hours."

A few train cars away, Kahn mentioned, some of the Cleveland Indians were drinking hard. Mays shrugged. "You think I could play like I been playing if I was drinking? No way."

Kahn was impressed. Drinking and carousing were so prevalent—among players as well as sportswriters—that Mays's rectitude was quaint, even jarring. Mays also discussed his development as a player, starting in Alabama, and acknowledged the importance of his instructors, including Durocher. But Mays's real edge had nothing to do with coaching: "Leo is a friend of mine, and he says this and that, but nobody can teach you nothing. Not me or nobody and nobody can write a book that will teach you. You got to learn for yourself and you got to do it your way. If you love the game, you can do it."

Later that spring, Mays was playing an exhibition game, and Tris Speaker, considered one of the greatest defensive center fielders of all time, was in the stands. After the game, he was asked about a throw of Mays's that had cut down a runner at the plate. "Well, it wasn't that good a throw," he said, "because it was too high. It couldn't have been cut off."

Mays, who'd always given a loft to his throw, heard about the comment, and he started lowering his pegs. "By the time the season started," *Sport* noted, "he was throwing them so hard and low the infielders were having trouble handling them."

Durocher spoke to him, and some of the loft returned.

Mays rarely talked about racial incidents, but during that exhibition season he was involved in two on consecutive days, one in Las Vegas and the other in Los Angeles. They are reminders that while Mays never drew attention to racial indignities, he knew them all too well.

The Giants and the Indians had an exhibition game in Las Vegas on a gray afternoon. After the game, the Giants had arranged for a bus to take the team to the New Frontier Hotel and Casino on the Las Vegas strip, where they'd get a free dinner and a show. A second bus was to take them to the airport at 11 P.M.

Mays, joined by Kahn, ate roast beef and watched Robert Merrill, the operatic baritone, sing an aria from *Pagliacci* in which Canio, the clown, sings of having to make people laugh, though his own heart is broken. At the conclusion, Mays, genuinely moved, said to Kahn, "You know, that's a very nice song."

He soon went to the gambling room and stood with a group of people at a dice table. Other Giants, including Monte Irvin, Whitey Lockman, and Sal Maglie, were trying their luck at blackjack or the slots or just watching the action. Kahn also showed up, chatted briefly with Mays, and moved on. On his way to the roulette table, a short, burly man grabbed his arm and pointed at Mays. "That guy a friend of yours?"

"I know him," Kahn said.

"Well, get him away from the dice tables."

"What?"

"You heard me. Get him the hell away from the dice tables. We don't want him mixing with the white guests."

"Do you know who he is?"

"Yeah, I know who he is. He's a nigger. Get that nigger away from the white guests."

Kahn determined that he was a security officer and noticed a significant bulge on his left hip. "Do you know this is America?" he asked. "Do you know that fellow just got out of the army?"

"That don't mean nothing. I was in the army myself."

"You bastards invited him down to your hotel."

"Who you calling a bastard?"

The argument continued. Garry Schumacher arrived and tried to defuse the matter. Kahn finally pulled out his press card, showed it to the security officer, and said triumphantly, "I really have to thank you. You've given me one helluva story for the Sunday *New York Herald Tribune*."

The officer retreated, and Kahn walked over to Irvin, the senior black on the ball club (he was thirty-five), and told him about the incident.

"When did this happen?" Irvin asked.

"Right now."

"Where's Willie?"

"Still at the dice table, I guess."

"He'll only get hurt," Irvin said. "I'm going to get him."

Without another word, Irvin found Mays and led him toward the nearest exit.

Mays didn't want to go. "Plane ain't gonna leave for two hours, roomie," he said. "What we gotta leave for?"

"Come on, Willie," Irvin said. "We'll get the bus lights on and you and me can play some cards."

Kahn was soon approached by two hotel officials, a vice president in a buckskin jacket, Maury, and his young assistant, Shana, who was "attractive in a hard-faced sort of way," and they repaired to a bar for a drink. Maury explained they didn't have anything against Negroes, but the dice tables were different. "There's a lot of body touching around the crap tables," Shana said. "People brushing against each other real close." Maury explained that customers shooting dice, particularly those from Texas, didn't want Negroes brushing up against their women. He said they were really a very liberal place—Lena Horne had performed there—and he invited Kahn to stay the night, eat, drink, and "Shana was free." The quid pro quo was understood. Kahn was tempted, but after one dance with Shana, he stepped away, made it to the bus, and was on the Giants' plane to Los Angeles that night.

He was going to write the story, but Irvin pleaded with him to reconsider. "This is something that Jackie Robinson handles all the time," he said. "But if you write what happened, you could put Willie in the middle of a huge racial storm. I think that would be too much for the kid. If you don't absolutely need to write what happened, I'd appreciate it, and I know Willie will appreciate it in time."

Kahn agreed. He included a sanitized version of the anecdote in a profile of Mays in *Sport* in 1956. He revived the incident for the same magazine in 1969, which included the racist language. A complete account appeared in his 1997 memoir, *Memories of Summer*.

Irvin confirms that he asked Kahn to hold the story. His job, he says, was to protect Willie. "I thought Willie wouldn't have liked it much, the racial comments," he says.

In 1996, Kahn visited Mays in Atherton, California, and he broached the Las Vegas incident for the first time. Mays told him that Durocher had filled him in shortly after it occurred. Kahn complained that he didn't get to write the story for his paper or take a shower with the girl.

"What can I tell you?" Mays laughed. "You're on your own." But then he turned serious. "There is something I can tell you. One word. Thanks. I wasn't much for controversy. Not then. Not now either. I guess not ever."

The day after the Las Vegas misadventure, the Giants were in Los Angeles for another exhibition game, and Mays again discovered the value of having protectors, particularly Academy Award winners. This time the team was at the Biltmore Hotel, with Mays sharing a room with Irvin. A cousin of Mays's called and asked if she and a girlfriend could stop by. Mays said yes. Five minutes after they got to the room, the phone rang. It was the house detective, who told Mays that he could not have any women in his room, and if he did, he would have to leave the door open.

"What the hell are you talking about?" Mays asked. He explained the guests were his cousin and a friend of hers. "You want me to keep my door ajar? Are you out of your mind?"

The door stayed shut. Several minutes later, there was a knock. Mays opened the door to the house detective.

"You can't have a female in this room with the door shut," he said.

Mays asked how he even knew anyone was in the room.

"I trailed her," the detective said.

"Do you trail everyone?"

"This is the way it is."

At that point, Mays's cousin said she didn't want to get him in trouble, and she and her friend left. Later that day, Irvin told Durocher what had happened. Durocher had plenty of friends in Hollywood, and the next day one of them showed up—Frank Sinatra, who had just won the Academy Award for best supporting actor in *From Here to Eternity*. He apologized profusely to Mays for the embarrassment and said he would make sure such a thing never happened again. The hotel manager apologized as well.

Mays thanked Sinatra for his help.

"If I played baseball like you, I'd be the happiest guy in the world," Sinatra said.

In countless interviews and two ghostwritten autobiographies, Mays never mentioned the casino or the Biltmore. In his mind, controversy was kryptonite, and any brush with it, no matter how innocent his own involvement, could damage him irreparably.

The major leagues that Willie Mays returned to was different in one important respect. Saddled with declining revenues, old stadiums, and waning fan interest, the teams were now on the move. In 1953, the Boston Braves settled in Milwaukee and played in the new County Stadium, the first to be built with public money. In 1954, the St. Louis Browns went to Baltimore, were renamed the Orioles, and played in Memorial Stadium, where an upper deck had been added. And in 1955 the Philadelphia Athletics migrated to Kansas City. The Ice Age of big league baseball, in which all the teams had been frozen in place since the turn of the century, had ended.

Greed was not the issue. It was survival. In 1948, the league's attendance had peaked just shy of 21 million and had been in decline ever
since, reaching 14.4 million in 1953. Television was part of the problem,
but so too were dingy ballparks ill suited for suburban fans increasingly
reliant on cars. The clubs needed modern stadiums in new markets, and
they found them. The Braves were Exhibit A. In their last year in Boston,
they drew 281,278 fans. Their first year in Milwaukee, they attracted more
than 1.8 million. The next year, 2.1 million. The other teams took note. Far
from dying, baseball was in demand by second-tier cities that were willing to confer subsidies and tax breaks for the cachet of a big league team.

Attention inevitably focused on the Giants, by far the weakest financially of the three New York clubs. By the end of 1953, the Giants had lost
money for five straight years; the Dodgers were profitable in four out of
five years, and the Yankees were in the black each year. In addition to the
Polo Grounds' poor condition, the stadium had a large number of cheap
seats and relatively few expensive box seats. The fear of crime, particularly
at night, also kept fans away—white fans. Those fears, legitimate or otherwise, were inflamed after a game on July 4, 1950, when a spectator was
shot dead by a youth who fired a .22-caliber gun in a haphazard fashion
from the edge of Coogan's Bluff.

Rumors of the Giants' departure began to circulate in 1954, fueled in
part by Durocher, who said they ought to move to San Francisco. Speculation about the Dodgers was equally rampant: their efforts to get government money for a new stadium had been unsuccessful, and they were
convinced that Ebbets Field was not viable economically.

Horace Stoneham, in an interview in the *Sporting News* in November,
stanched the rumors of the Giants' leaving town. He said the team had a
lease on the property until 1963 and there was "no chance for a shift." The
Sporting News seemed to agree, noting that "Stoneham is as much a New
York man as Durocher is a Hollywood lover."

The Giants' financial struggles were the furthest thing from Willie Mays's
mind on Opening Day at the Polo Grounds on April 13, 1954—in effect,
his second debut. He knew full well how much success the city's two other
center fielders had enjoyed in his absence. Duke Snider, at twenty-seven,
was the elder statesman of the trio. He was also in his prime. In 1953, the
sweet-swinging left-hander had crashed 42 home runs, driven in 126,
and hit .336, with a league-leading .627 slugging percentage and 132 runs
scored. Mickey Mantle, five months younger than Mays, was blossoming
in his own right. Over the past two years, he had 44 home runs and 179
RBIs, with a .303 batting average. Both Snider and Mantle had helped

lead their teams to pennants. Mays did not like being third seat in a three-piece orchestra.

Before the first pitch against the Dodgers, the Giants paraded behind Major Francis Sutherland's Seventh Regiment band to the center field flagpole, where they watched a Marine Corps color guard raise the flag. Then the players marched back, and Mayor Robert F. Wagner, a southpaw, threw out the first ball. The crowd of 32,397 included General Douglas MacArthur, Robert Wagner, and Jerry Lewis. Willie Mays gave them a show.

In the sixth inning, with the score tied 3–3, he came to the plate, dug his back foot in, waved the bat a couple of times, and glared at the pitcher. He was a study of balance and leverage, free of extraneous movement, and when he swung, his hips opened, and his massive arms and supple wrists created a vicious whiplash effect. Unfazed by two-strike counts, he never shortened up or choked up. "If there was a machine to measure each swing of a bat," Branch Rickey said, "it would be proven that Mays swings with more power and bat speed, pitch for pitch, than any other player."

He was facing Carl Erskine, a compact right-hander who threw one over the plate. Mays unleashed his thirty-four-ounce bat, hitting the ball with the savagery of a man denied for almost two years the pleasures of a major league fastball. The result was breathtaking: the ball traveled on a straight line into the upper deck just over the 414 marker. Arnold Hano estimated that the ball would have traveled 600 feet had it not hit the stadium. It was hit so hard, said columnist Frank Graham, "that it was still soaring when it crashed into the seats."

The Giants won, 4–3. Now, Mays thought, it was his turn to show Mickey and the Duke something.

The homer was both the climax to all of the preseason hype and the opening salvo of a yearlong publicity binge. The *New York Post* columnist Jimmy Cannon, perhaps the most influential sportswriter of his generation, framed Mays's unrivaled connection to the city in his tribute the next day.

"You're Willie Mays of Fairfield, Ala., who is part of the small talk of New York," Cannon wrote. "This shall be your city as long as your talent lasts. . . . Kids forget the squalor of their childhood as they emulate the shambling urgency of your gait. They speak as though you lived on the same block with them." Cannon said Mays did far more than entertain the fans at the Polo Grounds. "Strangers, aching with loneliness, spoke to those who sat along side of them. And they mentioned your name. . . . You brought people together in the bantering arguments of sports. You made time pass for the bored with a bright rush. It is a fine accomplishment in a terrible age." What was most important about Mays, Cannon wrote, was not the achievement but the specter, the myth. "Your frantic image dashed across the screens of television sets in living rooms decorated with splendor you wouldn't believe. You've become a metropolitan fable, told in saloons and pool rooms and related on street corners, in home and playground."

The headline was: YOU'RE WILLIE MAYS—A YOUNG LEGEND. Three weeks later, he turned twenty-three.

The Giants were not supposed to be competitive in 1954, having finished thirty-five games out of first place the previous year. Besides Mays, the Giants' only other meaningful addition was thought to have been pitcher Johnny Antonelli, who cost the team its best power hitter, Bobby Thomson. The pennant was expected to be a battle between the Dodgers and Thomson's new team, the Milwaukee Braves, which was fielding a rookie outfielder, Hank Aaron.

After the Giants' 1953 collapse, Stoneham publicly rebuked Durocher for his constant lineup changes and insisted that this year the team stick with one group of regulars until changes were necessary. Durocher ignored the injunction, beginning the season with twelve different lineups in twenty games. The juggling didn't work—the Giants lost eleven times—but there was reason for hope. They shut out the Phillies in three consecutive games, highlighting the team's strength—starting pitching, led by Antonelli, Maglie, and Ruben Gomez.

The biggest disappointment that first month was Mays. In Arizona, Durocher had predicted that he'd hit .300, a reasonable goal in light of the media hoopla. In the first twenty games, he showed some power—four homers and nineteen RBIs—but he was batting only .247. The looming concern about Mays—a great glove and arm, terrific speed, but a mediocre bat—might be true. The Giants were in fifth place.

Durocher, as he had done before, pulled Mays aside, told him that he had reverted to trying to pull everything, and urged him to go to right field.

The next game, on May 8 in Pittsburgh, Mays hit a home run and a single, and the Giants won, 2–1. All Durocher said to Mays was, "I told ya."

That day, Durocher also announced he would now stick with one lineup, with Mays batting fifth, behind Irvin and before Don Mueller. Stoneham had presumably pressured him to make up his mind. The Giants promptly won thirteen out of their next twenty, Mays being the difference. He hit .449, whacked nine homers and four triples, and drove in twenty-five runs. Some of his feats were memorable. On May 24, in Philadelphia, he came to bat in the seventh inning and smashed a ball into the lower left field deck. An inning later, he crushed one onto the left field roof with a man on base, giving the Giants a 5–4 win. Mays had three hits, drove in four, and threw out Earl Torgeson at home plate when he tried to score on a fly ball.

The Giants reached the .500 mark on May 21, and by June 9, they were ten games over, at 30–20. They took over first place on June 15 in the midst of a terrific month, winning twenty-three out of twenty-seven. They kept winning and on July 21 peaked at thirty-two games over .500, seven games in first place.

As with any winning team, many players contributed. Don Mueller, a left-hander known for his scientific place-hitting, would lead the league in hits with 212. Alvin Dark, the captain, hit a solid .293 and was steady at short. The starting troika of Antonelli, Maglie, and Gomez would win fifty-two times, register thirty-seven complete games, and lead the Giants to a league-best ERA of 3.09.

But the catalyst for the Giants was as predicted. By June 1, Mays had raised his average to .300. On June 21, he hit his twentieth home run, equaling his total from his rookie season. He was a more patient hitter and could make adjustments at the plate. In the second week of June, for example, in a four-game series against Milwaukee, he went 0-for-12 (though he drew five walks). Two weeks later, in three games against the same team, he went 5-for-11, with four homers and nine RBIs.

The next series was against the Chicago Cubs at the Polo Grounds, and on June 25, Mays entered the game with five homers in the past six contests. His first time up, his blast to left field rebounded off the grandstand wall and bounced away from the outfielders, and Mays dashed around the bases for an inside-the-park home run. Woozy from the heat, he sunk to his knees in center field after the start of the next inning. He gathered himself, however, and stayed in the game, driving in another run on a forceout.

The baseball world began to notice. When Mays hit his home run that day, his twenty-fourth of the year, the public address announcer at Ebbets Field, Tex Rickards, said to the crowd: "Dodger fans, we thought you would want to know that Willie Mays just hit another homer." The crowd cheered, but the Dodger players came to the top step of the dugout to convey their unhappiness with Rickards, who was later confronted by Pee Wee Reese, the Dodger captain. "Who in the hell wrote that one for you?" he asked.

"Mr. O'Malley," he whispered, referring to the team's owner, Walter O'Malley, who later told reporters: "I thought Mays hitting another homer was a point of interest to the fans."

What he really wanted, of course, was to encourage the fans to come see Mays. Reporters could not recall the Dodgers' ever promoting an opponent on the loudspeaker, particularly someone from the Giants. But Mays transcended the deep wounds of an ancient rivalry. Even Dodger fans wanted to watch him.

The next time the Giants played at Ebbets Field, for three games starting on July 6, Mays hit four homers and drove in nine runs.

Mays now had thirty home runs in eighty games, already surpassing the top individual total for any Giant in 1953—Bobby Thomson with twenty-six. He also had at least one long clout in every National League city except Milwaukee. Pitchers increasingly knocked him down. "But his reflexes are so sharp he can get out of the way of the close pitch," the *Sporting News* reported. "He has hit the dirt often, but he does not complain." Other teams were riveted. One reporter noted, "Even the Yankees themselves spend half their time talking about Mays and what he does."

They had good reason to talk. Mays was on pace to break Babe Ruth's record of sixty homers in a season. Since the Babe had reached that milestone in 1927, only two other players had challenged it—Jimmie Foxx (fifty-eight in 1932) and Hank Greenberg (fifty-eight in 1938). No one had exceeded even fifty home runs since 1938. Sixty home runs was the most prestigious record in baseball: it combined the singular achievement of the long ball with Ruth's heroic qualities; his early death, at fifty-three in 1948, only added to the public's longing for him.

As both Roger Maris and Hank Aaron later learned, challenging a baseball god involves crippling pressures, and in July 1954, it appeared to be Willie Mays's turn. The *Sporting News* published a graph, with photo insets of the two principals, showing Mays ahead of Ruth as of July 11: Mays hit his thirty-first home run eleven days before Ruth hit his. An illustration, stretching the entire length of the page, was also telling. At the bottom was Mays, standing on top of a globe, swinging a bat, driving a ball through some clouds to the top of the page, where an oversized Babe is resting with a crown on his head and, inscribed on his chest, "The Immortal Ruth." The ball knocks the crown ajar, and the Babe, bug-eyed, looks down at Willie as if to ask, "Who is this wannabe?"

The comparison ruffled Mays. After he hit two home runs against the Dodgers on July 8, reporters cornered him in the clubhouse and asked if he knew how many Ruth had. "Of course I know," he said, eyes flaring. "Everybody knows. He hit sixty." Asked how he felt about being ahead of Ruth's pace, Mays bridled: "Wish you wouldn't ask that. I won't think about that, not at all. When you think about home runs, you go up an swing too hard and it's a strikeout. If you don't think about home runs, you swing right and maybe you can get a home run." Noting that, in June, he was one swing away from tying a Giant record for the most homers in consecutive games, Mays continued: "They told me about having a chance to tie one home run record, and I got thinking about it and I didn't come close. No, sir. I'm not thinking about Babe Ruth. I'm not even thinking about home runs."

Mays later said that, at the time, he didn't appreciate the magnitude of Ruth's record, but even if he had, it wouldn't have mattered. He always insisted that he never played for personal records. In retirement, he joked that if he had known how meaningful records were, he would have gone for them.

Mays did read the newspaper stories that compared him to Ruth and, for that matter, Ty Cobb, Tris Speaker, and other greats, but he always seemed more mystified than impressed. "That's funny stuff," he'd say, "real funny stuff." But he also acknowledged that he felt the pressure. "For the first time," he later said, "I had the feeling that people were going to be disappointed in me if I didn't do something. I felt defensive."

After the tense interview at Ebbets Field, Mays hit only three home runs over the next eleven games, and Frank Forbes noticed the connection. "When reporters started asking him a lot of statistical things like will he break Babe Ruth's record and things like that," he recalled, "he didn't come out and say anything, but these questions put things in his head, and I noticed that week he was trying for the long ball more often, and so he was striking out more than usual."

The routine was broken up by the All-Star Game in Cleveland on July 13. Mays was selected for the first time, and he, like most of his peers, took the game as seriously as any regular-season contest. To play with and against the best players was an honor, a responsibility. In his first game, Mays came off the bench and singled in two at-bats, but his presence alone had an impact. Braves manager Charlie Grimm said after the game, "Willie Mays is the only ballplayer who can help a team just by riding on the bus with them."

But the best line of the year went to a sportswriter from St. Louis who, noticing a shiny object on the grass in center field, said, "Look, Mays just lost his halo."

If 1954 marked some of Mays's greatest achievements, it also represented one of his saddest moments. His aunt Sarah had developed cervical cancer five years earlier, and she battled it bravely as Willie followed her condition at a distance. When the cancer spread to her lungs, she could no longer fight it. Willie knew Sarah was in the hospital and, before a game on July 17 in St. Louis, asked Eddie Brannick, the traveling secretary, to stay apprised of her condition. After the game began, Brannick got the news that she had died. He told Durocher, and Durocher decided to tell Willie, who broke down and cried in the dugout. Mays did not take the field in the fourth inning, marking his first rest of the season.

Aunt Sarah was thirty-six. The adult who was most responsible for raising Willie, who took him under her wing when she was thirteen, never got to see him reach the top of his profession, but she saw him realize his greatest dream and knew that the family's lofty expectations would not be denied. Not long before she passed away, she was asked about her de facto son. "Willie is wonderful to me," she said. "He's always sending me money and things. Only trouble he ever gave me raising him was when he used to run off and play ball and leave the dishes he was supposed to wash and dry. At night, if I told him to be home, he was never late."

Her funeral was not held immediately, so Mays went to Cincinnati and played four games in three days. Then, accompanied by Forbes, he went home to Fairfield. The moment he entered his aunt's house, he wept. Sarah, active in her church and the community, had a large network of friends and relatives, and they all came by to pay their respects. Forbes estimated that over several days, he saw a thousand people pass through the house, cars and bodies jamming the unpaved road in front.

But few of them saw Willie, who was in his bedroom in his pajamas and robe. People went to his door to greet him, console him, or give him a note, but he kept the door closed, unwilling to open it except to get a glass of water. And when he saw the crush of people, he asked someone to get the water for him. Recalled Forbes, "He was a captive of his hometown admirers, the halt, the lame, the old snuff-chewers, and the drugstore cowboys."

The funeral service, on July 22 at Jones Chapel A.M.E., began at 2 P.M., the hottest part of the day. The church held five hundred, but people were standing four or five deep in the rear. Beautifully wreathed flowers covered the coffin as tributes were spoken by friends and family; Forbes spoke on behalf of Horace Stoneham and the Giants. Despite temperatures exceeding 100 degrees, the funeral lasted over three hours, including a sermon of an hour and twenty minutes.

Mays left early. The Alabama heat almost caused him to faint, and Forbes took him back to the house. He never went to the cemetery because he was too upset. Forbes noted another reason he stayed home. "There were people who wanted to exploit him," he said. Two radio stations wanted to interview him, but Forbes said Willie was too bereaved to cooperate.

Mays's experience in Fairfield centered on a heartrending event, but the pattern was played out many times. When the masses wanted him, even well-wishers and admirers, he found comfort in isolation. When a friend or loved one died, he could not confront the sadness of the cemetery. And when he was at his most vulnerable, he had to be wary of those who might exploit him.

The day after the funeral, Stoneham called Forbes and said that Durocher was clamoring for Mays to return. Mays had only missed two games, but Durocher saw no reason why the death of a beloved aunt should keep him away. So Mays and Forbes flew to Milwaukee, where the Giants had a night game, but they did not arrive at the stadium until the ninth inning. It was too late: Giants relief pitcher Hoyt Wilhelm gave up a game-winning hit to Bobby Thomson. Afterward, according to one reporter, "Durocher divided his energy between bawling out Wilhelm for feeding Thomson a fat pitch and gently rubbing Willie's neck, as a gambler rubs a lucky coin. 'Willie's back,' he seemed to be saying. 'Everything's going to be all right.'"

For all his emotional trauma, Mays continued to perform. In a double-header in Cincinnati, before he went home, he had five hits, including his thirty-third home run. His first game back, he hit another homer off Warren Spahn and dazzled on the bases. In the fourth inning, on first base with two outs, Mays raced to third on a sharp single to right. The throw came in to second baseman Danny O'Connell, who wheeled and faked a throw to third. He feinted several more times, then Mays bolted for home, barely scoring under the infielder's high throw.

Mays said that baseball revived him—he would hit two more home runs over the next four games—but the Giants went into a tailspin, and their grieving center fielder was implicated. In the thirteen games that followed Aunt Sarah's death, the Giants lost nine. Even with Mays back in the lineup, the Giants lost seven of ten. The drought represented the first real losing streak of the year and one of only two in the entire season. What happened? "The inevitable conclusion," Arnold Hano wrote, was "that Mays's bat was there along with his speed and daring, but his spirit had been crimped by his aunt's death. This leaden-spirited Mays was not quite the same young man, and the wonderful contagion this time was a grim ailment."

Mays discounts the speculation—every team suffers losing streaks— but the comments highlighted the nearly magical powers imputed to him.

At his emotional nadir, Mays achieved the apex of his standing as an iconic figure in American life, appearing on the cover of *Time* on July 26. In an era that preceded television's dominance of the news, *Time* was America's preeminent newsweekly, its cover, the most valuable real estate in journalism. Only newsmakers, historical figures, and the occasional legend appeared there. J. Robert Oppenheimer, Joseph McCarthy, and Humphrey Bogart were so honored in 1954. Jackie Robinson, in 1947; Martin Luther King, Jr., in 1957.

Mays, at the time, was the youngest African American to appear on *Time*'s cover. It showed him with his bat cocked, his biceps rippling, his right thumb extended. It also emphasized a quirk in his batting style. Most hitters stand at the plate with their eyeballs fixated straight ahead. Not Mays. As shown on the cover, his pupils strained all the way to the left, as if to reduce the distance between them and the pitcher. He was a portrait of concentration, of strength, but his soft black face also showed youth, vulnerability, even sweetness. The story was a flattering, if by now familiar, account of an emerging boy wonder—"a smooth-muscled athlete with a broad, guileless face, he plays baseball with a boy's glee, a pro's sureness and a champion's flair." Oddly, Mays himself is quoted only once: "When you tag 'em good, they'll go over the roof of any park." Otherwise, his protectors—Durocher, Forbes, Dark—do his talking. The reader is left to assume that Mays is to be appreciated, even glorified, but not heard.

The cover was part of Mays's new role as a cultural phenomenon. Television loved him. In July, he appeared on three network shows in one weekend, including as the Mystery Guest on *What's My Line?*, and was on fifteen other radio and television shows. Ben Gross, the television critic for the *Daily News,* wrote that Mays was a "TV natural. He spoke his lines with the ease and friendly charm of a professional." *Sport* said, "Whenever [Mays] has been on TV, he has been loose and smiling. The cameras don't frighten him." When the *Today* show featured him, its camera crew spent the day with him in Harlem. The Giants played that night, and the crew members asked Mays if he would get a hit early in the game so they could go home. Mays hit one out of the park his first time up.

Mays also had cameo roles on sitcoms. In the 1960s, he appeared on the *Donna Reed Show* as well as *Bewitched,* in which he played a "warlock." In 1954, in preparation for another television show, the director asked how he was going to play himself. Mays, puzzled by the question, replied, "I don't know. Just turn those cameras on, and if it ain't me, let me know."

His life was described in serial form in two newspapers and was carried by a national wire service. Reporters hounded him. "It has gotten to the point the last couple of weeks," Garry Schumacher said, "that Willie couldn't take a shower without some reporter waiting to get in with him." A headline in *Newsweek* read: WILLIE MAYS: THE HOTTEST THING

SINCE BABE RUTH. The *New York Times Book Review* opined on what people were talking about these days: "Topic A is either the hydrogen bomb, sex, where-shall-I-go-on-my-vacation, or Willie Mays." In August, *Vogue* called him "The Joy Boy of The New York Giants [who plays with] a kind of physical intuition, backed by almost perfect reflexes, [which] tells him where the ball is coming from." That same month, Ethel Barrymore, in a profile in the *New York Times,* asked, "Isn't Willie Mays wonderful?"

The *Washington Post* wrote: "It's hard to pick up a paper these days (unless you start with Page 1 or the comics) without having the name of Willie Mays hit you in the face. Willie is easily the most publicized athlete since Jackie Robinson who made good and is still doing a fair job."

Sports Illustrated, in declaring that the "golden age" of sports was right now—the summer of 1954—said: "Willie, by himself, is almost enough to make it that. At twenty-three, Willie is already being talked of as one of the all-time greats. It is not only Willie's performance on the field and at the bat; it is Willie's Way. For Willie is, above all, happy to be playing baseball and he makes everyone who sees him feel happy too. And it is important to remember that in no other age of sport could Willie play on a big-league ball team. Indeed, less than twenty years ago, a Willie Mays could not have purchased a ticket to sit in the grandstand in many major league parks. No Negro could."

The most enduring off-field image of Mays emerged in 1954—his playing stickball on St. Nicholas Place with kids from Harlem. He also played basketball and hopscotch, jumped rope, and even participated in hide-and-seek, but it was stickball that captured the public's imagination. The game's charm was its simplicity and resourcefulness: hitters used a broom handle, pitchers threw a pink rubber ball, home plate was a manhole cover. So was second base. First and third bases were fenders of parked cars. One strike, or one foul, was an out.

Mays played regularly during his first several years in New York. He didn't spend much time with the older players—even in 1954, the Giants' next youngest player was three years older than Mays. He would play stickball in the afternoon before night games, or he'd play in the evening when the Giants had a day game. New York sewers are reportedly placed about thirty yards apart. A two-sewer hitter was pretty good, but Mays was a mind-blowing five-sewer slugger. Could he really hit a rubber ball 450 feet? Who knows, but a report that he could hit the ball six sewers was a definite exaggeration. Monte Irvin thought Mays was going to damage his swing, but Mays thought the thinner bat and smaller ball helped his hand-eye coordination.

Mrs. Goosby watched Mays from the window of her first-floor apart-

Nicknamed "Buck Duck," Willie knew as a boy that his athletic skills were his ticket out of Alabama.
(Courtesy of Willie Mays)

Cat Mays, a good ballplayer in his own right, worked in the steel mills and as a Pullman porter so his son could pursue his dreams on the baseball field.
(© Bettman/CORBIS)

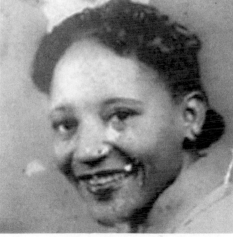

Willie's aunt Sarah, only thirteen when she became his principal caretaker, demanded respect, hard work, and excellence.
(Courtesy of Loretta Richardson)

A star at Fairfield Industrial High School, Willie (bottom row, fifth from the right) was probably better in football than baseball, but black quarterbacks had few professional opportunities. (Courtesy of Willie Mays)

Willie (bottom row, fourth from the left) was only fifteen when he played briefly for the Chattanooga Choo Choos. (Courtesy of Willie Mays)

This classic photograph, taken after the Birmingham
Black Barons won a championship in 1948, captures
the camaraderie of the Negro Leagues and the innocence
of their youngest player (back row, middle).

(Courtesy of Panopticon, Inc.)

Mays was a dazzling presence
with the Minneapolis Millers,
and when the Giants called him up
after only thirty-five games, they formally
apologized to Miller fans.

(© Bettmann/CORBIS)

The New York Giants' abrasive,
flamboyant manager, Leo Durocher,
became a trusted father figure
for the insecure Mays.

(Courtesy of the Anspach Collection)

Durocher won more than two thousand games as an
MLB manager, but his greatest contribution may have been
his mentoring of his young center fielder.
(Courtesy of the San Francisco History Center, San Francisco Public Library)

Mays brought energy and laughs to a club of veterans, including
Alvin Dark, Monte Irvin, and Wes Westrum. (© Bettmann/CORBIS)

In the 1951 World Series, the Giants fielded the first black outfield:
Irvin, Mays, and Hank Thompson. (Courtesy of the Anspach Collection)

Mays lost almost two
seasons in the army,
though his main job
for the military was
playing baseball.
(© Bettmann/CORBIS)

The Catch was the turning point of the 1954 World Series.
With 23 million television viewers, it helped create the Willie Mays brand.
(Courtesy of AP/Wide World Photos)

Mays believes most people miss the artistry of the Catch,
unaware of the many elements that had to be synthesized in a few seconds.
(© Bettmann/CORBIS)

Mays loved fashion and cut a stylish
figure off the field.
(Courtesy of Willie Mays)

Always a fan favorite, Mays obliged
autograph seekers throughout his career.
(Courtesy of the Anspach Collection)

Though Mays insists he
never actually said "Say Hey,"
he did chant the phrase for
a song recorded in 1954.
(Courtesy of the San Francisco History
Center, San Francisco Public Library)

ment and called him in for dinner, but she couldn't always keep him on schedule. As a rookie, he once lost track of time, and with a real game about to start, Durocher sent Forbes to look for him. He found Willie on a manhole cover.

His neighborhood diversion would have gone unnoticed, but one day a newspaper photographer showed up and took his picture swinging the broomstick. A new angle on America's newest hero! No fewer than six national magazines, including *Time* and *Newsweek,* soon ran stories or photographs of Mays playing stickball. *Collier's* ran a four-page photo essay on the subject. The headline: WILLIE'S BEST HITS AREN'T FOR THE GIANTS.

The game itself reflected the gritty resolve of the participants. They played in the Harlem streets, after all, because there were no parks nearby. They used a broomstick, sawed off six inches, with tape at the end for a handle, because they had no bats. They used manhole covers because they had no fields with actual bases.

The stories reaffirmed the existing stereotype of Mays—a childlike man with childlike tastes—while adding to his cult status. Though a full-blown celebrity, he was still of the city, part of the streetscape, approachable and engaging. As described in *Collier's*, one night a patrolman yelled to him, "Cut that out, Mays. I'm a Dodger fan and I don't want you practicing nights!" Mays giggled and sang out, "You a Dodger fan? Man, I'm sorry for you!"

The coverage showed Mays's legitimate fondness for children and his recognition of their needs. A nine-year-old named Gabriel Moses told *Collier's*: "Willie will play catch with us younger kids when the big fellers aren't around. He's always telling us, 'Throw harder, throw harder. How do you expect to be a big leaguer if you don't throw hard?' He's nice to us kids, takes us for sodas and all that. No swelled head with Willie." Added fourteen-year-old Carl Martin: "He doesn't let us think he's too great. He's a nice, friendly guy."

Collier's swooned:

> Willie's influence for good on the small fry of Harlem, not only in stickball but in his casual contacts with them, is almost immeasurable. The most completely unaffected athlete to come along in a generation, Willie is friendly as a kitten and gracious almost to the point of ceremonious politeness. Besides, how would you feel, as a kid, if you had a real big leaguer on your block who played ball with you, chatted with you, joked with you and treated you as an equal? Boys are hero worshipers, but few of them get a close-up of their idol the way the kids do along St. Nicholas Place.

To millions of American kids, *Collier's* concluded, Mays "already has replaced Superman and Captain Video."

Mays's inroad with adults was also strong. From the time he was a rookie, he had been represented by Art Flynn Associates, an advertising and publicity firm, whose principal was Stoneham's friend. "I want my boy well protected," Stoneham told Flynn in 1951. "Can you handle it?"

Flynn, having represented Ty Cobb and Joe DiMaggio, certainly could. Among other things, he developed an orange brochure touting the "Amazin' Willie Mays," and by 1954 he was charging between $500 and $1,000 for each radio and television appearance. He had also arranged endorsements for Minute Maid Frozen Juices ($700), Foster Grant sunglasses ($3,000), and Grove Furniture ($750). Wheaties, Polaroid cameras, and MacGregor sporting goods soon followed. Flynn said that no second-year player in history—including Ty Cobb, Babe Ruth, Ted Williams, Joe DiMaggio, and Stan Musial—had been in such demand. Speaking requests poured in from unlikely outposts. The publisher of the *Lethbridge Herald,* in Alberta, Canada, for example, invited Mays to speak at the annual Kinsmen's Sportsman's dinner, but the Kinsmen's Club couldn't pay the $1,000 fee.

Musical tributes raised Mays's profile even further—three songs about him were released in 1954, including "Amazing Willie Mays" by the King Odom Quartet and "Say Hey Willie Mays" by the Wanderers. The most famous, "Say Hey (The Willie Mays Song)" by the Treniers, a rhythm and blues group from Mobile, Alabama, featured Mays himself with several lines; the recording session was supervised by a young Quincy Jones. At the beginning of the song, Mays settles an argument among fans over whose ball it is. "It's Monte Irvin's!" Mays cries. At the end of "Whaddya say?" Mays chimes in gleefully: "Say hey!" The upbeat lyric captured the moment and the man and became the audio corollary—heard in most any documentary about Mays—to the images of his World Series catch.

The actress Tallulah Bankhead reflected on Mays's dramatic qualities in a *Look* essay, "What Is So Rare About Willie Mays." Bankhead acknowledges that she's a rabid Giants fan, in part because she finds all the other teams lacking. Who would root for the harmless Cubs? she asks. "The Cubs are cute. Or the Dodgers? I have never dodged anything in my life. Cincinnati? Too many Republicans."

Her greatest passion was number 24: "Everything he does on the field has a theatrical quality. Even when he strikes out, he can put on a show. In the terms of my trade, Willie lifts the mortgage five minutes before the curtain falls. He rescues the heroine from the railroad tracks just as she's about to be sliced up by the midnight express. He routs the villain when all seems lost." Bankhead also noted: "There have been two geniuses, Willie Mays and Willie Shakespeare."

Mays's image of youth, bordering on gullibility or callowness, was deeply embedded in the media coverage, and in some ways he was complicit. The *Herald Tribune,* for example, published a lengthy story in September by Mays, as told to a reporter: "I'd Play for Nothing." Mays not only said he would "play for nothing," but "I'd play ball even if they charged me"—an endearing comment, perhaps, but one that made him look like a naif. Mays recounted his signing of his contract on the first day of spring training that year. Giant officials gave him his contract, Mays explained, and all he asked for was a pen.

"Aren't you even going to see how much we're paying you?" Durocher asked.

"I don't care nothing about that," Mays quoted himself as saying. "If you say it's okay to sign, I'll sign. I'm only interested in playing."

He elaborated on his feelings about baseball. Playing it reminded him of a fellow he once saw in a show: "He was a tap dancer and how he could make his feet fly! He was having so much fun at his work and enjoying himself so much. I never saw anything like it. When the folks applauded him, he just kept dancing away. All he'd do was laugh and say, 'It's a shame to take the money.' Of course, he said it to get a laugh, but I could tell he meant it all the same. And that's sort of the way I feel about baseball."

Mays spoke from the heart. He did trust Durocher with his contract. He probably would have played for free. His greatest joy, like that of the dancer, was to entertain. His attitude pleased fans, particularly those who expected obedience from minorities. But the image of the smiling black dancer or ballplayer who was just grateful to perform, regardless of compensation, conjured up the worst stereotypes of Negro servitude. Moreover, it was a discordant note in the emerging civil rights movement, highlighted that year in the Supreme Court's unanimous ruling in *Brown v. Board of Education* that racial segregation in public schools was illegal.

What's most striking about this very public phase of Mays's life is how opaque he really was. In his television appearances, he spoke in the fluid, superficial platitudes of the medium; the dozens of articles on him rarely revealed his inner life or what he thought of his own improbable celebrity. Most hewed to the narrative of Mays as the "uncomplicated" Negro, the "uncalculating lad," or—as *Sport* called him—"this playful laughing boy from the steel-mill country of Alabama." Mays himself was not one to volunteer information except on baseball and the Giants. He was physically expressive but not communicative. *Sport* described him: "You get to know him and learn things about him because his emotions are on the surface, showing through his face and eyes and quick smile. You look at him and you can almost tell what he is thinking. You ask him about a recent great play and he starts talking, then suddenly stops as if he is thinking the rest of it to himself. He [doesn't] finish the experience for you."

Mays censored himself out of fear of misspeaking or stumbling into controversy. He reveled in the adulation but despised the scrutiny. In one instance, almost mistakenly, he did reveal part of himself.

In a *New York Times Magazine* story on July 11, a headline read: "NATURAL BOY" OF THE GIANTS: "In a dour age, Willie Mays fulfills the specifications of Jean-Jacques Rousseau in temperament and Leo Durocher in talent." The story, written by the magazine's Gilbert Millstein, adopted a patronizing, if conventional tone: it claimed that Mays, like Rousseau's "Natural Man," was good and simple, but only because he had not been corrupted by society.

"Since Mays is a Natural Man in an unquestionably naughty world," Millstein wrote, "he has had to be tended with great care, his instincts being basically sound but, like those of all Natural Men, somewhat protected."

While Mays had been protected, he had not lived in a vacuum for twenty-three years. He had traveled around the country, had been schooled by wise and cynical men, and had silently endured the racism of the day. The reporter interpreted Mays's reticence, his high voice, and his dialect for immaturity. But the story had at least one virtue: Mays described his ambivalence about his sudden fame and the intense pressures it had imposed.

"Sometimes I feel sorry I'm in this," Mays said. "Guys come to you and say, 'Do this, do that.' Sometimes I wish it hadn't happened, but I guess it just had to be. When I'm playing ball, I don't think about nothing but playing ball. It's just my way. I sometimes don't like to talk. I don't come out to the ballpark to talk to a lot of guys at once."

Mays wasn't a Natural Boy. He was a shy young man trying to please everyone in a world that wanted more than he could give. His refuge, his solace, was between the lines, and in 1954 he gave more than anyone could have imagined.

CHAPTER TWELVE

THE CATCH

Leo Durocher had been thinking. Before a game against the Cardinals on July 27, he called Mays into his office and closed the door.

"Willie, I want you to do something for me and the ball club," he said.

"What's up?"

"I want you to stop going for home runs." He explained that many of his home runs were with the bases empty, so if he got more hits and were on base more often, the team could produce more runs with Irvin or Thompson driving him in.

That night, Durocher moved Mays to the third spot in the order. He also told Mays that he'd have a chance to win the batting title—at the time, he was hitting .326, a strong average, but well below the league leaders, Duke Snider of the Dodgers and his teammate Don Mueller.

Mays needed little convincing, having felt the stress surrounding Babe Ruth's record. He wouldn't miss that, and if more base hits meant more wins, who could argue? Durocher asked him to change his stance as well. He had been hitting with his legs spread wide apart in a slight crouch. Durocher had him stand straighter with his feet closer together. Pitchers knew his power had been against high inside deliveries, so they were keeping the ball down and away. This new stance allowed Mays to more easily drive those pitches to right center and right field.

The strategy worked. Mays hit his thirty-sixth home run on July 28, but in the next fifty-five games, he hit only five more, one of which was inside the park. He also hit .379 over that stretch, including a twenty-one-game hitting streak, putting himself in the thick of the batting race.

Mays has always insisted that his transformation that year, from a slugger to a high-percentage hitter, was Durocher's doing. It's also possible that pitchers made adjustments and forced Mays to hit to the opposite field. By throwing outside, they prevented Mays from pulling cheap home runs down the left field line, and he was content to slash the ball the other way.

A more intriguing question is whether Durocher urged Mays to change his batting style to protect him. He surely recognized the emotional toll that the Ruth chase had already taken on Mays. Durocher's rationale for altering Mays's stance was flimsy at best: even as a home run hitter, Mays was batting .326. There was no reason to sacrifice home runs for a few more singles—unless, of course, the stress to hit those home runs would reduce their frequency.

Durocher knew that if Mays continued his assault on Ruth, the pressure would intensify. Having played with Ruth, Durocher appreciated his hold on the country, and he also understood America's racial divisions. He may well have foreseen the ugliness that would confront Hank Aaron, who received death threats when he broke Ruth's career home run record twenty years later.

Durocher protected Willie like a father, and he concluded that Willie was better off gunning for a batting crown than toppling the Babe.

The Giants had several near-collapses, but they proved resilient. After they lost six in a row at the end of July, their lead was down to two games, but they won seven out of their next eight. On August 15, after losing three to the Dodgers, they were in first by only half a game, but they peeled off seven straight wins. On August 29, the Giants were in first by only one and a half games, but four straight wins returned them to a comfortable margin.

Mays's excessive deference, particularly in his youth, to white authority may not have sat well with every African American, but he was still embraced by the black community. That was evident on August 8, when the *Amsterdam News,* a black newspaper in New York, sponsored Willie Mays Day at the Polo Grounds. This was already Mays's second "Day," though his first in New York. It began with a parade through Harlem and ended with a ceremony on the field, with Mays telling the crowd: "All my life, I've been dreaming and living for a day like this." He received plenty of goodies: a television, an air conditioner, jewelry, some cash, and—from a real estate agent—a plot of land in New Jersey. The ballpark ushers chipped in for a new portable record player; his teammates gave him a record cutter, which he could use to make his own acetate recordings. The sexy Rheingold girls (named for the beer) gave him some luggage; the Grace Del Marco models, wearing very tiny baseball uniforms, paraded with a sign: WILLIE IS OUR BOY!; the Chesterfield cover girl smiled sweetly.

Black dignitaries were also on the field, all of whom were pleased to be seen with the man of the hour. There was a state senator, the borough president of Manhattan, some Broadway figures, and a newspaper columnist. Also in the gathering was Thurgood Marshall, a future associate justice of the Supreme Court who, at the time, was a celebrated NAACP lawyer. He had represented the plaintiffs in *Brown v. Board of Education* and, less than three months earlier, had won the case. In a group photograph at the Polo Grounds, Marshall, tall and strapping, wearing a dark suit and a serious expression, stands right next to the smiling Mays. The other men all have their arms at their sides, but Marshall's right hand is draped tightly across Mays's shoulder.

Willie Mays knew nothing of Thurgood Marshall, but Thurgood Marshall knew all about Willie Mays.

The Giants won the pennant on September 20, the last Monday of the season, at Ebbets Field and finished the season at 97–57, five games ahead of the Dodgers. In the clubhouse, amid the popping champagne corks and sprays of beer, Mays told a reporter: "I had a big lucky year—not a real good year—but you got to have luck in this game."

Mays's regular season, however, wasn't over. He'd had three hits in the clinching game and now, for the first time, was in the batting lead. He had missed only three games and needed a rest, but with two Giants and a Dodger—Mays, Mueller, and Snider—vying for the title, all hovering in the .340s, Durocher thought it only fair that Mays and Mueller remain in the lineup for the remaining six games.

The competition, for Mays, was partly for bragging rights. He began the year as New York's third-best center fielder. Mantle was having his best season of his young career (.300, 27 homers, 102 RBIs), but it was easily exceeded by Mays's. Snider was having a superb year and finished with 40 homers, 130 RBIs, and a .647 slugging percentage. If Snider won the batting title, he could also claim the center field crown.

For Don Mueller, the competition with Mays was far more personal. Though only twenty-seven, Mueller had been with Giants for seven years. He choked up high on the bat, allowing his deft, left-handed stroke to spray balls to all fields and earning him the nickname "Mandrake the Magician." But he was one-dimensional: he couldn't hit the long ball, was a slow runner, and was a below-par fielder. Durocher wanted him to hit more home runs, and each spring he would try to replace Mueller in right field. Durocher and Mueller held each other in contempt, and the animosity intensified before the 1954 season when Durocher told Mueller to let Mays catch any ball he could in right field. The other outfielders accepted this directive. Monte Irvin, who had never fully regained his speed after breaking his ankle, gladly ceded balls to Mays. But Mueller was insulted by Mays's annexation of his territory. "He'd be miffed whenever a ball was just a little to his right, and I'd be calling for it," Mays said.

Mueller also resented Durocher's obvious favoritism. While the manager openly cheered on Mays, he all but ignored Mueller except for an occasional unflattering remark about his fielding. Mays's giddy acclaim, combined with the fawning reporters who interviewed him each day, created inevitable jealousies. Several Giants, including Mueller, lived in the same hotel and would pick Mays apart over their morning coffee. One reporter described it: "Sure, Willie was a bouncing, bubbly boy when he was hitting, they'd say, but he'd break down and cry when he was in a slump. Sure, he threw out a lot of runners with that booming arm of his, but his throws would sometimes come in so high that the cutoff man was helpless to stop a runner from taking an extra base. Sure, he knocked in a lot of runs, but when a hit was needed to pull out a game, he was just another guy with a bat in his hand." Roger Kahn said that by midseason, "there were resentments on the club so obvious that even the casual observer noticed . . . a coterie of detractors, small but bitter."

Most of the Giants were grateful to have Mays. As Whitey Lockman, decades later, says, "Once you got to know how good he was and what he meant to the team, you couldn't really be jealous of Willie's fame. I wish I could have been that good, for God's sake. Nobody was."

At the time, Durocher kept insisting that Willie put money in all their pockets, but for Mueller, a batting title would avenge the slights and rebalance the credit for the team's success.

Going into the final four-game series against the Phillies, Mays led the race by seven points and didn't slow down. He went 4-for-12 in his next three games, but Mueller went 7-for-13 and Snider, 4-for-7. Suddenly, on the last day of the season, Mueller held a one-tenth-of-a-point edge on Snider and four-tenths on Mays. Mueller was hitting .3426; Snider, who had led the race for most of the season, was at .3425; and Mays, .3422. The odds favored Mueller or Snider. The Giants were facing Robin Roberts, a right-hander who would lead the National League in wins (23), complete games (26), and strikeouts (160). Mueller, a left-hander, would have the advantage over Mays. Since the pennant race was over, the Dodger manager, Walter Alston, had tried to preserve Snider's narrow lead by sitting him against left-handed starters. For the final game, the Dodgers faced a Pittsburgh right-hander named Jake Thies, who had a 3–8 record, and Snider was in the lineup.

He went 0-for-3 as Thies gave up only four hits in the game; Snider finished at .341.

In Philadelphia, the Giants were keeping tabs on Snider on a telephone in their dugout. New York's game went eleven innings, giving Mueller, batting third, and Mays, fifth, ample opportunity. Both players singled their first time up; both made outs their second time. Third time up, Mueller flied out, but Mays tripled. Next time around, Mueller again flied out, but

Mays doubled. His hits reflected the success of his batting approach over the past two months. His first was to left off an inside fastball, while his extra-base hits came on outside curveballs slammed to right center.

Mueller doubled in the tenth inning, and with one out, the Phillies intentionally walked Mays. He did not come to the plate again; Mueller made one more out in the eleventh. Mays finished 3-for-4; Mueller, 2-for-6.

Final batting averages: Mays, .3451; Mueller, .3425.

As predicted by Durocher, Mays won the batting title, the Giants' first since Bill Terry hit .401 in 1930. On the train ride back to New York, Leo said, "I told you so." And at gatherings in the off-season, he introduced Mueller as "the man who lost the hitting title to Willie Mays."

With 41 home runs (second in the National League, behind Gil Hodges), Mays was the first player in more than thirty years to lead the league in batting average and hit more than 40 long balls. He finished first in the league in triples (13) and slugging percentage (.667), fifth in on-base percentage (.415), sixth in RBIs (110), and tenth in doubles (33). His most noteworthy achievement may have been in the outfield, where his thirteen assists included nine that were part of double plays, a phenomenal number. In comparison, the highest single-season total that strong-armed Carl Furillo ever had in this category—assists that were part of double plays—was six. Neither Roberto Clemente nor Mickey Mantle nor Joe DiMaggio ever had more than five; Duke Snider's best year, three.

Mays's final day of the 1954 season ended with a madcap evening in the celebrity vortex. He agreed to appear, wearing his home uniform, on both Ed Sullivan's *Toast of the Town,* on CBS, and the *Colgate Comedy Hour,* with Dean Martin and Jerry Lewis, on NBC. The shows appeared at the same time on Sunday nights, but Mays tried to accommodate both. When he and an associate of Art Flynn's arrived at the Sullivan studio at about 7:25 P.M., they realized that the Giants uniform had been sent to the Colgate studio. So they had to take a cab from Fifty-seventh and Eighth to Fifty-third and Broadway, get the uniform, and race back. Mays appeared with Sullivan from 8:10 to 8:20. He then jumped back in the cab and made it to NBC in time to appear at 8:35.

The next morning, Mays was a guest on the *Today* show with Dave Garroway, and that evening, Steve Allen interviewed him on *The Tonight Show.*

In many of these appearances, Mays's competition with his own teammate was the obvious angle. Ed Sullivan asked him what it was like to beat out another Giant. "If I hadn't won it," Mays said, "I would have wanted him to."

The goodwill did not last long. The following day, the Giants were at the Polo Grounds for a team photograph, and Mueller walked past Mays as he was tying his shoes. "Hey, Willie," he asked, "is it true you're the best center fielder in baseball?"

"The best right fielder too," he said. He never looked up.

After the photo, the Giants rode in fifteen open cars down Broadway to City Hall, cheered by a half-million fans beneath showers of ticker-tape confetti. The last two World Series had been between the Yankees and the Dodgers, but the Cleveland Indians won the American League pennant in 1954, so New York could rally around one team. Mayor Robert F. Wagner described the celebration as "equal to the receptions for Eisenhower, Lindbergh, and MacArthur." Not everyone celebrated. New York City's council president, Abe Stark, was a Brooklyn fan. He took the microphone and cried, "Wait till next year!" The crowd booed.

Riding in the first car was Alvin Dark, because he was the team captain, and Willie Mays, because he was Willie Mays. According to the *Sporting News*, "When the players were introduced individually after the parade, Willie drew the most applause."

Durocher addressed the crowd, and when he said, "Willie Mays is the greatest player I ever laid eyes on," he brought tears to his favorite player's eyes.

Few people gave the Giants a chance against the Indians, who had just completed one of the finest regular seasons in baseball history. Their 111 wins was an American League record; the 1927 Yankees, often cited as the greatest team ever, had won 110. (The Chicago Cubs' 116 victories in 1906 is the highest single-season total in a 154-game season.) The Indians' winning percentage of .721 remains an American League record. Cleveland lost four consecutive games only once all season. Otherwise, the Indians never slumped—nor could they, as the Yankees won 103 games, which represented Casey Stengel's best record in his twelve seasons as their manager.

The Indians were also heavily favored because the American League had been so dominant, winning seven consecutive World Series, six by the Yankees and one by Cleveland, in 1948. The Giants had won ninety-seven games in 1954, but their past disappointments in the Fall Classic— thirteen appearances and only four championships—hardened opinion against them.

The Indians' strength lay in their starting pitchers, which included three future Hall of Famers: Bob Lemon, Early Wynn, and Bob Feller; the fourth starter was Mike Garcia. Collectively, they had forty-six years of experience in the major leagues, and their combined ERA of 2.78 that year set an

American League record. The number one starter was Lemon, who with Wynn tied for the league best in victories—twenty-three. Garcia had perhaps the most freakish statistic: 259 innings pitched; only six home runs allowed. The Giants' best pitcher that year, Johnny Antonelli, also pitched 259 innings and gave up twenty-two homers.

The Indians could hit as well. Second baseman Bobby Avila, with a .341 average, was the American League batting champion. Outfielder Larry Doby led the league in home runs, with thirty-two. Third baseman Al Rosen had won the MVP in the previous season and finished the year with a .300 average and 102 RBIs. If the Indians won the World Series decisively, as expected, they would be remembered as one of the best teams in history.

The Giants, however, were not intimidated. Because both teams trained in Arizona, they had played twenty-one exhibition games together. The Giants had won more than they lost, believed they had the edge defensively, were better on the bases, and saw no reason to be unnerved. Willie Mays also thought Cleveland drank too much.

The Series again featured the advantages of racial and ethnic diversity: the Giants had, in addition to Mays, Irvin, and Thompson, pitcher Ruben Gomez, born in Puerto Rico, starting in Game Three; the Indians, meanwhile, had two African Americans in the starting lineup, outfielders Larry Doby and Al Smith, plus a black reserve, Dave Pope; Avila was born in Mexico; and Mike Garcia was of Mexican descent.

Mays had hit poorly in the 1951 postseason. He did not carry the performance of one game or one series into the next, so he added no extra pressure on himself for the '54 Series. But unlike in his rookie season, he was now the centerpiece of the Giants' attack—he would bat fourth—and he knew he'd have to perform far better if the Giants were to have a chance.

The first two contests were at the Polo Grounds, Game One on September 29. In the coming decades, the World Series would begin almost a month later, in the frigid night air before fans huddled in parkas, ski caps, and mittens. But in 1954 the games started in the hazy autumn sunshine, with men in sports coats and ties, women in dresses and pearls. Today, a gentle breeze drifted through the park, and the grass was moist with dew. The Polo Grounds was swept, scrubbed, and decked in bunting, a dowager in finery. The capacity crowd of 52,751 sat shoulder to shoulder—Laraine Day with Spencer Tracy; the wives of Lou Gehrig and John McGraw; Jackie Gleason, Don Ameche, Danny Kaye, and Perry Como, who would sing the national anthem; and the white-shoe bankers, the well-connected politicians, and the great swarm of humanity that brought with them, in Don DeLillo's words, "the body heat of a great city."

As the teams warmed up, a band with a female vocalist stationed in center field played "Say Hey." Mays himself posed for photographs, laughing and smiling, with his fellow batting champion, Avila.

The *Herald Tribune* wrote, "The Polo Grounds was a place to see and to be seen and call friendly greetings. But as the game approached everyone grew hushed with expectations."

Right-hander Sal Maglie started the game for the Giants. His career had appeared over the previous season, undone by a back injury. But he went to a chiropractor and was fitted with a rubber lift an eighth of an inch thick, which he put in the heel of one shoe. "My pelvis is tilted," Maglie explained. "The lift evens up my legs." A rebalanced Maglie went 14–6 in '54 and posted a 3.26 ERA. Mays liked Maglie because he had a penchant for throwing high inside fastballs, designed to move batters off the plate as well as to protect his own hitters. His tight pitches, plus his menacing stare and heavy beard—one writer called him God's gift to Gillette—contributed to his nickname, "the Barber." Stand too close to the plate, and he'll shave you.

The first batter of the World Series was Al Smith, and Maglie hit him in the back.

Avila followed with a single, which was booted by Mueller, allowing Smith to go to third. After the next two batters were retired, Vic Wertz boomed a triple to right, scoring the game's first two runs and beginning the most memorable day of Wertz's career.

NBC was televising the game, and viewers who had never seen Mays in action got their first glimpse of his abilities in the third inning. With Bob Lemon pitching, the Giants had already scored a run and had a man on first when Mays came to the plate. He walked, making it first and second. The next batter, Hank Thompson, hit a sharp ground ball to the right side. Mays had to freeze until the ball passed him, then he took off for second. Despite the delay, Mays skittered around the diamond for third. Right fielder Dave Philley had a strong arm—he had twenty-two assists one year—and his throw was right on target, but Mays narrowly beat it with a hook slide just as his hat flew off.

With the score tied 2–2, Maglie and Lemon settled into a pitcher's duel, the Indians getting the better chances. The problem for Maglie was Wertz. After his triple, he singled to left in the fourth and, in the sixth, ripped another hit to right. Mueller tried to throw behind Wertz at first but missed everyone for an error. Wertz ended up at second with one out, but the Indians stranded him.

By the seventh, the game had already lasted nearly two hours—long for that era—and the sun hovered over the grandstand behind first base, casting shadows past the right field foul line. It was still warm, the morning haze long since burned off.

The Indians went down in order in the seventh, and the Giants failed to score as well, with Mays, unable to read Lemon, making the final out. The score remained 2–2, Cleveland shut out since the first. There was little doubt that the next team to score would win.

The first hitter in the eighth, Larry Doby, was nursing a sore shoulder, but he was still the Indians' most dangerous threat. Maglie may have been too fine with him or maybe just tired, but he walked Doby, his first freebie of the game. The next hitter, Al Rosen, batting cleanup, hit a ground ball sharply to the left side. Shortstop Alvin Dark ranged to his right and stuck out his bare hand but could not field the ball cleanly.

Two on, nobody out, and Vic Wertz was the batter.

He was in many ways a prototype of the stodgy long-ball era— "muscular men not long in grace nor noted for acceleration, but men who commanded large salaries for occasional home runs," according to Bill James. Wertz was 6 feet tall and 186 pounds, a big man for his day, with a burly torso, quick wrists, and a chaw of tobacco in his mouth. By 1954, he had been a three-time All-Star with the Detroit Tigers and may have been the most grateful player in the World Series. He had begun the season with the Orioles and was traded to the Indians after twenty-nine games. The Orioles lost a hundred times and finished fifty-seven games out of first place.

Wertz was an outfielder, but Cleveland had no openings in the outfield. Rescued from baseball purgatory, he would have been satisfied pinch-hitting, but Indian manager Al Lopez had other ideas. He was without a quality first baseman, so he plugged in his brawny newcomer. Defensively, Wertz was barely adequate, but he gave the Indians another potent bat in the middle of the lineup.

The Giants wished he had stayed in purgatory. New York had a good read on all the Indians thanks to spring training, but they had never seen the left-handed-hitting Wertz. His three hits, all smoked, had come off a high fastball, a slider down and away, and an outside fastball.

Durocher was not going to let Maglie face Wertz again, so he dispatched his coach, Freddie Fitzsimmons, to the mound to change pitchers. Maglie, tall and brooding, took his long walk across the outfield to the clubhouse and was replaced by Don Liddle, a southpaw not quite 5-foot-10, with a narrow, pallid face and quick motion. He had come with Johnny Antonelli in the Bobby Thomson trade and had performed admirably as a spot starter and reliever, with nine wins and a 3.04 ERA. His best pitch was his curveball.

Mays knew that, so he was cheating in. Hitters tended to pound Liddle's curveball into the ground, and Mays wanted to cut down the runner at the plate on a single. He was shading him to right and assumed that Wertz, like most hitters, would be swinging at the reliever's first pitch.

Wertz indeed swung but missed, and Liddle was soon ahead in the count: one ball, two strikes. Wertz guessed he would see a high, tight fastball, which is what most lefties threw him with that count—drive him off the plate to set up the curveball. Liddle threw his fastball but aimed it poorly. The ball stayed over the plate, almost at the shoulders. Wertz extended his thick arms, rotated his wrists, and hit the ball squarely.

Ball game, thought Roger Kahn, who was standing in the lower deck between third and home.

Wertz thought so too as he watched his blazing line drive sail just to the right of second base. He put his head down and began pumping his stubby legs, confident he would end up on second or third or, if the center fielder misplayed it, all the way back at home.

Alvin Dark spun to his left. At shortstop, his first reaction on any ball hit straightaway was to spin and look over his left shoulder at the center fielder. In his fourteen years in the majors, Mays was the only center fielder who would be in full stride the moment he peered over his shoulder. (All other fielders were still picking up speed.)

Now Dark saw Mays at full speed and thought, two runs. The ball's distance wasn't the only problem. Mays had no angle on it. The ball was winging directly over his head, which is one of the toughest catches in baseball.

Al Rosen, nearing second base, was certain he would score.

Monte Irvin sprinted over from left field to prepare for the carom off the wall, hoping to deter an inside-the-park home run.

Liddle jogged, head down, toward the third base line to back up any errant throws to third or home.

The Giants in the dugout stood on the top step.

Leo Durocher retained hope, believing that any ball that stayed in the yard could be caught by Mays. He just wasn't certain if the outfield was big enough.

Arnold Hano, sitting in the right field bleachers, later wrote that the ball was hit "about as hard as I have ever seen a ball hit," but he was not immediately "perturbed" because it was hit to the deepest part of the Polo Grounds, Mays's territory. He had seen other center fielders catch majestic drives in those distant recesses.

"Then I looked at Willie," Hano wrote, "and alarm raced through me, peril flaring against my heart. To my utter astonishment, the young Giant center fielder—the inimitable Mays, most skilled of outfielders, unique for his ability to scent the length and direction of any drive and then turn and move to the final destination of the ball—Mays was turned full head around, head down, running as hard as he could, straight toward the runway between the two bleacher sections. I knew then that I had underestimated—badly underestimated—the length of Wertz's blow."

Watching this powerful tracer forty feet above Mays's head, Hano reached a quick, mournful conclusion: it will beat him to the wall.

Rosen had pushed ahead and reached second base, but Doby, himself a center fielder, had hesitated and begun to retreat to second. He realized the ball could be caught, and if so, he would still have time to tag up and score.

Mays, barreling toward the bleacher wall, looked over his left shoulder, slowing a bit, then continued with his head straight, arms thrashing, legs churning.

The center field wall, at its deepest, is 483 feet. This area is an alcove, created by a gap in the center field bleachers, and in the alcove are the stairs that lead to the two clubhouses. The bleachers themselves did not have markers on them; their distance has been estimated from 450 to 460 feet. Wertz's drive was not the farthest to have been hit to center field in the Polo Grounds. At least one ball had been hit into the bleachers, and two others had been caught at the foot of the clubhouse stairs.

What made Wertz's hit so startling was its low, tailing trajectory. No ball, it seemed, had ever traveled so far on such a low arc.

The bleacher wall was 8½ feet high, concrete with no padding, but the image on television made it appear that Mays was running toward something much bigger. To create a dark green background for hitters, large screens were attached to the top of the concrete wall closest to the alcove. On television, the wall and the screen were indistinguishable, so it looked as if Mays were just running toward an impenetrable barrier.

He ran past the farthest edge of the outfield grass, veering slightly to his right as his spikes touched the narrow cinder strip near the base of the wall. At the last moment, he looked up, extended his arms like a wide receiver, and opened his Rawlings Model HH glove. The ball fell gently inside. He had ten feet to spare.

Jack Brickhouse, the usually understated announcer who was calling the game for NBC, conveyed his surprise in his call: *"There's a long drive . . . way back at center field . . . way back, way back, it is a—Oh, my! Caught by Mays! Willie Mays just brought this crowd to its feet with a catch which must have been an optical illusion to a lot of people. Boy!"* The film clip shows a fan slapping his forehead, mouthing the words "Oh, my God."

But the play wasn't over.

Doby, seeing Mays's catch, completed his retreat to second, touched the bag, and took off for third. With Mays on the fringe, his momentum carrying him away from the plate, Doby, a fast runner, could score by advancing two bases.

But Mays whirled and threw "like some olden statue of a Greek javelin hurler, his head twisted away to the left as his right arm swept out and around," Hano wrote. His hat flew off in perfect sync with the corkscrew motion, and it was "the throw of a giant, the throw of a howitzer made human, arriving at second base . . . just as Doby was pulling into third and as Rosen was scampering back to first."

Second base umpire Jocko Conlan saw the ball coming in and said to himself, "This has to be the best throw anybody could ever make."

Television viewers at the time, and the millions who watched the film clip in years to come, couldn't admire the throw; it had been hurled out of the frame. But they saw something just as good: Mays from the ground, propped up by his arms, hatless, clean cut, his eyes squinting, scanning, trying to determine if his catch and throw had restored order to the infield.

It had, for Doby stopped at third. Rosen later said, "Normally, an outfielder has to make two or three more steps, but not Willie."

Vic Wertz never saw the catch. In all the crazy movements of baserunners and cutoff men and amid the gasps and cheers of the fans, he had passed the retreating Rosen and, finally at second base, saw the incoming throw and realized what had happened. He looked at Mays in disbelief, returned to the dugout, cursed, and kicked the water cooler.

No one thought about the historical significance of the catch. All it meant was that the Indians were now on first and third with one out.

Cleveland manager Al Lopez sent up right-handed pinch hitter Hank Majeski, so Durocher countered with right-hander Marv Grissom, a screwball pitcher. Liddle was done after one hitter. On his way off the mound, he said something to Grissom, which was reported as: "I got my man." (Liddle's son, Craig, later said that his father would never have made such a comment on the field but said it to Durocher in the clubhouse.)

Lopez then pinch-hit Dale Mitchell, who walked to load the bases. Another pinch hitter, Dave Pope, now had a chance to render Mays's catch meaningless, but he struck out. The next batter, catcher Jim Hegan, pulled a fly ball into left field, where the short fence and an overhanging facade allowed cheap home runs. Irvin ran to the 315-foot marker and a grand slam appeared imminent, but the ball dropped into his glove. Hano swore that the slight breeze had "developed a backbone" and pushed the ball back into play.

As Irvin jogged off the field with Mays, Irvin said, "That was a helluva catch, roomie. I didn't think you'd make it."

Mays said, "I had it all the way."

The game continued, but neither team could push a run across. Extra innings followed, and Wertz led off the tenth.

Grissom, still in the game, threw several screwballs low and away, forcing Wertz to foul them down the left field line. But the next screwball got too much of the plate, and Wertz shot it into left center, between the outfielders, down for extra bases. Mays raced to cut the ball off as it scooted toward the wall. Irvin had no chance for it. Mays had to decide: should he try to intercept the ball before it reached the wall and possibly hold Wertz to a long double—a strong throw would still be needed—or should he play it off the wall for a triple. If he tried to cut it off and missed, he would be out of position to retrieve it, and Wertz, given the deep alleys and angled wall that would kick the ball toward center, would circle the bases.

Mays gambled. He ran straight across the outfield, homed in on the ball, bent down, and scooped and hurled it in one flawless motion to third base, where Hank Thompson caught it on the fly one step before the bag. At least this time Wertz could watch Mays. He later recalled, "Willie came running in and grabbed it off the grass as he was skidding to the ground" and stopped him at second—a four-hundred-foot double.

Mays later said that play was as good if not even better than the catch because it required an instant calculation—could he or couldn't he reach the ball?—and Wertz himself said, "I think Willie may have made a better play on me in the tenth."

Hano wrote, "At this point, I think, the Indians quit. It is not fair to say they quit in the eighth when Mays made his catch. They still had clawed away, stopping the Giants in the eighth and ninth, and they opened the tenth (or at least Wertz had) full of vinegar. But when Mays again indicated he was not Mays, but Superman—they must have known they were through."

Wertz was through, replaced by a pinch runner, who was sacrificed to third. But the next hitter struck out. Next at bat was Bob Lemon, who was allowed to swing even though he had already pitched nine innings in the heat. He was, however, a solid hitter, swinging left-handed, and he smacked a line drive—right to the first baseman for the final out.

In the bottom of the tenth, Mays was due up second. The Indians had a new catcher, Mickey Grasso, a thirty-four-year-old career minor leaguer who had been in only four major league games that year. The usual backup catcher, Hal Naragon, had played in forty-six games, but he was only twenty-five, and Lopez wanted more experience behind the plate.

Mays, watching Grasso warm up Lemon, noticed that his return throws were weak, and after the practice pitches, he only lobbed the ball to second base. Mays figured Grasso for a sore arm, so he asked Durocher for the green light to steal if he reached first. Mays was not yet a good base stealer. He had only eight for the year and was thrown out five times. But Durocher said yes.

With one out, Mays came to the plate. He was 0-for-3 with a walk and hadn't hit the ball hard all day. But Lemon, perhaps tiring in the third hour of the game, walked him. On first, Mays took a lead and broke with the first pitch. He did not get a good jump, breaking well after Lemon had committed himself to throw. Hank Thompson took the pitch. Grasso jumped from his squat, grabbed the ball from his mitt, and threw it so low that it skipped fifteen feet in front of second base. Mays slid in safely.

With Mays in scoring position, the Indians intentionally walked Thompson to set up a double play. The next hitter was Irvin, but Durocher pinch-hit James "Dusty" Rhodes, one of the more colorful players on the team. The Alabaman was well qualified to be one of Stoneham's drinking buddies. His father, Rhodes would explain, was a corn farmer: "He used to raise two hundred gallons." Rhodes was a lousy outfielder, and knew it. Asked what position he played, he would say, "Me and Willie play left field."

But Rhodes earned his keep at the plate, batting .341 with fifteen home runs as a spot starter and pinch hitter.

The first pitch from Lemon, Rhodes popped a fly ball down the right field line. Second baseman Avila ran after it, but the ball, aided by the wind, drifted toward the wall. Dave Pope gave chase and reached the track. Would so cheap a hit make it to the wall? Would it win the game? The fielder leaped. The ball fell into the first row of the stands above a sign marked 257 feet. The home run traveled 200 feet less than Wertz's mighty clout.

Mays, tagging up at second, saw umpire Larry Napp signal the homer, and he began jumping and clapping in glee. He suddenly realized that Thompson was right on his heels, running hard, apparently unaware of Napp's signal—the ball had bounced off a fan's chest and rolled back onto the field. Mays, like a traffic cop, began madly signaling to Thompson while watching that both Thompson and Rhodes touched all the bases. Everyone made it around the diamond, and the Giants won, 5–2.

In the clubhouse, Lopez said, "It was the longest out and the shortest homer of the year."

Mays's catch was the talk of the game.

Joe DiMaggio, who watched it from the press box, said what made it remarkable was Mays's courage in coming so close to the wall, refusing to slow down until he grabbed the ball. He called the catch "greater than Al Gionfriddo's in the 1947 Series," referring to the Dodger left fielder's brilliant grab of a DiMaggio hit deep in the corner at Yankee Stadium.

A reporter asked Durocher if it was the greatest catch he'd ever seen, and Durocher used the question to make it clear, however crudely, that Mays was not a one-catch wonder: "What the fuck are you talking about? Willie makes fucking catches like that every day. Do you keep your fucking eyes closed in the press box?"

When Lopez heard Durocher's comments, he grew indignant, saying, "I've been playing ball since I was a kid. I've been around the major leagues for thirty years. That was the greatest catch I've ever seen. Just the catch, mind you. Now put it all together. The catch. The throw. The pressure on the kid. I'd say that was the best play anybody ever made in baseball."

Al Rosen later said, "Nobody else could've made that play at that venue at that time. It was a catch for the ages."

Not every Indian was so generous. Bob Feller said bitterly, "We knew Willie had it all the way . . . he was a great actor." Larry Doby, who would have scored had he anticipated the play at the outset, said that he would have made the catch as well "and without making it look so hard."

Several months later, Durocher claimed that Mays said after the game, "I don't rank 'em, I just catch 'em." These words cannot be found in a sampling of game stories, and Mays contends he never said them. In postgame interviews, he did convey a combination of confidence and humility. "I had the ball all the way," he said. "There was nothing too hard about that one. Did that save the game? Well, maybe it did. But what about my hitting? I wasn't any help up there at the plate."

He did, of course, contribute at the plate, with two walks, a run scored, and a pivotal stolen base, but he dwelled on his need to improve.

The game's aftermath included one other noteworthy moment. To get to the Giants' clubhouse, reporters and photographers had to walk past the steps that led to the showers. After Game One, Mays ambled out of the steamy room with his towel draped around his waist. The photographers yelled for him: "Wait! Look at the cameras! Smile!" Willie at first appeared dazed by the deafening gibberish, but just before the cameras snapped, he dropped his white cover. The bulbs flashed, and Mays, naked, laughed uproariously in his high-pitched squeal.

Mays loved a good prank, but all Robert Creamer, with *Sports Illustrated,* could think was: "This was the most perfectly sculpted, most beautiful human being I've ever seen—like a Roman god." Mays's glistening skin wasn't really black or even brown. It was a mottled gray brown. "It looked like marble," Creamer recalls. With careful modesty, Mays retrieved his towel, the photographers pleaded with him to cooperate, and just as they prepared to snap their next round of pictures, he dropped his towel again. He was having fun.

Finally Mays showed them mercy and allowed the photograph to be taken with the towel around his waist. What became of the other negatives is unknown. "That picture," Creamer says, "would be worth a million bucks today."

The Catch has a rich but complicated legacy. Mays's claim that he had it all the way is not false modesty. He had a fielding tic in which he would tap his glove when he knew he would catch a ball, and the replay shows him doing just that on his sprint to the wall. Mays also says that he didn't have to contend with other variables that cause mayhem in the outfield: he didn't have to worry about colliding with other players; he didn't have a difficult sky, strong winds, or rain; he didn't have wet grass or a slippery ball; he didn't have to jump over a wall, against ivy, or around a batting cage. It was a pure play, and he made it.

Mays regrets that his greatest plays, such as his Morgan catch at the base of the wall at Ebbets Field, were not preserved on film, so his "signature catch" is actually something less than his best work. What made the Catch legendary, he says, was not the catch but the atmospherics—it was on television before 23 million viewers at a decisive moment in a World Series game. It bothers Mays when he hears that he threw the ball back by "instinct." Most people, he believes, miss the artistry of the play, unaware of the many elements—including the ball's sound against the bat—that had to be synthesized in a few fleeting seconds. As he later recalled it:

"I'm playing a shallow center field. It's the eighth inning, score is tied, and I don't want Larry Doby scoring from second base. One run could be the ball game. The ball game could be the Series. You never know.

"Wertz hits it. A solid sound. I learn a lot from the sound of the ball on the bat. Always did. I could tell from the sound whether to come in or go back. This time I'm going back, a long way back, but there is never any doubt in my mind. I am going to catch this ball. I turn and run for the bleachers. But I got it. Maybe you didn't know that, but I knew it. Soon as it got hit, I knew I'd catch this ball.

"But that wasn't the problem. The problem was Larry Doby on second base. On a deep fly to center field at the Polo Grounds, a runner could score all the way from second. I've done that myself and more than once. So if I make the catch, which I will, and Larry scores from second, they still get the run that puts them ahead.

"All the time I'm running back, I'm thinking, 'Willie, you've got to get this ball back to the infield.'

"I run 50 or 75 yards—right to the warning track—and I take the ball a little over my left shoulder. Suppose I stop and turn and throw. I will get nothing on the ball. No momentum going into my throw. What I have to do is this: after I make the catch, turn. Put all my momentum into that turn. To keep my momentum, to get it working for me, I have to turn very hard and short and throw the ball from exactly the point that I caught it. The momentum goes into my turn and up through my legs and into my throw.

"That's what I did. I got my momentum and my legs into that throw. Larry Doby ran to third but couldn't score. Al Rosen didn't even advance from first.

"All the while I'm runnin' back, I was planning how to get off that throw.

"Then some of them wrote, 'he made that throw by instinct.'"

Television defined the Catch as Mays's iconic image, and the grainy film footage, run endlessly on ESPN and other sports channels as well as Internet sites, has become Mays's most tangible connection to future generations. The black-and-white photographs showing Mays in four frames have been reproduced countless times in books and magazines to the same effect. It's appropriate that a film clip or an image, not a statistic, defines him. Unlike other great players, who are associated with numbers—56, .406, 61, 714, 755—Mays holds no record with historical resonance. His brilliance was in how he played the game, and the Catch evokes the awe and wonder of those skills.

Ironically, the film clip does not capture its true magnificence. For all of Mays's efforts to downplay the Catch's value, virtually all who saw it recognized its greatness. But the scratchy kinescope replay makes it appear as if Mays simply ran back and caught the ball, not unlike any ESPN Web Gem shown every night of the season. There is no depth perception in the footage, no sense of how hard and low the ball was hit or how far and fast Mays had to run.

Bob Costas said, "It was more than just a great catch. It was a catch no one had ever seen before. . . . When the ball left Vic Wertz's bat in the massive Polo Grounds, where it was headed, where Mays was standing, there was only one possibility. Could he get to it before it was an inside-the-park home run? Could he hold it to a triple? Catching it was out of the question. He turned and ran to a place where no one can go to get that ball, starting where he started with the ball hit as it was hit. So, it was more than just a great acrobatic play. It was a play that until that point was outside the realm of possibility."

The Catch didn't surprise Mays's cousin Loretta, who watched it on television at Fairfield Industrial High School. E. J. Oliver had brought the students together to watch Willie play in the World Series. They cheered their hero when he grabbed the ball, but Loretta had seen it before. "When Willie would wash dishes," Loretta says, "he would throw them up and reach out for them and dive and catch them. That's where he got that catch from."

The rest of the World Series was anticlimactic. No other game could match the drama (or length) of the first contest. Game Two opened well for the Indians, with leadoff hitter Al Smith swinging for a home run on the first pitch, but it was Cleveland's only run. Vic Wertz had another good day, on base three times with a single and two walks, and Johnny Antonelli would repeatedly find himself in jams—the Indians stranded thirteen on eight hits. The Giants could muster only four safeties off Early Wynn, but once again, Durocher made the right move in pinch-hitting Dusty Rhodes for Monte Irvin in the fifth inning. Rhodes delivered the game-tying hit, driving in Mays, who had walked. The go-ahead run scored on a forceout, and Rhodes provided an insurance run with a homer in the seventh. The Giants prevailed, 3–1.

There were no days off in the 1954 World Series. The teams completed Game Two at the Polo Grounds, were bused over to the airport, flew to Cleveland, and were ready for Game Three the next day. The Indians were hoping that a hometown crowd of 71,555 would turn their luck, but the game was never in doubt. Mays saw to that. On the flight to Cleveland, Durocher told him that he had reverted to his previous batting stance and was again trying to pull the ball, which accounted for his lack of production. He instructed Mays to resume the style that had served him well down the stretch. In the first inning of Game Three, Mays got his first hit and RBI on a single to right field, then scored another run in the third. Incredibly, in the third inning Rhodes again pinch-hit for Irvin, and he again delivered—this time, a two-run single. The Giants laid down sacrifice bunts and ran the bases aggressively while Mays went 3-for-5 and drove in two runs. Two of his hits were to right field. The Indians, meanwhile, committed two errors in a listless performance. The only player with a pulse seemed to be Wertz, who hit a home run. With Ruben Gomez pitching, the Giants won, 6–2.

Cleveland's fourth pitcher was Bob Feller, who at thirty-five was still formidable—pitching once a week, he was 13–3 with a 3.09 ERA—but he was no longer the ace. Facing a deciding Game Four, Lopez came back with Lemon, even though he'd only had two days off after throwing ten innings in New York. The Giants weren't worried. Before the game, they ordered a repainting of their plane's fuselage—from "National League Pennant Winners 1954" to "World Champions 1954."

Lopez's move backfired. The Giants riddled Lemon for six runs and seven hits in four innings, and they led, 7–0, before any Indian crossed the plate. Irvin finally played the entire game and got two hits and drove in two runs. The Giants executed three sacrifice bunts and two sacrifice flies, and Durocher deftly juggled his pitchers. Don Liddle, who relieved in Game One, started Game Four and pitched into the seventh, and Johnny Antonelli, who started Game Two, relieved in Game Four and pitched the final inning and two-thirds. Mays went 1-for-4 with a double, an RBI, and a run scored. The Giants won, 7–4.

Vic Wertz went 2-for-4.

The Giants' championship was one of the greatest upsets in World Series history. The 1906 Chicago Cubs, who won 116 games, also blew the championship, but at least they won two World Series games. The Giants' sweep was stunning. Two of the Indians' best hitters, Doby and Rosen, played with injuries, but that alone could not really explain their futility. Lopez offered one possibility. "Losing the first game hurt us the most," he said. "We had so many chances when a hit or a long fly would have scored someone. Willie Mays made that great catch on Wertz's drive, and after that we never were the same."

This view became part of the Willie Mays mystique—that his catch had crushed the spirit of the mighty Indians, that his supernatural skills had crippled their resistance. The perception of invincibility loomed among the Cleveland faithful. In the fourth game, after Mays had caught the third out of an inning, he threw to the plate on the mistaken belief that there were only two outs. The *Cleveland Press* sportswriter Frank Gibbons leaped to his feet and screamed, "We finally found his weakness—he can't count!"

Mays himself accepts that the catch was the turning point, but he offers a more pragmatic explanation for its influence. "If Cleveland had won Game One, then they come back with Feller in Game Four and Lemon in Game Five," he says. "A different Series."

There were many victors. After eighteen years as owner, Horace Stoneham finally won a World Series, vindicating him as worthy of his inheritance. It was a triumph for Leo Durocher, his first championship in fifteen years as manager, placing him in the record books with John McGraw. Dusty Rhodes was the storybook hitting star. Johnny Antonelli picked up one win (on a complete game) and one save. The City of New York preserved its baseball dominance. The faded Polo Grounds reclaimed its glory.

The oddest loser was Vic Wertz, who was 8-for-16 in the Series, with two doubles, a triple, and a home run. He was, at the time, only the tenth player in World Series history to play every game and hit .500 or better. Many great hitting performances have been forgotten, but Wertz suffered a greater perversion. No one remembers his stupendous hitting. All they remember is his *out*. But infamy had its benefits. After the Series, the American League sent Wertz the film footage of the games, and he played the Catch when he gave speeches around the country. After he retired in 1963, he opened a beer distributorship in the Detroit area, but he could never escape Willie Mays. He told the *Sporting News* in 1973: "Even now, wherever I go, I'd say 90 percent of the people who recognize me ask me about the Catch. It really has given me a name. Heck, if the ball had gone over Willie's head, I might have gotten an inside-the-park home run, and it would have given me 5-for-5 in a World Series game. But who'd have remembered? It really wouldn't have meant a helluva lot."

Mays himself, after a slow start, hit well enough in a Series dominated by pitching. He went 4-for-14 (.285) and drove in three runs, but of the eleven innings in which the Giants scored, he was on base in eight of them.

Other Giants may have chafed at the fuss surrounding a single play in a single game, but ultimately the Catch made the 1954 World Series. Five decades later, how many people can even name the teams in, say, the 1957 Series? But fans know that the Giants won in '54 because of Mays's mad dash to straightaway center.

The Catch began the Willie Mays brand. Few sports images have been reproduced as often or have as much iconic appeal as number 24's reaching out and corralling the ball. To this day, when a kid on a sandlot or a big leaguer under the lights reaches over his shoulder for a ball on the dead run, the cry is heard—"a Willie Mays catch!" No explanation is needed.

The footage of the Catch helped shape Mays's legacy by placing him in a particular time and place. In Ken Burns's epic documentary *Baseball*, highlights are shown from the 1955 World Series, which was noteworthy only because it was the one Series won by the Brooklyn Dodgers. But the film is in color, which creates a startling contrast to the black-and-white highlights from 1954. In a single year, baseball seemed to have moved from one era to the next, from the old and hidebound to the glitzy and modern. The transition to the "modern" era of baseball occurred over many years and had no clear demarcation, but Mays played the bulk of his career in what's been considered the "modern" era—defined by the expansion of the leagues, the inroads of television, and jet travel.

Yet the Catch came from the age of black-and-white images, a very different era, when professional athletes were part of their communities, when teams were tied to their cities, when All-Stars performed for meager wages, when ushers gave their hero a portable record player, and when World Series games began in the warm autumn sunshine.

Willie Mays, in film if not in reality, will always be of that era.

In 1954, Mays won the MVP, making him the only player to win the award in his first full season. Twenty-four sportswriters voted, sixteen giving him first-place ballots, though some voters were curiously unimpressed. Mays received one fifth-, one sixth-, and one seventh-place vote. A black player had now won the National League MVP in four of six straight years.

Mays was named the *Sporting News* number one player of the year and was named baseball player of the year by the *Los Angeles Times*. He received the B'nai B'rith Sports Lodge Award and was named New York's most popular player by the Catholic Youth Organization. He was honored at separate dinners by the Boston baseball writers and the Metropolitan baseball writers in New York. He won the Ray Hickok $10,000 diamond-studded belt as Professional Athlete of the Year, and he won the Associated Press's Male Athlete of the Year, though it clearly reflected the AP's preference for fellow Americans. Mays beat Roger Bannister, the English trackman who broke the four-minute-mile barrier, a truly historic feat. The *Sporting News*, showing its bias for baseball and Americans, selected the Catch as the year's "greatest sports thrill," with Bannister's "miracle mile" second. Mays received some seventy awards for his 1954 season.

He was now readily compared to some of the greatest center fielders in history, including Tris Speaker, Joe DiMaggio, and Terry Moore. Dan Daniel wrote in the *Sporting News*: "I doubt very much if they ever before had so pronounced a standout Player of the Year as Mays made himself for 1954. The complete Mays story is not to be sought in the averages. . . . He became the most talked about ballplayer in years, the most everyday spectacular cynosure, The Arm, The Swing, The Speed, The Pennant Producer."

But these tributes also included the seeds of a downfall, as many celebrated Mays for his youth and innocence. According to *Sport*, "The Willie Mays that exists for [fans] is part Prince Valiant, part the dead Giant heroes of the past and part Peter Pan." After the World Series, Arthur Daley of the *New York Times* wrote: "The only thing which could possibly prevent Willie the Wonder from becoming the biggest box office attraction since Babe Ruth would be for him to lose his simplicity and his little boy's outlook on life."

Those were the expectations and the burdens. No matter how many home runs and catches and thrills he would offer in the future, some would begrudge him an unavoidable sin. Willie Mays would never be twenty-three again.

CHAPTER THIRTEEN

"OLE MIRA!"

Willie Mays was exhausted. He had played about 175 games, including the exhibition season and the World Series, in seven months. Virtually everyone in the major leagues played hard, but Mays competed with a boundless intensity. Roger Angell said Mays was more "into the game" than any player he'd ever seen. Always alert mentally, he positioned players from center field, studied pitchers, dissected the practice throws of opposing fielders, tried to anticipate the next bounce or ricochet, and agonized over letting down the fans. Physically, he covered the gaps, bowled over catchers, slammed into fences, and hit the dirt hard to avoid fastballs at his head.

He even warmed up with greater purpose. Before the first game of the World Series, the outfielders were making practice throws in their usual perfunctory manner. Then it was Mays's turn. As Arnold Hano described it, his first throw, to third base, was on a low line that never bounced, striking the infielder's glove two inches to the inside of the bag—a "magnificent throw," Hano marveled. Then he realized that a third baseman prefers that throw on the outside of the bag so it doesn't collide with the sliding runner. Mays's next bullet painted the outer edge of third base on a fly. Mays then threw two home without a bounce—the first, waist high, directly over the plate; the second, slightly lower, hit the catcher's mitt ankle high, the tip of the glove resting on home plate. "I do not believe I ever saw a more impressive display in my baseball life," Hano said. Mays "appeared superhuman."

Baseball simply meant more to him. The *Sporting News* wrote in 1958, "Mays attacks a ball game—any game, one that doesn't count as well as one that figures importantly in the standings—as if history for the ages depended on that score. . . . He vibrates with urgency. Of course that can be called showmanship . . . but that only stems from his aggressiveness. He actually registers belligerence towards a simple grounder directed his way. He handles it like a Panzer sortie sweeping a flank. It's an enemy; it's got to be wiped out. Any time Willie faces a critical situation at bat, with a glove or on the bases, the spectator has to get the idea that this one play represents the difference between dawn over Olympus and Stygian gloom. It does to Willie."

Mays aptly described his approach one spring training when a fan asked him if players worked as hard in an exhibition game as in the regular season. "I don't know about other players," Mays said, "I only know about myself."

"Well, do you?"

Mays nodded slowly. "Yes, I do. Don't make no difference about what kind of game it is. I always work as hard as I can." He pondered the thought. "That's the onliest way," he concluded, "I even know how to play ball."

That passion was always part of his appeal, but it also contributed to his fatigue. Even as a teenager, he'd collapse on the field from exhaustion in front of his father, and he would again, more than once, as a professional. Instead of resting during the season or even afterward, he pushed himself to play more—or, as in 1954, was prodded to stay on the field.

After the season, Mays could have made decent money with endorsements and appearances. He was even offered part of a nightclub act in Las Vegas. But the Giants, fearing predators as well as temptations, wanted him out of New York and certainly not in Las Vegas. Mays was never a man about town, but he wasn't a choirboy either. Frank Forbes said that his biggest challenge was keeping the young women away from Willie and keeping Willie away from the young women.

That was evident during the 1954 season, when a pregnant woman approached Mays with the claim that he was the father of her baby and demanded money for child support. Mays vehemently denied the claim. When the baby was born in early October, the woman's lawyer demanded a cash payment. Mays sought assistance from the Giants, and all parties agreed that a blood test would be used to determine if Mays was the father. Conducted by Dr. Philip Levine, a pioneering researcher whose discovery of the Rh factor in human blood was used to identify paternity, the test confirmed that Mays was not the father. The incident was kept out of the newspapers, but Stoneham was eager to remove his star as far as possible from harm's way.

He asked Mays to play winter ball in Puerto Rico, where he would still be in the Giants' orbit: Giant coach Herman Franks was managing the Santurce Cangrejeros (Crabbers) in San Juan. Stoneham also wanted to return a favor to Pedrin Zorilla, who had founded the Crabbers in the 1930s and had helped deliver Ruben Gomez, a native of Puerto Rico, to the Giants in 1953.

Over the years, Zorilla had recruited several standout black players

from America, including Josh Gibson, Roy Campanella, and Ray Dandridge, who were all embraced by Puerto Rico's delirious baseball fans.
Zorilla had never lured a player of Mays's skill or status; in fact, no major
league MVP had ever played in Puerto Rico. With attendance sagging,
Zorilla knew that Mays would electrify the island. He just needed Stoneham and Franks to convince him.

Franks made a practical appeal. He said that he already had a very good
team, which included Gomez; Negro League star Bob Thurman; future
All-Star George Crowe; and Don Zimmer, who had been a rookie shortstop for Brooklyn. Franks said he had one other player of note, a young
Puerto Rican who had just completed his first year in the Dodger farm
system: Roberto Clemente.

Mays told Franks that he was tired, but Franks said that this team, if he
joined it, could win the Caribbean World Series, which would mean more
money for all.

When Mays agreed, the announcement surprised Puerto Rico's baseball fans, some of whom made wagers on whether he would actually
arrive. On the morning of October 16, about a thousand people showed
up at San Juan's Isla Grande Airport either to greet Mays or collect on their
bets. Mays had fallen asleep while the Clipper was taxiing on the runway
in New York. Despite a passing hurricane, he did not wake up until the
plane landed in San Juan in a gray drizzle at 6:45 A.M. He couldn't believe
the crowd.

That day, Mays agreed to a contract that would pay him $1,000 a month.
He signed it with a pen and also marked it with his fingerprint.

Santurce played at Sixto Escobar Stadium, and at his first game Mays
met the team's batboy, an eighteen-year-old named Orlando Cepeda,
whose father, Pedro Cepeda, was one of the island's most prominent players. Neither Mays nor Cepeda could have imagined that in just a few
years they would be teammates. At the time, Cepeda literally stood in awe
before games as he positioned himself near the pitcher's mound to take
throws from the outfield—Mays in center, Clemente in right or left.

Mays played an unintentional, though significant, role in Clemente's
career. In 1954, Clemente was nineteen years old and attracting attention from five major league teams, including the Dodgers and the Giants.
He wanted to play in New York, where he had friends and relatives in the
city's large Puerto Rican community. The Giants believed he needed at
least one year in the minors, so they would not exceed the $6,000 bonus
limit, which would require keeping him on the major league roster for
his first two years. The Dodgers concurred that he needed more experience but still offered a $10,000 bonus. Clemente accepted and was sent to

the Dodgers' top farm club, in Montreal. As a result, he was left unprotected in the "rule 5" draft of minor league players: over two rounds that ran from the club with the worst record to the one with the best, any big league team can select any unprotected minor league player, which that winter included Clemente. The Pittsburgh Pirates chose him as their first draft pick.

Why did the Dodgers sign Clemente if they were not going to protect him? They feared the Giants were going to sign him. "We didn't want the Giants to have Willie Mays and Clemente in the same outfield and be the big attraction in New York," Dodger executive Buzzie Bavasi said later. "It was a cheap deal for us any way you figure it."

Mays and Clemente played together on numerous All-Star teams, but the only time they played together on a continuous basis was on Santurce. Clemente respected Mays but idolized another black Giant, Monte Irvin, who had played in the Puerto Rican winter league in 1945. While Mays and Clemente were never close, they pushed each other as Santurce teammates and were the backbone of a team that also included future major league catcher Valmy Thomas; Buster Clarkson, who had played in the Negro Leagues and the big leagues; Bob Thurman, a talented Negro League player who would reach the majors at the end of his career; and aging Puerto Rican stars Luis Olmo and Pepe Lucas St. Clair. "I always said that was the greatest winter league team ever assembled," Don Zimmer later said. "Can you imagine Mays, Clemente, and Thurman in the outfield? And Orlando Cepeda just hanging around, a big kid just stumbling all over himself because he was growing so fast."

Mays hadn't picked up a bat in more than two weeks, and Franks offered to use him only as a pinch hitter at the outset. But Mays said he was ready to play, striking out in his first two at-bats, then rapping two hits. Before the game, Franks was asked if Durocher had given him any instructions on handling Mays, and Franks looked surprised: "Instructions? What could you tell Willie? He doesn't drink and he doesn't smoke and he loves to sleep, so you don't have to worry about him being out of shape. Maybe he shouldn't go after that first pitch so often, but that's the way he is. Maybe his throwing might be more disciplined, but his one idea is to get the ball and fire it home as quickly as possible. If Willie lets a fellow get an extra base once in a while because of his throws, it's nothing compared to the extra bases he takes away from 'em."

Mays played well, hitting safely in his first five games. The first pitcher to shut him down was a Dodger left-hander named Tom Lasorda, who gained fame as the Dodgers' garrulous manager from 1976 to 1996. But he liked to talk even as a young pitcher in Puerto Rico, telling people that he had discovered Mays's weakness: he swung on the first pitch, which led to easy outs on balls outside the strike zone. Mays was a free swinger who often cut on the first offering, but that didn't make him a soft out. After thirteen games without a home run, Mays finally got one. The pitcher? Tom Lasorda. Mays then homered in four consecutive contests. After thirty-nine games over two months, Mays was leading the league in hitting with a .423 average, and he had twenty-eight RBIs. The fans loved him, initially singing out "Ole mira!"—the Spanish equivalent of "Say Hey!"—but in time they chanted, "Say Hey!" whenever he came to bat.

His desire to excel seemed to always shine through. One night in Caguas, a Santurce pitcher who was going to throw batting practice had no one to warm up with. Mays grabbed a catcher's mitt and took the preliminary tosses, then threw a strike to second base to nail an imaginary runner. Branch Rickey, Jr., whose father signed Jackie Robinson, was now working for his father as the farm system director of the Pittsburgh Pirates. Watching Mays from the stands, he said, "Look at that boy. He just can't wait to get things started. I've always maintained you can learn more about a ballplayer by watching him two days in the winter leagues than you can by watching him for two weeks in the States. Down here, you can tell who likes to play."

Off the field it wasn't as easy. Mays lived in a three-room apartment across the street from the ballpark, and the ever-present Frank Forbes, who helped Mays settle in, noticed that his first few days were difficult. "He had a real nice apartment, but he just couldn't get over the fact that when he came home at night, there was nobody there to say 'Hello' to him," Forbes said.

Mays felt adrift. The night after his first game, he appeared on a television show with a bilingual host, and the next day he discovered that the show was sponsored by a milk company. He was mortified, as he was already committed to a competitor in the States. Mays took loyalty to an extreme, even to a dairy products firm, and he was so distressed that he wouldn't pose for any pictures for days for fear they would be used commercially. He spoke no Spanish and had no interest in it. Regardless of language, he was careful about talking to strangers, was cautious with teammates, and missed New York. (Franks permitted some trips home as long as the team was in first place.) "Perhaps to some people it seemed I had changed, that I wasn't as easygoing as I had been," he later said. Actually, he was just growing up.

Fortunately, one of his teammates was an old friend from the Birmingham Black Barons, Bill Greason; they lived in the same apartment building, and Greason's wife cooked for them. Mays sometimes ventured into

town, sampling local dishes at restaurants and going to movies, grateful
that the sound track was in English. He once joined his teammates for a pig
roast at Zorilla's beach house. A photograph, published in *Collier's*, shows
the stylistic difference between Mays and his peers. A half dozen players
and coaches, including Zorilla, are standing around the pig on the spit.
The men are wearing wrinkled button-ups and baggy slacks, a portrait
of disheveled disinterest; Mays is wearing khaki pants, perfectly creased,
with pleats, cuffs, and a matching belt, plus a fitted blue gray short-sleeve
shirt with a white collar and white trim. Even at a Puerto Rican pig roast,
he looked like a million bucks.

Mays's time with Santurce appeared to come to an ugly end in one of
the more bizarre incidents of his career. On January 11 Mays got into a
fight with Ruben Gomez, his teammate on the Crabbers as well as the
Giants, creating a furor in both San Juan and New York. The *New York
Times* ran a two-column story about it, and the headline and subhead
merited five lines. It all began when Mays was waiting to hit for batting
practice, and Gomez, according to the *Times*, jumped in front of him.
Mays and Gomez argued over the hitting order, so Gomez decided to sit
on the plate and refused to budge.

Gomez, a wiry right-hander, had a temper. As a Giant, he once hit Braves
first baseman Joe Adcock in the arm with a pitch. By the time Adcock
decided to charge the mound, the ball had been returned to Gomez, so
he fired it again at the onrushing batter, hitting him in the thigh. The
Braves then chased Gomez into his dugout, where he picked up an ice
pick, which was used on hot days. Gomez yelled at Adcock and threatened to give him a second navel. Umpire Jocko Conlan tried to intervene.
"Give me the ice pick," Conlan told him. "If you don't give it to me, you'll
be suspended for life. And you have children, Ruben."

In Puerto Rico, with Gomez sitting on home plate, Mays stood a few
feet to the side and wouldn't move either. He told the pitcher, Milton Ralat,
to start throwing. Ralat's first pitch was a fastball at Mays's head. Now
Mays began screaming at Ralat, who, like Gomez, was Puerto Rican. Mays
wasn't a bully, but he never backed down either. From Fairfield to Newport News, he had gotten into scraps with guys bigger than he. So when
Ralat threw his next pitch, Mays caught it with his bare hand and fired
it back, hitting Ralat in the shoulder. Ralat cursed him in Spanish, and
Mays began walking toward the mound. Then Gomez, bat in hand, stood
up and joined the fray—he later said he was trying to stop the fight. But
Mays thought Gomez was trying to defend his fellow Puerto Rican, so
Gomez and Mays ended up wrestling, with Mays knocking him down
with a punch. Herman Franks and George Crowe finally broke it up, but

when Gomez headed off the field, he threw several bats at Mays, and Mays threw them right back. When Franks told Mays to "take it easy," Mays asked, "Are you on the Puerto Ricans' side?"

In the locker room, Mays told Franks that he was leaving. He had recently told a television interviewer that he had played baseball without any rest since March 1 and was too tired to last the rest of the winter. Zorilla met with Mays and Franks and called Stoneham, and a compromise was reached: Mays could go to New York in a few days so long as he returned for the playoffs in February.

Gomez, having won Game Three of the World Series, was a national hero in his own right, so when Mays came to bat the following day, he was booed. He had rarely been jeered, certainly never by hometown fans, and he felt he had done nothing to warrant the sudden disfavor. But he didn't show his anger or hurt. When he got to the plate, he hit a triple and came home on an outfielder's error. All was forgiven. Mays and Gomez reconciled and were good friends for many years, and when the season ended two weeks later, Mays led the league in hitting with a .395 average, and despite missing games, he also led it in total bases, triples, and slugging percentage. Clemente was also spectacular, hitting .344 and leading the league in hits (ninety-four) and runs scored (sixty-five).

Santurce made it to the Caribbean World Series in Caracas, Venezuela, where the modern University City Stadium was jammed with forty thousand rabid fans to watch a four-team round robin of flagwinners in Cuba, Panama, Puerto Rico, and Venezuela. But the main attraction was Mays, as shown by a headline in *El Nacional*: You just HAVE TO SEE him. But just as he struggled offensively at the start of the World Series, Mays made outs in his first twelve at-bats in Caracas. Unlike the crowds back home, these fans were unforgiving, and the Venezuelan "fanaticos" booed him lustily. Mays had now played in more than 220 games in less than a year, and his grim face showed tension and weariness.

But in Santurce's third game, with the score tied 2–2, Mays came to the plate in the eleventh inning with Clemente on base. He dug in, took a huge swing, and watched his miseries sail over the fence for the game-winner. Moments later, after leaping on home plate, he rode high on his teammates' shoulders, his arms raised in joy. The homer, according to Peter Bjarkman, an authority on Latin American baseball, "remains one of the most dramatic clouts in Caribbean series history." Mays then went on a rampage, collecting eleven hits in thirteen at-bats, including two home runs and two triples. His .440 average and nine RBIs were tops in the Series. The smile returned. His spirits lifted. Caracas was his.

Santurce won its third straight World Series, cementing Zorilla's relationship with the Giants, which would bear fruit in years to come. Mays said that the next year he wasn't going to play winter baseball in the Caribbean. The demands were too great, and a winning share of the Series was only $450. But Mays had proven that his stardom was not confined to the United States or to those who spoke English, and he would play in Latin America again. He never learned Spanish, but neither baseball nor Willie Mays ever needed translation.

CHAPTER FOURTEEN

A NEW ARCHETYPE

Willie Mays entered the big leagues after it had experienced two very different eras of play since the turn of the century—the dead-ball era and the live-ball—and opinions were sharply divided on which was superior. Each style had its own specialists: slap-hitting speedsters or slugging behemoths, and each approach had its own baseball icon as its leader. But Willie Mays created a category unto himself.

The game's dead-ball era prevailed in the 1900s and 1910s and was the heyday of "scientific baseball." It emphasized speed and strategy, with teams relying on steals, double steals, bunts, squeeze plays, and the hit-and-run—anything to advance a runner one base to push across a deciding tally. The era marked the apogee of the stolen base: between 1909 and 1916, the league leaders stole more than seventy bases a year; in 1915, almost 2.7 bases were swiped per game. Even when "small ball" came back in vogue in the 1970s and 1980s, the big leagues never saw more than 1.7 bases stolen per game in a season.

The dead-ball era's slap-and-dash style in part reflected the game's deep animus toward home runs, which were seen as selfish, unproductive, almost immoral. Big swings led to strikeouts, so home run hitters seemed to place individual glory ahead of the team. The baseball statistics in Sunday sports sections included batting averages, sacrifices, and stolen bases, but not homers, whose leaders sometimes would not break into double digits. The glory, and the contracts, went to those who excelled in scientific baseball, and its foremost practitioner was Ty Cobb, whose career average of .366 from 1905 to 1928 made him the dominant player of his time. Books and magazines promoted his skills: how to read opponents, how to deceive them, how to draw them out of position with fake bunts, steals, or place hitting. From 1907 to 1917, he led the American League in stolen bases five times, including a record ninety-six in 1915; for his career, he stole home fifty times.

The small-ball era began to fade with baseball's discovery that the home run was actually a crowd-pleaser: if you hit it damn far, they will come. The nuances of scientific baseball could not compete with the brute strength, virile showmanship, and instant gratification of the round-tripper, and the bellwether of brawn, of course, was Babe Ruth. His breakout season as a hitter was 1919, when his twenty-nine homers more than doubled those of the league leader in 1917. In 1920, when Ruth hit fifty-four, the American League smacked 396 homers compared to ninety-six in 1918. Offense in general flourished. In 1921, fifteen players had one hundred or more RBIs; before then, it was rare for two or three players to reach that milestone.

The live-ball era had arrived. Many believed the balls really were more "alive" because they supposedly were more tightly wound. Major League Baseball outlawed spitballs and other trick pitches and were more willing to replace scuffed balls with new ones. These moves were driven in part by tragedy: in 1920, Cleveland shortstop Ray Chapman was killed when he was struck in the head by a spitball. Hitters clearly needed more protection, which dovetailed with the game's new, free-swinging ethos. More offense meant more excitement and more fans, and in Babe Ruth, baseball had the perfect outsized personality to match the era's outsized home runs.

Ruth, and the musclemen who followed, recalibrated how baseball was played. The stolen base was once seen as a necessary skill for all players, but it was now deemed a foolish gambit that only specialists should attempt. Why risk getting thrown out when the hitter could plate two runs with one mighty swing? The entire risk-reward ratio of scientific baseball—bunting, hitting behind runners, the hit-and-run—had been shredded. Leonard Koppett wrote: "The emphasis shifted from maximum *advance* to maximum *men on*. It became more important to have as many men as possible safely on base when the home run did come up than to risk losing some of them for the sake of an extra base. It would be a double loss: not only would a runner be wiped out, but another out would be recorded, which might keep a home run hitter from getting another swipe later in the game."

Baseball purists, led by Ty Cobb, were scandalized, but they could not put the Ruthian genie back in the bottle. In 1929, the number of home runs per game eclipsed the number of stolen bases per game, and by the middle 1930s, most big leaguers had little experience in swiping bases. Baseball had speed merchants, but stealing was for niche players and certainly not for the great ones. Joe DiMaggio was fast, but he never stole more than six bases in one year; Stan Musial, never more than nine; Ted Williams, four. None was known for daring baserunning.

In 1950, the stolen base was at its nadir, with only about half a base stolen per game, and baseball, in Bill James's view, resembled a ticking time bomb: get a man on base and wait for a home run. But the live-ball era had also ended. The narrow focus on the long ball, at the expense of speed and strategy, had caused run production to decline. In 1922, the National League hit 520 home runs and scored 6,194 runs. By 1956, home runs had increased by 130 percent, to 1,219, but scoring had *declined* by 15 percent, to 5,275. Runs fell in part because stolen bases had declined by 51 percent—from 765 to 371. The American League numbers, while not as dramatic, reflect the same trend.

Jackie Robinson was the first of the pioneering black players who pushed the action. Roger Kahn said the most exciting play he ever saw was Robinson in a rundown, and Robinson's theft of home in the 1955 World Series was a signature moment in his career and a radiant signal of how the game was changing. The black players' most obvious influence was their dominance in stealing bases. In his rookie season, Robinson topped all National League players with twenty-nine steals. Two years later, in 1949, his thirty-seven steals were the most in the National League in nineteen years. The Braves' Sam "the Jet" Jethroe and Bill Bruton were not great hitters, but Jethroe led the league in steals in 1950 and 1951 while Bruton took the honor from 1953 to 1955. In the American League, Minnie Minoso won the base stealing crown his first three years in the majors, from 1951 to 1953.

Baseball's integration also brought in a new group of power hitters, including Larry Doby, Roy Campanella, and Monte Irvin. African Americans could not be typecast, but they did tend to fall into the traditional categories, speedster and slugger, that Ty Cobb and Babe Ruth had represented.

Willie Mays changed all that. A new archetype, he blended both styles, possessing the skills of the two greatest players in baseball history. His first two full seasons (1951 and 1952 combined, plus 1954) established his long-ball credentials, but he stole only nineteen bases in twenty-nine attempts. Nineteen fifty-five brought forth the full range of his talents. He hit fifty-one home runs, making him the youngest to surpass fifty and only the seventh player overall to reach that milestone. He also stole twenty-four bases in only thirty attempts, finishing two behind the league leader. Since 1900, only four other players had hit twenty homers and stolen twenty bases in the same year.

The following season, 1956, Mays reached a new milestone, topping the league with forty steals, the highest since 1929; it was also Mays's career best. He was only thrown out ten times, and he stole third base thirteen times in thirteen attempts. He also stroked thirty-six homers, becoming the first player in the league's eighty-year history to reach 30–30 in homers and steals. The closest player to reach that plateau had been Mays himself, the previous year, with 51–24. In fact, no National League player had ever reached thirty in both categories even in different seasons.

Mays would lead the major leagues in stolen bases for three consecutive years—1956 to 1958, while hitting more than thirty homers in each of those seasons except the last, when he had twenty-nine. In 1957, Mays also led the league in triples (twenty), and became the fourth player in league history to hit twenty or more homers, doubles, and triples in one season. He was so strong, Bill Rigney recalled, "that the ball sounded a little different than it sounded off of any other bat. In St. Louis, Mays hit the light tower behind the scoreboard, and he said to me, 'I hit that ball so hard, it scared me.' "

His breathtaking power made his baserunning all the more surprising. Mays says he did not begin stealing bases to break new ground in baseball or to prove any points. He did so because the Giants' offense was in decline, age and injury having caught up with some of their best players. Mays felt he had to contribute more, as he showed on May 6, 1956, his twenty-fifth birthday. The Giants played in St. Louis against a hard-throwing left-hander named Wilmer "Vinegar Bend" Mizell. Mays led off the second with a single but did not get a good read on Mizell's move; he made no attempt to run and was erased on a double play. Mays studied the pitcher from the bench. Left-handers were tougher to decipher, but he thought they all had one vulnerability: their eyes signaled their intentions. He also found a tip-off in Mizell's delivery. With a speedy runner on first base, Mizell assumed, like most pitchers, that his fastball would give his catcher a better chance on an attempted steal. But Mays saw that Mizell kicked his right leg higher on a fastball, making that the ideal pitch on which to run.

Mays's next time at bat, in the fourth, resulted in a walk, and he took a new measure of the pitcher. This time, he got a running jump and stole second, and on the next pitch he stole third. In the sixth, Mays walked again but knew the element of surprise was gone. It didn't matter. He stole second—and could feel the angry, frustrated stares of both Mizell and the catcher, Bill Sarni. In the ninth, with the Giants losing by one, Mays led off with a single. Mizell tried to hold him with several throws, but Mays ran on the first pitch and beat the peg—four steals in one game. He considered stealing third, though with none out, the attempt would have carried undue risk. He scored anyway when the next hitter doubled. Informed after the game that he had fallen one stolen base short of the single-game record, Mays said, "If I knew I was near a record, I could have taken third base easy." The Giants won, 5–4.

Mays proved that a player could steal bases without sacrificing power, but he never saw those skills as contradictory. They were, for him, the fulfillment of his father's dictum that the more things he excelled in, the longer he'd play. His base-stealing skills had developed in the Negro Leagues, out of necessity. There, most squads had fewer than twenty members, so versatility was required, and pinch runners were an unaffordable luxury.

What seemed natural or obvious to Mays seemed heedless to others. Why would a long-ball hitter who had already been compared to Babe Ruth risk injury by stealing bases? Hard slides caused many injuries, some irreparable. After Monte Irvin broke his ankle sliding into third base, he was never the same. Though Mickey Mantle was probably faster than Mays early in his career, the most bases he ever stole was twenty-one, and he broke into double digits only six times in his career.

Some of Mays's friends urged similar caution. Roy Campanella, after his own career was cut short by a car accident in 1958, tried to counsel Mays. "Willie runs too much," he said in his autobiography. "He's foolish. . . . Every once in a while during the winter, he visits me in the liquor store in Harlem. We go down in the basement and we talk. I told Willie, 'You know every time you steal a base, you're gambling on your career.' I used to talk and talk. I'd tell him, 'Look, Willie, you don't get paid for stealing bases. You get paid for hitting the ball over the fence.' You know what Willie answers? Nothing. He just sits there and doesn't say a word. Finally, I'd give up. What's the use? He's not going to change. He just plays one way. He don't know any other way."

Stolen bases were the easiest way to quantify Mays's running skills, but he also accumulated extra bases through speed, cunning, and force of will. In this area, more than any other, he imported the Negro League philosophy of daring, exuberance, and pugnacity.

Opening Day 1955, the Giants played the Pirates, and in the eighth inning Mays was on second base with the score tied. The hitter rapped a ground ball to shortstop Dick Groat, who lobbed the ball to first base. Mays was moving on contact and never slowed down. When he saw Groat's languid throw, he steamed toward home plate. The first baseman's peg beat him to the plate, catcher Dan Kravitz applied the tag, and umpire Larry Goetz called him out. But Mays had slammed into Kravitz with 180 pounds of rage, and the ball came out. He scored the winning run.

Baseball is a game of predictable calculations, but Mays seemed to run the bases with a completely different algorithm. He would go from first to third on an infield out or would score from first base on a hit-and-run single. Modern baseball has seen only two occasions in which a man scored from first base on a single to left—both times it was Mays, once when he was twenty-four, again when he was thirty. He once scored from first base on a bunt, without a fielding error. Willie McCovey, a left-handed power hitter, bunted the ball down the third base line. With the fielders pulled to the right side, the ball rolled into short left field. Mays never stopped, and McCovey got a double.

Mays would dance off the bag, taunt pitchers, try to draw throws. On a typical play in 1961, the *Sporting News* described what happened when Mays, on first, headed for second on a single: "Mays rounded second, feinted an all-out run into third, then feinted back toward second and provoked a throw to second by Wally Moon. As soon as Moon lifted his arm to make the fatal mistake of throwing behind Willie, Mays lit out for third and made it sliding."

Mays took responsibility for his own ventures. He says he never watched the third base coach but learned to round third base "backwards" by observing Jackie Robinson. His self-reliance was evident on the base-paths or in the field. He could look at a fly ball just once to determine its flight path; if runners were on base, he could then keep an eye on them. Mays didn't want to depend on his teammates to tell him what to do.

While he made his own decisions, they were grounded in preparation. Mays would sit in the dugout during pregame warm-ups and watch opposing fielders throw the ball. He never kept a notebook, but he thought he knew the strength and accuracy of every arm in the field. The same keen vision that helped him track long flies allowed him to see, while at full speed on the bases, the alignment of the ball, the outfielder, and the cut-off man. If a ball was hit in the corner or the gap, he saw—in Bob Costas's words—"the geometric possibilities of the play." Mays ran with his head on a swivel, absorbing information and recalibrating the risks. He tried to exploit any lapse, no matter how slight. If the cutoff man dropped his throwing arm after receiving the ball or if an outfielder lobbed a ball into the infield—those were green lights to advance another base. One outfielder, stunned at the sight of Mays bolting for home plate, was simply paralyzed, which allowed the man on first to reach second.

Mays was also a runner who wouldn't take no for an answer. In a 1961 game against Cincinnati, the Giants had the bases loaded with the score tied and Mays on third. The hitter grounded the ball to the first baseman, who touched the bag for the second out, then threw home. Bad move. The catcher was a twenty-six-year-old Nebraskan named Jerry Zimmerman who had played only a dozen games in the big leagues. Because the force play was no longer in order, he was going to have to tag the human wrecking ball that was bearing down on him. "Zimmerman exploded upon contact," Charles Einstein wrote. "The ball, the glove, the mask, and several pieces of Zimmerman appeared to disassemble in midair, like the cat in a Looney Tunes cartoon. By the time things fell back to earth, Mays had scored, a teammate had scored, and a third Giant was on third base, whence he would score a moment later."

Mays's creativity on the basepaths was boundless. On one play at home plate against the Dodgers, Roy Campanella was already holding the ball, so Mays went airborne. "I was kind of using his head as a fulcrum or something," he said, "and actually kind of ran up one side of him and down the other, and his hand with the ball kept aiming for me but never did touch me."

The umpire saw it differently, or maybe didn't see it at all, and ruled Mays out. Durocher stormed out of the dugout and tried to re-create Mays's acrobatics.

The ump wasn't buying it. "You're telling me he did the impossible," he said.

"He did!"

"Well, I ain't fixin' to believe it."

Mays also did things defensively that no one had ever seen before. Giant coach Tommy Henrich said, "I've seen him go up in the air trying for a catch with his left hand, miss it, then turn in the air and pick the ball off the wall with his right hand, all set for the throw. How anybody could have that kind of coordination, I don't know, but Willie has it."

Mays borrowed from other sports. As a kid, he watched newsreels of Don Hutson, the Alabama All-American who played wide receiver for the Green Bay Packers. He saw how Hutson would twist his body while catching a pass to elude defenders or how quickly Hutson could stop and reverse direction. So Mays practiced the same thing. On deep flies, he would twist his body to avoid slamming into the fence or would run full tilt toward the wall and try to stop right before impact. The moves further separated him from his peers.

And then there was his arm. Umpire Jocko Conlan said Mays was "the only player I ever saw who could run hard one way and throw hard the other." In a game in St. Louis, with the Giants leading by a run and the Cardinals hitting with a man on first, the batter drove the ball to the outfield fence. Bill Rigney recalled, "Those two rabbits started running and it appeared the Cards would tie the score. But do you know what happened? The moment Willie got his hand on the ball, they stopped and started looking for a base. It was just like musical chairs, when the music stopped. And it won us the game."

Joe DiMaggio said Mays had the greatest arm he ever saw, and some throws seemed to defy credibility. In 1955, in a game at the Polo Grounds, the Braves' Billy Bruton was on third with no one out. A fly ball came to Mays about 320 feet from home plate. Bruton was the fastest man in the league, so when the ball was caught, he assumed he would score easily. He took off from third and crossed the plate standing up. Only problem was, the moment he touched the plate, catcher Wes Westrum's glove came down hard on his shoulder, the ball in his mitt. How Mays had gotten the ball home so quickly, no one quite knew. It might have been the greatest throw of his career, and it caught home plate umpire Art Gore by surprise. He shook his head, as if to clear it, and then made a very odd call: "*Just* safe!"

Either "You're out!" or "You're safe!"—but "Just safe"? That suggests an uncertainty, a disbelief, in what you've seen.

His best catches seemed to be guided by some divine spirit. Whitey Lockman, in 2001, recalled Mays's making a bare-handed catch in Pittsburgh off Roberto Clemente. "A line drive," Lockman said. "He stuck up his hand. Remember the play that [Kevin] Mitchell made a few years ago? It was better than that. Mitchell's was a foul ball, a fly ball in the left field corner. But Mays's was a shot off Clemente's bat in left center. I mean, it was going, and Mays was racing, with his back to everything, and reached up with his right hand and caught it. I thought, 'Oh, my God, that's not *human.*'"

Mays's mental data book on opposing players was its own kind of weapon. In later years, teams used computers to develop sophisticated profiles on players and to create comprehensive scouting books. But Mays committed everything to memory, and he shared his insights with teammates. Joey Amalfitano, for example, was a twenty-one-year-old benchwarmer in 1955 when he entered a game in Cincinnati to replace an injured player. He got his first hit of his career, then he was to lead off the tenth inning against Gerry Staley. Mays called him back to the bat rack and told him that Staley would make him hit a curveball, so be ready. Amalfitano stepped into the batter's box and took the first pitch, a sinker, for a strike. The next pitch was a curveball, and he hit it off the left center field wall for a double. Mays later knocked him in for the winning run.

"I didn't play much those first couple of years," Amalfitano says, "but Willie would always sit next to me when the Giants were hitting and tell me things about the pitchers."

Ty Cobb noticed Mays's baserunning gifts. After he retired, he continued to follow the game and, in 1957, as paraphrased by the *Sporting News*, he described Mays as "a brilliant base stealer" who could lead the "revival" of the running style that he, Cobb, had perfected. That Cobb saw Mays as a possible heir was fitting. While Mays's power often led to comparisons of him with Ruth, he more closely resembled Cobb in style and aggressiveness (if not in personality). Tom Stanton wrote of Cobb, "He was the game's premier warrior, fiercest competitor, smartest hitter, most ingenious player, strongest drawing card, highest-paid performer, and brightest basepath terror and an inspiration to boys throughout the nation." The same could have been written of Mays.

By combining the best of Cobb and Ruth, Willie Mays forged his own era by creating a new standard—"the five-tool player." Mays had never heard the phrase until it was applied to him, but it became part of the lexicon, used to describe multitalented contemporaries like Hank Aaron, Roberto Clemente, and Frank Robinson. Just as Cobb and Ruth were the exemplars of their eras, Mays was the paragon of his.

CHAPTER FIFTEEN

JACKIE, WILLIE, AND ALL DELIBERATE SPEED

During spring training of 1955, *Sports Illustrated* wanted Willie Mays on its cover, an obvious choice given his previous season. What wasn't so obvious was who was photographed with him: Leo Durocher and his wife, Laraine Day. Durocher's celebrity was at its zenith, but the arrangement was still unusual, for the magazine had no story about the three, just a baseball preview. Mays doesn't know how the alignment came about, but it's safe to assume that Durocher, who reviewed most media requests for Mays and did not mind the envy of others, was behind it. To be on the front of a national magazine with an elegant actress who was his wife and the country's most dynamic athlete who was his devoted subaltern was impressive.

Laraine Day adored Mays. In her memoir, she said that while she interviewed many athletes on her television show, "the favorite of all is Willie Mays, who suffers tortures on the air and yet wins the heart of everybody."

On this day, the trio stood on the grass at Phoenix Municipal Stadium, the green outfield fence in the background. Mays and Durocher wore their home white uniforms, with black letters and orange trim, while Day wore a high-collared patterned dress with a hemline below the knees. Her feet, in open high-heeled shoes, looked dainty next to the massive black spikes of her companions. Her short auburn hair glistened in the sunlight. Her white earrings, red lipstick, and red nail polish accented her delicate features. She looked like a classy, middle-age PTA mom, except instead of walking her children to the bus stop, she stood between Leo Durocher and Willie Mays.

Taking the picture was Hy Peskin, *Sports Illustrated*'s first staff photographer, who produced some of the most memorable sports images in the twentieth century: Joe DiMaggio completing a swing, Jim Brown glaring from the field, Ben Hogan swinging a one-iron. In 1953, Peskin had photographed Senator John Kennedy sailing with his fiancée, Jacqueline Bouvier; the picture appeared on the cover of *Life* and helped promote Kennedy as a national figure.

Mays doesn't recall what Peskin said for that spring training photograph, but at some point Day put one hand on her husband's shoulder and the other hand on Mays's. All three looked cheerful. Peskin clicked his camera, and *Sports Illustrated* put the image on its cover of April 11, 1955.

The magazine was less than a year old. In time it would publish groundbreaking stories on sports and race in America, but in 1955 it stayed clear of social issues and didn't use its cover for any agenda beyond showing a good photograph. Whether Peskin had any ulterior motives is unknown, but according to Robert Creamer, then a writer at the magazine, "It wasn't until the letters came in that we knew of any controversy."

Sports Illustrated had shattered a great taboo: a white woman was touching a black man, surely a first for the front of any mainstream national magazine.[*] White supremacists had long raised the specter of predatory black "savages" deflowering helpless white women as grounds for segregation, incarceration, and violent oppression. The volatile mix of race and sex had triggered devastating riots, rallied lynch mobs, and turned innocents into martyrs—such as Emmitt Till, a fourteen-year-old African American who that very year was murdered after he spoke to or whistled at a white woman in a small Mississippi town. (The acquittal of two defendants would energize the nascent civil rights movement.)

In the mainstream media, the barrier between white women and black men could not be breached, but now Laraine Day was placing her willful right hand on Willie Mays's muscular right shoulder, with pleasant smiles on both their faces. The image chipped away at the corrupt armature of Jim Crow, and *Sports Illustrated*'s outraged readers sent their letters, some of which were published on April 25.

F. M. Odom of Shreveport, La.: *Up until now I have not found anything in particularly bad taste in SI, but by golly, when you print a picture on the cover in full color, of a white woman embracing a negro (with a small letter) man, you make it evident that even in a magazine supposedly devoted to healthful and innocent sports you have to engage in South-baiting. . . . I care nothing about those three people as individuals, but I care a heck of a lot about the proof the picture gives that SI is part of the giant plan to flaunt all decency, so long as the conquered of 1865 can be reminded of their eternal defeat.*

Edward F. Webb of Nashville, Tenn.: *To tell you that I was shocked at SI's*

---

[*] In August 1955, *Ebony* also published a cover photograph of Day standing between Durocher and Mays at the Polo Grounds. This time, Day is not touching Mays.

cover would be putting it mildly. . . . *The informative note inside the magazine tells me that this is Mrs. Leo Durocher, a white woman, with her arm affectionately around the neck of Willie Mays, a Negro ballplayer. . . . Let me say to you, Sir, the most appalling blow ever struck at this country, the most disastrous thing that ever happened to the people of America, was the recent decision of the Supreme Court declaring segregation unconstitutional.*

T. B. Kelso of Fort Worth, Tex.: *Please cancel my subscription. . . . This is an insult to every decent white woman everywhere.*

A. C. Dunn of New Orleans: *Such disgusting racial propaganda is not fit for people who are trying to build a stronger nation based on racial integrity.*

Those letters generated their own responses, which were published on May 2.

Norwood W. Pope of Jackson Heights, N.Y.: *I am embarrassed beyond words and infuriated to the point of battle, concerning those letters from the good Americans in Tennessee, Louisiana and Texas who thought your cover was "racial propaganda" and "an insult to white women." . . . Willie Mays is an American baseball player first, last and always. He waves no flags, he stirs no trouble, his teammates like him, he has no axes to grind. He is the personification of liberty, initiative, democracy and fair play. Willie is a topnotch baseball player; his only discriminations are against opposing pitchers, his only philosophy is to play good, clean baseball.*

A.P.L. Knott, Jr., of New Haven, Conn.: *I was shocked to see that such strong negative reactions to SI's April 11 cover should prevail in this great democratic country of ours. . . . I am quite sure that when SI printed the cover there was no intention of South-baiting, recollecting the Civil War, insulting any women or spreading racial propaganda on the part of the editors, as these gentlemen claimed.*

Steve Kraisler of Long Beach, N.Y.: *I have never written to a magazine before, but I consider it my duty to do so at this time. I was disgusted at the letters concerning the cover of Willie Mays and Mrs. Leo Durocher. I may be only 15 years old but I have more common sense than any adult with those ideas.*

Though unintended, *Sports Illustrated* had prompted a conversation about race. What's noteworthy is not the vitriol of the southern bigots but the naiveté of the northern liberals, including the magazine's editors—their shock that these racist views were even held, let alone tightly embraced, by others. Anyone reading the exchange would have gained insights into America's racial schism and recognized how fierce the opposition would be to integration.

And what did Mays think? He thought the cover was cool and knew nothing of the controversy.

• • •

The modern civil rights movement had no official beginning, but two events are usually cited as its launching point: the *Brown v. Board of Education* decision, handed down on May 17, 1954; and more than a year later, on December 1, 1955, in Montgomery, Alabama, Rosa Parks's refusal to give up her bus seat to a white passenger, which led to her arrest but also mobilized blacks to boycott the city's buses. One year later, the law that required segregated busing was abolished. These victories catapulted the careers of Thurgood Marshall, who represented the petitioners in *Brown*, and Martin Luther King, Jr., a young Montgomery pastor who led the bus boycott. As the scholar Charles Ogletree pointed out in *All Deliberate Speed*, Marshall and King had very different approaches to ending segregation. Marshall believed in change through the court system, or legal challenges, while King advocated nonviolent political protests, or extralegal challenges. Both approaches were needed, for resistance to integration was pervasive: from President Eisenhower, who privately disagreed with *Brown* and, when he did speak out, emphasized that integration should happen slowly; to congressional members from the South, 90 percent of whom signed a "Southern Manifesto," which vowed to reverse *Brown*; to the Supreme Court itself, which one year after *Brown* refused to rule that schools desegregate immediately but should do so "with all deliberate speed."

Grassroots opposition was also intense, including the White Citizens' Councils in the South, which publicly renounced violence in favor of economic tactics, but still contributed to hostilities against blacks. In Birmingham, resistance to *Brown* quickly surfaced. Before the decision, the city commissioners had abolished the ordinance that had prohibited blacks and whites from sharing any recreational activity. The commission unanimously amended the law so blacks and whites could play spectator sports together, including baseball, which would have more easily allowed Willie Mays to play exhibitions in his hometown. But two weeks after *Brown*, Birmingham voters resegregated baseball, among other sports, by a margin of 3–1. Throughout the South, local and state legislatures asserted their right to block the federal government from dismantling Jim Crow, and by the end of 1956, southern legislatures had approved of more than a hundred new segregation statutes.

The great milestones of *Brown* and the Montgomery boycott simply marked the beginning of a long struggle, and while Marshall and King would lead the battle in America's courtrooms and streets, there was a third assault on segregation, and it came from our national pastime. Racial attitudes don't change by judicial fiat or adamant protests. But they can be changed by events that challenge assumptions and biases, thus creating an opposing narrative to the outright lies embedded in white supremacy. Baseball created that opposing narrative, giving its black pioneers the perfect stage to defy and inspire.

Tallulah Bankhead said in 1954, "The Negro stars have certainly done something for baseball . . . and baseball has done something for the Negroes too. If nothing else, it's *unbigoted* some bigots."

Baseball wasn't the only sport to play a role. Boxers contributed, specifically Joe Louis, who was not only a champion fighter but a soft-spoken patriot. His defeat of the German Max Schmeling in 1938 and his fundraising for the U.S. war effort made him immensely popular with white fans. So too was Jesse Owens, whose four gold medals in the 1936 Olympics in Berlin discredited Hitler's racist ideology.

But baseball, with its deep roots in America, was different. Raw ability was not enough. It's a team game that requires collaboration, intelligence, and finesse—attributes that Major League Baseball had in fact cited to justify its color barrier. In 1946, the National and American leagues established a steering committee to evaluate integration, among other things, and concluded: "A major league baseball player must have something besides great natural ability. He must possess the technique, the coordination, the competitive attitude and the discipline, which is usually acquired only after years of training in the minor leagues." Since blacks never had a chance to play in the minors, according to the report's circular logic, "comparatively few young Negro players are being developed."

Branch Rickey rejected this sophistry, promoting Jackie Robinson the next year, but the report's patronizing language reflected common attitudes. An influential 1925 report for the army, for example, was blunter in its rationale for segregation. Because of Negroes' "smaller cranium, lighter brain, [and] cowardly and immoral character," they were lower on the evolutionary scale.*

By the early 1950s, blacks had succeeded in business, law, academia, and the arts, as well as the military, but by virtue of baseball's popularity, it fell to its Negro pioneers to shatter racist stereotypes, and it's no insult to Thurgood Marshall or Martin Luther King to say that Jackie Robinson deserves a place in the pantheon of great civil rights leaders. King himself recognized this. One month before he was assassinated, he visited Don Newcombe and said at the dinner table, "Don, you and Jackie and Roy will never know how easy you made it to do my job."

---

* President Truman's decision to integrate the armed services in 1948 defied the country's military leaders, including George Marshall and Dwight Eisenhower.

• • •

Willie Mays was often compared to Robinson, for good reason. They were America's two most prominent black athletes in the 1950s, and they were both fast, intense competitors who imported the Negro League style of aggressive play. They also shared certain habits, such as their shunning of tobacco and alcohol.

But their backgrounds and personalities, as well as their views on social issues, could not have been more different. Everything about the young Mays—apprehensive, amicable, fearful of controversy—Robinson contradicted. Eleven years older than Mays, Robinson grew up amid affluence in Pasadena, California, on a mostly white block in a working-class part of town. Even as a boy, he had a quick temper—he threw rocks at the father of a girl who called him "nigger"—and he channeled his anger through sports. He attended UCLA for two years, and though he didn't graduate, he was at least immersed in a world of inquiry and analysis. Unlike Mays, he could not abide blacks' second-class status, which led to repeated confrontations. After he was drafted, he refused to move to the back of a bus at Camp Hood, the army base in Texas where he was stationed. He got into an argument and was arrested, though found not guilty in a military trial.

Branch Rickey saw Robinson's defiance as a source of strength, which he would need to endure the slurs, the threats, and the isolation of baseball's "great experiment." But after suppressing his emotions for two years with the Dodgers, Robinson's simmering rage could no longer be contained, causing friction with opponents, the National League, and his own club. Robinson was one of the few blacks who openly protested segregated housing during spring training. On his expense account, along with the usual items such as meals, rent, and transportation, he inserted "humiliation," without specifying an amount, and suggested the Dodgers quantify the indignities he had suffered.

His frequent confrontations with the umpires prompted one, Jocko Conlan, to say that Robinson "was the most difficult ballplayer I had to deal with. . . . Jackie was one of those players who could never accept a decision. . . . Almost every time he was called out on strikes or on a close play on the bases, there seemed to be a few words."

Mays, by contrast, rarely argued with umpires, would greet them as he jogged to center field, and was never ejected from a game—not once in twenty-two seasons. He says he couldn't help the team from the clubhouse. Nor did he publicly complain about segregated housing during spring training, though he eventually rebelled against the treatment. At some point, the Giants could all stay in the same hotel in Phoenix, but the blacks and Latins could not eat in the restaurant. So Mays, motivated more by the inconvenience than moral outrage, moved to another hotel that was owned by a friend. The public never knew.

Where Robinson bitterly opposed discrimination, Mays turned segregation into a profit center. In St. Louis, baseball teams stayed at the Chase Hotel, which banned black patrons. Robinson demanded that the Chase drop its racial barrier, and in 1954 the hotel finally relented on a limited basis: blacks could sleep there but could not use the dining room, the swimming pool, or loiter in the lobby.

Mays didn't care about the Chase; he preferred staying in a black hotel. The Giants gave him the cash to cover the expenses for all the minority players, but the hotel waived their bill as long as they hung out in the dining room and bar—it was great publicity—and Mays divvied up the surplus cash among himself and the other banned players. That ended once the Chase was integrated.

As Robinson's career continued, he became more public and more strident in his demands for racial progress, and he was met with a backlash. "I was a martyred hero to a lot of people who seemed to have sympathy for the underdog," he wrote in *I Never Had It Made*. "But the minute I began to answer, to argue, to protest—the minute I began to sound off—I became a swellhead, a wise guy, an 'uppity' nigger." Robinson resented veteran black players like Larry Doby, Roy Campanella, and Monte Irvin for not speaking out with him, and his crusading spirit only intensified in retirement. Jimmy Cannon wrote that Robinson used "anger as a confederate," and Don Newcombe said, "He was the kind of man who had to make his presence felt. He sometimes overdid it. Like a boiler, he could not keep it all inside him."

While that smoldering intensity was part of Robinson's greatness, Mays concealed all his hurts with his joyous veneer and his honest belief that he was fortunate to play the sport he cherished. Robinson's game was an act of politics; for Mays, it was one of love. Donald Honig said, "Robinson, by virtue of seething pride, unforgiving resentments, his belligerency, and his outspokenness, was always the symbol of racial progress and aspiration. For some blacks, the innocent, laughing young Mays seemed too close to stereotype. Where Robinson threatened the social order, Willie approximated a comfortable fit."

Mays often had the ear of the most powerful people in the country. In July 1955, he was one of thirty-two "sports leaders" invited to the White House for a meeting with President Eisenhower on how to interest youngsters in competitive sports. Archie Moore, the boxer, gave such an inspiring talk on how to stop juvenile delinquency that Eisenhower suggested he run for Congress. Mays also had a platform. As the group prepared for a photograph on the White House lawn, reporters swarmed him. "What do you want to know, cats?" he asked. "Sure I go for this recreation business. We haven't got half enough parks for the kids in New York." Asked if he would give the president any suggestions, Mays said, "Naw, I don't go for that, but I'm with the program."

Mays showed a bit more spunk in a brief conversation with Vice President Nixon, who gave Willie some advice on working through a recent slump. "Keep your spirit up—that's the main thing," Nixon said. "You have the natural ability. After a good year, you usually have a bad one to settle down a bit and then you come up again."

Mays respectfully disagreed. "I don't believe that," he told Nixon. "A good player's got to play good all the time."

Mays's desire to please may have struck some as "too close to stereotype," but the ease with which white America could embrace Mays was invaluable at a time when the slightest challenge to the status quo—witness the *Sports Illustrated* cover—sent tremors. Mays was a transformative player, but he shunned the language of transformation or even triumph and hewed to a nonthreatening script of humility and respect.

After the 1954 season, Durocher launched one of his glowing riffs on Willie, claiming he could "out run, out throw, and out field" Stan Musial, and "he can out hit him as well and has so much power."

This caused a stir. Musial had already won three MVPs and six batting championships, and he was still near the peak of his Hall of Fame career. For Durocher to assert that a relative newcomer was his superior was heresy, the more so because Musial was a consummate gentleman who shied away from self-promotion.

Several weeks after Durocher's comments, Mays traveled to Rochester, New York, to accept the Ray Hickok Belt as the Professional Athlete of the Year. In a speech before 550 people, he bluntly contradicted his own manager. "I appreciate the nice things Leo said about me, but Musial has many great seasons in the records, while I am only starting," he said. "I hope I can become as great as Stan. . . . I'd like to be able to win this [award] three more times. I'm lucky I'm young enough to try. But most of all, I'd like to hit like Stan Musial."

By defending Musial's name and honor, "Mays stole the show," said Russ Hodges, who was in the crowd. Mays always knew his place.

Mays felt good about his comments, in part because Musial was such a fine person. One or two years later, Mays found himself on a plane with Musial on the way to an All-Star Game. Several black players were in the rear, playing cards, and Musial walked up to them and stood there.

"I'm for playing the game," he told Mays.

"Stan," he said, "you can't play with us. We're all black."

"I want to play."

So Musial sat down and joined them. Mays recalls, "That told me how classy he was, and I never forgot that."

Willie Mays was rarely asked about civil rights in the 1950s. Both he and the movement were young. He was insulated from criticism, but when he was asked about it, he urged patience. "I'm from the South," he told the *Saturday Evening Post* in 1957. "I understand these things. It won't change overnight. The old generation can't ever change. You have to wait for the young generation. I think sports have helped a lot. I think sports will help even more."

His critics later ridiculed his timidity, but ask any white youngster of that era who cheered for him, imitated him, or wept for him, and his contributions are undeniable.

Bill Littlefield, for example, grew up in Montclair, New Jersey, and his passion for sports led to his career as host of National Public Radio's weekly show *Only a Game*. As a kid, Bill was a Giants fan. He isn't sure why but assumes it had to do with his undiluted love for Willie Mays—he was six years old when Willie won his first MVP. Bill saw occasional games at the Polo Grounds and on television, but he also followed Willie in the newspaper that his father brought home each night and on his portable transistor radio, which he would take to his tree house to listen to games. It wasn't sufficient for him to root for Willie, he had to *be* Willie. One Halloween, he dressed up in a Giants uniform with number 24 on the back, blacked out his face with burnt cork, and went to his school, which had only white students. He then stopped by his neighbor's house. "They had a black maid," Littlefield recalls. "I don't know what she thought, except she laughed until I thought she was going to fall down."

He had no racial consciousness about Mays or, for that matter, the world around him. Bill had heard that Willie was looking for a house, so when he discovered the people next door were moving, he naturally thought it would be wonderful for Willie to move in next to him. "I thought he could help me out," he says. "I had no recognition at all that a black man couldn't just move into the neighborhood."

All Bill knew about or cared about was his hero's special greatness on the field. It transcended race, team loyalty, even baseball itself. He later commented, "His achievement beyond excellence was that he seemed to perform with such joy that he conveyed the impression that he was meant to do what he was doing. When you were watching him, you were watching the confluence of talent, concentration, and enthusiasm that not only allowed the suspension of disbelief—because who could believe that anybody could do some of the things Willie Mays did?—but that also encouraged the mad notion that a world where such grace was possible must be a pretty terrific place."

To some of Mays's fans, his blackness added a new layer, a different dimension, to the experience of watching him. Jim Bouton, for example, born in 1939, grew up in the blue-collar town of Rochelle Park, New Jersey. He pitched for the New York Yankees in the 1960s but gained his greatest fame by writing *Ball Four,* his controversial memoir on the foibles of the major leagues. As a boy, he rooted for the Giants, and on special occasions he went to the Polo Grounds, where he watched Willie Mays. "I saw him his rookie year, one of his first games, and he hit a line drive down the right field line, a triple, and boy, watching him fly around the bases, it was tremendously electrifying," Bouton recalls. "When he was on the bases, you had to lean forward in your seat. There was a feeling that at any moment, [there would be] a burst of action."

Mays's skin color "was part of the mystique," he says. "He looked different than everyone else, and that difference thrilled us." Jim got to one game three hours early to get Mays's signature. When Mays got out of a taxi, he was mobbed by fans but still signed their programs, including Jim's, and when Jim played stickball with his brother, he would imitate the batting stances of each Giant, including their tics in the batter's box. What was Willie's tic? Bouton pauses, then says, "He smiled." (Mays didn't smile in the box, but to a kid, it must have seemed that way.)

Bouton reached the majors in 1962 but, unlike most players of his era, he had gone to college and was far more aware of the world outside baseball. He believes Mays was "a tremendous help in civil rights," citing his own experience as proof. He recalls no racial hostilities in his town. There were also no black people. His exposure to race came mainly through baseball, where he noticed that few blacks sat on the bench. "They were the better players," Bouton says. And Willie was the best. "There were a lot of kids like me," he says, "who learned to love him before anybody told us we couldn't."

Television magnified Mays's appeal, allowing, among others, a ten-year-old southern white kid named Bill Clinton to become a fan. Born in Hope, Arkansas, in 1946, Bill tried to be home on the Saturday afternoons when the Giants played on *Game of the Week.* "Willie was the greatest player playing," Clinton says. "I saw him make those plays, and I just loved it." Those experiences contributed to his own interest in the nexus of sports and race in America. In Arkansas, like the rest of the South, the integration of schools proceeded slowly, if at all. In 1957, President Eisenhower had to enlist the Arkansas National Guard and send in army troops to allow nine black students to enter Central High School in Little Rock.

Clinton notes that opposition to civil rights was widespread, but many of those same opponents also followed Willie Mays. "Just watching him on TV, seeing what he did and the way he treated people, it had an effect on people even if they weren't aware," he says. Most teenagers and children were too young to understand the intellectual basis for civil rights, too inexperienced to appreciate the great speeches or the spirited debates over integration. But Willie Mays they watched, they understood, and they embraced.

As president, Clinton became a golfing buddy of Mays's, but even as a kid, he says, he recognized that Mays was different from the other players. "He had that personality that drew people to him," he says, and suggests that Mays did something important, beyond the score card, each time he took the field, something that helped pave the way for social change: "When you see someone doing something you admire"—like Willie Mays—"the image of that makes a mockery of all forms of bigotry."

By the time Mays reached the majors, one of the central fears about integration had already been dispelled—that black players would damage the value of a baseball franchise by alienating white fans. The experience of the Brooklyn Dodgers and Cleveland Indians had proven that false. Performance, not race, mattered. The year 1951 was critical for baseball's integration, in part because Branch Rickey and Bill Veeck, the executives with the Dodgers and the Indians who opened the door to blacks, went to the Pittsburgh Pirates and the St. Louis Browns, committing two more teams to the bandwagon. But Mays's arrival also accelerated integration. His popularity proved that black players were economic assets—Mays was baseball's biggest attraction. After watching him play, Dan Daniel of the *New York World Telegram* wrote: "We wonder how the magnates kept the Negro out so long." The Giants were to play an exhibition game on April 13, 1956, against the Washington Senators in the nation's capital. Mays was to be given the day off, but the Senators, citing large advance sales, appealed to him. Mays agreed to play, and the game drew 13,712; Washington had drawn 6,709 two nights earlier in an exhibition game against the Dodgers. With a triple, a single, and a fine catch, Mays delivered as promised.

Mays's broad appeal contributed to the pressures on those teams without black players. In September 1953, the Philadelphia Athletics and Chicago Cubs put African Americans on their rosters for the first time, with Ernie Banks joining the Cubs. On Opening Day 1954, the Pittsburgh

Pirates, Cincinnati Reds, Washington Senators, and St. Louis Cardinals had their first black players. Over several months, the number of integrated teams had doubled to twelve. The Yankees fell in line the following year, and by 1959 the remaining three teams—the Phillies, the Detroit Tigers, and the Red Sox—had purged the final vestiges of Jim Crow.

Jackie Robinson often spoke highly of Mays as a ballplayer, but he had little respect for him personally. He didn't publicly criticize Mays until the 1960s, when the civil rights movement assumed more urgency and Robinson denounced Mays's silence. In the 1950s, when they competed against each other, Robinson viewed Mays as a younger Campanella or Irvin or Doby—docile, uneducated blacks who accepted the corrupt status quo. Robinson saw Mays, according to Roger Kahn, as an "Uncle Tom."

The two men were going to be teammates, or so people thought, when in December 1956 the Dodgers announced that they had traded Robinson to the Giants. Robinson was thirty-seven and had just completed his tenth year in the majors. The last two seasons saw his performance decline. He was slower, thicker in the waist, and prone to injury, but he could still contribute. In his final season, his average, on-base percentage, and slugging percentage, compared to his career numbers, were .275/.311, .382/.409, and .412/.474.

Mays was excited about the trade. He craved mentors and believed that Robinson, still one of his heroes, could play that role. The Giants planned to make them roommates. No matter how much his physical skills had diminished, Robinson could surely teach Mays a few things about the game. The Giants, for their part, had no illusions about Robinson's eroding abilities. Chub Feeney later acknowledged that the principal motive behind the trade was the expected boost in attendance from the fans in Harlem.

The trade never happened. Robinson promptly announced his retirement, taking a position at Chock full o' Nuts instead. The Giants begged him to reconsider, but his playing days were over. Baseball pundits have speculated that Robinson quit because he didn't want to play second fiddle to Willie Mays or perhaps because he didn't want to join the team that had always been his sworn enemy.

Neither consideration likely played a role. Robinson, who had been feuding with Dodger management, had lined up his position at Chock full o' Nuts before the trade was proposed. His health was likely a significant factor in his decision. In 1957, Robinson was diagnosed with diabetes, but he had probably suffered from high blood sugar for a while. His doctor, at the time of the diagnosis, said that for someone who'd played sports and didn't drink or smoke, he had "never seen a body so badly deteriorated."

One can only speculate what would have happened had Robinson and Mays been teammates, as well as roommates, for a year. What impact, if any, would either have had on the other? In fact, Mays says he and Robinson never had a significant encounter or even a meaningful conversation. Their worlds rarely overlapped, and Robinson remained a distant hero. It might have been for the best.

CHAPTER SIXTEEN

"WILLIE MAYS DOESN'T NEED HELP FROM ANYONE"

As soon as spring training began in 1955, Willie Mays knew something was wrong. Leo Durocher, instead of basking in his World Series triumph, seemed distracted. Stories were circulating that he and Horace Stoneham had had a falling out, which wasn't unusual. Those stories had been around for years—at best, their relationship had always been an uneasy partnership forged out of mutual need, not respect. But an incident in the off-season had deepened the divide.

Durocher was given a testimonial dinner at the Hillcrest Country Club in Los Angeles, where his Hollywood friends—including George Burns, Jack Benny, Bob Hope, Frank Sinatra, and Milton Berle—auditioned their latest one-liners, and Danny Kaye served up an imitation of a besotted Horace Stoneham. Before Kaye began, he gathered the empty bottles, dishes, and utensils around him. Then he stood up, his shirt pulled out, his pants unzipped, his hair disheveled, and he went sprawling across the table, sending glasses, knives, and forks everywhere. He pulled himself up, teetered, screwed up his face, and asked, "Where can a guy take a piss?"

Stoneham was not amused. *Variety* reviewed the performance approvingly, and the *Sporting News* said, "They'll be talking about it from Toots Shor's to the Stork Club for weeks." Durocher did nothing to soften Stoneham's fury when the owner heard that his manager had almost died laughing.

The World Series was their doom, Stoneham and Durocher each believing the other was assuming too much credit. Mays knew that Durocher had talked about quitting baseball to work in television and that Stoneham preferred members of the "Giants' family"—retired players like Bill Terry and Mel Ott—to manage his clubs. Nonetheless, as Mays prepared for the season, he was no less dependent on Durocher than he had been as a rookie. When he was playing winter ball in Puerto Rico, Stoneham visited him with a new contract. It called for $25,000, roughly double what Mays

236

had started at in 1954, though he'd received bonus checks along the way. Before Mays signed it, he told Stoneham he needed to speak to the boss.

"What do you mean, 'boss'?" he asked. "I'm the boss."

"No, I mean Mr. Leo," Mays said.

Stoneham smiled and called Durocher at his home in Los Angeles. After Mays spoke to him, Stoneham wanted to know what he had said.

"He said you should give me $5,000 more." Which Stoneham did.

On another occasion before the season began, Mays was picked up for speeding in Woodbury, New Jersey. In the courthouse, he saw a man with four kids who had also been nabbed. The man couldn't pay the thirty-dollar fine, so Mays, feeling sorry for the kids, paid it. The grateful father asked where to send a check. Mays shrugged. "Just send it, 'Care of the skipper, New York Giants,'" he said. "I'll get it."

Mays had ties to other members of Durocher's family. In addition to Laraine Day, Leo and Laraine's adopted son, Chris, was part of Mays's life. Chris, six years old in Willie's rookie season, watched games from the dugout, his right foot on the top step, just like his father. "I remember Willie was always very friendly and outgoing with me," Chris recalls. "He had time for me whereas a lot of the players couldn't be bothered." Mays would get him gloves, bats, and autographed balls. "I knew Willie would do anything for me."

When Chris traveled with the team, he sometimes stayed with Mays. At first Willie thought he was babysitting for the boy until he realized that the boy was probably there to babysit for him. They would read comic books, watch cartoons, go to movies, and just as Mays took white ballplayers in the army to black neighborhoods, he would take Chris to black restaurants and homes for chitterlings, black-eyed peas, and cornbread. His father laughed when he discovered his son's new interest in soul food. One time in Cincinnati, Willie and Chris were driving through town when a police officer pulled them over. Mays tried to explain who he was and why he had a white boy in his car. The officer called the hotel to confirm that Durocher knew where his son was. Mays was allowed to drive on.

As Chris saw it, Willie was like his older brother because his father treated Willie just like a son. "He kept Willie under his wing and made sure he didn't go astray," Chris says. "My father looking out for Willie is what made him a great ballplayer." They were one big happy family. "Life was never so sweet," Chris recalls, "as during those years."

Mays couldn't imagine the family breaking up, but he also knew that 1955 was the final year of Durocher's contract. The Giants were heavily favored to win another World Series, which was probably the only thing that could save Durocher's job.

The team, however, was aging, and with age came injuries and ailments. In 1955 alone, second baseman Davey Williams, suffering back pains, was diagnosed with "spinal arthritis" and had to retire after eighty-two games. His double-play partner, Al Dark, missed forty games with a separated shoulder and a broken rib. Sal Maglie, at thirty-eight, was traded midway through the year to Cleveland. Johnny Antonelli had arm problems and was briefly suspended by Durocher when he complained about getting pulled from a game. Hank Thompson was only twenty-nine, but his preference for alcohol caught up with him, and he was out of baseball the following year. Wes Westrum, at thirty-two, lasted three more years but would never again play as many as seventy games in a season.

And then there was Monte Irvin. The Giants thought that Irvin, at thirty-six, had one more season in him, but he began the year slowly and was soon platooning. He was hitting .253 when the Giants played an exhibition game against their Minneapolis farm club. After the game, Durocher approached him in the locker room.

"Monte, you're not swinging the bat like you used to," he said. "We're going to leave you here."

Irvin was stunned. "It's just a matter of time before I hit my stride again," he said.

Durocher said no, and that was it—his career as a Giant was over. At least if Durocher had told him before the trip, he could have packed his belongings. Instead, he had to send for his clothes. It was a heartless move against a man who had brought nothing but honor to the Giants. Irvin didn't sulk but finished out the season with Minneapolis: in seventy-five games, he hit .352, with fourteen home runs and fifty-two RBIs. The following year he was signed by the Cubs, and in 111 games, he hit a respectable .271, smacked fifteen homers, and drove in fifty. Having proved that he could still play, he retired.

Mays lost his roommate, his best friend on the team, and one of his principal protectors. Irvin describes Mays as "upset" when he got the news of his demotion, but he remained philosophical for reporters. "I'll miss Monte," he told them. "He was like a father to me. Guess I'll be rooming by myself awhile now. You gotta keep on laughing. That's the true champion, I guess. Takes the downs with the ups. There's an awful lot of frontrunners in this world."

Like any father, Durocher sometimes had to discipline even his most gifted son, and in 1955 he benched Mays for the first time. While the year would be one of his best ever, Mays hit under .300 during the first three months. It was considered a disaster, in light of the pundits' spring training expectations that he could hit .400. (Mays always insisted he couldn't.) When Mays, with a batting average of .279, came to the ballpark in Milwaukee on June 18, his name was not in the lineup, and he thought Durocher was playing a joke. He asked Freddie Fitzsimmons about it. The coach told him to talk to the manager.

Earlier in the season, Durocher had pulled Mays aside and urged him to try for home runs, the exact opposite of the advice he'd given him the previous year. But Durocher told him the team didn't have enough power. Mays obliged, hitting seventeen long balls and driving in forty-two runs by the middle of June. But now he had only three hits in the last seven games, had recently been picked off a base, and had run into a double play. Durocher told reporters that Mays seemed to be "confused." His misplays had followed some early lapses when he had missed cutoff men and thrown to the wrong base.

So Mays silently watched the contest from the bench, a Giant loss that he later described as the longest game of his life. He was on the bench the next night as well, and the Giants lost again. Durocher spoke to him after the game and chastised him, as he had in previous years, for trying to pull so many balls. Pitchers were throwing down and away, and Mays was getting himself out on weak ground balls to the left side. His average had fallen by almost seventy points from last year's.

Durocher's psychological gamesmanship with Mays always centered on building his confidence, cajoling and pleading, exhibiting more faith in Willie than Willie had in himself, convincing him of his own greatness. He told Mays he could drive the ball to the opposite field and still hit it out of the park. "If you hit the ball to right field, you'll become one of the greatest hitters of all time!" he implored.

"Okay, Mr. Leo, I'll go to right field," he said.

"You better, or I'm not going to put you back in there."

Mays kept hitting home runs, to right and everywhere else, but he also experienced his single worst moment, to date, as a Giant.

On August 19, against the Dodgers in the Polo Grounds, Mays charged a base hit from center field, missed the ball, and failed to run after it. The hitter, Duke Snider, circled the bases. Mays had committed errors or miscues before, but they usually occurred from excessive effort—trying to take one base too many, overthrowing an infielder, bumping into another outfielder. Never had he been guilty of indifference, of giving up. For the first time, the home crowd booed Willie Mays, and they booed loudly. After the game, he tried to justify his action. "In our field, if you miss it in center, it's gone," he said. "Why bother about it? You can't get anybody out if you miss it." His excuse was roundly criticized by reporters as well as Durocher, all of whom noted that the failure to hustle could never be justified. He had committed not just a physical error but a baseball sin. Suddenly, Mays seemed not so fresh and naive. As the *Sporting News* lectured: "Willie had better grow up."

Mays discovered that every lapse was magnified. Several weeks before a June series in Cincinnati, he was asked to appear at an instructional clinic for kids. He said he would try to attend. The day the noon clinic began, the Giants had arrived late the previous night from Milwaukee and Mays missed it. He said he had never confirmed his attendance. There was no written invitation or confirmation. But it was front-page news—Willie Mays had disappointed the children.

Since Mays had arrived in New York, everything he did seemed to work out, but it couldn't last forever. Some financial setbacks occurred. He and Monte Irvin wanted to open a liquor store in Harlem, which Roy Campanella had done in 1951. Irvin approached a New York lawyer named Howard Cosell, who had assisted other athletes as well as actors, to help them. After the 1954 season, Irvin and Mays used most of their World Series winnings, about $11,000 apiece, to purchase a liquor store, in Brooklyn, with the intention of transferring the license to Harlem. But a licensing agent with the New York Liquor Authority was caught taking bribes, and all transfers were frozen. Irvin and Mays were saddled with a money-losing store, and the enterprise ended badly for all concerned. They never got the license for Harlem, and Irvin, after using additional money from his wife, said he lost between $25,000 and $30,000 on the business, which he sold in 1957. He says that Mays "just walked away from it." Mays, however, in an appeal to the state liquor authority to reinstate his license, alleged that the store had been sold without his consent. The authority rejected his appeal, leaving him with nothing to show for his investment. Mays and Irvin remained friends, but it was their last business venture together.

Even more costly, for Mays, were the fraudulent promises he received for commercial endorsements. Through his agent, Art Flynn, in 1955 he agreed to endorse a firm called the American Heritage Investment Company in Houston. He was to receive a base salary of $37,000 spread out over five years, plus "2% of gross premium income on a semi-annual basis from April 10, 1956," according to a letter from Flynn. But by the end of 1957, Mays had received nothing.

Flynn had been snookered, and it apparently took him two years to realize it. In a letter dated November 27, 1957, to the company's "Mr. J. B. Salas," Flynn wrote: "Inasmuch as you had not formed the company in February 1957 when you wrote, we would appreciate knowing if and when the company was formed." Alas, Flynn had gotten Mays a very lucrative business deal with a company that didn't exist.

Mays says he has no recollection of that deal but says that many arrangements fell through. His outside income, compared to that of most athletes, was not insignificant. In 1956, his earnings from "Royalties, Testimonials & TV Appearances" were $8,421, according to Flynn's records. That included two royalty checks from his ghostwritten autobiography for $122.32 and $218.66, and $1,000 for attending a Masquerade Party for Wolf Productions.

Those were respectable earnings in a year when the average take-home pay was $3,600 but a pittance compared to what New York's other marquee baseball player was making. In 1956, Mickey Mantle made $70,000 in endorsements. To be sure, he was at the height of his stardom, having won the MVP that year, but the disparity between him and Mays threw into sharp relief the different commercial opportunities for white and black athletes. Some of Mays's friends, including Irvin, believe that Mays was unhappy with the wide gap between his outside earnings and Mantle's, but Mays says he wasn't. He insists that the disparity in endorsements reflected the added commercial value that all Yankees were given. Race, he says, was not a factor.

There probably was a "Yankee premium," but race obviously played a role in shutting out Mays and all black players. In 1957, Hank Aaron won the MVP award and appeared in his third consecutive All-Star Game, but that didn't translate into endorsements. "I played in a small town in Milwaukee, but it was definitely related to race," Aaron says. "Willie got a few endorsements, but not as many as he should have." On one occasion in the 1950s, according to the *Sporting News*, a "food outfit" in Cincinnati wanted to use "all-star" squads from the National and American leagues for an advertising campaign. When Frank Scott, the business representative of MLB's players, recommended four blacks on the National League team, including Mays, "the reaction of the company's advertising manager was indeed unusual," he said. "He called up, shouting indignation. He demanded that I line up four white National replacements." Scott refused, and the deal was called off.

That Mays publicly discounts race as a drag on his outside income is consistent with his refusal to ever cite race on any matter. He will never play that card. To do so is to invite controversy, to appear the victim, to arouse sympathy for a man who disdains pity. On some issues, Mays is so steadfast, so intractable, that his public and private views have probably merged. He undoubtedly believes that both he and Mantle got what they deserved.

• • •

With Durocher protecting him and providing for him, 1955 was Mays's last year of baseball innocence. Mays visited Durocher at his mansion in Beverly Hills, where at elegant soirees Leo introduced him to the biggest names in Hollywood—Lauren Bacall, Humphrey Bogart, Gary Cooper, Doris Day, Glenn Ford, and Jerry Lewis. Mays, at ease with his fellow entertainers, made a good impression. "Movieland," the *Sporting News* wrote, "seems as 'gone' about Willie as fans everywhere he plays."

Mays wasn't loved by everyone, particularly by those who resented his special treatment, but his generosity became almost as storied as his play. Irvin, while rooming with Mays in Cincinnati, once got a call from a man who asked to see Willie, who said to let him up. The visitor said that he had lost his job, needed a loan, and would pay it back. Mays gave him a bill. Afterward, he said to Irvin, "That's another twenty down the drain."

"So why did you give your money away?"

"I used to play ball with him," Mays said. "He's all right."

The *Saturday Evening Post,* in 1957, noted that Mays would "carry up to $1,000 around in his pockets and hand money around almost upon request." His favorite restaurant was the Red Rooster in Harlem, and according to the *Post,* "Almost everybody at the Red Rooster—including the guy who sweeps up—has at least one of Willie's monogrammed sports shirts. Willie buys them in lots. To admire a Mays shirt is to get it hot off his back." When a Red Rooster manager complained that her watch didn't work, "Willie whipped off his own and insisted that she take it, although it was a specially engraved watch that *Look* magazine had awarded him for being picked on its all-star team."

Mays sent clothes back to his boyhood pals and money to his half-siblings; in 1952, when he was barnstorming through the South and was called to his draft board in Birmingham, his teammate and former manager Piper Davis entrusted him with money to deliver to his wife. When Davis finally returned to Birmingham, he discovered that Mays had given her *more* money than Davis had handed over.

Mays was never quoted or cited in the *Post* story as a source for any of these anecdotes. Others spoke for him. "Willie is the greatest, just the greatest," said Jimmy Hall, the bartender. "He's just a big, generous, over-grown kid."

The Red Rooster's owner, George Woods, himself a big Giants fan, called Mays "the baby," a reference to his youth, not his maturity. Mays would always order a soft drink with six cherries, a straw, and a piece of lemon, and the bartender would tease him that the cherries would get him drunk. Woods roped off a table for Mays, but that could not keep the masses at bay. "Everybody seems to be after him," he said in 1955. "He can't sit down to eat before he's wanted on the phone. Some newspaper man wants an interview; his agent wants to see him; somebody wants pictures; he's got to rush off for a TV show. It goes on that way all night. The fellow has little time to himself. How does he take it? Better than Babe Ruth—and I knew him too."

Desperate to meet Mays, women, from bobby-soxers to dowagers, went to the Red Rooster and watched the Giants game on a large television. Each passing inning, each out, would raise the excitement level. Finally, the game would end, and their golden boy would soon appear. "They start gathering early in the afternoon," Woods said. "They know Willie comes here for dinner, and these girls open up with me, hoping for seats that will provide a good vantage point of Mays having a meal."

But the adulation didn't make him boastful. According to Woods, Mays always credited Durocher or Dusty Rhodes for winning the World Series, and whenever anyone asked him about himself, his response was the same: "You got to ask the other guys."

Woods captured the essential paradox of Mays. He was "the happy-go-lucky player people see doing amazing things in a ball game." But he was also "a serious young man who keeps his business to himself." He loved the company, the attention, the noise, the sea of strangers and sycophants and starlets who engulfed him each night, yet he disclosed nothing about himself. His most aggressive admirers would literally rip pieces of clothing off his body. A young woman at the Polo Grounds once jumped over the wall and onto the field, driven, she said, by an irresistible urge to pat Willie Mays on the shoulder. The drop was fifteen feet, and she was carried off the field with a broken leg. Mays protected his privacy with maddening efficiency. Woods once drove him to Richmond, Virginia, to be interviewed by a newspaper friend, but Mays would only talk about others. "He was running true to form," Woods said. The interview "didn't work." As the author Joe David Brown once wrote: "Willie volunteers about as much information as a brass Buddha."

Mays thought nothing odd of his reticence. His father had been the same—a tactic to guard against misstatement, to protect himself. But Willie made a revealing comment to George Woods. One night, surrounded by young women, he confided, "They ain't kidding me. If I was just plain Joe Doakes, they wouldn't even bother to look at me."

This insecurity is common for celebrities—do they love me for what I do or for who I really am? Most celebrities don't care as long as they reap the benefits of their fame. But Mays did care. He wanted to be liked and accepted. The irony is that he never allowed the public to get to know him. Instead, he maintained that shell of privacy, which only hardened over time.

The Giants finished the 1955 season with a respectable record, 80–74, but they were never in the race. The Dodgers got off to a blazing start and finished 18½ games ahead of New York. Mays's failure to hustle earlier in the season proved an aberration. On September 21, the Giants played a meaningless doubleheader against the Pirates. Mays started both games, and in the first inning of the nightcap, he sprinted to the right center field bleacher wall, just beyond where he'd caught Vic Wertz's drive, trying to make a catch. He rarely crashed into walls but in fact did just that, ending up on the ground for several minutes. He didn't catch the ball either. He was taken off the field on a stretcher and, at Presbyterian Medical Center, he was diagnosed with a severe hip bruise and strained ligaments in his back. The Giants had the next day off, but Mays was back in the lineup the following day.

It was the final series of the year, against the Phillies, the season ending with a Sunday doubleheader. Mays had fifty home runs, one behind Johnny Mize's single-season record for the Giants. In the first game, he faced Robin Roberts, whose good control helped him win games but not without high home run totals, and in the first inning Mays hit one out to tie Mize's record.

During the second game, Mays was already beginning to think about his off-season barnstorming plans when Durocher called him over. They went into a tunnel between the dugout and the stands and squeezed into a small bathroom for the players. Durocher placed both his hands on Mays's shoulders.

"I want to tell you something," he began. "You know I love you, so I'm prejudiced. But you're the best ballplayer I ever saw. There are other great ones, sure. But to me you're the best ever. Having you on my team made everything worthwhile. I'm telling you this now, because I won't be back next season."

Mays had known about the rumors but couldn't comprehend it. "How can you leave?" he finally asked. He said he had only been back from the army for two years and they were just getting started.

Durocher said that Stoneham had made the change and that Bill Rigney would be the new manager. "I already talked to Rigney about how to treat you," he said. "Besides, you know I'll always be looking out for you. If there's anything you ever want or need, all you have to do is call me."

Mays had tears in his eyes. "But Mr. Leo, it's going to be different with you gone. You won't be here to help me."

Then Durocher told him something he would never forget. "Willie Mays doesn't need help from anyone," he said, then leaned over and kissed him on the cheek.

Mays later described it as his saddest moment in baseball.

The Giants released a statement saying that Durocher had "resigned," but no one believed it. Because his contract had expired, he had nothing to resign from. He left the Polo Grounds gracefully, shaking hands with Stoneham for the photographers, praising all of his players, and discussing his new career with NBC. Some of the fans, perhaps the very ones who'd despised him when he first arrived seven years earlier, yelled, "We want Leo!"

It turned out that Durocher was better at schmoozing with television stars than being one. Without his baseball uniform, he was just a short, balding white guy who was uncomfortable in front of the camera. He returned to baseball, first as a bench coach with the Dodgers in 1961, then, in 1966, as the manager for the Cubs. That lasted six years with little success, after which he managed the Houston Astros for two more years.

By the time he retired, he had managed in the major leagues in five different decades and had won more than two thousand games, placing him fifth on the list for most wins. (He is now tenth.) Durocher lived until 1991, but the Veterans Committee of the Baseball Hall of Fame waited until he was dead before electing him into the Hall, in 1994.

Whatever his shortcomings as a person, Durocher's development of Mays stands as a monumental contribution to baseball. Mays believes that in 1951, every other manager in the big leagues would have sent him back to the minors. That's what any responsible manager would do with any young player in the throes of despair. Mickey Mantle, to take one example, was sent down as a rookie. Mays was so depressed, he didn't even want to go to Minneapolis. He wanted to quit altogether.

Had Mays returned to Minneapolis, his self-image shattered, his vulnerabilities exposed, the arc of his career would have been quite different. He was only twenty, but he applied so much pressure to himself, took failure so hard, he would have required considerable time and nurturing to regain confidence. He also would have faced additional racial barriers, as black players were less likely to get second or third chances. Mays's hiatus from the majors could have been quite long.

Without Durocher, would Mays have fulfilled his potential as a big leaguer? Would he have retreated to the safety of the Negro Leagues or, haunted by failure, stalled out as a career minor leaguer?

Mays accepts those as real possibilities. When his career ended, he said, he "probably wouldn't have made it" without Durocher. "Leo made me believe in myself. He forced me to. He wasn't only my manager, he was my friend. . . . He put words in my mouth and ideas in my head."

Durocher shared that view. In 1958, he told the *American Weekly:* "If I had fined instead of fathered Willie Mays, he today might be one of the best ballplayers in Minneapolis."

His handling of Mays had its critics. Durocher, they said, pampered him in a way that led to his feeling entitled for the rest of his career, and Durocher invoked troubling stereotypes of Mays as a helpless farmhand at the mercy of a benevolent plantation owner. Both views have some merit, though not with Mays, who bristles at the notion that Durocher always treated him with kid gloves. Durocher, Mays notes, did bench him for two games, but he never gushed over another player as he did Willie.

Some of Mays's friends also believe Durocher simply used him as a meal ticket—1954 was his only World Series championship as a manager—but that sells him short. Durocher's affection for Mays was real. As a desperate manager, it was Mays who helped him win the Series. As an inveterate cynic, it was Mays who lifted his spirits and made him laugh, even in his darkest moods. Noted *Sport* in 1954: "Building a baseball myth is something Leo does well. His enthusiasms run hot and cold, and he has heaped extravagant praise on so many that you can never be sure how much of it he believes himself. Yet . . . you still get the feeling that Leo has a strong sentimental attachment to Willie. It is doubtful he has ever had the feeling before."

As Roger Kahn says, "To the extent that Leo Ernest Durocher could love anyone not named Leo Ernest Durocher, he loved Willie."

The feeling was mutual, for Mays never trusted another manager, or maybe anyone, as much as he'd trusted Durocher. "His departure," Mays said, "was a source of regret that would stay with me for the rest of my big league career." Mays now had to look to others for guidance, or maybe even himself. That prospect was frightening, and those around him noticed. "It was a big change," said publicist Garry Schumacher. "When Leo left, it was the end of Willie's carefree youth."

CHAPTER SEVENTEEN

THE END OF AN ERA

She caught Willie's eye at the Red Rooster, a stunning, light-skinned black woman with high cheekbones, a fashionable dress, and perfectly tipped fingernails, a portrait of glamour and sophistication. Her name was Marghuerite Wendell,* though some press accounts identified her as Marghuerite Wendell Kenny Chapman, a name that traced the contours of her complicated personal life.

Willie and Marghuerite were introduced in May of 1955 by the famed composer Oscar Hammerstein II, a Red Rooster patron whose family had roots in Harlem. Mays called her shortly thereafter and asked her to a drive-in movie. They had several things in common. They both avoided alcohol and didn't care for large parties or big crowds, they both loved poodles, they both had a sense of style and a taste for luxury, and they both knew about the harsh glare of celebrity.

But Marghuerite was very different from her suitor. She was born and raised in St. Louis, studied "domestic science" in high school, and briefly worked as a cook for the vice president of Bell Telephone Company. But she had other interests. She moved to New York before she was twenty and in 1946 had a baby girl. She told Bill Kenny, the lead singer with the Ink Spots, a popular rhythm and blues group, that he was the father, and the couple married. Kenny, however, later concluded that he was not the father, and the couple divorced in 1949. In 1954, she married a wealthy Detroit doctor, Roland Chapman, but that marriage lasted less than a year.

She was said to be two years older than Willie, though one report said she was over thirty. At least to Willie's friends, the age difference seemed significant. "Margie," as some called her, was part of Negro café society, knowledgeable about the entertainment business, comfortable in nightclubs, worldly, a woman who made an impression. She counted among her acquaintances the jazz greats Louis Armstrong, Duke Ellington, and Earl "Fatha" Hines. She was friends with the boxers Johnny Bratton and

---

* News reports also spelled her name as Wendel and Wendelle.

Joe Louis, who introduced her to her first husband. There were conflicting reports that she had been a New York model or a Chicago showgirl. Miles Davis, another friend, praised Marghuerite as "one of the hippest women I've ever met." A gossip magazine described her as "America's leading dusky playgirl [who] commuted between New York and Los Angeles with the regularity of an airline host."

But a big baseball fan she wasn't, though she admired Joe DiMaggio— "He was Mr. Baseball to me," she said. Even after meeting Willie, she saw only two or three of his games that year. "Oh, sure, I knew that three strikes meant you were out, and four balls meant that a man could take a base," she said, "but that was all baseball meant to me. Until Willie."

Though he was famous, handsome, and single, Mays's personal life generated relatively few tabloid headlines. Race may have diminished interest, or perhaps there just wasn't much to write about. But his relationship with Marghuerite Wendell received some notice. The *Pittsburgh Courier*, a black newspaper, wrote, "For many months, there had been much newspaper and street corner speculation about whether or not the baseball phenom would wed the shapely divorcee. More and more they had been seen exclusively in each other's company."

They weren't with each other exclusively. Mays's travels allowed Marghuerite to date others, and he didn't like that. "He got to the point," Monte Irvin says, "where he liked what he had, and she would be seen with other men here or there, and she told him, 'Willie, you don't have any rings on my fingers, so I can date whoever I want to.' That really got to him."

On Valentine's Day of 1956, two weeks before spring training, Willie and Marghuerite, joined by several friends and relatives, drove to Elkton, Maryland, to get married. Willie never formally proposed to Marghuerite because, he said, "I don't believe in that." But they went to the Elkton courthouse because they could obtain a marriage license there without delay; it was also the courthouse where Marghuerite had married her first husband. (Her marriage license with Willie said her second divorce had been on June 27 of the previous year.) Mays drove his light green Cadillac too fast and was ticketed for speeding, adding fifteen dollars to the day's expenses and providing fodder to news reports about his headlong rush to matrimony.

When Willie and Marghuerite returned, they were shocked to see her home surrounded by photographers, camera crews, and reporters. Someone had leaked the news. They were also surprised by the public's unfavorable reception of the marriage, as if his fans didn't want to see him grow up. According to the *Saturday Evening Post*: "Willie suddenly felt the outside world's snarl." One reporter went to their house and asked if they had to get married. Another reporter, from a black publication, was so caustic that Willie refused to let him in, prompting the charge that he was "anti-Negro."

In truth, most of Mays's friends urged him not to marry. He barely knew Marghuerite, and she had traveled in very different circles than he had. When she visited Willie's friends and family in Fairfield, it felt as if she had come from a different planet. How else to explain her spandex outfits? "Marghuerite came down and went out with my wife and me," Herman Boykin recalls. "She was okay, but she had covered some territory and knew about places he knew nothing about." Another friend, William Richardson, says, "Sometimes a country boy needs to be with a country girl."

Horace Stoneham asked Roy Campanella to try to talk Mays out of the marriage; Campanella declined. The most vocal opposition came from Frank Forbes, who had long warned Willie about financial predators and who saw his principal job as protecting him from seductresses. He wasn't the only one who believed that Willie's new wife was interested in his money, but he was the most adamant. Look at her track record. A singer, a doctor, and now a baseball player. But the warnings just strengthened Mays's resolve, and when he defied Forbes, the break between the two was so complete that they stopped talking to each other.

Several days after the marriage, Roger Kahn, seeking an interview, visited Mays at his new home, the one Marghuerite already owned in the East Elmhurst section of Queens. It was midday, and Marghuerite received him—"a beautiful woman," Kahn wrote, "who stared hard and knowing when she said hello." She told him that Willie had not come down yet. Kahn mounted the stairs and found Willie sitting in the center of a large bed, wearing pale ivory monogrammed pajamas. He rested against a red satin headboard, with a stylish tan telephone on his nightstand and a booming twenty-one-inch television near his feet. Three trophies were lined across the top of the set; the largest, for winning the MVP, featured bright gilt figurines of ballplayers running, batting, and throwing. His closet door, slightly ajar, revealed a vast assortment of suits.

"Man, I've been busy," Mays said. "But it's time for me to be settling down. I'm twenty-four years old."

He still had that face-splitting smile and uniquely eager expression, though the faint outlines of jowls were now visible. The telephone didn't so much ring as toll softly, and the interview was interrupted by a caller who wanted to sign him for a newsreel. Mays asked if there was any money in it; he heard the response and told the caller to contact Art Flynn.

After the call, Kahn told Mays there was no money in newsreels. Mays said he knew that. "But Art Flynn, he tells me if they use my picture for advertising, there should be something in it for me. I don't know. I just let him handle it for me, things like that."

He retained a maddening innocence, particularly about business, including baseball. At one point, when talking about contracts, he said he disapproved of players who worried about salary. "You shouldn't fight about how much you gonna get," he said. "You love the game and practice it and play it good and you don't have to worry. The money, it'll come."

The money did come to Mays, but most teams paid their players as little as possible. In 1955, Giant pitcher Johnny Antonelli won fourteen games and posted a 3.33 ERA, but his salary was cut by 25 percent, from $28,000 to $21,000. The Giants said he could restore his lost wages by winning at least twenty games, as he had in 1954. He won twenty in 1956. Players also knew they would be discarded as soon as they lost their usefulness. During spring training of 1958, the wife of shortstop Eddie Bressoud suddenly took ill. Three days later, she had surgery for a brain tumor; she died on the operating table. Bressoud took only one day off, he later said, in large part because "there was no security in the major leagues at that point unless you were a star. They expected you back."

Mays was protected from those pressures, and he bore no grudges against Stoneham for firing Durocher. "I been lucky," he told Kahn. "Mr. Stoneham is my friend. . . . We never argue how much I'm gonna get. Whatever he says is right is okay with me, because he's my friend."

Mays was too trusting. Within two years, he fired Art Flynn after concluding that he was spending Willie's money for his own purposes. Then there was Marghuerite. As delicately as possible, Kahn mentioned the "impression" that his wife was trying to take his money—or, as he wrote in *Sport*, it appeared that "Willie is a child in the hands of a femme fatale." Surprisingly, Mays parried with a quick, candid answer.

"Look," he said, "I don't know what's gonna be for sure, but I think Marghuerite can help me and I can help her, so we can help each other. Sure, they're gonna talk about her and me. Same people was talking and writing columns last summer how I was gonna marry this girl and that girl. Well, they was wrong then like they is wrong now. Oh, I don't know for sure, but I think I know and I think it's gonna work out."

Then Mays pointed to his chest with a mixture of defiance and pride. "I'm the only guy," he said, "who knows what's in here."

Marghuerite, in an interview with the *Pittsburgh Courier*, defended herself. "They told me I was too old for Willie," she said. "They kept emphasizing that I had been married twice before. These things haven't meant anything to Willie and me. I've never before loved anybody but him, and he knows it. . . . We don't need or like a lot of people around. In fact, we're both halfway antisocial."

Not everyone who met the couple disapproved. Edward Linn, who often wrote perceptively about Mays, said, "Mrs. Marghuerite Mays seems to be a very charming, very sweet woman. The feeling of those who finally got to meet her was that Willie had done very well for himself."

The marriage, for Mays, did not defy logic. Her beauty, and the intimacy she offered, was part of her appeal, but so too was her experience. She could show him a world, even around New York, that he had never seen. Her age, her travels, and her connections were an asset, not a liability. Leo was gone. Monte was gone. His aunt Sarah and his mother had been gone for several years. Now, so too were Frank Forbes and Mrs. Goosby.

His father was still with him. Willie had moved Cat Mays to New York in 1954, rented an apartment for him in Harlem, and found him a job as a security guard at a supermarket. Father and son were together again, but Cat, now in his forties, no longer saw himself as a guardian or even a confidant. All his efforts—pushing young Willie to excel in sports, instructing him on how to behave, calling him in the minor leagues—were to prepare him to be a professional ballplayer. Now he was done. He stopped calling Willie after he joined the Giants in 1951, though he would receive updates from Durocher. Even after he moved to Harlem, he rarely went to the Polo Grounds but listened to the games on the radio. He still saw Willie regularly, but he didn't join him at the Red Rooster or on excursions into the city. Cat remained what he had always been—a loving father and a fount of goodwill but a complete mystery. Willie has no memories of Cat's celebrating any of his son's achievements or of his communicating any of his feelings. "It wasn't like that," Willie says. "He didn't talk that way."

There was a vacuum in Mays's life, and it was persuasively filled by Marghuerite Wendell Kenny Chapman Mays. "He's the most wonderful human being I've ever known," she told a reporter. "If he were any better, I'm afraid he'd be a saint."

Mays's life on the baseball field was about to change as well. Spring training of 1956 marked the first time he had put on a Giant uniform without Durocher as his manager. That Bill Rigney struggled to connect with Mays at the beginning was probably inevitable. No one could replace Durocher, but Rigney made a point of not even trying.

Rigney was a good man, respected by players and reporters, the kind of company loyalist that Stoneham long favored as a manager. He grew up in California, the son of a tile setter, and he had to scrape his way to the majors. His rail-thin body, even as an adult, was often described as "gaunt" and "frail." One writer said he was not much bigger than "a eucalyptus sapling." His eyeglasses gave him a professorial look, and he turned gray prematurely. He began his professional career in the Pacific Coast League, one year playing all 180 games without missing an inning. He spent six years in the minors, three more in the military, and was twenty-eight before he finally reached the majors with the Giants in 1946—the first big league game he ever saw, he played in.

"Rig," as they called him, joined the team as a middle infielder known more for his bench jockeying than his physical skills. But no one questioned his courage. In one game, when he was playing shortstop, Phillie catcher Andy Seminick slid wide of the bag to break up a double play. Though he was forty pounds lighter, Rigney tore off his glasses and swarmed his burly adversary.

From the outset of his playing career, Rigney was labeled a future manager, and when he retired in 1953, he was promptly named manager of the Minneapolis club. In 1955, the Millers took first place in the American Association, and Rigney was named the league's manager of the year. In the final weeks of the season, Stoneham told him that he'd be managing the Giants the next year.

Rigney and Mays overlapped in Willie's first two seasons in New York, and the new manager needed no lecture on his center fielder's abilities. But he knew that some players remained angry at Durocher's favoritism of Mays. Rigney wanted to establish his own authority, to create a different culture, so he vowed to treat all the players the same. On the first day of spring training, he said, "Aside from center field, shortstop, and right field, every position is up for grabs. And if anyone can show me enough to move out Willie, Alvin [Dark], or Don [Mueller], even those spots may not be safe." Rigney declared that it was now a "new era."

Mays didn't think there was anything wrong with the old era and thought that he never had to worry about his job. Rigney wanted to show that no player was above criticism, so the first time that Mays overthrew a cutoff man, Rigney stopped play to censure him. On another day, he benched Mays for a practice game. Sitting out of uniform in the stands, he saw Mays pacing in the dugout. "I don't think I could have made him sit down if I had been on the bench," he later said. "Even where I was sitting in left field, I was conscious of that glare he sent my way."

Durocher had reprimanded or corrected Mays aplenty but had done so privately, and with a smile, or in a way that left Mays encouraged and motivated. Those subtleties were lost on Rigney; Mays found him remote and cheerless.

Rigney's instincts weren't necessarily wrong. He needed to restore the morale of some of his neglected players but not at the expense of the one Giant who was most sensitive to criticism. Besides, the notion that all the players should be treated the same was nonsense. As one Giant official said, "Rigney was out to prove that Willie was just one of twenty-five guys. You could see Willie looking at him out of the corner of his eye for a couple of kind words, but Rig never even had a smile for him. Well, Willie ain't one of twenty-five. If it helps him to tell him how good he is, why not tell him how good he is? That's what I always thought leadership meant."

Mays did not dispute that he needed compliments. "There is some general truth to that, particularly about me wanting to be praised, because it always seemed to me that when the fans cheered, I did better," he said. "I believe this is true of every ballplayer who's ever lived."

Marguerite saw how upset Willie was and, after spring training, she called Durocher, even though they had never met. Maybe he could help. Durocher already knew of the problems. He had given Rigney a single piece of advice: "The one thing you must never do is holler at Willie." Which Rigney did the first day. After Marguerite spoke to Durocher, he called Willie and told him that Rigney's style might be different, but he appreciated him every bit as much. "Actually," Durocher recalled, "I thought Rigney was being stupid. But I didn't tell that to Willie."

Winning would have alleviated some of the managerial tensions, but the Giants were no longer a winning team. With few exceptions, their veterans were all past their prime. Hank Thompson missed half the year in part because of a beaning; it was his last season. Don Mueller's batting average slipped below .300 for the first time in four years; he finished at .269. There was little magic left in Dusty Rhodes's bat.

The Giants had some talented players in the minors, but they needed more experience, and Stoneham was unwilling to bring in high-priced players for their immediate needs. As the losses piled up, familiar faces left the team. Alvin Dark and Whitey Lockman were traded. Sal Maglie had been dispatched the previous year. Johnny Antonelli threw well but would be the only starting pitcher with a winning record. A humiliating low point occurred when the Dodgers' Carl Erskine threw a no-hitter against the Giants on May 12 in a nationally televised game. It was Mays's first year in which the Giants lost more games than they won and finished in the second division. Attendance dwindled.

Mays looked around one day and realized that, with all the turnover, he barely knew half his teammates. They had been his family, and now many were gone. "You don't lose players that are part of a winning tradition, such as Dark and Lockman, without feeling an emptiness," he said.

Tensions between Mays and Rigney came to a head just after the All-Star break. In a game in St. Louis, Mays hit a pop fly behind home plate and stood there, expecting the ball to be caught in foul territory. But the wind blew it back, and the catcher was in fair ground when he gloved it. When Mays returned to the dugout, Rigney said, "I'm fining you a hundred dollars for not running."

Mays sulked, and after the game he approached Rigney and asked about the fine.

"You know why," he said.

Mays said it was a fluke. When was the last time he'd not run out a fair ball? He said he was guilty of misjudgment, not lack of effort.

"That's just the way it's going to be," Rigney said. "No exceptions, you or anybody else."

Mays was still steamed. He thought Rigney was trying too hard to manage him, giving him too many signs, too much instruction. Durocher just let him play and then corrected him when bad habits formed. And he never fined Mays. He gave him money. The incident in St. Louis angered Mays so much that he called Durocher, who told him there was nothing Willie could do but accept it.

The season only got worse. The Giants won eight out of twenty in July, due in part to one of the worst slumps of Mays's career. A reassessment was in order: yes, Mays put up terrific numbers, but he was an unusually streaky hitter, and when he didn't hit, the Giants didn't win. (Durocher told reporters that all hitters are streak hitters.) Rigney began touting rookie outfielder Jackie Brandt, a blond, baby-faced slugger acquired midseason, as if he were the next Willie Mays. The real one simmered.

The Giants finished in sixth place, 67–87, and twenty-six games behind the Dodgers, who won the pennant in the final weekend of the season. Mays was no longer the Giants' lucky charm, and while he led the league in stolen bases with 40 and was the first 30–30 National League player (he had 36 homers), his average fell to .296, the first time he had finished below .300 for a full season.

Meanwhile, across the Harlem River, Mickey Mantle had enjoyed one of the greatest offensive years in baseball history (.353 average, 52 homers, 130 RBIs), good for both the MVP and the Triple Crown. The Yankees beat the Dodgers in the World Series, 4–3, with Mantle slugging three home runs. In the competition among Willie, Mickey, and the Duke—or just between Mays and Mantle—the Yankee won decisively.

Reporters speculating on what caused Mays's midseason slump, or his "off-year" in general, cited two factors: he couldn't play without Durocher, or he couldn't play as a married man. The speculation annoyed him. Mays did not concede that he had a bad year and felt underappreciated. He played in 152 games, six more than the team's next highest player, shortstop Daryl Spencer, who hit only .221 with fourteen home runs. Why wasn't anyone complaining about him? Mays, however, did acknowledge that "in some ways, it was one of my most difficult seasons."

Many professional athletes have lost money through financial fraud or crackpot business deals or poor investments. They've been misled, duped, cheated; they've paid the price for getting too rich, too young, too fast. Mays's financial problems overlapped some of these themes. There were unfulfilled promises, bad advice, loans not repaid, and lousy business ventures. But most of his economic difficulties were self-inflicted, and they began in New York. He always enjoyed spending money on creature comforts—the new cars, the $250 suits, the silk ties. As a kid, he saw that the most respected men in Fairfield drove the best automobiles, wore the finest clothes, and carried the most cash. As a young player, he saw Durocher's profligate spending, on homes, apparel, and furnishings, as evidence of success and sophistication. He liked that, though if he had looked closer, he might also have seen Durocher's huge debts. Now married, Mays had a wife who also enjoyed luxury.

They bought a home at 502 West 168th Street, in the Washington Heights section of Manhattan. The building, three stories high but only eighteen feet wide, had been rebuilt and refurbished "until it looked like a doll house," wrote Dan Daniel. "It's painted black in front with white trimmings. Inside are ornate furnishings the likes of which no ballplayer ever before had lived with."

The dining room featured one wall covered with mirrors. A heavy chandelier, with crystal-like diamonds, hovered over the table, which had a thin glass top and curved marble legs. Heavy drapes marched across the wall; a large potted plant filled a corner. In the game room stood upsidedown wineglasses with delicate stems, baskets of Italian wines, barstools, and a velvet-smooth pool table. The bedroom had brocaded drapes and bedspreads, yet another ornate chandelier, and another wall of mirrors. (Mirrors were prominent in Mays's homes throughout his life.)

The home was gorgeous, ostentatious—and unaffordable, and rumors that Mays was broke began to spread. In an interview with the *Pittsburgh Courier,* Marghuerite insisted they were saving money, but the newspaper was skeptical: "Among the things she speaks of is a lavish home upon which was spent some $35,000 for furnishings and the services of contractors. The three-story domicile is completely air-conditioned, from top to bottom, and it might be stated rather candidly that Mrs. Mays did not satisfy her luxurious tastes in decor at a neighborhood hardware store."

Mays was broke. He had gone to Stoneham for advances, or loans, on his future salary. Stoneham was generous to a fault, occasionally giving Mays thousand-dollar "bonuses" during the season. In 1955, Mays bought a Cadillac for $5,900 and billed the Giants, asking them to take it out of his salary. At the end of the season, Stoneham simply made a present of the car. By 1957, Mays's official salary was just under $50,000 a year, making him the highest-paid Giant in history. Still, Stoneham acquiesced to Mays's requests for advances, and by the early 1960s, Mays owed the Giants more than $65,000. He made no effort to pass the blame. He later acknowledged, "The problem wasn't bad investments, in stocks or ventures. . . . It was buying a new car bigger or sooner than you had to, or 20 tailor-made suits instead of half a dozen you could buy off the rack, or paying retail for the most expensive pool table you ever saw, or getting married and throwing thousands into drapes and carpet and even wallpaper—that was me."

Mays did not dig himself out of debt until the mid-1960s, and he was so consumed by his losses that money surpassed almost everything else as a source of worry.

In 1957, the relationship between Rigney and Mays improved. They seemed to have recognized they were stuck with each other so they might as well make the most of it. With one year under his belt, Rigney didn't have to prove his authority. At spring training, he stopped dwelling on Mays's shortcomings and made sure the young players were aware of his skills. "When they hit it to him," he told his infielders, "please go to a base. Don't confuse the issue by asking me why. Just be there. He knows."

One of the players asked, "What does he know, skip?"

Rigney briefly pondered the question, then snapped, "I don't know what he knows, but Willie knows. So just get your ass to a base."

According to Mays, Rigney stopped overmanaging him. "He told me to go out and play my game," he said. "Nothing more, nothing less. And I did."

The two still had their disagreements. When Mays, battling a midseason slump, was taking batting practice, Rigney tried to give him some advice; Mays loudly rejected it, saying he should be left alone while swinging. "It was one of the few displays of temper by Mays as a Giant," the *Sporting News* reported, calling it a "prima donna outburst."

But Rigney finally understood that Mays responded to carrots, not sticks, and he embraced him almost as extravagantly as Durocher had.

"All I can say is that he is the greatest player I have ever seen, bar none," he told reporters in 1959. "When he's around it makes me feel good just to walk into the locker room and start suiting up. I know then I have a chance."

In an interview after he retired, Rigney said he eventually realized that Mays did not need a manager so much as a father figure. "He thought I didn't care about him," Rigney said. "Well, I did care about him." His style was simply different than Durocher's. The problem was not that Mays didn't like the manager but that he didn't know whether the manager liked him. Rigney acknowledged, "If I had to do it over again, I think I would have been a little more active in his life."

The reconciliation between Mays and Rigney could not save the Giants in 1957. They lost three young players to the military draft: first baseman Bill White, who had twenty-two home runs in his rookie season the previous year; and two outfielders, rookie Willie Kirkland and Jackie Brandt. On the first day of spring training, the Giants' projected starting catcher, Bill Sarni, walked onto the field and dropped straight to the ground, suffering a heart attack at twenty-nine; he survived, but his playing career was over. The Giants had to wait another year before they could rebuild. Instead, they brought back former stars—Bobby Thomson from Milwaukee, Whitey Lockman from St. Louis—as if to revive a play that had long been shut down. Stoneham liked reuniting his Giant family, which was a noble sentiment, but nostalgia doesn't win games. On May 3, the Giants were in sixth place, and they stayed there the rest of the year. Rigney looked tortured, his gray hair now turning white, his body looking more emaciated, his cigarettes piling up in ashtrays, his ulcers worsening, a man who had not turned forty but whose nickname—"Old Bones"—fit him well. His team had quit on him. After losses, wrote one reporter, "the ballplayers dressed in silence or sat, heads down, eyes absently pointed either to a questionable future or a happier past. Men walked aimlessly about, barefoot, or sat reading their scant fan mail or else they hurried to get out of the dank sepulchral clubhouse." The players said their lethargy mirrored the empty cavern in which they performed. "Playing before crowds of twelve hundred in the Polo Grounds," Lockman said, "was like walking through a morgue."

Mays didn't quit, and for that reason alone 1957 may have been his finest year. He had more ground than ever to cover in the outfield. In right was plodding Don Mueller, who at thirty had slowed down even further but was still a spring chicken compared to left fielder Hank Sauer. The heavy-legged slugger, who arrived in the off-season, was forty. And on the bases Mays was never better. In a game against the Phillies on April 21, he performed one of his most exhilarating excursions. With the score tied 1–1 in the ninth, he came to bat with one out against Robin Roberts. He chopped the ball to short and slid under the wide throw. The ball bounced away, so Mays tried for second and slid in safely. He then stole third with another slide under the tag. Then, on a short hit to right, he slid safely home with the winning run. Mays had slid around the entire diamond.

A month later, at Wrigley Field, he went from first to third on a ground-out and then stole home. On several occasions, he scored from second on groundouts. Infielders began committing errors on hurried throws when-ever Mays was on base—a valuable contribution but impossible to record. He also executed one of his finest, and most dangerous, catches that year at Forbes Field in Pittsburgh. The center field fence was so far away—462 feet—that the Pirates stationed an enclosed batting cage there because they figured no one could hit the ball that far. But against the Giants, Roberto Clemente did just that. Mays ran headlong to the cage, leaped, and caught the ball. "We thought from the bench, 'Here's the end of Wil-lie,'" pitcher Mike McCormick recalls. "But he kept his feet the whole time."

Young fans found in Mays a role model for their own aspirations. Most kids don't make it to the majors, but John Curtis did, and his dreams began when he walked into the Polo Grounds as a small boy from Long Island. Sitting in the upper deck, he saw "that expansive green grass field and the perfect symmetry of the [diamond]—it was like seeing Oz for the first time." He watched in awe as the players took their warm-ups, "aghast" that even a pop fly, appearing so easy to handle on television, required so much skill and judgment to actually catch. And then Mays came out, and everything he did looked so easy. Loping across the field to catch fly balls. Throwing perfect strikes to home plate from three hundred feet. Spray-ing line drives to all parts of the ballpark. "And during the game," Curtis recalled, "he was so colorful and so full of energy. He just seemed at that moment to symbolize what that whole game was about. The harnessing of immense talent. And from that moment on, I knew that that was what I wanted to do. If I was going to grow into a baseball player, I wanted to be someone with the authority and grace of Willie."

Starting in 1970, Curtis played in the major leagues for sixteen years, a respectable left-handed pitcher (lifetime ERA, 3.96) praised as much for his verbal eloquence as his fastball.

The fans showed their appreciation of Mays in 1957 by voting him as the All-Star center fielder—they tried to, anyway. He was leading the vote until the end, when the commissioner's office received a sudden ground-swell of 550,000 ballots from Cincinnati. If counted, the starting team for the National League would have consisted of seven players from Cincinnati, quite a showing for a fourth-place team. (Only Stan Musial survived the ballot stuffing.) The prospect of Gus Bell starting ahead of Willie Mays was too much to bear for Commissioner Ford C. Frick. He rejected the late Cincinnati votes, securing Mays's starting berth. (The next year, he transferred voting responsibilities to the players, coaches, and managers; not until 1970 would fans cast ballots again.)

In the All-Star Game, Mays hit cleanup behind Aaron and Musial, and in two late-inning rallies, he delivered a single and a triple, with an RBI and two runs scored. But the American League won, 6–5.

From the beginning of spring training, speculation had intensified that both the Dodgers and the Giants would be leaving, raising the possibility that New York would be without a National League team. Over the past five years, the Braves, Browns, and Athletics had all moved to new cities, confirming a fundamental shift in the game. Baseball teams were no longer simply sources of community pride or family touchstones that connected the generations. They were hard financial assets to be leveraged, bargained, and maximized, capable of being moved around the country like pieces on a chess board.

But the asset itself—the baseball team—was only as valuable as its players, and by 1957 both the Dodgers and the Giants were declining teams with only one megastar between them. With or without Willie Mays, baseball's transcontinental expansion would occur, but Mays was the source of New York's deepest sorrow and California's greatest hope.

The Dodgers, like the Giants, had an aging ballpark with inadequate parking for an increasingly suburban fan base that could now watch games on television. The difference was that the Dodgers were both popular and highly profitable. The Giants were neither.

In 1956, the Giants drew 629,179 fans, dead last in the National League and a decline of 46 percent since 1954. Not since 1943, during World War II, had so few people attended Giant games. In 1956 and 1957, only the Washington Senators drew fewer fans than the Giants. Unlike their money-losing years from 1948 to 1953, the Giants did squeak out profits, but they could not keep pace with their Gotham rivals. Between 1947 and 1956, the Giants earned $405,926; the Dodgers earned $3.5 million, and the Yankees, $3.6 million.

On the field and at the gate, the Giants were a woebegone third in a three-team town. They made money only because of their increasing media revenue, receiving $600,000 a year for their television rights. That income, combined with Stoneham's insistence in years past that the Giants would never leave New York, convinced some people that the team would stay but find another stadium. What everyone acknowledged was that the Giants would be out of the Polo Grounds by 1962, when the team's lease expired.

While Stoneham made relatively few public statements, Dodger owner Walter O'Malley was more outspoken. For several years, he had demanded public support for a new domed stadium at the intersection of Flatbush and Atlantic avenues in Brooklyn. At the same time, he'd been flirting with the city fathers of Los Angeles, who were pleading with him to move the Dodgers there. O'Malley sold Ebbets Field in 1956, and the following February, as spring training was to begin, he acquired the territorial rights to Los Angeles from the Chicago Cubs, which had a minor league team there. O'Malley continued to insist that he wanted to stay in New York, but he was laying the groundwork to move.

By spring training, Stoneham had already decided to move the team to Minneapolis and had begun enlarging his minor-league stadium there. In March, O'Malley met with him to discuss the Dodgers' consideration of Los Angeles, and he asked Stoneham if he would consider San Francisco instead of Minneapolis. O'Malley knew that San Francisco was eager for a team, and it made more sense to transport two National League teams to California—and a historic rivalry at that—than one team.

Stoneham initially said he wasn't interested, but it wasn't long before San Francisco Mayor George Christopher began taking secret weekend shuttles to New York to meet with Stoneham. "Getting a major league team into San Francisco," Christopher said, "is a crusade with us." He pledged that the city would build a new park with 40,000 to 50,000 seats; parking lots and concession deals would be part of the package. The mayor predicted annual profits of $200,000 to $300,000 for the Giants. While O'Malley continued to stall and haggle, Stoneham was sold. In May, he called Russ Hodges into his office and asked, "Do you want to move to California?" (He did.) Stoneham said the Giants would be going to the West Coast with or without the Dodgers.

Had Stoneham wanted to stay in New York, he had one more valuable chip to play. In June, the St. Louis Cardinals made him a $1 million offer ($750,000 in cash plus several players) for Willie Mays. He seriously considered the deal but didn't pull the trigger because of the club's pending transfer to San Francisco. Cardinal general manager Frank Lane told the *St. Louis Globe Democrat* that he made four separate offers for Mays, to no avail. Chub Feeney told Lane that if the Giants traded Mays and then moved to San Francisco, the people in that region would throw him into the San Francisco Bay.

Only the formalities of the Giants' move remained. In May, the National League voted in favor of a resolution allowing the Dodgers and the Giants to leave New York, and on July 18, Stoneham held a press conference at the Polo Grounds, overlooking the elevated railroad that had brought hundreds of thousands of fans to Giant games since 1890. "There is no longer any chance to survive here," he said. "I have been in this city fifty years and am more sentimental about New York and the Giants than any of my board of directors, but I must recommend to them that we can no longer hold the Polo Grounds."

New York City's council president, Abe Stark, condemned San Francisco's mayor as a "pirate," but Stoneham blamed the fans. The Polo Grounds drew more than 20,000 fans only twice in the entire season. "We're sorry to disappoint the kids of New York," he said, "but we didn't see many of their parents out there at the Polo Grounds in recent years."

On August 19, in an 8–1 vote, the Giants' board made the move official, though the vote was only for show. Stoneham could have overruled it. He and his sister, Mary Aufderhar, held a controlling interest in the National Exhibition Company, which owned the franchise. Stoneham, who received a salary of $70,000 a year, cited no personal responsibility for the team's hardship, but he was not blameless. For years he failed to invest adequately in either his team or the stadium, nor had he pursued alternative stadium options. But between 1952 and 1956, the Giants were one of only two National League teams that paid dividends. As the principal shareholders in the Giants, Stoneham and his sister received the bulk of those payments. (Horace's son, Pete, was also on the payroll.)

The one dissenting voice was that of Joan Whitney Payson, a fifty-four-year-old heiress who had acquired a 9 percent stake in the Giants. She was American royalty: her mother, Helen Hay Whitney, was the daughter of John Hay, who was an aide to President Lincoln and secretary of state for President William McKinley. Her father, the industrialist Payne Whitney, was the son of William C. Whitney, secretary of the navy for President Grover Cleveland. Her brother, John Hay "Jock" Whitney, owned four newspapers, including the *New York Herald Tribune* and *Newsday*. In 1927, she inherited, along with her brother, her father's estate, with an estimated value of $239 million, the largest then recorded in the United States. She was one of America's richest women.

Joan Payson loved horses, fine paintings, and miniature antique furniture. And she loved Willie Mays. A Giants fan since the age of six, she was so enthralled with Mays that she not only watched him at the Polo

Grounds but would take the train to Philadelphia to watch him there. Desperate to keep him, and the Giants, in New York, she offered to buy the team from Stoneham. He refused. But Payson vowed—somehow, some way—to bring Mays back to New York.

On October 8, the Dodgers officially notified the National League of their intention to move to Los Angeles.

In later years, the person who was most closely associated with the two teams' leaving New York, and who remained the most vilified, was Walter O'Malley; perhaps there was more sympathy for Stoneham because his plight in Harlem seemed beyond repair or because the Giants were not as integrated into the community as the Dodgers were in Brooklyn. But Stoneham still broke the hearts of fans who couldn't believe that the Giants, one of the founding clubs of the National League, would leave the city they had played in since 1883. "Horace, one of New York's own, will have to adapt himself to the way and the habits, and the manner of life, of a city more than 3,000 miles away from Toots Shor's," Dan Daniel wrote.

Willie Mays never believed the rumors that the Giants might leave New York. Couldn't believe them. The team had simply been there too long. So the news shocked him as much as it did most everyone else. And the prospects were disconcerting. He knew nothing about San Francisco. New York was home: everything was familiar; the fans loved him. He didn't particularly want to say good-bye to New York, and New York certainly didn't want to say good-bye to him.

A letter writer to the *Sporting News* said, "I don't mind the Giants, as a club, moving, but what kind of justice is it that would move Willie Mays? . . . Let the rest go anywhere they please, but leave us Willie." Gay Talese, with characteristic verve, wrote in the *New York Times*: "Undoubtedly, the exportation from New York to San Francisco of the 180-pound package of rare tenderloin labeled Willie Mays Jr. must be recognized by Manhattan historians as a grave event."

Mays turned twenty-six that year, and by most appearances, he looked and played as he had since he arrived in New York. But he was no longer the unstudied Alabama youth who showed up in 1951. He had outgrown the playful little brother role, the brunt of teammate jokes. His laughter and smile were not as conspicuous, the pepper games less frequent. The Say Hey Kid was no longer a kid. Even his cap didn't fly off as much, though that was due to adjustments by the manufacturer. "Willie's lid flew off so easily because of his receding forehead," cap maker Tim McAuliff said, "so I just reversed the sweatband and it made for more friction, which keeps his hat in place. Or at least more than it used to."

Bill Rigney, in an interview with *Sport* in 1958, said the first time he noticed a real change in Mays was the year before. "Willie was talking to some reporters while we were waiting for a plane, and he was dressed well and he spoke well," Rigney said. "He's still the same good-natured, lovable guy he always was, but he's no longer naive. I suddenly realized that Willie of 1951 was gone forever."

The stickball games were also gone. Marghuerite believed they further drained his energy. "I don't like him to do it," she said. "Nobody knows how much a game takes out of Willie, because he gives so much to it, but show him a piece of wood and ball, and that's it."

She had a point. The game did take a lot out of Mays, physically and emotionally, and 1957 saw him hospitalized during the season for undisclosed reasons. He rested for three days at Harkness Pavilion in the first of four or five vaguely defined hospitalizations—"exhaustion" was usually cited—during his career. But the first incident should have been a warning about the unrelenting pressures on him.

It was always a silent struggle for Mays to meet expectations that could never be satisfied, and the one person who understood it was Jackie Robinson. Whatever their differences politically, Robinson recognized the monumental challenge that confronted someone so young and unprepared. On Opening Day 1955, at a game between the Giants and the Dodgers, Robinson said, "I don't envy Willie. He'll be playing under the most terrific pressure all year, more than he can handle. Everybody is expecting him to duplicate or better his great season of 1954. They won't settle for anything less. Look what happened today. Every time he came to bat, the fans started yelling for a home run. Every place, every time, it's 'We want Willie. We want Willie.' Wherever the team goes, Willie is the center of attention. Sure he's great, maybe the greatest, but he's still a kid."

Mays's bubbly media image persisted long after it could be accurately applied to him. Bill White, for example, lived with Willie and Marghuerite when he joined the Giants in 1956. "I never saw the stickball-in-the-street phase," he said. "I never heard him say, 'Say Hey,' except in television commercials. All I saw was a man with a good baseball mind. It used to take us about forty-five minutes to drive to the park, and every day Willie would talk to me about the pitchers we were going to face: what they threw, what their ball did, what to expect in the clutch. He would tell me who you could steal off and who you couldn't, pitchers and catchers both. He would even tell me how to play the different batters at first base. And this was when he was in his 'larky' stage as far as the press was concerned."

White adds in an interview five decades later: "The 'Say Hey Kid' helped his image, but there was a man under there that they never saw, a man of great pride, intelligence, and integrity."

Even his given name—Willie—may have reinforced a disparaging image. Unlike, say, "William" or "Willard," "Willie" was a child's name, and according to Bill White, it was a name that newspapers often gave rookie black players. In his own case, the *Sporting News* announced his promotion to the Giants by describing him as "Willie White . . . a fast, powerful Negro first baseman." White told reporters that he was "Bill."

If Mays was seen only as one-dimensional—a supernova in center field who brought joy to the Polo Grounds—that was more than enough for any Giant fan. In 1957, he laid to rest any notion that either a new wife or a new manager would doom him. His .333 average was the third best of his career, while his .407 on-base percentage was his second best. He had a twenty-one-game hitting streak, which equaled one he'd had in 1954 and was a career high. He led the league in triples (twenty), slugging percentage (.629), and stolen bases (thirty-eight), and he was the first player in National League history to hit at least twenty doubles, triples, and home runs in one year. In December, he received the Gold Glove from the *Sporting News,* the first year the award was given. He was the only National League outfielder chosen; in subsequent years, three outfielders from each league were selected.

It was fitting that he ended in a blaze of glory. Though he was a New York Giant for only five full seasons, the memory of his greatness was seared so deeply that he was always associated with that team, in that town, at that time, and New York fans would always claim him as their own.

The final day at the Polo Grounds, September 29, was cool and gray, the flags whipping in the wind. Ray Robinson, a sportswriter, said he was "one of 11,606 pallbearers" who attended; his bleacher ticket cost seventy-five cents. Before the game, Bobby Thomson stood for the photographers, pointing to the left field seats. Matty Schwab, the head of the grounds crew who lived in a small apartment at the Polo Grounds, escorted Bill Rigney to center field, where they cut out a big piece of grass. Schwab wrapped it up and planted it in the outfield of the Giants' next ballpark in San Francisco. Giant old-timers were introduced to the crowd—men who had played for John McGraw, such as Carl Hubbell, as well as later Giants, such as Monte Irvin and Sal Maglie. They all stood with grim faces, as if they were at a wake—which, in a way, they were.

The most elegant honoree was Blanche McGraw, John's widow, who still went south with the team every spring and rarely missed a home game in Section 19. She was presented with a bouquet of roses and wept softly into her corsage.

In tribute to past glories, Rigney started all his players who had been on the 1954 championship team: Johnny Antonelli on the mound, Wes Westrum catching, Whitey Lockman at first, and Don Mueller, Dusty Rhodes, and Willie Mays in the outfield.

The game was a hapless affair against the Pirates. Roger Angell, sitting in the upper deck with his daughter, said it was the quietest crowd he had ever heard at any game. In between innings, a man stood with a sign: GIANT FAN 55 YEARS. Another sign said: GO, GIANTS, GO. Another: STAY, WILLIE, STAY. Gallows humor was in order. "If the Giants don't win," said one fan, "nobody will show up tomorrow."

But Mays demonstrated his virtuoso skills. In the first inning, the Pirates' Bob Skinner drove a ball into deep left center that rolled all the way to the wall. Rhodes gave chase while Mays positioned himself in medium left center. Rhodes finally reached the ball, picked it up, and threw it to Mays. But the ball came in low, skipping several feet in front of him. Mays bent down and trapped it with his back to home plate, rose, whirled, and fired. Skinner was trying for an inside-the-park homer, but the throw was a one-hop strike to the catcher—not as balletic as the Throw in 1951, not as dramatic as the throw after the Catch in 1954—but fierce and graceful nonetheless. The runner was out.

In the bottom of the seventh, Mays came to bat with the Giants on their way to losing, 9–1. The defeat would leave them with a season record of 69–85, twenty-six games out of first place. There was not much riding on this particular at-bat. Mays grounded the ball to third base—a routine grounder, an easy play—and third baseman Gene Freese fielded the ball cleanly. Then he got lazy, and he relaxed and floated the ball to first. It was accurate and ordinary—but too late. Mays had blown past the bag for an infield hit, running as though the pennant were at stake. "It was my first time in my thirty-five-plus years of watching ball games I had ever seen a man beat out a routine ground ball that had been fielded cleanly," Arnold Hano wrote. It was Mays's second hit of the game.

Mays came to bat for a final time with one out in the bottom of the ninth. The fans cheered when he stepped into the box. He kept his head down, adjusted his feet, then focused on the hurler. He took the first pitch and then another, but the applause never stopped. Instead, it gained momentum and strength, the fans standing and roaring with undiluted passion, the noise rising from the ancient concrete stanchions until Mays finally had to acknowledge it. He stepped out of the box and reached toward his cap and touched the bill as though he were going to lift it in thanks—then he froze. He lowered his hand, gripped the bat again, and stepped back in.

After the game, Mays said he was going to doff his hat but checked the impulse. He feared it would have been seen as showboating.

In Ted Williams's last at-bat at Fenway Park, he hit a home run, but he refused to tip his cap to the cheering fans. Williams, however, was not motivated by humility. As John Updike famously wrote, "Gods do not answer letters."

Mays would have liked such a farewell, a home run in his final at-bat, but he grounded out. Nevertheless, he was cheered again as he returned to the dugout.

"I never felt so nervous," he said after the game. "My hands were shaking. It was worse than any World Series game. I got a home run my first at-bat in the Polo Grounds and I wanted to bow out with another. I tried very hard to show them how I felt. I wanted to do something for the fans."

Watching the game was twelve-year-old Lanny Davis, who had come with his father to say farewell to Willie. The boy found consolation in his last at-bat. "My hero hustled to the very end," he later recalled. The game ended. "All of a sudden," Davis said, "I saw number 24 literally leap up the steps of the Giants' dugout, right in front of me, so close I almost touched him, and there he was, tearing full speed toward center field to the safety of the clubhouse. As soon as I saw Willie lead the way out of the dugout, I had only one thought: I have to shake Willie's hand and thank him and say good-bye. I have to! Without the slightest hesitation, I jumped over the rail and ran after him."

He had plenty of company. Though the voice on the loudspeaker asked people to stay off the field, thousands swarmed onto the grounds, a whirlwind of affection, nostalgia, anger, and excitement. They pulled out the home plates on the diamond and in the bullpen. They uprooted the bases and the pitcher's rubber, which had been nailed into the ground with eighteen-inch spikes; a girl with a penknife sliced it to pieces and shared them with friends. They ripped down the canopy over the bullpen, tore it apart, and dispersed the shreds. They yanked out telephones and flung telephone books and snipped the green foam rubber covering the fences. They dug up large clunks of sod and dirt and carried them out in cans and boxes. Lanny Davis, who in time became a prominent Washington lawyer and special counsel to President Clinton, stuffed dirt in his pockets and kept it in a paper cup in a desk drawer for years.

Members of the grounds crew, some of whom had been tending the green lawn there for more than thirty years, stood along the third base line. They had wanted to say good-bye to the players, the coaches, and maybe even the sacred terrain, but they could only watch in silent horror.

Before the game, Rigney had warned his players that seething fans were going to rush the field, and he instructed them to drop their hats and gloves and just make it to the clubhouse. Most of the players did that, though Mays held on to his cap. Clutching it against his chest, he had to avoid so many people that even Dusty Rhodes beat him. All over the field, the fans were cheering: "We want Willie! We want Willie!" Then hundreds gathered at the foot of the clubhouse, and leading the serenade was Lanny Davis: "We want Willie!"

Mays heard the cheers and was deeply moved—he recalled other times, in '51 and '54, when fans stood in the same spot and chanted his name and he returned their adoration with waves and smiles—but Rigney had instructed all the players to stay inside. Still they called his name. Mays quickly changed his clothes and figured it was the last time he would sit in front of his battered wooden locker, see the faded green concrete walls, and smell the room's pungent blend of sweat, liniment, and tobacco.

Outside, Lanny suddenly realized something was wrong. He couldn't find his father. At first he wasn't afraid, but as the mob grew in size and the yelling became more urgent, he grew frightened, panicked. Then he felt a hand on his shoulder. It was his father.

"How did you know where I was?" he asked.

"I knew where you'd be."

Then Willie came out, just briefly, and waved to the fans. "He looked down the stairs," Davis said more than fifty years later. "He looked at me, and he pointed his finger at me, as if to say, 'Hi, kid; bye, kid.' To this day, I am certain he was talking to me, only me."

All of the players were soon out the door, but according to one report, "Willie, alone of all the Giants, left with the cheer of the crowd in his ear."

The mood turned uglier outside. Instead of pining for Willie, they called for the owner: "We want Stoneham! We want Stoneham—with a rope around his neck!" Stoneham had not been seen at the ballpark all day.

At least Walter O'Malley attended the Dodgers' final game at Ebbets Field, where it was announced to the crowd that the year's attendance was 1,026,158—"the thirteenth straight year over a million. And the only team to leave after doing it."

Gladys Gooding, the organist for sixteen years, played "Don't Ask Me Why I'm Leaving," "May the Good Lord Bless and Keep You," and "Auld Lang Syne."

• • •

New York had no National League champion in 1957. The Milwaukee Braves, led by the young stars Hank Aaron and Eddie Mathews, won the first of two consecutive pennants.

An era had ended, and at the Giants' final game at the Polo Grounds, Blanche McGraw was the last to leave, still clutching her red roses. "I still can't believe it," she said as she was helped to her car. "New York can never be the same to me."

No more Giants. No more National League. No more Willie. For any New Yorker, it was hard to grasp. "I didn't feel anything," Roger Angell wrote. "Nothing at all. I guess I just couldn't believe it. But it's true, all right. The flags are down, the lights in the temple are out, and the Harlem River flows lonely to the sea."

CHAPTER EIGHTEEN

MIRALOMA DRIVE

Few American cities have inspired more rapturous prose than San Francisco. Described as "the City of Shining Hills" and "the Paris of the West," it lies on a thumb-shaped peninsula over forty-two rolling hills, with the Pacific Ocean on one side and a bay on the other. The California Coast Ranges serve as a rugged backdrop. The city has a distinctive, almost lyrical climate—the swirling afternoon winds, the pale autumnal sunshine, the hazy trademark fog, celebrated as "wistfully curling tendrils" that envelop the city in romance and mystery. The San Andreas Fault adds a subterranean peril. In 1958, its history could be plumbed for both triumph and tragedy: the riches of the storied Gold Rush (1849) and the heartbreak of a staggering earthquake (1906); the splendor of the Golden Gate Bridge (1937) and the hedonism of a port catering to its seafarers (every night). San Francisco was a magnet for writers, poets, and musicians, a haven for various Bohemian movements since the 1840s, all of which created a satisfying image of tolerance and sophistication.

Long before the Giants arrived, it was also a baseball town. The San Francisco Seals were a charter member of the Pacific Coast League in 1903, the mild climate allowing for a longer season than even the majors played. In 1931, the team moved into its own ballpark, Seals Stadium, in the Mission District, and the following year fans saw for the first time the eighteen-year-old son of an Italian fisherman who grew up on the North Shore. Joe DiMaggio, in his second year with the Seals, hit .340, had a hitting streak of sixty-one games, and created a standard by which all future center fielders in San Francisco would be compared.

The Seals were winners, racking up championships every decade, and they long flourished under manager Lefty O'Doul, a former major league player who was a San Francisco native and fan favorite. In its final season, 1957, the team won its fourteenth title before being dispatched to Phoenix, where it became a minor league affiliate of the Giants. The ball that recorded the final out of the San Francisco Seals was sent to Cooperstown.

Joe DiMaggio wasn't San Francisco's only connection to the major leagues. The city had produced quite a few star players, including Joe's brothers Vince and Dom. Also from the area were pitcher Lefty Gomez, catcher Ernie Lombardi, and shortstop Joe Cronin, all future Hall of Famers, as well as second baseman Tony Lazzeri, who was part of the Yankees' Murderers' Row, and first baseman Dolph Camilli, who was the National League MVP in 1941.

Baseball had deep roots in San Francisco, and the fans did not consider themselves novices. Pro football arrived in 1946, when the 49ers became the first major league professional sports team in the Bay Area. This breakthrough affirmed the area's rising economic power in the postwar boom years, but without a big league baseball team, San Francisco was still a minor league town. Major League Baseball, for its part, needed San Francisco as well as Los Angeles as much as those cities needed the big leagues. As early as 1947, a monograph was prepared for the majors that described the country's demographic shift to the west and the big leagues' current geographic imbalance. The major leagues had one team in Cincinnati, the twentieth largest city in the United States and Canada, and two teams in St. Louis, the tenth largest city, but there were no teams in Los Angeles and San Francisco, the third and ninth largest, respectively. Fear of air travel was one impediment. United Airlines had introduced the DC-6 in 1946, so a team could fly from New York to Los Angeles in less than half the time it took to reach St. Louis by train. But most major league executives, fearing that an entire team could be lost in one disaster, preferred the rails. By the late 1950s, those fears had receded.

San Francisco aggressively pursued big league baseball even before it had a specific team in sight. In 1954, the voters approved a $5 million general obligation bond to provide for the construction of a new stadium. A two-thirds majority was needed. All four daily newspapers supported it, as did the entire business community, and that commitment helped persuade Horace Stoneham to scrap his plan to go to Minneapolis and move to San Francisco instead. One potential problem: Stoneham feared that "San Francisco" had too many letters to fit on the team's road uniform. There was plenty of space.

While San Francisco celebrated its new team, the Giants still had to make a strong first impression and convince the loyal Seals fans that they were worthy. For that matter, the Dodgers had to win over Los Angeles as well. The problem was, neither team was particularly good. In 1957, the Dodgers finished in third place, eleven games out of first place, and their stars were gone or old. Jackie Robinson had retired; Roy Campanella's career was over. Other aging Dodger luminaries—Don Newcombe (thirty-two), Gil Hodges (thirty-four), Pee Wee Reese (thirty-nine)—were past their prime. The team still had Duke Snider and a young fireballer, Don Drysdale, who had won seventeen games in 1957, not to mention an undeveloped pitcher named Sandy Koufax, but the Boys of Summer were past their moment in the sun.

The Giants, buried in the standings for two years, may have been in worse shape. By 1958, most of the top players from the 1954 championship were gone. The Opening Day roster had six rookies, four of whom were in the starting lineup. By all rights, Stoneham should have been the team's most effective promoter; he could have owned the city. But, separated from his wife for many years and reclusive by nature, he was a solitary figure who never immersed himself in San Francisco's social or philanthropic circles, so he proved painfully inept as the franchise headliner. At his first public event in the city, at a dinner of about 150 former ballplayers from the semipro ranks, he received a hero's welcome amid a steady flow of beer. Then he tried to address the crowd. He stood up and rambled, at times incoherently, before finally sinking into his chair and mumbling, "Some of us drink too much."

All was not lost. The Giants still had Willie Mays. At twenty-six, he hadn't even reached his prime. His was the face of baseball's westward expansion.

WILLIE MAYS GOES WEST, cried the cover blurb of *Look* on April 29, 1958. (Winston Churchill appeared on the cover as well.) The story on Mays featured fifteen photographs across five pages showing his first visit to his new city as a Giant: standing at Seal Rocks to glimpse the sea lions, viewing the Golden Gate Bridge shrouded in fog, stepping off a cable car, visiting Fisherman's Wharf, chatting with Mayor Christopher, selecting Dungeness crab at an open market, and strolling across the lonely outfield of Seals Stadium.

On April 28, the cover of *Life* featured Mays, in a dark suit, white shirt, white tie, and white kerchief, riding in a convertible during San Francisco's parade welcoming the Giants. Mays was the only Giant on the cover. The actual story isn't about Mays at all; called "California Goes Big League in a Big Way," it's about Los Angeles and San Francisco welcoming the major leagues, but Mays carried the banner for both cities. The *Sporting News* told its readers: "When he goes to L.A., Mays will be more the hero than all the Dodgers. In his exhibition forays into L.A. in recent years, Willie performed such prodigious feats that the Angelinos probably would settle for Mays as a major league club all by himself."

This media focus served the Giants well. Stoneham never believed in marketing; he thought if his team won enough games or hit enough home runs, the fans would come in droves. But he had to make some efforts in his new town, so he relied on his star. Mays was the only Giant player in San Francisco in the off-season, and he stayed busy. He attended a "Welcome Willie" dinner that raised money for the Urban League of the Bay Area; he spoke at a benefit for police widows and orphans; he appeared at three Macy's stores, where he gave out autographed pictures of himself; he met with politicians and business leaders and was photographed as the first Giant putting on his new San Francisco cap.

He said all the right things. In 1957, when a Pittsburgh reporter raised the possibility of Mays's playing a "dirty trick" and not moving to California, he responded, "Mister, I like to play ball and I'd walk barefooted to San Francisco just to get into the lineup." The quote was published in the *San Francisco Examiner*.

In January, Mays was the center of one of the more unusual press conferences in baseball history. The Giants wanted to promote the signing of his 1958 contract, which would pay him $67,500, placing him third behind Ted Williams ($100,000) and Stan Musial ($80,000). Mays, Stoneham, and Rigney met with the press at Seals Stadium; without a press office, they convened in the ladies' powder room (it became a media room by Opening Day). Surrounded by fuchsia walls, lipstick mirrors, pink drapes, and—according to the *Sporting News*—"feminine paraphernalia," the men stood before television cameras and photographers to discuss batting streaks ("When I'm in a slump, anybody can get me out," Willie said. "Two years ago, I went 0-for-30 against the Cubs") and using San Francisco's hills for winter training (Mays said he wasn't "much of a hiker"). Also in the room was Marghuerite, wearing a stunning, full-length mink coat, and their white poodle, Pepi, who was battling the flu. "He's just fine now," Willie said.

The local press began its tributes to Mays at the end of the 1957 season, when several newspapers sent reporters to the Polo Grounds. On August 13, the *San Francisco Chronicle* reported: "San Franciscans who have been worrying out loud whether the sixth place Giants are good enough for the city should have been here Sunday to watch Willie Mays, baseball's greatest one man show. As long as the Giants have Willie, you have to welcome them west."

Reporters interviewed New York sportswriters, who reaffirmed Mays's singular abilities. "When San Francisco fans see Willie Mays, they'll forget about everybody else," New York writer Jim McCulley told the *Examiner*. Kenny Smith, who'd been covering the Giants since John McGraw was manager, said, Mays is "the greatest. And there'll come a time when Mays walking on the field is as important as the score."

All the while, the Giant officials did their part to drum up interest—and ticket sales—by making extravagant predictions about Mays. On February 16, *Parade* published a story by Bill Rigney, "Mays will hit 61 HOMERS." Rigney explained that the Polo Grounds, with the alleys at 450 feet and center field at 480 feet, was a terrible park for Mays, whose power was between left center and right center. He estimated that in 1957, Mays hit at least ten balls more than 460 feet that were caught; in any other park, they would have been home runs. To avoid long outs, Mays tried to pull the ball over the short fence in the left field corner, which led to bad habits.

Seals Stadium was perfect for Mays, according to his manager. Dead center was only 414 feet, while left center ranged from 370 to 404 feet. The long outs in the Polo Grounds would now be homers. "Willie Mays, either this season or during a season soon to come, will belt sixty-one homers—and maybe even more—for a new big league record," he concluded.

The park's dimensions, Rigney wrote, were only part of a new, ascendant Mays. In Seals Stadium, the wind blows to left center, Mays's sweet spot, and the weather itself would be a boon—the heat and humidity in the East are brutal, whereas San Francisco is "delightfully cool," which will preserve Willie's strength. Mays always plays hard, Rigney assured readers, but the empty stands at the Polo Grounds drained everyone's energy, and even Willie "can't help but try harder for west coast fans who have shown such great enthusiasm for the Giants." Rigney himself was going to give his star some help by not overusing him in spring training—last year, he played almost every game for six or seven innings, and he wore down during the season.

"Willie stands 5'11", weighs 185 pounds, and there isn't an ounce of fat on him. He has tremendous stamina and he's not injury-prone. . . . He's only 26. Ruth didn't hit his 60 homers till he was 32. Willie, in other words, has at least five or six more seasons to shoot for the record. . . . I predict [San Francisco] will not only help my center fielder hit 61 home runs, it also will help him—the season he does break the record—to hit .380 and drive in 150 runs." In the *Sporting News,* Rigney predicted that Mays would win the Triple Crown as well.

These predictions didn't seem outlandish in light of Mays's recent barnstorming visit to San Francisco. After the 1957 season, he had led a black troupe there in November, and his squad played two games against the local minor leaguers. During one at-bat, a retired Pacific Coast League pitcher knocked Mays to the dirt with a high, sailing fastball. On the next pitch, Mays hit a 450-foot drive over the clock in left center, one of the longest homers ever seen in Seals Stadium. In two games, Mays collected two homers and four singles in nine at-bats.

Nonetheless, Mays didn't care for Rigney's predictions; he had always ridiculed speculation that he could break Ruth's record. It wasn't that important to him, and the media scrutiny made him uncomfortable. Offensively, he strove for consistency, which meant a .300 average, 100 RBIs, and 100 runs scored. Rigney created a set of expectations that he didn't share or even covet.

Familiar with such hype, Mays had been cast in the savior's role before, but San Franciscans wanted to see for themselves if their transplanted New Yorker really could walk on (Pacific) water. Proud and provincial, the city didn't need East Coast writers to designate their heroes, and the only player in San Francisco history who'd ever posted the kind of numbers that Rigney had projected was Joe DiMaggio, playing for the Seals. The town might not be big enough for two baseball legends.

Mays had no interest in toppling sacred records or revered icons. Adjusting to a new ballpark would be challenge enough. He just wanted to play ball, and while he felt he would miss the familiar surroundings of New York and the unconditional love of the fans, he was excited about the opportunity. Maybe a new city—a new uniform, new stadium, new fans— would end the Giants' doldrums; the team needed a fresh start, and Mays himself might benefit from a different kind of life. But even before he put on a San Francisco uniform, he found himself in the center of a controversy that involved race, housing, and the city's cherished self-image.

Shortly after Mays completed his barnstorming tour, he and Marghuerite went house hunting in San Francisco. They quickly found something they liked, and on November 7, Willie paid a $100 binder as part of an offer to a real estate agent. There was no response. Mays was about to make a second offer when the house was mysteriously taken off the market. Someone had tipped off the *Chronicle* to these events, and word began to spread. Edward Howden, the director of the Council of Civic Unity of San Francisco, formed after World War II to combat racial inequality, received a call from Mays's broker, Charles Turner. But neither the *Chronicle* nor Howden could confirm that Mays had been victimized. Mays himself didn't want to draw attention to his efforts, and no public comment was made. (The timing of such a story would have been embarrassing for San Francisco, which was hosting a UNESCO conference, with prominent Americans and Asians in attendance.)

Willie and Marghuerite finally found a new, two-story home at 175 Miraloma Drive, next to the exclusive planned community of St. Francis Wood. Only three miles from Seals Stadium, the neighborhood was one of the highest points in the city and known as "the flossiest part" of town. The brick and redwood house had three bedrooms, a den, and a two-car garage. Set on a steep, winding hill, its most distinctive feature was a span of large glass windows that offered a sweeping view of the Pacific Ocean. Marghuerite toured the house with the builder, after which Willie offered $37,500 in cash—the asking price. The couple then waited. One day passed, but neither the builder nor his broker returned their calls. Once again, Turner reached out to Howden. At least this time the house was still on the market; it simply wasn't available to Willie Mays. Howden called the developer.

Walter A. Gnesdiloff was a builder who earned most of his money working for other contractors. He agreed to see Howden, and in a lengthy Sunday meeting, he said that he wanted to sell the house to Mays and had no objections on racial grounds. However, not long after he received Mays's offer, he and his wife began receiving phone calls from agitated residents in the Miraloma neighborhood. Some identified themselves; others were anonymous. Their message was the same: Gnesdiloff would be doing a "terrible thing" if he accepted Mays's offer because a Negro family would lower property values for the entire neighborhood. He also received calls from the lawyer of a builder who lived in that neighborhood and from a second builder who had several houses on the market in the vicinity. No direct threats had been issued, he told Howden, but these calls made him fear that his own livelihood would be in danger if he went through with the sale to Mays. He explained that "improvement groups," which can disapprove new buildings, would reject his future construction plans, and the builders for whom he worked wouldn't hire him.

Gnesdiloff said he had one other problem. His real estate broker, Peter Morgan, the owner of Village Realty, had told him that his firm would have nothing to do with a sale to a Negro and would not even accept Mays's offer.

Howden found Gnesdiloff credible but naive. At no point did the builder display any sign of racial animus, and he was clearly shaken by the barrage of phone calls. But he also had no understanding of this matter's significance. Willie Mays was an American hero whose arrival in San Francisco marked a watershed moment in the city's history. If he wasn't allowed to buy a house because of his race, the rejection would mock San Francisco's image of tolerance and sophistication while making it unworthy of its big league aspirations.

Howden explained that it would produce embarrassing headlines across the country and pleaded with him on the grounds of civic pride and patriotism. He also presented evidence that refuted the claims that Negroes moving into white neighborhoods lowered property values. Gnesdiloff expressed particular concern about the next-door neighbor. At Howden's suggestion, he called the neighbor and asked if they could meet with her that evening. She agreed, but when they arrived, she did not answer the bell, nor did she respond the next day to a note left for her.

That Monday, Howden worked the phones, speaking with Mays's broker and Gnesdiloff, seeking a way to make the transaction succeed while keeping the matter out of the press. Someone suggested that the builder sell the house to a third party, who would then sell it to Mays, but Howden wanted the immediate parties to work out their differences. Gnesdiloff remained noncommittal, so Howden placed a call to Mayor Christopher and asked one of his aides if the mayor would speak to Gnesdiloff. Christopher learned of the crisis that evening when he returned from an overseas trip.

By Tuesday, city supervisor Francis McCarty, who had also worked hard to bring the Giants to San Francisco, had spoken to Gnesdiloff; members of the mayor's staff had left messages for him as well. Meanwhile, Willie and Marghuerite were told by their broker that another home had been found, but they said they weren't interested. They insisted on the Miraloma house.

It became clear by Wednesday that city officials believed the solution was to find another house, any house, that the Mayses would accept. Marghuerite actually looked at one but wasn't impressed. The mayor's office was now receiving complaints about Christopher's intervention. His aides continued to scramble, and they found yet another house, later described by Howden as "in a good neighborhood but on a short street which has become heavily Negro in ownership." Again, the Mayses weren't interested, and tensions began to rise. While Willie showed little emotion, Marghuerite was insulted at the narrow choices, but the mayor's office found her too selective. Howden later wrote, "Not everyone in official circles understood why Mrs. Mays did not respond enthusiastically to the implication that this was the only street in their price bracket where they could have a home."

Gnesdiloff provided no help, citing complaints from two builders as a reason for not selling to Mays. Howden again warned him of the imminent public relations disaster for the entire city. They agreed to see the principal objector, a builder named Martin Gaehwiler, who also lived in the Miraloma neighborhood. Before the meeting, Howden and Gnesdiloff visited Willie and Marghuerite for the first time. The couple made it clear that only the Miraloma house—and the house they had originally bid on—appealed to them. Howden recalled, "They had no taste for a fight, but neither were they inclined to back away from the reported opposition. Mays said he hardly anticipated much in the way of neighborly contact but added . . . that when the kids came around to talk baseball, he would not be turning them away."

Howden and Gnesdiloff then met with Gaehwiler and his wife. In their mid to late thirties, they apparently had done well as builders, producing and selling about four high-priced houses a year. They planned on selling the Miraloma house in which they were now living and had others on the market, or about to be completed, in the neighborhood. Gaehwiler told Howden that a sale to Mays would cause them grievous financial harm, and he was quite candid in his denunciation of "colored people." When Howden reminded him that at least one Chinese and one Filipino family already lived in the area, Gaehwiler "drew a sharp distinction between these and the allegedly undesirable Negro," Howden recalled. "We went at it from every conceivable angle, but found no indication that the couple might reconsider their position."

Before Howden and Gnesdiloff left, Howden flatly predicted that Willie Mays would not adversely affect sale prices in the neighborhood and gently suggested that Gaehwiler consult with his religious adviser.

That night, Howden was told that the *Chronicle* would be publishing a story the next day, November 14, on Mays's inability to buy a house. (The *Chronicle* was the city's only daily newspaper with a black reporter.) Howden made one last plea to Gnesdiloff to change his position to give the Giants' "opening story a happy ending." It didn't work.

The front-page article was indeed a bombshell. Gnesdiloff tried to explain why he turned down the asking price for his house. "I'm just a union working man," he said. "I'd never get another job if I sold this house to that baseball player. I feel sorry for him and, if the neighbors said it was okay, I would do it."

But the neighbors said it wasn't okay. Gaehwiler told the newspaper: "I happen to have quite a few pieces of property in that area and I stand to lose a lot if colored people move in. . . . I certainly wouldn't like to have a colored family near me. . . . I told [Gnesdiloff] to use his own conscience, but that he'd get a bad name if he went through with this."

Howden's was the voice of outrage: "This shocking rejection of Mr. and Mrs. Mays as neighbors by a handful of Miraloma residents is nothing less than a civic disgrace. Regrettably, it is typical of practices in large portions of the private housing market."

The politicians tried to control the damage, though they weren't exactly rushing to Willie's aid. "I don't believe this incident typifies the feeling of the overwhelming majority of our people," Supervisor McCarty said. "I feel confident that there will be a number of offers to sell a home to Willie Mays and his family." Mayor Christopher didn't know whose side to be on. "San Francisco is a very understanding city, and it's not our practice to preclude anyone from living where he wants to, regardless of his race," he said. "On the other hand, no law requires an owner to dispose of his property."

Mays conveyed some hurt but also showed his pride and his capacity to forgive. "I'd sure like to live in San Francisco," he said. "But I didn't want to make an issue of it. I've never been through this kind of stuff before, and I'm not even mad about it now. I figure if a guy has his own problems, he's to lick them himself, and if neighbors don't want you, what's the good of buying? But they'll talk about a thing like this all over the world, and it sure looks bad for our country." He said he and Marghuerite might keep their home in Manhattan, "but this is where I'm going to play ball, and I'd sure like to live here too."

Marghuerite was less conciliatory: "Down in Alabama, where we come from, you know your place, and that's something, at least. But up here, it's all a lot of camouflage. They grin in your face and then deceive you." (Willie, not Marghuerite, was from Alabama, but her point still held.)

Newspaper and radio reporters and television crews descended on the Mayses, who were staying at a friend's house. By day's end, they had received several offers of new homes for sale, and Mayor Christopher magnanimously offered his own residence as a temporary domicile should Willie and Marghuerite find themselves without shelter.

Reporters were also calling Gnesdiloff, who finally realized the severity of the firestorm he had ignited. He contacted Howden but still wasn't certain what to do. He asked if there might be "alternative offers" for the house matching that of Mays. Howden said Gnesdiloff would have a moral obligation to Mays, since his was first, and his broker would have surely submitted another offer had there been one.

The media pressure was too great. Gnesdiloff told Howden to inform Mays that he would accept the bid, and if his broker wouldn't represent him, he would cancel his contract. Howden tried calling Mays, but the phone lines were jammed. After twenty minutes, he finally got through. Willie and Marghuerite were staying with Herbert Henderson, a dentist, and the house was filled with reporters in their dark suits and ties, bulky cameras, microphones, and bright lights. No offer to sell a two-story house had ever received so much coverage. The developments were reported in the afternoon newspapers and carried on radio and television newscasts throughout the rest of the day.

Then Gnesdiloff appeared to have second thoughts. Shortly after the announcement, he went to speak to Gaehwiler, but Gaehwiler held firm. Gnesdiloff then asked Howden to come to his house, where he was to meet his broker, Peter Morgan. The television cameras were also heading there.

Morgan didn't show up, but while Gnesdiloff waited with the press corps in his living room, an unexpected visitor did arrive—Martin Gaehwiler, who demanded an urgent, last-ditch conference in private with Gnesdiloff and his wife. The two men started yelling at each other so that some of the exchanges were quoted in the *Chronicle*.

"Do you realize how much money you'll lose?" Gaehwiler demanded. "There's thousands of dollars."

Gnesdiloff replied, "But just think of what you're trying to do to San Francisco. It looks bad."

The men finally emerged. Gnesdiloff tried again to call his broker but failed to reach him, so he telephoned Willie Mays directly. As the television cameras rolled, he said, "Mr. Mays, I want to tell you my decision personally. I am very happy to have you buy my home. The majority of the people of San Francisco want it that way, and I want it too." To the reporters, he said, "San Francisco is proud to have Willie Mays here, and I will be proud to have him in the house I built. . . . I'm relieved now that the pressure is over. The people of San Francisco seem to be behind me, and I hope some of the neighbors will be too."

He was visibly relieved, though his wife was still tense. "She seemed to feel guilty of a wrong against the Miraloma residents," Howden later said, "and she was worried too about possible business retaliation against her husband."

The day still wasn't over. Mays and Gnesdiloff had to sign papers to complete the transaction, and that was to occur back at the Hendersons' house. Gnesdiloff called Morgan's office and left word that if the broker did not show up at the Hendersons' in one hour, he would assume that Morgan did not want his commission.

So the newsmen and cameras returned to Henderson's house, where Gnesdiloff and Mays renewed their greetings. There was genuine warmth between the two, and they talked easily about furnishings and home building. They discussed what type of woods and finishes would be appropriate for one of the rooms in the new house. Mays signed Gnesdiloff's teenage daughter's autograph book. Marghuerite privately told him that she had received a call from a large developer, offering to sell her a home, and she had secured a promise from him to offer Gnesdiloff work should he need it as a result of selling this house to them. Mays's attorney arrived, the standard forms were filled in, a deposit check was written, and signatures were affixed—all at acceptable angles for the cameras.

Mays smiled wanly. "I'm glad this is over," he said. "I didn't want any trouble in the first place. All I wanted was a nice house in this town where I'll be playing ball. And I don't think the neighbors will make any trouble either. They'll calm down now that it's over."

Marghuerite retained her edge. "Sure they'll calm down," she said. "We're not planning to have tea and crumpets with them."

Shortly after everything was signed, Peter Morgan arrived, spoke privately with Gnesdiloff, and returned his brokerage contract. He preferred to forgo his $1,125 commission than do business with a black man.

After the last reporters left, Gnesdiloff said he thought that he and his wife would get away for a few days. Howden, driving home for dinner, heard a radio commentator in Los Angeles say that the Soviet Union would find the first part of this story, the rejection of Mays, quite useful, while ignoring the second part, the favorable conclusion.

In the coming weeks, Gnesdiloff received a couple dozen letters from as far away as Denver, New York, and Miami. Most were from the Bay Area and most were supportive, though a few were filled with racist and anti-Semitic language. Whenever Mays was asked about the incident, he always defended Gnesdiloff as a man who was trying to protect his business and who ultimately did the right thing.

Mayor Christopher said that the outcome "vindicated" San Francisco, which was nonsense. As predicted, the controversy brought scorn to the city and was a reminder of racial inequities outside the South. The *Washington Post* said in an editorial: "It is shameful that a handful of bigots should have clouded a city's welcome to the brilliant center fielder of the San Francisco Giants. . . . Plainly, the North and West can take little pride in this shabby incident, which dramatizes the ambiguous treatment accorded minorities outside the South." Edward P. Morgan, a commentator on ABC, was more caustic: "It seems that some of the citizens of San Francisco, often called the country's most sophisticated city, dwell behind picture windows which do not conceal their prejudices. For them, apparently, neighborliness consists of encouraging Willie Mays at home plate but when the Giants' Negro star moves next door, his welcome is the rude counsel to get farther away than the outfield."

In fact, the crisis ended favorably only because Mays was a celebrity, and not just any celebrity, but the very cornerstone of San Francisco's efforts to become an elite city. Almost any other African American would have had no recourse. The incident, far from vindicating San Francisco, lay bare the insidious but standard practice among Realtors, builders, and banks to prevent home buyers of color from entering certain neighborhoods. In that sense, Mays was a catalyst for citywide introspection. The *Chronicle* editorialized: "The pressures brought to bear upon Gnesdiloff are irrefutable evidence that some intolerance, some racial bigotry, still reside in cosmopolitan, enlightened, understanding San Francisco. The proof may sadden but ought not to surprise us."

It was also a defining event in Mays's career, for it placed a clear light on him as an African American. His reluctance to talk about race—or, more specifically, to discuss his experiences with racism—bleached out his black identity. He was always the nonthreatening superstar who was embraced by all and who seemed insulated from racial hostilities. He simply floated above the fray without complaint or concern.

The incident was a reminder that Mays did not live in some postracial nirvana, and his friends always pointed to this experience—even when Mays himself wouldn't—as evidence that he too suffered the sharp sting of discrimination.

Mays takes pride in how he handled the matter. He could have denounced the builder, decried the city's racist housing practices, and found another home. But he believes that he and Marguerite made a contribution by integrating that neighborhood. Asked by reporters at the time if he thought the controversy would help lower barriers for other home buyers, Mays said, "I think it will. I mean, I can say this: I know that the next fellow who wants to buy a home, they will think twice before saying, 'I can't sell it to you.' I will say that, yes."

Mays soon brought out his five televisions, his raft of trophies, his pool table, and his white Cadillac convertible, and by February the Gray Line's deluxe No. 1 tour bus would swing through the St. Francis Wood neighborhood, push up the steep roads, and stop, allowing excited tourists to glimpse the newest homeowner on Miraloma Drive.

CHAPTER NINETEEN

WELCOME TO SAN FRANCISCO

When the San Francisco Giants took the field in 1958, they were unlike any other team that had ever played in the league. They were, of course, the first major league squad from the Bay Area, but that didn't make them distinctive. They had six rookies, but they weren't the story. What was most striking was the team's racial and ethnic composition. In 1958, the Giants fielded four blacks and six Latins. The Dodgers that year had four blacks and no Latins. It was the Giants, not the Dodgers, who now set the standard for integration. They were Major League Baseball's melting pot, and their outreach brought in some of the finest players of the era while creating a vibrant—and at times divisive—backdrop for Mays's long tenure in San Francisco.

Mays himself played an indirect role in the team's changing demographic. In his rookie season, Stoneham was still adhering to the informal quota on the number of nonwhites on the roster. But that year was pivotal, for Mays's instant stardom coincided with Stoneham's decision to hire as a full-time scout a colorful baseball impresario named Alejandro "Alex" Pompez. His job: to find talent in the Caribbean. Stoneham had a long history with Pompez and may have eventually hired him anyway, but Mays's success alleviated his concerns about the white fans' support of minorities.

Pompez was a central figure in the remaking of the Giants. The son of a cigarmaker in Cuba, he grew up in Florida and moved to New York after World War I, where in Harlem he became the king of the numbers racket, a kind of lottery, illegal but lucrative. He also had legitimate business interests involving sports. He bought Dyckman Oval, a park in Harlem about two miles from the Polo Grounds, where he sponsored boxing and wrestling matches and motorcycle races. He also founded the New York Cuban Stars, which won the Eastern Color League title in 1924. When the league foundered, the Cuban Stars survived as barnstormers. Pompez's shadow business dealings caught up with him in the 1930s; he fled the country for a number of years to escape government prosecution, but he returned in 1937 and agreed to testify against figures in organized crime.

Pompez resumed the operations of the New York Cubans but needed a ballpark, so he leased the Polo Grounds from Stoneham. When Jackie Robinson broke into the majors, Pompez foresaw a new opportunity—providing players of color to big league teams. In 1947, he invited major league executives to a Negro League All-Star Game at the Polo Grounds. Most declined, but Stoneham showed up, and their friendship deepened. Stoneham would forgive Pompez his rent when he couldn't pay, and Pompez helped Stoneham sign Cuban catcher Ray Noble as well as Ray Dandridge and David Barnhill. With extensive contacts in the Negro Leagues and throughout the Caribbean, Pompez became a valuable scout, providing a direct line to huge pools of talent.

In 1955, Pompez helped sign Orlando Cepeda, the seventeen-year-old slugger from Puerto Rico. At Cepeda's first spring training in Melbourne, Florida, the team's director of scouting wanted to cut him, but, according to Cepeda, Pompez fought to keep him, and he soon emerged as the hottest prospect in the Giants' system. Jose Pagan was also signed out of Puerto Rico in 1955. The following year, Felipe Alou, the first of the Alou brothers, came out of the Dominican Republic, to be followed by Matty Alou and Manny Mota, then Juan Marichal and Jesus Alou. Out of the Bahamas came Andre Rodgers; out of Venezuela, Raymond Monzant. Pompez's native country, Cuba, delivered Jose Cardenal and Tito Fuentes. Cuba would have produced more players except that Fidel Castro, after seizing power in 1959, locked out all U.S. baseball teams.

Pompez also helped to scout black players, and he was in charge of all black and Latin prospects during spring training. He bunked them by nationality (Dominicans with Dominicans, etc.) and supervised their food, manners (no hats when eating), and dress. "When they first start out," he said, "I tell my boys, 'If you want to stay in organized baseball, you got to do things a little bit better. You got to fight, play hard, and hustle.' And they do. They're more ambitious, and they're hungry."

They also came on the cheap. At a time that Stoneham paid a $60,000 signing bonus to a white pitcher, Mike McCormick, he paid signing bonuses of $500 to Cepeda, $500 to Willie McCovey, $500 to Felipe Alou, and $4,000 to Juan Marichal.

Nevertheless, they and others created a pipeline of talent that fed the Giants for years to come.

Whatever misgivings the Giants had about their acceptance were dispelled almost immediately. On April 14, two days before their home opener, the team landed in San Francisco on a late-night flight from Omaha and was met by four hundred fans at the airport. All the players were taken to a downtown hotel except Mays, who returned to his house. The following day, the city threw a ticker-tape parade for the Giants through the financial district down Montgomery Street; the police estimated that hundreds of thousands lined the roads and watched from office buildings. Behind a marching marine band and cheerleaders with S F GIANTS on their sweaters, sparkling new convertibles carried various dignitaries: the mayors of San Francisco and Los Angeles, the commissioner of baseball and the president of the National League, Stoneham and Blanche McGraw. The former child movie star Shirley Temple Black was the parade queen. Finally, the players arrived, their names attached to the doors so the fans would know who they were screaming for. Five hundred pounds of rose-petal confetti, ticker tape, and punch cards fell from the top floors of the buildings.

The last car was occupied by Willie Mays and Hank Sauer, whom the Giants had acquired the previous year in a desperate attempt for a power hitter. When they came into view, hundreds of balloons descended on them, and Mays, smiling, grabbed one and waved it. Kids ran up to his car, pleading for autographs. Their parents did as well. At Montgomery and California streets, two twelve-year-old boys asked Mays if they could get in the car; he agreed, and they rode together for four blocks.

The parade reminded Mays of the one in New York after the Giants won the World Series. Even without a championship, San Francisco was showing its love—this was important to Mays if he was going to perform his best. "You felt that no one could ever top New York," he recalled. "Then you came out here and saw all the people. They shut down the businesses, they threw out paper. It was just a wonderful experience. . . . I needed that because sometimes when you go to new surroundings, you don't know what's going to happen. It was a good feeling."

A luncheon at the Sheraton-Palace Hotel drew a thousand fans, who showed their knowledge of Giants history, and their grace, in reserving their one standing ovation for Blanche McGraw. Bill Rigney received a key to the city, and San Francisco preened. "The Giants . . . have given us all a notable civic strut," wrote the *Chronicle*'s Charles McCabe. "San Francisco has been saying for decades that it is big league. In its secret heart, it has never been quite sure. These days it is."

Seals Stadium was nestled on the corner of 16th and Bryant streets, one of the warmest belts of the city and relatively free of fog. It was a gem of a park, a single-deck structure that held twenty-three thousand fans and featured a memorable sign over its clock in left center field: DAPHNE FUNER-ALS—EVENTUALLY. But not anymore. With the arrival of the Giants, the sign was replaced with one for Longines watches. The stadium's facade was repainted forest green; its front office windowsills were adorned with flower boxes. The smallest park in either league, its fans sat so close to the field, said Ruben Gomez, "it was like you were sitting in the same kitchen together, eating at the same table. Everyone was so close you could look at their faces and remember them." The fans at Seals Stadium, like those at the Polo Grounds, were allowed to come onto the field after the game, depart through an opening in center field, and visit, if they were so inclined, three neighborhood saloons—Double Play Bar, Third-Base, and Lou's.

But Seals Stadium had a quirky, fragrant beauty all its own. The visiting clubhouse overlooked a bakery, which dispensed a lovely aroma of fresh cinnamon rolls, crusty bread, and pastries. The players couldn't open their clubhouse window without feeling pangs of hunger.

Two breweries, meanwhile, were across the street; one of them, Hamm's, erected a flashing mug high above the stands, and the glass would gradually fill with beer to its foam-covered top, flash on and off three times, and then start over again. Occasionally, a player would become so entranced by the image that he would lose his concentration and commit an error. When the beer was brewing, tufts of foam were released from their buildings and wafted over the left field grandstand, descending gently into the bullpen. "There is nothing quite like the smell of new beer in the morning after a night on Frisco town," pitcher Jim Brosnan said.

Opening Day, April 15, was a warm, breezy afternoon, and the Giants faced the Dodgers. A downtown billboard read: WELCOME SF GIANTS. SWAT THEM BUMS. Joseph Magnin Company, a fine department store, distributed booklets to women that explained how baseball was played and offered tips on what to wear. Macy's dressed its mannequins in Giants uniforms. A sellout crowd of 23,449 was on hand, with several dozen more watching from a hill on Franklin Square beyond the right field bleachers. Scalpers were getting as much as $15 for a $3.50 reserved seat. Red, white, and blue bunting was draped around the diamond, from one foul pole around home plate to the other.

To celebrate the new era, the mayor of Los Angeles, Norris Poulson, stepped into the batter's box to face his San Francisco counterpart, Mayor Christopher. Two of the four pitches were wild, one bounced on the plate, and the fourth was hit by Poulson, who promptly ran to third base. During the introduction of the players, Willie Mays received the loudest ovation, though opposing players Gil Hodges, Pee Wee Reese, and Duke Snider were also cheered enthusiastically. At 1:34 P.M., the Giants' Ruben Gomez threw the first pitch and quickly struck out Gino Cimoli.

Don Drysdale, the young ace who had won seventeen games the year before, pitched for the Dodgers, but he didn't make it through four innings, and the Giants won handily, 8–0. Their muscular rookie, Orlando Cepeda, hit a home run, and Gomez went the distance. The game was covered by 110 reporters, the most ever for a regular-season contest, and the reviews, even among the New York scribes, were favorable. Joe King of the *New York World-Telegram* wrote, "It is sad for most of the old Giant fans to see their team depart, but the wrench is eased [by knowing] it has a new home in the city which keeps alive the spirit of old New York in which the great Giants prospered."

Mays, batting fourth, chipped in two singles and two RBIs and lost his cap chasing a fly ball. "It's like a World Series," he said after the game. He received a surprise visit from a long-ago acquaintance—Eddie Montague, the scout who signed him with the Giants. He now lived in San Francisco, and he went into the locker room so his nine-year-old son, Ed, could meet Willie. The boy also met the actor Jeff Chandler, but Chandler didn't leave nearly the impression that Willie did. "It was such a thrill," recalls Montague, who became a National League umpire. "My dad introduced me . . . and Willie had that high-pitched voice. He pulled a brand-new glove with his name embroidered on it, and he gave it to me. I remember holding it out the window [on the way home] saying, 'This is Willie Mays's glove.' "

For the team at large, the transition to San Francisco went smoothly with only a few minor exceptions. The *Oakland Tribune,* miffed that the arrival of the Giants forced the minor league Oakland Oaks to leave town, refused to print the words "San Francisco" in its Giant stories, datelines, or standings. The words magically came back the following year. At times, Russ Hodges inadvertently called the team "the New York Giants," and sometimes even newspaper boys cried out that "the New York Giants" had won the game.

Meanwhile, the real New York Giant fans had not been completely abandoned. After the Giants and Dodgers left town, WINS in New York wanted to use Western Union ticker tape to re-create the games of one of the displaced teams. Announcer Les Keiter figured Willie Mays could attract the largest audience, so he chose the Giants, and for the next three years, the fans could maintain their connection to Willie through Keiter's late-night broadcasts.

What most helped the Giants in San Francisco was their play on the field. Predicted to be a second-division team, the youthful squad got off to a hot start and at the end of May was tied for first place, with a 27–17 record. Even their losses won over fans. In a home game on May 5, the Giants were losing to the Pirates, 11–1, going into the bottom of the ninth.

They then staged a remarkable rally, which included a pinch-hit double by pitcher Johnny Antonelli, and they had the bases loaded with the score 11–10 when the final out was recorded.

Leading the charge was Willie Mays, who was hitting .397 at the end of April. On May 13, in one game against the Dodgers at the Coliseum, he led the Giants to a 16–9 win with two home runs, two triples, a single, four RBIs, and four runs scored. The Coliseum itself was an odd baseball venue: it was so vast that fans brought transistor radios to help them follow the action. Mays was amused but not distracted. In the four-game series, he hit .709. To Rigney, Mays's talents were no longer confined to the ball field. "Willie Mays is the world's greatest athlete," Rigney said. "His motions are so smooth. I even get a kick out of the silky way he puts on his coat."

For the first time, Mays also played the role of peacemaker on the field, defusing a brawl that was spiraling out of control. Ruben Gomez, not surprisingly, was in the middle. In September of the previous year, Gomez had hit Pirate pitcher Vernon Law on the left ear with a pitch, rupturing his eardrum and knocking him out for the season. The first time Gomez pitched against the Pirates in 1958, he hit catcher Hank Foiles in the arm, forcing him to leave the game. A Pirate pitcher knocked down a Giant hitter the following day.

Tensions finally exploded the next time Gomez pitched against the Pirates, on May 25 in Pittsburgh. In the fourth inning, second baseman Bill Mazeroski crushed an 0–2 curveball over the fence but foul. The next pitch was a high, tight fastball, which Mazeroski deflected with his left hand; the Pirates later said the ball would have hit his head. Mazeroski began cursing Gomez while his manager, Danny Murtaugh, charged from the dugout to check on his hitter as well as to bark at Gomez. Umpire Frank Dascoli warned Gomez, which drew Rigney out of the dugout to protect his pitcher.

Gomez came to bat the next inning—against the recovered Vernon Law. Before he stepped in, Dascoli sent Gomez back to the bench for a helmet. It was the first game of a doubleheader, and the Sunday afternoon crowd of 35,797, the largest in two years, booed him noisily. Gomez stepped back into the box, and with a runner on first, he squared to bunt. A high fastball sent him sprawling. Now Dascoli marched out to warn Law, which prompted Murtaugh to race to the mound to protect his pitcher. But the fiery Irishman veered toward the plate, said something to Gomez, and pointed to his own forehead, apparently indicating that the ball would soon hit him there. Gomez yelled back at the manager, who wheeled and started for him. Third base coach Herman Franks ran down the line and intercepted Murtaugh while Gomez swung his bat. Murtaugh ducked, causing his hat to fall off and just eluding the bat. "This guy's crazy!" he shouted.

Both benches emptied, some wild punches were thrown, and the players pushed and tugged at one another. But one player couldn't be controlled—Orlando Cepeda. Both Cepeda and Gomez were from Puerto Rico, and while the veteran Gomez was a mentor to all of the young Latin players, he was a father figure to Cepeda. The young first baseman even lived with Gomez and his wife, Maria.

Cepeda became enraged when he saw his friend in trouble. "He was like a mad bull," wrote the *Examiner*. "He tore his way out of one group and then another, finally dashing toward the Giant dugout where he had spied a bat."

Cepeda snared the bat and intended to beat the hell out of any Pirate who got in his way. "I was from a Puerto Rico slum," he said, "and I was used to grabbing the nearest thing to protect myself." He was ready to swing the bat, according to the *Sporting News*, "like a sugar cane machete."

But Mays saw him, raced his way, and tackled his 210-pound teammate. Mays was thirty pounds lighter, but with Hank Sauer's help, he pinned him down until order was restored. In all the chaos, Mays doubted that many people had even noticed, but they had. Mays's next time at the plate, the fans gave him a big hand.

Mays was often cheered in opposing ballparks, but his flying tackle was something completely apart. His "quick thinking . . . probably averted a full-scale riot at Forbes Field," *Pittsburgh Press* reporter Les Biederman wrote. Dascoli gave equal praise to the police and to Mays for "stopping the incipient riot." Murtaugh was the only one thrown out; Gomez, despite swinging his bat at Murtaugh, pitched a complete game for the win. Rigney was pleased with the near-riot. "That thing woke up Gomez," he said after the game. "He really pitched well after that."

National League president Warren Giles wasn't quite so forgiving of using a bat as a weapon. He fined Cepeda, Gomez, and Murtaugh $100 apiece but sent a telegram of commendation to Mays: "The umpires . . . report that your timely restraint of Cepeda prevented what might have become a very serious incident and I commend you for your clear thinking and quick action."

Cepeda was indeed fortunate. Had he skulled another player, his season and even his career could have been in jeopardy. At a minimum, photographs of such an assault, with blood smeared across the victim's head and uniform, the bat dangling in the perpetrator's hand, would have overshadowed all the other accomplishments of what in fact was a Hall of

Fame career. In saving Cepeda from himself—and in preventing a violent melee—Mays demonstrated familiar skills: excellent vision, unerring instincts, brute strength. "In the corner of my eye, I saw Cepeda charge out of the dugout with a bat," he said. "I'm saying to myself, 'No, no, that can't happen,' so I tackled him." He also moved quickly, he said, because he knew if Cepeda had bashed an opponent, he'd be thrown out of the game, and he'd be useless to the team in the dugout.

One might take Mays's actions for granted, as something any conscientious player would do. But no other player did do it. It was Mays who prevented the riot, and he played a similar role later in his career, on a larger stage and with higher stakes. Then and there, the full meaning of his peacemaking would be understood.

Mays's torrid hitting continued. In five games in June, he went on a 15-for-22 tear, which on June 6 pushed his average to .433. Opposing pitchers tried to disrupt him by knocking him down, a common practice for years, and Mays was hitting the dirt once a game. His remarkable start renewed speculation about a record-breaking year. "If Babe Ruth's home run record is broken, Mays is going to break it here," Cincinnati manager Birdie Tebbetts told the *Sporting News*. The magazine said Mays's feats belonged "on a higher adjective plateau—none but words like incomparable, breathtaking, electrifying, matchless, explosive, and dynamic will do." For his part, Mays intentionally aimed for a high average, not homers, believing that getting on base frequently was the quickest way to win over fans. With the team playing well, his line drives falling in, and the crowds supporting him, he couldn't have been happier. It was like a dream.

Then he stopped hitting. Mays had always hit in streaks, but in 1958 they were more exaggerated. Starting on June 7, he went 0-for-4, 0-for-4, 0-for-4, 1-for-4, 0-for-3, and 0-for-4. Always a free-swinger, he was now chasing pitches out of the strike zone while allowing good ones to pass by. The Giants lost five in a row, and the fans began to conclude that if Mays didn't hit, the team would lose. Mays's struggles continued, and in nineteen games, his average fell sixty-two points, to .371.

Mays knew he couldn't hit .433 for the entire year, that eventually he'd taper off, but this slump was different. He began to feel tired, and his health worried him. He told Rigney on June 19, when the Giants were in Pittsburgh, that he felt poorly. At the time, he had had five hits in his last forty at-bats. The previous season, Mays had checked into Harkness Pavilion under similar circumstances, so he now returned there, where the same physician, Dr. Stewart Cosgriff, examined him. According to press reports, the doctor indicated there was nothing "organically" wrong, and Mays was given vitamins and told to rest. He missed two games and rejoined the team in Philadelphia on June 22.

San Francisco Giant games in Philadelphia would long draw the New York press as well as a fair number of New York fans. Mostly, they came to cheer Willie. On this night, he was in good spirits, smiling and laughing before the game, a familiar image of boyish fun. But when reporters asked him about his health, he went into a shell. The interview, as reported by Dick Young, put him under siege.

"How do you feel?"

"All right now."

"How did you feel when you went into the hospital?"

"Tired."

"Did you feel any pain or anything?"

"No, jes tired."

"Do you mean tired physically, or mentally, or what?"

"I don't know. Tired, that's all."

"Have they given you any pills or medicine to take?"

"No, nothing like that."

"Whose idea was it that you go into the hospital—yours or the club's?"

"I don't know. Why don't you ask Rigney these questions? I don't want to get into no trouble."

Dick Young, known for his caustic opinions, was a fan of Mays's, but he was highly offended by his answers. "Willie wasn't examined," Young wrote in a huff. "He was brainwashed."

In an interview the following year, Mays emphatically denied that there was anything seriously wrong with him. "They ask me, am I physically tired or mentally tired, and I guess it's a little of both," he said. "In the hospital, the doctor tells me I'm run down, and he gives me those vitamin shots, and I rest for a day or two. That's all I seem to need when it happens, one or two days off."

But it wasn't the medical care that Mays needed. It was the privacy. "When I'm in a slump, people ask me so many questions that I go into the hospital and nobody bothers me," he said. "If I could get that same privacy somewhere else, just a complete rest, I wouldn't go into the hospital."

It was a rare acknowledgment of the stress that his own celebrity had created. All the hype created obvious pressures, but new ones emerged as well. At twenty-seven, he was now considered a team leader, even an elder statesman. He found himself bracketed by rookies in left and right— Felipe Alou, Willie Kirkland, and Leon Wagner, all of whom needed guidance both on and off the field. Wagner said that Mays showed him and

Kirkland around town and introduced them to the right people. "Mays always looked out for us," he said.

Mays had fun with the rookies. The first time he saw Wagner, he walked up to him. "So you're Wagner, huh?"

"That's right, that's me," Wagner said.

Mays sat down, looked at him, and then started to laugh. He walked over again.

"So you're Wagner, huh?" Wagner nodded. Again Mays walked away. The rookie had no idea what was going on.

Mays came over one more time. "Watch me," he told Wagner. "I'm the leader. You get outta line, I might have to trade you."

"I ain't like those other rookies," Wagner said. "I can pole."

"You can what?"

"I can pole. I can pole the ball."

Mays, amused by the rookie's brashness, keeled over with joy. Wagner recalled, "He laughed so hard he had tears in his eyes."

Wagner returned the barbs by calling Mays names like "Square" or "Chump," which Willie loved, and the veteran gave him clothes and watches. "He used to give me his best stuff," Wagner said. "Man, he gave me three or four silk suits, eight or nine alpaca sweaters, $55 slacks. He'd get a batch of sweaters or something, and I'd say I wanted a particular one and he'd scream and say, 'No, no, that's the best one, that's the one I want. Oh, no, you can't have it.' But he'd always end up giving it to me."

The Giants were already using Mays as an example to young players, though their motives were not strictly to improve their play. In 1956, Willie Kirkland, still in the minors, threatened not to report to Minneapolis unless he was paid more than $600 a month. In a letter to Kirkland, the Giants' director of the team's farm system, Jack Schwarz, said he didn't deserve more than $600 a month. He also told the twenty-two-year-old that he was a streak hitter. "Even Willie Mays is a streak hitter," Schwarz wrote.

> However, Willie is not a streak outfielder. He is a great outfielder all the time. When he makes a bad play in the outfield, it is so unusual that the writers are on him for ten days afterward. At times you make the exceptional plays in the outfield, and at times you do not look too good on the ordinary chances. . . . I have very high hopes for you, and think it would be a terrible mistake for you not to be in that Minneapolis camp in high gear.

And Kirkland was.

But while Mays had the star power and enjoyed the camaraderie, he was not a natural mentor. If asked, he would do anything for a team-mate, but he didn't impose himself on others, didn't pry or invade. Never a cheerleader, he led by quiet example. "He was a laid-back guy," recalled Billy O'Dell, who pitched for the Giants in the 1960s. "You'd have to look around sometimes to see he was there. What Mays had already done in his career, and how he still worked hard to accomplish more, was what inspired the other players." Added Johnny Antonelli: "He didn't get up in the clubhouse and make speeches. Willie always led by performance."

What others didn't appreciate was that Mays felt isolated in his new city with new teammates. The team was not only younger, but its New York bloodlines had been thinned out. During spring training of 1958, the Giants parted ways with New York stalwarts Don Mueller and Bobby Thomson, and Dusty Rhodes spent the year in Phoenix. In addition to Mays, only three players remained from the 1954 championship team. He roomed alone on the road, traveled to and from Seals Stadium by himself, and rarely socialized with his teammates. Moreover, he himself still craved a mentor, some older adult whom he trusted and—particularly now—who could help him with his batting stroke. His frustrations spilled out to Jimmy Cannon in an interview that ran in the *New York Post* a week after he left the hospital.

"I've been playing lousy ball for three weeks," he said. "I don't know what it is. I don't know what to make of it. I'm just bad."

He thought he knew what could help. "I need some older fellow to watch me. I mean, someone who knows me and knows all about me and what I did when I started and how I was when I came up." He knew who that was. "The best thing would be to have Jackie Robinson for one year. I mean for Jackie to play with me for just one year and tell me things. He'd tell me. . . . He knew me when I came up and what I did." Except for Hank Sauer, he said, none of his teammates had suggested how to end his hitting woes. "They're afraid to tell me. Nobody tells me. What are they afraid of? They must think I would resent it."

Cannon later wrote that Mays sounded as if "he were an obscure kid trying to hold on to a job he wasn't certain he could fill."

At the time, Mays was hitting .372 and leading the league. But that wasn't good enough for him. "Some guys hit .350 but they don't care," Mays told Cannon. "But I love this game. I got so much to learn about it. That's why I want some older fellow to tell me when I'm doing wrong."

The comments incensed Rigney, who called a clubhouse meeting and asked Mays if he was trying to show up his teammates and coaches. Mays said he wasn't.

• • •

That Mays sought a New York columnist to explain his difficulties was not coincidental. He would open up only to reporters he knew, such as Milton Gross, Roger Kahn, and Ed Linn, as well as Cannon. At his best, he could be engaging and insightful and was usually respectful, but in general he was a reluctant interview and instinctively wary of journalists he didn't know. Some reporters didn't like him. He would miss interview appointments, offer painfully short answers, and be dismissive or petulant toward those he believed—rightly or wrongly—were trying to embarrass him. But few professional athletes faced as much media attention as he did, and beyond baseball, he feared scrutiny.

Tensions emerged almost immediately between Mays and the West Coast journalists. "Some California sportswriters are not always finding him receptive," the *New York Times* reported from spring training, "and Mays has irked a few already." What bothered them was Mays's spending time with the writers from New York instead of with them. "Do they want me to talk to them like I would to old friends?" Mays asked. "Well, first we got to become old friends. . . . I want to know how he writes before I answer some questions. I don't like to be put on the spot."

Mays also got ensnared in San Francisco's newspaper rivalries. He agreed to publish a daily ghostwritten column in the *Call-Bulletin,* one of the four dailies. Immediately after a game, the newspaper's beat reporter, Jim McGee, grabbed Mays, leaving the competing writers outraged. "That irritated the rest of us," recalled Dan Hruby, who in 1958 was a first-year baseball writer in San Francisco. "I still believe most of the writers resented the column idea and, perhaps subconsciously, repeatedly threw digs into Mays in print."

Mays was criticized on two points: he wasn't worth his high salary, and he was responsible for the Giants' losses. "Mays's still-high batting average is a misleading thing," wrote the *Examiner's* Prescott Sullivan in early August. "Willie got his hits in bunches at the start of the season. . . . For the greater part of the season, he has been hitting closer to the .200 pace and, moreover, most of his hits have been of the dribbler variety. . . . With so little assistance from their key man, the wonder of it is that the Giants have remained in contention this long [given that the team has] to 'carry' the one player it had counted on for its scoring punch. . . . As we figure it, [Mays] has about $50,000 more baseball to play in order to earn his 70 G's."

Some attacks evoked images of racial hostility. Bud Spencer, the sports editor of the *San Francisco News,* wrote that "the general press box appraisal" of Mays was that he was "an All American knothead. . . . Willie's trouble is that he needs to be driven. Anybody got a whip?"

Actually, Mays had just as many admirers in the press who affirmed his supremacy on the field and his decency off. During his slump, Curley Grieve, the sports editor of the *Examiner,* wrote: "Possibly no one uses up as much energy in the course of a game as Willie. He goes all out every effort. . . . After every game, there's a small handful of youngsters waiting for him at the dressing room door for his autograph. He never disappoints them. He's such a gentle soul that he can't even get angry at the pitchers who are trying to drill holes in his head."

Bob Stevens of the *Chronicle,* disputing press accounts that Mays was selfish, recounted a game in which Mays came to bat in the ninth inning with the score tied and a man on second. He ripped a drive off the center field wall. As the winning run chugged home, Mays could have jogged to second for a double, which would have helped his slugging percentage. (He had led the league in slugging percentage in three of the four previous years; it was a coveted title.) But he stopped at first, sacrificing his double. "The Giants had won and that was good enough for Willie," Stevens wrote.

Jack McDonald, a veteran sports editor in San Francisco, described Mays as one of the classiest gentlemen he'd ever met in sports. "Willie must know he's a great ballplayer, but he never lets on," McDonald wrote in the *Sporting News* in July 1958. "And when you gain his confidence, he'll tell you everything—even though he may ask you not to print it."

Jim Murray, the future Hall of Fame sportswriter for the *Los Angeles Times,* wrote in 1962: "So far as is known, [Mays] has never done an unkind thing in his career."

In July, Mays hit .264, which would cause no alarm for any other player, but for him, the mere hint of mortality defied all expectations.

In one sense, Mays wasn't the same ballplayer—something had been lost at Seals Stadium. For all its charm, it was still a minor league park, where high flies were lost in substandard lights, the crosswinds were tricky, and the grass was tall. "I got to learn to play center field all over again," Mays said. What's more, the close fences, while perhaps suitable for home runs, negated the most exciting part of Mays's game—his defense. Compared to the expanse of the Polo Grounds, he had no place to roam. Balls that he once caught over his shoulder now sailed over the fence. Gone also was the unique visual drama caused by his shallow positioning. At the Polo Grounds, Mays tempted disaster by charging every hard ground ball or sinking drive; with the endless tundra behind him, a miscue meant the ball would roll forever. In Seals Stadium, it simply meant an extra base. Mays would never be mistaken for an ordinary player, but Seals Stadium confined his greatness.

Mays's acceptance in his new city was complicated by his New York roots. While the Giants wanted to make him the showpiece of the franchise, San Francisco didn't need a packaged icon from the East Coast. It wanted to find its own heroes. And it did, in "the Baby Bull."

Orlando Cepeda knew something about legends. His father, Pedro Cepeda, was a baseball superstar in Puerto Rico. Nicknamed "the Bull," Pedro gave his son both his strength and his temper (he was also called "the Babe Cobb of Puerto Rico"). Orlando Cepeda was so daunting physically that during spring training in 1958, Rigney gushed that he looked like "a bronze statue standing at dress parade."

When Rigney asked Whitey Lockman what he thought of the kid, Lockman said, "It's too bad he's a year away."

"A year away from what?"

"The Hall of Fame."

He was an immediate favorite in San Francisco. He hit for power and average, and with a broad smile and outgoing personality, he would joke and laugh with the fans and mill about the Mission District, near the park, which had a large Puerto Rican community. He liked to wear his sleeves high to expose his muscles, and he was visible on the nightclub circuit: the Copacabana for Latin music, the Blackhawk for jazz, and the Jazz Workshop, which initially wouldn't let him in—he was too young—but soon capitulated to the town's hottest new celebrity. Attracting dates was not a problem.

Cepeda was to San Francisco what Willie Mays, in his rookie season, had been to New York—young, accessible, and mesmerizing. Cepeda would also be Rookie of the Year and, like Mays, even carried around a portable record player. The rhetorical flourishes describing Cepeda had a familiar echo. "He is the very personification of power," the *Sporting News* said in 1958, "as he stands at the plate with his bat cocked, a magnificent athletic specimen and a challenge to any pitcher. We never see him standing there with a bat in his hands without thinking that a great artist or sculptor, wishing to put the theme 'Power at the Plate' on canvas, or into bronze or marble, would need to look no further than Cepeda as the greatest living model for such a work."

Cepeda also benefited by hitting fourth, behind Mays, whose .419 onbase percentage was the second highest of his career. Mays led the league with thirty-one steals as well, so Cepeda received an inordinate number of fastballs while Mays's running also created holes in the defense. Cepeda later said, "I was in the right place at the right time."

While Baby Bull heard the cheers, Mays, struggling to find his stroke, heard the boos. He had been booed once before, in the Polo Grounds, but that was for a single misplay. In this case, the *Sporting News* said, he had "been the target for more than just some isolated booing in the heretofore tolerant Seals Stadium. Fans just can't conceive of Mays getting anything less than a single every time he comes to the plate. . . . Willie himself confided to friends that it would take a superman to live up to such laudatory clippings."

Jim Murray wrote: "They didn't expect Willie Mays to land there; they expected the waters of the Golden Gate to part and let him walk ashore."

Some San Franciscans thought they deserved a new franchise, just as the 49ers had been new, and an American League franchise at that—the Yankees had been the most popular major league team in the Bay Area. The Giants were warmed-over National Leaguers, and Willie Mays, the most prominent among them, suffered one other demerit. His New York boosters insisted that he was every bit equal to, if not better than, Joe DiMaggio. But just as Mickey Mantle could never fill DiMaggio's shoes in Yankee Stadium, neither could Mays in San Francisco.

All of these passions led to impetuous attacks. On August 11, *Sports Illustrated* published an article by Richard Pollard, identified as a "San Francisco fan" who traveled with the Giants for a week. Noting that Mays was a loner, he wrote: "This can be irritating, particularly when the star is not performing with distinction." After the Giants were swept in four games, he wrote: "The weak hitting of Mr. Willie Mays, combined with inept relief pitching and a leaky infield, was too great a burden to carry into a decisive series." Actually, the Giants scored only five runs in four games—nobody hit well—but only Mays was cited.

His teammates, including Cepeda, understood his untenable situation. "I didn't have the disadvantage Willie Mays had," Cepeda recalled. "When Willie came here, the press built him up so high. The fans figured that every time he came up to the plate, he'd hit a home run, or steal a base, and never make an error. And when he'd strike out or whatever, I was doing well."

Mays's teammates from New York were particularly sympathetic. "Willie is the one guy I felt a little sorry for because he was such an icon in New York," Lockman says. "He, Mantle, Snider—they owned that place. Then he got to San Francisco, and he just wasn't the same to Giant fans there as he was to those in New York."

Mays believes his reception primarily reflected San Francisco's resentment of anyone who could be compared to the Yankee Clipper. "This was Joe DiMaggio's town," he later said. "Joe was great. He was one of my idols. I didn't come out here to show him up. I only hoped I could prove to San Francisco that I could play ball." The boos were jarring for a player who, with rare exception, had heard nothing but cheers at home and on the road. "On the road," he said, "you expect boos. But I think all players want to feel the hometown fan is his friend."

If Mays was supposed to get more rest, he got little help from Rigney. The Giants played doubleheaders on July 27 in Pittsburgh and July 28 in Phila-delphia. Two cities; two days; four games. Mays played every inning. On Labor Day, September 1, the Giants and Dodgers played a split double-header at Seals Stadium. The first game, at 10 A.M., lasted two hours and thirty-four minutes. The crowd then left, new fans entered, and the sec-ond game began around 2:30. That one lasted sixteen innings and took four hours and thirty-five minutes. All told, the players were at the park for eleven hours and fifteen minutes. Mays never sat out. With the exception of the two games he missed when he was hospitalized, he played in all other 152 games, more than anyone else. If he was around, he was on the field.

Mays's marriage had always been fodder for the gossip columnists, but the attention grew sharper, and less welcome, his first year in San Francisco. Margueritc cut a striking image about town. At a fundraiser for an edu-cational television station, she modeled a pink fox stole over a pink satin evening gown. When she tried on a $12,000 fur coat, she murmured to Willie, "I wish I could have it, it's so beautiful." A photograph captured Willie's petrified look. In September, *Ebony* placed Willie and Marguerite on its cover, he wearing an open pea-green sweater and yellow cotton shirt while holding their white poodle, she in a high-collared pink flowered dress, pink heels, and pearls, both of them leaning against the broad front fender of a shiny pink Thunderbird with a pink steering wheel. Other photographs showed the couple viewing the ocean from their large liv-ing room windows and cuddling in a tender embrace on their white sofa.

But behind the blissful image were rumors about dissension and divorce. Newspaper reporters from as far as Chicago, Pittsburgh, and New York, as well as San Francisco, were asking so many questions that the couple's lawyer, Terry Francois, issued a statement in September that there was "absolutely no basis for Willie Mays divorce rumors." Francois had recently spoken to Marguerite, and "she was shocked and amazed at such rumors." Willie, asked before a game in St. Louis about his mar-riage, said, "What is all the fuss about anyway? What do you want me to say?" He denied the rumors but noted that "every marriage isn't peaches and cream."

When a hospital treated Marguerite for a bruised forehead and a cut finger, a newspaper suggested that Willie may have struck her. "He hit her like he owned her," quipped one newspaper. Both parties vehemently denied it. "My wife slipped and fell down the stairs of our home in Frisco," Willie said. "That's the truth, but I know people don't like to believe it because it's more interesting to believe the other thing. They say I knocked her down, and everything. She just tripped and fell. It was a nasty fall. She went down head first. Her face and her side and her back were all sore."

Marghuerite said, "That rumor was started by a so-called friend of Willie's. If anybody, even my father, beat me up, I wouldn't live with him. I'd know he didn't love me, and I'd leave him."

Reporters seemed less inclined to ask Mays about his marriage when he was hitting .400, but now they connected his slump to his domestic life. Asked if she was responsible, Marghuerite said, "When Willie is going good, how come they never blame that on me?"

The Giants' unlikely playoff hopes effectively ended the first week of August, when they lost ten out of eleven games, giving them a 55–53 record, nine games behind the Braves. Poor pitching and inexperience had caught up with them. In one game three rookies, Alou, Cepeda, and Wagner, ignored Herman Franks's stop signs at third base and ran into outs. The crowd booed Franks, who then blasted the fans for having "no conception of the game."

But midway through the losing streak, on August 4 at Wrigley Field, Mays broke his slump with three hits, including his first home run since July 2 and his first RBI in sixteen games. And he kept hitting. In one four-game stretch against the Dodgers, he went 10-for-16 (.625), including seven consecutive hits, four homers (one in each game), two doubles, a triple, nine RBIs, and eight runs scored.

While the Giants won only ten of twenty-two in September, Mays roared to the finish line, batting .445, and was named National League player of the month. He started the final game in San Francisco, on September 28, batting .3445, close behind league leader Richie Ashburn, at .3469.

Before the game, a ceremony was held to award the Giants' MVP, as determined in a poll sponsored by the *Examiner*. Mays finished the season as the team leader in batting average, on-base percentage, slugging percentage, runs, hits, total bases, triples, home runs, and stolen bases. He won the Gold Glove and tied Orlando Cepeda for RBIs.

But the fans voted Cepeda the MVP, giving him 18,701 votes to 11,510 for Mays. Cepeda had had a wonderful year (.312 average, 25 homers, 96 RBIs), but he was not the team's most valuable player.

It was, for Mays, a fitting last snub to a tumultuous year. But if he couldn't win the hearts of fans in San Francisco, he might be able to win the batting crown.

Ashburn didn't cooperate. He went 3-for-4, all singles, and finished the year at .350. The Phillies had completed their game by the time the Giants began theirs against the Cardinals. Mays needed to go 5-for-5 to tie Ashburn, so Rigney had him lead off for extra at-bats. Fearing he would be undone by the added pressure, the Giants instructed the public address announcer not to reveal Ashburn's batting line, but someone told Mays anyway. He got off to a good start, hitting a double, but he flied out his next time up. He then hit a homer, his twenty-ninth, made another out, and then beat out an infield hit. His 3-for-5 day gave him a .347 average, the highest of his career, two points better than the year he won the batting title.

The Giants won the game, 7–2, ending the season in third place, twelve games behind the Braves but with eighty wins, an improvement by ten from the previous year. The more dramatic improvement was at the gate: the Giants drew 1,272,625 fans, almost double their last year's attendance in New York and the most since 1948. To show their appreciation, the Giants gave "the millionth fan," a photo engraver named Vaughn Santoian, an all-expense trip to Reno, a down payment on a Thunderbird, television and radio sets, free dinners, and a lady's nightgown.

The Giants were a success in San Francisco, but for all the change, the man who still defined the team—who still inspired reverence and awe—was their center fielder from New York. The most spectacular moment of the year, according to the *Call-Bulletin,* occurred at Wrigley Field, with Mays flanked by Wagner and Kirkland. As Wagner described the play:

> Willie told both of us to guard the line, so here's Mays playing practically the entire outfield. Man, he had two blocks to cover! Then Ernie Banks unloads a real blast, and I start going back toward the wall. I figure I'm gonna run into the ivy and that the ball is going into the seats. Then I hear footsteps, and here comes Willie! He came running up to me, full speed, and leaped on me. His feet went off my chest, and he shot straight up and caught that ball! And he did it without spiking me. I still can't figure out how I didn't get cut. He ran right up me and scared me to death. He made the damndest catch I've ever seen, and I still don't know how he did it. I couldn't believe it. I told him I didn't know if he was good, or just crazy.

The *Sporting News* said Mays missed Wagner by "the margin of a honey bee's stinger."

For all the anxiety over his hitting—the *Examiner* concluded that his "was the most prolonged slump for a name player in modern history"— Mays had for him a typical, which is to say brilliant, season. He led the league in runs scored (121), stolen bases (31), and OPS (on-base plus slugging percentage, 1.002). His only regret was not having gone for home runs; twenty-nine marked his lowest total to date for a full season.

Theories to explain his midseason doldrums percolated for months, even years—his wife, his physical condition, the pressure to satisfy impatient fans—but the most obvious answer was often ignored. Baseball is a game of failure, with even its best hitters failing close to 70 percent of the time. Mays's slump was the evening of a long season—his average hit bottom at .327 on August 27—yet somehow he was supposed to defy the sport's brutal arithmetic.

Mays himself kept perspective. After the last game, he sent Richie Ashburn a telegram to congratulate him on the batting title. When reporters asked Mays if he was disappointed, he said, "No, I'm not disappointed. If I hit .347 every year, I'll be satisfied."

CHAPTER TWENTY

BLACK BARNSTORMERS

Just as Willie Mays was one of the last great products of the Negro Leagues, he was also a luminous figure of another circuit that no longer exists. Professional ballplayers had "barnstormed" since the early 1900s, performing in the off-season in small towns and rural counties. Before television, barnstorming was the only way that large swaths of America could see major league players. Negro Leaguers barnstormed as well, playing against whites as early as 1907. Racially mixed crowds increased the gate receipts, and interracial teams were assembled even before Jackie Robinson broke the color barrier.

The actual term "barnstormer" is derived from the rural aspect of the game and the rapid movement from town to town. Stunt pilots were also known as barnstormers, flying over small towns and using farm fields, near barns, as runways. Like the aviators, the ballplayers had to whip up excitement and do something remarkable to bring out the crowds. Babe Ruth and Satchel Paige, both popular barnstormers, had that sort of charisma. So too did Jackie Robinson, who in 1947 led a group of African American players on a tour that allowed black fans to see their new hero. Called Jackie Robinson's All-Stars, the squad began a tradition of a team, comprising mostly black major leaguers, that played against top Negro League players in towns across the South. As long as the troupe had a marquee name, the crowds would follow.

In 1954, Robinson didn't play in the off-season, so the barnstormers were called Roy Campanella's All-Stars. In 1955, the torch was passed to Willie Mays. While his years as a barnstormer are often overlooked, it was a meaningful part of Mays's career. It represented a vast extension of the Willie Mays brand: he entered fresh markets in the United States and Latin America, forged bonds with new consumers, and created powerful memories that would be passed on to future generations.

Mays played for the same reason everyone else did—the money. Barnstorming could produce a decent income, and most players, white or black, had to work second jobs in the off-season anyway. The gate receipts for the black barnstorming games were divided between the two teams, but the major leaguers received 90 percent of the money. They, after all, were the drawing card. In Mays's first year, the six-week tour paid each player $3,000 to $4,000, or about half what most of them earned in a season. As the team leader around whom the games were promoted, Mays received even more.

Mays's team in 1955 might have been the finest club in baseball history. It had four future Hall of Famers—just in the outfield! Henry Aaron, Larry Doby, Monte Irvin, and Mays divided the playing time; future Hall of Famers Roy Campanella and Ernie Banks were at catcher and shortstop. Former Rookies of the Year Junior Gilliam and Joe Black played short and pitched; their best pitcher was Don Newcombe, who would win the MVP in 1956. Other solid players, including pitchers Sam Jones and Brooks Lawrence and first baseman George Crowe, rounded out the team.

The tour began right after the season in New York, and the players, traveling in cars, caravanned through the Carolinas, veered west in Georgia, rumbled through the Deep South, bisected Texas, and barreled all the way to Southern California. Whether in Albany, Georgia; Hazlehurst, Mississippi; or Beaumont, Texas, they won, going 28–0 that winter. (Five games were rained out.) Granted, they weren't playing major leaguers, but as Hank Aaron said, "I don't think it would have mattered who we played. That might have been the best team ever assembled."

Mays drove Aaron in his Cadillac. The two were always friendly rivals, competing against each other for almost two decades in individual games as well as for home run records. But they were also teammates in All-Star contests and as barnstormers. On that first tour Aaron was only twenty-one, a fellow Alabaman (Mobile), and he discovered that Mays's celebrity was more powerful than the South's racial customs. In Birmingham, they went to a men's store to buy some clothes, and when Mays pulled out a roll of hundred-dollar bills, a store clerk started to call the police. The store, and perhaps all of Birmingham, might have been embarrassed had a national hero been harassed in his own hometown, but all was forgotten once Mays identified himself to the manager.

Mays never mentioned the incident—just one more slight he would ignore. But Aaron remembered it and the lesson he learned. "It was okay to be black," he concluded in his autobiography, "as long as you were Willie Mays."

No matter the game or the circumstance, Mays always tried to give the fans something to talk about, even barnstorming across the South. "As the big star of the troupe, Mays more than filled the bill with his performance at bat and in the field," the *Sporting News* reported. "In the game, he smashed one of the longest homers seen in Atlanta, blasting the ball 460 feet up the vine-colored bank in center field at Ponce de Leon Park." In Columbus, Georgia, "Mays smashed one of the longest homers ever hit at Golden Park to thrill a crowd of 1,260. The wallop cleared the light pole towering over the left field stands." In Memphis, Tennessee, "Mays sparkled in the field." In Asheville, North Carolina, in Little Rock, Arkansas, in the Texas towns of Austin and Victoria, Mays hit home runs. In Longview, Texas, the game was delayed twenty-five minutes to allow all the fans, lined up around the block, to enter; 4,174 paid to watch. Mays, the *Sporting News* said, "rewarded the turnout by smashing a single, a triple, and a homer [and] made a tremendous throw from the 400-foot wall in deep center to nail a runner at third."

More than a hundred thousand fans, mostly African Americans, in more than two dozen towns saw Mays play that winter. He was promoted in newspapers and on radio, interviewed by reporters, invited into homes for dinner, and mobbed by fans. The games were only exhibitions, but not to Mays. Said Ernie Banks: "Willie was playing his usual reckless game, and Monte reminded him to take it easy, that his career with the Giants was more important. Willie said, 'This is the only way I can play.' "

That style caught up to him during the following year's barnstorming tour, which was, in general, far less successful. Attendance for the games—across four time zones in five weeks—fell significantly, and Mays's team found itself playing in near-empty ballparks. In Corpus Christi, Texas, for example, 820 fans attended the game, compared to 5,000 the previous year. There were only 683 in Memphis. Interest had fallen for two reasons. Black fans in the South tended to root for the Dodgers, and this team had no one from Brooklyn; Campanella and Newcombe were playing exhibition games with the Dodgers in Japan. More important was television. As sets became more common, fans could watch big leaguers without leaving their homes. The major leagues feared that their own attendance would suffer. That didn't happen, but it did suppress fan support for minor league games and exhibitions.

The direct effect on Mays and his team was less income, but they continued to win, for yet another future Hall of Famer, Frank Robinson, joined the team. Mays was still the headliner: in Little Rock, he twice got into rundowns, intentionally, between third and home, and twice he escaped while allowing the runners behind him to advance. But the games began to wear: driving in the dead of night, playing in the rain and cold, taking the field before empty seats, pocketing the tiny purses—the vagabond romance of Mays's Negro League days seemed far away. Then in Austin, Texas, he hurt his shoulder while sliding, and the following night he had to sit out a game in Victoria. The team lost, snapping a forty-nine-game winning streak dating from the previous year. Mays had to limit himself to pinch-hitting for several games, but that didn't prevent him from stealing home in Corpus Christi.

By the end of the tour, seven games had been canceled for weather, and the paid attendance marked a decline of about 67 percent from 1955. Based on the gate receipts, Mays's teammates each received $1,226.31, less $400 for travel expenses; Mays got a few hundred dollars more.

Shortly afterward, Mays conceded in an interview that the players had become a bit "tired" and "stale" by the end. Still, he expressed surprise at the waning fan interest: "Imagine that. People getting tired of baseball. I just can't understand it." He said the barnstormers would have better luck the next winter but perhaps without him. "I think if you play 154 games in the majors, you should not play winter ball," he said. "It's too much. Too much physically and too much mentally, because you live too much of the year in the same atmosphere."

But Mays didn't stop barnstorming. Given his spending habits, he needed the extra cash, but he also played in the off-season because playing baseball was what he did. In 1957, the barnstormers tried something different. They went to Latin America, starting with Mexico, where they played a team of national stars led by Cleveland's Bobby Avila. Like the Puerto Ricans, the Mexicans were passionate about baseball; they followed the American game, and they knew Willie Mays, who was more prepared for his reception after his tour in Puerto Rico. But even he was surprised when several thousand fans in Mexico City welcomed his team at the airport on October 11. They rushed through five games in three days, drawing more than 51,000 people. At a night game at Social Security Stadium in Mexico City, before a near-sellout of 23,659, fans would periodically rush the field for autographs from Mays and Wes Covington, a left fielder who had starred for the Braves in the World Series. In Veracruz, Mays had three hits, including a homer, and in Puebla he "drew cheers from a crowd of 7,465" for three sensational throws, according to the *Sporting News,* which continued: "The correspondent for *La Afición,* Mexico City's sports paper, said one of the heaves traveled 400 feet."

The next stop was the Dominican Republic, where Mays's All-Stars were met by so many at the airport in Ciudad Trujillo, the team's traveling secretary said, "They must have declared a holiday." Four games drew almost 30,000 fans. They soon played three games in Managua, Nicaragua, marking the first appearance of major leaguers in that country. The final leg of the trip was in Panama City, where the Americans won the last of three games, 2–1, with Mays stealing home.

It was a triumphant tour, with Mays's team winning fourteen of fifteen games and drawing 117,766 fans. The barnstormers played nine more games in the United States, including games in the U.S. and Mexico on the same day. On November 7, they played a day game in El Centro, California, and that evening they squared off in Mexicali, south of the border. Mays's team won both contests.

The barnstormers repeated their performance in 1958, playing twenty games in Mexico. But the following year, Stoneham asked Mays not to participate because he was recovering from a broken finger suffered in August. Mays agreed.

In 1960, Mays didn't barnstorm but did travel to Japan, where the San Francisco Giants played a series against the Yomiuri Giants. American teams had been playing in Japan since the 1930s and, after World War II, resumed in the early 1950s. The two governments had reestablished diplomatic ties, but for Japan's citizens to enthusiastically receive the American players so soon after Hiroshima was testament to baseball's universal appeal.

Not that the Japanese embraced everyone equally. Like fans everywhere, they wanted to see the biggest stars. So Mickey Mantle went there in 1955, Roy Campanella in 1956, Stan Musial in 1958. They finally got Willie Mays in 1960.

Mays knew hero worship, but this response was beyond compare. The team landed in Tokyo on October 20 in a driving rain and fierce winds. Several hundred dripping wet schoolchildren screamed and waved flags as the Giants walked down the ramp, Japanese starlets handing them flowers and gifts. The players then rode in a ten-mile motorcade to their hotel with the tops up on their convertibles. The cheering fans, hunkered under umbrellas, had to stoop to peek into the windows. A deluge of ticker tape and confetti greeted the procession in the downtown business district. About halfway through, a traffic jam brought the caravan to a halt, and a lunchtime crowd, some waving "Welcome Giants" flags, began circling the tiny red sports car that carried Mays. Shouting, "Say Hey," they clamored for autographs and began to rock the car. Panic briefly swept Mays, who kept the windows shut and the doors locked. Then policemen on motorcycles cleared a path and allowed the cars to proceed safely.

At a press conference later that day, Mays was nearly trampled by reporters in their eagerness to interview him, and he was introduced to the Japanese on national television. "I'll try my best on the field," he said. "I heard so much about Japan and am thrilled to see it for myself. I was surprised it was so cold for our arrival. I hope it warms up so I can see all those shrines and pagodas."

The Giants were to play sixteen games in Japan, each program featuring a cover photo of Mays leaping in the air, his left arm reaching high above his head, his outstretched glove catching the ball while exposing the heel of his hand. But on the field, Mays felt under the weather. His stomach was upset, and later his gums swelled up. After seven games, he was batting .227, with only one home run and five hits. "I've disappointed the Japanese fans," he said. "I hope I can snap out of the slump." As a team, the Giants lost two of their first three, an embarrassing start that gave the Japanese sports commentators a chance to rebuke the Americans. "The only thing impressive," one said, "is Willie Mays's $85,000 salary."

But Mays rallied. In the next four games he had nine hits, including two homers. The Giants traveled by overnight train to Toyama for two games and again by overnight train to Osaka, where they were again met by a ticker-tape parade. They played in ten cities in all, including Hiroshima, where Stoneham placed flowers at the Atomic Bomb Memorial Shrine.

The Giants reclaimed their respect in Japan, finishing with eleven wins, four losses, and a tie. Mays hit .393, with seven home runs. That was second best to Willie McCovey, who hit .423 and had eight homers, but Mays was named the Most Valuable Player. He may not have deserved it, but he was given a new Datsun Bluebird, which Nissan Motor could advertise as a car driven by Willie Mays. He was also given a Kobe bull.

"What am I going to do?" Mays asked. "My suitcase isn't big enough for a car or a bull?" He decided to sell them both, which, as far as the Datsun was concerned, was just as well. The steering wheel was on the wrong side.

With Mays in Japan, the Negro barnstormers who played in the United States and Latin America drew negligible crowds. Even though the team had brilliant players—Aaron, Robinson, Banks—none matched Mays's star power, and the team lost money.

The following year, 1961, the group's traveling secretary, Curtis Leak, announced that for the first time since 1947, no team of black major leaguers would barnstorm in the off-season. "We will not barnstorm this year for the simple reason that we could not get Willie Mays to sign up," Leak said. "To have a successful barnstorming tour, you must have some semblance of a good attraction, and Mays still is about the most colorful player around."

CHAPTER TWENTY-ONE

CHEERS FOR KHRUSHCHEV

In seven seasons, Mays had missed only eleven games, but he suffered his first serious injury during spring training in 1959. The circumstances were typical. In a lousy exhibition contest against the Red Sox, Mays, on second base, broke for third on an attempted steal. The batter hit a slow roller to the shortstop, who had no play, but Mays, instead of holding at third, rounded the bag and tried to score. The shortstop's throw was off the line, forcing the catcher, Sammy White, to reach high, leaving his left leg dangling a few inches off the ground. At that moment, Mays's sliding right leg crashed into the pointed end of White's shin guard, which cut through Mays's pant leg and ripped open his flesh to the bone. (He scored the run.)

Mays saw his bloody pant leg but didn't say anything. He got up, shook off the dust, and jogged off the field. He thought he would be fine, but the trainer, Doc Bowman, told him he'd have to go to the hospital, and Curt Barclay, a pitcher, drove them to the emergency room in his own car. Bowman described it as a "ragged, ugly wound": it required thirty-five stitches and a tetanus shot, and Mays was sidelined for two weeks.

The time off was a blessing. After the 1958 season, Willie and Marguerite had adopted a five-day-old baby and named him Michael. The family was together during spring training in Phoenix, where they rented a house in the city's Negro district; after the injury, Willie had extra time to spend with the baby. He enjoyed his duties. When Michael couldn't fall asleep, Willie would put him in his car and drive around the block until he nodded off. He even learned how to change diapers.

Mays described this period as P.M.—post Michael—and he often spoke of the bond he had with his young son, which was confirmed by reporters. When Milton Gross interviewed Mays in Phoenix two years later for the *Saturday Evening Post*, he noted how Michael would "toddle" beside his father, chattering, "Michael go bye-bye," as he was leaving with his mother. Gross wrote: "Willie fondled him lovingly. It's obvious he adores the child."

Mays was in the Opening Day lineup in 1959, but the spring training injury proved to be a bad omen, for both himself and opposing catchers. On June 1 in Milwaukee, trying to score from first on a double, Mays barreled into Del Rice, breaking the catcher's left leg. Mays had to leave the game as well with badly bruised shins. The previous inning, the benches had emptied after Rice applied a hard tag to a sliding runner—too hard, in the Giants' view. The umpires intervened before any blows could be thrown. After the game, several Braves believed Mays had "overdone" his slide to exact revenge. The play happened in the eighth inning in an 11–2 rout for the Giants; the game had already been decided when Mays broke Rice's leg.

Rice, however, defended Mays. "It wasn't his fault," he said. "He's got to slide. He was just trying to get home and I was trying to keep him from getting there. It's all part of the game." Mays said he tries to score every time he's on base, regardless of the circumstances; on this play, he was safe.

Three days later, he injured his shoulder on another home plate collision in Milwaukee, this time with catcher Del Crandall. He played four more games in three days, including every inning of a doubleheader, before finally sitting out the start of a game on June 8. Called to pinchhit in the eighth, he singled, stayed in, and singled again in the ninth. He then stole second, with the catcher's throw hitting him flush on an existing bruise in his back. Now hobbling, Mays played until the game ended in eleven innings. The next five games, he was available only for pinchhitting.

Even when Mays was supposed to rest, he often didn't. On July 24 against the Cubs, a stiff neck kept him out of the starting lineup, but he pinch-hit in the eighth and, carrying the potential winning run, tried to score on a squeeze play. With his spikes high, he smashed into Earl Averill, tearing the catcher's pants above the knee. Averill yelled at Mays, and the two had words, but home plate umpire Ken Burkhart averted a scuffle by shoving Mays toward the dugout. Mays, who was called out, ended up with a bruise on his thigh.

The Giants were supposed to be in their new ballpark in 1959, but construction delays kept them in Seals Stadium. The year was reminiscent of the previous season. The Giants again exceeded expectations—they were nineteen games over .500 on August 25—and they were again led by a young player who would win the Rookie of the Year. Willie McCovey, from Mobile, Alabama, was a quiet, leonine strongman whose left-handed swing generated as much power as any in baseball. Veteran baseball announcer Jack Buck said the hardest ball he ever saw hit was McCovey's—he golfed a low fastball that was sinking on a line when it cleared the center field fence. His nickname was "Stretch," for his long, 6-foot-4-inch reach at first base. He lacked Cepeda's charisma and confidence, but the humble twenty-one-year-old had no trouble endearing himself to the fans. In his first game on July 30, he faced the Phillies' Robin Roberts and went 4-for-4, with two singles and two triples. Major league pitchers were actually easier, he thought, because minor leaguers were so wild. He was another one of the team's "kids," an original San Francisco Giant, whom the fans could call their own.

McCovey's arrival gave the Giants two first basemen—McCovey and Cepeda—and trying to determine who to play where frustrated the team for years. At various times, both men would rotate through the outfield, forcing Mays to adjust his own play. In one of Cepeda's first games in left field, at Wrigley Field on August 10, he called for a fly ball in left center but missed it. The batter reached third. Mays was asked after the game if he could have caught it. "I could have caught that, easy," he said. Asked why he didn't call off Cepeda, he said, "I don't want to show anybody up. Orlando thought he could catch it. I don't want to hurt anybody's confidence."

In other respects, the season was all too familiar for Mays. He was hitting .339 at the end of May and then cooled off—his average dipped to .291 in early August—and he again faced a disapproving press. Some reporters believed that Mays, now twenty-eight, was nearing the end of his career. "Wonderful Willie Mays is in a slump again—and there are some who believe it may become permanent," wrote UPI on July 23. A fatal flaw had been discovered in his batting style: he stepped in the bucket, his front foot pointed toward third base, leaving him vulnerable to the breaking ball. Some stories sounded almost like a eulogy. "There was a growing solicitude today among S.F. writers . . . for Rigney because Willie Mays appears to be diminishing as a longball clutch slugger," wrote the *San Francisco News* on July 15. "In sorrow rather than anger, this is what the Giants' players say: 'We'd be six, seven games out in front if Willie had been cracking the long ball when it counted as he did when the club was in New York.'" At the time, he was hitting .307 with fifteen home runs.

Mays's salary increasingly drew attention. Fans have always been interested in players' salaries, and the incomes for such stars as Ruth and DiMaggio were staples for the press. But the fixation on Mays's salary seemed extreme. Game stories that had nothing to do with player incomes routinely mentioned Mays's income as if it were a defining part of his character; some broadcasts did as well. His high salary provided another justification for disapproval, and for some fans, his race surely intensified those resentments.

"There goes an $80,000 pop-up," a broadcaster muttered early in the season.

Never mind that Mays was hardest on himself. During an exhibition game, he dropped a fly ball that was ruled a double; according to the official scorer, any ball that Mays didn't catch was a hit. In between innings, Harry Jupiter, a reporter with the *Examiner,* saw Mays in the clubhouse.

"How can they call that a double when I dropped the ball?" he asked. Jupiter explained the reasoning. Then Mays asked, "Do you know anybody who wants this?" He threw Jupiter his glove. Angry about the play, Mays had ripped his mitt and now had no use for it. Jupiter kept it for himself.

For Mays, pleasing the San Francisco fans remained a struggle. The low point came on May 7 at home against the Dodgers. Mays was having a fine game, collecting a single, a double, and a triple, as well as two stolen bases and a run scored. Then he came up in the eighth with runners on second and third and one out, the Giants down by a run. The Dodgers decided to walk him intentionally, but on the fourth pitch Mays leaned over the plate, reached out, and swung. He popped out to the catcher, prompting a torrent of angry boos. The Giants didn't score and lost the game.

"The boner of the year!" roared one newspaper. "The boo-boo of the decade," said another. The play crystallized the view, already held by some critics, that Mays was more interested in his own success than the good of the team. "He is not entitled to be a law unto himself," an *Examiner* columnist lectured. "It is something you can't condone. I've known dozens of managers who would have punched Mays right on the ball field." The columnist said the play was "sure to become part of the Giants' San Francisco legend."

After the game, Mays sat despondently in front of his locker. "What can I say?" he said in a whisper. "I wanted a hit—I wanted to get those runs home. But Rig said it was a bad play, so I guess it was. Who am I to argue with the boss? So I guess I'm a blankety-blank player again."

Hank Sauer, Mays's closest friend on the team, said, "Nobody feels worse about it than Willie does. He's different from a lot of guys. He'll do anything to win. I thought he was going to cry for a minute when he came into the locker room."

While Mays didn't drive in the run, it was not an unreasonable play. Hitting behind Mays was Willie Kirkland, who was batting .200 and had already failed in three opportunities that day with runners in scoring position. Also, while superior batsmen like Stan Musial and Ted Williams looked for pitches in certain zones, Mays hacked at anything he could reach, often getting hits on pitches out of the strike zone. His chances of driving in a run by swinging at ball four were probably no worse than

Kirkland's chance of driving in a run with the bases loaded. (After Mays popped out, Kirkland ended the inning on a tap back to the mound.)

Mays was also criticized for his reluctance to bunt, even though he had never been a bunter, nor should he have. It made no sense to take the bat out of the hands of the team's best power hitter. But in San Francisco, the fans and reporters were used to the Pacific Coast League, where speed, bunting, and "small ball" were all emphasized. Home runs, hard to come by, were individual accomplishments, but games were ultimately won through teamwork. Hence Mays's aversion to bunting bespoke a deeper flaw in his character: he didn't like to "sacrifice."

"The fans here boo him on occasion—and Willie bruises easily," UPI wrote. "Mays seems to hit better when on the road than he does . . . at Seals Stadium."

Mays later said, "[The boos] were hard to understand, but I never let on that they hurt me."

Others were puzzled as well. Frank Coniff, an editor for the Hearst newspapers, visited San Francisco in September, the same month that the city welcomed the premier of the Soviet Union. "This is the damnedest city I ever saw in my life," Coniff said. "They cheer Khrushchev and boo Willie Mays."

The ballpark wasn't the only place Mays experienced problems. A far more frightening moment occurred at one-thirty in the morning on June 22, when a Coke bottle was hurled through the 6-by-8-foot window at his house on Miraloma Drive. Mays was asleep; also in the house was his visiting brother-in-law. Marghuerite had taken Michael to New York to attend her daughter's graduation from parochial school. According to the police, it appeared that one or more perpetrators drove up to the house, flung the bottle through the window, and raced off. Mays told the police that the bottle contained a note with a racist message, but he threw it out. The incident received little attention, which was how Mays wanted it. He told reporters that he didn't believe the attack reflected badly on the neighborhood because he assumed the perpetrators were from another part of town. In two subsequent autobiographies, he makes only one fleeting reference to the attack.

Mays, of course, was desperate to stay out of the headlines for anything controversial, even when he had been victimized. Given the media frenzy surrounding the purchase of the house, the last thing he wanted was to draw attention to his residence. Perhaps his lack of complaint explains why there was no public outcry and why the media were so cavalier. The act itself was designed to intimidate, to spread terror, to send a message—

literally and figuratively—to one black family and, by extension, to all blacks who would dare to live in a white neighborhood. That the bottle was thrown into a home where a baby lived made it all the more reprehensible. Yet the *Examiner* blithely wrote: "An incensed Giants fan threw a Coke bottle through Willie Mays' front window early yesterday. . . . The tosser's aim would have done credit to a major league center fielder. From the street, it took a throw of about 60 feet and deeply uphill to smash the middle pane of a plate glass picture window. . . . [The note] made a reference to his race and demanded that the Giants regain first place in the National League by beating the Braves, the police said. Not even this helped the Giants, who were pasted by Milwaukee yesterday, 13 to 3."

Whether the *Examiner* would have been similarly amused had the victims been white is unclear, but in this case, a criminal act had the same standing as a baseball game.

For Mays, the injuries continued to pile up. On August 7, in a home game against Cincinnati, he took a wide turn on a single and had to dive back into first base. His pinkie on his right hand hit the bag, and—he later said—"this one hurt." He stayed in the game. Later, the finger swelled up, and Bowman figured it was broken. Mays knew it was broken, but he refused to get it X-rayed. He assumed the doctors would put it in a splint or cast and keep him out of the lineup. Telling reporters that his finger was only a little sore, he didn't want the severity of the injury disclosed. If pitchers knew of it, they would jam him with inside fastballs. Mays was used as a pinch hitter in the next two games, then Rigney returned him to the starting lineup.

On September 11, the *Chronicle* wrote that Mays might be playing with a broken finger, which he had refused to have X-rayed. "I want no alibis," he said. "The finger is still a little sore and at times bothers me when I swing, but it's been that way for a month." And not a bad month either: he had pounded eleven home runs.

The boos. The injuries. The bottle through his window. Fatherhood. The pressures were changing Mays's outlook on baseball, and life. The work ethic was the same, but the context was different. "He invariably is among the first to arrive at the ballpark and among the last to leave," *Sports Illustrated* wrote in April 1959. "Sportswriters who follow the Giants around are agreed that Willie is one of the hardest working players they have ever seen. [But] Willie rarely clowns in pepper games. He loftily eschews gleeful locker-room pranks. It's unusual for him to provide a spirited and jeering exchange with one of his teammates. . . . He hustles as energetically as any of his teammates and bustles more thrillingly than most of them put together. The big difference is that Willie is now the star instead of the fondly regarded mascot."

Vin Scully, who'd seen Mays in all his youthful exuberance, interviewed him after a game in Los Angeles on August 28. Mays had just finished a bravura performance. The previous day, he had played all eighteen innings of a doubleheader in Philadelphia. The Giants then flew across the country, woke up in Los Angeles, and straggled onto the field against the Dodgers. Mays hit a double in the first inning and a home run in the second, knocking out Don Drysdale. He later notched a single and drove in three and scored two for the day. He also chased down a deep fly ball in left center by Wally Moon and, with a man on second, trapped a sinking drive so cleanly that the runner barely beat the throw to third. The Giants won, 5–0.

So, Vin Scully asked Willie on his radio show afterward, is baseball still just a game, or is it more of a business?

Asked about baseball over the years, Mays had always expressed his undiluted love, the game being his source of fulfillment and renewal. But now, jet-lagged from the road trip, bruised from various collisions, depleted by the long season, he said, "It's a business, Vin. When you've got a family, you've got to think of other things."

It was easy to grow nostalgic for the Say Hey Kid who happily pledged that he would play the game for free. But it was an expectation of eternal innocence, and the public begrudged its passing. At the season's end, the *Sporting News* voted Mays the most exciting player in baseball for the second year in a row, but in an editorial it said, "Willie Mays was once a carefree young ballplayer [but] of late, Mays doesn't seem quite as happy about it all. There are times when he seems to be brooding. Many factors enter into this. Whatever it is, one hopes that Willie some way, somehow can return to his carefree days."

The *Saturday Evening Post* soon suggested that he had outgrown his name: "Maybe it's about time to call him Bill."

During the season, the newspapers reported that Mays had had a fight with Giant outfielder Jackie Brandt, though the stories did not identify their sources and both Mays and Brandt denied the accounts. But according to Lon Simmons, the Giants' radio announcer, there were tensions. "Brandt was outspoken, and he was always criticizing Mays," Simmons says. "Willie was always willing to help others, but Brandt always thought Willie was trying to help him to make Willie look better." After the season, Brandt was traded to the Baltimore Orioles. "He wasn't good enough to stick around and bitch about Willie all the time," Simmons says. Brandt disputes that account.

In 1959, one of the better lines written about Mays appeared. In the All-Star Game in Pittsburgh, he hit a game-winning triple in the eighth inning. Bob Stevens, who had followed Mays the previous two years for the *Chronicle,* wrote: "Harvey Kuenn gave it honest pursuit, but the only center fielder in baseball who could have caught it hit it."

With the addition of two veteran starting pitchers—Sam Jones and Jack Sanford—and the midseason promotion of McCovey, the Giants assumed first place in early July and remained there, but could not stretch the lead to more than 3½ games. On September 17, they played the Braves at home and were one game ahead of the defending champions. The Giants faced Warren Spahn, a nineteen-game winner who had already beaten the Giants four times that year. Billed as the biggest game in the Giants' brief tenure in San Francisco, it proved to be Mays's finest performance to date in his new town. He singled in the first and second innings; in the fourth, with two men on base, he hit a tremendous home run high into the left field pavilion seats; he walked in the sixth and capped a clinching three-run rally with another RBI single in the seventh. He drove in five runs, and his four hits in four official at-bats put him over the .300 mark, to .303. The Giants won, 13–6.

The fans went crazy for Mays, his performance all the more heroic in light of his physical condition. The *Sporting News* said, "Willie was playing while virtually patched together with adhesive tape. The day before, in the series opener, he slammed into the right field cement barrier to make a spectacular catch of Ed Mathews's long drive. He paid for his leap with sore ribs. His left shoulder was already sore and he had a three-inch square abrasion on his left thigh, the results of previous collisions with the fences. Additionally, a swollen little finger on his right hand may be broken. But Mays refuses to have it X-rayed. 'I don't want them to take me out of the lineup until we clinch the pennant,' he said."

The Giants had a two-game lead with eight to go, and a World Series seemed likely, though it would have been a mixed blessing for San Francisco. The new ballpark still wasn't complete, so the games would be played in Seals Stadium, which would draw scorn from the national press. Even more troubling, the American Medical Association had scheduled its annual convention in San Francisco at that time, and the major hotels were booked solid.

Alas, the Giants promptly lost the next three games at home to the Dodgers, who took over first. Mays went 3-for-10, which drew a smattering of boos. The Giants then went on the road for their final five games, but they were spent—except for Mays. First in Chicago and then St. Louis, he pounded ten hits in eighteen at-bats, including three homers and two doubles. The Giants still lost four of five and finished in third place, three games behind the Dodgers and Braves.

The Dodgers won the playoff and went on to prevail in the World Series, making them the first major league team in California to win a championship.

Mays's second season in San Francisco was like his first, though he believed, given his injuries, that 1959 was superior. His batting average fell 34 points, to .313, but he had more home runs (34) and RBIs (104). His 125 runs scored were a career high, and he again led the league in stolen bases. He won the Gold Glove and led the Giants in home runs, runs, steals, on-base percentage, and slugging percentage. He played in all but three games, and in the last fourteen games, he hit .460. The fans voted Sam Jones (21–15) the team's MVP.

After the season, Willie and Marghuerite decided to sell their house on Miraloma Drive and move back to New York; Willie would rent a small house during the season. After all the hurdles in buying the home, they stayed for less than two years. Neither of them cited the Coke bottle incident, though that was a factor. Weighing heavily on Marghuerite was a feeling of isolation. By her own admission, she was never that social, but she still felt removed and concluded that this wasn't the place to raise their son. "I didn't know any of my neighbors," Marghuerite said.

Willie was resigned to events. He wasn't bitter; after all, Negroes couldn't live wherever they wanted in New York, so why should San Francisco be different? What's more, he wasn't particularly attached to the Miraloma house when they decided to buy it, but once he faced resistance, he had to go through with the purchase or be seen as weak. It was no different than baseball. If a pitcher knocks you down, you don't go back to the dugout— you stay at the plate and try to hit a home run. So they lived at the house and integrated the neighborhood; now it was time to go. Asked several years later about projections of plunging property values if he bought the house, Willie said dryly, "They ran sightseeing buses to point out where I lived, and the value went up."

The Mayses' move to New York attracted little attention in the press. Edward Howden, who had played such a main role in helping them buy the house, didn't even know they had moved until many years later. He was also unaware of the bottle incident. That's what happens, he says, when you don't read the sports pages.

No one imputed any larger significance to the family's leaving the city. The *Sporting News*, which published stories by the beat reporters in San

Francisco, noted that some residents had protested Willie's buying the house: "However, the only incident since then occurred when a bottle containing a note was thrown through a window of Mays's home"—as if it were a mere inconvenience.

Willie and Marghuerite bought a rambling, Normandy-style stone house for $75,000 in New Rochelle. A definite step up, the home included seven bedrooms, five bathrooms, a solarium of rare tropical plants, and servants' quarters over a four-car garage. New Rochelle is a fashionable part of Westchester County, and the house was in a quiet, predominantly white neighborhood, where the UN ambassadors of Indonesia and Ghana also lived. The Mayses moved in without incident, but Willie himself was no more visible in his new neighborhood than in his old.

His neighbors shouldn't have been surprised. Willie was once asked why he didn't reach out more to friends, relatives, reporters, and fans. He pondered the question, shrugged, and said, "I don't pursue people."

HEADWINDS

It was all about the parking. Horace Stoneham didn't have to build a new stadium. The $5 million in bond money already approved for a new park could have been used to give Seals Stadium a second level. The "double-decker" option had several strong advocates, including Lefty O'Doul and the popular columnist Herb Caen. It was a crime, they felt, to tear down America's most beautiful ballpark. But Seals Stadium had very little parking, and Stoneham retained bitter memories of the Polo Grounds—its inability to accommodate cars assured its demise. In his negotiations with officials in San Francisco, Stoneham was promised a new stadium with ten thousand parking spaces. Even when it became clear that the project was going to cost more than $5 million, Stoneham insisted on getting his stadium and his parking.

The Giants' new home, seven miles south of downtown, was on a tiny peninsula jutting into the San Francisco Bay. The land was called Candlestick Point, due to—take your pick—a bird of the same name that was once prevalent in the Bay Area or its rock formations, which loosely resembled candlesticks. Regardless, parking would not be a problem. What would be a problem was that the envisioned space was mostly underwater. The builder had to gouge more than 5 million cubic yards of dirt from adjacent Bayview Park Hill to create a sixty-acre landfill. "Taking down a mountain to fill a sea, a stupendous job," marveled Westbrook Pegler, another columnist.

Stoneham got his parking spaces (about eighty-five hundred), and Candlestick Park, the second stadium built since the Great Depression, became the first of eight large ballparks constructed in the 1960s. The "Stick" appeared to have some promising features. The electronic scoreboard, powered by six thousand lamps, was the world's largest; the seats, at twenty-one inches, were wider than usual and had comfortable wooden backs and armrests; a rounded shield at the top of the upper deck would block the wind. Those benefits paled in comparison to the most ambitious effort: radiant heating, in which hot water would flow from a central boiler through wrought-iron pipes in a concrete slab beneath the box seats. No outdoor site had ever tried such a thing. On frigid nights, fans would be able to watch the games in warmth and comfort. The architect, John Bolles, said the park was designed to endure "as long as the Coliseum in Rome."

Best of all, Candlestick Park was going to be a boon for Willie Mays. So promised Bill Rigney, who never missed an opportunity to rouse expectations. "Willie should have his greatest year, both at bat and in the field," he said. Candlestick had deeper fences—420 feet to center, 397 feet in the alleys—than those at Seals Stadium, so Mays would now have more room to make catches. "He'll hit more doubles and triples," Rigney promised. "A lot of Willie's line drives to left center hit the Seals Stadium fence so hard that outfielders were able to hold him to a single."

Mays agreed. "The new park will give me a chance to show what I can do."

True enough. Mays played more games in Candlestick, almost nine hundred, than in any other ballpark. That alone deserves commendation, for Candlestick may have been the worst park in the history of Major League Baseball—it was certainly the most ridiculed—and right-handed hitters suffered more than lefties. The gale-force winds that swept left to right constantly knocked down long hits that should have been homers while the swirling gusts, bone-chilling cold, and damp grass complicated every aspect of the game. That Mays remained baseball's finest player, despite those conditions, amazed his peers.

"Until I played at Candlestick," Ozzie Smith said, "I never realized how great Willie Mays was. My god, what would he have done in a real ballpark?"

There were warnings before it was built. The *Chronicle*'s outdoor columnist, Bud Boyd, said the site was a major source of pollution. "The area stinks, literally," he wrote. Actually, the whole project smelled. The man who sold the city the land for $2.7 million, Charles Harney, was also the stadium's contractor, and he was then made a director of a nonprofit organization to arrange additional financing. Public outcry forced him to step down. A grand jury investigated the stadium's funding and million-dollar cost overruns; the Stick ultimately cost $15 million. A Teamsters' strike delayed the installation of the seats. The City Fire Prevention Bureau called the park a "fire trap."

Most of those problems could be fixed. What could not be changed was the weather. Stoneham had visited Candlestick Point on a calm summer morning in 1957, the story goes, and was impressed. Then construction began, and one afternoon Chub Feeney stopped by and saw cardboard boxes fly past him.

"Does the wind always blow like this?" he asked.

"Only between the hours of one and five," said the worker.

Opening Day, on April 12, 1960, was warm and bright, and the game drew a near-capacity crowd of 42,269. There were few mishaps, though the public address announcer did alert the crowd that someone's boat was adrift. Ty Cobb, who lived in nearby Atherton, was in attendance, and Vice President Nixon, casting for votes in the coming presidential election, threw out the first pitch. In the clubhouse, veteran pitcher Billy Loes asked him, "Would you please take care of our fucking income taxes?"

The following night, however, turned cold, and the heaters in the stands were turned on. Only smoke came out. The pipes were too far away from the concrete slabs or the slabs were too thick, so the system was useless. The dugout was also supposed to be heated, but that didn't work either. Rigney didn't wear a jacket to persuade his team that it really wasn't that cold. The players still froze. The reporters couldn't see home plate from the press box, though the fans could see an exposed toilet in the dugout. (That was quickly fixed.) As predicted, the smell of sewage hung in the air. The stadium had parking spaces, but the fans were forced to climb a long hill to the front gates, and the hill was implicated in a rash of fatal heart attacks. The ballpark was not simply uncomfortable or unsightly, it was a serial killer. "Candlestick Park claimed its sixth heart attack fatality in 19 games," the *Sporting News* intoned. "William Smith, a deputy sheriff, had just climbed up 'Cardiac Hill.' . . . He was pronounced dead on arrival at the park's emergency dispensary." By 1962, Cardiac Hill had claimed sixteen victims.

The Stick's most infamous feature was the howling winds that whipped off San Francisco Bay and struck the Bayview Park Hill, just beyond the park's third base side. The ballpark's designers believed the slope would deflect the gales away from the stadium. Instead, the winds came over the hill, swooped down into the park, rushed across the outfield, caught the overhang of the stands along the right field line, swung back toward home, and blew past third. Candlestick was not so much a capricious wind tunnel as a ruthless vortex. At times, a player's shirt would be blowing one way and his pants the opposite. "You'd start the game and the wind would be in your face," recalled pitcher Mike McCormick. "In the third or fourth inning, it would hit you from the third base side, and then, if you survived, later in the game it would come at you from behind. We'd all know it was the same wind, but how in the hell it would do all those kinds of crazy things, I never knew."

The heavy grass added to the players' woes. Dampness from the early-morning fog soaked the grass, so the players' feet were wet and cold. Thick fog added surreal touches. One time, a high pop foul went into the fog, and the ball was never seen again. The sluggish air masses contributed to the bleak image of windswept badlands, the ground strewn with debris, the players blowing into their hands, the fans shivering beneath parkas. "I thought I was going to die," Ruben Gomez said. To limit the dust swirls, the infield was doused with oil until the earth became so hard and rocky that ground balls became treacherous. Before games, McCormick would put his glove against the right field fence and let go. The glove stayed on the fence "for a couple of extra seconds" before falling. After games, Doc Bowman would say, "Well, the cleanup crew is gonna go out there and pick up those telephone books off the fence." High over the scoreboard in right center was a large clock; on occasion, the minute hand, in its courageous push toward the 12, would find a gale-force wind, stop, quiver, and plunge back to the 6.

In 1961, San Francisco welcomed the All-Star Game to showcase the newest stadium. It did not go well. In the early innings, the heat caused nearly a hundred fans to seek medical attention. Then, without warning, the winds came, and one gust blew a pitcher off the mound, which wouldn't have been so embarrassing except it was a Giant pitcher. Stu Miller was a little guy—when Eddie Stanky first saw him, he asked, "Who's the stenographer?"—and that made him vulnerable. "The wind blew me off the mound," he told reporters after the game. "It was the worst I've ever seen it here. I had taken my stretch and checked the runners when a gust moved me just before I made the pitch." In fairness, Miller later insisted that the wind didn't actually blow him off the mound; it simply nudged him. Regardless, this Midsummer Classic was all about the elements. "The wind, you have to feel it to believe it," said Baltimore Oriole manager Paul Richards. "Conditions were as near impossible as anything I've seen."

The fans were no less miserable, so many enjoyed the spectacle of Melvin Belli, the flamboyant attorney known for his personal injury cases, suing Stoneham over the Stick's tormented heating system. Belli argued that he had bought season tickets with the expectation of being warm, and a jury awarded him damages of $1,598. When Stoneham was slow to pay him, Belli demanded custody of Willie Mays and asked the sheriff to guard him as well as the "movable items" at the park, including the Scotch in the front office. Law enforcement officials said they were familiar with "attachment writs" on horses but not star baseball players. Belli said, "We're not going to put Willie in the sheriff's warehouse. Maybe we should. It's a lot warmer than Candlestick." Stoneham eventually paid Belli and then printed a legal waiver in the game program, disavowing responsibility for the heater.

Stoneham's own haste to complete the park before the Dodgers built theirs was probably his greatest fault. A consulting firm, Medtronics Associates, later said that had the stadium been built only a few hundred yards in a different direction, the winds would not have been nearly as severe. Medtronics concluded that the weather conditions had not been checked before construction, and at this point, the best you could do at Candlestick is affect the direction of the wind but not the velocity. (That information cost Stoneham $55,000.)

Dodger Stadium, meanwhile, funded entirely with private money, opened in Chavez Ravine in 1962 and remains one of the major league's best parks. It has sixteen thousand parking spaces.

The Stick was indeed a laughingstock. Herb Caen said that you couldn't blame the architect for the ballpark—"after all, it was his first one." Just two months after it opened, *The Californian*, a monthly magazine, published a story, "The Giants Ballpark: A $15 Million Swindle." *Harper's* published an article the following year: "How Not to Build a Ballpark." Among players and coaches, there was no shortage of complaints.

"The Candlestick weather leaves you depressed," Eddie Bressoud said.

Rocky Colavito, who played in the 1961 All-Star Game: "If I had to play here, I'd think seriously about quitting."

Roger Maris: "The trouble with this ballpark is that they built it alongside the bay. They should have built it under the bay."

Jim Wohlford: "The only difference between Candlestick and San Quentin is that at Candlestick they let you go home at night."

When asked what would improve Candlestick, Jack Clark said, "Dynamite."

Willie Mays began 1960 with renewed hopes and increased expectations. Signing for $85,000, he was now the highest paid player in the major leagues; both Stan Musial and Mickey Mantle, coming off subpar years, had taken pay cuts. Mays's status as top wage earner was meaningful as a sign of respect, even if it gave his critics more ammunition against him. Also pleased the Giants were getting their new ballpark, Mays assumed that Candlestick would be built to take advantage of the team's strength—its young, right-handed power hitters: Cepeda, Alou, and himself. Yankee Stadium had been built with a short right field porch for Babe Ruth, and Mays figured the Giants would do the same for their best players. He also believed a different stadium would be a fresh start for him. Seals Stadium now lay in rubble. Perhaps at the Stick, he would not have to compete with the ghost of Joe DiMaggio.

Mays entered Candlestick for the first time the day before the opener, and his first thought was: if Seals Stadium was too small, this is too big. His power was to the alleys, but the alleys at Candlestick were almost 400 feet away. He'll always remember his first swing in batting practice. Leaning against the winds, he hit the ball and broke his bat. How does that happen in batting practice? He assumed the gale had something to do with it.

The conditions didn't bother Mays much at Seals Stadium. Appearing on a Bob Hope show in 1958, he was asked about the weather. "It's not bad," Mays said, "when you can see it through the fog."

But Candlestick was entirely different. How would he catch fly balls? A stadium architect told him that he'd have to use all his speed to track down routine flies that would twist and turn in the wind, and he soon saw that weird stuff happened on balls in the air. A high pop-up by McCovey that was called by the second baseman hit a jet stream and sailed over the fence. Other pop-ups that were called by the first baseman would be caught in foul territory behind third.

Mays thought he could dominate a park physically; he always felt in control. But one of his strengths—the ability to instantly determine the flight of the baseball—was now negated by hits that fluttered like Ping-Pong balls. He would call for hits in center that he would end up catching in right or close to the infield. One hit that he thought would be a home run fell in front of him for a single.

In his first year at the new stadium, Mays discovered the secret to playing fly balls, which he'd use for the rest of his career. When a ball was hit, he wouldn't move. Instead, he would count to five, then he would give chase. Each day, he would also try to measure the wind, and he considered his efforts a science that even an airplane engineer could not have solved. In some instances, the weather conditions created opportunities for breathtaking catches. In 1961, Stan Musial blasted a ball more than four hundred feet into "the howlingest winds in Candlestick history." Mays leaped high against the eight-foot fence, a wire gashing his left knee. Musial, in his twentieth year in the majors, was flabbergasted. "It was a great catch," he said. "The greatest."

Mays didn't ridicule Candlestick, as others did, but when asked about it, he said, "The people who built the ballpark just didn't know what they were doing, but we had to play there, so what could we do?" He made adjustments at the plate. Unable to consistently pull the ball over the fence, he tried hitting to right center, which reinstated the stroke he had used earlier at Durocher's request. When he went on the road, he returned to his natural swing, but the adjustments were tricky. "I had to stay on the road a week or two before I got my timing back again," he said. "Then the road trip was over and I had to go back to Candlestick and start hitting to right again. This messed me up." Of Mays's twenty-nine homers his first year at the Stick, only twelve came at home.

Over the years, those numbers evened out, but each season he still hit long balls to left that were knocked down by the wind. National League umpire Doug Harvey, who began his career in 1962 and worked about a dozen games a year at Candlestick, says he saw many balls hit by Mays in which the left fielder would turn and run back, then have to run forward to make the catch. "Willie was always swinging to hit the long ball," Harvey says. "He never choked up. What was hard on Willie was Candlestick."

Estimates vary on how much Candlestick affected Mays's home run totals over the twelve years he played there. Some statisticians have calculated that the winds cost him some 165 home runs; others say it was half that. Mays places the number somewhere in between. What is clear is that he made the adjustments, often hitting the ball to the opposite field, and accumulated 202 homers at the Stick, compared to 193 on the road. He also led the league in homers three times during that period.

What may have hurt Mays even more at Candlestick was how much room the fielders had to catch foul balls. That cost him an unknown number of at-bats every year. All of the new parks in the 1960s—and seven were in the National League—moved the fans farther away from the field, giving fielders more room for pop fouls.

These are important factors when considering Mays's career numbers, particularly when compared to the likes of Babe Ruth or Barry Bonds. He did not play in home ballparks, nor in an era, that favored hitters. Hitting had been in decline since the 1930s, but the trend accelerated in the 1960s. In addition to the larger ballparks, the strike zone was expanded in 1963 in response to Maris's breaking of Ruth's single-season home run record in 1961. The consequences were dramatic. In 1963, home runs dropped by 10 percent while batting averages fell by twelve points. Other trends—bigger gloves for fielders, a more sophisticated use of the bullpen, the emergence of the "slider"—all favored the pitchers. The *New York Times'* Arthur Daley contended that modern baseball—night games and cross-country flights—had cursed the hitters who had to play every day: "Baseball was once a leisurely, delightful pastime that permitted athletes to stick to the set routine that afternoon play provided. Their lives are now totally disrupted with violent switches from afternoon to night to twilight-night games and other atrocities. On top of this, expansion to the Pacific Coast has introduced time zones as much as three hours apart. The players eat at crazy hours, sleep at crazy hours and live on a catch-as-catch-can basis. Their finely tuned physical condition is jolted repeatedly. Sharpness disappears."

The 1960s saw some of the finest pitching performances in history: Sandy Koufax's four no-hitters (including one perfect game), Bob Gibson's 1.12 ERA in 1968, Denny McLain's 31–6 record in 1968, Juan Marichal's seven consecutive seasons in which his ERA did not exceed 2.76.

Willie Mays, in short, had to play more than half of his career in what Bill James calls "baseball's second dead-ball era," and the Stick was one more headwind to overcome.

The Giants were favored to the win the pennant in 1960, and they notched fifteen victories in their first twenty-two games. Mays, still adjusting to Candlestick, only had two home runs in the first month but was hitting .425. Then, before a home game on June 18, a grim and pale Chub Feeney approached Rigney on the field. The manager smiled weakly. "It looks like you've got something to tell me you don't want to tell me," he said. Feeney said that Stoneham had just fired him. Rigney, misty-eyed, headed for the clubhouse.

At the time, the Giants were 33–25, in second place and only four games behind. Mays was shocked and saddened. For all of their early problems, he had gotten along fine with Rigney in recent years, and he couldn't believe a manager would be fired in June when the team had a good record. But the Giants had just lost three straight home games to the first-place Pirates, which gave Stoneham the excuse he needed. The owner held Rigney responsible for the previous year's collapse, and Rigney was balking at Stoneham's demands to change the lineup. Moreover, the fans had begun to pillory Stoneham for Candlestick and the public funds that had been squandered, and they booed the team during its recent losses. Change was needed.

"It was Rig's job to arouse the players," Stoneham said. "This he did not do."

Mays knew better. "Horace felt pressured into making a decision that he thought would make everyone else happy," he said, "when actually the only thing necessary was to keep going as we were."

Most of the players were angered by the change, though Rigney gained some vindication. He managed the Los Angeles Angels in their first year, 1961, and, after finishing a surprising third, was named manager of the year.

Replacing Rigney was Tom Sheehan, a massive, bespectacled old-timer who had played his first game in the majors in 1915 and now, at sixty-six, would be making his debut as a manager. Stoneham wouldn't say if Sheehan was a permanent replacement, an interim, or what. His official title had been chief scout, though his unofficial role was Stoneham's loyal drinking buddy, a lively raconteur whose stint with the Yankees had given him a trove of stories about Babe Ruth's sexual adventures. Perhaps because Sheehan had once been the house detective for a hotel, his unlikely move to the dugout fueled suspicions that he had been Stoneham's clubhouse spy and had engineered Rigney's ouster.

It was clear that Sheehan was unfit for the job in every sense. He was so overweight that he didn't have a uniform for four days. "I think Omar the tentmaker had to make it," Stu Miller quipped. The players called him "Santa"—not a compliment. He was capable of denouncing his players' late-night card games while tolerating undisciplined play on the field. He couldn't motivate his players or win their respect. Once, when he went to replace Jack Sanford, the pitcher bolted from the mound before the manager could get there. Sanford was fined $200. Sheehan had few friends in the press and didn't help his image by conducting interviews in his underwear in his hotel room. Dick Young called him "an engaging old windbag."

Mays felt a measure of sympathy for him but was frustrated by his passivity and ineptitude. "He was in uniform in body only," he said. Sheehan, for example, would use his left-handed starters, Mike McCormick and Billy O'Dell, in Los Angeles, even though the Coliseum had a short left field fence and the Dodgers had a long lineup of right-handed hitters. Mays urged Sheehan to go with his right-handed starters, but he refused. "If a guy can pitch, he can pitch anywhere," he told Mays. The Giants lost five of eight in Los Angeles.

Mays had a more serious dispute with Sheehan late in the season, after the Giants had been eliminated from the pennant race. On September 13, after a game in Pittsburgh, Mays asked Sheehan for the next night off, in Philadelphia, so he could visit his family in New Rochelle. Sheehan said he could visit his family but had to return in time for the game. An angry Mays stormed out and threatened not to return at all. Sheehan said he would fine him heavily if he missed the game.

No one knew if Mays was going to be at Connie Mack Stadium the next evening. Was it actually possible that he would quit the team? But when the team bus rolled up at 6:30 P.M., Mays was in the clubhouse, waiting. He had gotten home at 2 A.M. and left for Philadelphia that afternoon. He was still upset, but after the game—in which he picked up two hits and an RBI in a losing effort—he had settled down. Reporters asked if he'd really considered quitting, and Mays spoke, for him, at unusual length about his dedication to the game and the financial imperatives that he faced.

"I guess the old man wants me to play every game, so I play every game," he said. "That's all there is to it. What's this talk about quitting? That doesn't make sense. I'm happy playing here. Everybody on this club has been very good to me—Mr. Stoneham, Chub Feeney, everybody—and I want to keep on playing. I'm getting good money. I can't afford to quit. It's my life. If they want me to quit, they'll have to pull the uniform off me."

Mays acknowledged the stress of renting a house in San Francisco during the season while his family was in New York, but said, "I'm getting paid good money to play ball, so I'll play ball." Asked if he was worried about his standing with the Giants, he said, "When you start worrying, it's time to get out. I just want to do the best I can. We've still got twelve games—that's all I'm thinking about."

Mays played in 153 out of 154 games that year, and under the circumstances it was an exceptional season. The Giants had had worse teams in his career, but perhaps none that were more disappointing. They went 46–50 under Sheehan and finished in fifth place, sixteen games out of first. The players, knowing that the hapless manager would soon be gone, routinely broke curfew and played in all-night card games (Mays was not among them); the team's motto was supposedly "Shut up and deal." Meanwhile, they performed with listless detachment on the field. In one inning alone, in a game against the Dodgers, their five errors led to eight unearned runs.

It cannot be said that Mays hustled on every play during the year, but his individual effort was memorable. Twice in 1960, for example, he scored from first base on a single, though neither time was he running on the pitch. The Giants won both games by a single run. In one instance, against Chicago, Mays took advantage of the right fielder's lackadaisical throw into second base to score in the ninth. The right fielder, Bob Will, said he wanted to hold the runner on first to set up the double play. Strictly speaking, that was the right decision, but Mays didn't go by the book. "I made up my mind if the throw went to second," he said defiantly afterward, "I was going home." In that same series, Mays made a catch, on a sinking, tailing line drive in right center off the bat of Ed Bouchee, that was considered one of his finest. A photograph shows Mays stretched out, reaching for the ball, his glove halfway off his hand. The catch demonstrated a basic difference between Mays and his peers. Most outfielders, as they try to close on a ball after a long run, tend to lose control, resulting in sloppy dives. Mays rarely lost control, usually kept his feet, and seemed to generate more momentum, more power, as he lunged for the catch. In this case, the San Francisco crowd gave him a standing ovation.

In one game in Cincinnati, he hit two home runs and a single, stole home, and recorded ten putouts, two shy of the record, and in an eleven-inning game in Philadelphia, he tied another record by hitting three triples. Perhaps most remarkable, at least for some of his critics in San Francisco, Mays bunted safely three times, which won him a necktie from Russ Hodges; the announcer had wagered that Mays couldn't get three bunt hits in one year. All told, Mays was the team's only player to hit over .300 (.319), and he led the squad in every offensive category except doubles. That included home runs (29), RBIs (103), and runs scored (107).

Sheehan's dismissal was announced while he was touring with the team in Japan. He took the news in stride. "General Douglas MacArthur and me have something in common," he said. "We were both relieved of command in Japan."

The disappointing year brought into focus the racial tensions on the club, though the tensions may have involved the white reporters who covered the team as much as the players themselves. The relatively high number of black and Latin Giants always made race and ethnicity a subtext. While most San Franciscans welcomed the nonwhite players, others wrote hate mail to the Giants complaining about "Rig's jigs" and then "Sheehan's shines." Rigney himself stopped opening his mail because of the bigoted comments.

As long as the team was competitive, race was not a public issue, but that ended in 1960. After the season, the publisher of the *Sporting News*, J. G. Taylor Spink, visited San Francisco to conduct an autopsy on what had happened to the squad. After his interviews, his story enumerated the problems, which included "too many Negroes." Spink cited other issues, such as the lack of leadership, the players' resentment of Candlestick, and the bullpen. But according to him, the problem "most frequently mentioned as the cause of the Giants' downfall [was] too many Negro players." Spink's sources, presumably other writers and Giants executives, didn't say that the Negroes had performed badly. There were just too many of them. Spink himself made no effort to verify or disprove the claim.

Sports Illustrated, on September 26, elaborated on this theme. "In private," the article said:

there are several dozen players, coaches, managers, writers and executives who will tell you what is really wrong with the Giants: too many Negroes. They said it last year and they are saying it now, out of the corners of their mouths, after looking warily around. Sometimes half a dozen people will be looking around and speaking out of the corners of their mouths in one small room at the same time. "That's the real reason the Giants are losing," they will say, "but, of course, you can't print it."

Even a cursory assessment of the Giants would reveal the claim as false. In 1960, the Giants had five African Americans, including Mays. The pitcher with the most wins, Sam Jones, was also black; he went 18–14, with a 3.19 ERA. Starting outfielder Willie Kirkland had the third-most hits, and his .252 average was twelve points higher than his career average. The one African American who had a poor season was Willie McCovey, whose sophomore swoon resulted in a brief return to the minors. The fans booed him mercilessly, and he finished the year with a .238 average and thirteen home runs. The Giants also had a black player from the Bahamas, Andre Rodgers, and four Latins, including Juan Marichal, who was called up in July and went 6–2, with a 2.66 ERA.

Whether the consensus that the Giants had "too many Negroes" was shorthand for all nonwhite players or just African Americans is unclear, but *Sports Illustrated* repudiated the spurious charge that the Negroes had done the team in. "What the Giants lack is leadership—and the responsibility here must be shouldered by the whites. The best ballplayers on the club are Negroes, yet the Negroes, even if they chose to, could not lead because the whites would refuse to follow."

Mays was asked directly about the issue during spring training the following year. "When baseball people were asked what was wrong with the Giants," Milton Gross said, "they'd answer, 'Too many Negroes.'"

"If that was the case," Mays said, "why is everybody looking for colored boys? Mr. Stoneham, he doesn't care what color you are if you can play ball. Every year, Mr. Stoneham brings up four or five colored boys from our farm system."

Mays also discounted the claim that Sheehan had failed to inspire the Negroes and that dissension existed among the colored players. "It happens with every club," he said. "Everybody has different hangouts, but I don't think we had cliques. We played cards a lot together, but nothing you could make a big thing about."

Mays's view that "everybody" was "looking for colored boys" was probably an overstatement. Only the smart teams were looking for them. By 1960, fifty-seven blacks were in the major leagues, and they had become a dominant force. In the previous decade, they had won eight MVP awards, six Rookie of the Year trophies, three batting championships, and nine base-stealing titles. Mays, along with Hank Aaron, Ernie Banks, and Frank Robinson, were four of the best players in the game, all under thirty, and a wave of younger black stars was right behind them. Every team should have been stricken with "too many Negroes."

A more accurate assessment was that too many bigots complained about too many Negroes and then relied on too many reporters to protect them.

Charles Einstein was a talented sportswriter, novelist, and screenwriter whose father was a radio comedian and whose half-brother was the actor Albert Brooks. Charlie's own prose was infused with a droll wit; he once described Doc Bowman as "so short-legged that when he sits down he looks like a comma." Einstein first covered Mays in New York and continued his reportage when he took a job in San Francisco for the *Examiner*. He was the ghostwriter for two of Mays's autobiographies and, more than any other journalist, dedicated his news columns to celebrating "a man named Mays" (one of his favorite phrases).

One late night in Philadelphia, Einstein walked into a hotel bar and heard three white Giant players making racist comments about Mays as part of a larger argument that he was overrated. Outraged, Einstein tried to defend Mays but failed. Said one of the players: "That's what you think. And don't go putting this in the paper, you son of a bitch."

The conversation took a different turn when another player pointed to a black man in the bar. "Who's the nigger?"

"A writer," Einstein said.

"Nigger paper?"

"He writes for the *New York Times*."

"I'll be a dirty bastard," said the player, who had heard the *Times* had sympathetic views on race. "It figures."

Einstein recounted the exchange two years later in his book about the Giants, *A Flag for San Francisco*. However, he didn't name the bigots and never wrote a newspaper story about the incident or anything specific about the racial climate on the team. Such an article might have shed light on why the Negroes were roundly implicated for the Giants' misfortunes, why unnamed sources freely disparaged their mere presence, and why Mays himself, as the most prominent minority, was held to a different standard than all the other players.

But it was a different era. The teams typically paid for the reporters' travel expenses, food, and booze; the Giants would leave a bottle of whiskey in the writers' hotel rooms. Across the league, reporters and players rode together on the same trains and planes; played cards together, drank together, caroused together, and drank some more. The cozy relationship ensured that the players' misdeeds off the field would stay out of print. "I wasn't going to squeal," said San Diego sportswriter Phil Collier, who began his career around 1950. "I rode in the back of the plane and the bus with the guys. I went out and drank with them every night. I always said I was going to write a book and call it, *The Bases Are Loaded and So Was I*."

Einstein was a product of that era, and even his fierce loyalty to Mays was not enough to expose the team's racists, including those in the hotel bar. He knew that he had betrayed his hero and his friend, not to mention his readers. "I don't take these guys on," he lamented in his book. "I tell myself I'm not going to change them nohow. . . . I got no guts in me."

CHAPTER TWENTY-THREE

THERE'S A FEEL
IN THE AIR

The year 1961 began on a strange note. For the first time in Mays's career, Stoneham did not offer him a raise. He sent Mays a contract for the same salary, $85,000, as he had the previous year. Mays thought he deserved an increase. "Any time I knock in a hundred runs and score another hundred, I think I'm entitled to get more money," he said. But neither Mays nor any other player had any leverage. The reserve clause, which bound a player to the team that signed him, would remain intact for another fourteen years. Over time, some of the game's superstars, including Babe Ruth, Lou Gehrig, and Joe DiMaggio, had engaged in bitter holdouts to extract more money or—in Mickey Mantle's case in 1960— to reduce the size of his pay cut. Don Drysdale and Sandy Koufax would hold out in 1966. Ruth's demands in 1930, which resulted in his receiving an $80,000 salary ($5,000 more than President Hoover), prompted his most famous quip: "I had a better year." Holding out usually affected the start of spring training, but DiMaggio actually missed the beginning of the regular season in 1938. He wanted $40,000; the Yankees offered him $25,000. After twelve games, DiMaggio settled for $25,000, and the New York fans booed him his first time at bat.

Mays didn't like confrontation, so he had always been the dutiful son— the first Giant to sign his contract, often surrounded by reporters and photographers while he expressed his gratitude to Mr. Stoneham. But with no raise in 1961, Mays had reason to be less gracious. Not only did he post terrific numbers in 1960, but the Giants had their best year ever at the gate. Candlestick Park, for all its deficiencies, drew 1.7 million fans, a 26 percent increase from the year before and a 174 percent increase from their last year in New York. Stoneham received his taxpayer-funded stadium, which, in one year, generated more revenue than he had ever seen. To be sure, not all the business decisions had worked out. Stoneham had hoped to win a pay-for-view television contract, which envisioned putting actual coins in slots on TV sets to watch Giant games. That never happened, but Stoneham still had plenty of money. Among other things, he was building a $1.25 million baseball training facility near his winter home in Phoenix.

He could be generous with favorite players, particularly when hardship was involved, but Stoneham was usually stingy and occasionally petty, and after the 1960 season, he was piqued at his team's rotten play. He decided to give some of the low-paid younger players, such as Felipe Alou and Juan Marichal, small raises and maintain others at the same level while cutting the salaries of the underperformers. Sam Jones, the club's leading pitcher, was just grateful that his wages stayed the same—$35,000. Of Mays, Stoneham said, "He has had substantial raises in the past. Willie had a good year in 1960, but not a great one. And we finished fifth."

This view was unusually peevish, not only because Mays was his best player but because he remained the team's premier gate attraction. If Mays had ever had enough standing to hold out, 1961 would have been the year, but it didn't happen. Whatever lingering resentments he may have had, Mays kept them to himself. He was now part of baseball's establishment, and he would no more trigger a confrontation with the Giants, or denounce a corrupt system that turned ballplayers into chattel, than he would protest Jim Crow or any other injustice.

In the days leading up to spring training, an airline strike delayed some players, but Mays drove to Phoenix from San Francisco, arriving on time, his contract signed. He was eager to get started, for he was reuniting with an old friend.

As soon as Rigney was fired, speculation centered on the triumphant return of Leo Durocher to the Giants, and the rumors had some legitimacy. Stoneham had asked Durocher to evaluate the club early in 1960, in part to determine if dissension involving the black and Latin players was hindering the team. Durocher concluded that the team's main problem was that it wasn't as good as Stoneham thought it was, though he found room to criticize Rigney. (Durocher still believed Rig was too hard on Willie.) After Rigney was fired, Stoneham met Durocher in New York and asked if he was interested in returning. Durocher, who had been out of baseball since Stoneham had fired him, said he was quite interested. Certainly Mays would have celebrated his return, but given the bad blood between Durocher and Stoneham, it's questionable whether Stoneham was ever serious. Besides, he could choose one of Durocher's protégés, who could manage the club in the same aggressive fashion but without Leo's baggage.

While the team was touring in Japan, Stoneham announced that Alvin Dark, who had played for the Giants for seven years, would be the team's new manager. Dark had never managed before or even coached. In fact, he had just completed his thirteenth season as a player, and Stoneham had to trade Andre Rodgers to the Milwaukee Braves to get him. But Stoneham liked former Giant players serving in the front office or coaching. They knew the team's history and contributed to Stoneham's image as a patriarch whose club was part of his extended family. Even Durocher, who loved Dark's tenacity on the field and had made him a co-captain, had to acknowledge it was a terrific choice.

Dark, however, was not the most obvious selection for a team in San Francisco, whose fans still pined for Lefty O'Doul to take over the Giants. Dark was part of the New York Giants and, unlike Rigney, had never played or managed in the Pacific Coast League. In his first press conference, he explained that he was from Louisiana, a tithing Baptist who didn't smoke, drink, or swear. Noted Don Sherwood, San Francisco's leading disc jockey: "I've already counted eight insults to our city. There can't be any left."

Stoneham wanted to restore toughness and discipline, and Dark fit the bill. A former marine who served briefly in China at the end of the war, Dark was a star running back at Louisiana State University and was drafted by the Philadelphia Eagles, but he opted for baseball instead. Like Durocher, he was a middle infielder who was not afraid to use his fists; he once took out Jackie Robinson on a rolling slide, then popped up and was ready to tangle if Robinson wanted to. Durocher used to call him his "upside-down shortstop," because that's how he always seemed to end up. But Dark had talent as well. The Rookie of the Year in 1948, he amassed a career .289 average and twice hit more than twenty homers in a season, an anomaly for a shortstop. At 5-foot-11, he was more imposing than big. He had a shock of black hair, swarthy skin, and intense eyes; the sportswriter Leonard Koppett said he looked like a "Confederate army captain." Dark described himself as an "aggressive Christian," and his aggression could be destructive.

In his first year managing, after a 1–0 loss in which the Giants stranded twelve men, Dark stormed into the locker room. Two players who followed him in were chirping like a couple of hummingbirds, so Dark picked up a metal stool and threw it with all his strength against a wall. The chatter stopped. Dark then felt a twinge of pain in his finger. His pitching coach almost fainted. Dark looked down and saw that the tip of his little finger was lodged in the bottom of the stool. The bone was sticking out while blood spurted everywhere. The doctor stitched him up and assured him it wouldn't affect his golf swing. The players rescued the fingertip and pickled it in a jar.

No matter the game or the circumstance, Dark simply hated to lose. One time, playing bridge on a team flight to Chicago, he looked at his cards, then the score, and said, "The only hope now is if we crash." His players feared him. During his first spring training, three Giants (Jim Davenport, Harvey Kuenn, and Bob Schmidt) were out one night, and they were arrested and jailed on a drunk and disorderly charge after getting into an argument with a twenty-year-old. That they were drunk or disorderly was never firmly established, and they were allowed to leave the jailhouse after several hours. But according to their lawyer, they were reluctant to depart. When reporters asked why, the lawyer said, "They heard their manager was downstairs, and I think they'd just as soon stay up there."

Dark publicly defended his wayward trio though privately fined each of them $100, if only to set a precedent.

Dark had played with Mays for all or parts of five seasons and knew how sensitive he was to his own failings and how Durocher had bolstered his confidence. "The only player on the team who doubted Willie Mays's ability was Willie Mays," Dark said. "He wore his heart on his sleeve, and every time he had a bad day, he despaired." Dark was aghast when he went to San Francisco as a player and heard the crowd booing Mays. After he was named manager, one of his first acts was to write Mays a letter: "Just a note to say that knowing you will be playing for me is the greatest privilege any manager could ever hope to have." During spring training, he repeatedly told reporters what an honor it was to manage Mays, and when the season began, he taped a radio program in which he always found something that his center fielder did to help them win a game. "Without Willie, the Giants are just an ordinary team," he said on one show. "Willie's the greatest ballplayer I've ever seen, greater than Ted Williams, Stan Musial, or Mickey Mantle." Dark later claimed that he wasn't trying to build up Willie. "I was trying to give him the credit he deserved," he said. "Wake up San Francisco to the facts of life."

With or without Dark, Mays was happiest at spring training. His reunion with teammates, the warm weather, the prospects of a new season—all were a balm for his self-imposed pressures. But his optimism seemed to get the better of him during Dark's spring training debut. Mays predicted that the Giants were going to win the pennant, even though they had finished fifth the year before. Reporters asked why Mays was so confident.

"It's hard to say," he shrugged, "except there's a feel in the air."

Charlie Einstein saw Mays in the clubhouse afterward. "Why'd you give that guy that stuff about 'a feel in the air'?" he asked.

"Aw, he ain't gonna print it," Mays responded.

"The hell he ain't."

"Well, there *is* a feel in the air."

"That's what you said last year."

"Was a feel in the air last year."

"And the year before."

"Feel in the air then too."

"Matter of fact, you think this way every year around this time."

"I know it," Mays said.

"Well, why didn't you explain that to the poor writer?"

"He only asked about this year."

Mays felt he did have reason to be hopeful; the new manager was creating a different atmosphere. Dark was, in the tradition of Durocher, a strategist who thought he could outsmart the other teams and who tried mind games to help certain players. The previous season, Cepeda and McCovey each played about sixty games at first base, while Cepeda played another eighty-six games in left field. Dark anointed McCovey his full-time first baseman while deciding Cepeda would play *right field*. This appeared to make no sense, for Cepeda complained bitterly about playing left field, and left field was easier than right in Candlestick. Dark's thinking was, by putting him in right field to start the season, fans would have low expectations because he was learning a new position. Errors would be forgiven, and a relaxed Cepeda would hit better and would also not resent his return to left field. The approach seemed to work. In 1961, Cepeda had one of his finest seasons (.311 average, 46 homers, 142 RBIs) and finished second in the MVP race.

More than anything, Dark instilled competitiveness, as seen in an exhibition game in Scottsdale, which ended in a near sandstorm. The Giants' pitcher, a twenty-two-year-old rookie named Bobby Bolin, was on the mound in the ninth with the bases loaded and the score tied. A close pitch was called ball four, sending home the winning run. Grateful the game had ended, everyone ran off the field except for Dark, who was running in the opposite direction. He started arguing with the umpire, and there, on the empty field, amid the swirling dust and sand, Dark, his rookie pitcher, and the umpire stood yelling at one another about the final pitch. "Dark knew that Bolin was fighting to make the team," Mays recalled, "and Dark was out there fighting with him. That showed us, very early, that he was a manager who would fight for his players." (Bolin did make the team, appearing in thirty-seven games and posting a 3.19 ERA.)

Mays called Dark "Cap," a reference to his former captaincy, and his comfort rose further with the addition of three new coaches—Whitey

Lockman, Wes Westrum, and Larry Jansen. All had been Giants in 1951, and they, as well as Mays and Dark, had been in the lineup the day Bobby Thomson hit his famous home run. Together again, the five of them replayed that game over and over in camp. Their reminiscing fueled the nostalgia of the reporters from New York, who were eager to relive the glory of the Giants. This only antagonized the Bay Area writers. Dark's refusal to drink with them, or anyone else, created further distance with the local press, who were also provoked when Dark made it clear that Lefty O'Doul was no longer welcome. O'Doul had been the Giants' batting coach since the team moved to San Francisco, but with Dark at the helm, he stayed only a week or so.

Mays, who had felt the New York–California divide more deeply than anyone, lamented these developments. Though he was beginning his fourth year in San Francisco, he was not yet part of that city. "I had the feeling that I was on one side of the Golden Gate Bridge— the side closer to New York—and that the rest of the Giants, the new ones who had joined the team since the move in 1958—were on the other side, along with the local writers."

That Willie and Marguerite were having difficulties was hardly a surprise, but in January, the first concrete evidence of their growing estrangement was reported. Willie packed his clothes and his record player and left their home in New Rochelle. The house itself now held five people. In addition to Willie, Marguerite, and Michael, Marguerite's daughter, Billy, was there. So too was one of Willie's half-brothers, William McMorris, whom Willie and Marguerite raised for a number of years.

After Willie left the house, Marguerite conceded to reporters that there had been some "frictions" between them, but she would not say if they were divorcing. She had little information about her husband. "I don't know where Willie is," she said. "I don't know where to tell you to look for him. If you want any details, ask him. I don't expect to see him— at least not very soon."

Mays had gone to Birmingham, where he lived in a hotel for a month, spent time with his friends, and tried to clear his head. He did not consult with his father, who had followed his son to San Francisco in 1958 and was living in an apartment there. Willie kept in touch with Marguerite, and by spring training they decided to reunite, with Marguerite and Michael traveling to Phoenix. Willie tried to defuse speculation about his marriage in a *Saturday Evening Post* interview.

"Why is it every time my wife and I have a fight, rumors start we're getting divorced?" he asked. "For four years, all I've read and heard is that our marriage is over, and I think these stories ought to stop. If married people don't fight, they don't love each other. I don't even believe in separation. If you're going to have a separation, get a divorce and get it over with."

He said that he went to Birmingham only because Marghuerite's family was spending so much time at the house; leaving was his way of conveying his desire to be with her. News reports suggested that Willie was upset at Marghuerite's expensive tastes, so Willie was asked if she spent too much. "I think all wives do," he said, "but in my case, it's been my own fault. I would say I'm just growing up. I've always been the type of guy who would say, 'Fine,' whenever she said she wanted something. I was making money. It would come easy and go easy."

Mays, who would turn thirty in a few months, said his free spending could no longer be sustained. "I'm beginning to realize that I'm only going to play maybe five, six more years. I've got to start accumulating money right now and begin adjusting myself to a lower bracket. A lot of money was wasted. I had people always trying to live off me." He said his house in New Rochelle was part of the problem. "It's too big for us," he said. "It's $150 a month just to get the grass cut on an acre and a half. Fifteen rooms and seven bedrooms for five people is too much."

The surplus rooms were a metaphor for the marriage. Willie and Marghuerite liked watching television but different shows. He preferred Westerns and action; she, mysteries and love stories. So they watched on separate TVs in separate rooms. Their worlds rarely overlapped, and there was no reconciliation.

On July 10, Marghuerite filed a "maintenance suit" in Superior Court in San Francisco, seeking to live "separate and apart from William Howard Mays." The separation would not come cheap. She asked for $3,500 a month to support herself and their son, plus $15,000 for lawyers' fees, $3,000 for the cost of the suit and accounting expenses, and all community property, including their home in New Rochelle and their rented house on Spruce Street, where Willie lived during the season. She also wanted sole custody of Michael and a restraining order on the Giants' paying Willie his salary. In her suit, she charged that Willie was "guilty of extreme cruelty and acted in an indifferent, hostile, and arrogant manner." The suit said that Willie had "ignored her presence in the home and has spent almost all of his evenings away from home."

Marghuerite talked to the press in her lawyer's San Francisco office, where she complained that her well-tailored gray suit, red hat, and matching red gloves were three years old, and virtually all that Willie had given her for almost half of their marriage was food money—"when he's home."

"This has been building up almost from the time we were married on

Valentine's Day, 1955," she said. Her lawsuit contended that she had been "a loyal and devoted wife but has been rebuffed on each occasion when she has attempted to talk to him." Despite her years of suffering, she said, "I think I finally made up my mind last night" to take this action. She said she wanted "separate maintenance," but she was not seeking a divorce because, according to the *Los Angeles Examiner,* that was "against her Catholic principles."

The *San Francisco Examiner,* showing its capacity to turn a family tragedy into a clumsy joke, wrote in its front-page story: "Willie Mays, who scored the winning run in Tuesday's All-Star game, was thrown out at home yesterday. Credit for the putout goes to his wife of five years."

The following week, Willie appeared in court with his lawyer, Bergen Van Brunt, and during the hearing, the lawyer delivered some startling news. Willie was broke. Part of the problem, he said, was that Marghuerite "spends his money as fast as he earns it. . . . His wife is very extravagant. She orders things like $400 shoes and $8,000 mink coats and the like." (Marghuerite denied the claim.) Van Brunt said he had spoken to the Giants' treasurer, Edgar P. Feeley, who had reviewed Willie's finances. "I don't have the exact figures," Feeley told Van Brunt, "but it looks to me as if [Willie] doesn't have anything left."

In addition to Mays's salary, he was making about $15,000 in endorsements for such products as razors and syrup. How Mays could be broke on $100,000 a year was probably more newsworthy, and embarrassing, than the fracturing of his marriage.

Willie and Marghuerite agreed to certain temporary arrangements. The Giants would deduct $250 a week from Willie's paycheck for Marghuerite; Marghuerite could use the couple's 1961 Cadillac but would have to pay for the gas; Marghuerite, when in San Francisco, would occupy their home on Spruce Street, though Willie would pay the rent and the utilities. Marghuerite told reporters that Willie could stay in the house when he was in town, but in a separate bedroom. "This is a large house," she said. "He and I have been occupying separate bedrooms at opposite ends of the house for months and months."

Despite Marghuerite's criticism, Willie declined to return the attack or even to defend himself. "I wouldn't want to say a thing to hurt her," he said, "because she might want to get married in the future, and even if I did know something, I wouldn't say anything about her."

Mays did make it clear that he wanted a divorce. "I want a clean break. If we're going to separate, then let's separate." His main concern was their son, now two and a half years old. "He's growing up so fast, and soon now he'll want to come to the ballpark to see me play. I want him to be proud

of me, and I don't want to spoil that by saying anything about his mother."
He added, "I just want to make sure I'll be able to visit him and he'll be
able to spend some time with me. It's very important for a growing boy to
have a father around."

Another hearing was set for August, and Superior Court Judge Joseph
Karesh referred the parties to the Domestic Relations commissioner,
Mary Malone, but both Marghuerite and Willie said they were not inter-
ested in reconciliation.

After the July hearing, Mays went to Candlestick Park and hit a home
run in his first at-bat against the Phillies.

It turned out that Willie's financial problems were worse than initially
stated. In August, his lawyer and financial adviser in New York, Edward
Rosiny, testified before Judge Karesh that Willie was deep in debt. Over the
years, the Giants had been advancing him money against future income,
so he currently owed the team $65,200; he was also $8,641 in debt to the
federal government and to the states of New York and California.

Rosiny said that Mays had hired him in 1957 as his financial adviser,
but, "My job was more like that of a scorekeeper." For example, Rosiny
said, in 1957 Mays had a gross income of $42,555 and expenditures of
$34,234. (Presumably, that did not include the sale of Marghuerite's home
in New York and the purchase of the $37,500 house on Miraloma.) The
following year, he more than doubled his income—to $90,537—while
paying out $88,375. The increase in income, Rosiny said, resulted from
an advance from the Giants. The pattern continued. In 1959, Mays earned
$60,269 while spending $60,667; in 1960, his income was $108,582, out-
flow, $101,532.

Asked by Judge Karesh if the Mayses were living beyond their means,
Rosiny said, "Way, way beyond their means." He said the Giants were now
paying Willie $1,900 a month, out of which he gives Marghuerite $1,000
while paying the rent on his San Francisco home and the mortgage on
his New Rochelle residence. As the *Examiner* wrote: "This would seem to
leave Willie with little more than money with which to buy the gum that
he chews constantly while on the diamond."

Granted, Willie's lawyer and adviser were trying to paint the bleakest
picture possible to minimize his own financial exposure, though Marghuerite's lawyer apparently did not present any evidence to contradict
the image of a man on the financial brink. Whatever the precise numbers, the hardship was real, and Willie held the unfortunate distinction of
being the highest paid player in baseball while being in debt to his own
team as well as the government.

If Marghuerite thought the public hearings and her charges would gain her support, she was wrong. Newspaper articles referred to her as "sultry" and "fashion-conscious"; she "purred" on the telephone, lived in a "posh" home in New Rochelle, and had two previous divorces. In photographs, she looked regal but icy. Nothing suggested deprivation. She was also erratic. In September, she told the *Examiner* that she was withdrawing the "maintenance suit" and instead hoped to "work something out with Willie." Then, in January, she filed for a "Mexican divorce" in Juarez. These were popular at the time among celebrities, though their validity was always in dispute. Marghuerite appeared before the judge in Juarez wearing a full-length white mink coat and three diamond rings. She asked for a divorce on the grounds of "incompatibility of characters."

Marghuerite's jaunt to Mexico did little more than annoy Judge Karesh. Divorce papers were eventually filed in San Francisco. The maintenance suit was withdrawn, and a settlement was reached in May 1962. Under the agreement, Willie and Marghuerite would sell the house in New Rochelle to pay off debts. Willie would pay Marghuerite $15,000 a year—$10,000 in alimony and $5,000 in child support. (That figure was later reduced to $10,000 total when the judge gave Willie more time with Michael.) Willie absorbed other related costs, including more than $6,000 in fees and expenses for Marghuerite's lawyer and $950 for her financial counsel. In addition, he would cover a bill of $1,696.70 for her private eye. Willie was paying for the man who spied on him. He initially lost custody of their son but eventually got him half the time.

In later discussing the divorce, Mays said, "I don't blame anybody but ourselves for what went wrong—basically, Marghuerite had trouble adjusting to my way of living, and I guess I didn't adjust to hers—but being a celebrity is no help in either direction."

Through it all, Willie never said an unkind word about Marghuerite. Not then, not ever. His friends, who had warned him from the outset, were not as forgiving. Even privately, Willie rarely mentions the experience, and when he does, he tries to find something positive, such as that Marghuerite broadened his world by showing him places that he would have never seen.

But the divorce left him alone and shaken. "When I was first divorced," he said, "it was very lonely. The first two months, it was bad." Already wary of outsiders, always skeptical of their motives, Mays now had more reason to retreat. "When you trust someone and all of a sudden that someone betrays you," he says, "it leaves a bad taste in your mouth. It makes it hard for the next person to come along."

For all the references to Mays as a loner, he actually wanted family or friends nearby. A year after his divorce, he spoke openly about his desire to marry again because, he said, "I like that kind of life. I've always had a big family around me. I love kids around."

But the marriage had reinforced his insecurities about his own celebrity, raised doubts about why people actually liked him, and made him want to disassociate himself from his own fame. "Once I find the right kind of girl," he said, "a girl who wants to be with me because I'm *me*, not because I play ball, I feel I'll get married in a hurry."

He found someone soon enough, but it was a long time before he would trust again.

Whatever was happening to Mays off the field, he never brought it inside the ballpark. Few of his teammates knew anything of his personal life unless they read it in the newspaper, and Mays's performance was rarely impaired by the collapse of his marriage or his financial stress. "Lots of times," he later said, "when things were the worst for me personally, playing hard helped take my mind off my troubles."

In 1961, he was hoping for a blockbuster start to help Dark, but that caused him to press. At the end of April, the Giants traveled to Milwaukee for three games, and in the opener they faced Warren Spahn. Forty years old and in his nineteenth season, he was good as ever and threw a no-hitter. The Giants won the following game, rapping fifteen hits, but Mays took the collar and had struck out three times in the past two games. He was now in a 10-for-40 rut and was hitting .291. Whenever his batting average fell below .300, it was, in the eyes of some San Franciscans, a national emergency. He only had two home runs for the month.

Mays typically roomed alone, but Dark granted no favors, so he roomed with McCovey. After beating the Braves on a Saturday night, they took a walk and brought some barbecued spareribs back to the hotel, where they ate them for a midnight snack, watched some television, and turned in. But Mays woke up at 3 A.M., vomiting. He collapsed on the floor and briefly passed out. McCovey called Doc Bowman, who soon arrived. "I was really scared," McCovey recalls. "I was pleading not to let him die."

Bowman gave Mays some sleeping pills, and Willie made it through the night fitfully. When he went to County Stadium the next day, April 30, he felt horrible. Joe Amalfitano, the utility infielder for the Giants, saw how bad he looked.

"You going to play today?" he asked.

Mays said no. "I was up all night."

"If you play at 75 percent," Amalfitano said, "you're better than most."

"The way I've been playing, maybe I should take the day off."

Amalfitano had an idea. Each player had his own bats, and Mays's were thirty-four-ounce Adirondacks with a tapered handle and a thick barrel with the weight at the end. But Mays hadn't been using them because he thought they were too light and had been swinging a thirty-five-ounce bat instead. Amalfitano had been using the thirty-four-ouncer in batting practice and thought the ball jumped off the wood. So he handed one to Mays.

"Will, why don't you use this bat," he said. "It's got a lot of wood in it."

Dark then came along and asked Mays how he felt. Mays said not so great, but as long as he had a bat in his hand, he decided to take his cuts in the cage.

It seemed everything he hit went into the stands. "You can always tell if a bat has good wood in it," he later said. "It rings when you hit the ball well." He decided he would play. The game would be the 1,234th of his career, on a sunny day before 13,114 people, and it would be televised on NBC's *Game of the Week* (though blacked out in San Francisco).

Even if he'd been feeling well, Mays had no reason to believe he'd have a good day. In addition to his recent struggles at the plate, he'd never had much luck in County Stadium. Of the opposing ballparks that he'd played in at least six seasons through 1960, he had his second-worst home run total in Milwaukee. Only in Philadelphia had he hit fewer. And County Stadium, at 402 feet to center and 392 feet in the power alleys, was no bandbox.

Starting for the Braves was Lew Burdette, one of the league's better right-handed starters, who had averaged twenty wins over the past three seasons. He was a control pitcher who could throw a fastball, a curve, and a slider. He also had a spitter.

Mays, batting third, faced Burdette in the first inning with the bases empty. Burdette threw a slider, and Mays socked it 420 feet to dead center for a home run. In the bottom of the first, Hank Aaron, the Braves' center fielder, outdid his counterpart with a three-run homer. In the top of the fourth, shortstop Jose Pagan hit his first homer of the year; then Mays came to bat with a runner on first. This time, Burdette threw a hard sinker, and Mays scorched it 400 feet to left center for a two-run homer, which also gave the Giants the lead.

The Giants' pitcher, Billy Loes, settled down and retired fourteen in a row before giving up another hit—a second homer by Aaron. A player who hits two homers in one game might have merited attention, but not on this day.

The Giants went on a long-ball binge in the fourth inning. Orlando Cepeda and Felipe Alou both hit homers while Pagan knocked his second. Mays led off the fifth against Moe Drabowsky and lined out to center. But in the sixth, he came to the plate with runners on first and third, with Seth

Morehead now on the mound. The lefty tried to jam Mays with a slider, but the ball caught too much of the plate. Mays turned, and his thirty-four-ounce bat flashed across the strike zone—*crack!* It did indeed have good wood. The ball traveled over the highest row of the left field bleachers and landed in a picnic area beyond. The estimated distance: 480 feet. In his game story, Einstein breathlessly described it as "one of the longest home runs any human ever hit." Mays could remember only one other hit, in St. Louis, that might have gone farther.

Mays felt as though he were getting stronger as the day progressed. In the eighth, the Braves inserted Don McMahon, a right-hander, and Mays came to the plate with a runner on third. Three years before, when the front-running Giants came to Milwaukee in July, the Braves swept the series, and McMahon had struck out Mays with men on base to help secure one of the wins. He may have been thinking of that at-bat when first baseman Joe Adcock called time. "I walked to the mound," Adcock later recalled, "and I told McMahon, 'Don't let this guy hit the ball this time.' McMahon said, 'Don't worry. I got him.' So I got back to first base and on the next pitch, Mays hits the darnedest screaming line drive you ever saw." The ball sailed 430 feet into the top row of the bleachers. The Milwaukee fans cheered as Mays circled the bases.

An announcement came over the loudspeaker that with four home runs in one game, Mays had tied a major league record. Eight other players, including Lou Gehrig, had reached that mark. Mays knew that he was now part of baseball history, but if he got one more chance, he could hold the record by himself.

Mays was due up fifth in the top of the ninth, and George Brunet was pitching. The leadoff hitter, Pagan, singled, but the next two hitters were retired. Jim Davenport needed to reach base, but with Mays on deck, he grounded out. The crowd booed.

The Giants won, 14–4. They hit eight home runs, tying the major league record. Including Aaron's, there were ten in all, tying a National League record. The lead of the *Milwaukee Journal*'s game story read: "The best thing that could be said about the Braves Sunday was that none of them got hurt." The previous game, the Giants had hit five long balls in scoring seven runs. It was as if the Giants were avenging Spahn's no-hitter to start the series.

Mays's hitting line was 4-for-5, with four homers, four runs scored, and eight RBIs. He also made the best catch of the game. That it was seen on national television added to the moment. In interviews after the game, he could barely contain his joy. "Man, after you get two in a game, you don't start looking for a third one," he said. "I've hit two in a game before, and three once, but that was in an exhibition. . . . Sure, this was my best game and it was my biggest thrill in baseball too. . . . The biggest day for me before this? What difference does it make. Second best don't mean anything. . . . No, [my best game] wasn't one of those catches I made in the World Series because I don't count fielding. That's always been easy for me."

Asked about his near-opportunity in the ninth inning, Mays offered a revealing answer. "Honestly," he said, "I might not have done a thing. I knew what I had done. I heard it over the loudspeakers. I had the greatest day of my career. I probably will never have another like it. If I'd gone up again, I might have pressed—gone for the home run. And when you press, you're dead."

The day produced two memorable photographs, both from the Giants' locker room. One featured Mays, a huge smile on his face, holding four baseballs in his massive right hand. The other showed him eating his postgame meal—barbecued spareribs.

Mays used the magic bat in the next series in Chicago, but he broke it on a single. Amalfitano grabbed it and put it in his locker, but after the game it was gone. A search yielded nothing. Someone had stolen the historic bat. Amalfitano blamed himself, though Mays didn't hold him responsible. He was just glad that his teammate had helped him.

More than thirty years later, the two men saw each other at spring training, and while watching a game, Amalfitano reminded Mays of the mishap.

"I feel terrible about that bat," he said.

"That's okay," Mays said.

"Hey, what were you going to do with it anyway? Give it to the Hall of Fame?"

"No, I was going to give it to you."

Maybe it was the return of Alvin Dark and the other New York Giants or the increased presence of the New York writers, but Mays made several plays in 1961 that stirred memories of his earlier years. There was another big throw, like the peg ten years before that nailed Billy Cox at the plate, but this one, from three hundred feet, gunned down the Dodgers' Maury Wills, who was trying to score on a sacrifice. There was another over-the-shoulder catch, this one at Candlestick. A photograph shows Mays closing in on the fence, his number 24 facing home plate, his glove outstretched, in almost the exact same position as in 1954. Dark said this catch was better, and Mays, noting the wind, agreed (though no throw was necessary).

But the most poignant memories of yesteryear occurred when the Giants actually went to New York to play an exhibition game against the

Yankees. Four years after they left for California, their return was hailed as a homecoming, but in truth it was a rekindling of a baseball love affair. New Yorkers had tried to follow their Giants by listening to Les Keiter on the radio or by watching the occasional televised game. But now, finally, they could see Willie in person.

Fog rolled across New York on the night that the Giants were to fly in from Cincinnati, diverting their landing to Idlewild Airport (later named John F. Kennedy International Airport). They didn't reach their hotel until after 4 A.M., and they woke up on July 24 to a driving summer rainstorm. Mays assumed the weather would limit the crowd; further, the game was going to be televised. He was also uncertain about his reception. New York, he believed, was now Mickey's town. San Francisco wasn't Siberia, but he felt far removed from the country's media mecca, and he would be playing in Yankee Stadium, not the Polo Grounds.

The Yankees had scheduled a home run contest before the game— Mickey Mantle and Roger Maris against Cepeda and Mays. It might have been a dramatic way for Mays to reintroduce himself, but the rain canceled it, and the game itself, to start at 7:55 P.M., appeared in doubt. A delay had already been announced, and the club waited in the locker room.

"We'll never play tonight," Dark said. Someone told him if he stepped outside, he would change his mind, so he walked down the runway into the visiting dugout and looked. "Wow." He saw the people in the stands— there would be 47,346.

The rain finally turned to mist, and the game began an hour late. But first came the starting lineups.

"Ladies and gentlemen," said the Yankee announcer, "for the Giants at second base, number 14, Joe Amalfitano." The cheering started. "Number 7, Harvey Kuenn, right field." It got louder. "Number 41, Matty Alou, left field." And louder.

"Number 24, Wil—" The crowd stood and roared, drowning out the rest of the order. Einstein wrote: "An unbroken, throat-swelling peal of adulation sprang from the hearts of Giant-starved New Yorkers. It rolled and volleyed off the great tiering of this triple-decked palace and against the vague outline of the Bronx County courthouse, looming in the gray black mist out beyond the huge scoreboard in right center field.

"They rocked and tottered and shouted and stamped and sang. It was joy and love and welcome, and you never heard a cascade of sound quite like it."

Mays was frozen, overwhelmed, and in tears.

In the record books, 1961 is the year of Mays's four homers in one game, of leading the league in runs scored with 129, of his best home run (40) and RBI (123) totals in six seasons, of two All-Star games* and one Gold Glove and of helping Alvin Dark restore credibility to the Giants (85–69, for third place). It is also the year of the caustic fallout from a bad marriage, Mays's name ridiculed in newspapers and in court, his tongue forever silent. And it's the year that Willie Mays returned to New York, where he led the Giants to a 4–1 victory with a game-winning single. He "drew what amounted to a continuous ovation whenever he was on the field," the *Sporting News* wrote, "and at times it thundered louder than the turbulent storms which almost had washed away the game."

It was a glorious moment. "New York," Willie later said, "hadn't forgotten me."

* Major League Baseball played two All-Star games a year from 1959 to 1962.

CHAPTER TWENTY-FOUR

ACCEPTANCE, AT LAST

Walking into the batter's box is an act of faith, for in no other sport does a player rely on the sufferance, the mercy, of another as a hitter relies on a pitcher. Dangers are embedded in other sports—the wayward punch in boxing, the late hit in football—but nothing compares to the life-or-death peril of a rising fastball. In 1920 at the Polo Grounds, in one of the most infamous moments in baseball history, the Cleveland Indians' Ray Chapman faced Carl Mays, a submariner with the Yankees. An 0–1 fastball struck Chapman flush in the temple and fractured his skull, spilling blood out of his ears, nose, and mouth. He was rushed to a hospital and surgery was performed, but he died twelve hours later.

Beanballs and brushbacks were part of the game, but some of the dangers were lessened when batters began wearing helmets in 1952. By the early 1960s, most major leaguers wore the hard hat, which offered more safety but also had the perverse effect of increasing the number of knockdown pitches. After all, the hitter now had protection. But the pitchers were endangering so many batters that umpire Jocko Conlan commented that hitters should use some old Ty Cobb tricks—bunt the ball down the first base line and spike the pitcher as he fields it, or push a bunt to the right side, forcing the pitcher to cover first, then bulldoze him with a football block. "I don't see these things being done nowadays," Conlan told the *Saturday Evening Post* in 1961.

Willie Mays found the batting helmet uncomfortable and wouldn't wear one. He thought he hit better without it and was certain he could elude any pitch to his head. His stubbornness infuriated the Giants, who feared for his safety as well as their investment. No one tracks knockdown pitches, but there was little doubt in San Francisco about which player dodged the most heaters each year and who took the greatest risk every time he stepped into the box.

"The man who was in the dirt more than any other was Willie Mays," said Hobie Landrith, a catcher who played in the majors for fourteen years, three with the Giants. "He's up and down like a yo-yo," the *Examiner* wrote in 1962. "Nobody over a season is asked to eat more dirt."

Mays was targeted because he was so good, and no one aimed at him more often than Don Drysdale. In his rookie season, 1956, the tall right-hander threw a high hard one that Mays easily ducked. But the next pitch was another fastball at his chin, and Mays, who had dug in, barely avoided getting hit. Drysdale's teammate was Sal Maglie, who had instructed Drysdale on how to pitch Mays. "You have to throw at him twice," he had said. The first time, Mays anticipates it. The second time, he doesn't.

Drysdale's excuses were not terribly convincing. In a game in 1960, he knocked Mays down in the first and hit him in sixth. Afterward, he told reporters, "I was just wild. The wind had something to do with carrying my pitches off line." After Bill Rigney accused Maglie of throwing at Mays, Maglie said, "That's a damn lie. I never threw at Willie. Maybe I brushed him back with a hard one under the chin once in a while, but I never tried to flatten him. I wouldn't do a thing like that to Willie."

Mays believed that the brushbacks were a sign of respect and even said that if he were pitching, he would knock himself down as well. However, he wanted his own pitchers to protect him, and he became incensed when they didn't. On Opening Day 1966, a Cub pitcher threw at Mays's head. (The Cubs were now managed by Leo Durocher, who presumably ordered the knockdown.) Mays wanted his pitcher, Juan Marichal, to retaliate against Cub star Ernie Banks, but Marichal would only throw a looper over his head.

After the game, a Giant radio announcer wanted to interview Mays and Marichal together, but Mays said, "Fuck it. Use Marichal."

"You don't want to go on?" the announcer asked.

"Not with him," Mays said.

Marichal was coming off a suspension from the previous year and was in no position to start this one with a beanball. In time, Mays cooled down and apologized.

Mays never publicly accused other pitchers of throwing at him and would rarely yell at the pitcher or make a threatening gesture. Curley Grieve, the *Examiner*'s sports editor, wrote in 1961: "He's such a nice guy that he even refuses to complain when he spends half the game on the seat of his pants." A photograph of Mays from a 1961 game shows him on his butt in the batter's box, his cap off his head, his mouth wide open, as if he's screaming in shock. A fastball by the Dodgers' Larry Sherry had nearly brained him. The *Chronicle*'s Art Rosenbaum wrote: "Normally when Willie is decked, he bounces right up. This time, he backed off, shook his head, talked to the umpire and the catcher, walked over to the on-deck circle to discuss it with Willie McCovey, rosined his hands, and finally took his place in the batter's box. 'I was leaning in when the ball came at me,' Willie said later. 'Man, that was as close as they come.' "

Rather than impugning the pitcher, he blamed himself.

For all his self-confidence, Mays was lucky he was never beaned or seriously injured by a pitch. He had plenty of close calls, and during spring training in 1962, Dark required that Mays wear a helmet. Mays reluctantly complied. "I'll wear it until it falls off," he said. (Major League Baseball did not mandate helmets until 1971, though most players wore them by then. Earflaps were required in 1983.) It may be just a coincidence, but the first year that Mays wore the helmet he was hit by four pitches, which equaled the most times he'd been hit in a season.

The 1960s saw the major leagues continue to expand, not just into new markets but also with completely new franchises. For almost sixty years, both leagues had had eight teams, with an eastern bias. By the end of the 1960s, each league had two divisions with six clubs apiece, the National League with squads from Atlanta to San Diego to Montreal, the American League with entries in Oakland and Seattle.

But for Willie Mays, the most meaningful addition was the New York Mets, created in 1962, which brought the National League back to New York and one of Mays's most devoted fans back into the game. After Joan Whitney Payson, the heiress with a 9 percent stake in the Giants, failed to persuade Stoneham to sell her the team so she could keep it in New York, she promised to bring Willie back to New York. Just five years later, she was the principal owner of the New York Mets, whose uniforms paid homage to both the Dodgers and the Giants: the Mets' blue lettering was Dodger blue, their orange trim was Giant orange, and their curling NY cap logo evoked that of the Giants. The Mets even played in the Polo Grounds until their new stadium was built.

Payson, whose first love was actually horse racing, had retained her equity interest in the Giants but was required to dispose of it after becoming the principal owner of the Mets. So she offered Stoneham her stock, valued at $680,000, and in return she wanted Willie Mays.

Payson was not supposed to be involved in personnel decisions, but Met president George Weiss didn't object. "Who wouldn't approve of a deal for Mays?" he said. "I felt it would have been a ten-strike had we been able to get him."

Stoneham said no. The New York Hospital, on whose board of trustees Payson sat, got the stock instead, and San Francisco kept Mays.

· · ·

It was fitting that in the year New York returned to the National League, the Giants and the Dodgers restaged their storied pennant clash of 1951, and just as that year was Mays's debut in New York, 1962 was a break-through season for him with the San Francisco fans. But it was also a year when the pressures got the better of him.

Mays knocked a home run in his first at-bat but otherwise began the year tepidly, hitting under .270 when the day began on April 17. The Giants had a game at Candlestick against the Dodgers, but due to a court hearing for his divorce, Mays got to the stadium in the second inning. Dark decided to keep him on the bench. It was only the eighth game of the season, and the crowd had no idea why he wasn't playing. He finally pinch-hit in the seventh inning with the bases loaded, and struck out. Then, with two outs in the ninth and the Dodgers ahead, 8–7, Mays batted with the tying run on base but popped out to end the game. The fans booed him with gusto.

Leo Durocher, now a bench coach for the Dodgers, said after the game, "I don't want to manage Dark's club for him, but I gotta say that if I've got Mays in the ballpark, I've gotta play him. There were two balls we hit for extra bases that Willie would have caught. What do you want him on the bench for? There are too many ways he can beat you."

Asked why Mays was on the bench, Dark declined to comment. He knew that Mays was upset over the court proceedings, but, as Einstein noted, "If he had known how upset, he wouldn't have used him even as a pinch hitter."

The Giants then traveled to Milwaukee and Cincinnati, and in five games Mays went 3-for-18, dropping his average to .217. The pressure that Mays always put on himself was amplified, with his ongoing divorce and deteriorating finances. This was his fifth season in San Francisco, the equivalent of the time he had spent in New York, and the boos still cut him to the bone. He would dream about one of his most persistent hecklers, a guy who sat behind home plate who would always scream, "Hey, Pop-Up Mays!" On the road he roomed alone, and his solitude had always been a source of comfort. He could sleep late, avoid restaurants, invite in those he wanted to see, nap, revive. But after a game one night, he suddenly felt isolated and distraught. He thought about his son, his boy. How could he be a father to Michael as Cat had been to him? Maybe he should have fought for sole custody, but he was a ballplayer, on the road more than at home. What kind of life was that? Willie started to cry. He couldn't sleep. He got out of bed and called Dark.

"I have the shakes," Mays said.

Dark told him to come up to his room. When he arrived, Doc Bowman was there, and he gave Mays some sleeping pills. "Sleep here tonight in that other bed, Willie," Dark said. They talked for a bit and he fell asleep.

Dark later said, "I thought the pressure on Mays was greater that year than ever before in his career, even more than 1954 when we won the pennant. I don't think he felt like he was under much pressure then. We had other [leaders] on the club and he was much younger. But in 1962, he's a more mature guy, and now he's expected to carry the ball club."

Mays rebounded. After his average fell to .211 on April 27, he hit safely in ten straight games, ripping six home runs, two doubles, and a triple, with fourteen runs scored and fourteen RBIs. His average rose to .309. By May 26, the Giants were in first place with a record of 31–14. They were clearly a different team.

After Cepeda's big season the previous year, Dark decided to have him play first base and switch McCovey to the outfield, which was not without risk. The running gag was that McCovey didn't need a glove to play the outfield, just a blindfold and a cigarette. But even playing in only ninety-one games, he hit twenty home runs and was second on the club in slugging percentage (behind Mays); with the two Willies (Mays and McCovey), the Alou brothers (Felipe and Matty), and Harvey Kuenn, the Giants now had more lumber in the outfield than any team in baseball. Third baseman Jim Davenport, sportswriters said, was so quiet you forgot he was even there. A fifth-year starter, he had battled injuries throughout, from a broken collarbone to bleeding ulcers. But he stayed healthy in 1962, played in the All-Star Game, and won an overdue Gold Glove. The most frequent complaint of the Giants since moving to San Francisco was its lack of leadership, but the acquisitions of Kuenn and Ed Bailey in 1961, two veterans, eased that problem.

On the mound, Juan Marichal was trying to rebound from an injury-plagued sophomore season. During spring training, his homeland, the Dominican Republic, was in turmoil following the assassination of its ruler the previous year; among those in peril was Marichal's fiancée, Alma Rosa, and her entire family. Marichal asked if he could leave camp to marry her so he could bring her back to America. Dark agreed, even giving him two plane tickets. When Marichal returned, he asked Mays what he could do to compensate Dark.

"Win," Mays replied.

Marichal was the Giants' ace for the rest of the decade.

If Mays wasn't a vocal leader, he still provided a steadying hand, which he used to minimize the growing tensions between Dark and Cepeda. Cepeda had already clashed with Rigney, who after leaving the Giants had claimed that Cepeda's reluctance to play the outfield had cost the Giants one or possibly two pennants. Cepeda said Rigney "lacked the guts to be a manager."

When Dark took over, he made several moves that antagonized some of the black and Latin players. He believed the team's three factions—whites, blacks, and Latins—needed to spend more time together, so in spring training he changed the lockers so there was more intermingling. But the social engineering didn't go over well with the players, and Dark restored the previous locker assignments. Another idea of Dark's was even less popular. He posted a sign at spring training that read: SPEAK ENGLISH, YOU'RE IN AMERICA. He called a meeting of the Latin players behind second base and said that the other Giants were complaining that they didn't understand what the Latin players were saying. There were almost a dozen Latins, and many of them, including Cepeda, viewed the edict as an insult. The Alou brothers—there were now three in camp—thought it odd to speak among themselves in what was to them a foreign language. The rule was unenforceable, and Dark dropped that one as well.

Cepeda held out in spring training in 1962. He had earned $30,000 in 1961 and was demanding—the reports varied—either $50,000 or $60,000. He got $46,000. But the delay angered Dark, who, like other managers at the time, took holdouts personally. Cepeda, meanwhile, resented Dark's refusal to allow players to bring music into the clubhouse, believing it targeted the Latin players.

The simmering feud came to a head in Milwaukee on August 19, a Sunday. The Giants were to leave the Pfister Hotel by bus at 11:15 A.M. Shortly after eleven, most of the players, including Cepeda and Dark, were on the bus. Then Cepeda was told that some friends, a Puerto Rican family with whom he had lived in Minneapolis, were here to see him. Cepeda got off the bus and, as he recalls it, embraced his friends and kissed the daughter, who had a light complexion.

That Dark didn't approve of interracial dating or displays of affection was no secret to reporters. He openly threatened to separate such couples who were nuzzling on the street.

When Dark saw Cepeda kissing his friends' daughter, he got angry, according to Cepeda, and told the driver, "Let's go, bussy."

According to an eyewitness: "The driver cranked up the motor and that's when Willie Mays spoke up. He said, 'It's not time to leave yet. It's still early.' So the driver cut the engine, and Cepeda finally got back on. Most of the people on that bus didn't even notice what happened."

In his autobiography, *Baby Bull,* Cepeda criticized Mays for not speaking out on behalf of Latin players, but Mays's only concern was keeping the Giants focused and together. In this case, had the bus left Cepeda behind, the division between Dark and Cepeda (and probably the other Latin players) would have widened, damaging the team in the midst of a pennant race. Later, Dark said he didn't recall the bus incident. He did, however, scratch Cepeda from the starting lineup that day, which Cepeda viewed as retribution.

At thirty-one, Mays still weighed 185 pounds, with a thirty-two-inch waist and a finely honed body. "I've seen eight hundred guys with their shirts off," says Tim McCarver, whose major league career began in 1959, "and the two people who stood out were Willie Mays and Stan Musial. What defined their backs were the groups of muscles around their shoulders. They looked like they worked in the mines."

If Mays's size hadn't changed, he did look different. His face was no longer young, his Afro was longer. When he was happy, his eyes and smile still radiated joy, but when he was worried, every feature seemed to shift into a brooding, tight-lipped expression. Just as his mobile features exaggerated his innocence, they amplified his heartache. His high-pitched laughter could still pierce the air, but his glare could be intimidating.

To some in the press corps, Mays hadn't changed at all. When he made his first trip to the Polo Grounds to face the Mets on June 2, 1962, a reporter asked him if he could speak with him. Mays didn't understand the question.

"I used to have to ask Durocher if it was all right to ask you a question," the reporter explained.

"I can talk for myself now," Mays said.

His return to the Polo Grounds was an echo of the previous year's exhibition at Yankee Stadium. The fans carried SAY HEY WILLIE signs and brought their bugles and horns to cheer him. The Giant players had begun to call Cepeda "Big Man," so when Mays received a mighty roar before the game had even begun, Garry Schumacher, standing at the batting cage, nodded toward Cepeda and said, "The Big Man just discovered who the Big Man really is."

Mays responded by hitting three home runs in a four-game sweep. He found the experience strange—he had never been in the visitors' locker room before—but as Arthur Daley of the *New York Times* wrote: "The center field turf at the Polo Grounds looks normal this weekend for the first time in almost five years. Willie has come home. It matters not that he is in an alien uniform. Here is the unforgettable hero from the past, the darling of the gallery gods. They loved him then and that deep affection, smoldering during his absence, blazed into full flame at his return."

The first time the Dodgers played the Mets, Duke Snider was asked how it felt to play again in the Polo Grounds.

"The place is full of ghosts," he said.

Dead ghosts?

"Live ghosts," Snider said. "I keep looking up and seeing Willie catching a long one."

Mays got into one fight in his major league career. It occurred on May 27, 1962, at Candlestick, and it was over in seconds. It also could have ended his playing days.

The game was against the woebegone Mets. The day before, against the same team, Mays had three hits, including two homers, and three RBIs. In the first inning the following day, Met pitcher Roger Craig decked him twice. In the top of the seventh, Cepeda was playing first base when his throw to second for an attempted forceout hit the runner in the back of the head, sending him to the hospital for X-rays. In the bottom of the seventh, after Mays singled, Craig hit Cepeda with a pitch. Cepeda took several steps toward the mound, bat in hand, then stopped himself, threw the bat away, and headed for first, where Alvin Dark waited to calm him down. Cepeda and Craig continued to bait each other until Cepeda lit after him, but he was dragged down from behind by Dark, momentarily preventing a brawl.

When play resumed, Craig alternated throws to first and second, trying to pick off Cepeda or Mays. On his first throw to second, he rifled the ball right on the bag and narrowly missed Mays's head. On the next throw to second, Mays slid hard into shortstop Elio Chacon. As he was getting off the ground, the infielder began punching him.

Mays, according to Chacon, had spiked him the year before, and he said Mays had done it again, so he started the fight. Unfortunately for Chacon, he was only 5-foot-9 and 163 pounds. Dark said that Mays "eats guys like Chacon for breakfast." In this case, a four-photo sequence shows what happened. Mays was initially surprised by the punches, then the two men stood face-to-face as Mays clasped his right hand around Chacon's back. Next, he lifted Chacon off the ground like a sack of flour as second baseman Felix Mantilla came over to help, and then he drove Chacon into Mantilla, landing on top of them both. As the *Sporting News* reported: "Chacon bounced on the ground like a rag doll, Mays sprawling on top, fists still flying." Cepeda and Craig then began pummeling each other near second base as the dugouts and bullpens emptied. For triggering the donnybrook, Chacon was the only player ejected; he was also fined $100.

Mays said after the game: "Yeah, my first fight and I hope my last one. Heck, I didn't want to hurt the kid."

During the melee, however, somebody's spikes ripped through Mays's stockings and scraped across the Achilles tendon of the right heel.

"Willie," Doc Bowman said, "is a lucky boy. He was wearing two pair of white sanitary stockings and perhaps they saved him. A little bit deeper cut and Willie's Achilles tendon could have been severed. Those spikes had to be razor sharp to make that slash."

Mays also suffered an abrasion over his left eye when the Mets' Gil Hodges pulled him off Chacon. The game itself was the first of a double-header. Mays played in the nightcap and got two hits.

If any club seemed like a team of destiny, it was the Los Angeles Dodgers of 1962. It was their first season in beautiful Dodger Stadium, drawing 2.7 million fans, a major league record. Shortstop Maury Wills stole 104 bases, shattering Ty Cobb's 1915 single-season total of 96; the last time a National League player had swiped more than 50 a year was 1916. The Dodgers had the best young outfield in baseball—Tommy Davis, who (after Mays) was the league's best all-around performer; Willie Davis, perhaps the game's fastest runner; and Frank Howard, one of the game's biggest players (6-foot-7, 250 pounds). Leading the pitching staff was Don Drysdale, who with twenty-five wins would capture the Cy Young Award, and Sandy Koufax, in the second season of his brilliant six-year run.

Starting on May 10, the Dodgers and Giants would be numbers 1 and 2 in the standings for the rest of the year, but the Dodgers, winning seventeen of nineteen games during one stretch that began in May, appeared unstoppable. And they probably wouldn't have been stopped had Koufax not injured the index finger on his pitching hand on July 17. At the time, he was 14–4, with a 2.06 ERA, and was also leading the league in strikeouts, but he was lost for most of the rest of the year and didn't win another game.

With no other teams in contention, the first real Giant-Dodger showdown in California drew national attention. Across the state, according to David Plaut's definitive account of the race, the battle shared front-page headlines with the stock market's worst drop since 1929, Israel's execution of the Nazi war criminal Adolph Eichmann, and Project Mercury space flights. When the Giants swept three from the Dodgers in August—thanks in part to Alvin Dark's watering down of the basepaths at Candlestick—San Francisco narrowed the lead to 2½ games.

While Mays's average hovered around .300, his power numbers were on the rise. On September 10, he hit his forty-third home run and drove in his one hundred and twenty-third run. With seventeen games left, he had already exceeded his long-ball totals for all but one year and had equaled or exceeded his RBI numbers for all but one year. He was on his way to having one of his best seasons.

But the year was different in one respect. With expansion, Major League Baseball had added eight games, a total of 162, but the season began and ended at the same time. The extra games were therefore squeezed into the same number of days, and with New York and Houston joining the National League, the travel demands increased.

Mays never asked for a day off, and despite Dark's promises of rest, he played in every game. The legal proceedings for his divorce were still ongoing, and that pressure, combined with the lengthy, feverish pennant race, weighed heavily on Mays. He had worn down in past seasons, but not quite like this.

"It was getting hot in the pennant race," Mays said. "But none of us wanted to take a day off. I pushed myself as I always did. Then one day it got to me."

There were warnings. In early August, Mays told Milton Gross, "I've never been so tired." On Sunday, September 9, during a home game against the Cubs, he felt tired "every place in my body," and that fatigue stayed with him the next two days. After winning on September 11, the Giants began an eleven-game road trip, a half game behind the Dodgers. On the flight to Cincinnati, *Examiner* reporter Harry Jupiter saw how drained Mays looked. Mays said, "Next year, I ain't gonna play no more doubleheaders. I guess I need a day or two off from time to time now if I'm gonna keep playing another eight or nine years like I want to. All these games, with all this traveling, it takes something out of you, no matter how strong you may think you are."

They landed in Cincinnati in the middle of a heat wave. "The trip from the West Coast was a jolt for everyone used to playing in the cooler air of San Francisco and Los Angeles," rookie pitcher Gaylord Perry said. "I had to change shirts twice that night"—and he never even got into the game. "The sweat was pouring off me just sitting in the dugout before going out to the bullpen."

Mays normally sat in the dugout before the game, but on this night he cut his batting practice short and headed to the clubhouse. When the game began, he was feeling dizzy, and in the first inning he struck out. He continued to feel as though he were in a haze, but he didn't want to say anything. Finally, in the top of the third inning, he was sitting on the bench, waiting his turn to bat, when he slumped over, collapsed, and passed out. He was quickly surrounded by his teammates, and when Russ Hodges saw who it was from the radio booth, he had tears in his eyes. Mays was put on a stretcher and carried to the clubhouse, where Doc Bowman estimated that he was unconscious for "a few minutes." Others said it was closer to twenty minutes. Bowman used smelling salts to revive him, and when Mays opened his eyes, Bowman asked, "Do you know me?"

Mays replied, "Sure."

Bowman offered him some water.

"What's wrong with me?" Mays asked.

"It's all right, Buck. You just fainted. How do you feel now?"

"I just feel like I don't want to move. I can move, but I don't want to move."

The Reds' team physician, Dr. George Ballou, examined Mays and initially thought he just needed some rest, then decided he should go to Christ Hospital. Still, the doctor downplayed the severity of the incident. "Anybody who has played all these games would be tired," he said. "The Reds are tired. The Giants are tired. The managers, the coaches, they're all tired. I don't think [Mays's] condition is serious at all. I believe he'll be all right and should be playing tomorrow night."

But Mays didn't play the next night, or the night after that, or even the following night. He stayed in the hospital, where he was photographed lying in bed, his face drawn, his eyes sagging, a white identification band around his wrist—an image of bewildered despair. (Another photograph, however, showed a relaxed Mays with a smile on his face.) One headline in the *Chronicle* asked: WHAT IS WRONG WITH WILLIE? Dr. Ballou didn't help matters with his revised assessment. "It is not normal for a finely tuned athlete to black out for five or more minutes," he said. "It is a cause for concern."

Rumors flourished, some of which were printed. Mays had venereal disease, epilepsy, a heart attack, depression, a mental breakdown, or he drank a Mickey Finn. Herb Caen wrote that Mays had been punched by a teammate. Bigots used the incident to make racist jokes—one of "Dark's darkies" taking some time off—while the *Chronicle*'s Charles McCabe, a frequent critic, wrote: "It is an interesting speculation whether Mays's annual collapses are physical, or neurotic, or even conceivably feigned." (McCabe was not known for his light touch. He once compared Russ Hodges's signature description of a Giant hitting a homer—"Bye-bye, baby!"—to the sound of the sportscaster's having an orgasm.)

Pitcher Billy O'Dell described Mays "as friendly with everybody on the team," but they respected his privacy. Few of the players asked about his personal life, and they were not about to ask about his hospitalization. "After it happened," Billy Pierce later recalled, "nobody really discussed it." He said Mays's health issues were not "major."

But Alvin Dark, who knew Mays far better, said the cumulative pressures on him were more than any one man could handle.

"Willie doesn't know how tired he is," Dark said. "There is nothing wrong with him physically. He's simply exhausted mentally and doesn't know it. He leads such an unnatural life. In every city in the league and at home, he has precious little privacy. On the road, he can't open his door without having to fight his way through autograph seekers or writers scratching for a story. He can't go out in public. He's always in demand. Kids are always after him for autographs. Grown-ups are always calling him on the telephone. He has to eat in his room. He can't go to a movie or a theater. Finally things mount until the pressure is unendurable and something snaps. You black out. That's all that is wrong with Willie. He's tired."

While "exhaustion" may have seemed simplistic, Mays's contemporaries recognized the unique pressures he was under. Kareem Abdul-Jabbar, for example, recalls that when he was in the eighth grade, in 1960, he met Mays at a Harlem Globetrotter game at Madison Square Garden. Mays stopped by the locker room, and the reporters descended. "They just mobbed him, and they pushed him back until he fell backwards over some chairs," Abdul-Jabbar says. "They knocked him over literally. I was just amazed that he had to deal with that type of mania. Willie was like, 'Hey, you guys gotta back off and give me some space.' He wasn't there to do an interview. He got out of there in a hurry."

Mays's style on the field was another factor. His hell-bent approach, slamming into catchers or fences, exacted an obvious price, but what really took its toll was what happened in between pitches. Filled with nervous energy, Mays seemed incapable of relaxing in between the white lines. A Chicago White Sox scout named Charley Metro once spent an entire game looking at Mays through his binoculars. "You won't believe what I saw," Metro said afterward. "The man is never still out there." Noting how he repositioned players every batter and sometimes every pitch, Metro said, Mays "looks like the signalman on the *Yorktown*."

Yet to the casual fan, as well as to many reporters, Mays was forever described as a "natural" whose skills flowed effortlessly from his body. Hank Aaron says that "most African American players were jealous of Willie—they were jealous of his skills on the baseball field. Every day was a struggle to stay in the league, but things came easily to him." Even his peers didn't understand the stress Mays was under.

The day after he entered the hospital in Cincinnati, he was allowed to see three people, Dr. Ballou, Alvin Dark, and Harry Jupiter, all of whom had to walk past a police officer guarding the door because so many hospital employees had been interrupting the patient for his autograph. Fueled, perhaps, by the hospital photograph depicting Mays in such dire straits, some writers later speculated ominously that he suffered from depression or had a complete breakdown. But as Jupiter's story in the *Examiner* made clear, the reality was different. The headline was: LIVELY DAY IN HOSPITAL WITH MAYS.

Jupiter's first sight of Mays was alarming: he was being pushed to his room in a wheelchair after some X-rays. Then Mays grinned when he saw the reporter. "I don't need this chair," he said, "but my buddy"—he jerked his thumb at the hospital attendant—"told me he'd get in trouble if I didn't ride in the chair." Mays then walked into his room and sprawled on the bed in his hospital pajamas and looked at Jupiter with his chin on his left fist. "I'm feeling pretty good now," he said, "but Harry, I was just plain scared last night. I don't think it was indigestion. I just didn't eat that much. But, man, I've been tired, real tired, ever since we went to Los Angeles."

Another attendant knocked on the door, and Mays asked him to buy him a comb, toothbrush, toothpaste, and "a whole lot of magazines. All kinds of magazines. But don't buy any of the ones with my picture on the cover. I've got all of them."

He reached into the drawer of a small table next to the bed and handed the attendant a ten-dollar bill. When he left, Mays continued: "People think it's funny when a ballplayer says he's tired. I don't complain much, but I'm real tired. I'm not as tired as I was last night. I took a sleeping pill and went right to sleep." (Jupiter didn't ask why someone so tired needed a sedative, though it appears Mays's physicians were often eager to give him sleeping pills.)

He said he probably needed one more day of rest. "I ain't no good to the team when I'm tired anyway," he said. He wondered if he could have his contract changed so he didn't have to play both games of a double-header—"they leave me pooped for four or five days after"—and complained about the extensive tests in the hospital. "They've even stuck pins in my head checking my brain," he said. "Man, that stuff hurts. And they're gonna do it again tomorrow too. They took blood from two places. They stuck a pin in my finger and they stuck a needle in my arm."

Mays groaned when a nurse entered to give him a vitamin B$_{12}$ shot. When she moved toward his right arm, he stopped her. "Not that one. Put it in the left arm." Then he turned to Jupiter. "That's all right, Harry. These vitamin shots are good for you." Jupiter said he was still glad he wasn't getting one. Mays called out, "Hey, nurse, give Harry a shot. Might pep him up a little bit." Everyone laughed.

But Jupiter tried to turn the conversation to more serious matters. Was Willie concerned about his health?

"Ain't nothing worrying me except maybe winning the pennant," he said. He thought for a moment. "You know what I worry about? I worry about Stretch [McCovey]. He ought to get married. Do him good. I've been taking care of Stretch in the outfield. I tell him where to play and try to keep boostin' his confidence. He's done real nice. There are a lot of out-fielders in the league that ain't as good as Stretch."

He also commended Felipe Alou and Harvey Kuenn. "Those guys made it easier for me in center field," he said.

The attendant returned with the magazines and toiletries, and Mays tried to tip him another dollar. The young man declined the bill.

"Take it," Mays said. "I gotta make a living and so do you."

The attendant smiled, took the dollar, and turned at the door. "I'll be back," he said. "My girl said I had better get your autograph for her or not call her anymore."

Mays waved. "Anytime. I'll be here tomorrow."

He was released from the hospital after two nights and three days. Whenever asked about these episodes—and there were more—Mays cited the relentless demands of the long season. But other players were not hos-pitalized for three days because of tired legs. Mays, however, needed the break: he pushed himself up to and beyond his physical and emotional limits. Sometimes, it seemed, the burden of being Willie Mays was too much even for Willie Mays. He did acknowledge, in an Associated Press interview three weeks after his collapse, that his penchant for bottling up his emotions, for refusing to reach out to others, had hurt him.

"I had a lot of trouble last year," he said, referring to his divorce. "Every-body knows what it was, and I don't want to get into it. The doctor told me those things can store up in a person, especially one like me who keeps it inside him. Then, all of a sudden, it busts out all at once. I really believe that's what happened to me."

He continued: "I try not to think of anything but what's happening on the field. It's when I'm off the field that I start to think—and then I get tired."

Mays joined the team in Pittsburgh on September 14, but Dark scratched him from the lineup on that day as well as the following. He was clearly concerned. "Nobody, but nobody, wants to win a pennant more than I," he said, "but I'm not going to do it at the risk of shattering some-body's nerves, perhaps permanently."

Dark's caution was not simply humane but courageous. The Giants lost all four of the games that Mays missed, dropping from 1½ games behind the Dodgers to four, with only thirteen games left. It appeared that Mays's collapse, combined with Dark's concerns, would cost the Giants a chance at the pennant, but when pressed by reporters, Dark held his ground. "The tests taken of Willie in Cincinnati didn't show anything wrong with him, and yet I won't let him play," he said. "How, tell me, can tests tell what goes on inside a Kuenn, a Davenport, a Sanford, an Alou, or a Mays in a pennant fight such as this? . . . These players are human beings. They're individuals and no stethoscope or hypo needle or X-ray machine yet made can explore and detect that pressure."

While the team was in Pittsburgh, a wire service photograph showed a sad Giant player, wearing a warm-up jacket, sitting in the dugout at Forbes Field. The caption said that Mays was "Aching to Play," which was true, except the picture was of Carl Boles, a reserve outfielder who looked like Mays. Boles was accustomed to the confusion. The first time he walked onto the field at the Polo Grounds, the fans cheered. "Then when they saw my number, 14, they booed me," he said. "Crazy, man. When Willie appeared, they cheered for several minutes and then turned on me, booing me again."

Mulling on the importance of Mays, a reporter discovered that he had missed nineteen games in his career. The Giants lost each of those games. The *Chronicle*'s Will Connolly wrote: "There is a big hole in center field when Willie Mays is out. Not only in the Giants' lineup, but also in the National League and the whole of baseball."

In his first game back, on Sunday, September 16, Mays came to bat in the eighth inning with two on and the Giants trailing, 4–1. He hit a three-run homer, but the Giants lost in extra innings. They lost the next day as well, extending their losing streak to six. That day, the *Chronicle*'s Art Rosenbaum wrote: "Ticket applications for World Series seats at Candlestick went to season subscribers on Thursday last, the morning after Mays blacked out. Awkward timing to say the least. By now it seems a trifle late for miracles but the undying San Francisco fans will wait. Maybe a pennant was never intended anyway."

Some fans reminisced about the furious comeback in 1951, but nostalgia gave way to reality. The Giants split their next four games, leaving them, on September 22, four behind the Dodgers, with only seven games remaining. The Dodgers had already won one hundred games, their final six games were at home, and Koufax was back in the rotation. Dark was one of the few optimists remaining. "Willie, the Dodgers could have taken charge and they haven't," he said. "I think something's wrong down there in L.A." Dark told the rest of the team the same thing and predicted that the Giants would catch the Dodgers and beat them in the playoffs. "Everybody thought he was nuts," Carl Boles said.

He wasn't. The Dodgers lost two of three at home against the Houston

Colt .45s while the Giants were winning three of four. With three games left, the Dodgers were still leading by two games. They were to finish the season against the Cardinals; the Giants, against the Colt .45s.

On Friday, September 28, the Giants' game was rained out, and the Dodgers lost in extra innings, cutting their lead to 1½. Before the Giants' doubleheader the following day, Mays saw his old friend Joey Amalfitano, now playing for the Colt .45s, who had just won two out of three against the Dodgers. And Amalfitano said something strange to Mays: "Can you guys score a run? If you can score, you got the pennant. [The Dodgers] are never going to score another run."

The Dodgers had indeed gone into a slump. Except for one thirteen-run outburst, they had averaged 2.8 runs over the past ten games. The Cardinals, meanwhile, were plenty loose. Long out of contention, they loved playing in Los Angeles for its late-night diversions. The Cardinals "were staying out until three or four o'clock in the morning for day games, and they didn't care," Ron Fairly of the Dodgers said. "They were as free and easy as you please."

On the penultimate day of the regular season, the Giants won the first game of their doubleheader, 11–5, moving to one game out. In the night-cap, Juan Marichal, recovering from a twisted ankle, started his first game since September 5. He was still in pain but felt that Dark didn't believe him. He took the ball and lasted only four innings, and the Giants lost. After the game, the Latin players, including Cepeda and Alou, gathered around Marichal's locker and, according to one account, shot "wrathful glances over at Dark and the coaching staff," apparently upset that the manager would risk Marichal's career for one game. The following day, neither Cepeda nor Alou was in the starting lineup. It's possible that Dark simply preferred left-handed bats against a right-handed starter, but the Latin players thought it was another act of Dark's vengeance.

The Dodgers, in their second-to-last game, couldn't score against the Cardinals and lost again, setting up the final day of the regular season with a one-game lead.

Willie Mays had had a terrible stretch run. In his last four games, he had gone 1-for-14 with one RBI. He also committed one of his most embarrassing gaffes. In the last game before their final series, the Giants were losing, 7–1, when Mays reached third base with one out in the sixth inning. Cepeda struck out, and Mays walked off the bag, thinking it was the third out. He was tagged to end the inning. He told reporters after the game: "I just didn't realize how many outs there were. I guess it can happen to a guy, once in a lifetime."

He received little forgiveness. As the *Examiner*'s Curley Grieve wrote:

"Because he makes more money than anyone in baseball ($90,000), Mays isn't supposed to make mistakes. And this one was compounded by the fact that he fanned dismally for the last out with two on in the ninth." On the final day of the regular season, with the Giants trailing by one game before a packed house of 41,327, Mays came to bat in the first inning and was met with loud boos. He drew a walk, pacifying some people.

The Giants faced Colt .45 pitcher Dick Farrell, a hard-throwing right-hander who had beaten the Dodgers earlier that week. But the Giants had nineteen-game-winner Billy O'Dell on the mound, and the two staged a classic pitcher's duel. The Giants took a 1–0 lead on a home run by Ed Bailey in the fourth, but Houston tied it with a run in the seventh.

A Dodger victory would have made the Giants' game moot, but the Dodgers and Cardinals, whose game began an hour later, were locked in their own scoreless battle, which was monitored on the Giant scoreboard.

After Mays's walk, he struck out and popped out and was zero for his last ten. No one had more at stake in this game than Mays: if the Giants lost, he would be blamed. The columnists had already said as much. So too did the jeers of the fans. Never mind that Mays led the league with 49 home runs, drove in 141, scored 130, and hit .304, and his slugging percentage of .615 was his fourth best in his career. Hitting in front of McCovey, he had reduced his attempted steals to keep the hole open on the right side, but he still led the team with eighteen stolen bases, and he led the team in every offensive category except average, hits, and triples. What seemed to matter most, however, was that Mays's mysterious ailment had cost him and the Giants four games down the stretch.

The last time Farrell had pitched against the Giants, on July 24, Mays had nailed him for two home runs, both on fastballs, so today he was throwing mostly curves. Mays led off the eighth, and organist Lloyd Fox played a few bars of the Giants' fight song, "Bye Bye Baby." Mays took a big swing on the first pitch—a curve—and hit it far but foul into the right field stands. He guessed that on the next pitch, Farrell would try to slip a fastball by him, which is exactly what Farrell tried to do. Except the pitch didn't get by him. Mays swung and, as the *Chronicle*'s Bob Stevens wrote, the ball "became a blur of white, smashed through the noise of roaring throats, sailing high into the blue, and it gave San Francisco the best shot it has ever had at the long-awaited pennant." In what may have been the most important home run of Mays's career, the ball landed in the fourteenth row of the left field seats. Mays, restored as hero, had gone deep on his first swing of the regular season and his last. The Giants won the game.

Even Mays's critics had to acknowledge him. "Willie Mays is salaried at $90,000 a year," wrote the *Chronicle*'s Prescott Sullivan. "At times he is worth it."

But nothing yet had been won. Most of the crowd stayed at Candlestick—it was Fan Appreciation Day, and the Giants were giving away five cars. The fans could follow the Dodger game on the radio; Russ Hodges was using the Western Union tape to call the contest. The Giants clustered around their own radio in the locker room. The game remained scoreless until the top of the eighth, when Cardinal catcher Gene Oliver tagged Johnny Podres for a homer. Alvin Dark let out a soft "wahoo" while the crowd at Candlestick as well as Kezar Stadium in San Francisco—where the 49ers were playing the Vikings, but the fans were listening to baseball—went wild. The Dodgers lost, 1–0. After the final out, the fans at Candlestick threw seat cushions from the upper deck. Strangers hugged each other. Men and women danced. Everyone was yelling, and a long line had begun to form for playoff tickets.

The Dodgers had been shut out the last two games of the season and were scoreless in twenty-one consecutive innings. They had lost ten of their last thirteen, though the Giants had won only seven in that span. It was a far cry from the glorious run in 1951, but the San Francisco newspapers called it "a miracle." The longest regular season in baseball history had decided nothing in the National League, which would now have a three-game playoff.

Duke Snider, thinking back to 1951, said, "We owe the Giants something."

The playoff allowed the press to focus on baseball's radical changes over the previous eleven years—the expansion to the West Coast, the increase in the number of teams, the longer season, the resurgence of the stolen base. What had also changed was Willie Mays, from the bubbling rookie to the world-weary veteran. "I think I'm a better ballplayer," he said. "I'm older and wiser, but tireder." Mays was the only Giant who had played in New York, and Duke Snider was the only Dodger who had played in the 1951 Series. Leo Durocher was the Dodgers' third base coach, though he liked nothing more than ignoring Walter Alston's "take" sign and signaling the hit-and-run.

The first game of the playoff was at Candlestick, where Dark was up to his old tricks, instructing the grounds crew to soak the left side of the infield to slow down ground balls. The field was in bad shape, but it probably didn't matter, because everything went right for the Giants and for Mays. Koufax pitched for the Dodgers, but after his long layoff, he said he felt as though he were in the third week of spring training. In the first inning, Felipe Alou doubled, and Mays followed with a crushing blow over the right center field fence. Koufax lasted only one inning, giving up three, and was replaced by Ed Roebuck. In the third, Mays came up, and Roebuck threw one pitch behind him, then the next pitch knocked him down. Mays rapped the third pitch to left for a single. In the sixth, the Giants were still leading by only three, and the Dodgers again tried to rattle Mays. Larry Sherry fired a brushback. Mays dusted himself off and hit another homer, inspiring an even louder torrent of cheers. Asked after the game about the knockdown pitches, Mays said, "Maybe the ball got away—no trouble. I wasn't hit. Sometimes those pitches make you mad and you just dig in and try harder."

Giant pitcher Billy Pierce, who threw a shutout that day, detected a turning point for Mays with the second home run. "I think it was the moment where San Francisco fans finally took him to heart," he said. "They believed he was doing something for San Francisco—not the Giants—but San Francisco. He was doing something to try to bring a winner to the city. Willie heard those cheers, and he liked it."

The Giants won, 8–0, and Mays had a perfect day, going 3-for-3, with two homers, three runs scored, three RBIs, and a walk. "I think the fans are starting to warm up to me," he said.

The Dodgers had now gone thirty straight innings without scoring. Durocher, who had always been superstitious, was so desperate that for the next game, he wore the same T-shirt he had on when Bobby Thomson hit his home run. At least that's what he said. He also claimed to have the same underwear and socks. The Dodger fans, however, had lost confidence. Only 25,231 Angelinos, almost 30,000 short of capacity at Dodger Stadium, attended that game, and the city's lack of faith appeared to be warranted. The Giants took a 5–0 lead against Drysdale and had their best pitcher, twenty-four-game-winner Jack Sanford, on the mound. But Sanford, battling a cold, tired in the sixth inning and was knocked out as the Dodgers took the lead, 7–5, in the eighth. Davenport and Mays led off the ninth inning with back-to-back singles. Then Ed Bailey singled to center. Davenport scored and Mays, his hat flying off, tried for third, but Tommy Davis's throw arrived just as Mays's foot slid in. The umpire's arms appeared to signal safe, but Jocko Conlan called him out. Mays bounced off the ground in disbelief, jumped high in the air, and began to argue, joined by his equally animated third base coach, Whitey Lockman. It was the most emotion Mays had ever displayed over a call and was probably the closest he ever came to getting thrown out. He even complained, respectfully, after the game. "I let him know it was a bad call," he said. "That would have been a big play for us. It would have meant at least one run, and probably changed the complexion of the game." Lockman was less diplomatic, calling it "a joke decision. I doubt whether Conlan even saw the play. He just called it from memory."

Even with the out, the Giants still tied the score that inning, but the Dodgers got a run in the bottom of the ninth to win, 8–7. Mays wondered if Leo's underwear really did bring him luck.

The Dodgers' victory set up the decisive game in Los Angeles, on October 3—eleven years to the day that the two teams had met in their historic clash at the Polo Grounds. A reporter asked Dark if he had any good luck charms from 1951, as Durocher had.

"Only Willie Mays," Dark said.

On a sun-splashed day, the fans turned out wearing short sleeves and sundresses, with Doris Day, Rosalind Russell, and Frank Sinatra among the 45,693 in attendance. Marichal, rested but still nursing his ankle, pitched for the Giants while Johnny Podres, with only two days' rest, started for the Dodgers.

The Giants grabbed a 2–0 lead in the third and could have had more, but Cepeda grounded into a double play with the bases loaded. Snider scored a run for the Dodgers in the fourth. In the top of the sixth, the Giants had the bases loaded with none out. Reliever Ed Roebuck was called into the game, and he induced two ground balls, including a double play, to keep it a one-run game. The momentum swung back to the Dodgers, who promptly took the lead on a two-run homer by Tommy Davis. In the seventh, Maury Wills singled, stole second base, and then stole third. The throw to third was wild, and Wills galloped home, with Durocher running with him down the line. When Wills slid, so did Durocher. Both men were safe. "Durocher got up laughing," Felipe Alou recalled. "Right then he thought he had the game won. . . . I wanted to beat them after what Durocher did. Sliding. Like it was a show." The Dodgers led, 4–2.

Roebuck, a thirty-year-old right-hander, had been a workhorse all year; he had a 10–1 record and had pitched masterfully in the game. But it was muggy, with smog hanging over the park, and after he retired the side in the eighth, he had gone three innings and was spent. In the bottom of the eighth, the Dodgers loaded the bases with two outs and the pitcher was due up. It seemed like a good time for Alston to pinch-hit to try to seal the win, then use a fresh arm for the ninth. The Dodgers' Ron Perranoski, who led the team in saves, with twenty, was available. So was Don Drysdale, who had pitched only five innings the day before, or even Koufax. But Alston didn't want to lift Roebuck, who dragged his bat to the plate and made the final out.

The Giants now came to bat in the top of ninth, still down, 4–2—very close to the bottom-of-the-ninth score from 1951 (the Giants were losing, 4–1). Dark offered no words of inspiration. He just said, "Matty, get your bat." Matty Alou pinch-hit for the pitcher and ripped the second pitch for a single to right. The dugout suddenly stirred to life. The next batter, Harvey Kuenn, grounded into a forceout, leaving the Dodgers only two outs away from a pennant. Then Roebuck unraveled. He walked pinch hitter Willie McCovey, and he walked Felipe Alou to load the bases. The next hitter was Willie Mays. Alston went out to the mound to ask Roebuck how he felt.

Roebuck, who had kept Mays in check that year, wanted to finish the game one way or the other. He told Alston he felt fine.

As Mays watched the inning unfold, he recalled the rally from 1951, and as he waited in the on-deck circle, he thought about one thing: this time, he wanted to be at the plate. He was still embarrassed by the memory of his quivering fears in the on-deck circle with Bobby Thomson in the batter's box. History had repeated itself so he could prove himself in the clutch. With the bases loaded and down by two runs, a long hit could give the Giants the lead, though a double play would give the Dodgers the pennant. The stunned crowd was so quiet that the national television audience could hear the Giants calling out encouragement.

Roebuck, who normally had a good sinker, was hoping for a ground ball. He threw a pitch down on the inside part of the plate—a tough pitch to handle—and Mays swung, smashing a line drive toward the pitcher. Bob Broeg, the veteran sports columnist for the *St. Louis Post-Dispatch,* wrote seventeen years later: "Even the most famous player of his day might top that sinker into a double play. Instead, hitting straight away, Mays drove a torrid shot through the box, as hard as I ever saw." Accounts vary on whether the ball hit Roebuck's bare hand, his glove, or his leg—Durocher said the ball actually ripped the glove off Roebuck's hand—but what's known is that Mays's cannon shot bounced off the pitcher and rolled away. A run scored as Mays reached first on the single, and the bases remained loaded with the Dodgers still leading, 4–3.

Belatedly, Alston removed Roebuck, but instead of calling in Perranoski or Drysdale, he summoned starting pitcher Stan Williams, who had pitched effectively in 1⅔ innings of relief the day before but could be wild. He averaged one walk every two innings. "To be truthful," Roebuck said, "I was surprised to see Stanley coming in." Durocher thought Alston had lost his mind.

Except for the Giant fans, the rest of the inning was painful to watch. Cepeda hit a sacrifice fly to tie the score, Felipe Alou moving to third. Williams threw a wild pitch, allowing Mays to move to second. After intentionally walking Ed Bailey, Williams walked Jim Davenport, forcing in the go-ahead run. Perranoski finally replaced Williams, and he got Pagan to hit a grounder, but rookie second baseman Larry Burright kicked it, allowing another run to score. The inning ended with a strikeout, but the Giants had plated four runs on only two singles. "Worst inning I ever saw in my life," Durocher said.

The Giants led, 6–4, and Dark brought in Billy Pierce, the starting pitcher who had shut out the Dodgers only two days before. He hadn't recorded a save all year, but as Mays said, "Dark wasn't taking any chances." The first batter, Maury Wills, grounded out. Jim Gilliam then flew out to right field. The Dodgers' final hope was pinch hitter Lee Walls, and on a 1–1 pitch he hit a soft liner into right center. At first it appeared it might fall, which would bring up the tying run, but the ball hung up, and Mays was closing fast. When he pounded the pocket of his glove with his fist, his teammates knew the game was over. Mays caught the ball, but not with his usual basket catch. He grabbed it chest high. Asked why in the locker room, Mays laughed. "You crazy?" he squealed. "That was $15,000 a man!"

Before the final out, Mays had thought to himself that if he caught the ball, he would give it to Pierce, but in all the excitement, he flung it into the stands—a rare display of celebration. Throughout his career, Mays avoided the boisterous screams, hugs, and dances or—after winning a pennant or World Series—the spraying of champagne. On this occasion, the stadium crew had to wheel the victory champagne from one clubhouse to the next three different times, until finally settling in the Giants' clubhouse. Amid the crush of reporters and bulky television cameras and hot lights and joyous, rowdy teammates who were imbibing voraciously after their longest season, someone offered Mays a glass of champagne. He declined.

In the Dodger clubhouse, a black rage had taken over—players smashed beer bottles, ripped their uniforms, cursed Alston, and wept. They had won 102 games and had nothing to show for it. The World Series money— at least $12,000 a person—would have doubled the annual salary of some players. Podres accused Alston of stealing it. A Dodger passed around bottles of whiskey to every player, some of whom literally dropped to the floor, drunk. "I don't like to be around drunks," Johnny Roseboro recalled. "So I got dressed and left. It was the worst scene I ever saw with the Dodgers."

There was little time to celebrate—the World Series against the Yankees would begin the next day—but that didn't stop San Franciscans from enjoying the moment. In the financial district, ticker tape, torn telephone books, and papers were thrown from office buildings. Cable cars clanged, horns blared. Some streetcars were rocked, and trolleys were pulled off wires. Market Street was jammed until long past midnight. The police barred vehicles from Third to Eighth streets, and in North Beach howling fans demonstrated. The Yankees were already in town, staying at a town house on Market Street. Had the Dodgers won, the Yankees would have flown to Los Angeles that night, which might have been safer. Some unruly fans, according to the *Sporting News,* "burst into the town house and threw furniture around, but police finally restored order."

The city's delirious throng headed for San Francisco International Airport, where the Giants were due to arrive. No one on the plane could have predicted what happened next. The pilot, Orv Schmidt, made the announcement: "Fellows, there is a little disturbance down below. We're told that there are at least twenty-five thousand people down there—maybe it's seventy-five thousand—and they've blocked off the runway. They thought we were coming in on an earlier jet and they ran out on the landing strip to meet it. Then they ran to another jet. The police can't get them back out of the entranceways. We don't know if we can land. We may have to land in Oakland."

Groans were heard in the cabin, with someone saying, "What a way to end the day. First we win the pennant, and then we go up in flames."

The DC-7 banked east for Oakland, then turned around and continued to circle as the chaos unfolded below. Cars were jammed for miles along the Bayshore Freeway; some people simply abandoned their vehicles to join the crowd—later estimated at fifty thousand—at the airport. The police could not clear the runways. Almost forty minutes after the first announcement, Schmidt took the microphone again: "We can't go in. Two big jets are stalled down there. We'll have to land at the west runway."

The pilot had received clearance to land at an old United Air Lines maintenance base behind locked gates. Finally, the National League champions reached the ground to the polite cheers of the hangar police, maintenance men, switchboard attendants, and a bus driver. But their night wasn't over.

The bus was available; some players, however, simply started walking for the highway in search of a ride. According to Cepeda, "A lot of us ended up hitchhiking—Matty and Felipe Alou, Pierce, Marichal. People we'd never met in our lives pulled up, offered us rides, and we jumped in."

The others boarded the bus and headed to the main concourse, where the mob was waiting. Any hope of making an inconspicuous exit was quickly dashed. The fans, some of whom were waving signs and banners, broke through the police barricades and circled the vehicle. "Those folks meant well," Dark said, "but they really shook us up." The horde pushed ahead, rocked the bus, and shattered windows. "I really thought they were going to turn the thing over and crush some of the people," Billy O'Dell said. Added Ed Bailey, "That was as scared as I've ever been."

Fortunately, no one was hurt, and an episode that could have turned tragic was remembered as a defining moment of the Giants in San Francisco, the moment when the team and city became one. "Hysteria is not a Bay Area trait," wrote Art Rosenbaum and Bob Stevens. "Sedate enthusiasm is the proper role for a proper San Franciscan. The sophisticates would never have the bad taste to lose their heads over a baseball team [but] when the fans were trying to break through the windows, the Giants knew they were home."

And with the fans surrounding the bus, a chant could be heard, softer and then more loudly, a chant that echoed from the last game in the Polo Grounds to the runways of San Francisco: "We want Willie!"

At last—after five years, after a season of turmoil, after the booing and the sniping and the cold shoulders of a city that wouldn't quite accept him—they wanted Willie.

But Willie was gone. After the plane landed, one cab was at the maintenance base. It had been called from the airplane by Russ Hodges, for himself, but Mays found it first and took it. The man who always took pride in separating himself from the masses had once again struck out on his own. Under the circumstances, no one complained. When the crowd continued to call for Willie, Bob Nieman, a utility outfielder, spied Mays's look-alike and said, "Let's throw them Boles and get the hell out of here!"

The bus eventually left, and everyone made it home safely. When Mays reached his house, he answered some calls from friends who wanted World Series tickets, then went to sleep.

For the Giants, the World Series in 1962, as in 1951, felt like an anticlimax. They had the same opponent as before, and the Series began the day after the last playoff game. There was no time to rejuvenate. After their harrowing return to San Francisco, most of the players didn't get home until after midnight, and the first pitch of Game One was in the afternoon. Two hours before game time, Mays sat motionless at his locker. "Willie," a reporter asked, "are you as tense before this game as you were in 1951 and 1954?"

"Man," Mays said, "after that playoff in Los Angeles, I'm all out of tense."

Mays was actually in good shape physically compared to some of his teammates. Second baseman Chuck Hiller, spiked twice in the past week, had raw welts on his left shin, and his bruised right ankle was nearly black. Both Jack Sanford and Jim Davenport were battling colds. Davenport's ulcers were also flaring; he was supposed to avoid cigarettes, but by the start of the Series, he was smoking more than a pack a day. Tom Haller, the catcher, had been spiked in the second playoff game and had six inches of stitches in his left forearm. Jose Pagan's legs were completely bandaged, and in the first game, Felipe Alou had scraped his arm on the fence while trying to make a catch, leaving a four-inch welt.

The Yankees, despite winning nine fewer games than the Giants, were heavy favorites, having won nine out of the last fourteen World Series and thirteen out of the last fifteen pennants. The year 1962 featured the famed "M&M Boys," Mickey Mantle and Roger Maris. The previous year had been one of the most memorable in Yankee history, with Maris's sixty-one homers breaking Babe Ruth's record; the team had won 109 games and defeated the Reds in the World Series in five games. In 1962, their record wasn't as good (94–68), but they led the league in hitting, had six All-Stars across a deep veteran lineup, and Mantle won his third MVP award. The Yankees, having won the pennant by five games, were also rested.

Second-year Yankee manager Ralph Houk could barely hide his contempt for the Giants. Asked whether they impressed him, he had to take a long pause. Then he said, "Well, naturally—they have men—they have several players who naturally impress you."

The Series did bring the Fall Classic to San Francisco for the first time, which, according to Herb Caen, briefly put the city's much-maligned ballpark in a better light. "Even Candlestick Park," he wrote, "which sometimes gives the uncomfortable impression that a giant had taken the Embarcadero Freeway and bent it into a horseshoe, looked brighter than usual. Flags, banners, and splashy clothes on the overflow crowd, which included both people and politicians, gave the place the touches of color it too often lacks." Caen, however, was underwhelmed by the opponents. "The Yankees have twice as many prima donnas as the S. F. Opera Company."

With veteran Whitey Ford pitching—he had not allowed a run in his last thirty-one World Series innings—the Yankees won the first game, 6–2. Mays, who had had six hits in seven at-bats in All-Star games against Ford, stroked three singles, but the game validated expectations of a Yankee romp. The next day, however, Jack Sanford shut out the Yankees, 2–0, which included a McCovey home run off Ralph Terry. The victory revived the Giants. "If we lose now," Felipe Alou said after the game, "it's because they are the better team."

When the Series shifted to New York, the win-loss pattern continued: the Yankees won Game Three, lost Game Four, won Game Five. For the most part, the contests were close and low-scoring, with the heavy artillery on both teams kept mostly in check. Mantle hit .120, Maris, .174, Cepeda, .158. An unlikely hitting star emerged in Game Four, when Chuck Hiller cracked the first World Series grand slam ever by a National Leaguer, pacing the Giants to a 7–3 victory.

In New York, Mays chipped in only two singles in three games, and he vented his frustration during batting practice before Game Five. After the regulars completed their swings, catcher Ed Bailey, who was not starting that day, stepped in and took a practice swing. Unknown to Bailey, Mays came in behind him, hoping for a couple of extra swings, and Bailey's bat almost hit him. Mays yelled at Bailey, then stepped in the batter's box while Bailey stood in the opposite box waiting for the pitch. For a few seconds, neither man moved until Bailey finally deferred. The pitcher, however, threw the ball in the dirt. Mays picked it up, and as he fungoed it, he cursed the pitcher and walked away. "It was the one ugly moment in the Series, and a minor one at that," Arnold Hano wrote, "and you have to remember that all through the Series, Willie Mays kept saying, 'I'm so tired, I can't wait for this thing to end.'"

The 1962 Series is known less for any specific play than for the rain. A downpour delayed Game Five for one day, then, as the teams traveled back to San Francisco, a huge storm with gale-force winds swept across the northern California coast, causing five deaths. San Francisco absorbed nearly two inches of rain in less than one day before two more days of rain. It finally stopped, but the conditions exposed another liability of Candlestick—poor drainage. Stoneham hired three helicopters to dry the fields, but that didn't work. The Series experienced three rainouts and two travel days, and by October 14, everyone thought Commissioner Ford Frick would declare the field ready to play, if only because the delays had forced him to delay a trip to Japan. But he said the stadium needed another day to dry out.

NBC, which was broadcasting the Series, was apparently short on backup programming. During one delay, Mel Allen spoke on the air for an hour and a half. One journalist, desperate for copy, asked Willie Mays, "How do you feel about the nation's economy?"

Mays looked at him in disbelief. "You must be kidding," he said. "I don't even know how much money I got sitting in my pants."

Another reporter asked Mays what he'd had for breakfast that day. "I didn't eat breakfast this morning," he said. "Why? Number one, I ain't got a maid. Number two, I ain't got a wife anymore, and number three, I can't cook."

Play finally resumed on October 15. Orlando Cepeda had been 0-for-12 in the Series, 0-for-29 including All-Star games, leading to the criticism that he couldn't hit in big games. But the days off allowed him to regain his strength and move to a heavier bat, and against Whitey Ford in Game Six, he got a scratch hit his first time up. That seemed to relax him. He got two

more hits, including a double, drove in two runs, scored a run, and led the
Giants to a 5–2 win behind Billy Pierce's three-hitter.

That set up the seventh game. No team in major league history had ever
had a more grueling season than the Giants—172 games, with a World
Series that spanned twelve days and included two cross-country flights.
Thus far, Mays's most significant contributions were on the sodden outfield turf. As Hano wrote:

> Once he had gone into left center and, as he made a catch, hurdled Felipe
> Alou so that Alou slid under him. It was breathless, perfect synchroniza-
> tion. A second time he had gone into left centerfield, and this time Matty
> Alou had come over and made the catch, and Mays slid under Alou. They
> never touched; they never brushed. The Yankee outfielders played well all
> Series, but countless times they were banging together, committing last
> minute lunges, fighting wind, and looking a bit like novices. As did Kuenn,
> McCovey, and at times Felipe Alou, of the Giants. Only Mays was magnifi-
> cent in the outfield all Series long.

Game Seven was another duel between Sanford and Terry, both of
whom had pitched superbly in Game Two. Terry offered a compelling
subplot. In the seventh game of the 1960 World Series, he had surrendered
the game-winning home run to Bill Mazeroski in the ninth inning. In
1962, he went 23–12, with the most victories in the American League, but
he was still haunted by his previous failure. He told a writer before Game
Seven at Candlestick, "After that Mazeroski home run in 1960, the fact
that this team is letting me pitch the seventh game is like a tonic to me."

The game was scoreless until the fifth inning, when the Yankees pushed
across a run on a bases-loaded double play. The Giants didn't even get
their first baserunner until the sixth, when Sanford singled. Mays had bad
luck in the seventh: he hit the ball long and hard into left but right into the
teeth of the wind. The ball stayed in the park, and left fielder Tom Tresh
made a running one-handed "snow cone" catch. McCovey followed with
his own moon blast that stayed in the park and fell for a triple; he was
stranded when Cepeda struck out.

The Yankees appeared ready to break the game open in the eighth when
they loaded the bases with nobody out and had Maris at the plate. Relief
pitcher Billy O'Dell took over and promptly induced Maris to hit into a
forceout at the plate and Elston Howard to rap into a double play. Two
ground balls, and the Giants still had life.

Their bats, however, remained silent, and they trailed, 1–0, going into
the bottom of the ninth. Terry, working on a two-hitter, stayed in the game.

Dark needed a pinch hitter and chose Matty Alou, just as he had in the last playoff game when the Giants trailed in the ninth. Alou once again came through, this time dragging a bunt past Terry for a single. The crowd of 43,943, quiet for most of the afternoon, began to make noise. Houk peered nervously out of a silent dugout while Dark paced his own. The next hitter, Felipe Alou, tried to bunt his brother over, failed, and struck out.

With one out, Hiller was the batter. Dark was sometimes accused of "overmanaging," of not allowing his squad to simply play. In this case, he took the bat out of Hiller's hands and asked him to bunt as well. Even if he was successful, the Giants would be down to their last out. But Hiller couldn't get the bunt down and, with one swing left, also struck out.

The season came down to one hitter—Willie Mays. And he had one thing on his mind. "I was going for the bomb," he later said. "We needed a home run. I was going for it." Terry jammed him on two inside pitches, then blazed one on the outside part of the plate, knee high. "I felt I had real good stuff on it," Terry later said.

Mays was hoping for a pitch to pull. He didn't have time to adjust his stride but, just using his wrists, flicked his bat through the strike zone and hit the ball squarely. A line drive went down the right field line for an extra-base hit. The crowd roared as Alou, a speedy runner, put his head down, rounded second, headed for third, and looked for the signal from third base coach Whitey Lockman.

Right fielder Roger Maris was playing Mays to pull. At the crack of the bat, it appeared the ball would reach the fence, which would have scored Alou while giving Mays a triple. But the soggy outfield slowed the ball down. Though known as a slugger, Maris had also won a Gold Glove; he got a good jump on this hit and closed on it. A right-handed thrower, he was able to cut the ball off just shy of the warning track, pivot in one sweeping motion, and fire toward second baseman Bobby Richardson. Lockman saw the play, threw up his arms, and stopped Alou, with Mays pulling in at second.

Reporters and fans alike instantly questioned whether Lockman should have sent Alou, but the argument had to wait. The next hitter was Willie McCovey, who had already homered off Terry in Game Two and tripled off him today. Houk went to the mound to talk to his right-hander; most of the Giants assumed he was instructing Terry to walk McCovey to get to the next hitter, the right-handed Cepeda. The conference was brief; Terry later acknowledged flashbacks to 1960 and the hope for redemption. "A man," he said, "rarely gets a second chance like I did."

Surprisingly, Terry pitched to McCovey, who swung at the first pitch, a curve, and fouled it down the right field line. The second pitch was a fastball, and McCovey uncoiled his massive arms, swung ferociously, and sent a tracer to the right side. Mays took off with the expectation of scoring the winning run. The fans screamed. But the ball, a sinking line drive, sailed right to Richardson, who snared it, staggered, but held on. The Yankees won the World Series.

"A few inches," Alvin Dark muttered after the game. "That was twice as hard a line drive as any man can hit." When a reporter said that McCovey hit the ball so hard he doubted Mays would have scored, Dark said, "By the time they got the ball home, Mays would have been dressed."

McCovey, who was even more media-shy than Mays, spoke with pride. "A man hits the ball as hard as he can," he said. "He can't feel bad about what he does. Of course you want to win. Of course you'd rather hit one off the fists and break your bat and have it drop in, but if you hit it hard, that's all you can do. . . . We are a great team, and the Yankees know it too."

Mays didn't get the ring, but he laid to rest any doubt about his ability to deliver under pressure. In his last at-bat in the regular season, his homer had won the game. In his last at-bat in the playoff, his single drove in a run and extended the rally. And in his last at-bat in the World Series, his double nearly tied the game.

His double also generated the most controversy—should Lockman have sent Alou? Both Lockman and Dark defended the decision, as did Houk. "Matty would have been out by a mile," he said. Art Rosenbaum later wrote: "Most Yankees and Giants who had a clear look at the flight of Maris's throw and the advancement of Alou later agreed: it would have been suicide to send Matty home."

Mays was not among those "Yankees and Giants." He has never specifically criticized Lockman but reframes the argument by saying what he would have done had he been the runner. He notes all of the things that the Yankees had to do to make the out: Maris had to field the ball cleanly and throw it accurately, Richardson had to catch it and throw it on target, and Elston Howard had to catch it and make the tag. Each step in the sequence increased the possibility of a mishap, and indeed, Richardson's throw was up the line. McCovey's final out was a reminder of how deeply the odds are stacked against the hitter. For most batters, the probability of getting a hit is less than 30 percent, and even a scorching line drive doesn't guarantee success.

Mays's regret was not that Alou was held at third but that he had not been the runner. He would have ignored Lockman and sped for the plate. The prospect of a furious collision with a two-hundred-pound catcher didn't bother him one bit.

"Elston Howard and I," Mays said, "would have had some fun at home."

• • •

The Most Valuable Player Award stimulates a perennial debate: should it go to the best player on the best team—his value enhanced by virtue of his leading his team to a pennant—or should it simply go to the best player in the league? In 1962, the sportswriters who voted for the award tended to favor pennant-winners. Over the previous twelve years ending in 1961, eight of the MVPs in both leagues had also won pennant championships. In 1962, Mantle won the award while his teammate Bobby Richardson came in second place.

By those standards, it appeared that Mays would scoop up his second MVP in 1962. He led the league in homers (49), total bases (382), and put-outs by an outfielder (425); was second in RBIs (141) and runs (130); third in slugging percentage (.615); and he hit .303. The only player with comparable numbers was Dodger Tommy Davis (.346, 153 RBIs, 120 runs, 27 home runs). They each had 18 stolen bases, though Mays won the Gold Glove. Even if Davis had a slight statistical edge, Mays's contributions in winning the championship should have put him over.

Davis's teammate Maury Wills, however, won the MVP, with Mays coming in second and Davis third. Wills hit only .299, with 6 homers and 48 RBIs, and he scored the same number of runs as Mays, but his 104 stolen bases carried the day. The vote was close. Twenty writers cast ballots, and each was allowed to choose up to ten players, ranked 1 to 10, with number 1 receiving 14 points, number 2 receiving 9 points, and so on. Wills's point total was 209; Mays's was 202. (Mantle, by contrast, won 234–152.)

No one would dispute that Wills's 104 stolen bases was a magnificent achievement as well as unexpected: the previous year he had stolen 35. What's harder to defend is that out of twenty writers, Mays received five votes for third place and four for fourth place. Almost half the voters, in other words, did not believe that Mays was among the top two players in the league, while four writers inexplicably judged him fourth best.

In a column for the *Sporting News,* Dan Daniel noted that Maury Wills wasn't the best player in the league. He wasn't even the best player on the Dodgers. "I have the highest regard for Wills . . . but the Dodgers failed [to win the pennant]. The Giants won because they had, among them, one Willie Mays."

Why was Mays snubbed? His relationship with the men who did the voting, the writers, is the most plausible explanation. By any reading of the record, most reporters and columnists across the country, and by now in San Francisco, thought highly of Mays. In 1962, the *Los Angeles Times'* Jim Murray wrote that Mays "doesn't drink or smoke and scandal has never touched his life. He is a credit not to his race but to the human race." In

1964, the *New York Times*' Arthur Daley said that Mays "was unquestion-ably one of the best-liked men in baseball."

But Mays always had his critics. He rarely disclosed much except to his favorite reporters; he could be snappish if he didn't like a question or would stand up interviewers entirely. He was always his worst publicist. Some reporters took offense, and the possibility that several aggrieved writers cost Mays the league's top honor was given credence when a similar MVP race unfolded twelve years later. In 1974, the Cardinals' Lou Brock broke Wills's record with 118 steals, but the MVP went to the Dodgers' Steve Garvey, who won on the grounds that he was a more complete player than Brock and was the best performer on a pennant-winner. Granted, the sto-len base might have been devalued by 1974; but by the criteria that elected Garvey, Mays should also have won.

Mays was gracious in defeat. "I was glad to see Maury Wills get it," he told the *Sporting News* in December 1962. "He deserved it for having beaten Ty Cobb's long-standing stolen-base record." That Mays and Wills were good friends no doubt made the outcome easier for Mays, though he has always insisted that individual awards didn't matter to him, nor did records. Asked in 1968 about his goals, he said, "I never set goals. If I did, I might think I had to make them and then I'd be playing for myself, not the team." He was also asked about his biggest thrill. "I don't try to peg them either. The thrill that satisfies me most is hearing those fans happy in the stands after I do something [special], catch a ball, throw a man out, get a hit, or take an extra base.

"That makes me happiest," Mays said, "thinking I've made the fans happy."

Mays had little time to worry about the MVP after the 1962 season. Earlier in the year, he had agreed to go on one more barnstorming tour provided the Giants didn't win the pennant. When the Dodgers seemed comfort-ably ahead in the final two weeks, Mays allowed the promoters to book him on the ten-day tour. That was a mistake. "I committed myself to make the trip," he said after the season, "and now I wish I hadn't."

Before it began, the Giants insisted that Mays undergo another round of tests at Mount Zion Hospital in San Francisco. They confirmed that "simple exhaustion" had caused Mays's blackout, but his three days in the hospital allowed the staff and patients to form the Willie Mays Fan Club, which presented him, on his final day, with a two-layer cake with number 24 on top. On his way to the press room, Mays walked down the hallway of the pediatrics ward, which was lined with nurses and patients. Rolling the cake with him, Mays stopped and gave pieces to his friends. He spoke briefly to reporters, and "on his way out," the *Examiner* wrote, "baseball's highest salaried star stopped at virtually every bed to give a disabled kid a pat or a hug and a few cheering words." With regular news bulletins about his release, a huge crowd was waiting for him outside.

Mays caught up with the barnstormers in Wichita, Kansas. There had been no tour the year before, so this was one last effort to see if barnstorming was still viable. A backbreaking schedule was planned—ten games in seven states in nine days, all covered by car. Thirty major leaguers participated, including Tommy Davis, Willie McCovey, and Vada Pinson, but after Mays, the biggest name was Satchel Paige. Buck O'Neil managed one of the teams. Every player was supposed to get $100 a game except for Mays, who would get more.

The tour fizzled quickly. The first game in Wichita drew a decent crowd, 6,500, but the next game was supposed to be the following day in Monroe, Louisiana—a 650-mile all-night trip. The players, informed of the schedule, canceled that trip and headed for Kansas City, 200 miles away. That game drew fewer than a thousand fans. The next contest, in Little Rock, Arkansas, was also poorly attended, and the tour was finally canceled. BARNSTORM TOUR FLOPPO AT GATE, FOLDS EN ROUTE, reported the *Sporting News*. Mays, long accustomed to traveling in comfort and still trying to recover from the long season, was through with all forms of winter ball. He still needed the money, but his body needed the rest.

It was the final barnstorming tour. Fans in remote communities didn't need it anymore, with television bringing the major leagues into their homes. Expansion into new cities and the emergence of the Instructional Leagues in Florida also increased access to the best players. As Thomas Barthel describes in *Baseball Barnstorming and Exhibition Games*, the tours were doomed as well by the slow death of semipro teams and the Negro Leagues, whose players had provided opposition. With minor league teams also in decline, professional baseball was increasingly becoming a big-city attraction.

Willie Mays was one of the few players who straddled baseball's different eras, cultures, and communities. He was there in the glory days of the Negro Leagues, he was there at the height of the barnstorming tours, he was there in the trenches of the minor leagues, he was there in the exotica of foreign lands, and he was there in the golden age of New York, the sunshine of California, and the bright lights of the World Series, carving a legacy of depth and scope that few would rival.

CHAPTER TWENTY-FIVE

YOUTH IS SERVED

Willie Mays no longer played stickball in the street, but he was still accessible to his young fans. "Get me talking about kids," Mays once said, "and you've got me talking about one of my two favorite subjects. Baseball is the other." Plenty of athletes paid lip service to children; visiting them in the hospital was a time-honored tradition, the photographs indispensable to buffing a star's image.

Unlike Babe Ruth, whose image as the lovable galoot was crafted by a publicist named Christy Walsh, Mays had a genuine concern for children. Early in his career, he supposedly reached out to kids because he himself was just a big kid. But that missed the point. Mays always juxtaposed the innocence of children with what he saw as the corrupting influence of adults, a lesson from his own youth. He believed kids genuinely appreciated him while adults would support him only in good times.

In a 1955 article in *Coronet*, "What Kids Have Taught Me" (as told to the ubiquitous Charlie Einstein), Mays noted that he received tons of letters. "You can tell the big difference between a kid and a grown-up writing to you," he said, "because the mail from the grown-ups comes in big especially when you're going good. It's when you hit a slump that the mail from kids really picks up. 'Hang on there,' they tell you. 'You can do it.'"

Mays said that what "you can learn from kids is how to get along with people. They understand you, and they accept you as an equal." He described how the previous summer, when he had gone to Hempstead, Long Island, for a photo shoot, the cameraman's son had a ball and glove in the back seat. "Well, the next thing you know," he said, "we're having a pretty good game of catch, and here comes the camera director, hollering blue murder.

" 'Listen,' he said, 'we're all set up. This is important.'

" 'This is important too,' I told him. And of course it was."

For all the complaints about Mays as a recluse, he was frighteningly accessible to kids, even after he moved to San Francisco. One night in June 1961, a ten-year-old boy named Billy Knox was near Mays's house on Spruce Street, so he and a friend decided to ring the bell and ask for an autograph. Marghuerite answered and told him that Willie wasn't home but he could try back in the morning. Early next morning, the two boys returned and waited on the stoop until Mays walked out in a yellow cardigan and brown slacks. They asked for his autograph, and Mays complied. Then Billy had a wild idea.

"Hey, Willie," he said. "We got tickets to the game today, and we were gonna take the bus, but how about a ride out to the game?"

Mays told them to hop in the front of his Cadillac convertible.

As soon as he pulled out, the boys realized they had forgotten their tickets.

"Where do you live?" Mays asked.

Five blocks away, Billy's friend said, so Mays drove them to get their tickets. They were finally on their way to the game when Billy exclaimed, "Willie! My mother made us bag lunches for the game. She'll kill me if we don't pick up our stuff. She might even worry."

So Mays now had to drive to Billy's house. "To this day," Knox recalls almost forty years later, "I can still see my mom standing at our dining room picture window with her hands on her hips, mouth ajar, awestruck as the lime-green Cadillac sped off."

After Mays pulled into the players' lot at Candlestick Park, he turned to the boys. "Meet me here after the game," he said, "and I'll take you home." Billy soon met up with his older brother and his brother's friend and bragged about his magical ride. The older boys didn't believe it, so after the game they tagged along. In the parking lot, while the fans were mobbing Mays, Billy and his friend jumped into the front seat while the two older boys hid in the back. By the time Mays saw them, he was already on the road.

"Who the hell is that!"

Billy explained, and a forgiving Mays drove the four boys home.

Two weeks later, Billy was trying to convince a skeptical friend of what had happened. The friend wasn't buying it. So the next day, with tickets in hand, they showed up at Mays's stoop at 9 A.M. He saw them, sighed, and said, "Get in the car."

Knox says that years later, his mother was at a dinner party in San Francisco. Mays was there, holding court, regaling his audience about the time two ten-year-olds talked him into driving them to the game. He was enjoying himself.

Mays was most interested in helping children in need, and he made regular visits to hospitals as well as their homes, typically without media coverage. Lon Simmons, the Giants' Hall of Fame announcer, recalls when he and Mays visited an eight-year-old boy who was suffering from an incurable disease. They walked into the house, were met by the grateful parents, and were led to the child's room. On their way, Mays spotted the boy's older brother, about twelve years old, standing to the side, and went over to him.

"You and I have to work together," he said. "Here's the key to my trunk. You get my things." The youngster lit up, went to Mays's car, and brought in balls, bats, and gloves for both boys.

"I don't know what to say to kids who are ill," Simmons now says, "but Willie just walks over and has them laughing." In this instance, Mays could see how the illness was affecting the entire family and how the brother needed support as well. "Even though that older boy loved his little brother, he had that feeling that he was on the outside," Simmons says. "Willie was able to assess the situation and read the kids. It was amazing to me. I get tears in my eyes now just thinking about it."

More often than not, Mays's good deeds were revealed by others. The *Sporting News* wrote an editorial in September 1961 noting that "Mays has been accused of being a loner who resents any intrusion on his privacy." But it described how Mays had appeared at a state mental hospital in St. Louis to conduct a batting clinic: "Officials at the hospital said it was the best therapy patients could have. What is more important, Mays did not do this for publicity. Had it not been for a tip from a hospital official to a newspaper, no one would have known Willie had been there."

In the early months of 1963, *Pittsburgh Press* sports reporter Les Biederman spoke at the Western Pennsylvania School for the Blind. Afterward, the students asked if it would be possible for Willie Mays to visit when the Giants were in town. Biederman wrote to Mays but never heard back. The day the Giants arrived in Pittsburgh, however, Mays contacted Biederman and said he was ready to visit the school. "He simply isn't a letter writer," Biederman concluded.

He drove Mays to the school, and when he entered the auditorium, whispers rippled through the crowd of two hundred students. They may not have been able to see him clearly, but they knew he was there. "That's him now," one boy said. "He really came."

Mays was introduced, and he became—in Biederman's words—"the eyes of these sightless youngsters."

"It's nice to see you kids," Mays said. "Real nice to be here. They tell me you've got some questions, so let's get going."

Arms shot up. "Hey, Willie! Over here, Willie!"

"Take it easy, take it easy," Mays squeaked in a chuckling, high-pitched voice. "We got time, lots of time."

The students were rabid baseball fans. One boy asked him to compare Leo Durocher with Alvin Dark. Mays said, "Durocher was like a father to me. I don't think I could have made it without him." Dark had also been wonderful. "Both play good baseball. But I can get along with anybody. Alvin is very religious, and Leo, well, he's liable to do anything." The students laughed.

A student asked about Pirate outfielder Bill Virdon.

"You like him?" Mays asked.

"Yeah!" the assembly shouted.

"Well, I don't! He makes too many catches on me!"

"You ever play in the World Series, Willie?"

Mays raised his eyebrows. "I'm gonna have to send you a radio," he said.

"Who's the youngest player on the Giants?" a young girl asked.

"Well, let me see," Mays said. "We've got a fellow named Al Stanek, who is nineteen—but he's too old for you, honey." The girl smiled.

Mays was completely relaxed in front of the group, a natural. When he was asked if baseball was easy, his answer, reflecting on hard work and unappreciated sacrifices, resonated. "Nothing is easy," he said. "Too many people think a ballplayer's hours are just the time the game takes. They fail to realize we're at the ballpark two and three hours before a game and a good hour after the game. In between, we must get our rest. No man can do his best if he's tired mentally and physically. As for myself, I can't get enough sleep. A man wrote me saying he carried a lunch pail eight hours a day and how come I would get tired just playing ball. Well, I told him he doesn't have twenty thousand or twenty-five thousand people watching how he carries that lunch pail and his average isn't printed in the papers every day."

The audience welcomed the sentiment. Willie Mays trying to convince a group of handicapped children of the humanity of a baseball player.

Mays was also asked about his greatest thrill. "Being a big league ballplayer has always been a great thrill for me," he said. "But I'd have to say the answer to that question is just being here." The kids cheered.

After the talk, Mays waded into the group and touched the hands and arms of the students, who reached up and touched his face.

"I gave them only my time and a little bit of baseball," he told reporters afterward, "and they gave me their hearts."

Mays enjoyed being a mentor, playing the same role that so many others had played for him. Roy McKercher, for example, was fourteen years old when the Giants hired him as a batboy in 1958. On Opening Day, one of the first players he saw was Mays.

"Are you the batboy this year?" he asked.

"Yes, I am."

Mays extended his hand. "Welcome to the big leagues."

Unlike most of the players, Mays would ask McKercher how he was doing in school, how his parents were doing, and whether he had a girlfriend. Calling him "Red," Mays would urge him to bear down in school. When McKercher traveled with the team for the first time, Mays had him sit next to him on the plane so he could give him instructions. "Be sure to be polite and give autographs," he told him. "Be sure to leave a nice tip but don't overdo it. . . . And remember, you're always being watched because you're a Giant." In 1959, McKercher appeared on *What's My Line?*, the game show in which panelists tried to guess a contestant's profession. Afterward, Mays told him that a girl in Chicago wanted to meet him. "Take her out, take her to a nice place, and be a gentleman," he said. He emphasized that when you have "a little notoriety" you have to be careful.

Mays introduced McKercher to the girl in the lobby. She was a few years older. They went to dinner and a movie, and then she dropped him off back at the hotel. All went well until, according to McKercher, "Willie started spreading rumors that we were getting married."

"He was like the big brother I never had," says McKercher, who was a batboy for four years and later worked in law enforcement, becoming a San Mateo County sheriff's deputy. "Mostly, he taught me how to treat people." In time, Mays took great pride in telling others, "I helped raise that kid."

Over the years, newspaper columns and now Internet blogs have accused Mays of brushing off kids who wanted an autograph. Nothing infuriates McKercher more. "So many people idolized him because he was so friendly," he says. "He would stand there and sign autographs for two hours, say no to one person, and be accused of being a jerk."

In 1959, McKercher was assaulted in his high school and put in the hospital. Horace Stoneham offered to fly in specialists from the Mayo Clinic, though that wasn't necessary. The team sent over a basket of fruit, but a piece was missing. A note said: "Red, I owe you an apple. Get better. Willie Mays."

In 1961, a youth counselor at the Booker T. Washington Center in San Francisco called Mays about a fourteen-year-old kid from the slums who was a sensational athlete but was now in trouble with the law. A member of the Persian Warriors gang, he had been caught stealing from a liquor store.

The counselor told Mays that the boy could play football in college, but now that seemed in jeopardy. His name was O. J. Simpson.

After spending the weekend in San Francisco's Juvenile Hall, his mother took him home. He dozed off in his room and awoke to voices downstairs. He expected his father had come by to give him a whipping. He went down and looked in the living room. "So there in our crappy little project house was my hero," Simpson told *Sports Illustrated* in 1987. "Willie Mays—in my house!"

Simpson had first seen him several years earlier at Seals Stadium. "I never took my eyes off Willie Mays," Simpson said. "I had heard about his basket catch and the way his cap always fell off when he ran, and I watched for those things. He did them all. He even hit a home run for me. . . . I hate to go so far as to say that he was my god, because my family was religious, but it almost amounted to that. I could almost say that I worshiped Willie Mays."

Now, standing before him, Mays said, "You want to come out with me this afternoon?"

The two left the house. Simpson was expecting a lecture, but it never came. Mays had a day off, and he simply had the boy follow him around. They went to a dry cleaner's to pick up a couple of suits, an appliance store, and then to a friend's house, where plans were being made for a banquet. Mays also took him to his own house. He asked Simpson what he thought of the new Chrysler and who he thought was going to win the pennant. He never asked about his gang activities or his scuffle with the law, but he did suggest that playing college football in Los Angeles made more sense than Utah, which Simpson was considering. Closer to home and a bigger television market, Mays said. He had one other message: "Do not forget your mother if you should find success."

Mays later said that his goal was to show Simpson the kind of life he could have if he made the right choices. The boy got the message. "I had an entirely different outlook on everything after that day with Willie Mays," he said in 1987. "I can't really say that it turned my life around, just like that. . . . But that time with Mays made me realize that my dream was possible. Willie wasn't superhuman. He was an ordinary person, so there was a chance for me."

In 1994, after Simpson was charged with murdering his wife and Ronald Goldman, a member of his entourage called Mays to see if he would be a character witness for Simpson. Mays said no.

What's most striking about Mays is the contrast between his dealings with children and those with adults. One group he trusts; the other he doesn't. With one group, he is open and relaxed; the other, he is tight-lipped and wary. From one group, he expects nothing in return; from the other, he expects compensation. In the early 1960s, Mays began declining certain magazine interviews unless he was paid. Why should everyone else, he figured—the writer, editor, publisher—make money off his name? When he was invited to promote the opening of a new electronics store, he was offered one free television but demanded, and received, three. (He gave the other two away.) Certain that people were trying to take advantage of him, he became a tenacious negotiator for his cars, clothes, and furnishings.

He speaks in general terms about the money that he lent to friends and never got back, as he protects even those he believes have wronged him. Those betrayals, says Poo Johnson, his roommate from his army days and one of his closest friends, have caused him to calibrate every adult relationship. "I know Willie has helped out a lot of people financially who he should not have trusted," he says. "So Willie keeps friends on a short leash." Johnson concedes that "being Willie's friend can be a challenge," and his lack of trust "has deprived him of some real strong relationships with people who had good intentions." But, he says, "once Willie knows you have a good heart and knows you will take him when he has his highs and lows, he'll do anything for you."

Yet his faith in kids is unconditional, for in them he sees himself—innocent souls who need kind words and meaningful support, as he once did, to fulfill their dreams. So he is usually a soft touch when youth are involved. Consider this anecdote, recounted by Richard J. Martin in a 2001 letter to the Baseball Hall of Fame.

In 1965, Martin was the twenty-four-year-old director of the St. James' Center in Pittsburgh, an afterschool program for disadvantaged children that was part of President Johnson's War on Poverty. The center planned an awards ceremony one Saturday in June, and Martin wanted a sports celebrity to present the trophies. He checked the Pirates' schedule and saw they were playing the Giants, so he immediately thought of asking his hero, Willie Mays. Martin's colleagues thought he was crazy, but he called Bill Nunn, the editor of the *Pittsburgh Courier,* who said he would contact Mays.

The day before the Giants came to town, Nunn called Martin with one question: "How many kids will be there?"

"A couple hundred," Martin said.

"Willie will do it."

Martin was flabbergasted. "Are you kidding?"

"No, I'm not kidding, Mr. Martin. Willie just wanted to make sure the event was primarily for kids."

That Saturday, Martin drove to the Carlton House, where the Giants were staying, and asked for Willie Mays's room number. He assured the skeptical clerk that he was expected. Martin dialed the number, and a soft, tired voice answered.

"Mr. Mays. This is Dick Martin. I believe Mr. Nunn spoke to you about me and the program tonight?"

"Yeah, man. I'll be right down," Mays said.

He had played a game that day, but ten minutes later he walked across the lobby in a sharkskin suit and shook Martin's hand—he was much bigger than Martin had expected—and Martin felt everyone's eyes in the lobby. They got into his car and were soon driving to an obscure youth center in an impoverished neighborhood. When they arrived, Martin snuck Mays in through a fire escape in the back of the auditorium and immediately pulled aside the fourteen-year-old master of ceremonies—who almost fainted—and instructed him on how to introduce their guest. When the time came, the youngster walked onstage through drawn curtains and shakily announced: "And now, to present the Most Valuable Junior and Senior Softball Awards, possibly the greatest player of all time, Willie Mays!"

The curtain opened, and Willie walked out. The audience of two hundred, students and parents, sat in stunned silence. Then they realized it really was the Giant star, and they shouted, whistled, and clapped for several minutes.

Mays stepped to the microphone and said it was an honor and pleasure to be there. Then he said, "Some people may think that winning a softball award in some neighborhood youth league is no big thing, but I'm telling you that when you win the most valuable award in anything, you're doing something." He then called out the names of the winners, two brothers, William and John Moran, who mounted the stage with beaming smiles and had their photograph taken with Mays.

After his remarks, Martin whisked Mays back down the fire escape, where his sister took their picture, and drove him back to his hotel. Martin was in such shock that he never even asked Mays who had won the game that day.

Martin, who later became a teacher and high school principal in Arlington, Virginia, recalled, "I must have thanked him a dozen times for his exceptional generosity. One of the greatest athletes of all time did this for no money, no publicity, no conditions whatsoever. He did it just because he loved kids, plain and simple. What a selfless gesture, what an amazing human being."

The event had a tragic postscript. One of the winners, John Moran, was killed several years later in Vietnam. "As sad and tragic as this was to hear," Martin said, "I am heartened with the knowledge that John's picture with Willie was undoubtedly a highlight of his short-lived life and a memory which he took with him to the grave."

CHAPTER TWENTY-SIX

A MAN NAMED MAYS

After the 1962 season, Mays considered himself, for the first time, a San Franciscan. Wanting to make the city his permanent home, he bought a new house at 54 Mendosa Avenue, in the Forest Hill District, a liberal enclave with a heavy concentration of Jews and Catholics; California's governor, Edmund "Pat" Brown, lived there as well. Mays's house marked a fresh start for him in every way. Unlike his first home, this one was easily acquired. Some residents grumbled privately, but for the most part Mays was treated well while given a hero's welcome by the children. Even before he moved in on December 20, his mailbox was stuffed with unstamped letters.

"Dear Willie," one said. "I represent 'The Neighborhood Kids,' a bunch of boys on Ninth Avenue. We welcome you to our neighborhood and hope you enjoy it. David." Another, from Maurine, eleven: "We are happy you moved to our neighborhood and we hope you have a nice time." Barbara, twelve: "I watched your house go up. I live in the second house up the street. I hope to get to meet you and welcome you to our neighborhood. Well, so long, and may God bless you. P.S. You are my favorite ballplayer."

Once settled, Mays decided to have a housewarming—for the kids—and got a list of names from the Forest Hill Improvement Association. One mother dropped off nine children, all hers; also attending was nine-year-old Amy Irving, the future actress. Mays gave each child an auto-graphed picture and a record, and he served chips, punch, ice cream, and a cake decorated like a baseball diamond, with toy players on top. At one point, the host had to run out to buy more ice cream. "They didn't come to see me," he said. "They came to eat."

The Giants' 1963 yearbook printed photographs of the players with their families, an effort to personalize the men in uniform. Fans saw Jose Pagan hoisting his two pajama-clad boys above his shoulders, Harvey Kuenn's little boy sticking a cigar in his mouth, and Bob Garibaldi standing next to his new bride at the ballpark. And there was Willie Mays, holding the baseball cake at his housewarming, surrounded by thirty-one white children, eyes bright, mouths agape, having a blast.

The house itself, on a deep slope that overlooked the Golden Gate Bridge, allowed Mays to add another dimension to his life. He always loved innovation and style and was in restless pursuit of the spectacular. His modish clothes and deluxe cars bespoke these sensibilities; so too did his multitiered mansion on Mendosa Avenue.

The builder, Al Maisin, had a rags-to-riches story as compelling as Mays's. Penniless after World War II, he worked for years as a longshoreman before inching his way into the construction business. He bought and renovated some homes, became a major builder, and in 1965 was featured in a *Time* article, "How to Become a Millionaire (It Happens All the Time)."

Maisin had vision and moxie, which he needed to build a house on Mendosa Avenue. Eight architects turned him down—the hill was far too steep. But a ninth agreed, creating an angular building with a cocoa and white design, which stood on two steel and concrete beams on diagonals under it.

Once the house was built, Maisin looked for a buyer and found Mays, who purchased it for $85,000 and promptly made his own architectural imprint. He asked that a hole be cut in the living room floor for a circular staircase, which would run to the downstairs storage area that opened to the garage. This gave him access to his convertible without having to go outside.

Mays's greatest contributions, however, involved the decor: French Provincial color scheme—white and gold—and the furnishings. He had lost all his furniture in his divorce, so he was starting from scratch. "I felt everything should be something I really want to live with, so when I went shopping and saw something I liked, I bought it," he said. What he created was the most extravagant bachelor's pad in San Francisco.

He adhered to the white and gold motif throughout the house, though the master bedroom was accented in blue. ("I don't like a lot of colors.") A gold wool carpet at $20 a yard covered most of the first level, except in the entranceway, where steel gray porcelain flooring was exposed. Austrian white drapes, valued at $4,200, graced two-story windows in the entrance hall. An ironwood tree with decorator leafing stood near a wall switch, which raised and lowered the arch-string drapes in the foyer. A circular marble living room coffee table was set off by a burnished gold lion's head. The dining room had its own circular table; the white china plates with gold rims were monogrammed wm in Old English lettering. The same insignia also decorated his wine goblets and the glass doors of the showers in his master bathroom, the taps of which were gold-plated. Closet doors throughout were louvered.

Massive, antique-style lamps brightened the living room—"I like big lamps. I think they look better large"—while an oval mirror with a gold ornamental frame hung in the hall upstairs. The bedroom featured a king-sized bed ("I like a lot of room to thrash around") and a closet, running twenty feet, jammed with suits, sweaters, and sports coats. A small panel in the wall next to the headboard was the intercom outlet. The house had five white telephones, with one in the master bathroom, and six televisions, including a $900 color set. There was a glass-walled billiard room, an alcove for his many trophies, and a den that displayed an encyclopedia set, a Bible, and an unabridged Webster's dictionary. ("I'm a newspaper and magazine reader, not a book lover.")

Both the house and the occupant attracted droves of tourists and celebrity watchers. David Rapaport, who grew up in the neighborhood, recalls, "If I had a dollar for every time someone asked where Willie Mays's house was, I could have started Google."

Mays was featured in *Ebony* in August 1963. At the time, each issue of the magazine had a story about an athlete, who was shown on the football field, the baseball diamond, or in the boxing ring—images of grit, sweat, and brute force. *Ebony*'s article on Mays included a photograph of him swinging at the plate, but fourteen other pictures, splashed across eight pages, were of his sumptuous digs. Mays was in almost every one, always wearing perfectly creased, well-tailored clothes. The lead photograph was a wide-angle shot of Mays, alone, leaning on the rail of his front balcony, king of his castle, but the most stunning photograph showed him at the base of the circular staircase, looking up at the camera, a smile on his face, protected by a swirl of golden handrails.

The spread put Mays in a whole other category as a figure in American culture. To be sure, he had already appeared on the covers of several mainstream magazines, his taste in clothes and cars was known, and he was already revered by black Americans. When New York Yankee rookie pitcher Al Downing visited the Red Rooster in Harlem in 1963, the owner handed him a book to sign. It included autographs from Louis Armstrong, Count Basie, Cab Calloway, Duke Ellington, Ella Fitzgerald, Lionel Hampton, Earl Hines, Bill ("Bojangles") Robinson, and Sugar Ray Robinson. "The pages were so crowded with such celebrated names," wrote David Halberstam, "that it took Downing a long while to find a page with only one name, and he prepared to sign his name there. 'No! No! No!' said the owner. 'That's Willie Mays's page! No one else signs that page!'"

The sprawling profile in *Ebony,* however, seemed to raise new possibilities about success for African Americans, for few black people, let alone black athletes, had ever been depicted amid such opulence. Larry Lester, for example, was fourteen years old when he saw the magazine. He had already seen Mays play baseball on television and in newsreels, and he tried to emulate him as well as his other heroes, Jackie Robinson and Hank Aaron, when he took the field himself. He'd grown up in a hardscrabble section of Kansas City—his family was on welfare for a while and relied on food stamps—and when he saw the *Ebony* photographs, he glimpsed a world that he didn't know existed for black people. "Mays set a lifestyle standard," Lester recalls. "I said, 'When I grow up, I want everything in my house to be white and gold.' That was my hope. Then I got married, and my wife had different ideas." Lester got a college degree in business administration, spent more than twenty-nine years in corporate America, sent three daughters to college, and was one of the founders of the Negro Leagues Baseball Museum in Kansas City. Looking back, he says, those affluent images of Mays "had a big influence on how I lived my life."

Mays lived in that house until 1969, relying heavily on a domestic named Johnnie Alberta Wade, who had been recommended by Mays's dentist. She came to the house each day and kept it immaculate, washed and ironed his clothes, and cooked him 1½-inch steaks well done. Mays was usually kindest to the working class—the clubhouse attendants, bellhops, porters, drivers, waiters, and all-purpose domestics like Johnnie Wade. In an interview almost fifty years later, on the eve of her one hundredth birthday, Wade had warm and vivid memories of her six years with Mays.

"He treated me as if I was someone in the family," she says. "He paid me my salary and also paid my income taxes." Wade says Mays never criticized her cooking or said she was wrong about something. "One time I made some cornbread, and he said, 'You know, I like the other kind better.' He would never say he didn't like something." She didn't have to grocery shop as much as expected, because companies and friends were constantly sending him food; someone once sent him frogs' legs, which she cooked and he ate. Boxes of clothes were also regularly sent to him.

She recalls the crazy neighborhood parties—"he was in love with those children"—and Mays often invited over ballplayers from the Giants and other teams. But the house was more for show than comfort, with Mays spending much of his time in his bedroom. Asked if she could tell whether the Giants had won or lost when Willie came home, Wade says she had no idea. "He would go up those stairs and stay in his bedroom, and he stayed there until it was time to eat. And if it was just him, he'd come to the stairway and say, 'Johnnie, I'm ready to eat.'" Unless he had company, he would have his meal upstairs.

When Mays left San Francisco, he rarely saw or spoke to Wade again. He was not one to keep in touch; nor was she. What she remembers most about him is his kindness. "If you aren't a nice person," she says, "you can't pretend for six years."

In 1963, a brash young filmmaker named Lee Mendelson helped give Mays's image another boost. At KPIX in San Francisco, Mendelson had made documentaries describing the city's rich history, including the 1915 World's Fair and the Golden Gate Bridge. His work had won a Peabody Award, but his great love was baseball. He persuaded Joe DiMaggio, who had been retired for more than a decade, to do an interview for a story about San Franciscans who had made it to the Yankees. Mendelson also talked to him about a documentary, but there wasn't enough film footage of him on the field.

Mendelson left KPIX to start his own production company, but he soon found himself with nothing to do. "I thought I'd get all kinds of phone calls because I won the Peabody for best documentary, but the rest of the country didn't see it," he says. He happened to pick up a book on Willie Mays, which described how he had had to stay in separate hotels in the minor leagues. DiMaggio never had to go through that, Mendelson thought. He then noticed that the book's flap said the author, Charles Einstein, lived in nearby Marin County.

It occurred to him that if he couldn't do a documentary on DiMaggio, he could do one on Mays, so he called Einstein.

"How much money do you have?" Einstein asked.

"I don't have any money," Mendelson said. "All I've got is a cameraman." He explained to Einstein that they would have to ask Willie to work for nothing, but he would get a percentage of the proceeds if they sold the program.

Mendelson could be persuasive. He had convinced William Randolph Hearst, Jr., to be interviewed for a documentary on San Simeon; now, Mays was his target. Assisted by Einstein, a meeting was set up. The conversation began casually; Mays and Mendelson began by talking about all the San Franciscans who had played with the Yankees. They were soon swapping Joe and Dom DiMaggio stories. While many journalists hit a brick wall with Mays, Mendelson understood that building trust was his first requirement. No requests for cooperation could be made until that happened. Einstein's involvement was an obvious plus, but Mendelson's passion for baseball reassured Mays. Before long, Mays asked Mendelson what he had in mind for a documentary, and he explained that he wanted his cameraman to follow him around for several months during the baseball season. The footage would then be used to create a thirty-minute film. "We don't have any money," Mendelson said, "but we could sell it to a network if you're willing to take a chance on it."

At the time, camera crews were not allowed in locker rooms or dugouts. Mendelson said it was a small crew—Sheldon Fay controlled the camera and microphone, Charlie would conduct the interviews and narrate the film, and he was the producer—and they would be unobtrusive. The novelty appealed to Mays, and he agreed with one condition. "I'm willing to gamble on it if you guys are," he said, "but just be good to baseball."

Mays didn't appreciate how unlikely the gamble was. Network documentaries focused on serious matters: politics, international affairs, economics. Edward R. Murrow's *See It Now* series in the 1950s, which exposed Joseph McCarthy, was considered the model. Sports were peripheral, a harmless diversion. The prospect of a network documentary on an athlete—let alone a black athlete—would have been summarily dismissed had Mendelson actually proposed it. That the filmmaker himself, working out of his office in Burlingame, thought he could match Hollywood in production value was all the more reason to be skeptical.

Unfazed, Mendelson spent the first four months of the 1963 season following Mays, tracking him at home, on the diamond, in his car, and on the road in Milwaukee, Pittsburgh, and Los Angeles. The film would have no script but allowed Mays to talk freely into the camera, prompted by Einstein's questions. "No prepared documentary in the history of television ever did that before," Einstein later wrote. At the time, most of the film footage of baseball games came from the press box, taken by a camera with a long lens. But the Giants gave Mendelson access to the field, dugout, and locker room, allowing Fay to use his Bolex camera for close shots.

Fay knew almost nothing about baseball. When Mendelson told him to get a picture of the umpires walking in from right field, he asked, "Where's right field?" Another time, Fay was instructed to film Mays at the batting cage. He went inside the cage and began shooting until Mays asked what the hell he was doing.

"I was told to get you in the batting cage," he said.

"You better get out of the cage or else you're gonna get killed," Mays said.

Everything was improvised. Mendelson wanted to film Mays driving to Candlestick Park. "How can I talk and drive at the same time?" Mays asked. Mendelson said he was going to put Fay in the front seat; "Let's just try it." The film showed Mays trying to keep one eye on the road while turning to talk into the camera. Toward the end of the filming, Fay was sent to Fairfield, Alabama, to get a shot of Mays's home, but when he returned, Mays said he filmed the house next door. "What the hell," Mendelson said. "Nobody will know the difference."

Mays was not a passive subject. He suggested that they ask him about brushback pitches "because they're an important part of the game." He also told Mendelson: "Make sure you show me doing bad too. If you show me doing nothing but hitting home runs, that won't be it. That's not what I'm like." The documentary would show Mays's midseason slump, when his batting average fell to around .250.

Mendelson had no sense of Mays beyond his baseball skills, but the more time he spent with him, the more he admired him. "His innate intelligence got to me immediately," he recalls. "He said he regretted his lack of formal education, but I said to him, 'You have so much more basic intelligence, why do you worry about it?' He could spot right and wrong, good and bad, and he never badmouthed anybody."

Which made the racist phone calls all the more disturbing. Once Herb Caen wrote about Mendelson's efforts, the calls began. Some asked why Mendelson wasn't following Mantle or Maris around. Others were more blunt: "Nobody is going to show that nigger on our station," one said. Threats were made to the "camera crew." Recalls Mendelson: "It totally threw me for a loop, but it never gave me pause. I thought it was so ridiculous, I just set it aside." Mays never knew about the calls.

By July, Mendelson had created his thirty-minute story. He boarded a plane with 16mm film and flew to New York, his first time there. He initially met with CBS executives, who watched the tape and told Mendelson they really liked it. "I was so excited I almost wet my pants," he says. They offered him $25,000 and said they'd put it on their Saturday afternoon *Sports Spectacular* show. But they needed an answer that day.

Mendelson wanted to take it, but he had a meeting scheduled with NBC, so he told the CBS executives that he had to discuss it with Charlie and Willie and asked if he could get back in touch.

Mendelson met with NBC's Ed Friendly, who was in charge of special programming and later helped create such hits as *Rowan & Martin's Laugh-In* and *Little House on the Prairie*. Friendly also liked Mendelson's documentary but had a question.

"Why do you have this sportswriter as the narrator?" he asked.

"Because he was $100 and Willie trusts him," Mendelson said.

"That's good enough for me."

Friendly then asked if Mendelson could lengthen the program to sixty minutes.

"Absolutely!" Mendelson said.

"I'll trust you," he said. "We'll give you $50,000 and run it in prime time."

Recalls Mendelson: "I almost passed out." He didn't know how he was going to double the length, so he started shooting more film, including another car ride to Candlestick on August 25. Mays had hit 399 home runs in his career, and as the camera rolled, he predicted he would hit a home run that night against the Reds' left-hander Joe Nuxall, and he would do it before the fourth inning, after which the change in wind currents would make a long ball prohibitive.

Before a crowd of 31,553 and one Bolex camera, Mays hit his four hundredth home run that night, to right field, in the second inning. Mendelson decided that he couldn't include Mays's earlier comments because viewers would never believe them.

Several weeks before the program was to air, Mendelson received a call from a *New York Times* reporter who asked what it felt like to be going up against Taylor. Mendelson thought he was referring to Tony Taylor, a second baseman for the Phillies.

"No," the reporter said. "Elizabeth Taylor."

NBC had placed the Mays program against CBS's *Elizabeth Taylor in London,* a one-hour feature on October 6. *TV Guide* billed it as David vs. Goliath: a shoestring documentary of a Negro baseball player against a lavish half-million-dollar production of a major celebrity's tour through London. Mendelson kept his sense of humor. "Taylor," he said, "never played in the National League, where we should do well."

When Mendelson began the project, he had no idea that it would coincide with some of the most dramatic developments in black Americans' struggle for equality, nor could he have anticipated that his subject's hometown would be a deadly battleground of that struggle. But he never strayed from his topic, delivering what he had always promised—a story about a young man's rise from his humble roots in Alabama to his triumphant acclaim in New York, then to his struggle for acceptance in San Francisco. For some television viewers, that may have seemed wildly disconnected from what was happening in America, but for other viewers it was a soothing antidote to the country's bloody divisions.

In the civil rights movement, the momentum toward increasing violence had been building for years. In 1960, a sit-in at a segregated Woolworth's lunch counter in Greensboro, North Carolina, triggered nonviolent protests throughout the South. The following year saw the "freedom riders" taking bus trips through the region to challenge segregation in bus terminals and railway stations. The year 1962 was the first that a black student,

James Meredith, enrolled at the University of Mississippi, but each step toward equal rights was met with resistance; the riots surrounding Meredith's enrollment forced President Kennedy to dispatch five thousand federal troops to Mississippi. In Washington, civil rights legislation stalled, as the president feared alienating support from southern legislators, and Martin Luther King, Jr., declared that civil rights "no longer commanded the conscience of America."

In 1963, King targeted Birmingham to protest its continued segregation in shops and restaurants and its discrimination in employment. Birmingham, he said, was "America's most segregated city," and it was the site of at least a dozen unsolved bombings in black neighborhoods. King operated out of the Sixteenth Street Baptist Church, on the edge of Kelly Ingram Park, to rally the community through marches and sit-ins. They began in early April, with protesters carrying signs that read EQUAL OPPORTUNITY AND HUMAN DIGNITY and BIRMINGHAM MERCHANTS UNFAIR. The rallies increased in size, and a judge soon issued an injunction making any march illegal. On April 12, a mass arrest included King, and in a Birmingham jail, he wrote his 6,700-word letter that consecrated his reputation.

King was released on April 20, but the demonstrations continued, with hundreds of protesters jailed and the national media, both print and television, on the scene. Black youths, teenagers and younger, began demanding that they be allowed to protest, and on May 2, several dozen marched out of the Sixteenth Street Baptist Church down Fifth Avenue North, singing and dancing, defying orders to stop in the face of fire hoses. As the television cameras rolled, Police Commissioner Bull Connor gave the order. "The firemen kept their fogging nozzles on, misting their human targets as if they were prize flowers," wrote Diane McWhorter. She continued:

> Some marchers backed off. When a dozen plopped down on the sidewalk, the firemen switched to their monitor guns, fed by two hoses for maximum pressure. The sound of the hose spray shattered the singing like automatic-gun fire. The children flung their hands to their faces and then embraced, holding their ground for a few seconds before sprawling across the sidewalk. Those trying to flee were pinned against doorways, and a group leader took the high-powered spray until his shirt was ripped from his body. The marchers who continued to pour out of Sixteenth Street church were sent skittering down the gutters. One girl surfaced with a bloody nose, another with scratches around her eyes.

Next, before photographers and news cameras, German police dogs were set loose, biting the protesters' arms, ripping their clothes, and knocking them over. Pictures of the attacks, including one of a police dog lunging at a Negro woman, became front-page news. The grim film footage dominated the evening news, turning the clash, and Bull Connor, into a symbol of white resistance against an innocent adversary.

The protesters seemed to score a historic victory. On May 11, the authorities announced that lunch counters, restrooms, and drinking fountains would be desegregated within ninety days and the arrested demonstrators would be released. King would later declare that "the black people of Birmingham, Alabama, aroused the conscience of this nation and brought into being the Civil Rights bill. . . . And there was a power there which Bull Connor couldn't adjust to, and so we ended up transforming Bull into a steer."

But in response, the Ku Klux Klan held a rally in Birmingham, and firebombs were used to blast the home of the Reverend A. D. King, Martin's brother. The same night, the Gaston Motel, the city's principal Negro hotel, was also bombed in an apparent attempt on King's life. Angry black mobs took to the street, torching a grocery store and a taxi in a night of rioting.

The mayhem caught the attention of Jackie Robinson, who went to Birmingham with Floyd Patterson. "I can't explain exactly how I feel," Robinson said when he saw the destruction. There was little he could do but bear witness.

The battle of Birmingham spurred dozens of additional demonstrations across the country. They culminated in the March on Washington on August 28, the emotional apex of the civil rights movement, when King delivered his "I Have a Dream" speech before a crowd of 250,000.

But there was only heartbreak in Birmingham, where the specter of desegregation ushered in more bloodshed. The Klansmen brought in new recruits and gave lessons in building bombs. Some police officers were issued submachine guns to keep the peace. Riots convulsed the city. Alabama's governor, George Wallace, peeved at Negro violence, told a *New York Times* reporter: "What this country needs is a few first-class funerals, and some political funerals as well." King sent a telegram to President Kennedy: "Something must be done to apprehend the bombers and curtail the irresponsible action of Governor George Wallace, or realism impels us to admit that Birmingham and Alabama will see the worst race riot in our nation's history."

On the morning of September 15, a Sunday, a loud explosion went off at the Sixteenth Street Baptist Church. The blast was dynamite. It was as if, McWhorter wrote, "someone had hit the world's largest washtub, followed by a ripping blast that sent a streak of fire above the church. Closed doors flew open, and the walls shook. As a stale-smelling white fog filled the church, a blizzard of debris—brick, stone, wire, glass—pelted the neighborhood. Some of those inside believed the Russians were coming." Four girls in a basement restroom, Addie Mae Collins, Denise McNair, Carole Robertson, and Cynthia Wesley, from eleven to fourteen years old, were crushed—all four were killed, one decapitated. King wired President Kennedy that "unless immediate federal steps are taken," the "worst racial holocaust this country has ever seen" would be upon Alabama. In another telegram, he told Governor Wallace, "The blood of our little children is on your hands."

Three weeks later, *A Man Named Mays* appeared on NBC. Mendelson had shot more than twenty-five thousand feet of film, but not one frame included a reference to the country's racial tumult. The only mention of Birmingham was that Mays had grown up nearby and played for the Black Barons. Mendelson says he had promised to create a documentary about Mays's life as a ballplayer, which he had done. The narrow focus suited Mays as well as NBC.

Mays remembers that he saw the dogs attacking the protesters on television and recalls hearing the news about the church bombing. It was all upsetting, he says, but he was never tempted to go to Birmingham or make a public statement. Neither his celebrity nor his hometown ties, he believes, would have made a difference. "What could I have done at that particular time to stop all that?" he asks. "I'm not a politician. Even if I had gone down there, what was I going to do?"

The irony was that he did do something in spite of himself.

A Man Named Mays told the story of the American dream, and the leading man was an appealing hero. Mays was successful (his $105,000 salary was more than the president's), stylish (his elegant home was lovingly presented), impeccably dressed (a cream turtleneck and tan sports coat), fatherly (he carried his son on his shoulders), entrepreneurial (he was learning banking), and funny (when Einstein said, "In five years, when you become slower—" Mays chimed in, "Don't use that word!"). Comfortable in front of the camera, he spoke carefully, mindful never to offend; he was shy and even vulnerable. The footage repeatedly showed him getting knocked down or brushed back. Asked about those pitches, he said he relied on his own pitchers to protect him, but there was nothing he could do except duck. He was also deferential: Durocher, speaking confidently into the camera, noted that Willie always called him "Mr. Leo."

The documentary captured the stress and fatigue that Mays endured through the pennant race. In a game at Candlestick on September 2, he fell helplessly to his knees at home plate. The film showed him being assisted off the field, and Einstein noted that this was the second consecutive year that such a collapse, caused by tiredness, had occurred. Mays was back in the lineup four days later.

The camera was also there for Mays's address to the blind children in Pittsburgh. There was no sound, but the images were sufficient. As Willie stood before them in a suit and tie, the students faced him with expressions of awe.

Mays emerged as an inspiring figure of hope and unity. In one sequence, he came to the plate as different demographic groups throughout San Francisco huddled around their radios: construction workers on break and men sitting at a bar, Chinese dishwashers in a steamy kitchen, an elderly white man in a hospital, a white woman in a beauty parlor, young parents bathing their child, teenagers at the beach—all ages, races, and backgrounds, and they were all cheering for Willie, a soothing balm for a country's deep wounds.

The documentary held its own against the competition. *TV Guide* reported that Elizabeth Taylor's show attracted 55 percent of the viewing audience. "Viewers saw a lot more of Miss Taylor's architecture than London's," it said. The Mays program, however, "attracted a very respectable 28 percent share. And those who watched it were treated to an expert documentary featuring the elements which were so woefully lacking in the Taylor show: a good script, imaginative camera work and film editing, and an unpretentious approach to its subject. And all for one-tenth of the cost of Liz's lemon."

Again, Mendelson thought his success would lead to all kinds of opportunities, but the phone never rang. Without work, he happened to be reading the *Peanuts* comic strip one day and noted that Charlie Brown was Mays's opposite in baseball. Mendelson thought, if I could do a documentary on the best baseball player in the country, why not one on the worst player? He called Charles Schulz, the creator of *Peanuts,* which led to his producing *A Charlie Brown Christmas.* An instant sensation, it led to a long collaboration between Mendelson and Schulz.

But the documentary on Mays was also a milestone. While some might criticize it for its failure to acknowledge the traumas outside baseball, in its own way it delivered a powerful message. That was made evident by where it wasn't seen: Birmingham, Alabama. In that riot-torn city, where any display of black achievement, acceptance, or adulation would defy a crumbling social order, where the fears of the ruling class trumped the love of a hometown hero, the NBC affiliate blacked out *A Man Named Mays.*

CHAPTER TWENTY-SEVEN

BEFRIENDED
BY A BANKER

Ever since Orlando Cepeda joined the Giants, he and Mays formed the best power-hitting duo in baseball. Between 1958 and 1964 they hit 488 home runs, nine more than Hank Aaron and Eddie Mathews hit for the Braves during that span. On the Giants, Cepeda and Mays were also the most prominent Latin and black players, respectively, but their positions were not equal. Cepeda was the budding star in line to succeed Mays as the team's MVP and perhaps the league's. In 1959, *Look* magazine asked the question directly in its story, "Orlando Cepeda: Will He Pass Willie Mays?"

The notion of the temperamental prince usurping the proud king caused some stress. Cepeda later wrote: "It's not a secret that Willie Mays and I didn't get on that well. . . . Willie began to distance himself from me almost immediately. . . . Willie was a private person and a loner, so it was hard to figure out what he was thinking. I was hurt when he didn't congratulate me on being named the Giants' MVP and the National League Rookie of the Year." In a subsequent interview, Cepeda says he now regards Mays as a friend. "That's just the way Willie is—I don't think he's close to anybody. But most players are like that. I'm not close to McCovey either. That's the way we are. Very seldom do you see good ballplayers close. I don't know why."

Mays has always denied any friction between him and Cepeda, and when they were teammates, he repeatedly commended him in the press. Asked in 1961 about an alleged beef with Cepeda, he said, "I've never had an argument with him about anything. I've tried to help him"—in playing the outfield and adjusting to the major leagues—"and I did help him, but I don't want any credit for it, because he's a wonderful ballplayer."

Besides, Mays's relationship with his teammates was the least of the Giants' problems. For five years, the team had four future Hall of Famers on the field at one time: Cepeda, Marichal, Mays, and McCovey. A fifth, Gaylord Perry, pitched in his first game for the Giants in 1962. Hav-

398

ing come so close to winning a World Series, the Giants should have been focused on finding that one missing piece to push them over. A championship? Hell, they should have had a dynasty. For Mays, the tragedy was not that he lacked close friends on the team but that he was drawn into an ethnic and racial maelstrom that undermined such a talented club.

Cepeda's troubles with Alvin Dark resurfaced at the end of 1962, with the publication of an article in *Look* that Cepeda thought would describe him as the best right-handed hitter in baseball. The article, however, was called: ORLANDO CEPEDA: CAN HE SLUG HIS WAY OUT OF THE DOGHOUSE? In it, Dark described his heretofore secret grading system for players. Unhappy with such conventional measures as batting average, home runs, errors, and stolen bases, he wanted to evaluate more precisely how players contributed to winning games, so he devised his own system of pluses and minuses. Thus, a home run in the first inning might get one plus while a homer in the ninth that won a game might get four. There were pluses and minuses for everything. But the system was highly subjective, and no one besides Dark understood it. Regardless, he explained to *Look* that Mays graded out the best and Jim Davenport was second. But Cepeda? "He had more minuses than anybody," Dark said.

Cepeda did slump during the stretch drive in 1962, but given his numbers (.306, 35 homers, 114 RBIs) as well as his track record (four consecutive All-Star games), Dark's evaluation was hard to fathom. In 1966, when Mays testified in a libel suit that Cepeda brought against *Look,* he was asked if Cepeda was a team player. "When you hit over .300 and bat in over a hundred runs," he said, "you have to be."

Cepeda, meanwhile, was convinced that Dark was "trying to destroy [me] emotionally." The hostilities escalated during spring training when Cepeda held out, which he had done in past years, but this time Dark held a press conference to reiterate his harsh views about Cepeda's "productive value." Cepeda ended his holdout after securing a $1,000 raise, but any hope for a reconciliation between him and Dark was gone.

By the start of the 1963 season, Mays had his new house, and his divorce proceedings were complete; but his personal problems were far from over. His finances were a mess, and personal bankruptcy loomed as a possibility. Plenty of athletes and entertainers have plunged themselves into debt without ever recovering, and black stars have suffered disproportionately. The most famous, and perhaps most tragic, was Joe Louis, who died in 1981 owing the federal government more than $2 million.

Mays managed to avoid that fate. In 1962 he met a banker who played a central role in rescuing him. This relationship was one of several that he forged over the years with San Francisco businessmen who helped him gain access to country clubs and social clubs and win broader acceptance in the city. As the years passed and he approached retirement, Mays reached out to other businessmen to help with his life after baseball. These patrons were not entirely altruistic. Whether you ran a bank, a hotel, an insurance company, or a car dealership, your association with a sports legend was good for customer relations, and Mays helped the owners of all those businesses. But many of his advisers were also motivated by a genuine desire to help someone who needed both guidance and protection, and no one was more devoted than Jacob Shemano.

His was the classic immigrant success story. Jacob was two years old when his family moved to America from Russia. They settled in San Francisco, and his father worked as a barber on Golden Gate Avenue. Jacob attended San Francisco State College, pumping gas to the pay his tuition. After school, he got into the installment credit and finance business, married, had two sons, and became involved in civic activities. Mayor Christopher appointed him to the San Francisco Housing Authority in 1957. What Shemano really wanted was his own bank, but in the 1940s and '50s, few if any Jews in California were given charters for state banks.

An opportunity, however, arose when John Kennedy entered the White House in 1961. Shemano had gone to high school with Kennedy's press secretary, Pierre Salinger; in Washington on a business trip, he told his old friend about his struggles in getting a state-chartered bank. Before long, Shemano received a call from the White House: the president wanted to see him. Shemano met the president and was given a federal charter. At the age of forty-nine, he opened Golden Gate National Bank on Montgomery Street in San Francisco's financial district. Shemano, according to one news account, looked "more like a Hollywood Buddha than a banker," for he favored green velvet shirts and smoked English Ovals. But true to his roots, he kept the doors open on Saturdays so working-class customers could meet with bank officers. His friendship with the mayor also helped: the city deposited $1 million with the new bank, and the mayor himself purchased more than 1,600 shares of stock in the company.

One day in 1962, Jake Shemano's teenage son, Gary, was invited to Candlestick Park to shag flies and pitch batting practice with the Giants. "The only guy who was nice to me in the clubhouse was Willie," Gary recalls. "Amazingly enough. The superstar of all superstars." His father came down to see Gary, and in the clubhouse he was introduced to Mays, and the two struck up a conversation. Shemano loved sports, and like many Jewish immigrants, he got along with African Americans; he took the unusual step, for example, of hiring black tellers for his bank. Mays thought he found a man he could trust and met with Shemano privately at the end of the year. "From a business standpoint," Mays later said, "it was the most important single moment of my life."

Mays told Shemano that he had been advised to declare for personal bankruptcy, which would protect him from his creditors. His advisers said it was his only way out.

Shemano, who hadn't reviewed Mays's finances yet, looked at him. "Well," he said, "it's good advice. It can be the way out for you. Except for one thing."

"What's the one thing?"

"If you file for bankruptcy, I will say again that it can be the sound and logical move in the shape you're in—but if you do, then I want nothing to do with it."

Shemano understood that while companies can file for bankruptcy protection, reorganize, and emerge as viable, a baseball player had to protect something besides his assets. He had to protect his image. Filing for personal bankruptcy carried a heavy stigma, and in Mays's case, it would forever redefine him. "You're a baseball player, not some slick corporate executive somewhere, living off of stock options and pension plans and all the other stunts," Shemano said. "Kids look up to you."

"I know that," Mays said.

"Do you know it?" he said. "You made $90,000 last year. You'll make better than $100,000 next year. What does it look like to a kid who finds out that Willie Mays, his idol, makes $100,000 and can't pay his taxes?"

Actually, Mays's problems were even worse. Given his debt to the Giants, the club began deducting money from his paycheck. It was possible that his actual take-home pay would be less than his state and federal taxes, and he already owed the State of California and the federal government $8,641. He owed as well $15,000 a year in alimony and child support payments. Following bad advice, he had made costly investments in some real estate and restaurant deals, which he called "the quick way to find your way to the soup kitchen." Yet he continued to spend money freely on his new home and its extravagant decor.

As far as Mays was concerned, a bankruptcy filing didn't really matter. "I'm down here in the pit," he told Shemano. "If I can't climb out of it, I'm not much of an idol to the kids that way either, am I?"

Shemano was familiar with hard times, including some of his own making. "I can tell you one thing," he said. "There was a time when I was in worse shape than you. And they weren't even my own obligations. I'd underwritten some things for other people, and they went sour. I was three times worse off than you are now. But I came out of it."

"Then come out of it with me," Mays said.

"Not if you're talking bankruptcy," he responded. "If you are, you can clear out right now."

Mays said he wasn't talking bankruptcy, his adviser was. Shemano said he would help on one condition: he had to follow his advice to the letter. Mays agreed.

In 1963, Mays signed a contract for $105,000, making him the highest paid player in baseball. (Mickey Mantle earned $100,000.) But Shemano negotiated an installment plan with Stoneham that deferred income. Presumably the deferral, which allowed Stoneham to retain capital for his own purposes, was used to increase Mays's ultimate payout. By 1966, when Mays's finances had stabilized, more than half his income was deferred. According to his contract, Mays signed for $125,000, but only $50,000 was to be paid during the year. Some $30,000 would be paid in 1970; $30,000 more would be allocated in 1971; and the last $15,000, in 1972. By then Mays would be forty-one. Shemano not only wanted him to avoid squandering money but may also have been considering his retirement needs.

Mays had often had father figures, but Shemano was the first one not associated with baseball. In 1963 Mays agreed to deposit every dollar of his current income into the trust department of Shemano's bank, which started paying off Mays's debts while giving Mays an allowance. Shemano did not provide investment advice but found him a lawyer and an accountant. He also gave him an office on the fifth floor of his bank, down the hall from his own. He gave him some introductory books on finance and arranged for him to do some public relations work. Mays sat in on some customer meetings, signed baseballs, and spoke to groups of kids in the boardroom. Shemano set up lunch meetings with the likes of California's attorney general, Stanley Mosk, and he reviewed business deals for Mays with Gillette and other sponsors. He and his wife also took Mays and a girlfriend to the theater.

Shemano told *Sports Illustrated* in 1964: "Willie has been taken in by more people that he had confidence in. He has a good searching mind, but he has never paid any attention. He cared only about being a ballplayer. When I took him on, I did it only with the understanding that he would also have the finest legal advice and the finest public accountant. I am not his financial adviser. I'm just the keeper of the keys. We've put Willie on a budget. We have made him prepare himself to live under a limited income, as he will have to do when he is through playing."

Mays was always self-conscious about his lack of formal education, and Shemano noticed how quickly he seized on that with children. "He'll meet a kid," he said, "and the first thing he'll say is, 'What school do you go to and what grade are you in?' And you know, now he talks about saving money too. When his son was out here this winter, he was playing catch one day, and I asked him what he wanted to do when he grew up. Right away, like most kids, he said he wanted to be a ballplayer. Willie came over and patted him on the head. 'No, Michael,' he said. 'Be a doctor. We need them.' What has happened is that he has changed from Willie Mays the young man to Willie Mays the man."

Mays said in 1964, "If I had met Jake ten years ago, I'd be a millionaire today. He and his family are the best friends I've ever had in my life. They're wonderful people."

Mays developed a strong rapport with Jake's two sons, Richard and Gary. When Richard decided to get married, the first person he told was Mays. Gary played football for Lowell High School, and Mays was a surprise visitor at one of his rallies; he would also go out to Kezar Stadium to root for him. When Gary missed an extra point in a game against St. Ignatius, he was heartbroken. Mays cheered him up with a gift: his autographed bat from the 1962 World Series. Gary went on to the University of Southern California, and when Mays was in Los Angeles to play the Dodgers, Gary would go with Mays and his friends to the city's black neighborhoods, or Mays would stop by his dorm room.

When Gary took a girl to a ball game at Candlestick, he would devise a plan with Mays to impress his guest. Before the game, Mays would jog past their seats behind the Giants' dugout and yell, "Hey, Gary! Hey, Gary!"

"Hi, Willie!" he'd respond.

"I got something for you." Mays would throw him a baseball, and Gary would hand it to his date. The ball was inscribed: "Julie, Gary's friend. Willie Mays."

Gary recalls, "You can't put a price tag on that."

For all their closeness, the relationship between Mays and the Shemanos was not entirely about family love, nor was it altogether reciprocal. Jake Shemano never charged Mays for his services, but he recognized Mays's commercial value as the ambassador for his fledgling bank. Other businessmen who befriended Mays, such as the hotelier Mel Swig, the insurance executive Richard Goldman, and the architect who designed his house, Al Maisin, were all drawn to Mays by his personal appeal as well as his star power. "If Willie wasn't the greatest ballplayer in the world, would they have felt the same way about him? Probably not," Gary Shemano says. "But they felt Willie was vulnerable, and they wanted to protect him."

Mays welcomed their friendship, but he always kept a certain distance, even with the Shemanos. It was usually Jake or his sons who called Willie, and while Willie would share a laugh with them and help in any way, he would never reveal his fears, his dreams, or his soul. "I don't think I ever had a serious conversation with Willie," Gary says. "He never opened up." The reserve was evident not just in conversation. "I come from a hugging family," he says, "and I would give Willie a hug. It was not comfortable for him."

Over the years, Mays developed a habit of promising to show up at a dinner or a function and fail to appear. Rhoda Shemano used to complain to her husband, but Jake defended him. Mays didn't like the spotlight. He's always traveling. He was tired. And he never had a better friend than Jacob Shemano. "My father's life," Gary says, "was dedicated to his family, to his religion, to his shareholders, and to Willie Mays."

Pitching dominated 1963, with the Giants involved in some memorable duels. Sandy Koufax threw a no-hitter against them on May 11 and had a perfect game into the eighth; the lefty threw eleven shutouts in the year, which no pitcher except Bob Gibson has matched. Juan Marichal also threw a no-hitter in 1963—two walks shy of a perfect game—against the Houston Colt .45s. But the finest pitching showcase occurred at Candlestick Park on July 2, when Marichal faced Warren Spahn of the Milwaukee Braves. Neither team could score through nine innings, and both Marichal and Spahn continued working. In that era, clubs paid little concern to overusing a pitcher, and going the distance was expected, particularly from an ace. On this day, Dark wanted to lift Marichal, who refused. "In the twelfth or thirteenth, he wanted to take me out, and I said, 'Please, please. Let me stay,'" Marichal recalled. "Then in the fourteenth, he said, 'No more for you.' And I said, 'Do you see that man on the mound?' And I was pointing to Warren. 'That man is forty-two, and I'm twenty-five. I'm not ready for you to take me out.'"

By the time Mays came to bat in the bottom of the sixteenth with one out, he had gone 0-for-5, with a walk. But Spahn, after 276 pitches, finally made a mistake—a screwball that "didn't break worth a damn"—and Mays hit it over the left field fence, ending the four-hour, ten-minute marathon. He says it was one of his biggest homers: it allowed Marichal to win a historic duel. (Among his other all-time homers, Mays counts his very first, also off Spahn, and his four in one day in Milwaukee in 1961.)

The blast also helped Mays secure a record that will never be challenged. By the time he retired, he had hit a homer in every inning from one to sixteen. It's such a freakish mark—how many players even have a hit in every inning from one to sixteen? how many players even have an at-bat?—that not much is made of it, but it's an achievement that defines Mays's essential qualities: his durability, his power, and his clutch hitting.

Notwithstanding his sixteenth-inning long ball, Mays got off to a miserable start in 1963, hitting .233 in April and .257 in May. Jose Pagan sought divine intervention. "In the dugout, every time Willie comes up, I pray for him," he said in early June. "He is a good fellow. He laughs and he jokes, but I know inside him he is dying because he is not hitting." Dark and Feeney worried about his eyesight but, fearing his wrath, were unwilling to ask if he had had his eyes examined during his physical. So they asked Charlie Einstein.

"You could just mention it in passing," Feeney told him in Dark's office before a game. "You know, just in passing."

"Kind of like an idle question," Dark said. "It's like if it comes from you, it's not official. It's like that he won't know you've been talking to us."

Einstein went through the tunnel, walked onto the field, and fell in alongside Mays at the batting cage. "Say, Buck," he said. "You notice how many players are wearing glasses this year?"

"Like who?" he said.

"Well, Howard—Frank Howard. He's got glasses."

"He ain't hitting either," Mays said.

Mays, in fact, did have his eyes checked and was told they were fine. He never had any explanation for his streaks, though in this case, one of his longtime chroniclers, Arnold Hano, had a theory. In spring training, he watched the Giants play the Cleveland Indians, and after McCovey hit a homer, pitcher Jim Perry (brother of Gaylord) threw a thunderbolt at Mays's head, flattening him. Mays cautiously stood up, got back into the box, and was immediately decked on the next pitch. A few innings later, McCovey hit another home run, and Perry again threw a fastball at Mays's left ear. "It is the closest I've seen a man come to being killed, without actually being touched," Hano wrote. "Mays got up again, took a toehold, and swung furiously at the next pitch. He missed because he was swinging out of anger, and he was overswinging."

Mays, of course, had been thrown at for years, but Hano believed that word had spread among the pitchers that Mays could be intimidated. Now he said, "Every game you knew that some pitch would come flying in at his ear and send him spinning to the ground." There was a grain of truth in Met relief pitcher Larry Bearnarth's comment that the "only way to get Willie out is to hit him in the back, then pick him off first base." In Lee Mendelson's documentary, Mays acknowledged that no batter hits as well when he's been thrown at or expects to be thrown at. Perhaps all the knockdown pitches were taking their toll, though at least Mays's reflexes remained sharp—he was hit only twice during the season.

His slump also renewed concerns about his age, a source of quiet rumblings for several years. On May 6, he turned thirty-two. Conventional wisdom held that a batter peaks between twenty-eight and thirty-two, but some players' skills begin to erode before then. After Willie had endured an 0-for-18 stretch in May, an unnamed Giant executive suggested in the press that he was through. Mays was too proud, too sensitive, to ignore the slight, which offended him as deeply as the boos. "Here we go again," he said. "It just seems that some guys wait until me or somebody else goes bad and they knock us down and kick us. Believe me, nobody knows better than me that my batting average is low. I sleep with it. . . . It hurts when we don't win, and it hurts when I don't help."

Retirement terrified Mays. Baseball was his life, and few observers believed his career was truly winding down. He still had a thirty-two-inch waist, and while he may have lost a step, he was still one of the better runners in the game. Bob Stevens wrote: "The 32-year-old superstar is about as washed up as General Motors."

New York continued its romancing of its long-lost center fielder. With the Giants in town, May 3 was declared Willie Mays Night at the Polo Grounds. He was given a gold key to the city and a wide assortment of gifts, including a bicycle, a year's supply of coffee, and—from the New York Chapter of the Baseball Writers' Association—a typewriter. Mays donated the gifts to the New York City Police Athletic Association. Bill Shea, the lawyer who helped bring the National League back to New York, told the crowd: "We want to know, Mr. Stoneham, Horace Stoneham, president of the Giants—when are you going to give us back our Willie Mays?"

Just before taking the field, Mays received a telegram from the White House. It read:

> I would like to join the many loyal fans at the Polo Grounds tonight honoring your achievements in the world of baseball. This honor is well deserved and I know we can look forward to many years of the exciting spectacle of Willie Mays at bat and in the field. My very best wishes to all of your friends tonight. (Signed) John F. Kennedy

The players were still selecting the starters for the 1963 All-Star Game, and when Mays received his ballot, two weeks before the July 9 contest, he voted for Vada Pinson in center field. Though he wanted to start, Pinson was having the better year. Mays's peers, however, voted for him, giving him his eleventh consecutive start in an All-Star Game and returning him to Cleveland Stadium, where he had made his All-Star debut in 1954. Mays always reveled in the Midsummer Classic's attention and drama as well as the camaraderie. When he arrived, he found a message for him, in heavy black crayon, from Whitey Ford, who had been in Cleveland two days earlier with the Yankees. "Willie: Sorry I didn't make the team, but [manager Ralph Houk] didn't want me to make you look bad. Whitey." Mays had had six hits in seven at-bats against Ford in previous All-Star games.

This year's contest was different in one respect. Reporters asked Mays if he thought he was getting too old. Mays left his answer on the field. He collected a single, which tied Stan Musial's All-Star record of twenty hits while lifting his average to .417 in fourteen All-Star games. He also walked, stole two bases, scored two runs, and drove in two runs (one on the single, one on an infield out). He made the defensive play of the game as well. In the eighth inning, with the National League up by a run, he raced back on a long drive by Joe Pepitone, snaring the ball just before his right foot got caught beneath the wire fence. Mays did a brief war dance of pain and hobbled off, but the play snuffed a possible rally, and the Nationals won, 5–3.

His performance was so complete, so flawless, that *Pittsburgh Press* reporter Les Biederman was moved to write: "He's a once in a lifetime ball player, and we may never see his equal in this generation. Whatever he does, he does to perfection."

Mays said, "I just play the game."

Mays entered the All-Star break hitting .276. Soon, he went on a tear as if he were making up for lost time. He hit .322 in July, .387 in August, and .378 in September. During one fifteen-game span from July 21 to August 6, he scored twenty-two runs, knocked in twenty, and smacked nine homers. During one week in August, he hit four balls that struck the top of the center field fence in Candlestick, giving him four doubles instead of four more home runs.

He also turned in some of his finest single-day performances, few better than his game against the Braves on August 22. It began with a first-inning walk, which kept the inning alive and allowed Cepeda to drive home two runs. In the third, the Braves' Lee Maye hit a line drive into right center. The ball was actually past Mays when he reached out and gloved it as he tumbled to the ground. He broke his fall with his glove hand, dug his left shoulder into the ground, then flipped on his back. "It was such a spectacular spill the worst was feared," the *Examiner* reported. "The players, Dark, the trainer—all rushed out. The crowd in the stands would have been there too except for the gate." The game was delayed for ten minutes, but Mays stayed in the game. On base again in the bottom of the inning, he broke up a sure double play with a rolling block into the shortstop, which allowed Felipe Alou to bat, and he hit a three-run homer. Mays later drove in what proved to be the winning run with a single, and after advancing to third, he bolted for home plate on a ball that rolled four or five feet behind catcher Del Crandall. Mays slid in just beneath the throw.

Reporters stopped asking him if was too old to play.

The Giants played better than .500 ball all year but couldn't close the gap with the Dodgers, and Dark's frustrations showed, his temper also marked by pettiness. He once gave Pagan a fifty-dollar bill and told him to "take the boys to supper," which meant the Latin players. Several days later, Dark told Pagan that he was being fined for his failure to hustle.

"How much?" Pagan asked.

"Fifty dollars," Dark said.

McCovey later said, "Alvin managed percentages, not people."

During losing streaks, Dark would call clubhouse meetings and sprinkle his lectures with political references and biblical injunctions. He shared his admiration of Barry Goldwater and once said that Jesus was the only man in the history of the world who was perfect. Dark was accustomed to giving "Christian testimonies," mostly about tithing, for church groups and other gatherings, and he carried that spirit into the clubhouse.

But the clubhouse was a baseball sanctum, and the players had little interest in Dark's views beyond the ball field. A married man, Dark may have had more authority if he hadn't been having an affair with a flight attendant, which he later wrote about in his autobiography. "Perhaps if we had not been Christians, with strong beliefs about right and wrong, it would have been easy," he wrote of his trysts. "We didn't want to be found out. We didn't want anyone to know. On the road, we were prisoners in our hotel rooms." Imprisoned or otherwise, he could not keep the affair a secret, which made his moralizing all the more ridiculous. Mays said, "He didn't convert anyone to his politics or his religion, and, actually, no one took him seriously when he started to talk like that."

Mays himself had his first confrontation with Dark on August 2, in Chicago. With the Giants leading, 11–5, in the eighth, a Cub hit a ball to deep center that Mays failed to chase. It went off the wall for a hit, and the Cubs rallied to win. After the game, Dark snapped at Mays: "You laid down on me."

"I didn't cost you no seven runs," Mays yelled back. He knew he was wrong for not hustling but didn't think he should be reprimanded in front of his teammates. He and Dark didn't speak for several days, then all was forgotten.

While Mays never took criticism well, he rarely shirked responsibility. In a game against the Dodgers on September 7, he dropped a fly ball.

While he averaged eight or nine errors a year, most were on overthrows or booting grounders. His misplay against the Dodgers was his first dropped fly in four years. Afterward, he explained that he lost the ball in the sun and couldn't find it no matter how many times he flipped his sunglasses up and down. A reporter asked, "Could Felipe Alou have come across in time to catch it if you hollered to tell him you couldn't see it?"

Mays responded quickly: "Listen, the ball was in my territory. Don't go trying to give another man my error."

Thanks to his furious rush in the final months of the season, Mays finished with a .314 average, his highest in three years. For the first time since 1954, he did not lead the league in any major offensive categories, but that didn't bother him. He was second in slugging average (.582) and runs scored (115), and his 38 home runs was third best. He also drove in 115. What did decline was his stolen bases—he had 8, the first time since 1954 that he was in single digits.

The Giants won eleven fewer games than they had the previous year and finished eleven games behind the Dodgers. Despite missing four games after his collapse on September 2, Mays played in 157, which meant he was otherwise given one day off the rest of the season. He led the team in games played.

And 1963 also marked the last games at the Polo Grounds. Shea Stadium opened the following year. Just before Opening Day, a huge crane rumbled beneath Coogan's Bluff and took aim at the condemned edifice with a two-ton iron ball. In time, a low-rent housing project stood on the turf where McGraw had snarled at umpires, Ott had lifted his leg, and Mays had made the Catch. With the scoreboard clock frozen at 10:24, there was only the swirl of dust and debris and memory, and as the iron ball crashed against the concrete wall to make its first gaping hole, the workmen doffed their steel helmets in silent tribute. The back of their shirts read: WRECKING CORP. OF AMERICA. The front: GIANTS.

By the time the last piece of steel had slowly fallen from a light tower and sheets of tin flapped gently in the breeze, the wrecking company's vice president, Harry Avirom, could only admire what once had been.

"Very well built," he said. "It could have lasted forever."

CHAPTER TWENTY-EIGHT

CAPTAIN MAYS

Willie Mays took up golf after the 1963 season. At first he found it difficult to hit a stationary ball, but he became a diehard player who would crush his drives three hundred yards, practice his putting on his living room carpet—he'd line up twenty balls at a time—and carry a 4 handicap. Over the years, the game allowed him to break color barriers at country clubs while opening doors for himself socially and in business, and his skills on the links were as stupefying as they were on the diamond. Art Rosenbaum, a longtime San Francisco sportswriter and editor, once played with Mays in a foursome. "We came to a par-3 hole, about two hundred yards," he recalled, "and he gets up and takes a terrific swing, but tops the ball. It skims along the ground and hits a tee box, and comes right back at him at about 110 miles an hour. He catches the ball, and with one, flowing motion puts it back on the tee and hits it onto the green. It was the most athletic feat I ever saw."

When Mays had his finest start ever in 1964, Jake Shemano credited golf; according to his theory, Mays's golf swing was smoothing out his stroke to right center. Mays could no more explain his streaks than he could his slumps, but after one month he was hitting .497, with a slugging percentage of over 1.000 (he had more total bases than at-bats).

His early-season success led to an important milestone for baseball and for race relations, and Mays, free of domestic concerns and his finances stabilized, should have had a triumphant season. Instead, he found himself in the middle of several controversies that were not of his making, altercations that would contribute to a chaotic season that would end with doubts about his supremacy as a player.

Mays's torrid start left baseball fans turning on their radios in the morning to find out what he had done the night before. He hit six homers in his first six games and twenty by the middle of June while also amassing a twenty-game hitting streak. The hitting spree led to speculation that he would be the first .400 hitter since Ted Williams finished at .406 in 1941. Mays didn't care for the added scrutiny in 1954, when he threatened Ruth's record, and he tried to tamp down expectations ten years later, referring to .400 hitters as "extinct animals." The game had simply changed too much—against hitters—to ever make it realistic. Thirteen players had hit .400, but only two since 1925, and by the early 1960s, barely a dozen players in each league were even hitting .300. The night games, the bigger gloves, the deeper pitching staffs, and the development of the slider were all part of the difference, but Mays, in a diary he kept for *Sport*, cited travel and scheduling as the biggest deterrents.

When Williams hit .406, Mays wrote, "there was no 162-game schedule and if you traveled overnight, you slept in a bed while you were doing it. The worst time-zone difference was a difference of one hour. Nobody ever heard of checking into a hotel in a new city at 3 A.M. (Nowadays, it seems like there isn't any other check-in hour *except* 3 A.M.) Even on home stands, the hours are crazy. Here in San Francisco, we play night games Tuesdays and Fridays, with day games Wednesdays and Saturdays. Sit down with yourself and try to see how you'd schedule three meals a day at that rate." Even days off weren't days off, Mays wrote. After the Giants recently played a doubleheader in May at Candlestick, they flew to Tacoma, Washington, to play an exhibition game against a farm team, then flew all night on a chartered DC-7 to St. Louis, checking in at 8 A.M. They arrived at the ballpark and suited up, only to wait out a rain delay until the game was finally called. It was rescheduled for later in the year on what should have been an off day for travel.

Injury did not force Mays out either. In a game at Dodger Stadium, he pulled his hamstring chasing a fly ball. The next inning, he limped out of the dugout and stopped at first base, where he played the rest of the game. "A man doesn't have to move around that much at first base," Dark said. Mays got two hits, including a home run, had six putouts, an assist, and no errors. He said he enjoyed talking to the runners.

Doubleheaders depleted him, but on May 24 he played all eighteen innings of a doubleheader at Candlestick. A week later, on May 31, the Giants had a doubleheader in New York. Mays played nine innings in the first game, which the Giants won. They were leading, 6–1, in the second game, but the Mets tied it in the seventh, sending the contest into extra innings. And extra innings they played. Gaylord Perry took the mound in the twelfth and pitched ten shutout innings, but still the game went on. When the Giants ran out of infielders, Mays played three innings at shortstop, then returned to center field. Finally, in the top of the twenty-third, San Francisco scored two runs and held on to win, 8–6. Mays had played thirty-two innings in nine hours and fifty-two minutes—it was called "baseball's longest day." He was the only Giant to play every inning of both games.

"They told me afterward I played three innings at shortstop," he wrote in his diary, "but I have trouble even remembering that. All I remember is that the bat kept getting heavier and heavier."

He began the day batting .383. After going 2-for-13, he was at .364. Speculation about .400 was over.

In May, Jackie Robinson's *Baseball Has Done It* was published, featuring lengthy interviews with players and coaches as part of a celebration of the sport's role in civil rights. While Robinson later lashed out at baseball's slow pace of integration, the book was mostly a tribute. Retired Dodger pitcher Carl Erskine, for example, said, "When you're on a club with a Negro, you know the guy is flesh and blood, and eats and sleeps, rides a train with you, and sweats with you out there on the field, and he helps your club more than anybody else, and then you walk into a restaurant and they say everybody can eat but him, then you really *understand* what it's like to be a Negro."

Alvin Dark also weighed in on the subject. "Since I was born in the South," he said,

> I know that everyone thinks that Southerners dislike Negroes or even being with them. The majority of the people in the South, especially the Christian people that I have associated with, have really and truly liked the colored people. As for socializing with them on different levels, there is a line drawn in the South, and I think it's going to be a number of years before this is corrected, or may never be corrected.
>
> The way I feel, the colored boys who are baseball players are the ones I know best, and there isn't any of them that I don't like. . . . I never had any trouble with any of them. In fact, I felt that because I was from the South— and we from the South actually take care of the colored people, I think, better than they're taken care of in the North—I felt when I was playing with them it was a responsibility for me. I liked the idea that I was pushed to take care of them and make them feel at home and to help them out any way possible that I could in playing baseball the way that you can win pennants.

Dark then offered his thoughts on integration:

> I think it's being handled a little wrong in that people in the South, and I think I know them because I've lived with them. . . . I feel too many people

are trying to solve the Southerners' problems in the North. . . . The majority of people in the South like colored people. They consider them as human beings, but right now it's being rushed too fast.

The best thing that could be said for Dark was that his views reflected the majority opinion in the South, which was how Mays interpreted his views. While civil rights activists, reporters, and Horace Stoneham all denounced the comments, Mays kept quiet, but he later said, "I knew what Dark was saying. I was from the South, and so was he. I understood what he was talking about. But it seemed nobody else did."

With the book controversy bubbling, Dark called Mays into his office at Candlestick on May 21 before a game against the Phillies.

"Willie, I'm making you captain of the Giants," Dark said.

Mays stared at him.

"You deserve it," Dark continued. "You should have had it long before this."

Mays's first feeling was admiration for Dark. The major leagues had never had a black captain, and if Mays accepted, it would be a meaningful breakthrough, placing an African American in a position of authority. Granted, a captain's authority is largely symbolic, but a black captain would bring baseball one step closer to something truly monumental—a black manager. The issue riveted the sport in the 1960s: a black manager would mark baseball's next step toward equality while sending a powerful message to the country at large:

Blacks could command whites.

Bench them.

Fine them.

Cut their white ass if they so dared to even look the wrong way—in front of television cameras, if need be. For many, a Negro manager would drastically invert long-held racial assumptions, and a Negro captain inched them closer to that possibility.

"Will you take the job?" Dark asked.

"Yes, Cap," he said. "I will. But you don't have to do it."

"Never mind what I have to do. I'm doing it."

Mays understood that the timing, on the heels of Dark's controversial comments in Robinson's book, would be seen as intended to give Dark cover. Naming a captain in the middle of the season was strange, and it wasn't as if the Giants typically had one. Oddly enough, the last Giant captain, in 1956, had been Alvin Dark. But Mays had nothing to apologize for. He believed he got the job because he deserved to be captain, the quiet elder statesman who each year logged the most innings, positioned the players, gave away the sweaters, dress shirts, and neckties that companies sent him, and—as McCovey says—"laughed at our jokes even when they weren't funny." The previous year, Dark had established a players' committee to help team members with issues they didn't want to take to Dark. Mays was chairman of that committee.

This year, Mays was off to his big start, and the Giants were in first place. In that sense, the move did not smack of desperation. And if Dark was having problems communicating with the players, Mays believed he could help him. The appointment also paid him $500.

Dark called a meeting before the game to tell the players, and in comments to reporters, he noted that Mays was "managerial material." Then Mays executed his first chore as captain, taking the lineup card to the umpires. Ed Sudol was working the plate.

"Okay, twenty-four, let's go over the ground rules," he said. "If the ball hits the scoreboard and sticks in one of the slots, what do we give the batter?"

Mays laughed. "Give him the scoreboard," he said.

Once the game started, the captain hit two homers, drove home three, and scored three in the Giants' 9–4 win.

Several days later, the *Chronicle*'s Charles McCabe, who was not a sports columnist but still found time to criticize Mays regularly, was in high dudgeon. "I had not intended to make any comment on Mr. Alvin Dark's comments on the Negro in baseball," he wrote,

> believing that every man is entitled to one really huge goof a year in his public life. Mr. Dark's views are those of an educated, committed Christian Southerner. They are terrible.
>
> The only reason I bring them up is that the manager of the San Francisco Giants, a largely Negro ball club, recently named Willie Mays to be "captain" of his club. And "managerial material."
>
> Willie Mays has as much reason to be captain of the Giants, even if in name only, as I have to be placed in charge of our space program. His naming to a fictitious job was, apparently, a public relations gimmick to becalm the Negroes of this area, many of whom are rightly enraged by Mr. Dark's odd views on the race question.

McCabe's valid criticism of Dark's racial views was obscured by his own regrettable views. The Giants were not a "largely Negro ball club," with only three blacks among the twenty-four players that Dark mostly used (unless McCabe was including the five Latins). And his disparagement of Mays, with no evidence, reeked of condescension and was as offensive as anything Dark had said.

But McCabe's article brought to the fore what others were saying privately—Dark was using Mays—and the two men discussed the matter.

"I told you something like this might happen," Mays said, referring to the column.

"Just so long as you don't believe it," Dark said.

Mays continued to trust Dark. He remained noncommittal about his managerial aspirations. "It's too early to think about managing," he told reporters. "I hope to have four or five more years of playing before I think about managing." In September *Argosy*, a men's magazine, published a story, "Will Willie Super-Mays Be Baseball's First Negro Manager?" Both Monte Irvin and Roy Campanella thought he would be a good skipper. "He knows the game and is a keen student," Campanella said. "I think if he wanted to manage, he'd be successful because he'd have harmony among his players."

Taking a very different view was Jackie Robinson, who until that year appears not to have criticized Mays in public. But by 1964 Robinson, at forty-five, had become increasingly bitter about disappointments in his own life and in the country. His position at Chock full o' Nuts was coming to a close, and he did not have a similar job lined up. In the coming years, his efforts in banking, public relations, life insurance, real estate, and broadcasting were met with limited success. He had become more active politically, and he supported for president New York's governor, Nelson Rockefeller, who headed the liberal wing of the Republican Party. (He had supported Richard Nixon in 1960.) Rockefeller lost the nomination to Barry Goldwater, the conservative Arizona senator, whom Robinson described as "a bigot, an advocate of white supremacy."

Robinson was mired in a jumble of contradictions. He feared a white backlash against the growing Negro militancy—witness the June murders in Mississippi of three civil rights workers, James Chaney, Andrew Goodman, and Michael Schwerner—while he also sympathized with the growing resentment among young blacks. He believed the new leaders of the movement, Muhammad Ali and Malcolm X, were divisive figures, but he was also frustrated by the slow rate of progress engineered by mainstream spokesmen. The landmark Civil Rights Act was passed into law in July 1964, but in March Robinson expressed his view that no Negro would have it made until "the last Negro in the Deep South has it made." Where Robinson should have remained a revered figure—with the Dodgers—he had become isolated; his relationship with the team began to deteriorate after Branch Rickey left the organization in 1950. Finally, at home, Robinson had become estranged from his son, Jackie Jr., and in 1961 he was devastated by the death of Branch Rickey's son, Branch Jr., who died from diabetic complications at the age of forty-seven. This event seemed to fore-shadow Robinson's own fate. Robinson's poorly controlled diabetes was destroying his vision, imperiling every organ, and hastening his decline.

In that context, his remarks about Mays were tinged with the mordancy of a man whose life, health, and dreams had all been thrown into doubt. In his book, he lashed out at both Mays and Maury Wills for declining to be interviewed. "Both might have contributed revealing facts and offered helpful suggestions," Robinson wrote.

> No doubt they did not wish to stir things up. But there's no escape, not even for Willie or Maury, from being a Negro, which is more than enough to stir things up when bigots are around.
>
> Willie is the highest paid star in baseball. He is a certain future member of the Hall of Fame. . . . I hope Willie hasn't forgotten his shotgun house in Birmingham's slums, wind whistling through its clapboards, as he sits in his $85,000 mansion in San Francisco's fashionable Forest Hills. Or the concentration camp atmosphere of the Shacktown of his boyhood. We would like to have heard how he reacted to his liberation in baseball, and to his elevation to nationwide fame. And about his relations with his managers, coaches, fellow players and his many loyal friends, black and white. . . . Willie didn't exactly refuse to speak. He said he didn't know what to say. I hope that he will think about the Negro inside Willie Mays's uniform, and tell us one day.

The distortions—"Birmingham's slums," "the concentration camp atmosphere," "his liberation in baseball"—only highlighted Robinson's intemperateness, and his disdain for Mays continued in his interview with *Argosy*. Mays's captaincy, Robinson said, "is a step in the right direction, but it doesn't really have any impact. It merely means Willie is the oldest player on the club in terms of service. . . . He'll never become the first Negro manager. He's personable and has great talent, but he's never matured. He continues to ignore the most important issue of our time. He's never really had any decent guidance in these matters and probably keeps looking only to his own security as a great star. It's just a damn shame he's never taken part. He doesn't realize he wouldn't be where he is today without the battles that others have fought. He thinks it's not his concern. But it is."

It appeared as if Robinson's own rage had got the better of him: he concluded that Mays would never manage because he was not more active in the civil rights movement—a complete non sequitur.

Mays believed that Robinson was bitter because he had never been asked to manage, and now his unworthy heir was in line to wear that crown. Nonetheless, Mays didn't respond to the attacks and made no reference to them in his 1966 autobiography. He had faced plenty of criticism, but these rebukes came from his hero. "It hurt him a lot," McCovey says. "I just know it hurt him." Four years passed before Mays, once again denigrated by Robinson, defended himself.

Alvin Dark began the year on notice. The previous season, Stoneham had called him into his office, said he knew about his girlfriend, and demanded that he end the relationship. Stoneham was no moralist, but his manager's hypocrisy was hurting the team. Dark fined any player $250 if a woman was caught in his hotel room, and he would alert house detectives to watch the players most apt to violate the rule. Stoneham was also unhappy with the team's play. Despite winning the pennant in 1962, he thought the Giants backed into it through the Dodgers' collapse. The following year, a terrible August cost them a chance at another pennant, and by 1964 even a championship wouldn't protect Dark's job. Dark continued his affair with the flight attendant, Jackie Rockwood, though he eventually divorced his wife and married her.

Dark never tried to rationalize his own hypocrisy, but he believed Stoneham also resented him because, unlike past managers and coaches, he didn't drink with him.

Fortunately, the Giants were winning, and on July 1 were in first place, with a 46–28 record. But in the middle of the month, they lost five in a row, and on July 21 were in second place. Edgy in the best of times, Dark began to seethe until, in an interview before a game at Candlestick, his anger boiled over.

Stan Isaacs, a reporter for *Newsday* on Long Island, had asked to interview Dark. Unknown to the manager, sportswriting was in the midst of a revolution. The day was about to end when journalists and athletes had effectively been partners in creating heroes and protecting rogues, and a new era dawned in which scribes questioned, contested, and analyzed their subjects. A new professionalism emerged, which meant that teams could no longer ensure favorable coverage with free travel, meals, and booze. Prodded by television, sports journalists had to dig for news, find fresh angles, and apply the same standards as the rest of the newspaper. The change was slow, but it was led by a group of young reporters—irreverent, ambitious, and intrusive—eager to push aside the old guard.

One such writer was Isaacs, who asked questions that no other reporter had ever considered. In the 1962 World Series, he was curious about the feeding habits of Ralph Terry's new baby. "Breast or bottle?" Isaacs asked the pitcher.

Now Isaacs had traveled to San Francisco en route to covering another event in Los Angeles. He interviewed Dark, whose answers appeared in two columns, the first of which appeared on July 23. The columns' gist was that the Giants continued to squander great talent with dumb mistakes. Dark concurred, and he had identified the cause. "We have trouble because we have so many Negro and Spanish-speaking players on this team," he said. "They are just not able to perform up to the white ball player when it comes to mental alertness."

Isaacs noted that Dark's views were also held "by other brains of the major league trenches." What set Dark apart was his willingness to discuss his opinions openly, a subject, he told Isaacs, "which you New York writers and I disagree on."

Dark said, "You can't make most Negro and Spanish players have the pride in their team that you can get from white players. And they just aren't as sharp mentally. They aren't able to adjust to situations because they don't have the mental alertness."

Some Negro players, like Mays and Robinson, were exceptions, he allowed, but "you would have to be here day in and day out to see what happens. They are not the kind of thing a manager can correct—missed signs and such—but they are inabilities to cope with game situations when they come up. And one of the biggest things is that you can't make them subordinate themselves to the best interests of the team. You don't find the pride in them that you get in the white player."

Told by Isaacs that the Boston Celtics had been quite successful with black players, Dark shrugged, saying, "I only know what I've seen on this team and other baseball teams. If I'm wrong, then I have been getting an awful number of the slow ones."

In the age of the Internet and cable television, these comments would have been a national story in seconds, but in 1964 it took a full week for the *Newsday* columns to reach the Giants. When they did, Dark denied that he had made the statements (Isaacs acknowledged that he didn't use a tape recorder) and pledged to sue, but he withdrew the threat when he was told that his private life would be made public in any trial. Charlie Einstein later wrote: "Those of us who were accustomed to the way Dark punctuated his agitation with negatives might have been less apt to publish his words, but when Isaacs did publish them they came as no surprise."

The Giants were in Pittsburgh when they learned of the interview, and Mays had a revolt on his hands. Most of the black and Latin players came to his room at the Carlton House. Mays was not in the best condition. Suffering from a bad cold, he had an inhaler, which he would periodically hold to his nose. His body ached and his eyes were watery, but he saw the anger in his teammates and knew he had to restore calm.

"Shut up!" he told them. "Just shut up."

"You don't tell me to shut up," Cepeda said. "I'm not going to play another game for that son of a bitch."

"Oh yes you are," Mays told him. "And let me tell you why."

He said that Stoneham was so upset that he was planning to fly to Cincinnati the next week and fire Dark—which would be a disaster by turning him into a martyr. Mays said that he, Chub Feeney, and Herman Franks were all trying to persuade Stoneham to hold off. "I tell you for a fact, he is not going to be back next year," Mays said. "Don't let the rednecks make a hero out of him."

Mays also had a practical reason. Fire Dark now—or quit on him—and their pennant chances disappear. They were two games out of first, and Dark gave them the best chance to win. "I don't say it'll happen, but it's money if we do, and we ought to take our best shot. We changed managers in the middle of 1960 and look where that left us."

Mays noted as well that Dark didn't discriminate when he filled out the lineup. Though both Cepeda and Marichal had complained about incidents to the contrary, Mays's point could be supported. Dark played more black and Latin players than any other manager in baseball. Mays went back a long way with Dark and told the players he knew him better than anyone there. "I know when he helped me and I know why," he said. "The why is that he's the same as me and everybody else in this room: he likes money. That preacher talk that goes with it he can shove up his ass. I'm telling you he helped me. And he's helped everybody here. I'm not playing Tom to him when I say that. He helps us because he wants to win, and he wants the money that goes with winning. Ain't nothing wrong with that."

Mays used the same argument that Durocher had used in the spring of 1947 when the Dodger players had circulated a petition objecting to Jackie Robinson. Money trumped all else. In this case, Cepeda mildly objected, but Mays reiterated that Dark was color blind when necessary. "Suppose him and a lady friend went to a picture show together in Birmingham, where I'm from, and one of them passes out. And somebody shouts, 'Is there a doctor in the house?' And it turns out the only doctor is colored. You think Dark's gonna turn him away?"

Willie McCovey, standing beside the window, said, "Be awhile for him to get there, that doctor, seeing as he'd have to make his way down from the balcony."

That broke the tension. Mays had quelled the uprising. Cepeda later said that he wished Mays had spoken out against Dark, but Mays worked from within. The team would carry on.

The Giants' next stop was New York, where Commissioner Frick met Dark for lunch and recommended that he call a press conference. When the team arrived at the clubhouse at Shea Stadium on August 4, copies of the *Newsday* columns were waiting in envelopes for the black and Latin players. Before the game, Dark spoke to about thirty-five reporters, who discovered that communication was not his strength. "I was definitely misquoted on some things, and other statements were deformed," he said. Dark tried to defend himself by noting that he started seven Latins and blacks and had replaced several white players with minorities, such as Jim Ray Hart for Jim Davenport at third.

Then he said, "I thought I proved my feelings when I named Willie Mays captain. If I thought Negroes were inferior, would I have done that?"

When Mays read these words the following day, he later said, "I was actively sick." In his view, the comment indicated that Dark had made him captain to protect himself.

It was their last night in New York, and Mays's cold had worsened. When he got to the clubhouse, Dark handed him the lineup to take to the umpires, and his name wasn't on it. Dark was going to let him rest. But Mays made a different calculation. If he sat out, he might be accused of bailing out on a manager who had effectively embarrassed him in public. That could hurt Mays's reputation as well as Dark's. Einstein asserted that if Mays had sat out, it would be seen as a protest, and Dark's managerial career would have ended right then.

Mays took the lineup card, considered the options, and wrote in his name. He hit two home runs and the Giants won, 4–2.

The Giants stayed in contention, but the Cardinals, winning nine out of their last eleven, edged the Reds and the Phillies by one game. The Giants finished in fourth, three games out. Stoneham fired Dark in the sixth inning of the final game.

Dark was incensed. With ninety wins, the Giants had improved by two games on the previous season, and he thought he had weathered the racial storm. He was not without his supporters, including Jackie Robinson, who was unperturbed by Dark's racist comments. "I have known Dark for many years," he told the *New York Times*, "and my relationships with him have always been exceptional. I have found him to be a gentleman and, above all, unbiased."

The circumstances of his firing could have been far worse had Mays not suppressed the players' uprising or had he criticized Dark for what he considered to be his betrayal. Dark's career suffered little. He was managing again in two years and managed nine more years with four teams, winning the World Series with the Oakland Athletics in 1974. More than three decades after he retired from managing, Dark says Mays "is the greatest player to have ever put on a uniform." Mays is equally generous in thanking Dark for his mentoring in the early 1950s and his support of Mays as manager. But the two men stopped talking to each other after Dark's New York press conference in 1964 and have rarely spoken since.

Mays's defense was as good as ever in 1964, and included one of the most acrobatic catches of his career. On September 4 in Philadelphia, he was playing unusually shallow against light-hitting Ruben Amaro, but Amaro drove the ball deep toward the scoreboard. Mays ran full bore until he reached the fence, then jumped, left arm extended, and grabbed the ball—but his momentum was carrying him forward, so he had to throw his legs out straight to prevent his face from smashing into the fence. His legs hit it hard, with his body suspended in midair, then he crashed to the ground on his back. He stood up and flipped the ball to the right fielder as the Philadelphia fans gave him a standing ovation. Hano, who wrote the book on the Catch, had now seen one better: "It is my own opinion that you cannot make a better play than that one—the run, the catch, the improvised thrusting of legs at the board to break the immediate impact, the daring of the boards, the holding of the ball despite the heavy crash to the ground."

Mays, wearing a brace, had to sit out one game, but he was back the following day.

After his brilliant start, Mays ended up hitting under .300 .296—for the first time in eight years. He still had, by any measure, an exceptional year, easily leading the league in home runs (47, fourteen ahead of Billy Williams), slugging percentage (.607), OPS (.990), and placing second in runs scored (121) and RBIs (111). In July he passed Eddie Mathews as the leading all-time home run hitter among active National League players. He ended the year with 453, one behind Mickey Mantle in his last significant home run campaign. Ahead of the two sluggers lay Stan Musial, who retired in 1963, with 475, Lou Gehrig with 493, Mel Ott with 511, Ted Williams with 521, Jimmie Foxx with 534, and then the Babe with 714.

But 1964 marked the first time that Mays's batting average declined each month (excluding October)—from .488 in April to .189 in September. For all the improvements in his personal life, he still took sleeping pills on the road. "I have a lot of tension," he explained. "I'd rather take a pill and relax myself than stay awake and do nothing." Since Mays joined the club in 1951, he had missed only 25 games out of a possible 1,892. In 1964, he appeared in 157 games, the most of any Giant. He did not collapse on the field as he had the past two seasons, but on September 3 he was so weary that he was lifted for a pinch hitter for only the second time in his career (the first occurred the previous year when he collapsed at the plate). Mays was given the following night off.

Coach Herman Franks said, "I've spent a lot of time with Willie on the road off and on since 1951. I've seen him become exhausted before but not as completely as late last season."

If Mays wore down that completely at thirty-three—and his average declined in lockstep—it was easy to conclude that his best years were behind him. Maybe his good years as well. Mays himself would never acknowledge such a possibility. Never. But he made some concessions. After the second game of the twenty-three-inning Met doubleheader, he was asked if he still liked to play.

"I love it," he said. "But the way it is these days, the name of the game is money."

CHAPTER TWENTY-NINE

THE PEACEMAKER

If Willie Mays was celebrated as an athlete, he was often underestimated as a speaker and rarely given credit for his intelligence. The perception was understandable when Mays was a scared twenty-year-old with a squeaky voice, but in a view often applied to black athletes of that era, he was frozen in his adolescence. Dick Young, in criticizing the Giant players' response to Alvin Dark in September of 1964, described Mays "as a very mixed up little boy." Mays was thirty-three.

The patronizing was not consistent with how Mays actually presented himself. He was still nervous before audiences, but on television, whether on *The Ed Sullivan Show,* in a home run derby against Mickey Mantle, or in his own documentary, he never sounded uneducated or flighty, and he would occasionally turn a wonderful phrase. Once asked by a reporter about his supposed difficulties in playing under pressure, he said, "I'm always more aggressive then. Even through high school, I played my best basketball in the pressure games. *I like that kind of weather.*"

Mays also had a quick wit and a biting sense of humor; with his clever razzing of opponents, Tim McCarver called him "a stand-up comic." Mays once had to fill out a medical card during spring training. One question asked: "Have you ever suffered from fainting spells?"

Mays wrote: "Periodically."

"And what," a nurse asked, "does that mean?"

"Every time I think of my income taxes," he said, "I faint."

On another occasion, Charlie Einstein was the master of ceremonies at a boosters' club luncheon, and he warmed up the audience with a Mays fable from the Giants' tour in Tokyo. With the bases loaded, Einstein explained, a hitter drove the ball to deep center field, but the wind carried it clear out of the park. Mays, however, noticed that the exit gate was open, so he raced through it, reached a tree-shaded avenue, jumped aboard a fire engine answering an alarm, and, three blocks farther, reached up with his glove and caught the ball. One fireman turned to another and said, "Home run in the Polo Grounds."

After Einstein's introduction, Mays spoke, and toward the end of his presentation, a member of the audience earnestly asked, "About the time you caught the ball while you were riding on the fire engine in Japan, did the guy on third score after the catch, or was your throw in time to get him?"

Mays didn't miss a beat. "I didn't make any throw," he deadpanned. "Didn't have to. There were two outs at the time."

Mays could be underestimated by his friends as well. In January 1965, he was given a testimonial dinner at the Fairmont Hotel in San Francisco. Nearly a thousand people, at $25 a plate, attended, with the proceeds going to a charity for underprivileged children. After the testimonials were over (Don Drysdale: "I flew up here from Los Angeles because I thought I was attending Willie's retirement dinner. Learning that it isn't, I'm disappointed"), the event's chairman, Alan Browne, president of San Francisco Stadium Incorporated, drew the evening to a close: "Good night and thank you."

But Mays, resplendent in tuxedo and black tie, rose quickly and took the microphone. "Wait a minute," he said. "Everybody please sit down. I've got something to say." As the big room quieted, he began. "I'm scared. But I can't let you fine people go without thanking you for what you've done tonight in helping a lot of kids."

Mays was disappointed he hadn't been asked to speak, and he said as much: "Every time I go to a dinner, they think I don't want to talk, but at my own testimonial, I think I should say something. For myself, I want to say everyone here has been wonderful to me, and I hope I can show my thanks by playing four or five more good years—"

"You've got ten more years, Willie!" someone in the audience yelled, and the crowd cheered.

Mays had now played more games as a San Francisco Giant than as a New York Giant, a milestone he noted. "When I first came here, you had a great ballplayer in one of my idols, Joe DiMaggio," Mays said, "and I don't blame you for saying, 'Show me.' When I was a boy, my dad once told me to keep my mouth shut and just try my best to produce. That's what I did my best to do. It was nice of that gentleman in the audience to say I can go on probably for ten more years, but that's like asking me to go back and be a boy again. I'm no longer a boy.

"San Francisco," he concluded, "feels like home to me."

There it was—straightforward, without any notes, and from the heart. The crowd gave him a standing ovation, a fine prelude to a season in which his skills, and his character, were never more in evidence.

• • •

In 1964, Mays had led the Giants in games played (157), hits (171), triples (9), homers (47), walks (82), RBIs (111), runs scored (121), and stolen bases (19), and was the only Giant to win a Gold Glove. So for 1965, his salary was increased by . . . zero. An unnamed front office executive told the *Sporting News* that Mays had tailed off the last months of the season; according to the reporter, "It might be said that Mays earned $90,000 of his $105,000 salary in April, May, June and part of July, and only about $15,000 in August and September." It was a "Jekyll and Hyde season," but despite Mays's erratic performance, the Giant executive said, "We never for a moment considered cutting Willie's pay."

Mays knew he deserved better but assumed he was in no position to complain. No player was. When Koufax and Drysdale held out the following year, they figured they had leverage as a tandem. They didn't. The Dodgers broke them, and the pitchers reported the last weekend of the exhibition season without getting close to the salaries they had demanded. (Their spare time allowed them to begin filming the movie *Warning Shot,* which prompted Bill Russell of the Boston Celtics to observe: "Suppose it had been Mays and McCovey—do you think they would have gotten a movie contract?")

Though Mays and Mantle were the game's highest paid players, Mays had not received a raise in three years, but as long as the reserve clause was in effect—and the owners could artificially control wages—the players were all supposed to be grateful that their salaries weren't cut. As the Giant executive told the *Sporting News,* "We had some players who were paid substantial money in 1964, beyond what they actually earned." Their salaries would be slashed, he said, but "we've never asked any of our players to take a full 25 percent cut and won't this year."

The media's breathless attention on Mays's salary, combined with their management bias, always put Mays on the defensive. The *Sporting News* asserted that Mays's stagnant salary "works no hardship on Willie [because] a raise would boost his income taxes. Actually, he does better financially at $105,000 than he would with a small hike in pay."

The real story, in fact, was how vastly underpaid Mays was. Had players the basic right to receive market wages, owners would have had to determine which players generated the most revenue in ticket sales and television and radio fees and pay them accordingly. It's possible that in a true free market, some players would have fared only marginally better, but it's clear who would have fared the best. As Horace Stoneham himself was fond of saying, "I'd pay my way into a ballpark to see Willie play."

• • •

Mays always felt good during spring training, and 1965 was no exception—not simply because "there was something in the air." Late in the '64 season, when Dark was still managing, Mays met with Stoneham about replacements, and Stoneham asked Mays about Herman Franks. Mays knew him well and liked him. Franks was a protégé of Leo Durocher's who, as a coach for Durocher, had befriended Mays; the two would get into soapsuds fights at the Polo Grounds. Franks had managed Mays in the Caribbean League in 1954 and had coached him under Rigney and Dark. Mays told Stoneham that Franks could speak Spanish and had a good relationship with the Latin players, and he thought Franks could relieve the tension among the black, Latin, and white players. Franks fit Stoneham's mold for a manager—a player or coach with long ties to the organization, a Durocher disciple, and a friend of Willie Mays's. Franks was introduced as the new manager on the last day of the 1964 season.

Franks marked a new era of Giant baseball. The stylistic opposite of the handsome, God-fearing Dark, Franks was a portly forty-nine-year-old former third-string catcher with a receding hairline and a brusque personality. Emery boards were smoother. One writer said Franks "could cuss, chew tobacco, spit, and scratch." His habit of pulling his crotch before shaking hands did not endear him to reporters, for whom he had little regard anyway. The feeling was mutual. *Atlanta Journal* columnist Furman Bisher wrote: "Herman Franks is not the most unpleasant man I ever met. But he's close."

But many players, including Mays, believed he had an imaginative baseball mind and improved the clubhouse atmosphere with a more open style. The change began before his first spring training, when the team gathered at Buckhorn Hot Springs in Arizona. Franks invited the players to join him on a wild hog hunt. Most joined him, though Mays declined. ("I'm scared to death of guns," he explained. "Too many guys get hurt.") He stayed behind and enjoyed the sulfur baths.

Franks tried not to embarrass his players. He rarely called clubhouse meetings, which Dark had used to dress down his troops, and when a pitcher needed to be replaced, Franks would often send a coach to the mound because the struggling hurler could talk him out of it.

Other players, however, saw Franks as a crass good ol' boy who was mainly accessible to the stars and whose station-to-station offense failed to manufacture runs. He rarely bunted or used the hit-and-run, and the Giants' forty-seven stolen bases in 1965 ranked eighth out of ten National League teams' numbers. The following year, their twenty-nine stolen bases placed them dead last. (In fairness, Stoneham tried to stock his team with home run hitters.)

What most distinguished Franks, however, had nothing to do with baseball. Though he dropped out of college as a freshman, he began buying land in the late 1940s in his hometown of Salt Lake City, which led to interests in real estate development, mobile homes, hardware stores, supermarkets, and drugstores. By the time he became manager of the Giants, Franks was a rich man, which eased the pressures of the position. "I think it makes any job easier," he said, "if you don't need the money."

One thing was certain from the outset: he understood the value of Willie Mays and used some of the same tactics Durocher had to draw the most out of him. Mays no longer needed protection from reporters, but he needed protection nonetheless. In one of his first interviews, Franks said, "When the Giants are on the road, Willie's phone rings constantly. When he tells the hotel operator he's accepting no calls, they bang on his door—autograph seekers and people with deals. He doesn't get the proper rest. I may keep his room number a secret even from the telephone girl at the hotel next season. He'll be listed as being in room 312, say, but he'll be in 520."

Franks promised he'd give Mays more days off. "As for periodic rests, you do that automatically with most players, but Mays is so good defensively, the temptation is strong for any manager to keep him in there whether he gets a hit or not. I intend to resist that temptation. Nearly every time in the past, when Willie was tired and given a rest, he came back like gangbusters."

Mays also had new standing on the team, though it had been initiated by Stoneham, who wanted him to take on more responsibility—to be not just the captain but something like an assistant manager. Mays agreed, and Franks embraced the idea. "I'm going to put more responsibility on his shoulders," Franks said. "I can get only so close to a club. The coaches can get a little closer. But a player like Mays can get real close. I expect to have him in my office a lot and talk to him about the club. I won't hesitate to ask him if he thinks I should play this or that man. He's very smart. I'm not too proud to ask for suggestions."

Before most games, Mays would meet Franks and review the lineup—Mays says he kept players off the field if they did not heed his instructions on positioning. They also discussed how to pitch opposing hitters and where to play them. Mays had always been frustrated by his inability to talk to the pitcher while he was in center field, but he resolved that problem by naming second baseman Hal Lanier as the "infield captain." Mays and Lanier had a special relationship dating from Lanier's youth. Lanier's father, Max, had been Mays's teammate in 1952. Ten-year-old Hal would go to the Polo Grounds, where he and the other players' children would mill around the clubhouse. "All the players were friendly toward us, but Willie exceptionally so," Lanier recalls. "He would take us to center field and play catch and pepper with us."

When Lanier joined the Giants in 1964, Mays called him by his father's name, "Maxie," and took him under his wing. On the field, he would position him at second base and, before games, review the opposing pitcher—what he threw when he was ahead in the count and behind. On the road, Mays ate with Lanier, took him to menswear stores, and from his trove of freebies gave him golf equipment, sweaters, and suits. When Mays was asked to appear in a Coke commercial, he insisted that Lanier be included.

Mays's trust in Lanier made him a logical choice to be infield captain; his principal job was to talk to the pitcher when Mays thought he had lost his concentration or developed a bad rhythm. "I watch [Mays] in the outfield," Lanier told reporters, "and when he waves me to go talk to the pitcher, I go. The pitcher knows I'm coming in on Willie's order, and that's good enough for him."

More than four decades later, as manager of the Sussex Skyhawks, a minor league team in New Jersey, Lanier decorates his office with seven photographs of Mays. "He was like a second father," he says.

Mays's role as a mentor represented a subtle but meaningful change. While he had always given advice, in the past he had waited for teammates to ask him. Now he was more willing to approach players on his own and speak his mind, and he would hold others accountable. If a pitcher was supposed to throw a particular hitter fastballs outside but threw an inside curveball that Mays couldn't catch because he was out of position, he would chew out the pitcher and the catcher. They typically did not talk back. "Given the amount of ground that Willie covered in the outfield, the last thing that a pitcher would want to do is complain," hurler Mike McCormick recalls.

Mays also intervened in personal problems, none more directly than Jim Ray Hart's. Another in the line of black players that the Giants had developed, Hart was a powerful right-handed hitter who already knew about adversity: he grew up picking cotton in the dusty fields that surrounded Hookerton, North Carolina. He broke into the big leagues in July 1963, but he liked to crowd the plate, and in his second game a Bob Gibson fastball broke his shoulder blade. He returned to the lineup five weeks later and had played several games when he was beaned by Curt Simmons, ending his season. In spring training the following year, Alvin Dark threw pitches at him so he might learn to dodge them, and it appeared to work. Hart was hit only four times during the season, and he slugged thirty-one homers and finished second in the Rookie of the Year contest.

Off the field, however, Hart struggled with his own demons. He was so quiet, according to one reporter, that he considered "a nod a hello and a throaty chuckle an endless conversation." Whether due to loneliness or insecurity or some other reason, Hart liked to drink and break curfew, and in July of his sophomore season, Franks fined him and suspended him indefinitely. Mays got the suspension lifted after twenty-four hours. Hart was twenty-three, and Mays thought that he needed someone who'd talk to him, not scold him. He figured that Hart didn't even realize how much alcohol he consumed—drinking was probably rampant in his rural community. After Hart's suspension, Mays wanted him to acknowledge the problem.

Hart said, "I just got to have a little every now and then. If I don't drink some, then I get all tight and nervous."

Mays remembered how Durocher had dealt with Dusty Rhodes's drinking: he didn't forbid it and actually gave him money for it. In exchange, Rhodes agreed not to consume alcohol for the rest of that week. Then Durocher would give him money again and Rhodes would make the same pledge.

Mays told Hart: "If you play for me six days, I'll give you one." He explained that if Hart stopped by his locker every Monday morning, he would give him a bottle. They shook hands on it. Franks wasn't entirely pleased by the arrangement, but Mays reminded him of Durocher's solution. Mays bought a case of Old Crow, kept it in his locker, and each Monday for the rest of the season, Hart stopped by for his bottle.

On the road, Mays invited Hart into poker games that he organized in his hotel room. Sometimes he would select players based on his friendships; other times, on his desire to keep certain players under his eye. He would carry thousands of dollars in cash, securing the bills with rubber bands, and he would stake some of the players in his games, including Hart. Guys in the card game were in the starting lineup the next day.

Hart excelled under Mays's vigilance. When he was suspended, he had nine home runs. In the last sixty-eight games, he hit fourteen homers and ended with a .299 average and ninety-six RBIs. He also played in 160 games. When the season was over, Mays took five hundred-dollar bills out of his wallet and gave them to Hart. "It's for telling me the truth and playing every day," he said. Hart was an All-Star the following year and had a solid career that lasted twelve seasons.

• • •

In 1965, Mays once again began on a rampage. On May 18, after thirty-two games, he was batting .403, had clubbed fourteen homers, and had driven in thirty. More than half of his twenty-six hits had been for extra bases, and even his singles were mostly line drives. Franks allowed him to make his own schedule to reduce his fatigue. In lopsided games, Mays would sit out the last two or three innings, which over the course of the season added up to several days off. There were fifteen games in which he didn't start, though he was often used as a pinch hitter. The Giants played only six games in which he didn't appear, but the sight of Mays on the bench befuddled reporters, who surrounded him after an off day in June. "Why all the fuss?" Mays asked. "They don't run a racehorse every day. Other players get a day off, often two days, and nobody gets hot and bothered." Even sitting on the bench was not that restful for Mays—he was too invested emotionally. "If I'm in the park, I'm playing every play even if I'm not in the game," he said.

Age wasn't Mays's only motivation for more rest. He was also injured. Early in the season, he slipped in the outfield and tore muscles in his shoulder and leg. Wrapping the leg provided some comfort, and the trainer would rub hot ointment on his shoulder before each game. Daily whirlpools also helped. Mays could still run, but his throwing was impaired. He believed he had only a couple of good throws each game. The Giants never disclosed the injuries, so before each game, Mays would make one strong throw to third and one to home. Opponents saw that he still had his golden arm and respected it during the game. Mays continued throwing runners out, with thirteen assists during the year, but they mostly came from his outsmarting runners by throwing behind them.

The rest was clearly beneficial. After slumping at the end of May, he rebounded in the following month. On June 20, he stroked seven hits in a doubleheader sweep, raising his average to .342. Three days later, he hit his twenty-second homer of the year—number 475 of his career. On July 8, he hit number 476 to pass Stan Musial and place him sixth on the all-time home run list. But on June 30 he pulled a groin muscle against Houston and, to reduce his need to run, had to move to right field. He played a corner outfield position for several more games but was back in center against Philadelphia on July 10, the last game before the All-Star break.

In the first inning, Mays reached first on an infield single. The next batter grounded the ball to the third baseman, who threw wildly to first. Mays tore fearlessly around second and then third—one fan said he ran "as if his upper torso was chasing his legs." He wanted to score, but the first baseman threw the ball to catcher Pat Corrales, who caught it on his knees in front of the plate and turned to make the tag, but Mays had launched himself, feet first, toward the plate. A photograph shows him airborne and hatless, his body parallel to the ground, both arms extended like wings on a plane, his left foot smashing into the catcher's chest protector. The collision left both men on the ground. The umpire called Mays out, but then the ball rolled out of Corrales's glove. The umpire yelled safe. Corrales was given an error. Neither player returned to the game.

Mays now had a severely bruised thigh and hip, and, according to Ed Rumill of the *Christian Science Monitor,* "many assumed that he would miss the 36th All-Star game [in three days] at Minnesota." At thirty-four, Mays had played in fifteen consecutive All-Star games and had nothing more to prove. Prudence dictated rest. That's what other players had done in similar circumstances. Rumill noted, "Hadn't ballplayers, some no more than slightly injured, been 'begging out' of the midsummer engagement for years. If a fellow let his imagination ramble, he might even get the impression that some of the boys would rather go fishing than play in the National League versus American League classic."

The National League was in the midst of a dominating run. When Mays played in, and lost, his first All-Star Game in 1954, the National League's record was 8–13. The two leagues split the next six games. Then the National League won twenty out of the next twenty-two, with one game ending in a tie. The reason for its supremacy in the 1960s was no secret. The National League had integrated far more aggressively than the American League and therefore had superior black and Latin players. The 1965 team was representative. Its starters in the outfield were Mays, Hank Aaron, and Willie Stargell. Dick Allen opened at third, with Maury Wills at shortstop, Ernie Banks at first, and Marichal on the mound. Coming off the bench were Roberto Clemente, Frank Robinson, and Billy Williams. The closer? Bob Gibson. The American League's only minority starters were Willie Horton, Felix Mantilla (from Puerto Rico), and Vic Davalillo (from Venezuela).

Some years, the only black American League All-Star was Elston Howard, whereas every third National Leaguer was black. That created, for many players, an extra incentive. "The All-Star game meant a lot to us," Aaron wrote in his autobiography, "because the big difference between the National League and the American League was that we had the black players. . . . So it was a matter of pride with us. And we always knew we would win. . . . When people talk nowadays about the National League's domination of the All-Star game, they usually say that the National League always seemed to take the game more seriously. But they don't say why. Willie and Ernie and I know why." The additional motivation for black players, Aaron told *Ebony,* "was spiritual."

Mays did take the All-Star Game seriously, but unlike Aaron, he never looked at it, or baseball itself, through a racial prism. If National League victories brought credit to his race—and prodded American League owners to give more opportunities to black players—so much the better. But Mays strove for All-Star glory for his teammates and his league. Other considerations diluted the game's purity. He told reporters in 1965, the All-Star Game "means too much to a lot of people. It's bigger than any one player." It was also bigger than any one race.

But Mays, of course, was not just another All-Star. When he walked onto the field before the game in Minnesota, Elston Howard and Minnesota Twin catcher Earl Battey doffed their caps and shouted, "Here comes the king!" Despite his injury, Mays was in the starting lineup. "He's like Mantle," National League manager Gene Mauch said. "They can both limp into the Hall of Fame." To everyone's surprise, Mauch had Mays lead off, and in the first inning, Mays stepped in and promptly hit one over the fence, which gave him an All-Star record of twenty-one hits and three homers. He also scored two runs, extending that record to eighteen. In the eighth, after taking several steps in on a line drive, he reversed himself and made a leaping backhanded catch to preserve a 6–5 win. He played all nine innings.

The last two weeks of July were a disaster. Mays was limping from his collision in Philadelphia, and he had also hurt his thumb, forcing him to release the bat early. He didn't get a hit in twenty-four at-bats and went twenty-two days without driving in a run. He hit only two home runs in the month, and his average fell from .339 to .310. Mays stopped taking batting practice to preserve his strength and moved to a lighter bat, but it seemed that 1964 was going to repeat itself, with a protracted slump that would sink his average below .300 and assure the Giants' disappointment. The team had actually played beyond expectations. Cepeda missed most of the season with a knee injury, and the Giants had to carry two "bonus ballplayers," who contributed little. Franks had only nine pitchers on the roster, and besides Marichal, had only one other reliable starter, Bob Shaw. Out of desperation, the Giants even picked up forty-four-year-old Warren Spahn after the Mets released him; he won three and lost four, then retired after the season.

By August 1, the Giants were still in contention—in fourth place, four games out. But the Dodgers had better pitching, the Braves had superior hitting, and the Reds had more balance. They needed something close to a miracle; more specifically, they needed a month that no baseball player had ever had before. They had such a player in center field.

• • •

On August 5, Mays hit two homers in Cincinnati to give him twenty-seven for the year. He also drove in four runs and raised his average to .316. If he could avoid a drought, he would have another outstanding year and preempt speculation about his retirement. His hits against the Reds paced the Giants to victory, giving them three in a row and lifting them into second place, three behind the Dodgers. Two nights later in St. Louis, Mays went 3-for-3, with two more homers and five RBIs in another victory. He hit another long ball the next night, one of three hits.

Perhaps it was the additional rest, because instead of tapering, Mays was getting stronger. The Giants returned home on August 10 for a thirteen-game home stand, culminating with four games against the Dodgers. Mays kept hitting and the team kept winning. Between August 5 and 12, he hit seven homers in a seven-game streak. After going hitless for three games, he roped his eighth home run of the month on August 16, then another one on the eighteenth. Next came the Dodgers.

With Drysdale, Koufax, and Claude Osteen, the Dodgers held first place almost every day from April through August. But they hit poorly—their highest batting average among the starters was Maury Wills, at .286, and out of ten National League teams, they were eighth in scoring. With four teams in contention, their first-place margin was slim throughout the year, and when they arrived in Candlestick for four games, their lead was only 1½ games ahead of the Giants.

The hostilities between the Giants and Dodgers may have lessened somewhat when the clubs migrated to California, but a healthy rivalry still existed. The teams didn't divide neighbors as they had in New York, but they battled for the pennant every year. The two cities, each convinced of its own superiority, craved California bragging rights; and neither distance nor time could eliminate the bad blood, the beanballs, or the history.

In 1965 the sniping began early, in April, when the Giants played a series in Los Angeles and Don Drysdale knocked several players down, including Mays, in a 2–1 victory for the Dodgers. The losing pitcher was Juan Marichal, who said after the game, "If Drysdale ever comes close to one of our batters again, he better watch out."

Drysdale responded, "If he wants to get me, I'm only 60 feet, 6 inches away. But if he does, he better get me good, or I'll take four players with me, and I don't mean .220 hitters."

The series at Candlestick that began on August 19 was, by far, the year's most highly attended. The Giants averaged 19,087 fans a game in 1965. The opening contest against the Dodgers drew 35,901, and the next three games averaged 42,316. It was, indeed, a playoff atmosphere. In the first game, Mays's two-run homer in the first gave the Giants the lead, and Giant catcher Tom Haller's two-run blast in the ninth tied it, but the Dodgers won it in fifteen innings. The Giants evened the series in the second game, with Mays hitting another long ball. In the third game, Mays's homer in the eighth tied the contest, but the Dodgers won it in eleven innings.

Beyond the scores, a tense subplot was developing. In the fifth inning of the second game, Maury Wills came to the plate and squared around as if to bunt. Haller moved forward, but Wills then pulled his bat back, striking Haller's glove or mask. Catcher interference was called, and Wills was awarded first base. Wills had gotten four hits the previous day, and the fake-bunt ploy was an old trick of his that further antagonized the Giants. In response, Franks instructed his leadoff hitter in the fifth, Matty Alou, to do the same thing in the hope of hitting Dodger catcher Johnny Roseboro.

Roseboro, who replaced Roy Campanella, had been the Dodger receiver since the team had moved to Los Angeles. A lifetime .249 hitter, he was a stout, rugged Gold Glover who tried to unnerve hitters with his taunting and was unapologetic in his calling for knockdown pitches. "When a hitter is standing on top of the plate, fearless and swinging from his ass, you have to move him back," he said.

On this night, Alou squared to bunt and pulled the bat back, but no interference was called. The move, however, distracted Roseboro, and the pitch missed his glove and smacked him in the chest protector. Roseboro was outraged. "You weasel bastard!" he snarled. He told Alou that if he hurt him again, he'd regret it. Roseboro was going to get him.

From the bench, Franks and Marichal began barking at Roseboro. Franks was protecting his player. Marichal was defending his friend, a fellow Dominican. Roseboro was not one to back down. He yelled back, ridiculed Franks about his weight, and shouted, "You sonofabitch, if you have something to say, you come out here and say it to my face." Marichal yelled that Alou had only attempted what Wills had done. Roseboro blared, "The next time something like that happens, you're going to get hit in the head with the ball."

The game continued, but the dustup was not forgotten. The following day, Roseboro told his teammates Jim Gilliam and Lou Johnson that Marichal had better not get out of line, "because I won't take any guff from him."

Marichal was due to pitch against Koufax the very next day, August 22.

Baseball is an escape, an alternate universe, and rarely does a game echo the events of the outside world. But that's what happened in the final game of the Giant-Dodger series. It should have been a triumphant time for

African Americans—and for all Americans—for on August 6, President Johnson had signed into law the Voting Rights Act. Instead, less than a week later, in the midst of a Los Angeles heat wave, a race riot erupted in a community that few Americans had ever heard of. The mayhem began after a California highway patrolman stopped two black men in a car on the corner of 116th and Avalon, in a neighborhood called Watts. The driver was under suspicion of drunkenness. There was an argument, then a crowd, then a punch was thrown, and then a mob. The rioting lasted for six days, with raw television images, fed from a camera on a helicopter, delivered live to stations in Los Angeles and the networks. An army surplus store was soon aflame, igniting ammunition that engulfed adjacent stores. Burning cars were turned over, storefronts smashed, fire trucks were met by bricks, police cars by snipers, and the aerial shots, capturing waves of black smoke, provided an eerie cinematic quality. The destruction and bloodshed didn't end until the area was controlled by 12,242 National Guardsmen carrying .30-caliber machine guns. More than thirty people were killed, about nine hundred injured, and six hundred buildings damaged. There had been race riots before this one and after, from Newark to Detroit to cities beyond, but no word became more synonymous with the era's urban rage than Watts.

Johnny Roseboro lived near Watts, and he and his teammates continued to play at home through the riot, for Dodger Stadium was sufficiently removed from the unrest. By the time the players reached San Francisco, their televised games seemed to offer a reprieve from the seething tensions in their own city.

The most anticipated game was on Sunday, a warm afternoon with a high sky, which featured baseball's two most glamorous pitchers. Sandy Koufax was the left-handed fireballer whose later decision to observe Yom Kippur rather than pitch in a World Series game was a rare example of faith and perspective. Juan Marichal was the high-kicking flamethrower whose sweet temperament and snappy clothes had earned him the nickname "the Dominican Dandy." Koufax entered the contest 21–8, with a 2.10 ERA; Marichal was 19–9 with a 1.73 ERA. The winner might have the inside track on the Cy Young Award.

The game, however, had no bearing on any pitching awards. Maury Wills led off with a bunt single and scored on Ron Fairly's two-out double. Like other pitchers of that era, Marichal didn't like hitters bunting, so when Wills came to bat in the second, he flattened him with a high fastball. Wills glared out at Marichal, dusted himself off, and got back in the box. The at-bat ended uneventfully, but Roseboro wanted vengeance.

Wills was Roseboro's friend and roommate—black players always roomed together—and the leader of the team. Roseboro wanted Koufax to deliver the same message to Wills's equivalent on the Giants, Willie Mays, who led off in the second. When Mays stepped into the batter's box, Roseboro put his right hand between his legs and flipped his index finger—his signal for the pitcher to "flip" the hitter, knock him down. Roseboro thought Mays could be intimidated anyway and would often call for his pitchers to brush him back, but Koufax didn't like throwing at other people's heads. He sailed a fastball so far over Mays's helmet that, according to Roseboro, "Mays would have had to climb a ladder to get hit by it." Mays had been expecting the "courtesy" pitch and believed the message had now been sent.

But in the top of the third, Marichal moved Fairly off the plate with a tight one. The Giant right-hander later said that Fairly had made it look closer than it really was, but the Dodger dugout was now yelling at him, and Roseboro in particular was angry. Mays, in center field, could feel the tempers rising. The Dodgers led, 2–1, but that was secondary. In the bottom of the third, Marichal led off for the Giants. Roseboro believed it was payback time but had lost all hope in his pitcher. "Koufax was constitutionally incapable of throwing at anyone's head, so I decided to take matters into my own hands," he later said. (According to another account, both benches had been warned, so Koufax knew that a beanball would result in a suspension.)

Roseboro went to the mound and told Koufax to throw the ball down and in, which would position him to buzz Marichal from behind the plate. The first pitch was a strike, but the second was low and inside. Roseboro dropped the ball, picked it up, and fired it back to Koufax. Marichal later said that the ball nicked his ear, and it would have killed him if it had hit him squarely. Roseboro said it was two inches past his nose, but he readily acknowledged his intent—to scare the shit out of Marichal, which he did. Wills said, "When a hard-thrown ball goes past you that closely, it makes a noise like a bullet." Mays, watching from the bench, couldn't believe it. He had never seen a duster thrown by a catcher, and he knew something bad was going to happen.

Marichal turned around and yelled, "Why did you do that? You better not hit me with that ball!" According to him, Roseboro cursed his mother, which angered him all the more. Roseboro said he had already made up his mind that if Marichal protested, "I was going to annihilate him." When Marichal did protest, Roseboro started out of his crouch.

Marichal, at 6 feet, was taller than Roseboro but far less muscular, and he feared that Roseboro was going to maul him. As Roseboro came toward him, he backed up toward the pitcher. He later said that Roseboro took off his mask and appeared ready to use it against him. Perhaps he thought that's what happened. But according to the photographs, Marichal used his left arm to hold Roseboro at bay, shove his mask, and spin him toward Koufax, who was charging in from the mound with the ball still in his glove. The melee's most recognizable photograph shows Marichal holding his bat high above with his right hand, ready to land a blow on Roseboro's head, a stricken Koufax helplessly trying to separate them. By the time Koufax, third base coach Charlie Fox, and home plate umpire Shag Crawford could intervene, Marichal had struck Roseboro three times with glancing blows, and the Dodger was bleeding profusely from his head. Crawford stopped the swings by grabbing Marichal and throwing him to the ground. The Western Union ticker tape reported: "Game delayed, argument."

Most baseball fights follow a predictable rhythm. Triggered by some provocation—a brushback pitch, say, or a hard slide—two combatants encounter each other and tussle, but they are quickly swarmed by the other players, coaches, and umpires. If the principals have already fallen to the ground, a scrum is guaranteed. Some players may try to settle old scores, and some fights will produce secondary skirmishes, but most of the action peters out quickly, with guys standing around and watching as the two aggressors are separated. Serious injury is rare. Baseball fights offer the grand entrance of players and coaches rushing onto the field as if they are trying to catch a bus, and that sight alone usually elicits more excitement than any pugilistic feat. But the swamping of the field has a dampening effect, the teammates serving as protectors against bullies and defusing any spark that could ignite a true donnybrook.

This Candlestick brawl was different. The benches and bullpens emptied, but instead of order being restored, the hostilities increased. The Giants' on-deck batter was the twenty-one-year-old Cuban Tito Fuentes, who had made his big league debut just four days earlier. Perhaps unfamiliar with the customs of major league fights, he raced toward Marichal and Roseboro brandishing his bat. A photograph shows Fuentes poised to clobber Roseboro. Bolting from the dugout, meanwhile, was Orlando Cepeda, who was also carrying a bat, as he had in Pittsburgh in 1958. Fortunately, there were no accusations after the game, or evidence, that anyone other than Marichal had used a bat as a weapon.

The Dodgers wanted revenge. Outfielder Wally Moon, who was thirty pounds lighter than Cepeda and seven years younger, barreled into the Giant first baseman. Relief pitcher Howie Reed charged from the bullpen and, according to one account, "went berserk" and "turned into a 205-pound madman trying to pull players off Marichal so he could get at him." Rookie pitcher Mike Kekich had one arm around Marichal's neck but was not able to deliver a decisive punch. "I blew it," he said. Lou Johnson sprinted in from left field and threw wild punches into the maelstrom. "I was swinging at anybody in a white San Francisco home uniform," he explained. Coach Danny Ozark initially tried to separate the players but then tried to fight Marichal, who was taunting Roseboro. "He's a goddamn nut," Ozark said. "He was asking Roseboro to come and get some more, I guess. A guy like that would hit a woman."

Marichal's behavior surprised those who knew his mild personality, but he entered the game still on edge after his exchange with Roseboro two nights earlier. Matty Alou said, "Juan wanted to fight all day. He had the devil inside him that day." While Roseboro may have started the fight, Marichal's attempted bludgeoning of him violated the game's unwritten rules and created a very different dynamic. The *New York Times* reported: "In the melee that followed within a few seconds, peacemaking seemed desperately urgent, and there didn't seem to be the usual taking of sides. Everybody seemed horrified by the nature of the attack and by the sight of blood streaming down Roseboro's face." Adding to the mayhem was the belief that Roseboro had lost his eye. "I thought [the bat] had knocked Roseboro's eye out," Dodger manager Walter Alston said. "There was nothing but blood where his left eye should have been. A man might as well have used a gun as a bat."

For a moment, Watts had spilled over to the national pastime.

One person who would not be pacified was Johnny Roseboro, who had been given boxing gloves at a young age, later learned karate, and was known for his strength. One writer said, "When Johnny Roseboro comes at you, you should be entitled to call a priest." Roseboro lamented that once the battle with Marichal began, "I forgot all the fancy fighting I'd ever learned and went after him as if it was an alley fight. . . . I didn't see anything clearly. It was all confusion. My head didn't hurt much, but I had blood all over me and could see I was still bleeding. I was mad that he had hit me with a bat and mad that I'd only gotten in one blow, which I didn't think had hurt him. As Marichal ran toward the dugout, I chased him."

But Roseboro never made it there. A massive right hand grabbed his jersey, next to his chest protector, and began walking him to the Dodger dugout. The hand belonged to Willie Mays. "You're hurt, John, you're hurt," he said. "Stop the fighting. Your eye is out." On their way, Roseboro gave the finger to the fans, who booed him.

A photograph shows Mays, without his hat, pulling Roseboro along surrounded by nine Dodgers. Blood from Roseboro's face has splattered his chest protector. He is looking in disbelief at his right hand, also covered with blood. Flecks of blood are scattered on Mays's uniform as well.

When the fight began, Mays rushed onto the field and darted in and out of players, pulling them apart and removing the bat from Fuentes's hand. "This is crazy," he said to players on both teams. "You're too smart to get mixed up in it." Foremost in his mind was the fear that the fans would rush the field, which would set off a riot. His most important task was getting Roseboro into the dugout. Mays worried that his friend had lost his eye and knew he needed treatment. He also believed that as long as Roseboro was storming after Marichal or was close to any Giant, the fans would be tempted to jump the railing.

Mays took Roseboro to the dugout and sat down next to him, which defied all tradition and logic—a player, in the heat of a brawl, taking a seat on the enemy's bench. Mays used some towels to stanch the bleeding, then cradled Roseboro's head while the trainer, Bill Buhler, examined the injury. Roseboro had a two-inch wound on the left side of his head near the top of his scalp, allowing blood to pour into his eye, but the eye itself was fine. Roseboro reacted more with anger than relief. He started cursing Mays for holding him back and tried to rejoin the fray, but Mays restrained him. At some point, the Dodgers' Lou Johnson lit out for Shag Crawford. Mays jumped out of the dugout and grabbed him around the knees before other players piled on, but not before Mays took a knee to the head.

Like a spent windstorm, the brawl finally wound down, with both Marichal and Roseboro in their respective dugouts. Roseboro wanted to stay in the game, but his trainer and his manager told him to go to the clubhouse. To get there, he had to walk across the outfield. He was greeted with jeers, so he bent over and patted his rear end. In the clubhouse, the trainer wanted to stitch the wound, but it was in a difficult position and Roseboro didn't want the needle, so butterfly bandages were used.

The rest of the game was sullen and anticlimactic except for one at-bat. Crawford told Koufax, "Whatever you do, don't throw at anyone. We don't want a riot here." With police officers in the dugouts, it seemed a reasonable concern. When play resumed, a shaken Koufax walked two batters and then faced Mays. One of the lefty's best pitches to right-handers was his hard fastball just off the inside corner. Hitters would lean back and were then helpless as his next pitch, a big curve, snapped across the plate. But Koufax was now robbed of his "jammer," and Mays could crowd the dish. Koufax threw him a high fastball, and Mays crushed it 450 feet into the left center field bleachers for his thirty-eighth homer of the season. "I don't take much pride," Mays later said, "in the advantage I had over him."

The home run made it 4–2, and the Giants won, 4–3. After the game, Mays went into the Dodger clubhouse to check on Roseboro and assure him it was just another fight. But by then he was gone. Candlestick's security guards had feared for Roseboro's safety, so they had put a Giants cap on his head, hustled him out of the ballpark, and sent him to the airport with a police escort.

The Giants' victory put them a half game out of first, but the talk was of the fight—and of the man who now had a new title. "Willie Mays," said the *Sporting News,* "acted as the great peacemaker."

The Dodgers recognized his contribution.

Maury Wills: "I gained new respect for Willie after that."

Walter Alston: "Mays was the only player on either club who showed any sense."

So did his fellow Giants. "It was getting out of control," Gaylord Perry said. "Willie was there to try to take care of the situation. It would have been a lot worse if Willie hadn't gotten Roseboro to calm down."

Mays's efforts brought a redeeming quality to one of the ugliest incidents in baseball history. That was the assessment of the league's president, Warren Giles, who said, "This man was an example of the best in any of us."

Mays's peacemaking added a new dimension to his standing as the game's most complete player. "A leader in sports," said the *Pittsburgh Press,* "doesn't have to be the best player on the team, although it helps. A leader doesn't necessarily lead with his bat, his glove, or his arm: he can lead with his head and his heart, too. Willie Mays is such a leader. . . . He leads by inspiration, by deeds. Yet his quick thinking is also one of his great assets. . . . Mays helped break up the riot in San Francisco when he went into the pile of players and came out with John Roseboro, leading the Dodger catcher to the dugout."

Media adulation was not unusual for Mays, but he had now transcended the game. As the *Boston Record American* reported: "Except for the majestic presence of Willie Mays, several players could have been maimed. Willie was out of the dugout in a flash to help disarm Marichal and prevent several dukes-up situations. He has extrasensory perception, that Willie Mays. . . . He is so well respected that several belligerent combatants [were calmed] as Willie walked between them and among them. . . . This could be the year Mays wins the MVP award and Nobel Peace Prize, too." Added the *San Francisco Examiner*'s Prescott Sullivan: The brawl "might still be going on had it not been for [Mays's] intervention. . . . As a natural born peace-maker, he would be of far more value to his country in Vietnam."

It was Mays's finest moment on a baseball field. The most revealing glimpse of him occurred in the Dodgers' dugout, when he was gently ministering to Roseboro. Mays "cupped the enemy's head and surveyed his wounds," wrote *Sports Illustrated,* "with a deep anguish on his expressive face." Roseboro looked at Mays and saw that he was crying. "I guess Mays was more a ballplayer than he was a Giant," Roseboro later said. "He was a sensitive guy." The tears rolled down Mays's face, and they rolled down the television screens in Los Angeles, where viewers saw the image up close. And on newscasts that night and the following morning, Americans across the country beheld the same stirring image of a baseball icon— heroic, sentimental, proud, wounded.

Why did Mays cry? And, more important, why among some sixty players and coaches did he so distinguish himself amid the bedlam?

Mays answered those questions in part after the game. Shaking his head sadly, he said, "I hate to see good friends fighting like that."

Mays did consider many Dodgers—Drysdale, Jim Gilliam, Koufax, Roseboro, Wills—personal friends. But his feeling ran deeper. Mays played baseball for many reasons—for the money, for the competition, for the thrill of the game. But baseball was also his family. It's a quaint notion, but it applied. With the exception of his father, Mays had severed ties with most of his Alabama kin. He and his cousin Loretta had a falling-out over the sale of his aunt Sarah's house. The other cousin with whom he'd been raised, Arthur B, had been killed in a stabbing. His mother's death had cut his involvement with virtually all of his half-siblings, and his stepfather had died as well in a stabbing.

Mays had spent most of his adult life around baseball players. Regardless of their uniform, he trusted them. Much attention was paid to Mays's various homes, but his real home was always the clubhouse, where he was surrounded by the men who knew him best and where his loyalties rarely wavered. The Giant broadcaster Lon Simmons says, "Willie thought he was the head of a family."

So when the Dodgers and Giants staged their epic brawl, it was, to Mays, like a family being ripped apart. He did what most would do in a serious family disagreement. He tried to separate the belligerents. He tried to make peace. But the violence had occurred. So in the dugout, his hands holding a towel soaked with blood from the deepest of wounds, he wept.

In one regard, the brawl could have been worse. Had a white player used a bat against a black player, or vice versa, the images could have inflamed urban tensions even more. The pictures of Watts and Candlestick, however, were still intertwined. The *Christian Science Monitor* noted: "The rioting so far has been in the streets. But if baseball and all the other major spectator sports aren't careful, do not heed the red flags and act drastically and at once, they may also be faced with mob violence of the sort that could threaten their futures."

Though Roseboro admitted starting the fight, he wasn't disciplined. Marichal immediately apologized for using his bat and said he swung it in self-defense. President Giles fined him $1,750 and suspended him for eight playing days. It was the largest fine that Major League Baseball had ever levied against a player, and the suspension was one of the longest, though the punishment was seen by many as far too light.

Marichal was booed for the rest of the year whenever he pitched outside San Francisco, and wherever the Giants went—Pittsburgh, Philadelphia, New York—the players received threatening phone calls. Cepeda got a call saying that his body would be found in a river. When the Giants landed in Los Angeles, they were met by a police escort, and at Dodger Stadium the fans booed them loudly—until Mays stepped to the plate. He alone had been cheered in every city on the road trip. The fans knew what had happened at Candlestick. But the Los Angeles cheer—a raucous standing ovation by fans whose own player had been hammered by a Giant—meant even more. "I will always treasure the memory of the roaring welcome that Giant-hating crowd gave me when I came to bat for the first time," he later said. "It was a salute maybe to the hot pace I'd been going at, but much more, obviously, to my reputation as the 'peacemaker' in the Roseboro incident."

The fight, and the immediate aftermath, left Mays and the Giants drained. The team lost its next four games; Mays went hitless in three games and sat out another. But he hit a home run on August 26 in Pittsburgh, then traveled to New York, where he had a historic weekend. On Friday night, he hit his fortieth homer of the season, marking the sixth time in his career that he'd had at least forty long balls in a year. He wiped out the National League record of five seasons held by Ernie Banks, Ralph Kiner, and Duke Snider. (Babe Ruth had the Major League record, hitting forty or more in eleven seasons.) On Sunday, Mays hit another homer, which gave him seventeen for the month, breaking Kiner's National League mark. Kiner, who broke the record as a Pirate, was now a Met broadcaster, and he interviewed Mays on his star-of-the-game show.

"Are you sore?" Mays asked him.

"Sure I'm sore," Kiner said.

"I'm sorry, Ralph."

Kiner later said, "I've seen two of my records broken by Willie. Sure, it hurts a little. But if somebody had to break them, I'm glad Willie did."

Mays's last home run in New York was also number 494 for his career, passing Lou Gehrig and putting him fifth on the all-time home run list. He also moved closer to 500, which was a magic number in those days.

He had just completed his most memorable month in baseball: seventeen homers, twenty-nine RBIs, and a .363 average, plus his role as peacemaker. He was now followed by a growing number of reporters who wanted to chronicle his five-hundredth homer while he also battled for a pennant.

In early September, five teams were within three games of one another. Even without the suspended Marichal for a weekend series in Los Angeles, the Giants beat the Dodgers twice and reached first place for the first time all season. The Giants reeled off fourteen consecutive wins, seventeen out of eighteen, and were four games in front with only twelve to play. Mays led the way. On September 12, in the Astrodome at Houston, he led off the fourth inning with a 450-foot line drive into the center field runway for his five-hundredth home run, and as he jogged around the bases, the fans stood and chanted: "Willie! Willie!"

Warren Spahn greeted him in the dugout. "I threw you the first one and now I've seen the five-hundredth," he said. "Was it the same feeling?"

"Same feeling, same pitch," Mays replied.

Eddie Logan, the clubhouse manager, tracked down the woman who caught the historic ball and offered her an autographed baseball in exchange. She refused, but she gave Logan her phone number should Mays want to call her about it. "She can have it," Mays said.

The following night at the Astrodome was even more dramatic. The dome itself was a revolutionary structure that tried to transform the experience of watching a game. Astro home runs, for example, prompted the scoreboard circling the outfield to light up with Western cartoons featuring fireworks, rockets, snorting cattle, galloping horses, and gun-wielding cowboys; a home run by the visitors was greeted by a ticking time bomb flashing TILT. Going into the top of the ninth, the Astro's Bob Bruce held a 5–2 lead, but after he gave up a one-out walk, he was replaced by Claude Raymond, a small right-hander from Quebec with a good moving fastball. He retired the first hitter and was now one out from victory. But Jesus Alou (the youngest of the three Alou brothers) singled to right, making it 5–3. The next batter was Mays.

Mays usually didn't try for homers, but this situation was different, and everyone knew it. Though he led the league in home runs, Raymond didn't want to walk him, which would bring up McCovey, the go-ahead run. So he challenged Mays with fastballs. Twice Mays swung so hard that he fell to one knee. Both times he missed. Raymond couldn't find the strike zone and ran the count full. Mays dug in for the next delivery. Alou prepared to leave with the pitch. The Astros were in ninth place, twenty-four games out of first, and only 15,415 fans were in the cavernous dome. But they began to cheer as Raymond came to the stretch and fired. It was a fastball, and Mays nicked it foul. The crowd clapped louder as Raymond prepared for the next pitch. Alou took off, and Raymond threw another fastball. Again a tip foul. Now the fans were on their feet and screaming, but not for Raymond or the Astros or the Giants but for the man at the plate. Mays fouled it back again. Alou trudged back to first. The fans caught their breath. One more pitch came. Another fastball. Another foul. Perhaps Raymond thought about an off-speed pitch, but that might now seem . . . unmanly. "I kept waiting for a breaking ball," Mays said later. "A curve, a slider—something other than a fastball. But that's all he threw. Nothing but fastballs." They were two heavyweights throwing their best punches. On the bench, Herman Franks muttered, "It's like challenging God."

On the tenth pitch of the at-bat, with the fans still yelling and Alou still running, Raymond threw another fastball on the inside part of the plate. As he recalled, "Willie bailed out but opened up on the ball at the same time, the way only he could." Mays hit the ball squarely and lined it deep into left field. The Giant players jumped off the bench. Alou kept running. The fans gasped as the ball sailed over the fence.

TILT!

As Mays circled the bases, Marichal was so excited, he started pacing in the dugout, tossing seat cushions on the bench.

"What's he doing?" Franks asked coach Larry Jansen.

"I think he's looking for his glove," Jansen said.

"Why?"

"He wants to go in and pitch when they come out."

"He pitched nine innings yesterday," Franks fumed. "Is he out of his fucking mind?"

Mays was embraced when he got to the dugout. Then he tipped his cap to the still-cheering crowd.

The Giants won the game in the tenth on a two-run single by Jim Davenport, and in their jubilant locker room afterward, all anyone could discuss was Mays's at-bat. "Everyone in the stadium knew he was going for the home run," said Giant outfielder Len Gabrielson, "and he went and got it. Honest to God, Mays is the greatest thing I've ever seen in my life. And there's not one guy in the big leagues who thinks different."

Astro general manager Paul Richards approached Raymond after the game, commended him for staying with the fastball, and told him it was a great duel.

Indeed it was. When Roger Angell in 1991 asked Mays to name his favorite long ball, he said, "Home run against Claude Raymond. . . . That was the only dramatic-type home run I ever hit."

• • •

The Mays legend reached its zenith in 1965. *Life* ran an eight-page, thirteen-photograph essay on Mays's final month of the season, when he hit .360 and smashed another eleven home runs. "To his team he gives the best—and he gives baseball its finest hours," the magazine pronounced. Mays "drives himself almost demonically," and the Giants' opponents have been "outpaced, outclassed, and outplayed by the most brilliant virtuoso performance ever seen in baseball." A shirtless Mays shows the ten pounds of muscle he has gained since entering the big leagues. In one sequence of photos, he is shown sliding into home plate into the legs of an opposing player, tumbling over his shoulder in a cloud of dust, and then, on his back, screaming in pain as the wind is knocked out of him. The umpire punches him out—but Mays finishes the game, and the Giants win on his forty-ninth homer of the season.

But Mays's dramatics were not enough. After winning seventeen out of eighteen games, the Giants lost seven out of ten. They were still 23–10 the last five weeks of the season and finished with ninety-five wins, but they couldn't hold off the Dodgers, who won fifteen out of their last sixteen and beat the Giants by two games. The Dodgers won the World Series in seven games against Minnesota.

While the Giants had exceeded expectations, they would have almost certainly won the pennant but for the brawl. It was Marichal's best year—he finished with a 2.13 ERA, 10 shutouts, 24 complete games, and 240 strikeouts compared to 46 walks. But the suspension forced him to miss two or three starts, and when he returned, he wasn't the same, losing four out of seven games in the final month. Koufax, who pitched a perfect game in September, won the Cy Young.

Roseboro filed a civil suit against Marichal, which was settled out of court, and in some ways the fight overshadowed Marichal's career. Though he was the winningest pitcher of the 1960s, he was not elected to the Hall of Fame until his third try, and only after Roseboro posed with him at an old-timers' game. The two men did become friends, and when Roseboro died in 2002, Marichal eulogized him.

Mays won the MVP in 1965. His fifty-two home runs were a personal best, and his .317 average was his highest since 1960. He led the league in slugging percentage (.645) and was among the leaders in runs scored (118) and RBIs (112). He seemed to be getting stronger with age: in his first four years in San Francisco, he hit 133 homers; in the next four, he hit 186. With 504 career home runs, the records of both Mel Ott, the National

League champ (511), and Jimmie Foxx, the greatest right-handed home run hitter (534), were in sight. The real question was whether he could reach the Babe (714).

Anything seemed possible. After the documentary on Mays appeared in 1963, Lee Mendelson urged NBC to rerun it as soon as possible. "Don't forget," he said. "This is perishable, not Peter Pan."

After Mays's 1965 season, Mendelson wired NBC: "I take it back. He is Peter Pan."

CHAPTER THIRTY

A PIECE OF
WILLIE'S HEART

Like his MVP season in 1954, Mays's triumphant year in 1965 led to invitations outside baseball. He was invited to Washington to meet Vice President Hubert Humphrey, who asked him to visit Youth Job Corps Centers during the Christmas season. "Willie, the kids will listen to you," Humphrey said. "All you have to do is talk to them." Mays didn't think he could solve the problems of the world, but he could talk to kids. In Washington, he addressed fifty young "Job Corpsmen," including a boy who, during the question-and-answer period, vented his anger against the "theys" who wouldn't let him be what he wanted to be—a minister. The boy grew more and more agitated until he started sputtering.

Mays held up his hand. "Cool it, baby," he said. "I'm on your side." The boy calmed down.

"If you want to be a minister," he said, "you be a minister. Don't let anybody stop you. When I was twenty, I had one hit for twenty-four times at bat with the Giants. If I had taken a lot of advice, I'd have quit baseball then. If you want to be a minister, you keep on trying." The boy seemed convinced.

Throughout the mid 1960s, Mays appeared on television talk shows and variety hours, such as *The Hollywood Palace,* and continued to make cameos on sitcoms. He was introduced to Tony Owen, the television producer, who told Mays he was married to the actress Donna Reed. The name was unfamiliar at first, but then Mays recalled seeing her in Westerns and *From Here to Eternity.* He became friendly with the couple, and they told him that whenever he needed money, he could come on *The Donna Reed Show,* which featured a white middle-class family in a white midwestern town in white America. Mays did need the money, so he appeared in three different episodes, playing the only part he knew—himself. In one episode, he and Don Drysdale, also playing himself, competed to sign a hot prospect (Reed's son on the show). The youth shunned the riches of baseball and chose to continue his education. He was twice a mystery guest on *What's My Line?*, and in 1965 he was a contestant on *The Dating Game*. An actress, Judy Pace, questioned three bachelors hidden behind a screen and chose Willie Mays. The date was supposed to be in Ankara, Turkey, but after the show Mays said he didn't want to go to Turkey, so instead they went, properly chaperoned, to Nassau, in the Bahamas. The trip resulted in a spread of handsome photographs in *Ebony* but not much romance. Mays spent most of the time on the golf course and visiting his former teammate Andre Rodgers. Asked if she was disappointed, Pace said, "Not really. I love shopping and playing on the beach, and he did take me out to dinner." (One viewer of the show was Cardinal outfielder Curt Flood, who was so smitten with Pace that he spent almost a year trying to meet her and more than twenty years later married her.)

Mays was becoming part of the establishment, in baseball and in San Francisco. He was recruited to become the first black member of the Concordia-Argonaut men's club, which comprised mainly wealthy Jews, and Mays, along with Joe DiMaggio, were voted into the city's Press Club. To his surprise, Mays discovered that people would actually pay money to play golf with him. Mays also received a raise from the Giants. While news reports speculated that he was asking for $150,000, he signed a two-year contract for $125,000 a year. Koufax, after holding out, signed for the same amount in 1966.

Mays's off-season took a jarring turn in December, when he made his first stop on his tour for the Job Corps. Traveling with Jake Shemano, Mays was giving a talk in Salt Lake City when he had another fainting spell. "He said he was a little woozy," Ted Kirkmeyer, city manager for the Intermountain theaters, told a wire service reporter. "He was determined to speak, got up, and walked toward the stage. Then he said, 'I just can't make it,' and went and sat down." Mays couldn't deliver his speech. Leaving the theater, a reporter noticed tears in his eyes.

Herman Franks lived in Salt Lake City, so a police car took Mays to his home, where he stayed for a week. At Franks's insistence, he canceled the rest of his trip, which would have taken him to five cities in as many days. He was examined by a doctor, who, according to Mays, said he was suffering from exhaustion. In a telephone interview, Dick Young asked how he could be tired when he hadn't played baseball in more than two months.

"I know, but I've been going pretty good. Banquets and this Jobs Corps thing almost every day. I get tired. I'm gonna have to take a little rest."

"Willie, other people get tired, but they don't pass out."

"I know. That's what I can't figure out."

Mays never did figure it out. Nor did any doctor. Perhaps the specter of five consecutive nights of speeches or acting at the behest of the vice president raised his anxiety level, or perhaps even in the off-season he was not getting enough rest. In the meantime, Shemano returned to San Francisco, and Mays recuperated with Franks, who himself was recovering from surgery. The two had long conversations, and Franks expressed his concern for Mays's financial well-being. Mays still owed the IRS $16,240, and Franks didn't care for his current adviser.

"I don't think Shemano's doing a damn thing for you," he said. "For the next five years, you'll make more than a million bucks, and you'll end up broke."

Franks offered to make his own "tax man" available to Mays. He also encouraged Mays to invest his money with him, but he made a demand: "You have to quit Jake Shemano."

A war was on between two headstrong men, Franks and Shemano, over what was best for Mays. When Mays returned to San Francisco, he told Shemano about Franks's recommendation that he change accountants. Shemano had already provided him with one, and he said that Franks's accountant could not be trusted. Franks was also unhappy about Mays's deferred income, as negotiated by Shemano; Franks thought the income should be paid and invested. Both men had similar motives: they considered Mays their friend and wanted to help him, but they also recognized his value as their business partner. Just as Mays was an ambassador for Shemano's bank, Mays could help Franks recruit other ballplayers to invest their money with him.

In theory, both men could have worked with Mays, but the antagonism between them was personal. At one point, Franks went to Shemano's bank and argued bitterly with him over Mays's finances. Mays would have to choose between the man who saved him, financially, during one of the lowest points of his life, and the man who had shared a locker room with him off and on since 1951 and now promised him riches.

Mays chose Franks. Years later, he says the decision was practical. Franks was going to earn him money whereas Shemano could only take care of it. "Sometimes when you have a friend who's going to make you money, sometimes you have to lean on him," Mays says. But the baseball connection was also a factor. No matter how grateful Mays was to Shemano and his family, they could never have the same standing as his manager. Shemano felt betrayed, and the break was complete—Shemano stopped talking to Mays, who severed ties with Shemano's bank and returned his silence with silence.

The economic consequences of this decision are in dispute. In an interview several months before he died, Franks said Mays received outstanding returns on his real estate investments, though he offered no specifics, and he took credit for digging Mays out of his financial hole. Mays says he received checks for many years from those investments but is vague about details. Others believe he is protecting his friend. Sy Berger, a retired baseball card executive at the Topps Company who has known Mays since 1951 and is one of his closest friends, says, "I constantly told Willie, 'Herman did nothing for you. He lives off you. You don't live off Herman.' And he told me, 'No, no, no. Herman is a good guy.'"

What is clear is that when Mays retired, he was still living paycheck to paycheck, and Franks's overlapping roles—financial adviser, investment partner, and baseball manager—created conflicts of interest that would never be tolerated today.

The real tragedy, however, was not financial but personal. When Mayor Christopher left office in 1964, Jake Shemano lost his patron at City Hall. Business suffered, Golden Gate National Bank's stock price cratered, and the enterprise failed. "My father ended up losing everything," Jake's son Gary says.

Years passed, and Jake Shemano would not reach out to the man to whom he had once devoted so much of his life. Maybe he was too hurt; maybe he was embarrassed by his own financial setbacks. But the breach between the two men was never closed. In the 1970s, Shemano was stricken with prostate cancer; the treatments failed, and in 1977 he was in the hospital, dying, when he told his family he wanted to see Willie, to talk, to make amends.

Mays, retired from baseball, lived in the Bay Area, and Gary called the person who screened all of his requests. "My dad's got a couple of days left," Gary said, "and he would love to see Willie."

Mays never showed up. He sent a get-well card instead.

"It broke my heart," Gary says, "because I saw my dad's heart break. The only thing he asked for was that he wanted to see Willie." Now in his sixties, Gary acknowledges that the correct message may not have been forwarded to Mays, but the pain lingers. "I'll probably take it to my grave," he says.

Mays, when asked about the incident, says he has no recollection of getting a message about Shemano's illness, but even if he had, he would not have gone to the hospital because he never makes that kind of call. Visiting anonymous children was one thing, but he would not see acquaintances or intimates. "I was a guy who couldn't handle that," he says. "I couldn't handle someone dying who I really enjoyed being around. . . . Maybe [Shemano's family] didn't understand me at the time."

Mays talks about his need to be surrounded by "happy things," which is why he rarely goes to funerals, and when he does, he will not look in an open casket and will often leave early. When he is watching television, he will click to a different channel to avoid a scene that is particularly violent or sad. On one level, his ability to shield himself from hardships and forget past misfortunes has served him well. He does not drown in yesterday's sorrows. But on other matters he has a sharp memory—anyone who slights him will not return to his good graces. That may be understandable for a man who has often felt exploited, but nothing can justify his neglect of those who genuinely care for him.

His indifference toward Jake Shemano was one example, a reminder that Mays was never good at the intricacies of friendship. He takes pride in helping friends, and had Shemano asked for money, Mays would have sent it, in cash. But what Shemano needed—empathy, reconciliation, a piece of Willie's heart—Willie couldn't give.

Shemano's son Richard maintained his friendship with Mays, which led to arguments with his brother. But Richard died in 2003, and Gary, who runs an investment firm in San Francisco, has made his own peace with the man he idolized as a boy. Mays called him one day when he needed help assessing the value of his memorabilia. Gary sent his son, who's in the jewelry business. The ice was broken. A friendship was renewed. Gary now visits Mays at his home, he calls him on his birthday, and he worries about him. The two do not speak of his father.

The best thing that ever happened to Willie Mays was Mae Louise Allen, who could draw out his warmth and humanity as few others could. Ask a hundred people about Mae, and you'll hear a hundred glowing comments. The word "saint" is sometimes invoked, and if any man ever found one, Willie did in her.

The actual romance, had it been a Hollywood script, would have been rejected as a mawkish fable. It began with a chance encounter between a beautiful maiden's doting mother and a shy, handsome prince from the big city. Years later, the young girl miraculously meets her lonely idol; moving from coast to coast over the next two decades, they realize great success in their separate endeavors and forge a lasting bond but are unable to pledge their eternal love.

It pretty much happened that way.

Mae Allen's family lived in the racially integrated Homewood section of Pittsburgh. Mae's mother, Clara, was a tall, slender woman who loved fashion and cosmetics and sometimes modeled for Revlon. She was also a big sports fan, and when she traveled to New York in 1952 for Revlon, she visited the Red Rooster, hoping to secure an autograph from her hero,

Jackie Robinson. The owner told her that the Dodgers were out of town, but she might like an autograph from a young Giant who was going to be the next superstar. She met Willie Mays, who gave her an autographed picture of himself, and was impressed by the nice, clean-cut young man.

"You're going to marry my daughter someday," she said (a comment Mays had heard before).

Mae was only thirteen, and she was disappointed with the photograph. She had been expecting Jackie Robinson. An only child, she resembled her mother in height, physique, and beauty, with soft shoulder-length hair, high cheekbones, and caramel-colored skin, and she modeled at *Ebony* fashion fairs in Pittsburgh. She was not brash like her mother but was closer in temperament to her father, Emmett, a proud, soft-spoken man who was an excellent tennis player and hardworking chauffeur. He was also a baseball fan, and when the Giants were in town, he would take Mae to Forbes Field to watch the player whose signed photograph she possessed, the great Willie Mays.

Mae was an active, popular teenager who ran sprints for a YWCA track team, marched in her high school drum and bugle corps, worked as a camp counselor, and loved the outdoors. She attended the University of Pittsburgh, part of a small group of black students at the school in the late 1950s, and found a home as a member of the Alpha Kappa Alpha sorority; she earned her degree in sociology.

After graduating in 1960, she was allowed to take a vacation with two girlfriends to Atlantic City, where she was introduced to a rookie basketball player named Wilt Chamberlain, who played for the Philadelphia Warriors. "Wilt was just coming off a tour," Mae recalled. "He had the biggest Cadillac I ever saw and a big pocket full of money—like $10,000 in cash. We had a lot of fun and remained friends through the years."

The following year, on a Sunday night, Chamberlain was at Small's Paradise, a Harlem club he owned, when Willie Mays walked in. The previous Sunday he had hit four home runs in Milwaukee, so Ed Sullivan had invited him on his show. After his appearance on May 7, he had time to kill. When he saw Chamberlain, he said he was heading for Pittsburgh the following day.

"Man, do you know any girls there?" he asked.

"I know these girls I met last year," Chamberlain said. "This one girl is kind of square, but she has friends."

Mays took her phone number, and when he got to Pittsburgh, he called it.

Mae was home from graduate school at Howard University in Washington. She had just picked up a newspaper when the phone rang.

The caller asked for Mae Louise Allen.

"Speaking," she said.

"You don't know me, but I'm Willie Mays."

She assumed some prankster knew of her fondness for Mays—she considered herself "a super fan"—and was now playing a joke. She had no time for jokes. "Yes," she said, "and I'm Martha Washington."

She hung up and, as usual, the first section she pulled out of the paper was the sports page. The headline read: MAYS & CO. IN TOWN TO PLAY BUCS. Mae gasped, wondering if that could have possibly been him. If it was, what had she just done?

Willie called again, explained how he had her phone number, and asked if she liked baseball.

She said she did but was a fan of the Pirates and Dodgers.

Willie invited her to the game, and she went with her father and two girlfriends. They met him afterward and thanked him, with Mae's father scrutinizing him carefully. "He wasn't sure about him," Mae recalled.

Willie asked her out to dinner but said, being a ballplayer, he had a curfew.

"I have one too," she assured him.

Before he left town, he took her to dinner, and he brought McCovey along.

They stayed in touch as Mae returned to graduate school. After she received her master's degree in social work, she moved to San Francisco. Willie wasn't the only reason. Pittsburgh, the country's steel capital, offered few opportunities for a young, highly educated black woman, and Mae had always dreamed of moving to California. But Willie was the true draw.

"She thought Willie was her soul mate from the first time they met," says her cousin Judi Phillips. "She never dated another person, and needless to say, she had tons of admirers."

It was a difficult time. Willie was still going through his divorce and wasn't prepared to get seriously involved. "I couldn't figure out what he wanted with me," Mae recalled. "Willie is only seven years older than me, but at that time it seemed like a lot. He was also very famous. But he was shy, and I liked him."

Mae built her own life. She got an apartment and found a job as a child welfare worker in the adoption division of the San Francisco Department of Social Services. She became, according to the *Chronicle*, "a pioneer in getting single adoptions started in San Francisco."

Over the years, Willie's relationship with Mae ebbed and flowed, and he dated other women, but they were never apart for long. Though the women's movement was gaining steam, Willie was still a Depression product of the Deep South who clung to traditional views. He would forbid Mae, for example, to wear short skirts or show cleavage. In 1974, Mays appeared on Merv Griffin's show with the actress Marlo Thomas, and he was asked, "What do you think women's role should be?"

Mays said, "Women belong in the kitchen."

He was roundly booed, and Thomas, an outspoken feminist, was aghast.

"Hey, that's the way I feel about it," Mays said. "You asked me, so I told you." It was the last time he made such a comment in public.

The irony was that Willie loved a woman who did not stay in the kitchen but seemed to satisfy the feminist ideal—a financially independent professional who was not tethered to a man for her own happiness. Mae was his opposite in so many ways, possessing the very traits that he lacked and, in some cases, coveted. Mae had an advanced degree. She was expressive and spoke with precise diction and grammar. She was organized and careful with her budget. She was comfortable in front of strangers and courteous to a fault. She liked the arts. She trusted others. She hugged friends.

Willie never had to work that hard at courtship, which was just as well, for he disdained the whole process. Even the most innocuous gesture, such as holding hands, did not come naturally; Mae had to teach him the grammar of affection. When they started dating, they went out with their friends Jessie and Buddy Goins, and when Buddy held Jessie's hand, Mae exclaimed, "See, that's what you're supposed to do!"

Other times Mae put her arm around Willie, who said, "What are you doing, girl?"

"What do you mean?"

Willie shrugged. "Okay."

Or Mae teased him. "Come on, I dare you to kiss me in front of everybody."

"You're crazy," he responded.

Willie was so absorbed in baseball, so entrenched in a male world, that sometimes he simply forgot about Mae. On one occasion, he drove Mae to the ballpark, and after the game he headed to the parking lot, got into his car, and was getting ready to leave. He only stopped when he saw Mae running after him.

But Mae understood the pressures on Willie—those that he imposed on himself and those from the public—and she saw in him the quiet decency of a man who was trying to do the right thing. "He's not a symbol," she said. "Oh, he's sexy and all, a real man. But he's not like Joe Namath. He's the guy in the white hat." Says Gary Shemano, "She saw a side to his soul that was much more enduring than what we might see on the outside."

Their most obvious bond was baseball. Willie and Mae played catch, and to her friends' dismay, Willie threw the ball hard, but Mae held her ground and fired it right back. At Candlestick she bought seat cushions for $1.75 apiece and flung them in the air when Willie hit a home run. They were in lockstep literally: Willie walked fast through crowds—otherwise he'd be mobbed—and Mae, the high school sprinter, kept pace.

"Mae was his biggest fan, and she loved him uncontrollably," Jessie Goins says.

The feeling was mutual, for Mae's tenderness and devotion triggered a response in Willie that few had seen. "Mae was Willie's catalyst," says another friend, Phil Saddler. "He adored her. She'd walk into a room, and he'd light up."

Throughout the 1960s, the gossip columnists tried to track who Mays was dating, but unlike other celebrity bachelors, he shunned the nightlife and was hard to pin down. When reporters asked when or if he was going to remarry, he expressed a desire to do just that but offered no specifics. He never mentioned Mae's name or introduced her at any public event. The years passed, and no proposal was forthcoming. The decade ended, and Willie and Mae remained together but single.

Willie was scared. Whenever the topic of marriage came up, he would walk away, and Mae didn't pressure him. "I don't know if this will ever happen, marriage-wise," she told her cousin. "But I'll be patient." She knew that the wounds from his first marriage hadn't healed. "Oh my goodness," she said. "I don't know that he'll ever trust again."

CHAPTER THIRTY-ONE

MILESTONES
AND MISERIES

On the field, Mays's acrobatic plays garnered the most attention, but his style and grace—his carefully applied eyeblack, his black wristbands, his two-tone spikes, his creased hat, his sunglasses that he effortlessly flipped down with the ball in midflight—always set him apart. Tim McCarver said that Mays was the only player he ever saw at the plate with buffed fingernails. Even the most mundane tasks left indelible impressions. A Cincinnati radio announcer, describing Mays sliding into third, marveled, "Willie surrounded that base like he was kissing it."

David Rapaport, one of the kids on Mays's block, recalls how at Candlestick Mays would pick up four bats as he prepared to hit: "He would swing them from behind his right shoulder until he swished them through the imaginary hitting zone, and a small cloud of dirt and pebbles would rise from just beneath him. Then he would settle on one bat and with one additional firm practice swing, he would crack it through the air like an electric whip."

Rapaport would sneak down to the box seats in the late innings, and in those days, he says, "with no sound system pummeling you, you could sometimes hear Willie's shirt tighten around his muscles as he swung, the threads of his uniform stretching enough to make [clubhouse attendant] Mike Murphy take out his sewing kit. Then he would step in, and the sound of his bat hitting the ball—*crack*—was like a high-pitched rimshot."

At the plate, Mays didn't walk around the batter's box, tediously rub dirt in his hands, or knock debris out of his spikes. He stepped in and hit. Joe Torre, catching for the Braves, once tried to break his concentration by not putting down a sign and making him wait. "I know what you're doing," Mays told him. On another occasion, Torre tried to engage him in conversation. "As he's hitting the ball out of the ballpark," Torre recalls, "he's answering my question."

The writer George Plimpton once pitched to Mays in a postseason All-

Star exhibition at Yankee Stadium. Plimpton, seeking fodder for a book, threw in a pregame batting contest. He faced the first batter and then, standing on the mound, heard "a mounting roar from the stands" when Mays appeared from the dugout and walked forward purposefully. Mays, Plimpton wrote, "gets set quickly at the plate, hopping eagerly into the batter's box, where he nervously jiggles and stamps his feet in the dust, twisting on his rear foot to get it solidly placed, staring down at the plate in concentration to sense when his legs feel set, and when they do he reaches out and taps the plate, twice, three times, with the bat before he sweeps it back over his right shoulder and cocks it. Then for the first time he looks out at the pitcher."

Plimpton then confronted that odd blend of innocence and fury:

> Most batters tuck their chins down and glower out at the pitcher from under the brims of their batting helmets—which makes them look properly sinister and threatening. Mays, on the other hand, has a pleasant face to start with, and he looks out at the pitcher with a full, honest regard, his chin out, his eyes wide as if slightly myopic. He seems to inspect the pitcher as if he were a harmless but puzzling object recently deposited on the mound by the groundskeeper. Furthermore, when Mays's face is set in determination, his eyebrows arch up so that under the batter's helmet his expression is that of a lingering look of astonishment. But the deception is mild; you see the coiled power of his stance as he waits.

Mays swung at the first strike he saw. "As the bat came through into the pitch, I could sense the explosive power and I flinched," Plimpton wrote. Mays could only manage a pop-up, but Plimpton would always remember "feeling the sudden terror of Mays uncoiling his bat."

Mays appeared to be a trendsetter. In the early 1960s, when baggy baseball pants were the norm, Mays had his tapered to increase his running speed, and that soon became the standard. When Mays entered the big leagues, fielders kept all of their fingers inside their glove. But Mays realized that he could control the glove better by sticking his left index finger outside the mitt. He doesn't claim credit for starting the trend, but eventually most players had their index fingers outside as well.

Mays's physical abilities verged on the supernatural. On one occasion, with the Braves' Hank Aaron at first base, the hitter drove a ball into deep right center. Mays caught it with his back to the infield, forcing Aaron, who had already passed second base, to make a hasty retreat. A strong throw to first might have doubled him off, but Mays wheeled around and threw to second instead, where Tito Fuentes was standing. Mays motioned for him to step on the bag, and the umpire called Aaron out. Aaron had failed to touch second base on his way back to first, and the double play was completed.

After the game, Mays was asked how he could have possibly seen Aaron miss the base when he was in the deepest part of right center and his back was to the play. "I know the way he runs," he said.

Mays always said he didn't play for records, which was true but not the entire story. By the second half of his career, he was very much aware of the records and where he stood in relation to them. After he hit his five hundredth homer in 1965, he said he just wanted to keep winning and didn't really count his long balls. Then a reporter asked, "Do you know you're only eleven behind Mel Ott now?"

"Sure," Mays said. "It's Ott 511, then Ted Williams 521, then Jimmie Foxx 534, and then the Babe—he's too far in front. He's got 714."

In 1966, Mays became the second greatest power hitter in the history of the game while he also raised the possibility that he could challenge Ruth. But the year also marked the beginning of Mays's decline. He was still an outstanding player and could do things, on the bases and in the field, that his peers could only dream about, but hints of his baseball mortality would soon be evident.

Mays's assault on Mel Ott's 511 drew considerable attention; league achievements were taken more seriously in the days before free agency, which accelerated the players' movement between leagues. In addition to the television cameras and sportswriters, the quest attracted John Gregory Dunne, a writer who as a college student had seen Mays's first homer and now wanted to write about his record-breaker for the *Saturday Evening Post*.

Dunne's account broadened the lens on Mays's historic effort. In Houston, he described a brief anecdote at the swank Shamrock Hotel, where the Giants stayed but also where the Texas Butane Dealers Association was meeting. When Mays walked into the lobby amid the horde of butane dealers, one said loudly, "Who's the nigra?"

"That ain't no nigra," his friend said. "That's Willie Mays."

"Well, what do you know," the butane dealer said. "I've got to get his autograph." He went after Mays, calling, "Hey, boy."

Dunne wrote: "If Mays heard, he gave no notice."

Thanks to a blistering start, it appeared Mays would quickly overtake Ott. On April 24 in Houston, in the team's twelfth game, he hit his sixth home run of the year, which tied Ott at 511 and prompted the Astro fans to give him a standing ovation. Dunne described the scene in the clubhouse afterward, where a phalanx of reporters and photographers surrounded Mays, who sat naked at his locker except for a uniform shirt he had pulled on for those with cameras. Before the game, he had to ice his bruised left hand, and he skipped batting and fielding practice, which he no longer took on day games after night games. Now he submitted to the postgame ritual.

"Were you thinking of Ott when you circled the bases, Willie?"

"No."

"What were you thinking?"

"Tie score."

The Giants went on to win.

The spectator who caught the home run ball was a brakeman who'd driven 150 miles to the game. Afterward, he came to the clubhouse with the ball and wanted to sell it.

"A lot of foul balls went into the stands today," Herman Franks said. "How do I know this is the one?"

"You don't," the fan said. "You just gotta take my word for it."

"I'll give you fifty dollars for it," Franks said.

The brakeman took the money and counted it.

"Christ," Franks said. "He doesn't trust me."

Franks popped the cork on a bottle of champagne. Mays didn't drink it but put the glass to his lips for the cameras. A photographer then asked Franks to pour some of the bubbly on Mays's head.

"Not that picture again," Franks said. "Don't you guys ever get any new ideas?" With a disgusted look, Franks asked Mays if he minded. Mays shook his head, dutifully bent over, and absorbed the dunking.

By the time Mays could finally shower, the clubhouse was nearly empty. He was asked if he wanted ball number 511.

"Naw," he said. "It's Herman's fifty. Let him keep it. All it means to me is something else to dust."

The Giants were returning to San Francisco for ten games, which meant Mays would almost certainly break the record at home. In the photographer's booth at Candlestick, fifteen television crews settled in to record the milestone. The club announced that it would give $100 to the fan who caught the historic ball. A huge cake, inscribed with 512 in silver sugar beads, was prepared for the celebration. Then Mays stopped hitting. Not just home runs, but any kind of hits.

He started thinking about 512 and began pressing, first against the Braves and the Reds, then the Cardinals and finally the Dodgers. He found himself in one of his classic swoons. And he was sick. He came down with a cold, had an upset stomach, got diarrhea. He was taken out of one game against the Reds and ordered home. The next day, he returned to the park shortly before the game, but Franks sent him back home.

Mays was in the lineup the following day, but the reporters tried his patience. Asked if he was thinking about the record, Mays snapped, "How can I not think of the record. You guys remind me of it every time I turn around." Against the Cardinals, he stumbled over first base trying to beat out a hit and limped off the field. Wrote Bob Stevens: "For days, it really wasn't Mays at the plate. Bats slipped out of his hands; he lunged desperately at the ball, trying too hard. He was awkward, robbed of his rhythm by the torment in which he was living."

Not everyone despaired. A freelance cameraman, on hearing that in 1965 Mays had once gone seventeen games without hitting a homer, said, "I hope he never hits the son of a bitch. I get $82.50 a game every day I'm out here."

John Gregory Dunne, meanwhile, was having no luck at interviewing Mays. He knew that Mays had adopted a son, and Dunne and his wife, Joan Didion, had recently adopted a child as well, so he approached Mays during batting practice and told him about their common bond.

"How 'bout that," Mays said wearily. Nothing more was volunteered.

Dunne then tracked down one of Mays's good friends, the Reverend Peter Keegan, at St. Cecilia's Roman Catholic Church. It was May 4, and Father Keegan told Dunne that he had just had lunch with Mays and had given him some rosary beads and a St. Christopher's medal.

"For good luck?" Dunne asked.

"Actually, it's for his birthday Friday. But it won't do any harm, and if it works, I suppose you could call it a good-luck charm."

Dunne had another question: "Did you talk about the record?"

"I told him he's been pressing and he was going to hit it tonight."

"What did he say?"

"He said, 'I hope so, Father.'"

When Dunne saw Mays before the game, he said he'd met with Father Keegan.

"Boy," Mays said, shaking his head. "You guys are really following me around."

Only two games remained on the home stand, and that night, in front of 28,220, the Giants faced Claude Osteen, who had not surrendered a home run in ninety-two innings. He struck out Mays the first two times, but in the fifth he threw Mays a straight change—the first change Mays had seen in ages—which he hit over the right field fence. The fans stood for more than five minutes and screamed, "We want Willie!" Mays was engulfed by his teammates at the lip of the dugout but went back out to tip his cap. The crowd wouldn't be quiet, repeating its rhythmic "We want Willie" until Mays had to come out a second time. Not until he went to center field did the fans settle down, only to rise again when he came to bat.

Hal Lanier almost broke into tears when the ball cleared the fence. "My insides were shaking," he said. Giant rookie Ollie Brown said, "It was an honor to play in the same game." The *Chronicle* editorialized: "There is some belief that the prolonged outpouring of human emotion turned on by Willie Mays's bat amounted to the greatest ovation ever offered by this community. . . . It contained one other element of note. It contained affection—affection for Willie Mays, a popular hero of the first magnitude who once feared that San Francisco didn't like him."

Osteen grumbled: "It was just another home run . . . a lousy pitch."

Nine games had passed since 511; Mays had had only three hits in twenty-three at-bats; his average had tumbled from .348 to .277. "I know that reporters and TV guys have jobs to do," he said, "but there are times when I wish I could hide for a few hours, just to have some time for myself. I don't mean to gripe. It's just that I have more fun playing ball than I do giving interviews."

After the final out, Mays was interviewed on two postgame shows, then made it to the clubhouse, where for thirty minutes he stood before flashing bulbs, television lights, microphones, and quarreling journalists.

"What do you feel?" one asked.

"Relief," he said.

A cameraman told him, "I took a shot at every pitch you saw the past ten days."

"So did I," Mays said.

He smiled for the photographers, though the only time he seemed pleased was when a reporter said, "Willie, you're a great credit to the game of baseball."

"Why, thanks, man," Mays said.

The cake was rolled out. According to Dunne, it "was so stale that it crumbled like a tenement under the wrecker's ball." Mays held a piece to his mouth, was photographed, then threw it back on the table. Franks whispered to him that the fan who caught the ball was demanding $1,000.

"One thousand dollars?" Mays said. "He can keep it."

But Franks had heard wrong. The fan, seventeen-year-old Henry Garron, was in the clubhouse and had made his way to Mays's locker. It appeared his father thought the ball was worth more than the $100 that the Giants were offering. "I didn't ask for $1,000," he told Mays. "Will you sign it for me?"

"I'd be glad to," said the exhausted home run king. "Be my guest, and keep it."

• • •

Mays hit number 522 against Bob Gibson on June 27, which moved him past Ted Williams, with only Ruth and Jimmie Foxx ahead of him. The UPI's lead on its story of the game was: "When you're only No. 3, you have to try harder." Mays did, and at Candlestick on August 17, against the Cardinals' Ray Washburn, he passed Foxx at 534, making him the top right-handed home run hitter of all time. "That one," Mays said, "kind of sang itself out of the park." It's noteworthy that Mays's two landmark home runs at Candlestick, 512 and 535, were hit to right field, where Mays had been forced to redirect his power because of the winds. His four hundredth homer was also hit to right.

As he crossed the plate for 535, umpire Chris Pelekoudas, violating protocol and good sense, extended his hand, and Mays shook it. The umpire quickly realized his error and turned sheepishly to the Cardinal dugout, as if seeking dispensation. He later said, "We're supposed to be impartial, and I suppose an umpire shouldn't do a thing like that. But when a man reaches baseball immortality—well, I'm not sorry I did it."

Mays ended the season with thirty-seven homers, which was third best in the league, and he may be the only player in history to have hit homers in more parks (eleven) than there were teams (ten) in a given season. The Cardinals moved into their new stadium after the season began, and Mays had hit one out of both the old park and the new. In another rare feat, he threw out three runners in Los Angeles on May 17—one at home, first, and third. He would have had the throwing equivalent of a hitting cycle, except Tito Fuentes missed a tag at second base. "Mays threw so many baserunners out he may lead the entire Giant infield in assists," Jim Murray quipped in the *Los Angeles Times*.

Mays was again the leadoff hitter at the 1966 All-Star Game, played in St. Louis to celebrate the opening of Busch Memorial Stadium. The contest was primarily remembered for the heat—105 degrees. Hundreds of fans collapsed, and smelling salts and oxygen were required in the dugouts. Cruelly, the game went ten innings, with the National League finally winning, 2–1. Mays played every inning. So did several other players, though Mays was the oldest.

Thirty-seven years later, Major League Baseball, in conjunction with Fox Sports, tried to raise the stakes of the All-Star Game by giving home field advantage in the World Series to the victorious league. "This time it counts," fans were told.

Whenever Willie Mays took the field, it counted.

• • •

Orlando Cepeda, coming off a knee injury, didn't get along with Herman Franks any better than he did with Alvin Dark, and he was traded to the Cardinals nineteen games into the season. Heartbroken at first, Cepeda found the clubhouse atmosphere in St. Louis far more relaxed and, installed at first base, he thrived, leading the Cardinals to two pennants and one world championship while winning the MVP in 1967.

Mays was disappointed by the trade, in part because the Cardinals sent the Giants pitcher Ray Sadecki, whom Mays had always hit well.

Mays had lost a step by 1966, but that didn't deter his audacious baserunning, which was on full display when the Giants visited Los Angeles on September 7. So too was his showmanship.

Both teams, as usual, were battling for first place, and the Wednesday game drew 54,993 fans. Mays, hobbled by a pulled thigh muscle, started in right field for the second straight game, which went into the twelfth inning. Mays came to bat with two outs, and on a pitch in the dirt, Johnny Roseboro blocked the ball so it popped straight up. Mays stuck out his bat, caught the ball on the very tip, balanced it for several moments, then calmly flipped it back to Roseboro. The crowd roared at this impromptu but utterly natural act.

Mays then limped to first base on a walk, and the next hitter looped a single into right center, where the right fielder, Lou Johnson, chased it down. Johnson had no play on Mays at third, so he threw it to second, keeping the hitter at first and setting up a forceout. It was the right throw.

But Mays had his own calculation. It was extra innings, there were two outs, and the Giants' bullpen had already been taxed. So when second baseman Jim Lefebvre received the throw and looked up, Mays was hurtling toward the plate. Lefebvre threw home; Roseboro caught the ball and braced himself. Mays crashed into him, which left both men on the ground in a swirl of dirt. "Out!" yelled umpire Tony Venzon. But Mays sat up and pointed to the ground where the ball now lay. Venzon followed Mays's finger, then cried, "No, goddamn safe!"

Despite his scoring the go-ahead run, the Dodger fans applauded Mays as he limped to the dugout. Roseboro was charged with an error, and the Giants won on the unearned run. In the clubhouse, the reporters asked Mays how he could make that play on a bad leg.

The team had a plane to catch, he said.

The Giants flew out of Los Angeles a half game out of first, then lost three in a row and eight out of their next twelve, and were four games out when they left on their final road trip.

Then came more race riots. San Francisco experienced its own convulsions, and Mays's life again overlapped, but in a positive way, with the turmoil of the outside world.

On the evening of September 27, a black teenager who was pulled over for speeding fled from the vehicle, and a white police officer fired two shots. The officer later said they were meant as warning shots, but they struck the youth and killed him. Within minutes, the Hunters Point district, which is next to Candlestick, was a riot zone. Mobs looted stores, lit fires, and overturned cars. A curfew imposed by Mayor Jack Shelley was ignored, and 349 people were arrested. As the violence continued the following morning, the mayor concluded that force alone could not keep the rioters off the street. Maybe a baseball game would.

He asked the Giants if they would work with television station KTVU and another station in Atlanta, where the Giants were playing, to televise their contest that night. The arrangements were quickly made, and the afternoon papers put the agreement for the televised game on the front page. But someone was needed to make a direct appeal to the residents of the city to watch the game. That choice was obvious.

Mays was reached in his hotel room, informed of the crisis, and within twenty minutes, his taped message was on its way to ten different radio stations in the Bay Area. The script made no reference to the riots, raised no alarms, and implied no threats. All it carried was the moral authority of the messenger.

"This is Willie Mays," the announcement began. "Channel 2 is carrying a special program, a game against the Atlanta Braves at six o'clock. I, for one, wish and hope each and every one will be tuned in, wishing us well. I'll be out in center field trying to do my best."

The announcement aired almost three hundred times. An hour before the game, shooting broke out in Hunters Point and a large fire was set. But shortly after the broadcast started, the unrest diminished, and by the time the game ended, the rioting had come to a virtual halt. Both Mayor Shelley and the chief of police, Tom Cahill, said the broadcast played a major role in restoring peace, and the ratings supported that view: citywide, the telecast ranked number 1 with 33 percent of the market, and in the riot areas, the game captured a 42 percent share. Many people received credit, including the Giants' executives, who waived the fees, and Russ Hodges and Lon Simmons, who worked the telecast for free. Mays had played a supporting role in a frightening urban drama, and his contribution added to his standing as a peacemaker.

And the Giants won the game.

• • •

It was a great time to be a National League fan. In 1965, the six top teams entered September within 3½ games of one another. The following year, five teams vied for the pennant down the stretch. The Giants and Dodgers set all-time league records in 1965 for road attendance, which they surpassed the following year. Unfortunately for the Giants, the outcomes were the same. In 1966, they won eight out of their last nine games but came in second place for the third consecutive season. In Koufax's final year, the Dodgers won by 1½ games.

Mays did his part. He led the Giants in runs (99) and RBIs (103), and he had more than 300 total bases for the thirteenth straight year, tying Lou Gehrig's record. He also played in 152 games, marking his thirteenth consecutive year with more than 150 games, a record that still stands. (Cal Ripken, Jr.'s string of twelve was broken by the strike-shortened season of 1994.) But Mays hit .288, his lowest batting average since his abbreviated season in 1952, and he never had that one torrid streak that had lifted him in past years. His five stolen bases were also his lowest since 1952. Ironically, in a season of home run milestones, his drop in long balls may have been the clearest sign of aging. He still led the Giants with thirty-seven, but that was a 29 percent decline from the previous year and his lowest total since 1960.

No one knew it at the time, but 1966 was the final year that Mays closely resembled the player who had stood astride the league for so many years. He would never bat .300 again, or hit thirty homers, or reach triple figures in runs scored or RBIs, or play in 150 games. While he could not have foreseen all that, he was a realist, and he tried to dampen speculation about reaching 714. One hundred and seventy-two homers behind, he'd have to average more than thirty-four long balls a year for five more years. "I think that record is here to stay," he said. "I'm thirty-five."

In 1967, the Giants got off to their worst start since moving to San Francisco, losing seven out of eight, and Mays began just as badly. In the third game of the season, he tore a hamstring muscle on a wet field in Atlanta, which cost him five games. On June 7, nineteen-year-old rookie Gary Nolan struck him out four times, which had never happed to Mays before. (The next time they faced each other, in June, Mays did hit a home run.) Bill Singer, a twenty-three-year-old Dodger pitcher, struck out Mays three times in one game, and the next time Singer pitched against the Giants, he struck him out in the first inning, after which Mays took himself out of the game.

For the first time in thirteen All-Star games, Mays was not elected to start. His numbers were solid—batting .291, with thirteen homers and

forty-five RBIs—but the players, managers, and coaches voted for Lou
Brock to accompany Aaron and Clemente. Mays finished fourth and
for days was peppered with questions about his downgrade. Did he feel
slighted? Was he angry? Mays handled the questions with class. "Look,
time marches on," he said. "I'm honestly not disappointed at losing the
chance to be a starter. Let's face it. I'm not a kid anymore and there are so
many fine young outfielders coming up, and some are already here, that I
feel good just finishing as high in the voting as I did."

The All-Star Game did seem to represent a passing of an era, as both
Mays and Mantle entered the game as pinch hitters—and struck out.
Mays, however, stayed in, but he didn't look right and went 0-for-4 in the
National League's fifteen-inning victory. "He looked tired and weak and
sick," Ernie Banks said, "and he told me that was just how he felt."

Just how sick became clear several days later. July 14 was a cold night
at Candlestick, and before the game Mays began to shake. He had a fever
and told Franks he was better off in bed. Franks agreed but asked Mays to
hand in the lineup card and stay around for a while, so the Astros would
think he was available. Ty Cline started in Mays's place, but he pulled a
muscle hitting a first-inning double. Gaylord Perry had to pinch-run. The
only other extra outfielder was Jesus Alou, who had a leg injury, so the
next inning, Mays unbuttoned his jacket, grabbed his glove, and headed
for center field. But his legs were heavy, and the bat felt as if it weighed five
pounds. After he misplayed a line drive into a triple and struck out twice,
he took himself out of the game and went home.

The next day, Mays checked into St. Mary's Hospital in San Francisco,
where Stoneham placed him under the care of his personal physician, Dr.
Edmund Morrissey, a famed neurosurgeon. Initial reports indicated that
Mays had a bad flu, which he had been carrying for some time. Rest was
prescribed. Why a neurosurgeon was involved was never explained; but
the Giants were concerned about all aspects of Mays's health, and Stoneham trusted this particular doctor. Mays remained in the hospital for five
days, spurring another round of guesses. But there were no mysterious
ailments. The hospital was Mays's haven, in isolation from the public and
the press, where he could restore his strength. Later in the year, as his own
struggles and those of the Giants deepened, he said, "Some guys can go
0-for-4 the way I have and lose the way the Giants have and then go home
and sleep. Not me. I worry. They pay me to win, and when I don't win, I
worry and don't sleep." In the hospital he slept and had no worries, and he
could trust those nearby. Before he was released, as always, he visited the
pediatrics ward and distributed signed baseballs.

The Giants lost five of the six games that Mays missed. When he returned, he was supposed to be eased into the lineup, but in his first game back, on a hot day in Chicago, he played all twelve innings of an extra-inning contest, and he played all nine the next day. "I can't think just of myself," he said. "A lot of guys on this club don't make too much money, and I've got to think of them. If they can make money for finishing in fourth place, then I've got to help them make it."

He hadn't lost his passion for the game. Against the Dodgers on August 28, twenty-two-year-old right-hander Don Sutton hit Mays with a pitch, which prompted an angry stare. Mays soon found himself on second, and on a wild pitch he flew around third and headed home, trying to advance two bases on one errant pitch. Sutton ran to cover the plate. The ball and the runner, spikes high, were going to arrive at the same time. Sutton, wanting no part of this collision, stepped aside and let the throw sail past him. Mays slid home safely, but as he got up, he said, "I could have got you, kid."

As the season wore on, however, Mays couldn't regain his strength. After leaving St. Mary's, he only hit .227 for the rest of the season, and he had to take himself out of games. He was moved from second or third in the order to fifth. He would take twenty minutes of batting practice and not hit one ball over the fence. "Willie Mays," said Phillie manager Gene Mauch, "is not Willie Mays four times a game anymore."

On August 14, against the Braves, the Giants had a runner on third with one out and Jim Ray Hart was at the plate. Mays was on deck, and the unthinkable happened. The Braves intentionally walked Hart to get to Mays. "I was furious and embarrassed," Mays later said. "I was ready to tear down the stadium." He hit a single to right field instead.

It was a rare triumph in a dreary season. Though the Giants finished strong for second place, they were out of the race by the middle of August and ended 10½ games behind the Cardinals. Mays had the worst season of his career to date. In 141 games, he hit .263, drove in seventy, and scored eighty-three—all well below the .300/100/100 goal that he had established for himself. He hit twenty-two homers.

Sports Illustrated wrote a dolorous profile of Mays, "Say Hey No More." When a *Philadelphia Bulletin* columnist repeatedly asked Mays why he was sitting out, he refused to answer. "I'm keeping my thoughts to myself," he said. "You want a story, you write want you want." The columnist did just that: "Everybody thinks Willie Mays is nice, friendly, warm, sociable, fun-loving . . . a joy to be around. It will come as a shock to those out there in fantasyland that Willie Mays is cold, surly, suspicious, uncooperative. He is not an easy guy to talk to."

Other observers recognized that Mays's struggles disappointed his fans, including those in the press, because he was defying a perception that had taken deep root across the country. "Willie Mays," wrote the *Atlanta Constitution*'s Furman Bisher, "wasn't supposed to grow old. He was supposed to go on forever, his cap flying off as he broke the sound barrier on foot, face bright and two eyes twinkling like stars. Willie Mays was born for eternal youth. Age is acting in direct violation of that code."

This April 1955 cover of *Sports Illustrated,* with Mays, Durocher, and Laraine Day, led to a flood of angry letters.

(Courtesy of Getty Images)

Jackie Robinson praised Mays's athletic skills but bitterly criticized his unwillingness to speak out on civil rights.

(© Bettmann/CORBIS)

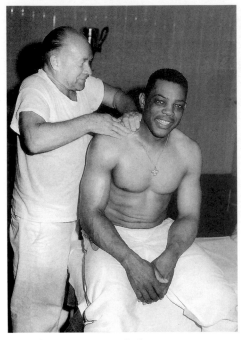

With Doc Bowman helping, Mays set a
record for durability by playing more than
150 games in thirteen consecutive years.
(Courtesy of Willie Mays)

Marghuerite Mays did not win much
public support when she told reporters
why she was divorcing Willie.
(Courtesy of the San Francisco History Center,
San Francisco Public Library)

To the delight of Giant owner Horace Stoneham (left) and manager
Bill Rigney, Willie was typically among the first to sign his contract.
(Courtesy of the San Francisco History Center, San Francisco Public Library)

The Giants' arrival in San Francisco in 1958 was celebrated as a watershed event in the evolution of a big league city.
(Courtesy of the San Francisco History Center, San Francisco Public Library)

Mays was the face of MLB's expansion to California, but it took several years for San Francisco to embrace him.
(Courtesy of the San Francisco History Center, San Francisco Public Library)

In the 1960s, the National League fielded far more black and Latin players than the American League, and future Hall of Famers such as Roberto Clemente, Mays, and Hank Aaron ensured the senior circuit's dominance in All-Star games. (Courtesy of Willie Mays)

The Giants were MLB's star-studded melting pot, as shown by Felipe Alou, Jim Davenport, Mays, Juan Marichal, and Orlando Cepeda, who were named to the 1962 All-Star Game. (Courtesy of the San Francisco History Center, San Francisco Public Library)

Mays's return to the Polo Grounds in 1962 renewed a love affair between player and city. (Courtesy of the San Francisco History Center, San Francisco Public Library)

Mays's furious baserunning often resulted in collisions, and more than a few opponents—in this case, Phillie catcher Pat Corrales—got the worst of it.
(© Bettmann/CORBIS)

Mays's finest moment on the baseball field occurred during a 1965 bat-wielding brawl at Candlestick, which ended only when Mays pulled Dodger catcher Johnny Roseboro off the field.
(Courtesy of Neil Leifer)

In an image that captures the sad end of his career, Mays pleads with umpire Augie Donatelli, who had called Bud Harrelson out at the plate in the 1973 World Series.
(© Bettmann/CORBIS)

Mays took great pride in his physical fitness, maintaining his body weight
and his thirty-two-inch waist throughout his career.

(Courtesy of FinalShot.com)

© J. Warren

Mae Allen Mays set aside her career as a social worker
to be Willie's life partner and soul mate.

(Courtesy of Willie Mays)

Mays's long history of helping children reflects his belief that kids, unlike adults, will always appreciate your efforts and will never betray you.
(Courtesy of Willie Mays)

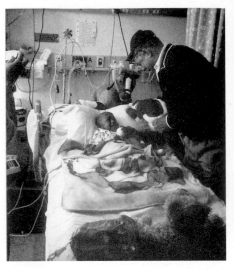

Beyond baseball, Mays wants his legacy to be his Say Hey Foundation, which is dedicated to supporting organizations for children.
(Courtesy of Willie Mays)

Mays met Senator Barack Obama even before he announced his candidacy for the White House. In fulfilling one more dream, Mays rode with President Obama on *Air Force One* to attend the 2009 All-Star Game in St. Louis.
(Courtesy of Willie Mays)

CHAPTER THIRTY-TWO

A DOCTRINE OF
BROTHERHOOD

During spring training of 1968, Jackie Robinson again put Willie Mays in his crosshairs. In a television interview in San Francisco, Robinson was asked if black Giant players had done enough for the civil rights movement. He said they hadn't and characterized Mays, Willie McCovey, and Jim Ray Hart as "do-nothing" Negroes. Mays in particular should have been more active, Robinson said, because he had been denied housing in San Francisco. The words echoed Robinson's criticism of Mays three years earlier, and talking with the *Los Angeles Times*, Robinson added a twist: "Willie Mays has a personality that is loved by white Americans, and I think he will be one of the first Negroes to move into a front office position."

It was not a compliment. As the *Chicago Daily Defender*'s A. S. "Doc" Young noted, "Any Negro who makes it in the white man's world is, automatically, an Uncle Tom."

Mays was twice awakened by reporters seeking a comment about Robinson's "do-nothing" claim, and he said he wanted to hold a press conference before a spring training game in Phoenix to "make my position clear." Now almost thirty-seven, he responded in part because he believed he had to stick up for McCovey and Hart, two of the shyest players on the team. Straddling a metal chair in Herman Franks's office, Mays spoke in a low, even voice—according to Bob Stevens, "his face clearly revealing the sincerity that was in his heart, and also some of the hurt that was in Robinson's finger pointing."

Mays began by paying tribute to Robinson, noting that he himself could not have done what Robinson had done in breaking the color barrier. "It took a special kind of man to do that, and Robinson had that quality," Mays said. "He had a college education and that helped." What Robinson began, others have built upon, Mays said. "Great progress has been made since Jackie broke in. Jackie is a great reason behind that progress. I really admire the guy."

Mays paused and breathed deeply. "But I don't think he should go around pointing accusing fingers at other guys, particularly nice guys like Willie and Jimmy Ray. Different people do things in different ways. I can't, for instance, go out and picket. I can't stand on a soapbox and preach. That simply isn't my nature. People like Mr. King and Mr. [Roy] Wilkins are better equipped than I am. But it's not true what Robinson said about my not doing anything about race relationships. I've worked for the Job Corps, and I don't know how many kids' groups I've addressed and will continue to address. In my own way, I believe I'm helping."

Mays mentioned McCovey and Hart again: "You know Willie and Jim Ray. They're quiet guys. Jim Ray is just a happy-go-lucky guy and McCovey is simply quiet. But in Willie's case, I believe he's gotta start speaking up more. When I leave the Giants, McCovey will be the number-one Giant, and he'll have to go out and talk to the people and get to know them, just like I've had to and enjoy doing.

"You see," he continued, "I've been doing things a long time along this line, but I want no credit. Everyone must do his own job in his own way, and in my heart, my way is just as important as Jackie Robinson's way. I believe understanding is the important thing. In my talks to kids, I've tried my best to get that message across. It makes no difference whether you are black or white because we are all God's children fighting for the same cause."

Mays pointed toward the dressing room, where the players were noisily preparing to take the field. "Let's talk about that progress for awhile. Just look around out there in the clubhouse. There are an awful lot of southern boys on this team. Yet we live and play together in harmony. It was not possible fifteen, sixteen years ago. Today's kids don't have the hardships Jackie and I had, and they realize it and appreciate it. Today, for instance, we play as many as five or six Negroes at the same time on our ball club, and once in Atlanta we had eight or nine in there at the same time, and Atlanta is a southern town." He added, "I believe that if a man wants to go with his Negro friends, he does no slight on the white players. I like to be alone a lot."

Mays said that even when he had been victimized, his tactful approach had opened doors for others. "Look, ten years ago, you remember I had a little difficulty buying a house in San Francisco. You can't blame the people or the city for what happened back then. It was the contractor. But you can't blame him either, because he has a family and has to make a living. Now I live in a better area and in a bigger and fancier house. I think that I have the respect of the people of San Francisco, and this is important for all of us. I play all the golf courses. I'm the first Negro to be a member of the Concordia Club. I also belong to the Press Club. Now you know that wasn't possible ten years ago. And I haven't done these things and gotten these things by 'doing nothing.' "

The reporters were stunned. Mays rarely talked at length about anything, let alone a subject as sensitive as race. His comments tried to strike a delicate balance. Had he criticized Robinson, he would have inflamed a dispute that could have scarred baseball—its two most consequential black players at each other's throat—and set off a media frenzy. But Mays's praise of Robinson showed his grace; his defense of his own conduct, his spirit and sensibilities. One journalist said Mays's press conference was one of his finest hours.

Several weeks later, Mays was asked if he had prepared his remarks or if anyone had coached him. He shook his head. "I didn't need any help," he said. "When you speak from the heart, you don't need to read a statement or ask for help. Words come easy."

But the dustup wasn't over. After reading Mays's comments, Robinson sent a stinging letter to the *San Francisco Examiner.* "It's tragic when one so popular as Willie," he wrote, "feels a contribution in race relations is measured by the clubs he belongs to or how many golf courses he is able to play. One does not have to get on soapboxes to be a man, and it should be obvious to him that he does not have it made until every Negro has it made. . . . It seems to me that Willie Mays has made himself a hero in your eyes and in the eyes of some white Americans who believe we should be seen catching baseballs but should be silent when the rights of our people are at stake."

Robinson could not recognize that any great social movement needed a continuum of voices—the militants who would prod a reluctant country to change, and the conciliators who tried to find common ground among hostile factions. The *Examiner*'s Jim McGee, who had ghostwritten Mays's column in 1958, published an open letter to Robinson. "As you know," he wrote, Mays

made a plea for understanding and patience. That's his way and always has been. . . . His statement was not that of a man detached from the problems of his race. It was that of a concerned man who has never lost sight of the fact that he is a black man. It was a statement of far more depth and perception than anybody else in baseball had realized. It convinced many that Mays, if he wanted, could be the first black major league manager. . . . If he felt it would advance the cause of his race, he'd jump at it for that reason alone. . . .

[Willie Mays] was not trying to refute you. He was simply stating his own case. He was not seeking white hero worship. He was talking man to man for the right to differ without recrimination. As I recall, he said, "There is neither black nor white. We are all God's children." A profound statement pointing out the infinitely loving defect in God. He is color-blind.

Mays's hopes for patience and understanding were quickly overwhelmed. On April 4, on the balcony of a motel in Memphis, an assassin's bullet ripped through the right cheek of Martin Luther King, Jr. He was declared dead an hour later. Mays had met King only once, briefly, at the Fairmount Hotel in San Francisco, but he later described him as "my president" and adopted some of King's rhetoric from his haunting final speech in Memphis, the evening before his assassination, when he declared, "I've been to the mountaintop . . . and I have seen the promised land!"

In later years, Mays told black groups that "Dr. King" got to the mountaintop, "but instead of going to the mountain and stopping, we need to go over the mountain. That's what progress means. If not, we're going to come back down and everything is going to repeat itself."

King's martyrdom ignited riots that swept through more than 150 cities, and militants such as Stokely Carmichael and Rap Brown urged violent retaliation as the only response to America's assault on black people. Further traumas ensued: Robert Kennedy's assassination, street warfare at the Democratic National Convention, mounting death tolls in Vietnam, and growing protests on campuses.

Most athletes, fearing that controversy would hurt their professional standing, shunned politics and said little about the country's anguish, but by the middle to late 1960s, a handful of prominent African American athletes were embracing the black power or antiwar movement. Muhammad Ali refused his induction into the military. Jim Brown and Bill Russell talked about the country's exploitation of black athletes. At the 1968 Olympics in Mexico City, sprinters Tommie Smith and John Carlos raised their black-gloved fists on the medal stand as a sign of defiance and unity. Several black athletes, including UCLA's basketball star Kareem Abdul-Jabbar (still known as Lew Alcindor), boycotted the Olympics entirely. Even Hank Aaron spoke out. In an interview with *Jet* in 1966, he ripped Major League Baseball for paying blacks less money and denying them opportunities to manage or work in the front office. (Shortly after the interview was published, Monte Irvin was appointed to a new position in the commissioner's office.)

The grievances of black players were given much broader play in *Sports Illustrated* in an ambitious five-part series that began in July 1968. The magazine set out to topple the conventional wisdom that sports had benefited Negro athletes at either the college or professional level. "Increasingly," *Sports Illustrated* reported, "black athletes are saying that sport is doing a disservice to their race by setting up false goals, perpetuating prejudice and establishing an insidious bondage all its own. . . . Almost to a man, they are dissatisfied, disgruntled, and disillusioned. [They are] treated like subhumans by Paleolithic coaches who regard them as watermelon-eating idiots."

Such a story needed a foil—an emblem of passivity who seemed to blissfully accept his own exploitation. That man was Willie Mays.

In one respect, *Sports Illustrated* said, Mays created a false promise for black youths. "A white kid tries to become president of the United States," said one high school coach, "and all the skills and knowledge he picks up on the way can be used in a thousand different jobs. A black kid tries to become Willie Mays, and all the tools he picks up on the way are useless to him if he doesn't become Willie Mays."

More troubling, Mays was the tool of white racists who profited from blacks on the field but discriminated against them off it. "The black athlete was the institutionalized Tom, the white man's nigger," thundered Harry Edwards, a sociology professor described as a "fanatical superblack" who was urging an "athletic black rebellion," including an Olympic boycott. Edwards, himself a charismatic speaker, reserved his harshest criticism for the blacks who refused to speak out. They were, he said, "house niggers" and were worse than Alabama governor George Wallace. "At least we know where Wallace stands," he told one audience. "As long as you have black athletes making it to the top and then shutting up like Uncle Willie Mays . . . then athletics has done very little for the black community. It has helped black individuals to delude themselves, this is all." Edwards had a poster of "Negro Traitors," with articles on Willie Mays attached to it.

Sports Illustrated opined that "the Negro star who refuses to take a firm stand on racial matters finds himself, at worst, ostracized by his race, consigned to . . . 'spiritual death,' or, at best, left in a kind of limbo between white and black. Some, like Willie Mays, try to take refuge in a passive role. . . . More and more, Willie Mays finds himself becoming what Mike Garrett of the Kansas City Chiefs calls 'a marginal man,' exciting the deep respect of neither race and, indeed, the outright dislike of some."

Mays could mount little defense for himself. "I'm a ballplayer," he said. "I am not a politician or a writer or a historian. I can do best for my people by doing what I do best."

Aaron never publicly criticized Mays but, in an interview forty years later, says, "If any part of me was not satisfied with Willie, it's that he didn't speak out enough. I couldn't understand that part of it. I never spoke to him about it. I just let it be." He adds, "I got to know Jackie, and it takes more than just one person to conquer a storm."

Mays found himself in the wrong decade. He was an authority figure when opposing authority was celebrated. He was a man of deference at a time of defiance. He dwelled on positives in an era of righteous indignation. He even lived in the wrong place, a conformist in the epicenter of the counterculture.

Some of the complaints, such as *Sports Illustrated*'s characterization of Mays as a despised, marginal figure bordering on spiritual necrosis, were clearly overblown. Mays was still a leading gate attraction—he rebounded with a good season in 1968—and was, according to the *Pittsburgh Press,* "no doubt the most popular player in the league." That Mays was called an Uncle Tom put him in good company. Given the climate in the late 1960s, virtually any black person who worked successfully within the system was given that designation. Sidney Poitier was called an Uncle Tom (he was too docile in his movies). So was Jackie Robinson (he was too close to Nelson Rockefeller).

While Mays was not an activist, he was still within the mainstream of black America. As the scholar Gerald Early notes, "Sometimes people misunderstand the civil rights era. Many think that every black person was in the streets demonstrating, but actually it was only a small minority of blacks who demonstrated. Most did not, as one would expect from any population. The activists are a relatively small number."

Mays was also subject to a double standard. No one ripped Mickey Mantle for not speaking out for poor rural whites or Sandy Koufax for not campaigning against anti-Semitism, and few complained that other black baseball stars—such as Ernie Banks, Frank Robinson, and Billy Williams—rarely voiced their opinions. Besides, Mays's performance on the field echoed beyond the foul lines. As the *San Francisco Examiner*'s Wells Twombly wrote: "The first time that it became obvious that racism was starting to slip in this country came one spring morning in 1966. On a Texas meadow here was this blue-eyed, freckle-faced grandson of a Klansman catching a fly ball in a Little League game and shouting, 'Look at me, I'm Willie Mays!' "

Mays was somewhat engaged politically. In the 1970s, he and his boyhood friend Herman Boykin drove to Montgomery, Alabama, to visit Governor Wallace. They arrived at the capitol unannounced, but when Wallace saw them, he canceled his appointments and spoke to them. Mays had seen the film footage of Wallace in 1963 standing outside the doors of the University of Alabama, trying to block the enrollment of black students. He failed, but Mays wanted to know why he tried.

Now paralyzed from the waist down from an assassin's bullet, Wallace eventually disavowed his segregationist past. Meeting with Mays, he said, "Willie, it wasn't me. It was the system at that time. I was the governor and I had to go with my duties." Mays, believing that politics, like business or any adult activity, was easily corrupted, accepted the answer.

Some criticism of Mays was valid. He was inclined to conceal his own experience while painting baseball in utopian colors. "Sure, it was different for the Negro when I broke in," he told the *Sporting News* in April 1968, "but I don't care to go into it. Everybody knows it is better now. I don't want to bring up all that stuff. I don't want to digress. All in all, baseball has been great to me. I owe it a lot. . . . There's no doubt that race relations are better and will continue to get better."

Such comments grated on Sam Lacy, the prominent black sports columnist who had ridden in the same train berths as Mays and had shared the same hotel rooms. "What Willie appears to have forgotten," Lacy wrote, "is that there have been MANY times since he's been a Giant that he has been made to understand the differences between black and white. . . . For instance, [in spring training] when he and Monty Irvin, Hank Thompson and Ray Noble were required to live in a third-class hotel, separated from the white members of the squad. . . . And on the annual spring sojourns into Dixie where he parted company at the airport or railroad terminal and caught a cab to 'colored town.' . . . And on those bus trips to New Mexico and southern Arizona when Willie—Monty—Hank and Company waited outside until a . . . white batboy brought out sandwiches from the restaurants in which the rest of the team was enjoying steaks."

Mays didn't have to enter the political fray or engage any enemies, Lacy explained. He simply had to talk about his own life.

But it wasn't to be. What emerges is a man who was bounded by the strictures of his southern roots and by the expectations to play a role for which he did not feel qualified. In fulfilling his dream, Mays had succeeded in the very society that his fellow blacks were now trying to reform, reshape, or topple. He could not join them. His own celebrity, he believed, was perishable, so he tried to avoid headlines for anything beyond baseball and found safety in his separation.

But that came at a price his critics never appreciated. In 1974, on his induction into the Black Athletes Hall of Fame, he gave a speech that acknowledged the hardship and shame he had experienced and suggested the deeper impact of his reserve.

"This award means a great deal to me," he said at the Americana Hotel in New York, "because the time that I broke into baseball, I was like a young Jackie Robinson. I broke into the Interstate League. I was at it by myself, and I had a lot of hardship that no one knows about. I don't like to speak about it because I was very ashamed of it. I've been told, 'Willie, you don't care about your people.' But that's a lie. The suffering that I received in the last, I would say, twenty-three years, I couldn't talk about because it was inside of me. I had to hold it. But this award here again tells me that the young blacks have a helluva chance. This award here tells me that we are getting together. As one man said, it may take a while, but we're coming."

Even his critics conceded that Mays was an activist of a different sort. Sam Lacy noted that Mays probably spent "more time with hospital inmates than any other six athletes in the professional sphere. Despite the fact that it is off-season for him, the annual Shrine Football Game in San Francisco in late December is occasion for Mays to be on hand to offer what inspiration he can to the crippled children for whose fund the game is played."

Willie may not have been in the streets or on the campuses, Lacy concluded, but "in his own quiet way (Willie shies away from discussing it), the finest baseball player of our time displays his own private doctrine of brotherhood."

CHAPTER THIRTY-THREE

THE WISDOM
OF THE YEARS

One night on a flight out of Atlanta, Mays sat down next to Jim McGee and asked, "What was the best catch you saw out there tonight?"

The Giants had beaten the Braves behind Gaylord Perry, but McGee, covering the game for the *Examiner,* could not remember any outstanding play. He suggested a one-handed catch against the fence by Giant outfielder Ken Henderson.

"No, that wasn't it," Mays said.

McGee said he couldn't think of any noteworthy grab.

"The catch I made off Tillman in the seventh," Mays said, referring to right-handed-hitting catcher Bob Tillman.

"That was routine," McGee responded. "You caught that ball right in front of you, just standing there."

"Yep," Mays said. "But did you notice what I did before Tillman swung? I moved ten feet toward left. If I hadn't done that, the ball would have gone through for a triple—I'd never have reached it—and we'd have lost."

"Why'd you shift left?"

"I figured, or that's the way it seemed to me, that Perry was losing something off his fastball. I figured he might be getting tired. And Tillman, as you know, hits the long ball, and he's a pull hitter. So I shifted to left, and that's where he hit it."

McGee knew that Mays enjoyed talking about those kinds of plays more than his athletic feats. For all the focus on his five tools, his intelligence and preparation were just as valuable, and they became even more essential as his physical skills declined. Ken Henderson had a close view of those intangibles.

When he joined the Giants in 1965, the nineteen-year-old was touted as the "next Willie Mays," which didn't please the existing Willie Mays. Perhaps feeling threatened, Mays said little to the kid. Henderson then spent much of the next three years in the minors but joined the team for good in 1969. By then, Mays knew he was in the final stages of his career and lent a hand to Henderson, but much of what the young player learned just came from watching.

"I felt like I was able to communicate with him," Henderson recalled, "and he helped me tremendously defensively. When I played next to him in left field, I'd always look over my left shoulder at him, and at times he would put his hands on his knees with that big, wide-open stance of his. And just before the pitch was made, he'd move. He'd sense something, and he'd move maybe a step toward left field. And I used to watch him, and I would sense when he would move, and I would try to move along with him. He might move five or six steps more to right field, then I would sense that and I would move that way. And it was just a matter of getting to know and to communicate without using any words. It was a sense, an instinct that we had together after playing for a while. And it was really kind of a beautiful thing."

Cardinal manager Johnny Keane used to tell his team that if Mays was on second base and a hit went into the outfield, the fielders should not try to throw him out unless it was the ninth inning or extra innings. Keane knew that Mays played possum on the bases, slowing down to draw throws so trailing runners could advance. Mike Shannon, who played with the Cardinals for nine years and has been broadcasting major league games for almost forty years, says Mays is the smartest player he's ever seen. When he slid, for example, he would use one foot to tag the base and the other to jar the ball loose. Or, after drawing a walk, he would limp down to first base, then steal, and laugh while he was dusting himself off. "He had to find ways to entertain himself," Shannon says.

He recalls one game in which Mays was on second base and a sinking line drive was hit to the outfield. When the second base umpire turned and ran out to get a better view, the third base umpire headed toward second to cover that base. The ball fell for a hit, and as Mays ran for third, he saw there was no umpire. So he cut several feet in front of the bag, saved some time, and scored. The third baseman, Ken Boyer, appealed the play. "The umpire calls him safe," Shannon says, "and Mays is on the bench laughing."

Sometimes it was the run that Mays didn't score that most impressed. In a game against the Pirates at Forbes Field, Mays was on second and the batter hit one off the right field wall. Everyone assumed he would score, but when he got halfway down the third base line, he abruptly stopped and retreated. He saw that Roberto Clemente, who had the best arm in baseball, had fielded the ball cleanly and had launched a perfect throw home. "You had the greatest baserunner against the greatest fielder," Gaylord Perry says. "Willie's play was very heads up. He would have been out."

Bob Stevens said the best play he ever saw by Mays had nothing to do with his physical skills. In a spring training game, the Dodgers had the bases loaded with nobody out and the batter hit a ball to deep center. Mays gave chase and then tapped his glove—the signal, now known by everyone, that he was going to catch it. The runners retreated, but the glove tap was a decoy. The ball hit the top of the fence. Mays fielded it on a hop, whirled, and threw. Only one runner scored on a hit that sailed more than four hundred feet.

Mays was also the consummate sign stealer, not only from second base—where he had a clear view of the catcher's signals—but also from first and third. He says he could tell by the muscle movement in the catcher's right forearm how many fingers he was putting down. Mays was also superstitious: running in from center field, he would step on first or third base on his way to the dugout. But he was always calculating. He says he would strike out intentionally in an early inning with the hope that he'd see the same pitch later with the game on the line.

After his dismal, flu-ridden season in 1967, Mays wanted to erase the speculation that he was ready to retire. He turned thirty-seven in 1968, and he knew that made him one year older than Joe DiMaggio when he retired. Mickey Mantle was still playing, but he had moved to first base the previous year (and retired after 1968). Duke Snider had called it quits in 1964 at thirty-seven.

Mays demonstrated that he was still one of the better players in the game. Compared to the figures in the rest of his career, his batting numbers were down in 1968, but offensive numbers were deflated across the majors. It would be known as "the Year of the Pitcher." Only six players hit .300. Not a single player scored a hundred runs. Only three hitters drove in a hundred. The Giants and the Cardinals threw back-to-back no-hitters at Candlestick, which might not have been so shocking if Marichal and Gibson had hurled them. Instead, it was Gaylord Perry and Ray Washburn. Perry could have lost the game—he faced Gibson and eked out a 1–0 victory. The All-Star Game typified the year and even the decade. Mays led off with a single, advanced to second on an errant pickoff throw, moved to third on a wild pitch, and scored on a double-play ball. The game ended 1–0, and Mays was named the game's MVP. The *Sporting News* declared: "Pitching is strangling the breath out of baseball."

Mays played in 148 games and had 573 at-bats, third on the team behind McCovey and Ron Hunt. His .289 average, 23 home runs, and 79 RBIs all ranked second. He also didn't wear down, hitting .311 in August and .377 in September, and he had nineteen game-winning hits, the most in the big leagues. Mays also won what would be the last of twelve consecutive Gold Gloves, and he devised new baserunning exploits. He was on first with McCovey at the plate and the Pirates using a shift. Maury Wills, now playing third for the Pirates, was the only player on the left side of the infield. Mays was running on a 3–2 pitch, and when McCovey walked, Wills helpfully threw up his hands to alert his friend that he need not slide. But Mays, seeing the left side of the infield empty, kept running so that he stole third base from first on one pitch. "I was trying to be nice and warn Mays," Wills said after the game, "but it cost us."

And 1968 introduced the Giants' most heralded rookie since Willie Mays. Bobby Bonds was a 6-foot-1, 190-pound free spirit, the California high school athlete of the year who long-jumped 25 feet, 3 inches, ran 100 yards in 9.5 seconds, and was awarded all-league honors in football (he was a touchdown machine at tailback) and basketball (he scored 38 points in one game).

Bonds also played the outfield, so it was natural that he was called "the next Willie Mays." He had been compared to Mays as a nineteen-year-old in the Western Carolina League, where he hit .323, banged twenty-five homers, and once ran over a catcher to score the winning run. His manager was Mays's former teammate Max Lanier, who said that his prodigy "could run faster than Mays ever thought of." Bonds had athletic bloodlines. His sister, Rosie, had been a hurdler in the 1964 Olympics, and his brother, Robert, played wide receiver for the Kansas City Chiefs.

Bonds grew up idolizing the Giant legend. "He didn't want to go to a team unless it was with Willie Mays," says Pat Bonds, Bobby's wife. Bobby said that when he went to spring training for the first time at eighteen, "Willie Mays had a locker near mine, and it took me one-half hour to get dressed because I kept watching him. He put his arm around me and said, 'I'm gonna teach you how to play ball.' He was my greatest asset in the game."

Mays was alternately tender and stern with Bonds, but always protective. When he didn't like the way a coach was trying to adjust the way Bonds held the bat, Mays ran him off. He lent Bobby money for his new house in San Carlos, and he gave him extra furniture from his own house. When Pat was pregnant with their third child, Bobby was supposed to leave home for spring training, but Mays told him to report late, that he would take care of things in Arizona. "When I had the baby," Pat recalls, "Willie and Bobby would play cards, and I think he let Bobby win the money to buy the crib."

Bonds made history in his very first game when he hit a grand slam, the first time that had happened in a rookie's debut in the twentieth century. Like Mays as a rookie, Bonds was talented but raw—in only eighty-one games, he led the team in stolen bases (sixteen) as well as strikeouts (eighty-four) while whacking nine homers. Pat says that Bobby was determined to be as good if not better than Willie, and his numbers bore out that relentless ambition. In his first full year, Bonds hit thirty-two homers and stole forty-five bases (in forty-nine attempts), but unwilling to shorten his swing, he hit .259 and struck out a staggering 187 times. (In Mays's first full year, by contrast, he struck out 57 times.)

The Giants were certain they had finally found Mays's successor, though Mays himself never cared much for the "next Willie Mays" hoopla. For one, he was still around, but he also thought the tag was unfair to the next in line, and he pleaded with reporters not to write so much about Bonds at such a young age. "It puts too much pressure on a kid who tries to live up to the notices," he said.

Some observers have speculated that the pressures on Bonds contributed to his personal problems, specifically his excessive drinking. Mays, aware of his taste for alcohol, urged him to take care of his body, but the pleas didn't work. Bonds's demons haunted him throughout his life.

His oldest son, Barry, was four years old when Bobby joined the Giants, and over the next several years, the boy would attend games and putter around the locker room. On Fathers' and Sons' Day, he would take the field, swat a beach ball with a plastic bat, and run around the bases. Like most kids in and around the clubhouse, Barry gravitated to Mays and would rummage through his stuff for gloves and baseballs and would hide on top of the locker. Mays obliged the boy and, when his parents asked, agreed to be his godfather.

For some years, Barry was estranged from his father, resenting him for his neglect as both a father and a husband, though he says they reconnected once he entered college and were close from then on. Barry had another father figure as well from a very young age. "Willie was always challenging me as a kid," he said. "I remember when he'd catch the ball, and he would just flick it and it would go all the way back into the infield. And I could barely reach the infield as a kid. And he would tease me: 'C'mon, how are you ever going to make the major leagues if you can't throw the ball to second base?' . . . He would laugh at me because I couldn't throw."

When Barry Bonds joined the Pirates in 1986, he wore number 24.

At the All-Star Game, Herman Franks announced that he would not return as manager unless the Giants won the pennant . . . and the Giants didn't win the pennant. For the fourth consecutive year under Franks, they finished second (the Cardinals again won), though with eighty-eight wins, it was their worst season under Franks. The team was always a pitcher or two short and, with the exception of center field, never that strong up the middle. In addition, both the Dodgers and Cardinals recognized the imperative of speed, stolen bases, and "small ball" to manufacture runs in a low-scoring era. Stoneham's fetish for home runs, embraced by Franks, was costly.

Financial problems also loomed, which eventually had a direct impact on Mays. The Giants' parent, the National Exhibition Company, also owned three minor league teams and a hotel and related recreational facilities in Casa Grande, Arizona. For 1968, the company posted an operating loss of $179,099, compared to an operating profit of $215,491 in 1967. Plunging attendance caused the red ink.

For the second straight season, the Giants were out of the race by the first day of August, but it was also the first year of the Oakland Athletics, who had migrated from Kansas City and now divided the Bay Area's fan base. The consequences for the Giants were devastating. In 1968, attendance fell 33 percent, to 837,220, from the previous year, marking the fewest fans they had drawn in their eleven years in San Francisco and less than half their record in 1960. It was also the first time they had fallen below 1 million since leaving New York. The Athletics, who finished in sixth place, drew 837,466 fans, virtually the same number as the Giants. The A's were eighth out of ten American League teams in attendance; the Giants, seventh in their own league.

The Giants did not face an immediate crisis, as each National League club reaped a $2 million windfall from the expansion teams in San Diego and Montreal, which would start in 1969. The Giants also received a million-dollar settlement over litigation stemming from the Polo Grounds. But the one-time gains did not obscure the cold emptiness of Candlestick Park, which for some games drew fewer than 2,500 fans. Stoneham's abysmal sales and marketing were hurting the team as well. Lon Simmons recalls a fan who wanted to buy season tickets, but the Giants didn't accept checks. He left without any tickets.

Fittingly, the 1968 Giants led the league in road attendance, drawing almost 1.6 million, setting the pace for the seventh time in the past eight years. Everyone knew the reason: the fans wanted to see Willie.

National Exhibition was a publicly traded company, and at its annual meeting in early 1969, Stoneham was asked about Mays's salary. At $125,000, he was the company's highest paid employee, though that was deceiving. Stoneham's salary of $80,300, which hadn't budged in years, did not include dividend payments. Stoneham said he expected Mays to again play for $125,000. Juan Marichal was also discussed. His $100,000 salary was second to Mays's, and in 1968, he had won twenty-six games, recorded an ERA of 2.43, and had thirty complete games (a mark never achieved by the decade's other top pitchers—Gibson, Koufax, and Denny McLain). Stoneham said Marichal might receive a raise.

News accounts do not indicate whether any shareholders complained about Mays's salary, but the issue was clearly in play. Unless Stoneham could turn around the company, the high-income stars would have to go, and the entire franchise could be in peril.

The Giants' next skipper was Clyde King, a soft-spoken North Carolinian who had been managing in the minors for thirteen years—most recently for the Giants' AAA club in Phoenix—and was promoted for one purpose: to break the Giants' second-place stalemate. In some ways, the forty-four-year-old former pitcher was a refreshing change from the abrasive Herman Franks, and his experience managing some of the younger players in Phoenix, who had felt neglected in Franks's star system, was a benefit. But King had never led a big league team before, and he was the first manager in Giants' history, besides Leo Durocher, who had not served in some capacity with the parent club. His lack of experience, on all counts, hurt him. He was unaccustomed to a twenty-five-man roster—his limit in Phoenix was twenty-one—and, fearful that he would run out of players at other positions, would only carry nine pitchers. He also apparently didn't understand how to "double switch" players to move the pitcher's spot in the order.

But his biggest difficulty was his relationship with Willie Mays, who as a rookie had actually faced King when he pitched for the Dodgers. (Mays struck out once and hit a home run another time.) But King had no history with Mays as a teammate or a coach and didn't know how other managers had handled him. Even as a veteran, Mays still needed encouragement and support and remained hypersensitive to slights. He had been doubly protected by Franks, his financial adviser, who allowed Mays to determine his own playing schedule.

Mays had now played more years in the majors than any active player, and he believed that he had earned special privileges and that both he and the club were the better for it. King thought otherwise, so troubles were inevitable. "In Willie, he inherits an institution," wrote the *Los Angeles Times*'s Mel Durslag. "It's as if a new conglomerate suddenly acquires the House of Rothschild."

In his first press conference, King declared that all the players, regardless of age or tenure, would be required to practice equally. Then in spring training, he announced that Mays was going to hit leadoff; he felt Mays's

speed would benefit the top of the lineup. It's possible that if King had suggested the idea to Mays so that Mays could claim some ownership of it, the
switch would have been easier. But King didn't. He thought he should treat
Mays like every other player, and Mays balked.

"Why do you want me to bat leadoff?" he asked. "I'm no kid, you know."

"I know that, but you're not hitting home runs like you used to," King
said.

"I can still hit twenty or more," Mays said. "That ought to be enough."

Mays thought the extra at-bats at leadoff would wear him out sooner
and he could help the team more by driving in runs in the three hole. He
didn't complain to the mainstream press, though he did tell the *Chicago
Daily Defender*, "I'm used to knocking in runs. If they want me to score
runs, I can, but I if I knock in fifty runs this year, it will be a miracle. [But]
I'm not going to fight with [King]. If he feels that's what I should do, then
I will. He's the manager."

Even without Franks seeking his guidance, Mays found ways to continue to control the field. On one play, he fielded a single to center and,
with a man at first, he overthrew the cutoff man in a vain attempt to cut
down the runner at third. On the overthrow, the hitter advanced to second. Sitting in the press box was Franks. "Look at him," Franks said. "He's
managing in place of King. He wanted that hitter to move up to second
base so first base would be open. Now they'll walk the next hitter on purpose. Then they'll get the next guy out and have the guy after him having
to lead off the next inning. That's the way Willie's got it planned."

Mays proved to be good at the top of the order, hitting .317 over the first
eleven games. But the Giants were 6–5 and had beaten only the expansion
San Diego Padres. In the next game, Mays was hitting third, with Bobby
Bonds leading off. Perhaps it was just a coincidence, but one day later the
Giants began a nine-game winning streak in which Mays hit .364.

On the field or in the dugout, Mays almost never lost control of his emotions, but it did happen. At Candlestick in September 1968, two fans along
the first base line kept heckling him, and when he came jogging to the
dugout after a good catch, one of them yelled, "Nice catch for a $100,000
bum! You're finally earning your money!" Mays had heard enough. He
changed course, headed for the stands, and tried to scale the railing. Herman Franks, among others, had to restrain him. The police escorted the
hecklers out of the ballpark. After the game, first base coach Charlie Fox
said, "Ordinarily, you don't mind needling from the fans, but these fellows
were really abusive right from the start of the game." Mays apologized:
"After all these years, I should have known better."

A more publicized blowup occurred the following year at the Astrodome with Clyde King. It was June 24, a Tuesday night game. Mays thought he was getting the night off, but before the game a teammate told him that his name was on the lineup card, which was posted in the dugout. Mays retreated to the clubhouse to take off his sweats and put on his uniform. King said when it was time to present the lineups, he couldn't find Mays and assumed he didn't want to play, so he erased his name from the card. Mays returned to the dugout, saw his named removed, and erupted. He thought King was trying to show him up—first putting him in the lineup, then taking him out. He barked at King, waved his arms, and appeared ready to charge him when McCovey, Perry, and Larry Jansen surrounded him. Mays continued to shake his finger at King, then settled down. In the second inning, Jim Ray Hart, playing the outfield, hurt his shoulder, and King asked Mays if he wanted to play.

"You're the manager," Mays said.

He played the rest of the game. Afterward, King told him that he would be fined.

The incident only crystallized the bad relations between the men. Mays didn't believe he was accorded enough respect, and King resented his attitude. "If I'm fined," Mays told him, "I quit."

Stoneham was not about to let that happen, and no fine was levied. Chub Feeney, citing the best interests of the team, urged Mays to apologize to King, which he did. Even his most ardent booster, Charlie Einstein, described Mays's behavior in the dugout as "unforgivable," but the *Examiner*'s Prescott Sullivan noted that the tantrum was the first for Mays "in some eighteen years as a professional player [and] he had us wondering if he'd ever get around to it. . . . It's only human to foul up now and then, and Willie, who had baseball's longest good conduct record going for him, finally did it."

Mays began the 1969 season needing only 13 home runs to reach 600. Pundits predicted that with a fast start, Mays would hit that plateau by Mother's Day. Though his knees troubled him throughout the year, he began well enough and had 9 homers on June 21. Then he went almost two months, to August 15, before he hit the tenth. He didn't hit his twelfth—599—until September 15. The chase for 600 didn't garner the media attention that accompanied 512, but the pressures were the same. Mays had also injured his knee on July 29 in a home plate collision with Cub catcher Randy Hundley, and the damage was evident. "People cringed in sympathy," Bob Stevens wrote, "when he went on defense and stumbled and wobbled and did not quite get to some baseballs he would have gobbled up two years ago. When he swung at the plate, the knee would cave in under him and rob the swing of the pure, terrifying power it once generated. Yet, Willie played."

The Giants battled the Braves down the stretch in September, and that they "won any games at all," Stevens wrote, "was because [Mays] was producing—hurting like all hell. But playing and producing." He drove in five game-winning runs in September and scored the game-winner four times.

But number 600 lingered. The Adirondack Bat Company had sent Frank Torre, the retired Braves' first baseman (and Joe's brother), to present Mays with some gifts when he hit the milestone homer. Torre followed Mays for six weeks, waiting for the moment. Mays wanted to hit number 600 in San Francisco during a ten-game home stand, but he never came close. Then, on September 22 in San Diego, he was given the night off. Municipal Stadium was nearly empty—there were 4,779 fans—and the public address announcer had advised the small crowd that the fan who caught Mays's six hundredth homer "tomorrow night would receive season's tickets for next season." But in the seventh inning with the score tied, King looked at Mays on the bench, and Mays looked back.

"I'm not tired," he said. "Just hurting a little bit."

"Grab a bat," King said.

Mays pinch-hit for rookie George Foster. With a runner on second, he just wanted a single against Mike Corkins, a rookie who was five years old when Mays broke in. His first pitch was a belt-high fastball. Ron Fimrite's story of the game suggested a redemptive quality to the blow that followed: "In the privacy of San Diego's Municipal Stadium, the great center fielder—staggered by injuries, haunted by the specter of old age and the taunts of critics who have been burying him for the better part of four years—lofted a 391-foot home run to the empty left field seats. . . . As Mays rounded the bases, the tiny crowd rose to its feet and gave him the reception that rightfully should have been his from a far greater multitude."

The ovation was expected. What Mays didn't anticipate was the scene at home plate, where all the Giants had raced from the dugout to greet him. He was genuinely touched by the reception. "It was my most satisfying home run," he said after the game, "because of all those guys waiting for me when I crossed home. There was nobody left on the bench. That really got to me."

Mays acknowledged that he had been trying too hard and the pressure had affected him, and he again waved off the possibility of reaching 714. He was just glad the team won. The only man happier than Mays was Frank Torre, who estimated that he had seen forty games, traveled 12,000 miles, and spent $4,200 waiting for the historic swing. Not expecting Mays to pinch-hit, he almost missed it entirely, but he scurried onto the field to present Mays with his awards: a trophy made up of three bats on a plaque with the number 600 tying the handles together at the top, a $12,500 Italian sports car, and a share of Adirondack stock for each foot the ball had traveled; at $9 a share, it was a $3,519 clout.

Said Mays, "I'm just glad Torre can go back to his family."

Mays stole six bases for the year, which made him the first player ever to hit at least three hundred homers and steal at least three hundred bases. He played in 117 games and had 459 at-bats, his lowest totals for a full season to date, but he finished with the third-best batting average on the Giants, .283 (second among the regulars), and the third most RBIs, with fifty-eight. While his thirteen homers marked the first time he'd hit fewer than twenty in a full season, they were still second highest on the club.

The leagues now had two divisions with six teams apiece. The Giants once again finished second, three games behind the Braves in the West Division. During the season, news reports claimed that Joan Whitney Payson, the owner of the Mets, was trying to trade for Mays. The Mets were young and talented but needed some veteran leadership. Stoneham said he had no intention of trading Mays. It didn't matter for the Mets. Founded only seven years earlier, the Miracle Mets won their division, the pennant, and the World Series.

Mays took some consolation when the *Sporting News* named him "Player of the Decade," an honor that Ted Williams and Stan Musial had held before him. Another publication chose Mays for a team called "Baseball's Greatest Living Players." At last he was with DiMaggio.

CHAPTER THIRTY-FOUR

BASEBALL ROYALTY

The twilight years of Mays's career saw a seismic shift in baseball: a serious challenge to the reserve clause, which led to its demise, and the strengthening of the labor union, which forced a players' strike. While baseball eras are vaguely defined, a new one had clearly begun in the early 1970s. Mays did not play a major role in the bitter disputes that seemed to threaten the very existence of the game, but his name was invoked by parties on all sides, and his surprising reaction to baseball's upheavals shed additional light on his character.

Money—especially from television—had changed baseball's landscape. In 1946, the Yankees were the first team to sell television rights to their games, which netted them $75,000. By 1970, television revenue for the entire league was $38 million. Expansion fees and higher ticket prices brought in even more. But the average salaries for the players, when adjusted for inflation, had changed little.

The Major League Baseball Players Association was formed in 1954 but for years did little for its members. Then in 1966 it hired Marvin Miller, who for more than a decade had helped lead the powerful United Steelworkers of America and who was now determined to convince professional ballplayers that baseball was a business. He achieved some incremental gains in short order—the owners agreed to raise the minimum wage, for example, and contribute to player pensions. But the owners' principal tool in keeping salaries low and maintaining a docile labor force was the reserve clause, which the U.S. Supreme Court upheld in 1922.

In 1970, after Curt Flood was traded to the Phillies, he sued Major League Baseball in an effort to overturn the reserve clause—in effect, to win his freedom. In an interview, Howard Cosell said to Flood, "It's been written, Curt, that you're a man who makes $90,000 a year, which isn't exactly slave wages. What's your retort to that?"

"A well-paid slave," Flood said, "is a slave nonetheless."

While the representatives of the players' union supported the suit, many of the game's high-salaried stars did not. Carl Yastrzemski said the suit, if successful, would ruin baseball. Harmon Killebrew, Frank Howard, Ron Santo, and Gaylord Perry all opposed Flood.

The game's most important voice belonged to Willie Mays, whose league-high salary—$150,000 in 1970—was cited by the owners as evidence of their fairness and generosity. On the *Tonight Show,* Johnny Carson asked Mays what he thought of Flood's case. Mays said, "If Curt is doing something he thinks is right, I think he should do it. I haven't really studied it too much. I don't know all the arguments that are going on, and I'm not going to get involved."

As Brad Snyder pointed out in his book on Flood's case, *A Well-Paid Slave,* five black future Hall of Famers—Hank Aaron, Ernie Banks, Frank Robinson, and Billy Williams, as well as Mays—failed to support Flood. All but Robinson had grown up in the South, and Aaron, Banks, and Mays had played in the Negro Leagues. "They succeeded by obeying the system," Snyder wrote. "They were not boat rockers. They feared retribution from the owners and did not want to jeopardize their salaries, their careers, and their futures in the game."

Nonetheless, Mays's comments got the most attention, including a reaction from Flood. In his 1970 book, *The Way It Is,* Flood wrote: "All but a very few major leaguers share my view of baseball reality. Among those who do not, the most prominent is the great Willie Mays, who reports from the privileged isolation of his huge success that he has absolutely nothing to complain about."

Flood lost his legal battle, but his efforts effectively opened the door for other challenges, and in 1975 a federal arbitrator ruled that two players, Andy Messersmith and Dave McNally, were free agents when their contracts expired. The reserve clause was dead.

The players' ability to receive market wages contributed to huge increases in salary, and as a matter of principle—the freedom to choose your own employer—the victory was long overdue. That is the consensus, but not for Mays, who believes something important was lost with free agency.

Mays wants to see players make as much money as possible, and while he has always felt aligned with the owners, he's never had any stake in their profits. Free agency, to Mays, was not simply about the dollars. It was about values. Mays prizes stability, order, and loyalty, and the reserve clause ensured that rosters were fairly stable and that teams could be kept together. Free agency, however, invited disruption for management while obliterating any pretense that the players were loyal to their teammates, their organizations, or their cities. They were now mercenaries whose only loyalty was to their checkbook.

As Mays said in *Say Hey*, "Once the arbitrator ruled that a player was free to make his own deal, many of the values that I treasured suddenly went down the drain. I believed in a family atmosphere in a club. . . . While I didn't play under free agency, I started to see a change in mutual respect. Oh, ballplayers always griped. I'm not saying we didn't. But there was also a . . . what's the word I want? . . . pride. Yes, pride, in being there, in being one of the few hundred ballplayers out of the tens of millions of Americans who dreamed one day of becoming a big leaguer."

Mays, to be sure, is not the most objective critic of free agency. When he was still playing, his high pay cushioned him against the inequities of the chattel system, and his close ties to Stoneham caused him to understate the owners' treatment of the players as disposable parts. But Mays's central point—that the demise of the reserve clause contributed to a freewheeling money culture, which has diminished the players' devotion to the game, fed their conceit about their self-worth, and raised self-aggrandizement to an art form—stands as a reasonable critique of the modern game.

What's more, Mays proved that he was no stooge of management in 1972, when the owners refused to bargain on insurance benefits, and the players, through their representatives, voted unanimously to strike. As it happened, Stoneham had traded the Giants' player rep (Hal Lanier) and alternate (Gaylord Perry) after the 1971 season, so Mays suddenly found himself representing the team at this critical time.

The strike itself, which began in spring training, would only succeed if the players remained unified, and as Opening Day approached, Marvin Miller was concerned that that unity was beginning to crack. Many of the players lived from paycheck to paycheck, and they had no experience with labor-management showdowns. The players' executive board met in New York, and Mays was asked to address it. His comments, recalled in Miller's autobiography, convey as much about Mays's commitment to baseball as they do about his support for the union.

"I know it's hard being away from the game and our paychecks and our normal life," Mays said. "I love this game. It's been my whole life. But we made a decision . . . to stick together, and until we're satisfied, we have to stay together. This could be my last year in baseball, and if the strike lasts the entire season and I've played my last game, well, it will be painful. But if we don't hang together, everything we've worked for will be lost."

Mays's words left the room silent. "My doubts" about our unity, Miller said, "disappeared like one of his towering home runs."

The players held firm. The strike lasted thirteen days and forced the cancellation of eighty-six games, but the owners agreed to add $500,000 in health care benefits. Their control over the players, even before the reserve clause was overturned, had ended.

Clyde King was abruptly fired after forty-two games in 1970. The Giants were only four games under .500, but Stoneham reportedly held King responsible for the Giants' failure to win the pennant the previous year, and despite King's background as a pitching coach, the team's ERA was 5.44. On his last day as manager, the Giants scored sixteen runs and still lost to the Padres, 17–16. Those reasons notwithstanding, King's inability to get along with Mays was an important reason for his dismissal. Mays's low assessment of King's managing skills was never contradicted; King had two more managing stints, with the Braves and the Yankees, but he'd hold those jobs for fewer games than he had with the Giants.

The Giants' next manager was Charlie Fox, a long-standing coach who had seen Mays thrive under Herman Franks and afforded him the same latitude. The team improved, going 67–53 for the rest of the year, and finished third.

That season produced one of the truly memorable images of Mays's career. In an April game at Candlestick, the Reds' Bobby Tolan smashed a ball into deep right center. Both Mays and Bobby Bonds sprinted to the track and leaped at the same time, their gloves reaching over the fence. In a sequence of four wire-service photographs, the two men collide in mid-air, with their legs entangled, their glove hands outstretched, with Mays's belt flush against Bonds's midsection. Next, their feet land, though their bodies are entwined as one. They then collapse to the ground, with Bonds on his left side, Mays flat on his back, the ball visible in his glove. Finally, Mays remains on the ground, the wind knocked out of him, as Bonds lifts himself up and reaches for the ball, which he held up for the umpires. It unfolded like a violent airborne dance. Watching the game was five-year-old Barry Bonds. "I believe I was crying, because anything that happened to Willie got to me," he says. It was the last out of the inning, and by the time Mays sat up, the Reds' outfielders, including Pete Rose, were looking over him. "Friends came out to see how I was doing," Mays recalled. "That's what made it special."

Mays was no longer the best player in the game or even one of the best, but at thirty-nine, he was surprisingly good. On June 7, he equaled his home run output from the previous season, thirteen, and passed it three days later. He flirted with .300, and his catch on Tolan's ball was one of several sensational defensive plays, including his cutting off a base hit in left center with his bare hand. In July, *Sports Illustrated* broke down Mays's game. He remained one of the best baserunners on the team who, running on 3-and-2, had gone first to third on a wild pitch. He could still throw strikes from the outfield and, using his knowledge of hitters and quick jumps, was still "the master of his position."

Mays always preferred off-speed pitches to fastballs and, with the rest of the league, struggled against Sandy Koufax, Bob Gibson, and Tom Seaver. Mays had other reasons to be scared of Gibson. The Cardinal pitcher, accompanied by teammate Bill White, once visited Mays at home.

"Is that Gibson?" Mays asked in disbelief. "You wear glasses? Man, you're going to kill somebody one of these days." Gibson wore glasses but did not use them when he played.

As Gibson recalled, "After that, he never leaned over the plate too much."

In 1970, Mays conveniently scheduled his off days when Gibson or Seaver pitched, but he made adjustments against hard throwers by bailing out, giving him the opportunity to turn on inside pitches, though his reflexes were fast enough to still reach outside deliveries. Mays, however, received his highest praise as a teammate who helped younger players. "He's a beautiful person," said Giant outfielder Frank Johnson. "I don't think anybody on the club dislikes him. If they do, they're crazy." Added Bobby Bonds, "He's the most nonchalant superstar you'll ever see. He acts just like he draws the minimum." (*Sports Illustrated* noted that Mays had never been that close to Juan Marichal, who in the off-season told a Dominican reporter that Mays should consider retiring. Marichal later said he was misunderstood and retracted the comment.)

Mays began the year needing 74 hits to reach 3,000, but unlike past home run chases, he went on a tear as he approached the milestone, going 10-for-23 to reach 2,999. Then, on July 18, in a sunny afternoon game at Candlestick, Mays came to bat in the first inning. When Montreal Expo hurler Mike Wegener walked him on four pitches, the crowd booed madly on each throw. In the second, Mays stepped to the plate again and, with an 0–2 count, cut on a low slider and chopped it through the infield on the left side—"every bounce," the *Examiner* wrote, "was lustrous with history." When Mays reached first base, he doffed his cap to the cheering crowd— he was only the tenth player in big league history to get 3,000 hits, Hank Aaron having reached the mark earlier in the season. Mays was soon surrounded by his teammates, and several Expos congratulated him as well. A ten-minute ceremony was led by Chub Feeney, now president of the National League. Also on the field were Stan Musial, who put his arm around Mays, and Monte Irvin, representing the commissioner's office.

After the game, Mays said he couldn't help but think about the record, given that two photographers were at his front door when he left for the park. "I don't feel excitement about this now," he said. "A reaction may set in later, but the main thing I wanted to do was help Gaylord Perry win a game. I don't like to talk about goals, but maybe I have a goal—to help the guys win."

He played 139 games and hit .291, with twenty-eight homers, eighty-three RBIs, and ninety-four runs scored. On the Giants, only three players hit for higher average and for more RBIs, and only two for more homers. On September 28, Mays entered another exclusive club—he had at-bat number 10,000 for his career. Only Ty Cobb (11,434) and Stan Musial (10,972) had more.

The cover of *Saturday Review* blared: "The Age of Willie Mays." The date was May 8, 1971, two days after Mays had turned forty, and the photo was one of Willie's favorites. Set in an ornate gold frame, it showed him at the plate, swinging the bat, his arms fully extended, his eyes on the ball. His uniform was skin tight, and what Mays loved about the picture was its display of his muscular thighs, torso, and arms—he had a few gray hairs on his temples and a slightly receding hairline, but he still had a thirty-two-inch waist, Herculean arms, and a sculpted physique. Charlie Fox noted that this was no accident. "In twenty-two years," he said, "Willie has gained a pound and a half. You spread a buffet for the team after a game, and young players will gobble everything in sight. Willie will take one stick of gum."

There was poetic symmetry in Mays's life. He had been born forty years earlier and had joined the Giants twenty years earlier. He had also achieved a kind of royal status, recognized by writers, players, and fans alike. In both 1970 and 1971, a poll of the players had ranked Mays as the fourth-best outfielder for the All-Star Game, but in 1970 the voting returned to the fans, who elected Mays to start. One time in Los Angeles, he was hit by a pitch in the small of his back. "The pitcher, Don Sutton, looked on in horror," Jim Murray wrote, "as if he had just thrown a dart through the Mona Lisa or cracked a statue of St. Francis with a well-aimed rock. . . . Sutton ran up like a Red Cross nurse. The crowd—a Dodger crowd, mind you—booed him."

The claim that this was "the Age of Mays" was a stretch. It was more like "the Age of Elegies," as wistful tributes for Willie tumbled in. The *Saturday Review*'s Peter Schrag wrote that Mays "should be well past his prime, an aging star dogged by fragile legs, trick knees, fatigue, and the other assorted aches and pains that the flesh of annuating athletes is supposed to suffer. But Mays moves with the grace of memory, defying time, defying the inexorable erosion of fantasies, defying age itself. He remains unequivocally our man. To see him now is like watching the instant replay of a generation, the crowds of twenty years, the old ballparks with their erratic dimensions and their even more erratic fans."

Schrag noted Mays's unpredictable moods and his coldness to reporters he didn't know, but those could be forgiven. Mays urged the young Giants to adopt his daring style, which the writer summarized as: "If you want to make money, don't play it safe." At a time of increasing corporate conformity, Schrag concluded, and "when baseball itself seemed to be dulled by tepid professionalism," Mays "appeared to us as the new romantic individualist, a man of the ritual, but a man who enriched it. He brought jazz to the game."

Milton Gross, Mays's longtime friend and confidant, wrote in the *New York Post*: "Mays is more than a man nearing middle age so far as baseball is concerned. He is an emotional experience. He is the tie that binds so many of us to our carefree days of the past and for the younger generation he is the legend that lives, the only authentic piece of active history which links baseball as it is to what it used to be."

Wells Twombly, a sports columnist for the *Examiner* with a literary flair, reprised the theme that Mays's aging violated nature's will. "As the greatest baseball player of his generation advances on home plate," he wrote, "carefully picking his steps on legs that are only slightly bowed, it is difficult to shirk the feeling that perhaps this is the only mortal time ever agreed to leave alone. It would be a sin to have him grow old. Indeed, there are moments, especially when he goes swooping after a fly ball in darkest center field like a peregrine falcon chasing a dove, when it seems he will still be playing this game two decades from now. . . . But the end moves closer with every inning, with every pitch. These bits and pieces, these broken shards, are nothing more than that. Nature has, in the final analysis, a ghastly sense of humor."

The veteran sportswriter Joe Falls lamented that Mays had never played a game in his city, Detroit, and he had never seen Mays play in person. So he flew to Cincinnati to watch him. Mays struck out twice and popped out twice, but he also went into deep center field for a towering fly, turned around, and—*plop!*—the ball fell into his glove for a basket catch. "The whole trip was worthwhile," Falls wrote.

He had an even better anecdote in 1971, when Mays finally played at Tiger Stadium in the All-Star Game. The next day, two young men dialed Falls with a story that highlighted the bond between Mays and his fans. Tim Hemming, nineteen, and Ron Salsido, twenty-one, placed a call to Mays's hotel room at 4 A.M. on the day of the game. Though half asleep, Mays answered and spoke to the guys, and he agreed to help them out. They had bleacher seats, and before the bottom of the first inning, one of them threw a baseball onto the field. Mays picked it up, signed it, and threw it back, setting off a mad scramble.

"I got a black eye out of it," Hemming said, "but I've got the ball."

On Mays's fortieth birthday, he was given a party similar to the celebration on his thirty-fifth. It was again held at the Fairmont Hotel (in the Grand Ball Room), it again raised money for a charity (the Hunters Point Fund), and it included a list of impressive dignitaries from the worlds of sports, entertainment, and politics. The price per plate had gone from $25 to $24, to match Mays's uniform number.

The ballroom was festooned with pennants from all twenty-four major league teams, symbolizing the event as a nationwide salute. That Mays was hitting .368 contributed to the theme of the star as a timeless wonder. Seven hundred celebrants showed up, and the front table consisted of a pretty fair outfield—Mays, Aaron, and DiMaggio. In one of his few public speeches, the fifty-six-year-old Yankee legend said, "I know you're going to wind up in the Hall of Fame, but I don't know if I'll be around to see you get in. There's a rule, you know, that you have to wait five years after you retire to be elected."

Chub Feeney said, "Those of us who saw him break in twenty years ago have all grown older, but he hasn't." Carl Reiner, the director, remarked, "Mays brings out the child in all of us that refuses to die." Albert Brooks did a ventriloquist act. Charlie Fox, in his finest Irish tenor, sang an altered rendition of "Danny Boy."

"Friends may forsake me; let them all forsake me; I still have you, Willie boy."

Horace Stoneham almost broke down praising Mays, and Dianne Feinstein—who, the *Sporting News* reported, "may be America's most attractive city supervisor"—gave Willie a plaque that read: "Mr. Mays, you are a very bright light in San Francisco."

The evening's most poignant moment occurred with the remembrance of Russ Hodges, who had died three weeks earlier of a heart attack at the age of sixty. He had been the voice of the Giants for twenty-two years and had seen all but three of Mays's home runs. Mays was one of the first to be notified of his death. "Willie broke up over the phone," a member of his family told the press. "He couldn't talk."

At the birthday celebration, Hodges's call of Mays's at-bat in Houston in 1965, when he kept fouling off fastballs until he finally hit the game-tying homer, was dramatically played to a tearful audience.

The party was like Mays's thirty-fifth in one other respect. Whoever planned it did not include Mays as a speaker. Lee Mendelson, who had filmed the documentary in 1963, was surprised when he picked up the program and noticed the omission. "I remember that very distinctly," he says more than thirty-five years later. "I went up to Stoneham or somebody and said, 'I haven't talked to Willie about this, but I think Willie would like to speak.' And somebody said, 'Do you think he wants to speak?' I think there were people around the Giants, the PR people, who didn't realize what a good speaker he was and were always trying to protect him."

Mays didn't need the protection. He wasn't completely relaxed in front of audiences, but he had tried to improve his diction and grammar and had worked on lowering his voice. After radio interviews, he would ask friends how he sounded. He continued to speak without notes, but his friends would hear him practicing his talks in a separate room in his house. On the night of his birthday, wearing a cream-colored suit, he gave a heartfelt speech with a surprise ending.

"All I've ever done is to try my best," Mays said. "America must be a beautiful country when someone like me can have the opportunity to do what everyone here this night has said." He hit familiar notes in describing what motivated him to play. "I don't play for myself," he said. "I play for the fans. If they enjoy my playing, I enjoy myself. . . . I'll be at Candlestick Park ready to play tomorrow night. People ask me when I'm going to retire. I'd like to say never . . . maybe I can be thirty-nine forever, like Jack Benny." Mays revealed a bit more than usual, however, when he talked about the struggles of celebrity and how tough it was "to live in a bowl." He also defended himself on racial matters. According to the *Examiner,* he said he "didn't care for the rap that he's an Uncle Tom, although he never used that expression."

Before he said his final thank-you, Mays said he wanted to make a special introduction. "She's always mentioning that wherever we go, she's never introduced, and she's gotten mad at me sometimes when I don't introduce her as my girl. But she has to understand that it is different when you are going around with a baseball player." He nodded to his partner. "I'd like to introduce Miss Mae Allen." Mae was completely surprised. She stood, took a bow, and wept.

Willie's acknowledgment was so uncharacteristic that the *Examiner* ran a sidebar, "Mae and Mays," and wondered if they'd "step up to the matrimonial plate soon?"

Not all the attention was favorable. Mays could still be uncomfortable with interviews, and that was clear when he appeared on Dick Cavett's show in January.

"Some people look at their fortieth birthday as a crisis," Cavett said. "How do you feel about that?"

Mays thought Cavett was suggesting that he was getting too old to play, and his reply was tetchy and defensive. "Hey, why does everybody want to ask me about my age?" he snapped. "I may play three or four more years."

Cavett: "George Blanda is forty-three and—"

Mays cut him off. "Blanda is only a placekicker. He comes and plays a few seconds once a week. I play every day. Are we going to discuss football or baseball?"

Cavett: "I sense I'm being put on here. Mr. Mays, you make me nervous."

The two staggered through the rest of the interview until Hank Aaron and Jim Bouton joined them.

By now, Mays received little criticism from San Francisco journalists, who recognized his unique status and knew how to approach him and what to expect. But he was subject to an unusually personal attack from a *Chronicle* columnist named Glenn Dickey, a screed so caustic that competing writers for the *Examiner* rose in Mays's defense.

Dickey's column was supposed to run the day after Mays's birthday, but as the *Sporting News* reported, it was held for three weeks on the theory that eviscerating a man on his birthday might offend some readers. Mays, Dickey wrote, "sheds his greatness like a cloak when he leaves the playing field. . . . You know the myth [of] the Say Hey kid, a happy-go-lucky fellow with a kind word for everyone. Try that on an autograph-seeking kid who has been brushed off, a sportswriter who has been cursed, a manager who has tried to exercise authority, a black who has tried to get Mays to speak out against racial inequities." Dickey described Mays as a "hypochondriac" who used his "famed fainting spells" to garner extra attention, and now, "when the Giants are looking for him, they check the hospitals first." Dickey's conclusion: "Occasionally, there is talk that Mays will be the first black manager, but he would bring only indolence, an uncertain intelligence and a petulant personality to the job. Better keep playing, Willie."

The timing of the attack was not particularly good. Three days earlier, Mays had hit a game-winning home run, breaking the National League record by scoring run number 1,950 of his career. For that, the grounds crew ceremoniously dug up home plate and gave it to him. The day before the column appeared, Mays had what the *Sporting News* said was "one of his most sensational days in San Francisco." Against the Mets, he hit a game-tying home run in the eighth. Replacing the injured McCovey, he made several game-saving plays at first in the ninth and tenth innings; then, in the eleventh, he was on second base with one out when the hitter chopped a bouncer to third baseman Tim Foli. Mays could have reached third easily if he had run fast. Instead, he slowed down so that Foli, glimpsing Mays out of the corner of his eye, believed he could tag him instead of getting the sure out at first—a high-risk baserunning gambit that required speed, improvisation, and an instant calculation of his chance for success. Mays avoided the lunging Foli and slid in safely at third, giving the Giants runners at the corners with one out instead of a man on third with two outs. Mays scored the game-winning run on a sacrifice fly.

The day that Dickey's harangue was published, Charlie Fox said of Mays, "I'd kiss him if Jim Bouton wouldn't put it in his next book," and Dickey's own newspaper wrote that Mays "should have been given the stadium."

The column set off a media firestorm, drawing scorn from radio talk show hosts as well as Lon Simmons during a game. The *Examiner* also pounced. Prescott Sullivan, who acknowledged that "we are not one of Mays's biggest boosters," described Mays as "a less than perfect human being, [but] with fewer faults than are necessary to the species." He asked *Examiner* photographer Charles Doherty if Mays was uncooperative. "Not at all," Doherty said. "Oh, there may have been a couple times over a period of thirteen years when he balked at posing for gag shots, but I'd say he had a pretty good record." He also asked Giant beat writers about Mays.

Bucky Walter: "He's okay. I've always gotten along with him." Jim McGee: "I've never had any trouble with Willie. It isn't easy to get a story out of him, though. He tries to avoid controversy."

Wells Twombly attacked the messenger, saying of Dickey, "Ambition doth make hatchet men of us all." Sarcastically calling him a fine newsman, Twombly wrote: "Confronted with the fact that his shirt slithered off his back at high noon when he left his air-conditioned hotel room, he immediately broke the news that it is humid in Houston in the summertime." Twombly also noted: "If Willie isn't the bubbly little creature that New York writers used to insist he was, he, at least, isn't surly. And these days, that is a blessing."

In a second column, Dickey said that many fans had written to him— "the kinder ones suggested I was mentally ill"—and the Giant players "threw me out of the clubhouse."

Mays himself never commented on the column, nor will he. He never dignifies his adversaries. But he was visibly upset when he read it, which confirmed his view that with rare exception, he should never trust a journalist.

A more creative attack came from a magazine called *Sport Scene,* which in 1971 published an article, "Willie Mays Is Hurting the Giants!" How so? "Usually no man wins or loses a pennant by himself, but an overreliance on Mays may very well have cost the Giants one or more flags." If only he had played for the Dodgers.

There were no second-place finishes for the Giants in 1971. They finally won something, the National League West, though even that they almost blew. They took over first place on April 12, were up by ten games in early June, and had an 8½-game lead on September 3. But they lost eight out of nine in one September stretch and had to win the final game of the season to hold off the Dodgers.

McCovey, hobbled by injuries at the age of thirty-three, played only 105 games. Bobby Bonds was now the star, hitting .288 with 33 homers, 102 RBIs, and 26 stolen bases. Younger players, including Ken Henderson, third baseman Al Gallagher, and rookie shortstop Chris Speier, rounded out a solid if unspectacular starting lineup—Bonds's .288 average was the highest on the team. Marichal and Perry anchored the starting staff, and reliever Jerry Johnson had a career year as closer (eighteen saves).

The hot bat that Mays took into his fortieth birthday cooled down as the summer progressed—he was hitting .289 by the end of June and, playing in 136 games, finished the season at .271. The year reflected his adjustments to his age. The most walks he ever had for a season was 82, in 1964, but in 1971 he drew 112 walks, giving him a team-best on-base percentage of .425. More surprising were Mays's stolen bases—twenty-three in twenty-six attempts, equaling his stolen bases for the three previous years combined. Mays says he ran more because McCovey missed so many games, reducing the need to keep the hole open on the right side, and it's probably true that Mays would have stolen far more bases in the 1960s with a different cleanup hitter. Regardless, in 1971 he showed that with his power numbers down, he could beat you in other ways.

There were, however, signs of decline. The most obvious were his strike-outs—123, by far the most of his career and the first time he had surpassed 100. Mays also had seventeen errors, another career high, but eleven of those were at first base. Perhaps the clearest indication of age occurred in September, when Dodger hurler Bill Singer hit Mays with a pitch, sidelining him for several days. "He couldn't get out of the way," McCovey recalls. "So we teased, 'You're slowing down.' That was kind of the beginning of it, really."

In the Giants' final game, against San Diego, Mays drove in the first run with a double and scored on rookie Dave Kingman's homer. San Francisco won, 5–1, triggering a celebration in the clubhouse as the players sprayed champagne, romped around, and happily denigrated the Dodgers. "They kept saying we were a dead horse," Marichal said. "Who's dead now?"

Mays sat slumped in the corner, subdued. He had received about ten cortisone shots during the year for various ailments, and the night before, Giant trainer Leo Hughes had wanted to give him another shot for the painful bursitis in his right shoulder, which had prevented him from holding his bat properly aloft. Mays refused, because he would have to wait twenty-four hours to play. He did, however, advise Bonds to take a cortisone shot for a pulled muscle in his left rib cage—so Bonds sat out the most important game of the season, but now he'd be ready for the playoffs.

Reporters clustered around Mays. When Kingman poured champagne over his head, all he could do was wipe it from his eyes. He spoke almost as if he were watching another team.

"Let them celebrate," he said. "That's for the kids. I'm really happy for them. We're not there yet. They don't think like me. We still got the Pirates to worry about."

He considered the broad sweep of his career. "Nineteen fifty-one, 1954, 1962. That's not many pennants when you play twenty years, and we don't have this one yet. The kids are happy because they just won the division. I won't be happy until we get into the World Series. I like to wait to do my celebrating."

Mays ran his hand over his sunken face. "Man, even this was a long time coming." Asked if he was tired, he could barely speak the words: "Oh, man, I've been so tired for the last month or so. Everybody on the team's known it, but I had to play. I had to be there. . . . Those kids need me. They come to me and I go to them with advice. Some of them look on me as their father."

McCovey, who had been spelled repeatedly by Mays, paid homage to his friend. "You know who I'm happiest for?" he said. "Willie. He played too much. He played when I couldn't because one of us had to be in there."

The Giants' inability to wrap up the division cost them dearly. The Pirates, led by Willie Stargell and Roberto Clemente, had won their division by seven games and were well rested. But Marichal had to pitch the last game of the season, which meant he could pitch only once in the five-game series against the Pirates, and not until the third game. Perry threw the opener in Candlestick and won, 5–4, but the Pirates won the next game, 9–4. In Pittsburgh, Marichal pitched well but lost, 2–1. The fourth game returned Perry to the mound against Steve Blass.

The playoff attracted writers from New York, including Jimmy Cannon, who had immortalized Mays years ago and now had a chance to rhapsodize about him again. "The face is young, but the lines of exhaustion age him," Cannon wrote.

He carries the skills across the autumn, and he reminds me of those summer days years ago on picnics. There was a race, and people would have to negotiate a measured distance holding a raw egg on a spoon. The ones who were careful, walking gingerly, won. Every step was important, and if the egg rolled off the spoon the race was over. This is Willie Mays now, going through a playoff with the egg of his skills on a spoon.

"It is just a helpless hurt," he told me. . . . "I can't even think about it."

Mays hit well in the opening games, going 3-for-7 with a home run and three RBIs. He got a single in game three, but neither he nor anyone else could stop the Pirates. The Giants were drained from the division race, and they could not overcome their many injuries; Bonds missed the second playoff game and was a nonfactor throughout. Mays went hitless in the fourth game, as the Pirates knocked out Perry in the sixth inning and won handily, 9–5. The series ended quickly.

The most-discussed play for Mays occurred in the third game, in the sixth inning, when he came to bat with Tito Fuentes on second, the game tied, and no one out. With the series at 1–1, it was a critical moment. On the first pitch, Mays squared and bunted it foul. The next pitch, he faked the bunt and took a ball. On the third pitch, he bunted, but the ball rolled only a couple of feet. He screamed to Fuentes, "Go! Go! Go!" But catcher Manny Sanguillen grabbed the ball, checked the runner back, and threw out Mays. The Giants failed to score.

For a player who had once been criticized for his unwillingness to bunt, Mays's play evoked both bewilderment and sadness. Had he been bunting for a hit—and with the element of surprise, he would have succeeded with a good bunt—the play would have been easy to justify. But he had already tipped his hand and was bunting to sacrifice. For most batters, that was a legitimate move—get the runner to third with less than two outs. But Mays had never been "most batters."

He was grilled with questions after the third and fourth games. Why did you bunt? He answered evenly, without rancor. He said he was trying to make it as easy as possible for the next hitters, McCovey and Bonds, to drive in the run. "I felt one of them could get Tito home and the way [Marichal] was pitching, another run could've meant the ball game, right?"

"Yes," someone challenged, "but that means you were giving up and saying you couldn't drive in Fuentes yourself."

"I resent anybody saying I'm giving up," Mays said calmly. "That run to me was an important run. I was thinking of the best way to get the run in, the best way to win. Another thing: I've played 137 games this year. I'm dead tired. I didn't feel that strong Tuesday. If I felt stronger, I'd never do that."

Mays didn't fly home with the team. He wanted to go by himself. Says Fuentes, "I believe he was hurt and embarrassed. It ate him alive, and he wanted to think about it."

It was, no doubt, a melancholy end to Mays's season, but it did not obscure his contributions. By now, his record as one of the greatest players in baseball history—if not the greatest—had been established, and if he had retired in 1971, his legacy would have included his durability and his fitness. At thirty-nine and forty, he easily outperformed Babe Ruth at those ages, who, bloated and ailing, had to retire after twenty-eight games in his fortieth year. Mickey Mantle and Joe DiMaggio both retired at thirty-six. Neither Ty Cobb nor Ted Williams played in as many games, at thirty-nine and forty, as Mays, and Stan Musial's numbers weren't as good at that age either.

Had Mays retired, he would be remembered for defying his own biology through a lifestyle that emphasized temperance, moderation, and rest, and the images that would have bracketed his career would have been the Catch in 1954 and his collide-and-catch with Bonds in 1970, two moments that captured the skill and spirit of the man. But Mays did not retire.

CHAPTER THIRTY-FIVE

NEW YORK, NEW YORK

One year before Willie introduced Mae at his birthday party, he took her out to dinner and seemed unusually serious. He told her how he felt. "I want to marry you," he said, "but give me a little time. I don't want to lose you." He slipped a ring on her finger.

Love, yes; commitment, apparently so; an actual wedding date, no. Mae continued to wait, though Willie himself had entered a new phase of his life. In 1969, he wanted to buy a home in Atherton, an exclusive community— said to have the highest per-capita income in California—about thirty-five miles south of San Francisco. Ty Cobb had lived there. So too had Alvin Dark. But Mays didn't have the money. Instead, he had friends. He had met Dinah Shore on the Pro-Am golf circuit. The actress was also from the South, and she seemed to understand Willie, who was fifteen years her junior, and would often tease him, "Hi, little boy, you need anything?"

"I don't need anything now," he'd say.

But one day Mays called her. "Dinah, I got to buy a house, and I don't know what to do."

"How much do you need?" she asked.

Mays also asked for help from Donna Reed, and she and Shore helped him cover the $67,000 down payment on the $165,000 house and also paid for new furniture. The house itself had eighteen rooms, including five bedrooms, a swimming pool, and a cabana, all on two acres of spacious lawns with tall redwoods and California oaks.

By November 1971, Willie finally decided, in his words, "to grow up a little," and also to fully trust again. He invited Mae to his house, and at midnight Mae called her friend, Jessie Goins.

"Willie wants to know," Mae said, "can you go to Mexico?"

Jessie, who had never been out of California, asked what for.

"Willie is talking about going to Mexico and getting married," Mae explained. She said Willie wanted to bring a group of friends.

"Whatever it takes," Jessie said. "When are we going?"

"Tomorrow morning."

The next day was Thanksgiving.

"No problem," Jessie said.

Willie's friends were used to his unpredictable travel whims—last-second decisions, say, to pack the car and drive to Vegas. But this seemed preposterous. Nine people would be traveling, including several who didn't have passports and one—Mae—who didn't have a wedding dress. At the airport, Willie bumped into one of his golfing partners, Bob Hope, who asked where he was going.

"Mexico—to get married," he said. Hope thought that was hilarious.

By now, Mays had become a savvy negotiator and knew how to leverage his celebrity for the best possible deals, be it for cars, clothes, or travel. He had also expanded his contacts in the corporate world, including American Airlines, and he persuaded the carrier to fly his party, free of charge, to Mexico City and then to Acapulco and to put them up in luxury hotels owned by the airline. But American Airlines got something in return. *Ebony* ran a glorious cover photo of Willie and Mae in Acapulco and published four pages of photographs of the couple's wedding and honeymoon. In the middle of those pages was a full-page ad from American Airlines promoting travel to—naturally—Mexico.

Willie had also resolved the passport issue. When they landed in Mexico City, they were met by Bernard Farat, an executive at the National Council of Tourism, who allowed them to enter without passports. Willie tried to tip him, but Farat said he couldn't accept money. Willie had another idea. He had given Jessie a "Willie Mays watch," which had his image on the face and which she was now wearing.

He showed Farat the watch. "Can you take this?" The executive said he'd be grateful for it. Willie gave it to him and replaced Jessie's when they returned.

In Mexico City, Mae bought a white lace wedding dress with white gloves and a veil, but a problem arose on the wedding day. Mae and Willie needed to submit a photograph of themselves to the judge, but they didn't have any. So they had to take a taxi to a photographer's studio—"It was out in the middle of nowhere," Jessie says—and once they arrived, the photographer recognized Willie and said he'd take the picture if Willie gave him an autograph, plus his usual fee. Willie got angry only after the camera broke and more time was wasted waiting for a new one. It was Saturday, and the couple had to be in a judge's private office by noon to take their vows or wait until Monday. Back in their hotel, they were hurriedly dressing for the ceremony when Willie's zipper broke, requiring someone with smaller fingers to get the damn thing on track. They barely made it to the judge on time. The brief ceremony was conducted in Spanish, which neither Willie nor Mae spoke, but Farat translated.

The whole traveling party went on the honeymoon, which suited Willie fine. He loved Mae, but he reveled in the companionship of men, with whom he could play golf while the women shopped and lounged on the beach. For his wife and his friends, Willie organized the trip just as he played baseball—it was spontaneous and flamboyant, and it gave them something to talk about.

Mae and Willie settled in. She put her career on hold and assumed the job of caring for Willie. She cooked, cleaned, answered his mail, packed his luggage, sent out the Christmas cards, paid the bills, took care of the new poodle, and helped with the raising of Michael. "The feminists will probably crucify me for this," she said, "but if you love the guy, it's worth it."

Her warmth and generosity were her greatest assets. She would give the police officers who patrolled the neighborhood pastries or autographed baseballs. But she also stood up to Willie. One time, he had promised to donate a golf bag to a charity, and when he forgot, a member of the charity came to the house and asked for it. Mae told the person, "You go out in the garage, pick out a bag, and if he says anything to you, you tell him to come see me."

She understood that baseball was Willie's first love and he could only give her so much of himself—Willie acknowledges that he does not share his deepest feelings with anyone. "Even your own wife shouldn't know everything about you," he says. "That's just the way it is. That's the way I am."

But his deeds won over Mae. On one occasion, her cousin Judi Phillips was visiting, and she was in the kitchen, crying. Willie came in and asked what was wrong. Judi said she was on the phone with her mother, and they'd had an argument. Willie pulled out his wallet and gave her a hundred-dollar bill.

"Wipe your eyes," he said. "Send her some flowers and tell her that you love her." He then walked out.

When Judi told Mae what had happened, Mae said, "He never ceases to amaze me." And he found ways to show his love. One Valentine's Day, he gave Mae a white Rolls-Royce with a burgundy interior.

Mae was thirty-two when she married, and in an interview at the time she talked about her stepson—"Michael is a wonderful boy"—and their intention to start their own family.

"We'd love to have a baby girl," Mae said. "They're so wonderful. And I think Willie needs a baby girl. We already have our boy."

"Two," said Willie, laughing.

• • •

By 1972, Mays was older than every National League ballpark except Wrigley Field. Five managers were younger than he. The itinerant Braves had moved from Boston to Milwaukee to Atlanta, and the game itself looked and felt different. There was AstroTurf (installed in Candlestick in 1970), bright, stretchy uniforms (not good for flabby pitching coaches), new markets (Arlington, Texas), and the push for a designated hitter (adopted by the American League the following year). No other player from Mays's rookie year remained active.

Mays began the season with a bad vibe. The year before, he had asked Stoneham for a ten-year contract for $750,000. He would finish his playing career over the next several years, then work for the Giants in some capacity. Stoneham rejected the offer, saying the board of directors had authorized him only to offer a five-year contract at $75,000 a year. Mays was both hurt and puzzled; in all their years together, Stoneham had never mentioned the board of directors. Mays turned down the offer and signed a two-year deal for $165,000 a season.

Mays also thought it odd that the Giants had never acknowledged his marriage—no calls, no gifts, nothing. He had a box at Candlestick right next to one used by Stoneham's son, Pete. Before, Pete's wife often chatted with Mae. Now there were no conversations.

Events on the field, with the Giants staggering out of the gate, were even more troubling. McCovey fractured his arm on a collision at first base, Marichal started 1–6, and the team lost fourteen out of its first twenty games. Mays started badly too. In nineteen games, he was 9-for-49 (.183), with seven singles and two doubles. Charlie Fox said the aborted spring training, due to the players' strike, had hurt Mays more than most, but he was also losing patience. On April 25, the Giants called up outfielder Garry Maddox, a lithe twenty-two-year-old Vietnam veteran who, after eleven games in the Pacific Coast League, was batting .438 with fourteen extra-base hits and twenty-two RBIs. He replaced Mays in center field, and comparisons were immediately made to another young center fielder who had joined the Giants long ago after an astonishing run in the minors. Maddox had grown up in Los Angeles but was, in fact, a Giant fan because he idolized Mays and would wear number 24 in Little League. He was now succeeding the real number 24.

Mays and Fox were soon at odds over playing time. Before the first game of a doubleheader in late April, Mays handed in the lineups, then left Candlestick. Both he and Fox later said he was ill, but Herman Franks showed up the next day and spoke with Fox about how best to use Mays.

After the Giants lost three games in New York, they traveled to Philadelphia, where, on May 5, Mays received a phone call from a reporter in New York and was told that the Giants were trying to trade him to the Mets. He was stunned. He knew that the Giants were going with a younger team, but he couldn't believe that Stoneham hadn't told him first. The organization that he had given his life to apparently didn't want him anymore. He took it personally. He felt betrayed. "I only regret that I wasn't told," he said to reporters at the ballpark. "I'm not mad at anybody. I'm just sad. They're mad at me. . . . I was told they were going with young players. But I've contributed as much as the youth. Why punish me? When your time is up, they tell you to go? That's not fair."

Mays's age was less the issue than his salary. The Giants were going broke, and Stoneham could no longer afford his high-priced players. Thanks to the team's division championship in 1971, attendance had surged 52 percent, to 1,122,786, and the Giants' parent company earned $460,000, but it eliminated all dividends on common and preferred shares. Stoneham retained his $80,000 salary, but his loss in dividend income cost him at least $47,000. The Giants' dwindling attendance in 1972, 647,744, ensured another year of red ink, and one by one—Perry, Lanier, and Dick Dietz (1971), then McCovey (1972) and Marichal (1973)—the team was dismantled.

On one level, the effort to trade Mays was a mournful exercise. Joan Whitney Payson, who had vowed to bring Willie back to New York, had bankrolled the Mets in part to ensure that Mays and the other Giants would play nine games a year in New York, and throughout the 1960s, she had offered Stoneham considerable sums for Mays. This public courtship led to George Carlin's joke in 1966 when he played sportscaster Biff Burns. "In the sport-light spotlight tonight," he said, "first, a baseball trade: the San Francisco Giants have traded outfielder Willie Mays to the New York Mets in exchange for the entire Mets team. The Giants will also receive $500,000 in cash, two Eskimos, and a kangaroo."

Payson never offered that much, but even in 1971, well after Mays's prime, Dick Young reported that she had bid $1 million for him. Stoneham concluded that he needed Mays to win a championship. In 1972, however, the Giants were reeling, so Mays was expendable. But with his average under .200, the market had changed.

Stoneham wanted the Mets to assume Mays's contract and offer him a long-term deal. But he also wanted some young players. He traveled to New York in early May, and in four days of negotiations, he pressed for infielder Ted Martinez and one of two pitchers—Jon Matlack or Jim McAndrew. He got none of them. The Mets, led by M. Donald Grant, Payson's stockbroker who served as the organization's chairman of the board, did not deem Mays worthy of a single major league player and certainly not $1 million. The negotiations stalled.

Mays's fans, including those in the press, just wanted the return of their hero in exile. Red Smith wrote: "Twenty-one years have taken something off the speed, the arm, the batting eye, the power and the bubbling joie de vivre that made him the most exciting player of his time, but he is still Willie, a beautiful man. It would be a joy to welcome him home."

Wrote Dick Young, "When there's a chance to get a Willie Mays, don't quibble about a decade or two."

They got their wish, and the trade was announced on May 11. Willie would go to the Mets for a minor league pitcher named Charlie Williams and cash, with reports speculating the sum to be $100,000. Stoneham, however, later acknowledged that he didn't accept any money. Ultimately, all that mattered was that Willie would be taken care of, and the Mets agreed to pay him $165,000 that year and the next. Mays said the Mets also agreed to pay him, on his retirement, $50,000 a year for ten years.

The announcement, at a press conference at the Mayfair House, caused Stoneham to tear up. "I never thought I would trade Willie," he said. "But with two teams in the Bay Area, our financial situation is such that we could not afford to keep Willie and his big salary as well as the Mets. The Mets are the only club that could take care of him. Don and Mrs. Payson are as much in love with Willie as I am."

By then, Stoneham had explained to Mays why he couldn't tell him about the trade talks. If the trade hadn't happened, then what? They were all blindsided by the leaks, and the trade may have been harder on the owner than the player. Stoneham was now seventy years old, and looked it. The financial stress, as well as the alcohol, had done him no favors. He sold the Giants in 1976, but even that wasn't his biggest loss.

As Pat Gallagher, a longtime Giant executive, later said, "Selling Willie was the great tragedy in Horace's life."

At the press conference, Grant conceded that the trade had little to do with improving the club. This was about helping Willie. "There was a lot of sentiment and pride" in bringing him back, Grant said. "Willie would be taken care of just as Mr. Stoneham would want him to be."

The comments were sad and paternalistic—Stoneham and Grant sounded like "plantation owners," wrote the *New York Times*'s Dave Anderson—but Mays, who was at the conference, found the words reassuring. The clubs were doing what you do in any family. "I really have to thank that man," Mays said, nodding to Stoneham. "He looked after me. He took care of me."

Typically, he concealed how he truly felt, but his wife told a reporter the following year how deeply he had been wounded. "No one, not even myself, really can imagine how badly Willie was hurt when he was traded," Mac said. "We're very close. But he wouldn't then, nor now, talk about it. He felt like a father to some of those" Giant players.

But Mays's ties with New York had now been restored. "I always liked San Francisco," he said, "but this is like coming back to paradise." Asked if playing in New York would give him a psychological edge, he noted, "I don't know that psychology can do anything for you when you're forty-one, but I can still run and I can still swing a bat."

The St. Francis Monastery of Manhattan, in its "Your Good Word for Today," had recorded: "New York has reason to rejoice these days. Willie Mays has returned. There is some heart in professional sports."

The Giants, and much of San Francisco, were devastated. Mayor Joseph Alioto said in a statement, "There is no joy in Frisco. The mighty Stoneham has struck out." Clubhouse attendant Mike Murphy cried. So did Tito Fuentes and Bobby Bonds. Charlie Fox, in a clubhouse meeting, told the players the trade was in Willie's best interests. "We should all get down on our knees tonight and pray to God that what has happened to Willie will happen to us when we're through." But that was no consolation to Bonds. "I don't think I've ever been so disappointed or hurt," he later said. "It was like they cut me down the middle and traded part of me. It was like only half of me was playing for the rest of the year."

Lon Simmons spoke with Mays on the phone for his pregame show. "What do you actually feel?" he asked.

"Well, first of all," Mays said, "it was very hard for me to leave San Francisco, leaving the guys I know so much, but once you get here and the feeling that you have here, it's just like you're going to another family."

Simmons asked a series of questions. Did he feel like he was returning to where it all began? Did he have any thoughts on how long he was going to play? Was he going to make San Francisco his home? Mays answered respectfully but cautiously. Then Simmons tried to draw Mays out of his shell.

"Willie, what are your thoughts now about San Francisco? Have they been good years for you out there?"

Simmons might have expected an answer that would reveal Mays's struggles and triumphs and the long journey that spanned fourteen years in which the city learned to love him and he learned to love her. But Willie does not reveal the secrets of his heart in radio interviews. "I think I had wonderful years in San Francisco," he said. "I have a lot of wonderful friends there. I'll be coming back there off and on, I know."

After the interview, Simmons played a clip of Mays scoring from first base on a McCovey bunt that rolled along the left field line, announced that the Giants were retiring number 24, and declared the end of an era. The first time Simmons saw Mays in an orange and blue Met uniform, he cried.

Mays had indeed come full circle. He had played for the New York Giants, the venerable patriarch from the league's earliest days; the San Francisco Giants, the defiant adventurer who opened the West; and now the Mets, in the vanguard of the upstart expansion teams that ultimately increased the majors from sixteen clubs to thirty. Mays's repatriation, however, was freighted with meaning beyond wins and losses, as his storybook return was seen as an antidote for baseball and New York. It was a bad time for both.

In baseball, the wounds were still deep from the players' strike, which was only a preview of battles to come. Curt Flood's lawsuit had left scars on players and owners alike, while an unusually bitter holdout by Oakland A's pitcher Vida Blue against his bombastic owner, Charlie Finley, had ended in a crossfire of accusations. Baseball itself had been surpassed by football as a television attraction, as the NFL now featured glamorous athletes like Joe Namath and O. J. Simpson. The average baseball attendance had fallen steadily throughout the 1960s—the game's meditative qualities were anachronistic in an era of instant gratification. A character's comment in the 1973 movie *Bang the Drum Slowly,* "Baseball is a dying game," seemed true enough.

The New York to which Mays was returning was no longer "the capital of baseball" and was not in "the golden age" of anything. The forces that had pushed the Giants out in the first place—suburban flight, crime, congestion, poverty—had only taken a deeper hold. New York was spinning toward bankruptcy, three years away from the *Daily News*'s famous headline: FORD TO CITY: DROP DEAD. Gotham's preeminence had been lost, its confidence shattered. In movies such as *Dog Day Afternoon, The French Connection, The Out-of-Towners,* and *The Taking of Pelham One Two Three,* New York was depicted as a relentless urban dystopia. And where the Polo Grounds once stood was a redbrick fortress of an apartment building— "the projects"—and center field was paved with an asphalt playground surrounded by wires for foul balls. WILLIE MAYS FIELD, proclaimed a forlorn sign. SOFTBALL PLAYING ONLY.

For many New Yorkers, the departure of the Dodgers and the Giants was seen as the symbolic beginning of the city's downward spiral. Now Willie Mays had returned to reverse it, and it began in his very first game.

• • •

Before the trade was made final, Grant and Yogi Berra, in his first season as the Mets' manager, had told Mays that he would be a role player, platooning with left-hander Ed Kranepool at first base and spelling Tommie Agee in center. His first game in New York was on May 12, when the Mets faced the Giants. Bonds and Fox sought him out before the game to shake his hand. When Maddox spoke to him, the new Giant center fielder said he needed a mitt. "Willie gave me his glove right there," Maddox recalls. "His name was written into it."

Mays didn't start the first game, and when a pinch-hitting opportunity arose in the eighth, the crowd booed when John Milner stepped into the on-deck circle. Mays didn't get in the first game of the series or the second, but in the final game, on Mother's Day, he started at first base and led off. Rain kept the attendance down to 35,505, but their cheers, Mays later said, gave him goose bumps. He took the field in the strange pin-striped uniform—he said it felt "a little awful"—but he had his familiar number. Jim Beauchamp, who had been number 24, now wore number 5. With the rain coming down, Mays faced Sam McDowell in the first inning. "It's kinda hard to consider Buck the enemy," McDowell later said. "There's just no way you can feel he's the enemy deep down inside you."

McDowell walked Mays in his first at-bat but struck him out the second time. Mays fielded some throws at first base and caught a pop-up, then in the fifth, came to bat with the score tied 4–4, with Don Carrithers pitching. Mays felt more relaxed than during his first at-bats, and he was thinking home run. The crowd, according to *Sport*, "cheered Mays with a fervor nearing desperation. . . . There were 40,000 who wanted it to happen, who were trying by a collective act of will to make it happen, just this once."

With the count full and the rain falling harder, Mays lined the pitch over the left field wall. It may have been his most dramatic swing ever. It was certainly his strangest trip around the bases. He got to first and passed Dave Kingman. Then standing around second base were Fuentes and Chris Speier, who wouldn't give Mays a direct path to the bag. "Get outta here!" Mays squealed. He nodded to Jim Ray Hart at third and, as he headed toward the plate, "I felt something in my leg," he recalled, "and I couldn't hardly get to home, and I happened to turn my head to the right, and I saw all the Giants in there clapping, and I got to home plate and made a half turn right before I realized it." Mays was heading to the wrong dugout. He stopped himself, turned left, and jogged to the correct one.

If it had rained any harder—if the heavens had opened up—there might have been a mass conversion in Shea Stadium to all faiths, one writer observed. Columnist Pete Hamill wrote: "Willie Mays ran the bases, carrying all those summers on the forty-one-year-old shoulders, jogging in silence, while people in the stands pumped their arms at the skies and hugged each other and even, here and there, cried. It was a glittering moment of repair, some peculiar sign that we might be able to erase what happened, eliminate the sense of cynicism that flooded the city in 1958 when the Giants and Dodgers left for the West. It was as if some forgotten promise had been kept."

The home run was the difference in the game, the Mets winning, 5–4.

Mays had joined a team that was still in despair from a tragedy. Three years earlier, the Mets had won the World Series with Gil Hodges as their manager. Tough, disciplined, and highly respected, he was recognized as one of the best managers in the big leagues. He also smoked three packs of cigarettes a day, and on April 2, 1972, just two days before he would have turned forty-eight, he dropped dead of a heart attack. His replacement, Yogi Berra, would always suffer by comparison. He had been a Met coach and in 1972 would be elected to the Hall of Fame for his career as a Yankee catcher. In his only other managing stint, he had been fired by the Yankees, who thought he had lost control of the team, and his efforts to prevent that from recurring led to clashes with several veterans, most notably Mays.

The Mets were a fairly young team, so while Berra may have envisioned Willie as a high-priced scrub, he was still a demigod in the locker room. Tommie Agee recalled playing with Mays in the 1966 All-Star Game in St. Louis. "When I went out in the outfield, I tried to stand in the same place Willie Mays had been standing," he said.

Met pitcher Jerry Koosman was nine years old when Mays broke into the majors. "Willie Mays had always been my hero," he said, and now having him "as your center fielder or first baseman—talk about giving you a pump!" They became friends and often ate meals together in Willie's hotel room, where Mays would strengthen his hands by squeezing a rubber ball. "We'd talk about baseball every night," Koosman said. "How to play the game, what to do in certain situations, what hitters looked for, what he looked for against certain pitchers."

No Met idolized Mays more than Cy Young winner Tom Seaver, who as a player at Fresno State College once sat next to Mays in the dugout when the Giants were there for an exhibition game. "I looked at him and the top button of his uniform was unbuttoned, so in the big leagues, I never buttoned my top button," Seaver says. "That's where I got it from."

The first time Mays played in center with Seaver pitching, he approached Seaver before the game with the opposing team's lineup, asked how he was going to pitch each batter and where should he play. "Part of me thinks, isn't this ironic, but the professional part of me thinks, this is spectacular," Seaver recalls. "So I went down the lineup. And then I said, 'If I want to move you, I'll turn around and move my glove that way, and you move until I lose eye contact, and that's it.' And then he said, 'We'll adjust the last six outs.' And I said, 'Absolutely.'"

Seaver, who pitched in the majors for twenty years, says Mays was the only position player who ever asked him how he was going to pitch to opposing hitters. "Nobody ever did that to me," he says. "Nobody."

There were still skeptics who viewed Mays's return to New York as one more bauble in Joan Whitney Payson's bejeweled life. Mays might be good for an occasional thrill and a few nostalgic riffs from aging journalists, but he was ultimately a museum piece who wouldn't do much to help the team. Mays proved them wrong.

Including his home run against the Giants, he got on base nineteen times in his first thirty-seven trips to the plate. He scored at least one run in each of the next six games he played and won three games with base hits—two homers and a fourteenth-inning single. New York had revived him.

As was always the case, the numbers alone did not reflect Mays's contributions. His teammates would talk about one play for years, a base-running ploy that defied age and reason. It occurred against the Expos on May 18, and Murray Kempton, whose baroque essays covered New York for more than three decades, wrote about it while on assignment for *Esquire*. Kempton initially observed Mays taking batting practice, noting that "there falls upon him in the cage a desperation like the prisoner's in his cell."

In the first inning, Mays dodged two close fastballs, tipped a pitch, and then walked. The next hitter, Ted Martinez, drove the ball into right center. Mays, Kempton wrote, "gunned around second and then, coming into third, quite suddenly slowed, became a runner on a frieze, and turned his head to watch the fielders. He was inducing a mental error; he had offered the illusion that he might be caught at home, which would give Ted Martinez time to get to third.

"And only then did Willie Mays come down the line like thunder, ending in a heap at home, with the catcher sprawled in helpless intermingling with him and the relay throw bouncing through an unprotected plate and into the Montreal dugout."

Mays jumped to his feet and pointed to the ball to ensure that the umpire knew to send Martinez home. The two runs, Kempton wrote, "were the unique possession of Willie Mays, who had hit nothing except one tipped foul."

Kempton compared his hesitation at third base to both the Delta blues and to Faulkner—a purely southern gambit that required a rhythmic defiance of all convention. "Willie Mays arraying himself of the charge—three pauses to assemble the irascible, occasionally even vicious dignity of the southern country boy's announcement that he is taking command of the city ones."

The Mets won, 2–1. After the game Berra said, "I think Willie timed that throw. I've seen him do that before. He slows down and tries to hit the plate at the same time as the throw to make it hard on the catcher."

Mays said, "Yogi lies a lot. You can't time no throw like that."

Mays may not have played stickball in Harlem anymore, but he was still visible outside the ballpark. In August he accepted an invitation to speak at Riker's Island, where he took some swings on a softball field and addressed about five hundred inmates, most of whom were black and Hispanic. "I wanted to come and talk to you fellas," he said. "I don't think my coming here is going to change anything for you and that things will be any different when I leave, but I want you to know that I'm very happy to be here just the same. I understand what's happening here."

Asked by a reporter what he meant, Mays said, "I can't explain it. It's something between me and them. But believe me, I can feel it in here." He pointed to his heart. A prisoner asked Mays for his baseball hat. "I'm sorry," Mays said. "I can't give it to you because it's the one I use in ball games. But if you'd like, I'd be happy to give you the vest I'm wearing." Mays took off his gold vest and handed it over.

"Wow," the inmate said, "right off his back. He's good people."

The Mets were 14–7 and in first place when Mays joined them, and they won nine in a row and fourteen out of eighteen. Then came the injuries. Right fielder Rusty Staub, whom the Mets had acquired in the off-season and was now the centerpiece of their offense, broke his thumb and didn't return until September. The Mets' other outfielders, Cleon Jones, Tommie Agee, and John Milner, also went down, as did second baseman Ken Boswell. The upshot was that Mays played more than he'd anticipated—in one three-week period, he started seventeen of twenty-three games, and it was too much. His left knee needed to be drained, he pulled his right thigh muscle, he injured a finger sliding into a base. Friction with Berra, only six years his senior, soon surfaced over playing time—Mays thought he was being overused, which was hurting his performance. Berra wanted Mays to take batting practice before each game and follow the same schedule as everyone else. But Mays had been setting his own schedule for years, and he wasn't prepared for the extra work. The strain was evident, with reporters variously describing him as "brooding" or "crotchety." "By the end of the season," *Sports Illustrated* wrote, "he could hardly drag himself to the plate."

The year began with Mays at 646 homers and Hank Aaron at 639. Aaron was thirty-eight years old, and Mays had known for several years that it was only a matter of time before Aaron would pass him. He did just that on June 10, with home run 649. Now Hank alone would chase the Babe.

With Mays on the team, the Mets made only one trip to San Francisco in 1972. They flew in from Los Angeles late on July 20; while walking through the San Francisco airport, Mays was so distracted that he bumped into a pillar. Berra had announced that he would not be in the starting lineup, but Mays asked to start and Berra agreed. Mays had never been in the visitors' clubhouse, and he had a funny feeling throughout the game. Only 18,117 fans were at Candlestick, the attendance curtailed by Berra's announcement. But they gave Mays a standing ovation when he hit a two-run homer in the fifth inning.

The Mets couldn't overcome their injuries or their lousy hitting and finished in third place, 13½ games out. Mays posted the lowest offensive numbers of his career, but he gave the Mets as much as they could have hoped for. He played in sixty-nine games, about 50 percent of the Mets' total once he joined. His .402 on-base percentage led the team, and his .267 average and .446 slugging percentage were second. His star power had not diminished. Though the Mets were not a pennant contender in the second half, they led the league in both home and road attendance.

Mays's improbable return, awash in remembrance and renewal, was hailed as a triumph. "Mays knows that we New York fans will not forget," Jeff Greenfield wrote at season's end. "And in turn, Willie Mays is reminding New York of our own best moments, and our own best hopes. He is there to convince us that it was not a dream—that time when New York was secure in its own vitality. The city is an unhappy land that needs a hero, but we are less unhappy now that Willie Mays is back where he belongs."

CHAPTER THIRTY-SIX

THE END OF
A LOVE AFFAIR

M ays had been worried about his finances for several years. His expenses were still high—and more so after he was traded to New York, where he bought a penthouse overlooking the Hudson in the Riverdale section of the Bronx—and his investments had provided little security. In 1971, playing in a golf tournament in Puerto Rico, he met Vernon Alden, the chairman of the Boston Company, a financial services firm. He asked to meet privately with Alden and told him he would be receiving only $50,000 a year from baseball after he retired. "I can't live on that," he said.

Alden pledged to help Mays find work as a corporate consultant and by the following year had arranged contracts for him to represent three large companies, including Colgate-Palmolive, for an annual income of $150,000. Alden advised Mays for years to come, but the significance of these early contracts was that Mays entered the 1973 season with new sources of income. The Mets were still paying him $165,000, but money alone wasn't the reason he returned for another year.

For the first time in his career, Mays showed up at a spring training camp that was not part of the Giants. As it happened, he wore a gold medallion around his neck engraved with the symbols of three religions. "Christian, Jewish, Muslim," he said. "I don't take any chances."

But he needed more than an amulet. In the off-season he had had his knees examined, and when he took the field for the first time, he wore leather and steel braces around both: one brace to support his bad left knee, the other to prevent him from favoring the good one. "It's simple," he said. "Either my knees will take another year or they won't." His throwing arm began to bother him as well and required a cortisone shot. He asked Dick Young to watch him play and give him an honest opinion. Young concluded he could play one more year.

Mays had been going to Arizona for spring training since the early

1950s. Now with the Mets, he was in St. Petersburg, where vestiges of Jim Crow remained. He wanted to rent a luxury condominium along the waterfront but was told none was available. An employee at the complex called a local newspaper and said that places were available, but Mays was turned down because he was black. Called by a reporter, the people in charge quickly backtracked and told Mays that a misunderstanding had occurred; he would now be welcomed. The incident appears to have been ignored by the New York press, and Mays didn't call attention to it. However, he told *Black Sports,* a monthly magazine, "The hell with the [condominium officials]. They can't hurt me, man. That sort of thing's been happening to me all my life, and I'm way past it now. The only thing I ever worry about is, if they'd turn me down like that, what would they do if one of our young black players went there looking for a place? A kid, somebody who wasn't famous. They're the people I'm concerned about."

Mays also had problems with Berra. He arrived a day late, then, one Thursday afternoon, flew back to California to see Mae. She wasn't feeling well, he said, and he was still miffed about the condo. He intended to return on Friday, an off day, but the flight was canceled and he didn't get back until Saturday, missing a practice. Mays hadn't told Berra he was leaving, and the manager fined him $1,000. Mays admitted he was wrong and apologized in the press, but the relationship between the two men soon deteriorated beyond repair. Berra, under pressure after the previous year's collapse, wanted to impose discipline; he fined Rusty Staub as well for violating a team rule.

As the season unfolded, Mays didn't make it easy for Berra—another unexcused absence, erratic demands for playing time, and chronic injuries souring his own mood. In one game, Berra ordered Mays to bunt twice, and both times he popped out. Afterward, Mays openly questioned his manager. "I think I sacrificed only ten times in my career," he said, "and never twice in one game."

Berra resented Mays's being there in the first place. Years later, he was discussing his problems as a Yankee manager when George Steinbrenner kept interfering with the roster. "It was not just one guy like Willie Mays when he came to the Mets in 1973," Berra said. "It was four or five guys who [Steinbrenner] wanted and the coaches and I didn't."

Mays began the season 0-for-7. In early May, he smashed into a wall and aggravated his already creaky shoulder. On one play in center field, he had to toss the ball underhand after he caught it, which allowed a runner to easily advance from first to second. In his youth as a Black Baron or in his prime at the Polo Grounds, Mays served as the cutoff man for his left fielder. Now, in a June game at Shea, Mays tracked down a ball to the left center field fence, turned, and unexpectedly flipped it to *his* left fielder. "His failings are now so cruel to watch that I am relieved when he is not in the lineup," Roger Angell wrote. "It is hard for the rest of us to fall apart quite on our own; heroes should depart."

Even opposing pitchers took pity. "I say to hell with all hitters," an unnamed hurler told the *New York Times*, "but I gotta admit I feel a little sorry for him. You don't want him to hit a home run off you or beat you, but you wouldn't mind too much if he got a base hit off you once in a while or at least hit a long drive. You have to remember, this is Willie Mays, and he's not even getting the ball out of the infield anymore."

Willie's knees had to be drained, and in May he went on the disabled list for the first time in his career for a pulled tendon in his right shoulder. He returned, sore and limping. "They're keeping the old warrior together with needles and bailing wire," the *Sporting News* wrote in July.

No one suffered more than Mae. "When he was batting, I felt I was up there at the plate with him," she later said. "When his powers started diminishing, I ached with him. It was very difficult to hear people say he wasn't what he used to be. That was agony. Sheer agony."

The possibility of his retirement moved beyond speculation. It was now assumed. The only question was when.

Hitting .214 at midseason, Mays was not elected to start the All-Star Game or placed on the twenty-eight-member team by manager Sparky Anderson. Mays had played in twenty-three consecutive Midsummer Classics, and Jack Lang of the *Long Island Press* persuaded the National League's commissioner, Chub Feeney, that Mays should play in this one. Feeney also wanted his friend in the game, so he huddled with his American League counterpart, Joe Cronin, and they agreed to enlarge the rosters to allow Mays on the team. Insulted, Mays initially declined but then agreed. "Some guys find a way to duck the game," he said, "but I always went because it meant something to me and to baseball."

Justice was served in the American League as well, where Oakland manager Dick Williams added Nolan Ryan, who had already thrown two no-hitters in the season.

Mays made an out in his one at-bat as a pinch hitter, which did little to dampen his claim as the finest All-Star performer in history. His at-bats (seventy-five), hits (twenty-three), total bases (forty), and runs (twenty) remain records to this day. He was also twice named captain.

The Mets were having other problems. Once again, they were devastated by injuries—at one point, Berra had only a dozen healthy players—and they were in last place on June 29 and were still there on August 30. As the Watergate hearings took center stage that summer, Met reliever Tug McGraw wondered aloud who would get fired first, President Nixon or Yogi. Donald Grant said he would not fire Berra "unless public opinion demands it." (It apparently didn't, at least not until Grant fired him in the middle of the 1975 season.)

The Mets began a West Coast trip on August 8. Mays still hadn't said anything about retirement, though the Mets had announced that Willie Mays Night would be held on September 25. The fans in other cities began giving him tributes, starting in Los Angeles, where Mays received a raucous cheer when he pinch-hit in the final game of the series. In San Francisco, he received one final standing ovation when he loped to the dugout after grounding out in his last at-bat. And so it went, from San Diego to St. Louis, from Montreal to Philadelphia.

On August 17, Mays hit his sixth homer of the season over the right center field fence at Shea Stadium. It was the last of his career, number 660.

Fortunately, there were no dominant teams in the Mets' division, and when their injured players returned, they began to win behind Seaver, Koosman, and Matlack, with Tug McGraw closing, and they narrowed the lead from 11½ games on August 5 to three games on September 9. That day, in a game in Montreal, Mays collided with a metal rail while chasing a foul ball and cracked two ribs. After a day off, he failed to show up for a game in Philadelphia and arrived the following day. Under growing criticism from the press, he had told Grant earlier in the summer that he would be retiring, but then he had second thoughts. Not anymore. He called his friend Sam Sirkis from his hotel room. Sirkis had been helping professional athletes with their investments since the late 1950s and gradually began negotiating contracts for them as well. He had met Mays in 1970 and had represented him ever since. "Willie was very sensitive to critical press," Sirkis recalls, "and finally he had enough. He wanted to announce his retirement."

Why didn't Mays retire earlier? News reports suggested it was money or willful denial or self-centeredness. (The headline of Wells Twombly's column read: TRAGIC EGO TRIP OF WILLIE MAYS.) A better answer was fear. Mays kept playing because it was all he had ever done and all he really knew. Baseball had given his life order, context, and community, and the prospect of life without it was too chilling to contemplate.

"I don't know what I'm going to do next," he said in May. "Would you believe me sitting behind a desk? I can't stand the idea of working in an office. I've got energy I have to work off, even at my age." He added,

"Money has nothing to do with it. Baseball is my life. It's not something you can just walk away from and say good-bye to."

His teammates understood his struggle. McGraw said, "Willie was forty-two and he was hurt a lot. He got down on himself after a while because he knew he was going to retire, and he wanted to help the club and also not embarrass himself. Sometimes he'd force himself to play, and then he'd hurt himself again while trying to do it. . . . I know he and Yogi had a tough time as far as the lineup went, and a lot of times maybe Willie didn't want to come to the park at all—so as not to cause trouble about whether he should be in the lineup. [But] he didn't go around second-guessing anybody in the clubhouse, and on the bus and plane he really made himself fit in. I mean, he was with us only two years, and he was twice as old as some of the guys, but you'd think he'd spent the whole twenty years in the bigs with them."

Says Tom Seaver, "There are individuals you know you're going to have to tear the uniform off of. It's like a battlefield and you're in the trench, and the mentality is exactly the same with baseball. You're going to fight and play until they tear the uniform off—or, on the battlefield, until they kill you. And you got that sense with Willie—they were going to have to tear the uniform off him. It's sad to see, but it's a beautiful thing too, because of the love he had for what he had done for some twenty-odd years."

Neither he nor any other Met was going to question Mays's judgment on retirement, Seaver says. "It's a god you'll never confront."

The Mets' front office, however, apparently did not share the players' high esteem for Mays. Sirkis took the news about his retirement announcement to Grant, but the meeting did not go well. "Grant was derogatory against Willie in every way," he says. "I never told Willie about it, but we had no support for Willie's retirement." Adds Sy Berger, the Topps executive and Mays's longtime friend, "The Mets didn't want him. It was her money. Payson wanted him. Willie knew that, but he would never tell you if it bothered him."

The Mets helped promote Willie Mays Night, but plans for the actual ceremony fell largely to Mays himself as well as Sirkis, who enlisted corporate donors for gifts and other contributions. It wasn't that hard. Willie, for example, wanted to present Mae with a fur, and at the offices of the American Fur Industry, he selected a white full-length ermine coat with a hood. When he asked what it cost, the owner, Irwin Katz, said, "This is my personal gift to you for all the joy you have given me."

Colgate, meanwhile, covered the expenses for a suite at the Roosevelt Hotel, where Mays and Sirkis did most of their planning. One afternoon, four or five members of an African American group called Mays and asked to see him. Mays, in his bathrobe, invited them up and heard their request: they wanted him to talk about "black power" during the celebration. But using baseball to deliver a political message, to Mays, was like diluting the finest wine with a brackish backwater.

"See that door," Mays told them. "See you later."

Mays still had to announce his retirement. He had a long relationship with NBC, so he decided to make his statement on the morning of September 20 on the *Today* show. That afternoon, he held a press conference at the Shea Stadium Diamond Club. About a hundred journalists showed up, as did Grant, Berra, and other members of the Mets' organization. The *Daily News* would run a triple headline on its front page the following day:

GARMENT EXEC KNIFED TO DEATH

NIXON, COX DEADLOCK ON TAPES

WILLIE GOES OUT AS GRACEFULLY AS EVER

Mays kept his composure as he spoke before a bank of cameras.

"I thought I'd be crying by now," he said, "but I see so many people here who are my friends, I can't. Maybe I'll cry tomorrow . . . or the next day."

He's retiring, he said, "because when you're forty-two and hitting .211, it's no fun. . . . I just feel that the people of America shouldn't have to see a guy play who can't produce."

He said he played this year only because he was in New York. "New York fans love me," he said. "They showed me that. You know New York—when they love you, they love you." He was modest—"I never considered myself a superstar. I considered myself a complete player"—but also cautious about his future. "Managing is hard work, and I don't want that," he said, flashing a smile at Berra, "and I don't want to be a coach and just stand out there like an Indian."

Mays hadn't played in eleven days, and his ribs were still healing. The Mets were two games under .500 but in third place, only a game and a half out of first. Would Willie ever play again? "I came in playing," he said, "and I'd like to go out playing." But he did not want to "get in the way of these kids who have made such a great comeback." Still, "if the Mets get in the World Series, I'm playing in it. I don't know how, but I'm playing."

Mays acknowledged that his retirement "is no surprise to most of you," but it was still a surprise to him. "Baseball and me, we had what you might call a love affair."

• • •

The Mets, behind the best pitching staff in baseball, continued to win. In 1969, they were the "Miracle Mets" for overcoming the Cubs' big lead. Now their motto was, "You gotta believe." They won eleven of thirteen games and moved from fifth place to first, where they stood on Willie's night, September 25. Mays drove to Shea Stadium with Mae, Michael, and Sirkis. Also with them was Cat Mays, who had come in from California. On other trips to Shea, Mays would sometimes stop at a park or a playground and play stickball. "Even at that age, he would do that," Sirkis recalls. But not this afternoon. Mays said nothing while in the car, and when he pulled up to Shea at around 4 P.M., thousands of fans had already gathered in and around the parking lot, screaming for Willie.

Attending the game were Dodgers (Branca, Reese, and Snider), icons (DiMaggio and Musial), barnstormers (Doby and Joe Black), and the man to whom history had tied him forever (Vic Wertz). Plenty of Giants were there, including Bobby Thomson, now a graying businessman. "I was the center fielder" in 1951, he told reporters. "I saw him once and I said, 'Bobby, you'd better get a new position.'"

Mayor John Lindsay declared September 25 Willie Mays Day. Dick Young said it was "a night the pennant race stood still." The *New York Times* editorialized that Mays was "the epitome of what all great athletes ought to be—a man of grace and dignity. His list of vices began and ended with the bedevilment of opposing pitchers."

More than fifty-three thousand fans packed Shea, and their feelings were captured in signs around the stadium.

WE WHO ARE ABOUT TO CRY, SALUTE YOU
A GIANT AMONG METS
BYE, WILLIE, WE HATE TO SEE YOU GO
SHALOM

Met broadcaster Lindsey Nelson served as the emcee, and at 8 P.M., he introduced Walter Curley, New York's commissioner of public events, who read a proclamation from Mayor Lindsay. The fans booed. Then Nelson said, "The man you came to honor tonight . . . Willie Mays."

Mays hopped out of the dugout and walked steadily to the platform set up at home plate, where he joined Mae and Michael. On this cool night, he was wearing his blue warm-up jacket with the large NY insignia across the left breast. He stood next to Mae and Michael, stuffed his hands in his pockets, wet his lips, and stared straight ahead with dark, melancholy eyes. The cheers rang out for six minutes. Nelson tried to stop them after three minutes by raising his hand, but he was booed. The scoreboard lights read 24: SO LONG, YES; GOODBYE, NEVER, and the waves of adulation—"naked love," one writer said—continued, muffling the roar of the jet planes that flew low out of La Guardia.

Next came the gifts, which told their own story of how much baseball had changed. In presents that harkened to a time when players and fans were neighbors, store owners gave Mays towels, sheets, bedspreads, golf clubs, luggage, records, a silver tray, shirts, and a typewriter. He even got a salami. But in gifts that heralded the coming of the multimillionaire professional athlete and the marriage of big-time sports with corporate behemoths, Chrysler gave Willie and Mae His-and-Her cars—a Chrysler Imperial and a Chrysler Sebring. Pan American Airlines gave him a trip around the world, and American Airlines gave him a week in Acapulco. He also got a boat, bottles of Teacher's Scotch and Moët Champagne, and a "private telephone system." Mae, in addition to her ermine coat, received a diamond watch.

Joe Frazier gave Willie a snowmobile. Horace Stoneham gave him a $17,000 Mercedes-Benz. Miles College gave him an honorary doctor of laws degree, and the *Amsterdam News* gave him a plaque.

The Mets gave him nothing.

Mays finally spoke, though his remarks were short. He was concerned that the ceremony was intruding on a pennant race.

"I apologize for taking up a lot of your time," he began, his words echoing back. "I say to the Met players, forgive me." He thanked New York for always supporting him and then bared a bit of his soul. "This is a sad day for me," he said, "to hear you cheer me and not do anything about it." He again spoke to his team. "I hope you go on to win the flag for the New York people. This is your night as well as mine. I also want to thank the Montreal ball club. I know this is a delay for you. But this is my farewell. I thought I'd never quit."

He dabbed his eyes twice as he reached a haunting conclusion: "I see these kids over here, and I see how these kids are fighting for a pennant, and to me it says one thing: Willie, say good-bye to America."

Willie, say good-bye to America? The sentence seemed to be spoken in the inverse. Should it not have been "America, say good-bye to Willie"— that is, America's baseball fans could no longer watch him on the field, so they had to say good-bye. But Mays was a public figure who could not envision any other public role for himself, an entertainer with no second act. "He stabbed us all," Larry Merchant wrote, "with his epitaph."

Mays waved his cap into the final roar of the crowd, and he hugged Mae and Michael. He then picked up a box of long-stemmed roses and walked them to the stands along the first base line. Joan Whitney Payson, now seventy years old and in a wheelchair, was bundled in a heavy coat. Willie handed her the roses, and she leaned forward and placed a kiss on his cheek streaked with tears. He disappeared through the dugout and into the runway.

Watching in the Met dugout was Cleon Jones. "I felt I wanted to cry," he said afterward. "I know how Willie must have felt to say he can't perform anymore. It got next to me. . . . I think I might have dropped one or two tears. It was one of those times when you cry inside."

The Mets won the game, giving them seven in a row and a first-place lead of 1½ games. But Mays felt there was nothing left for him. He was now a retired ballplayer. He hadn't played in more than two weeks, and he was ready to return to Atherton. He called Payson and told her his plan. She urged him to reconsider. "You can't go home now," she said. So he stayed.

The Mets won their next game, then flew to Chicago with a half-game lead for the final series of the regular season. Two doubleheaders were scheduled. They split the first one but still picked up half a game. On Monday, October 1, they needed to win only one of the two games. Seaver started the first and was staked to a five-run lead; McGraw threw the final three innings and picked up his twenty-fifth save of the year. The umpires canceled the second game, and the Mets celebrated in the locker room. "We began pouring it on," McGraw later said, "hollering and screaming and wondering what all the people who'd counted us out of the human race a couple of months earlier must have been thinking." At 82–79, the Mets' .509 winning percentage was the lowest to win a division or a pennant. They scored fewer runs than all but one team in the majors, and they had no hitter with a .300 average or a pitcher who won twenty games.

You gotta believe.

Mays was with the team but did not see any action. After the game, Seaver looked for him in the clubhouse.

"Where's Willie?" he asked.

"He took two sips of champagne," someone told him, "and he's passed out on the training table."

The Mets faced the Cincinnati Reds in the playoffs in what appeared to be a mismatch. The Reds had won ninety-nine games, played three future Hall of Famers in Johnny Bench, Joe Morgan, and Tony Perez, and had MVP Pete Rose. What's more, Seaver's arm was strained from overuse down the stretch.

But the Mets had depth at pitching, the great equalizer in baseball, and the teams split the first two games in Cincinnati, with Matlack throwing a shutout for the Met victory in the second game. Mays did not play in either contest. Back at Shea for the third game, he did take the field in a way that added to his unique portfolio of contributions.

The Mets were leading, 9–2, in the fifth when Rose, on first base, tried to break up a double play with a hard slide at second. He knocked down Bud Harrelson, who had broken his wrist on a similar slide by another player in June. The wiry shortstop quickly regained his feet and cursed Rose, who charged him. The benches and bullpens emptied, secondary skirmishes broke out, and a five-minute brawl ensued. Rose was known for his hell-bent aggression—embraced by Reds fans as "Charlie Hustle," despised by others as a dirty player. In a lopsided game, the Met fans saw Rose's slide as a cheap shot, and when he took left field in the bottom of the inning, he was pelted with debris. Vendors later described fans grabbing beer cans right off their trays and hurling them at Rose, who flung several right back. The inning continued, but when a whiskey bottle flew out of the stands and nearly hit Rose, he called time and headed for the dugout. Red manager Sparky Anderson took his entire team off the field and told the umpires they wouldn't return until it was safe. The umpires consulted with Chub Feeney, who informed Berra that the Mets would have to forfeit unless the fans could control themselves. The public address announcer delivered that warning, which only provoked more boos.

Feeney had an idea—why not send the most respected Met onto the field to talk to the fans in left field. "He chose Willie Mays as a designated peacemaker and asked Berra to serve as a Henry Kissinger in knickers," Red Smith wrote. So out of the dugout appeared Mays, like an apparition, who was promptly cheered by the crowd. He was joined by Berra as well as Cleon Jones, Seaver, and Staub. Mays gave the peace sign to the fans, who again applauded him. He made a straightforward appeal. "Look at the scoreboard!" he yelled. "We're ahead. Let 'em play the game."

The grounds crew had to sweep up the debris, but play resumed, with Rose back in left field. The Mets won, 9–2, and Mays had a coda to his legacy as a peacemaker.

After an extra-inning Reds victory in the fourth game, the series went to the fifth and final contest, in New York, Seaver against Jack Billingham. In the fourth game, Staub had separated his shoulder when he ran into the outfield wall, so Cleon Jones shifted from left to right and Ed Kranepool played left. Kranepool drove in two runs in the first, but the Reds chipped away and tied it. In the bottom of the fifth, the Mets went ahead, 3–2, and with the bases loaded, Kranepool was due to bat against a left-hander. Berra called for Mays to pinch hit, and the Reds countered with right hander Clay Carroll. Mays hadn't been to the plate in thirty-one days and hadn't had a hit in forty-two days. He swung on the first pitch and chopped the ball straight down, perhaps off the plate, and it bounded high in the air. Carroll grabbed it but had no play. An infield single—"the shortest heroic blow in memory," Roger Angell wrote—and a run batted in. Mays scored himself a few moments later.

The Mets won, 7–2, but the victory was overshadowed by the fans, estimated at five thousand, who crashed onto the field after the final out. METS' CLINCHER MARRED BY MANIAC MOB, read a *Sporting News* headline. Even before the game ended, the spectators pushing against the railing had trampled the wife of the Reds' trainer. The game had to be stopped so the other wives of Reds players could be escorted to safety. When the game ended, the 340 police officers on the field could do little against the stampede. Pete Rose, who was on base, had to run through the crowd like a halfback seeking the safety of the dugout, where his teammates stood with bats in their hands. Reporters sat aghast in the press box as the rioters tore down the fence, pulled up home plate, and ripped out the turf. "If those are Met fans," Rose said bitterly after the game, "they must let them out of the zoo before the game and then lock them up afterward."

One of the most harrowing photographs was of Mays, who was in center when the game ended. He took off his hat and tried to leave the grounds through the bullpen in right field. In the picture, he has almost reached the bullpen door, but a young man with thick hair has grabbed him from behind and is trying to tackle him. A Met player with his warm-up jacket on is throwing a block on a second fan who is also chasing Willie. They want his hat, but Mays clutches it tightly. The bullpen door is open, and two arms are reaching out, trying to rescue him.

The last time Mays ran off a New York baseball field like that, after the final game at the Polo Grounds, the fans pursued him with love and reverence. This time, they chased him with the angry zeal of a mugger.

Mays played in the World Series in his rookie season, and so too would he in his final year. "I came in a winner, and I'm going to leave a winner," he told reporters before Game One. He was also returning to the Bay Area, where the Mets would face the Oakland Athletics. The A's led the league in clubhouse squabbles, thick mustaches, and garish uniform combinations, but they had upset the Reds last year to win the World Series and had a great running game with Bert Campaneris and Billy North (though North was injured), three twenty-game winners led by Catfish Hunter, and relief ace Rollie Fingers. They also had MVP Reggie Jackson, though the "P" could have stood for "provocateur." "The Mets," he said, "have no name players."

The Mets' center fielder down the stretch had been Don Hahn, but with Staub's shoulder still ailing and lefty Ken Holtzman pitching the first game for the A's, Berra decided to move Hahn to right and start Mays in center. The move delighted the fans at sun-splashed Oakland–Alameda County Stadium, who gave Mays the longest pregame ovation of any player on either team. But Mays hadn't started a game in five weeks, and since then, had only played in the outfield the three innings of the final playoff game. Berra also had him hitting third.

Throwing out the first pitch was Hank Aaron, dressed in a light blue suit and red tie, the first time an active player was given that honor. With 713 homers, he was one behind Ruth, and his presence in the stadium, standing near Willie, was a visual reminder of the game's rich history: two players who began their careers in the Negro Leagues now stood as the second- and third-greatest home run hitters of all time.

Mays got the first hit of the Series, a clean single to left in the first inning. But as he rounded first base, he stumbled and had to scramble back. Later in the game, he booted a ground ball single in center field and was charged with an error. Joe Garagiola, the former catcher who was announcing the game on television, stepped out of his booth and said to Charlie Einstein, "It's got so you pray they won't hit a fly ball to him."

"Leave him alone," Einstein said. "He's retired."

"I know." Garagiola nodded. "So who was that who got the base hit to left?"

In a pitcher's duel the A's won, 2–1. Mays had one hit and no fly ball chances in the outfield.

Game Two was also played in the afternoon, with a brilliant sun and cloudless sky, and the outfield was a hazard. In Game One the A's Joe Rudi, who went on to win three Gold Gloves, lost a deep fly ball in the sun, which went for a double. The Mets had even more trouble. In the second game, Cleon Jones went to the track for a fly ball . . . and it dropped right in front of him. All day, fielders on both teams staggered under pop-ups.

The contest was remembered as one of the wackiest World Series games ever played, taking twelve innings and lasting four hours and thirteen minutes—at the time, a postseason record. Eleven pitchers were used, another record. Six errors were committed, five by the A's. Their second baseman, Mike Andrews, committed two errors in one inning, after which owner Charlie Finley tried to place him on the disabled list with a fabricated injury. Andrews's teammates threatened to strike unless Finley reinstated him, and they taped Andrews's number, 17, to their shoulder during a workout at Shea. Commissioner Bowie Kuhn, mortified at the spectacle, publicly denounced Finley and demanded that Andrews be returned—which he was, though his martyrdom made him a hero in New York. If that wasn't weird enough, A's manager Dick Williams told his team that he was quitting as soon as the Series ended, regardless of the outcome. Which he did.

Yet the 1973 Series is known primarily for one thing. In Game Two, Mays pinch-ran for Staub in the ninth inning with the Mets leading, 6–4. With banners and bedsheets reading WE LOVE WILLIE MAYS and THE AMAYSing METS, the crowd cheered the opportunity to see him one more time. Mays was on first when the next hitter singled to right, but as he rounded second, he stumbled to the ground. "Here's the unusual thing," said Tony Kubek for NBC, "one of baseball's all-time greatest runners had an easy shot going from first to third, and he fell." He was stranded at second.

Mays took the field in the bottom of the ninth. With Hahn in center, he thought he was to play right. The two Mets looked into the dugout and got their direction. Willie was to play center. With the late afternoon shadows now covering the batter's box, the first hitter, Deron Johnson, drove the ball into left center. Mays, his sunglasses turned upward, moved tentatively to his right, feeling his way, searching for the ball. But he couldn't see it. He staggered and at the last moment tried to lunge for it, but instead of pitching forward, his legs flew out from beneath him and he landed hard on the ground. His glove was outstretched, but the ball fell only inches from it and rolled to the wall. Mays's sunglasses flipped down from the fall, and as he got to his knees, he lifted them back up and turned his head helplessly in search of the action. Cleon Jones retrieved the ball, and Johnson was credited with a double.

Fans could only wince. As Kubek told his broadcast partner Curt Gowdy, "Boy, Curt, this is the thing I think all sports fans in all areas hate to see—a great one playing in his last years having this kind of trouble, standing up and falling down."

The misplay led to two runs to tie the game. In the top of the tenth, Mays again found himself in the center of the action. With runners on first and third and one out, he was in the on-deck circle, holding two bats. The hitter, Felix Millan, lofted a fly ball to medium left field. Rudi flipped down his glasses and caught it, and Harrelson tagged at third and sprinted home. Mays moved toward the plate to clear out Millan's bat. Rudi's throw, on one bounce, was up the line a bit. Mays, on one knee behind the plate, motioned to slide, but Harrelson thought he could avoid the tag by cutting inside catcher Ray Fosse and staying on his feet. Fosse caught the ball and swiped his glove at Harrelson. Umpire Augie Donatelli, expecting Harrelson to slide, was flat on his stomach, and he called Harrelson out. Mays, outraged, jumped to his feet, ran to the plate, and dropped to both knees. His batting helmet tumbled off, and the two bats fell to the ground. Mays looked up, spread his arms wide, and yelled at the ump. His words—"No way! He didn't touch him!"—were immaterial. It was the image, replayed on television and reproduced in photographs, that was heartbreaking. Mays was rarely seen complaining to umpires. Now he looked like a desperate supplicant, his face creased with anguish, his hair too long, his emotions exposed. He appeared like a character actor making a vain attempt to play Willie Mays.

Berra, Harrelson, and other Mets continued the argument.

"Where did he touch him?" Berra demanded. "Where did he touch him?"

"Right here," Donatelli said, touching Yogi's backside. "On the ass."

When Donatelli threatened to eject Harrelson, the Met shot back, "I'm not getting thrown out for your inadequacies!"

Donatelli had been in the majors one year longer than Mays, and during the argument Mays remembered that Donatelli would also be retiring after this season, and the question suddenly dawned on him: *What are we doing here?*

The instant replay showed that Harrelson was safe, but that would be forgotten. What remained was the photograph of Mays, so powerful that what actually happened on the play was twisted around. When Donatelli died on May 24, 1990, the *New York Times*'s obituary read: "In the 1973 series . . . Donatelli called Willie Mays of the New York Mets out at the plate, leading to another famous argument."

Mays found redemption in the twelfth. He came to bat with runners on first and third and two outs. The shadows had now reached second base while the outfield remained treacherous in the fading sunlight. Mays, chewing gum, took a slider from Rollie Fingers.

"I can't see, man," he told Fosse.

Fosse called for a fastball. If the old man can't see, then hard stuff, always his weakness, was the way to go.

Mays waved his bat and waited for the fastball. He got it, hitting a sharp one-hopper over Fingers's glove and into center field. He stumbled coming out of the box, his helmet falling off, and he ran gingerly to first base. But the go-ahead run crossed the plate. Mays, at first base, rubbed his right knee.

Met hurler Ray Sadecki, who had already pitched in the game, was watching the action on television in the clubhouse. He turned to Harry Parker, who had also pitched, and said, "He had to get a hit. This game was invented for Willie Mays a hundred years ago."

McGraw, who looked up to Mays like a father, was on second, and he and Mays advanced one base on a hit and then scored on an error. After Mays crossed the plate, McGraw shook his hand and tenderly wrapped his arm around Willie's shoulder. The Mets took a 10–6 lead.

Mays still wasn't finished. In the bottom of the twelfth, with the game now in prime time on the East Coast, Reggie Jackson led off with a deep fly into left center. Mays went back to the track, looking up, and touched the wall with his right hand. But he made no effort on the ball, which bounced chest high against the wall. Jones again retrieved it, and Jackson ended up on third. The A's scored only one run in the inning, and the Mets won to tie the Series.

In the raucous locker room afterward, NBC's Dick Schaap asked Seaver if he thought Mays was going to get a hit in his final at-bat, and Seaver described Mays's cunning.

"I think he had a good shot at it," he said. "I think he decoyed the catcher into thinking he couldn't see."

"How'd he do that?"

Seaver imitated Mays's high-pitched voice. " 'I can't see, man! I can't see. I can't see! The background is terrible.' So they threw the ball right down the pike and base hit." Seaver then laughed uproariously.

Most of the game stories, as well as longer articles in *Sports Illustrated* and the *New Yorker,* described Mays's misadventures as part of a roller-coaster day—high jinks and redemption—that were part of a whole comedy of errors from both teams. There was no suggestion that his misplays would have any historical traction. Red Smith began his *Times* column on Mays with his RBI single. He wrote: "So he lost the game in the ninth inning, won it in the twelfth, came perilously close to losing it again—and walked away from disaster grinning. Never another like him. Never in this world."

What Mays said then, and has always said, was that he lost the first ball in the sun, though he should have played it more safely. On the second ball, he didn't want to crash into the fence with a four-run lead and risk injury when the team was already shorthanded.

It does Mays little good to point out that he had barely played for the last six weeks, that the sun made other outfielders look just as bad, and that he did get the game's most important hit. He has become the poster boy for all athletes—or, for that matter, even entertainers or politicians—who don't know when to quit.

Did Mays play too long? Of course. But so did Ruth and Aaron and Mantle and Gibson and—in other sports—Unitas and Ali and Jordan and Gretzky and countless others who wanted to stretch their glory. But Mays is synonymous with this particular sin for one reason: he committed it in the World Series, on television. The very medium that was central to the legend, that broadcast his gifts to all corners of America—that made the Catch immortal—was the medium that recorded and preserved him at his nadir.

That wouldn't be so bad, except the images have cheated his legacy. If Mays had stumbled through the last years of his career, then his missteps in Oakland would befit his record, and the scorn, more than three decades later, would be deserved. But that wasn't his record. At thirty-eight, thirty-nine, and forty, he still performed at levels that equaled or exceeded those of most of his peers. That part of his legacy, however, and what he did to achieve it, has been obscured by those images of him chasing a few wayward fly balls in Oakland's cruel, glinting twilight.

The Series continued in New York, where the Mets took two out of three and Mays pinch-hit once for his only appearance. Game Six featured Seaver, and despite a tired arm, he gave up only two runs in seven innings. The Mets, however, could manage only one off Catfish Hunter. Mays didn't play.

The final contest pit Jon Matlack against Ken Holtzman, facing each other for the third time. The A's took control early. In the third inning, Campaneris and Jackson each launched two-run homers. The A's were leading, 5–1, in the sixth when Rollie Fingers relieved Holtzman and shut the Mets down until the ninth. Then a walk, a single, and an error made the score 5–2 with two runners on. There were two outs, and with left-hander Wayne Garrett due up, the A's brought in lefty Darold Knowles. Garrett, nicknamed "Red," had hit .265 during the season and had been the Mets' second-leading power hitter, with sixteen homers. He had gotten a single off Knowles in Game Six but was only 5-for-29 (.172) in the Series.

He was now the tying run. And Mays sat on the bench, hoping to be called on to pinch-hit. There were the percentages to play—a right-handed hitter would have a better chance than a lefty. And there was a storybook ending to write—the embattled icon, in his final swing, ties Game Seven in the ninth inning. Mays wanted that ending, or at least the chance. He thought he deserved it. Ever since he watched Bobby Thomson hit his home run, he wanted to be the man, and this was no exception. But Berra never looked his way. He had clearly lost confidence in him after the second game, and Mays was forgotten the rest of the way.

That he wasn't called to pinch-hit at the end might have been for the best; obviously rusty, he might have looked bad in his final at-bat. But his friends and fans regret that he didn't have the chance. "I don't care if he was in a body cast," Lon Simmons said. "I would have sent him to the plate—he was Willie Mays."

Garrett popped out to the shortstop. The Series was over. The Mets had scored two runs or fewer in five out of the seven games.

Mays dressed quickly. "I don't feel nothin' yet, man," he told reporters. "I probably won't feel nothin' until next spring training."

What he felt was anger, disrespect. He has few regrets in his life and puts a positive spin on almost all his memories. But not this one.

"Mae could tell you," he later said. "I went home so quick. Forgot my glove, my uniform, everything, and when I got home, Mae asked me, 'Where is your glove?' I said, 'I gave it away.' I didn't care. If I'm overlooked at that time, I said to myself, 'Go on home.' I left very quickly."

The love affair was over.

EPILOGUE

"For two years after I retired," Mays said, "I wouldn't think about anything but yesterday."

The present was too disheartening. Mays would wake up in the morning, ready to play ball. Or he would wake up in the middle of the night worrying about the game the next day. But there was no game. His responsibilities with the Mets were poorly defined, and he didn't know what to do with himself. He had too much passion for baseball to sit idly on the bench as others stumbled through the sport that he had excelled at for so long. His body may have faltered, but his competitive spirit was still blazing. So he would go to Shea, put on his uniform, mill around, talk to some of the players, pretend to be useful, and leave before the game started. The yesterdays were all he had.

His adjustment to corporate America wasn't any easier. For as long as he could remember, his baseball teams had made decisions for him. They told him when spring training started, when to get on the bus, when to play; they arranged for wake-up calls and paid for his travel, lodging, and meals. Mays was notorious for missing appointments and standing up interviewers. Now these problems worsened. The Mets once sent him to Visalia, California, where they have a farm club, but he didn't show up at the ballpark on the night advertised. He arrived the next night instead.

When Joan Payson died in 1975, Mays lost his most important ally with the Mets. The general manager, Bob Scheffing, who had been closely involved in the trade for Mays, was replaced by Joe McDonald. A new regime was in place. On Donald Grant's order, McDonald kept a log on Mays to document when he showed up at Shea and how long he stayed. The record did not reflect well on Mays, and the Mets threatened to terminate his contract. His lawyer intervened. So did Bowie Kuhn. A compromise was reached, and Mays's duties were spelled out more clearly. He now had to sit through home games for four innings.

• • •

533

Mays was still with the Mets in 1978, when he was elected to the Hall of Fame, receiving 409 votes out of a possible 432 from the Baseball Writers Association of America. No player has ever been elected unanimously, perhaps because, as Red Smith noted, "unanimity is a word some baseball writers can't spell." Nonetheless, the 94.6 percent result for Mays was the highest since 1936, when the first five players were enshrined and the three top players, Ty Cobb, Babe Ruth, and Honus Wagner, received at least 95 percent of the vote. (To be elected, a player must be named by 75 percent of the voters.) The one hundred and thirty-seventh player elected to the Hall, Mays was only the ninth to be chosen in his first year of eligibility. He was also the only living player inducted that year, entering with two deceased members, Hack Wilson and Warren Giles. Duke Snider, who finished sixteen votes shy of election, said, "It wouldn't be normal if you didn't feel disappointed, [but] Willie really more or less deserves to be in by himself." Snider was elected in 1980.

Cooperstown is forever described as quaint and picturesque, a community on the shores of Otsego Lake that calls itself a village and stands as a monument to America's pastoral roots. Everyone, it seems, should be so lucky as to "end up in Cooperstown," but only baseball's elite are so privileged.

Mays had long expected to get there, but that did not diminish the thrill. His induction ceremony took place on Sunday, August 5, 1979, a broiler of an afternoon that turned the top of Leo Durocher's bald head pink. The seventy-four-year-old had lost neither his sartorial panache nor his exuberant rhetoric. "The good Lord put me there when Willie came along," he said. "I never taught him anything. He taught me."

Twenty-eight Hall of Famers sat on the warm stage while more than five thousand friends, family, and fans filled out the lawns and terraces. Mays drew "the biggest and most raucous turnout of fans in forty years," according to Ritter Collett, the longtime sports columnist from Dayton, Ohio. The ceremony began with a moment of silence for deceased Hall of Famers as well as Thurman Munson, who had died three days earlier trying to land his airplane. But the somber mood lifted whenever Bowie Kuhn, in his introduction, mentioned Mays's name. "Willie!" the fans shouted. Kuhn said he enjoyed embellishing the achievements of inductees, but "Willie Mays needs no embroidery. From 1951 to 1973 he played for the fans." Then he introduced "a legend named Willie Mays." The fans stood and yelled, and Kuhn, nearly screaming, butchered his next line: "He never gave the fans a penny of short-change!"

Mays, now forty-eight, strode to the dais amid a rhythmic "Say Hey" chant. The lines on his face showed his age, but he was still taut and muscular in his solid blue suit. "Thank you very much," he said.

"Thank you very much," shouted a spectator.

"I'm not excited now," he said. "But I'll wake up tomorrow, turn to my wife, and I'll say, 'Hey, I'm in the Hall of Fame.'"

The crowd roared at Mays's unintentional echo of his nickname. He beamed as fans yelled, "Willie! Willie!" Someone held up an old newspaper showing photographs of Mays, young and smiling, a New York Giant celebrating the pennant in 1951.

Mays said he didn't have any notes. "I was laying in bed last night and thinking how they wanted me to write this out," he said. "How could I write it out? How can you put what I feel on paper?" He spoke for nearly thirty minutes, a rambling biography of fact and folklore that described what it was like "coming out of Birmingham and knowing nothing."

His youth, he said, was about the making of an athlete. "My uncle told me when I was ten, 'Boy, you have to be a ballplayer.' And my high school principal told me, 'We will put you out of school if you don't play sports.' And when I was in with the Black Barons as a kid, we had twenty-five guys on the club, and all twenty-five would put me to bed every night. I didn't get to meet many girls that way, but I got plenty of sleep. When I got to the minor leagues in 1950, I played for Trenton, and I was the only black guy in the Interstate League. When we went to Hagerstown in Maryland on a Friday, they were calling me every name they could think of. But by Sunday they were cheering me."

Mays talked about his years in New York and looked at Durocher when he said, "He brought out all I had in me." He acknowledged his struggles in San Francisco: "It took them about five years to get used to me there. They had another center fielder. His name was Joe DiMaggio." He thanked his owner. "Horace Stoneham was my backbone, and one of the only things about my career I'm sorry about was leaving him. When he told me he was sending me back home, that made it a little easier. There was only one place I wanted to go—New York City." He was contrite about his tenure with the Mets. "I couldn't play those last two years. The power was gone out of my arm. The last two years—they were a gift. Almost as if Mrs. Payson and baseball were saying, 'You gave us eighteen years, we're going to give you two.'" He was candid about his messy finances: "I was never good about handling money. I just got it and spent it. I never worried much about it. Mr. Stoneham helped me when I needed help." And he was confessional: "I give you one word—love. It means dedication. You have to sacrifice many things to play baseball. I sacrificed a bad marriage and I sacrificed a good marriage. But I'm here today because baseball is my number one love."

Toward the end, Mays showed that some wounds remained. "I am deeply upset the San Francisco Giants didn't send me a uniform to give you," he said. "After eighteen years, they didn't see fit. The people in the front office just don't realize I gave my life to baseball. I say this to you not with hate. Forgiveness is everywhere."

He then stood with Kuhn holding up a New York Mets uniform to present to the Hall. Mays's comment, it turned out, was in error. The Hall confirmed that it had received a uniform from the Giants; Mays simply didn't know. But the remark created a sour headline for the day.

A far worse breach was about to divide Mays and Major League Baseball.

It began when Mays received a call from Al Rosen, the former Cleveland Indian who was on first base when he made the Catch. Rosen had recently left his job as president of the New York Yankees to be an executive vice president at Bally's International, the hotel casino operator. Rosen's boss, Billy Weinberger, had previously hired Joe Louis to be a "greeter" at Caesars Palace in Las Vegas. Bally's was now opening its Park Place Hotel in Atlantic City, and Weinberger asked Rosen to recommend another sports figure who could fill that role. Rosen suggested Mays.

Just as Joe Louis had attracted high rollers to Caesars, Mays could do even more for Bally's. His celebrity was equal if not greater than Louis's, and he was in better health, which would allow him to play golf with patrons. Bally's offered Mays a ten-year contract for $100,000 a year.

Mays was still working for the Mets, and when Rosen notified Kuhn of Mays's job offer, Kuhn sent Mays a telegram telling him that if he accepted the job, he could no longer be employed by the Mets or any other Major League Baseball team. Mays was devastated. He had always assumed he'd work in some capacity in baseball, be it coaching younger players or simply serving as an ambassador for the game. But Bally's would pay him twice as much as the Mets. Which job should he choose?

"Willie faced this trauma two other times in his life," Mae told the *New York Times* on the day he made his announcement. "First when he was traded, and then when he retired. We sat around our apartment in Riverdale last night with Willie's lawyer and accountant, using them as a sounding board. Then Willie had a massage and we were in bed by midnight, but sleep did not come easily."

Mays met with Kuhn one more time and pleaded that he be allowed to work both jobs, but the commissioner wouldn't bend.

Mays accepted the job with Bally's, and on October 29, 1979, his contract with the Mets was terminated. Kuhn, offering few specifics, said, "It has long been my view that such associations by people in our game are inconsistent with its best interests."

Baseball had long been haunted by the Black Sox scandal of 1919, in which gamblers paid players to throw the World Series. Worried about baseball's image, Kuhn didn't want anyone associated with the game involved with gambling. He fancied himself the heir to Judge Kenesaw Mountain Landis, the game's first commissioner, who was responsible for cleaning up baseball after the scandal. Kuhn, as described by Red Smith, was "the game's upright scoutmaster," and perception was everything.

The reality was that Mays could in no way affect the outcome of a Major League Baseball game while schmoozing with patrons of a New Jersey casino. He wasn't working for a bookie. The casino had nothing to do with sports betting. All activities in the casino were legal, and under state law, Mays wasn't even permitted to gamble there. Part of his job involved going to schools, where he would urge kids not to smoke or drink. He also told them not to gamble.

Kuhn's decision reeked of hypocrisy. He owed his job to the major league owners and had worked for years as a National League lawyer protecting their cartel. He allowed several owners, including George Steinbrenner and the Galbreath family (which owned the Pirates), to have racehorses. Mays himself had worked in promotions for Suffolk Downs, a racetrack in Boston. That drew no objections. Somehow, blackjack was corrupt; Thoroughbreds were pure.

What made Kuhn's move so galling was that Mays himself had been such an exemplar. The *New York Post*'s Maury Allen wrote: "I know of a hundred ballplayers who have smoked marijuana. I know at least half a dozen who have snorted cocaine. I know of fifty who probably could be medically certified as alcoholics. I know of several hundred who have chased women, gambled excessively on horses, and given less than their best on the field on many days of their career. Willie Mays is not among them." If Kuhn cared about the game's image, Allen wrote, he should focus on those problems.

At a press conference, Mays could not conceal his pain. "I think anybody regrets it when his name is dragged through something like this," he said. "But what skills do I have outside of baseball? Only public relations, dealing with people. . . . Baseball has been good to me, but I've been good to baseball. You ask me if I'm upset and unhappy, I will say yes. I'm not going to challenge Bowie Kuhn. That's challenging baseball. I'm not here for that. . . . Baseball's my life. I love the game. But I have to protect my family."

When Mickey Mantle took a similar job at the Claridge Hotel and Casino in Atlantic City in 1983, it cost him his job as a Yankee batting coach. "I wasn't much of a batting coach anyway," Mantle said. "I could only teach 'em how to strike out." Together as rookies in 1951, Mays and Mantle were again united as banished legends.

Working at Bally's was the hardest thing Mays had ever done. Maybe because baseball had come so easily to him, any full-time job was going to be a struggle. The rhythm and responsibilities of corporate America were alien to him. He had little sense of deadlines, calendars, or even time itself. If a meeting was supposed to start at 11 A.M., that meant, well, he was supposed to be there at 11 A.M. "When you're the star of a ball club," he later said, "when you go to the park you do nothing. You're just there to play. Everything is done for you. But in the business world, it's different. You have to do things yourself, and I wasn't aware of that. But my new bosses at Bally's explained to me that they had to answer to other people, and I had to answer to them."

Most professional athletes struggle when they leave their protected bubble, but Mays's stumbles were magnified. The Giants, for example, finally wanted to have a Willie Mays Day in 1979 to formally retire his number. But Mays said he would participate only if he received money, which would be used for his Say Hey Foundation. Mays now understood—baseball's a business. If he's going to put tens of thousands of people into the stands, why shouldn't he receive something as well? The Giants withdrew the offer. Not until 1983 did Mays have such a day, though he got what he wanted—contributions to his foundation.

Old-timers' games were another minefield. Mays was allowed to play in them, and he took them seriously. Jackie Brandt recalls that when he and Mays were playing in the outfield at Seals Stadium in the late 1950s, he raced in front of Mays to catch a sinking line drive, and Mays yelled, "Jackie! There's twenty-two thousand people who came here to watch me catch that ball!" Some twenty years later, both men were in the outfield at Candlestick for an old-timers' game. The first batter hit a fly ball twenty feet from Brandt. Mays dashed across the field but couldn't reach it. Neither could Brandt, who was limping with a strained muscle in his leg. The ball fell for a hit.

"Goddammit, Jackie!" Mays yelled. "You gotta catch it!"

Brandt just looked at him. "There's fifty-five thousand people here," he said, "and they came to watch you catch that ball."

Mays's pride could get the better of him. In 1983, he agreed to play in an old-timers' game at RFK Stadium in Washington. He flew in from San

Francisco and warmed up before the game, but was then told he wouldn't start. "When they didn't put him in the starting lineup, he was really hurt," Monte Irvin told reporters. "Then they told him he would pinch-run. He just said he wouldn't do that. He didn't want to be hurt twice. He just went inside and showered and flew home."

"I really felt for him," Richie Ashburn said. "He came to play. That's Willie. He couldn't believe he wasn't starting."

The five-inning game ended with the crowd chanting, "We want Willie," who by then was on the last flight west.

Mays was implicated in a more serious matter in September 1985, during a federal trial of a Philadelphia man who was accused of selling cocaine to big league ballplayers. Retired player John Milner testified that he had used amphetamines when he played for the Mets in the early 1970s. He said the drug, an illegal stimulant, was so pervasive that when he went into the clubhouse, he often found the pills, or "greenies," waiting for him in his locker. He also said that Mays had "red juice" in his locker. This was, he said, a liquid form of the drug. Mays didn't give it to him, he testified, "but I went to his locker and got it." Milner said he didn't like the red juice and didn't try it again. He also said he never saw Mays drink it or hand it out.

Milner's charges created instant headlines and overwhelmed the details of the rest of the trial, the outcome of which has long been forgotten. Jim Bouton's *Ball Four* had already exposed Major League Baseball's widespread use of amphetamines, but Mays's alleged involvement raised the problem to another level. Mays denied the charges. He said he had received the liquid from his doctor in San Francisco, John Jackson, who appeared on *The CBS Evening News* to say the solution was a prescription drug called Phenergan VC, a cough syrup. He said he prescribed it for Mays's ongoing sinus problems and colds.

Mays was angry and hurt by the allegation. "Why am I going on trial for what [Milner] thinks he saw in my locker?" he said at the time. "If you're going to bring me into this, that's un-American."

Asked now about his use of amphetamines or any illegal drugs, Mays says, "I really didn't need anything. . . . My problem was if I could stay on the field. I would go to the doctor and would say to the doctor, 'Hey, I need something to keep me going. Could you give me some sort of vitamin?' I don't know what they put in there, and I never asked a question about anything."

For years, Milner's testimony was a footnote in Mays's career. Amphetamines had been widely used in the major leagues since the late 1940s, and other athletes have confirmed Bouton's description of the players' easy access to them. Darryl Strawberry said that nine out of ten players were taking amphetamines when he joined the Mets in 1983, and Jerry Remy, who played from 1975 to 1984, says, "We all took amphetamines, for chrissake. You almost have to, to make it through a season like that. But that was no big deal. Everybody knew it."

The Steroid Era, however, has again focused attention on amphetamines and, by extension, has put Willie Mays in the center of the controversy. Those who defend the players' use of anabolic steroids or other performance-enhancing drugs draw a moral equivalence with amphetamines. They say each generation of players uses whatever drugs are available, so if amphetamines have not cost any other player his Hall of Fame standing—and Willie Mays, as the most famous player who supposedly took amphetamines, is cited—then the juicers of today should not be punished or stigmatized.

It would be naive to think Mays never took amphetamines. Hank Aaron said he took one, didn't like it, and stopped. But citing amphetamines as a defense for steroids equates two very different drugs. Steroids, among other things, build muscle mass and enhance performance—clearly evidenced by the surge in home runs at the end of the 1990s and the beginning of the 2000s. Amphetamines restore energy and allow someone to perform at full strength. The medical experts debate to what extent, if at all, the drug increases one's natural ability, but the drug itself did not change the character of the game and certainly did not distort the record books. (In 2006, Major League Baseball banned amphetamines, and began testing for them, as part of a sweeping new policy against performance-enhancing drugs.)

Mays, of course, laments that his name is connected to any drug, past or present. He would never embarrass baseball knowingly or jeopardize his standing with children. "I've tried for years and years to be a hero to the kids of America," he said after Milner made his charges. "I hope the people won't take that one statement and crucify me."

Mays got the hang of his job at Bally's when he realized it was similar to playing center field. He was still a performer, but now he entertained by signing autographs, attending brunches, hitting golf balls, signing more autographs, going to dinners, and chatting about old times. Patrons would recall a game in, say, Philadelphia in 1955 or Chicago in 1966, and Mays would need only a couple of clues—the month of the game, the starting pitcher—and he could remember how many hits he got, the final score, and who made the error in the sixth inning that allowed the tying run to score. The same photogenic memory that he once used to scout opposing players now regaled gamblers and golfers. It was all in the performance. "I didn't like it when I started," he said in 1991. "I like it now because I know what I'm there for. I'm in the business world. I don't like to play golf, rush home, change clothes, go to a party. Because your mind is so run down, but you got to keep smiling all the time. Because if you don't smile, someone is going to say, 'Hey, what kind of guy is this?' You're onstage all the time in the corporate world."

But Mays's exile from baseball gnawed at him. One day in 1981, he was waiting for a flight at JFK airport in New York when a young man walked up and introduced himself. He said he was Larry Baer and he worked in marketing for the Giants. Baer had idolized Mays as a youth, and they struck up a conversation. They were both flying to San Francisco, and Mays told the flight attendant that he wanted Baer to sit with him in first class.

In the aftermath of the aborted "Willie Mays Day," some members in the Giants organization viewed Mays as a malcontent who wanted nothing to do with the team. So Baer was surprised when he said, "It's killing me not being associated with the Giants or baseball. It's killing me."

Baer said that the following week, the Giants were having a holiday party at Candlestick for low-income kids from Hunters Point, and Baer invited him to attend.

"I'll be there," Mays said.

"Really?"

"I'll be there," he insisted.

When Baer told his colleagues what had happened, no one believed him. But at 4 P.M. on the day of the party, Baer recalls, "Sure enough, Willie Mays walks in. We had current players there, but they were chopped liver. It was amazing."

In October 1984, Bowie Kuhn was replaced by Peter Ueberroth, fresh off his triumph as the maestro of the Summer Olympics in Los Angeles. Public relations was among his many skills, and what single move could improve baseball's image more than reinstating two of the most popular players of all time. WELCOME HOME! cried Sports Illustrated's cover for March 25, 1985. Ueberroth stood behind Mays and Mantle, all three beaming. At a press conference, the new commissioner assured everyone that "we are going to look for stronger, more clarified guidelines to keep gambling and baseball apart" and that Mays and Mantle "are exceptions to the current guidelines. I am bringing back two players who are more a part of baseball than perhaps anyone else."

Mays said, "This is a happy occasion for Mickey and me, to have that word 'ban' lifted. I don't think I did anything wrong to leave baseball. . . . I'm pleased I can keep my job and earn a living. Baseball made me."

• • •

The following year, Mays was back where he began, a "special assistant to the president and general manager" of the San Francisco Giants. He was hired by the man who had engineered his employment at Bally's, Al Rosen, who had left that company shortly after Mays had joined, returned to baseball, and had just been hired by the Giants. At the press conference, Mays said, "My wife knew that every day when I got up, I wanted to be part of a team. I left [March] open when I went to Atlantic City because I thought I'd be back in baseball someday."

Mays now had responsibilities with both the Giants and Bally's while also participating in the growing memorabilia and trade show market. As a player, he blithely gave away historic balls, gloves, equipment, and awards, but he had an epiphany in the 1980s when he gave one of his Gold Gloves to someone who said he was a museum curator, only to discover that he then sold it for $64,000. Whatever Mays endorsed or scribbled on, it seemed, had value. In the early 1990s, he was at a barbecue restaurant in Phoenix, and he doodled on a paper tablecloth. After he returned to his hotel, he was in the lobby when a young man entered waving the very same tablecloth. It was stained and dirty, but he announced that it had Willie Mays's doodles and the manager had sold it to him for $100. The awards that Mays had long since given away or somehow lost kept appreciating in value. The person who had his 1954 Silver Slugger trophy (for winning the batting title) auctioned it off in 2003 for $120,096.

Mickey Mantle's memorabilia was priced even higher; one of his old jerseys sold for $54,000. Both men received far more money signing their names than they had ever received playing baseball. If others were going to cash in on their names, why shouldn't they get a cut?

The value in the Mays and Mantle brands was evident in 1981, when their first names, along with Snider's, were the title of Terry Cashman's nostalgic ode to baseball's golden era, "Willie, Mickey and the Duke":

> They knew them all from Boston to Dubuque,
> Especially Willie, Mickey and the Duke.

Mays has now hoarded a massive trove of awards, photographs, gloves, jerseys, trading cards, fan mail, and other memorabilia, which will be part of his estate. He even has one of Joe DiMaggio's jock straps, inscribed with the number 5, given to him by Whitey Ford at an All-Star Game. What Joltin' Joe's undergarment is worth is anyone's guess, but Mays assumes it's appreciated in value.

• • •

The demands of his various jobs ensured Mays a chaotic lifestyle but matched his restless spirit. In 1987, Giants publicist Duffy Jennings described the challenge of corralling the fifty-six-year-old Mays for a game to celebrate the twenty-five-year anniversary of the 1962 pennant: "He's constantly on the road. My file on him for this game has phone numbers in New York, Atlantic City, Birmingham, Palm Springs, Scottsdale, St. Petersburg, and Atlanta. I'm always a day behind him. He's always on a plane to somewhere. The man has twenty telephones and fifteen cars and they're always in motion. It's an amazing process to watch."

Duffy did not exaggerate. Mays had four houses as well. When Duffy was asked what Mays did for the Giants, he said, "It would be real hard to write a job description for special assistant to the president and general manager, which is Willie's formal title. His real-life title is Willie Mays."

On bad days, he could be abrupt at signings, and during other personal appearances, and over the years, he squandered business opportunities by being unpredictable and prickly. He shunned most interview requests and, for those reporters who did break through, made little effort to win their affection. On a public stage for much of his life, he had neither the interest nor the need to give even more of himself. In doing so, he also created an emotional firewall that kept outsiders at bay and his fans bewildered.

But Mays's firewall is also his protection, for even the most innocent requests can be deceptive. Consider an incident described by Rick Zeller, an executive who worked with Mays at Bally's. In the early 1980s, they were to meet for a golf tournament at a country club in New Jersey. Zeller was standing outside the clubhouse when Mays drove up, got out of his Cadillac, and walked toward him. Two other men were standing near Zeller, and one said to the other, "Who's going to tell this nigger that deliveries go in the back?"

When Mays reached Zeller, they greeted each other warmly and chatted briefly. Then Mays left to park his car.

One of the men hurried up to Zeller and asked, "Who was that?"

"That's Willie Mays," Zeller said.

The two men bolted after Mays and asked him for his autograph; Mays obliged.

Later that day, Zeller told Mays what had happened, and Mays was more upset by the hypocrisy than the racism.

Mays himself, while confirming the anecdote, would never discuss such an experience. Even long after his playing days have ended—and even when he has been the victim—he does not want to trigger a contentious headline and does not want to appear as if he's been hurt. He will speak in general about how much he's endured, but he keeps the details, no matter how fresh or raw, inside. He has followed that course his entire life, and it served its purpose by averting any controversy that could derail his career.

But outsiders always ask, Why doesn't Willie Mays trust people?

The answer is: for good reason.

"He started out with pretty normal skin," Herman Boykin says, "but the skin toughened up."

Or, as Mays says, "You have to assume that everyone wants something from me because of who I am." It is why there are only three groups that he trusts: baseball players, children, and household pets. None will ever betray him.

Mays also never truly reconciled his own celebrity, which he discussed in 1991 when he was asked about his very public life.

"Well, it's good and bad," he said. "It's good when you go places and they recognize you and you can get most anything, and get the things you need in a hurry. Then sometimes it's bad, when you want to be by yourself and you can't. Because you're in a world where people love you so much and they just want to be part of you. I'm part of the people. Very few of us can say that. The world owns you. The way I try to get away with it is, I don't go out that much."

Asked if he had had more joy than sadness in his life, Mays paused. "I would have to say yes, overall," he said. "Because how many guys can say they played baseball starting at age fourteen and played until forty-three? Now in between you're always going to have some sadness." Then Mays, almost sixty years old at the time, affirmed how deeply baseball was carved into his soul.

"You go into a slump," he said, "and that's the worst sadness I've ever come across."

The Giants maintained a tenuous foothold in San Francisco. Stoneham sold the team to Labatt Breweries in Toronto, which planned to move the club to Canada. But San Francisco's mayor, George Moscone, blocked the sale with a temporary injunction, and the real estate mogul Bob Lurie led a group of investors to acquire the team. But the Giants continued to struggle financially, and voters rejected various initiatives to provide public money for a new stadium. In 1992, Lurie announced that he had agreed to sell the club to investors who were going to move it to Florida, but the sale was delayed until an investment group from San Francisco, led by Peter Magowan, the CEO of the Safeway Corporation, could buy it.

The new owners' first order of business was the courting of Barry Bonds, who had won his second MVP award in Pittsburgh and was now a free agent. By then, Mays's involvement with the team had been on the wane, but Magowan asked him to be part of the initial meeting with Bonds. At Bonds's first press conference as a Giant, he said, "This is the greatest moment of my entire life. Every time I step on that field, I know my godfather's in center field and my dad's in right field." He requested number 24 but was told that was not possible, so he settled for his father's old number, 25.

At the time, the Giants' star was the fiery Will Clark, and the owners were concerned he wouldn't get along with the temperamental Bonds. Mays intervened. According to Larry Baer, who was part of the new ownership: "Willie said, 'I got the answer for you. I'm going to put my locker in the clubhouse right between Barry and Will. There will be no problem.'"

Meanwhile, during spring training of 1993, Mays signed a lifetime contract with the Giants, and he played a role in helping build public support for a new downtown stadium (though what mattered more to voters was that it was privately financed). Pac Bell Park opened in 2000. Its name was changed to SBC Park, then to AT&T Park. What hasn't changed is the magnificent nine-foot bronze statue of Mays, shown after he has taken a mighty swing, or the twenty-four palm trees behind it, or the stadium address, 24 Willie Mays Plaza. Mays has a private box, where old teammates like Johnny Antonelli and Ray Sadecki will stop by, see how he's doing, still looking out for him. Mays attends spring training games, hobnobs with the club's investors, visits farm teams, and performs ceremonial functions. But he is happiest in the clubhouse before a game, razzing the players and maintaining ties with equipment managers like Mike Murphy, who has known Willie since 1958 and is moved to tears when he talks about him. Willie likes to say of "Murph": "I raised him."

The generational divide between Mays and the younger players is significant—the music, the BlackBerries, the tattoos—but he has always judged players by their contributions to the team. He is old-fashioned but not closed-minded. Asked if Major League Baseball is ready for an openly gay player, Mays asks, "Can he hit?"

For a number of years, Mays's most visible position with the Giants was as Barry Bonds's patron.

Bonds had been a divisive figure since entering the majors, winning acclaim for his superior talents while alienating the fans, the media, and his teammates by his truculence and egotism. None of those attributes changed in San Francisco. What did change was that he was now under the eye of both his father, who had been hired as the Giants' first base coach, and his godfather. Barry Bonds, at twenty-eight, had already distinguished himself as the rightful heir to Mays, having surpassed thirty homers and thirty stolen bases twice in one season. He had collected three Gold Gloves as well. But Mays pushed Bonds for more.

"He would always give me his blessing, but he did not allow me to get satisfied," Bonds says. " 'Boy,' is his favorite word—he still calls me that—and he would come to my locker and say, 'Boy, what the hell is wrong with you? Don't get happy because you hit two home runs. That second swing, you got lucky.' And I'd think, Can't you show me some love?" At other times, Mays would tell Bonds, "I have the vision of what you should do. I just can't do it anymore."

Bonds's first year in San Francisco was his best to date (.336, 46 homers, 123 RBIs), as he flourished before the two people who meant the most to him. "For me to satisfy my father and my godfather was more important than anything in baseball," he says. When his father died from lung cancer on August 23, 2003, at fifty-seven, Mays filled the void. He told Barry, for example, that he should not take too much time off. "I want him back on the field," he told a reporter. "He needs that. I don't want him to be lonely. I want him to be positive again. We know how sad he is. He needs to get back on the field and take it out on baseball."

Bonds could be churlish with reporters, fans, batboys, even teammates, but not with Mays. Giant broadcaster Jon Miller recalls one time when Mays was sitting in Mike Murphy's office before a game. "Barry came in, and they exchanged a few insults, had a few laughs," Miller says. "I never saw Barry as relaxed and impish as when he was around Willie."

It was a rapport born of respect. "I recall when Bonds was at five hundred home runs," Miller says, "and I asked if he was interested in Babe Ruth. Willie was right there. And Barry said, 'I'm really only interested in Willie's record. That's the only one I'm interested in, no disrespect to the Babe.' And Willie said, 'You better not be taking any days off, man. You better get busy.' "

Bonds entered the 2004 season one home run behind his godfather. In 2002, Mays had participated in a leg of the Olympic torch run and still had his torch, so he took it to a jeweler and inscribed it with diamonds: "660" and "661." Mays wanted to be at home plate when Bonds hit 660, so he traveled with the Giants as they opened with two road series. Bonds remained stuck on 659, but in the season opener in San Francisco, he pounded number 660 into McCovey Cove, and Mays gave him his sparkling torch at home plate.

Mays told reporters afterward, "I think it's appropriate that he did it in a Giants uniform. That's what I really wanted." Said Bonds, "I just feel right now I completed our family circle." Mays was not on the field, or visible to cameras, when Bonds passed him with number 661.

Bonds didn't follow all of Mays's advice. Mays recoiled at any headline that was not related to baseball, whereas Bonds seemed to court them. According to Miller, Mays encouraged Bonds to be less hostile to reporters.

"Be nice to those guys," Mays would say. "What's wrong with you?"

"I'm only happy if they don't like me," Bonds would explain.

"Well, give it a try." The pleas usually went for naught.

Bonds's triumphs on the field ultimately put Mays in an uncomfortable position. Bonds hit seventy-three homers in 2001 for the single-season record, then in 2007 he pursued Hank Aaron's all-time mark of 755. By then, he had testified to a grand jury that he had mistakenly used a steroid that had been given to him by his trainer. The congressional hearings investigating steroids stirred public outrage against a sport that seemed in permanent denial. Bonds was still loved in San Francisco, but he was vilified across the country as the juicer who held some of the game's most treasured records. While Aaron vacillated in his support of Bonds, Mays stood by his godson, literally and figuratively, as he was once again on the field to congratulate Bonds when he hit number 756.

In interviews, Mays was asked about steroids in general and in connection to Bonds, but there was no satisfactory answer. He could no more criticize another baseball player, let alone his godson, than he could repudiate a member of his own family. "I've always told Barry, 'Whatever you do, whether right or wrong, I'm here for you,'" he says.

But Mays's refusal to condemn those who would cheat the game was also disappointing. If Willie Mays won't defend baseball, who will?

Mays's tactic was to avoid interviews.

Bonds, who hasn't played baseball since 2007, is currently defending himself against federal perjury charges in connection with grand jury testimony from 2003. Asked if Mays has helped him "through his controversies," Bonds says, "If not for my father or for Willie, I wouldn't have been as strong as I was. Willie keeps me going because Willie keeps going."

Cat Mays had lived in California since 1958. He occasionally went to Candlestick and followed the rest of the games on radio or television. He had access to every modern technology but could never really shed his country roots, sometimes to his son's dismay. He would, for example, keep his surplus cash in the ice tray of his freezer. Willie asked him why.

"If I get robbed, they won't think to look there," he said.

"Okay, man, you do what you gotta do."

Cat's relationship with Willie remained one of unspoken love and immense pride—he was in the audience at his son's Hall of Fame induction ceremony—and just as the father once cared for and protected his son, the reverse would soon be true. In the 1960s, the Chrysler Corporation gave Willie a new car each year, and Willie would give it to his father until Cat's impaired vision prevented him from driving.

Cat developed glaucoma and moved to a nursing home in Atherton, near Willie. He remained physically fit and always looked sharp. Willie bought him the best clothes, and Cat's lady friends would arrange them on hangers so the outfits matched. Even when Cat became legally blind, he could make his way around his room and even prepare his own food (again, to Willie's dismay). Long after his son had retired, Cat enjoyed listening to the ball games on the radio.

In the late 1990s, Cat developed blood clots on his lung and had cardiac issues, and he was hospitalized several times in Redwood City. "When Willie would come to visit," Dr. Edward Anderson says, "he was the adoring son. Sometimes it was the unspoken word. Just touching him, grabbing his hand. 'How thing's going, Dad. How was your day. You look better. You look stronger.' He was just engaging him. And he wanted to make sure that all the people who were taking care of him knew that Mr. Mays Sr. was someone who deserved the utmost care and respect. He was not just an older blind gentleman. . . . He wanted skin care, nutrition, everything. Things that sometimes are neglected for an older African American in the hospital."

Cat died on August 27, 1999, at the age of eighty-eight. The funeral program featured a photograph of Cat, in his fifties, wearing an overcoat, a tie, and a fedora, with alert eyes and a smooth face. Willie wrote the eulogy, which reflected his love for the man who had made his life possible. But one line spoke volumes about his own life. He said of Cat:

"He and his son defied the odds."

Mae and Willie never had children of their own, though their house was often a refuge for family members. Mae was dealt a blow in 1997 when she was diagnosed with a form of dementia, which was later confirmed as Alzheimer's. Mae was only fifty-nine, at a young age to develop the disease, and she was a young fifty-nine—still trim and vivacious and beautiful. Willie eventually found help at the Institute on Aging, which sends caregivers to their home each day. Rene Anderson, Willie's personal assistant, and their friends help out as well. The progressive nature of the disease has inevitably diminished Mae's strength and her memory, but with help she stays active, jogging down the halls of the house and using the treadmill. Willie instructs her aides to brush Mae's hair in the morning, apply lipstick, and paint her nails, and Willie holds her elbow and walks with her around their grounds and talks to her in a soft, sweet voice.

"Every time he sees Mae, it's as though he's just seen her for the first time," Anderson says. "He wants to know her plan for the day, and her face brightens up. Sometimes she responds the right way, sometimes not. But Willie expects her to have a good day, and when he's gone, sometimes she'll ask about him."

Willie says he is doing for Mae what he tried to do for his father. "I try to do whatever I can," he says, "because it's hard to see her walk around and not be able to understand what we're talking about. But Rene says sometimes she can understand more than you think she understands. So I just do what I have to do and make sure that she's okay, and hope that I don't have to put her in a home or anything like that. As long as I'm around, I don't think that will happen."

Mae sleeps in a special hospital bed in her own room, but Willie listens for her. "I find myself getting up at four or five in the morning, going there, and making sure she's okay. . . . But it's difficult sometimes."

Before bedtime, Mae will watch a ball game on television, sitting in the dark, her eyes focusing and then fading, as if searching for a familiar figure. The game continues, and it's easy to believe that Mae is looking for Willie to come to the plate, bat in hand, eager to take his licks.

Willie himself was diagnosed with glaucoma in the 1990s and by 2005 had to stop driving his cars and playing golf. He still travels extensively, typically with Anderson and sometimes a friend, and he still uses a rubber band like a money clip for his thick roll of cash. Cash, he learned long ago, is the currency of respect. Willie uses it to shop (badgering the sales staff for lower prices on televisions, clothes, gifts for Mae, whatever) and to tip. He also uses it for those in need. When a friend of his died, he attended the funeral long enough to give the widow an envelope with $5,000 in cash.

Computers fascinate him. While he has difficulty reading small keyboards, he can download music, watch baseball videos, and check stats. Shopping satisfies his competitive spirit. If a friend has bought a new television, he'll try to buy the same one for less money. A common ploy: he'll tell the salesperson that he plans on buying two televisions and he expects a discount. When he receives it, he says he's changed his mind and wants only one—at the discounted price.

Whether in one of his homes or in a hotel suite, he is a loner who does not like to be alone. He prefers to be surrounded by friends who will tell their stories, laugh, and carry on. Willie will chip in his own light stories, his voice rising for comedic effect; sometimes he'll stand up and hop around to re-create a particular play. But he's also content to sit back and relax. In the 1990s, President Clinton invited him to spend a night at the White House. He declined, believing the bed and the television were too small. But one suspects he prefers familiar hotel suites, surrounded by familiar faces, to the august ambiance of the White House.

His friends bristle at the caricature of him as "a bitter old man." Mays is quite aware of the trajectory of his life, from a poor Depression-era black kid in the Deep South to someone who can go anywhere in America and be treated like royalty. "I could not have dreamt," he says, "the life that I've lived."

Like many older African Americans, he also could not have dreamed that he would see a black man in the White House. Mays met Barack Obama in 2006, before Obama had declared his candidacy for president. Once his campaign for the White House began, he found several ways to mention Mays in his stump speeches. When a news report suggested that Obama was a distant cousin of Dick Cheney's, he quipped, "Why couldn't I have been related to someone cool, like Willie Mays."

Mays had never followed presidential politics, but he closely tracked the 2008 race on television and stayed up until 5 A.M. watching the returns, and he wept when the results were clear. When he woke up, he told Anderson to send an e-mail to Obama:

> *Dear Mr. President,*
> *Move on in.*
> *Your Friend,*
> *Willie Mays*

One of Mays's few remaining personal goals was to fly on *Air Force One*, a message relayed to the president by a mutual friend. When Obama flew to St. Louis for the 2009 All-Star Game, he invited Mays to join him on his plane and to be his guest at the game. Asked afterward what his next goal was, Mays said, "Bowling in the White House."

What is most striking about Mays, in the twilight of his life, is the consistency of his values. When he had his hip replaced in 2004, for example, he was met at the curb by Judy Kaufman, the director of special patient services at Stanford Hospital and Clinics. She picked up one of the suitcases. It was so heavy she nearly dropped it.

"What's in here?" she asked.

"Baseballs," he said.

If Mays never mastered the language of affection and gratitude, baseballs gave him a vocabulary for his most vital emotions. A baseball, to Mays, retains a pureness and beauty that transcends any commercial value, and his signature is its gold-plated imprimatur. So he took a whole suitcase of them to the hospital, where he distributed them to surgeons, nurses, technicians, cooks, administrators—anyone involved in his care. Once he was back home, Mays decided to give signed balls to the kids at the Lucile Packard Children's Hospital at Stanford. He insisted that he see the sickest children, such as those with cancer or organ recipients. When Kaufman suggested that he sign the balls ahead of time, Mays said no. He wanted the children to see him sign them so they knew the signatures weren't fake.

Mays, of course, has been visiting kids his whole adult life, but the atmospherics are entirely different. He is now an old man with a paunch, a hearing aid, and eyeglasses teetering on his forehead, a complete stranger to these youngsters. But it doesn't matter. Mays sits in the tiny chairs in the arts and crafts room or sidles up next to the beds, and he asks the children, some connected to tubes and wires for life support, how they're feeling. He tells them to stay strong, and he says nothing about himself unless he is asked. Parents madly snap pictures with their cell phones. The children know that this is a special moment and that the baseball he hands over is a possession to be cherished.

Mays has now visited this hospital each Christmas since his surgery. One time a mother asked him to sign a ball, and he barked, "Who are you? This is for the kids." She said it was for her son, and Willie signed it. Another time, he saw the sibling of a patient and gave him a ball and a hat. "You need this too," he said.

Dr. Philip Pizzo, the dean of Stanford's medical school, believes that these visits are connected to the image Mays has of himself as a child. "I think in these kids," he says, "Willie sees the helplessness, the deprivation, the inability to do what he could do when he was young—to use his body to overcome adversity." He notes that Mays has to walk great distances through the hospital, that sometimes it's hard, but he does it with the stoic determination of an athlete. "It's not that easy for him, but to connect with someone who is more helpless touches something in his own heart. . . . He just wants to make people feel good. That's his gift."

Even as a septuagenarian, Mays defines himself by the player he once was. The license plates on his idle cars display some variation of "WM24" or "SayHey." His telephone numbers end in "2424." He was once riding in an elevator with a teenager who was wearing a basketball shirt with the number 24. Right there, Mays traded his baseball cap for the shirt.

Mays had no biological children, and Michael, who lives in New York, has no children of his own. Asked if he regrets not having grandchildren,

Mays says, "Not really. It happens if it happens. You can't make that happen." Then he switches to his own bloodlines. "I don't even know if my sperms are there to have kids. I never checked, never thought anything like that. . . . I guess that's why we adopted."

Mays admits to few sadnesses, and won't here, but the void is apparent. When he says, "If it had happened, it would have been my pleasure to take care of him," it's unclear if he's referring to a biological child or a grandchild, but the meaning is the same.

From his youth and throughout his adult life, Mays has had dogs—a police dog named Star was his favorite—and in the 1990s he adopted a white miniature poodle and named him Giant. When Giant was a puppy, Mays would stuff him in his coat pocket and take him to the ball game. He would wipe off Giant's wet feet when he came in from outside and would tell others, "This is Giant's house. He allows you to live here as long as you feed him." Indeed, when Giant barked, Willie got him a biscuit.

When Giant was fourteen, he developed cancer of the liver or kidney. Some in the house thought he should be put down, but Willie wanted to keep him alive, so he was given an operation and chemotherapy. He soldiered on for a few more months but then got sick, developed breathing problems, and had to be taken back in. The vet said Giant could no longer be treated, so Willie held the poodle, stroking his belly, as the vet prepared to stick in the catheter.

"You're okay, Giant," Willie told him softly. "You're a good boy and I'm so proud of you. I've got you. Don't be scared." The vet plunged in the needle. Giant gasped, and it was over. Willie had to leave the room before answering: cremation or burial? He later said, "I could feel the life leave his body."

He's adopted another white poodle, Giant Too, and is impressed by his ability to flip the top of the candy jar to get the chewing gum.

"All of these poodles," Mays says, "are very smart people."

In the movie *Manhattan*, Woody Allen said Willie Mays was one of the things that made life worth living, right after Groucho Marx but before "those incredible apples and pears by Cézanne."* Charles Schulz used Mays's name in his *Peanuts* strips more than any other because he "always symbolized perfection."

But was Mays the greatest player in the history of baseball?

Let it first be said that Mays, unlike DiMaggio, does not require his

* Allen, in an interview, says he never met Mays "in any coherent way," but in a celebrity softball game at Dodger Stadium, he caught a pop fly hit by Mays.

introduction to be preceded by "greatest living player," nor does he tout himself as such. But second, let it be said that, if you ask him, he does think he's the greatest. Or, as he will say in a soft voice, "I did things that no one else did."

In many debates, Mays is described as "the greatest all-around player" but is somehow excluded as "the greatest." This is nonsense. The phrase "greatest all-around player" is redundant—one's greatness is determined by performance in all aspects of the game. Anyone who designates Mays as "the greatest all-around player" has given him top billing as well.

What makes the assessment difficult is that baseball, more than any other sport, relies on statistics, but the game has gone through so many changes over the past hundred years—live-ball, dead-ball, integration, night games, cross country travel, expansion, changing pitching mounds, changing strike zones, steroids—that the numbers from era to era mean very different things, so true comparisons are impossible. Another problem is that the numbers, for all their elegance, capture only part of the game, and they disserve Mays by failing to reflect his strategic, intangible contributions (inducing bad throws, quick first steps in the outfield, positioning, knowledge of hitters, and so on). The "five-tool" designation understates his skills by ignoring his intelligence, preparation, and guile. Mays was always better than the box score.

The hard numbers tell a compelling story of power and speed (.302 average, 660 homers, 338 stolen bases), of consistency (Mays strove for 100 runs scored and 100 RBIs each year, and he ended his career with 2,062 and 1,903, respectively), and of untouchable defensive prowess (7,095 putouts, the most of any outfielder). The case for Mays as the game's greatest is easy to make but impossible to prove: he beat you in more ways than any other player. Unfortunately, the documentation erodes in the yellowing game summaries and in the fading memories of those who saw him.

Was he better than the Babe? Most polls, to be sure, would name Babe Ruth as the greatest. (On his numbers alone, Barry Bonds deserves consideration, but steroids have tainted those accomplishments.) Before becoming a full-time position player, Ruth was one of the league's top pitchers, and as a hitter he dominated the game like no player before or since. In 1927, he hit sixty home runs—more long balls than twelve out of the majors' other fifteen teams hit in total. Ted Williams may have been a better "pure" hitter, and others can make arguments for Cobb, Aaron, Musial, DiMaggio, and Mantle, but no player lorded over his competition like the Babe.

In that context, Ruth was baseball's most dominant player; Mays was its greatest master.

Mays's legacy would have been enhanced if he had beaten Ruth's all-time home run record, and Mays's supporters lament that his time in the army, plus his playing in two ballparks that were unfriendly to a right-handed hitter with gap power, denied him that opportunity. Mays believes he would have hit eight hundred homers if he had not gone into the military and had played in parks like Aaron's. But given what happened to Aaron when he approached 714—the death threats, the racial epithets, the unbearable stress—one should not be so quick to wish that on Mays. He suffered mightily when trying to pass Mel Ott's record. He could have passed Babe Ruth's, but his pursuit would have been a personal trauma.

If Mays's skills are underappreciated, his achievements have been given a boost by the Steroid Era, which has caused fans to pine for a game that they could still associate with honesty and innocence. Baseball has always been an imperfect institution, but as much as anyone, Mays evokes its highest ideals. His legacy, ultimately, will never be about his numbers, his records, or how he helped his team to win. It will be about the pure joy that he brought to fans and the loving memories that have been passed to future generations so they might know the magic and beauty of the game.

In his easy chair at home, Mays will doze off when the ball game is on, then he'll wake up in a start when he hears the announcer cry, "A Willie Mays catch!" He'll peer at the television, watch the replay, and grunt, "He made that with two outs. I made mine with one, and I had to make the throw."

Or he'll be watching a game and the announcer will pose some baseball trivia question.

"Me!" Mays will answer. Then he'll rest his eyes.

On Saturday, March 21, 2009, Willie Mays returns to Fairfield, Alabama, from spring training in Scottsdale. Over the years, he has not been all that visible in Fairfield or the Birmingham area, but he returns to make a contribution of $50,000 in baseball equipment, through his Say Hey Foundation, to kids who play in youth leagues as well as to Miles College and Fairfield High School.

The foundation itself has had a limited reach, but Mays is now seventy-eight, and he envisions it as part of his legacy. He wants to improve its financial footing and find ways for it to make an impact. His trip to Fairfield is one step in that direction.

In the mid-1980s, Fairfield had named a ball field Willie Mays Park, but it had fallen into disrepair. In the days leading up to the ceremony, volunteers in the community gave the park a makeover. They repainted the green stands, graded the outfield, applied fresh chalk along the foul lines, cleaned the barbecue pit, and sought donations for food and beverages. "It came from the heart of each and every one," says Clarissa Milano, a friend of Mays's who is on the foundation's advisory board. "In these tough times, you saw people give back, and that's what Willie wants people to do."

The ceremony commences on a sunny morning that draws Mays's Black Baron teammates James Zapp and the Reverend Bill Greason. Several hundred people are in the stands, and dozens of children, dressed in bright orange T-shirts, with a silk-screen picture of Willie Mays on the back, are lined up on the infield. They are prepared to accept their bags stuffed with, among other things, a bat, a mitt, a batting glove, and a videotape about Mays's life.

The Reverend Robert G. Twyman, pastor of the First Church of Fairfield, begins the event with an invocation. "We're grateful for this man who grew up in this community who's come to give back," he says. "Bless him in a special way."

Mayor Kenneth Coachman speaks next, welcoming Willie home, giving him a key to the city, and sharing an inspiration he had at four that morning—that the city should raise funds for a Willie Mays statue at his park, "somewhere in the area of the barbecue stand."

A young man sings the national anthem, and the emcee thanks a list of sponsors, from AT&T, PepsiCo, and Rawlings to the Fire House of Fairfield and Merita Bakery. Then Willie is introduced. He wears a Giants cap, a blue blazer, and dark pants. He's lost about ten pounds this year and looks good. As always, he has no notes but speaks from the heart.

"We got a lot of product for the kids," he says, "so you got to start clapping for these kids. Not for me, because I got mine a long time ago."

He describes how he was in Birmingham last year on business and was driven around Fairfield. "When I looked around, there was no convenience store where we used to steal stuff, so I knew something was wrong. . . . The first thing that I wanted to do was to give the kids something to look forward to. And this is why I wanted them to have a day of their own."

As Willie talks, the organizers nudge the children into a close-knit semicircle around him. "I talked to the mayor and I said, 'What is needed here?' And all he had to say was, 'Just look around, and you'll see for yourself that we need help.' "

Willie says he has good reason to help the people of Fairfield. "They're the ones that made me," he says. "They're the ones who said, 'Willie, you cannot have any drugs, you cannot smoke, we're gonna send you home at ten o'clock at night,' and they did. And I appreciate that, because when I went to New York, nobody had to tell me to be in the house, no one had to tell me to go home. I was there because of all you that saw me play football, basketball, and baseball in this town."

He acknowledges that returning home isn't easy. "I know I was kind of hesitant in coming and doing things here. I guess I wanted the kids around me. . . . That's what this is all about. It's not about me. I had my life. I had twenty-two years of baseball. Enjoyed every minute of it. These kids that are coming now need help. [Other people] say, 'Why are you going to Fairfield with the money that we give you?' and sometimes you have to say, 'This is my home, man. Help me. Do something for these kids. Make sure that they have a good life.' "

Then Mays does something odd. He notes that he is giving equipment to Miles College but has neglected Lawson State, a community college. "I know that my mother lived about five minutes from there," he says. "I know she would want me to help whoever I can, and next year, when I come here . . . I will make sure that everyone that's in sports, high school, college, or whatever it may be, will be supported in this program."

Mays never mentions his mother, but the reference is in the spirit of his homecoming. The previous day, Eric Fernandez, a friend who helps with the foundation, drove Mays around his old neighborhood and saw the emotion rising in him. "It's important that the people of Fairfield are proud of him not as a baseball player but as a man," Fernandez says. "He has a focus now on Willie Mays the person. That's what he wants his legacy to be. . . . Now he's saying I've come home to my parents. It's important to him, an internal check box. When he meets his parents in heaven, he can say with a straight face that I gave back to my community. I did what you wanted me to do."

When Mays finishes speaking, he helps distribute the equipment, signs balls, and wraps his massive arms around the children for photographs. Reporters, city council members, and friends all want his attention, all want his time. He chats and he smiles, but he can't stay long. He has to return to Scottsdale. The Giants have added some talent, a veteran lefty, a new shortstop, and a rookie third baseman with a big stick. Willie Mays wants to get back.

It's spring training, and there's a feel in the air.

AUTHOR'S NOTE

Over the years, many writers, agents, and publishers approached Willie Mays, seeking his cooperation on a biography, and Mays always said no. So how did someone who never saw him play, doesn't live in New York or San Francisco, and isn't even a Giants fan get that honor? Therein lies an author's note.

In 2000, I wrote my first book, on Rubin ("Hurricane") Carter, a very different black athlete of that same era, and after one of my talks, a stranger approached me and said I should really write a biography of Willie Mays. The idea immediately appealed to me. As a kid, I wanted to be a sports journalist because I thought my typewriter would be my ticket to all the games. Well, I was wrong about my career and wrong about the typewriter. What didn't change was my love for baseball, and while I never saw Mays play—I was born in 1962 and grew up in St. Louis—the name was magic for any fan.

My problem was that I didn't know anyone associated with the Giants or even Major League Baseball. In search of leads, I found a recent ESPN documentary about Mays. The program captured the arc of his remarkable career, celebrating the highlights and noting the disappointments. What was missing was . . . Willie Mays. He was interviewed but said very little. He was depicted, as a player and in retirement, as isolated and inscrutable. "No one really knows Willie Mays," Bill James said.

Mays might have been unknown, but he wasn't unknowable. Fortunately, the documentary featured an interview with an older gentleman who did seem to know him, Sy Berger. I learned that he had retired from the Topps Company, the maker of baseball cards, so I called Topps, which kindly gave me Berger's home number on Long Island. I called him, introduced myself, and said I'd like to talk to Willie Mays about a possible book.

Sy's voice was gravelly but gentle. He told me he's known Willie since 1951—they were both a couple of kids back then—and he had signed Willie to his first trading card contract, and they had been good friends ever since. He had also advised him on financial matters. "I'm one of the few people he trusts," he said proudly.

Sy was encouraging but skeptical. He very much wanted a biography of Willie because he believed his friend wasn't appreciated enough. His numbers didn't capture his greatness, and a book was needed to spell out, particularly for those who never saw him play, his true genius. But Sy warned me that Willie didn't like talking about himself and can be uncomfortable in social settings. He told me how he travels with Willie to Cooperstown for the Hall of Fame induction ceremonies, and while the parties are going on, Willie will stay in his hotel room, and everyone will want to know where he is. "Finally," Sy said, "he comes down, and he's the life of the party."

By now I had read about Willie's occasional run-ins with reporters, and I asked Sy about them. He said Willie didn't always handle situations the right way; he could ruffle feathers and could even make it difficult for his friends.

"So," I said, "what do you think of Willie?"

"Me?" he asked. He paused and chuckled a bit, and I'll never forget what he said next. "I love the guy."

That was good enough for me. We spoke for more than an hour, with Sy explaining that Willie had legitimate reasons to be wary of outsiders and that his gruffness toward strangers was his way of protecting himself. "But once he gets to know you," he said, "he'll tell you all the stories."

It was July, and Sy asked me to write him a letter with my request, which he would take to Willie at the Hall of Fame ceremonies later that month. He told me that convincing Willie was a long shot, but he would try to help. The day after Sy returned from Cooperstown, he called.

"He's not interested," he said. "Sorry, but that's Willie."

So I wrote another book but kept Sy's number, and two years later I called him again and reintroduced myself. He remembered me, and we had another long discussion about Willie, whom he was going to see in a few weeks in Cooperstown. Sy told me to send him another letter, and he would see what he could do. I dusted off my original note and sent it. Soon after he returned from Cooperstown, Sy called.

"Not interested," he said. "Sorry, but that's Willie."

So I wrote another book, and two years later I called Sy again. We again had a long talk about Willie, Sy again told me to send him a letter, and he would again see Willie at Cooperstown. A few days after the ceremonies, the call came.

"Still no luck," Sy said. "That's Willie."

I had a thin file on Willie Mays, including Sy's phone number, but when we moved to a new house, I tossed the file. Three strikes and you're out, I figured.

So I wrote another book. After I completed it, my agent, Todd Shuster, asked me what I was going to do next. I told him I was considering some other writing opportunities, "and frankly, the only topic that would still interest me is Willie Mays, but that didn't work out."

"You have to try again," Todd said. (This, of course, is what agents get paid to do—prod their authors to write another book when common sense says they should get a real job.)

It was now January of 2007. Seven years had passed since I first spoke to Sy. I no longer had his phone number and didn't even know if he was still alive. You can appreciate the tenuous life of a writer when his career hinges on the pulse of an octogenarian. Fortunately, the Topps Company again gave me Sy's number, and both Sy and his lovely wife, Gloria, were still very much alive. This being the winter, Sy would not be seeing Willie at Cooperstown, but he said he would call Willie for me and to please send a letter.

Days passed. Finally, Sy called back. "He'll talk to you," he told me. "I'll give you his phone number."

I promptly called the number but got what appeared to be a fax machine. I kept trying, with the same result. I called Sy back and asked him to check the number. He did and gave me the same one. I tried again but the call wouldn't go through. I called the operator and asked her to try, but she couldn't complete the call either. I called Sy back.

"Sy! That's not the right number. Please look again."

He fumbled around. The number he had given me had ended in "2422." Now he gave me another number—this one ended in "2424."

Of course.

I called Willie, and he told me I should stop by his house that weekend. I'm not sure he appreciated that I lived in the Boston area and he lived in California, but he was now giving me directions from the highway, and three days later I was ringing his doorbell.

It still took a full year for Willie to get comfortable with the idea and with me, and to find the right publisher, and to work out the details. The book is an "authorized biography": Willie agreed to cooperate with all of my efforts—granting interviews; directing me to friends, colleagues, and family members; and sharing documents, photographs, and other archival material. Willie read the manuscript (given his glaucoma, he had Rene Anderson read it to him), and he could correct any factual errors. With one exception, Willie did not ask me to change a single sentence, idea, or anecdote. (The exception: I described the fight that Willie had with Ruben

Gomez in Puerto Rico. Willie told me to add that he and Gomez resumed their friendship when they returned to the States.) I promised to keep his point of view front and center, but the conclusions and interpretations are my own. Willie and I are dividing the proceeds of the book, with much of his going to the Say Hey Foundation.

Why did Willie agree to cooperate on this project? He probably had several reasons, but I said to him at the outset that this book will try to define his legacy on and off the field. "You should look at the totality of your life—the achievements and the disappointments—and if you're satisfied with the balance, you should do this."

I didn't know it then, but Willie is extremely proud of his life, and I think he ultimately wanted a complete outsider to validate it. Toward that end, I interviewed more than 130 people (some of whom came from Willie, others I found on my own), reviewed more than four thousand newspaper and magazine articles and blogs, watched several documentaries on Mays, read more than 135 books, sorted through dozens of photographs, and found countless letters, contracts, and documents related to Willie— from his high school report card, to his father's employment records with the Pullman Company, to Ed Howden's detailed report describing Willie's efforts to buy his first house in San Francisco.

On one of my early visits with Willie, I was to meet him in his box at AT&T Park, and we would chat while the Giants were playing a game. I arrived an hour early and noticed that outside the park about fifteen people had lined up next to the gleaming Willie Mays statue so they could have their picture taken next to it. I then walked into the Borders bookstore across the street and checked out the sports aisle. There were biographies of Babe Ruth, Joe DiMaggio, Ted Williams, Jackie Robinson, Mickey Mantle, and Roberto Clemente. But there was none of Willie Mays.

When I went back outside, I saw that there were now twenty people waiting to have their photos taken next to the Mays statue. I realized then that it was my job to tell those people what was inside that bronze sculpture.

It was worth the wait.

CAREER STATS

SEASON	TEAM	G	AB	R	H	TB	2B	3B	HR	RBI	BB	IBB	SO	SB	CS	AVG	OBP	SLG	OPS
1951	NYG	121	464	59	127	219	22	5	20	68	57		60	7	4	.274	.356	.472	.828
1952	NYG	34	127	17	30	52	2	4	4	23	16		17	4	1	.236	.326	.409	.736
1954	NYG	151	565	119	195	377	33	13	41	110	66		57	8	5	.345	.411	.667	1.078
1955	NYG	152	580	123	185	382	18	13	51	127	79	13	60	24	4	.319	.400	.659	1.059
1956	NYG	152	578	101	171	322	27	8	36	84	68	20	65	40	10	.296	.369	.557	.926
1957	NYG	152	585	112	195	366	26	20	35	97	76	15	62	38	19	.333	.407	.626	1.033
1958	SF	152	600	121	208	350	33	11	29	96	78	12	56	31	6	.347	.419	.583	1.002
1959	SF	151	575	125	180	335	43	5	34	104	65	9	58	27	4	.313	.381	.583	.964
1960	SF	153	595	107	190	330	29	12	29	103	61	11	70	25	10	.319	.381	.555	.936
1961	SF	154	572	129	176	334	32	3	40	123	81	15	77	18	9	.308	.393	.584	.977
1962	SF	162	621	130	189	382	36	5	49	141	78	11	85	18	2	.304	.384	.615	.999
1963	SF	157	596	115	187	347	32	7	38	103	66	5	83	8	3	.314	.380	.582	.962
1964	SF	157	578	121	171	351	21	9	47	111	82	13	72	19	5	.296	.383	.607	.990
1965	SF	157	558	118	177	360	21	3	52	112	76	16	71	9	4	.317	.398	.645	1.043
1966	SF	152	552	99	159	307	29	4	37	103	70	11	81	5	1	.288	.368	.556	.924
1967	SF	141	486	83	128	220	22	2	22	70	51	7	92	6	0	.263	.334	.453	.787
1968	SF	148	498	84	144	243	20	5	23	79	67	7	81	12	6	.289	.372	.488	.860
1969	SF	117	403	64	114	176	17	3	13	58	49	7	71	6	2	.283	.362	.437	.798
1970	SF	139	478	94	139	242	15	2	28	83	79	3	90	5	0	.291	.390	.506	.897
1971	SF	136	417	82	113	201	24	1	18	61	112	11	123	23	3	.271	.425	.482	.907
1972	SF/NYM	88	244	35	61	98	11	1	8	22	60	6	48	4	5	.250	.400	.402	.802
1973	NYM	66	209	24	44	72	10	0	6	25	27	0	47	1	0	.211	.303	.344	.647
CAREER		2992	10881	2062	3283	6066	523	140	660	1903	1464	192	1526	338	103	.302	.384	.557	.941

ACKNOWLEDGMENTS

Every author relies on the kindness of strangers, but this book, more than most, relied on the goodwill of others. Willie is honest but guarded and only over time does he open up. His comments to me were ultimately invaluable, but by then a very clear portrait had already emerged. I've already described Sy Berger's contributions in my Author's Note, but several individuals deserve special recognition.

While Loretta Richardson hasn't spoken to Willie in many years, she generously shared her memories of their childhood in Alabama. Herman Boykin was also essential in my understanding of Willie's youth, and David Stokes became my personal guide to the history of Fairfield. James Zapp and Bill Greason still carry the torch for the Birmingham Black Barons, and I was honored to meet both men. James "Poo" Johnson lifted the veil on Willie's army years and spoke with unusual insight and candor about his good friend. Karl Zimmermann was my unfailing tutor on air and train travel in America. Roger Kahn gave me his time, and sent many e-mails, to help me understand Willie and his era. Monte Irvin has given many interviews over the years, but a conversation with him on Willie, the New York Giants, and the Negro Leagues still constitutes an excellent history lesson. Lon Simmons, a great source on Willie and the San Francisco Giants, spent many hours with me on the phone. Gary Shemano helped me understand the complex relationship between his father and Willie. Lee Mendelson, who has lost none of the passion for Willie that propelled his groundbreaking documentary, helped me at several stages in my research. Judi Phillips brought details and context to Mae's relationship with Willie. Jessie and Bud Goins and Phil Saddler all helped me understand the man behind the legend. Rick Swig supplied me with photographs, insights, and leads. Michael Jacobs was wonderfully generous in sharing his massive collection of Willie Mays memorabilia with me. Clarissa Milano and Eric Fernandez brought me up to date.

Bob Costas is really a baseball historian who happens to have a media gig, and I was grateful for his time; Bruce Cornblatt's assistance was also much appreciated.

If you write a book that allows you to talk to Bill Clinton, Woody Allen, Hank Aaron, Kareem Abdul-Jabbar, Sandy Koufax, and Tom Seaver, you've probably got a pretty good subject. These men are all in demand, and I thank them for their time.

Barry Bonds doesn't give many interviews these days, but he spoke with me by phone for a full hour and was cordial and respectful throughout. His mother, Pat, was also interviewed. I thank them both for sharing their thoughts on Willie.

The San Francisco Giants supported this project throughout. My deepest thanks to President Larry Baer, Senior Vice President Mario Alioto, retired executive Pat Gallagher, equipment manager Mike Murphy, and clubhouse attendant Harvey Hodgerney.

Diane McWhorter sent me a lengthy unpublished chapter from *Carry Me Home* on the history of Fairfield, Alabama. She gave me another lead as well on an obscure but very helpful book about Birmingham. Jane Leavy, the author of *Sandy Koufax* who was working on a Mickey Mantle book, also gave me some reporting guidance. Brad Snyder, the author of *A Well-Paid Slave,* opened some critical doors as well.

I would like to thank the following people who kindly spoke with me (and sincere apologies to anyone I've overlooked):

Bob Akers, Vernon Alden, Joe Amalfitano, Dave Anderson, Edward Anderson, Greg Anderson, Johnny Antonelli, Richard Arrington, Dusty Baker, Rick Barry, William Bell, Jim Bouton, Jackie Brandt, Eddie Bressoud, Willie Brown, Pete Carlson, Orlando Cepeda, Jimmy Clark, U. W. Clemon, Gladys Cofield, Ken Condon, Robert Creamer, Dink Cryer, Alvin Dark, Jim Davenport, Faye Davis, Ken Donnelly, Bill Dully, Chris Durocher, Gerald Early, Lee Elder, Frank Evans, Roy Face, Katy Feeney, Ron Fimrite, Tito Fuentes, Walter Gibbons, Redenia Gilliam-Mosee, Stanley Glenn, Clyde Golden, Richard Goldman, Rebecca Grisby, Arnold Hano, Doug Harvey, Edward Howden, Bill Howes, Larry Jansen, Hobie Landrith, Hal Lanier, Stuart Leeds, Larry Lester, Bill Littlefield, Ronnie Lott, Fred Lowell, David Kaufer, Judy Kaufman, Will Knox, Ed Kranepool, Harry Leppo, Garry Maddox, Richard J. Martin, Tim McCarver, Mike McCormick, Willie McCovey, Roy McKercher, Charlie McMorris, A. J. Mercado, Lenny Merullo, John Miles, Jon Miller, Jessie Mitchell, Ed Montague, Joe Morgan, Jo-Jo Perota, Gaylord Perry, Nick Peters, Philip Pizzo, Charley Pride, David Rapaport, William Richardson, Paula and Jon Roberts, Ray Robinson, Al Rosen, Ted Rosengarten, Bill Royer, Ray Sadecki, Art Santo Domingo, Virgil Saxon, Mike Shannon, Harold Shepherd, Tom Sherak, Walter Shorenstein, Chuck Smith, Eugene Smith, Robert Sockolov, Steve Sockolov, Don Stapley, Sam Stith, Adam Swig, Otis Tate, Valmy Thomas, Diane Turner, Johnnie Alberta Wade, Doris Ward, Michelle Watkins, Martha Whetstone, Bill White, Cecil Williams, Sydney Williams, Fred Williamson, Charles Willis, Maury Wills, and Rick Zeller.

I interviewed five people who have since passed away, and I want to acknowledge them separately: Herman Franks, Whitey Lockman, Dusty Rhodes, Sam Sirkus, and Jules Tygiel.

My thanks to Eamon Dolan, with whom I first discussed this project many years ago and who encouraged me to pursue it.

Richard Johnson, the curator of the Sports Museum of New England, happens to be a tenacious collector and a diehard Giant fan, and he kindly shared with me a huge trove of books, magazines, newspaper articles, programs, and yearbooks related to Willie Mays.

Taking mercy on their technology-challenged friend, Michael Seidman bailed me out of various computer jams, and Moshe Bar and Peter Mesnik provided additional IT support—all with good cheer. On predawn drives to the airport, Walter Curran provided me with hot coffee, sound baseball analysis, and lasting friendship.

Several libraries were extremely helpful: the A. Bartlett Giamatti Research Center at the National Baseball Hall of Fame and Museum, the Historical Department of the San Francisco Public Library, the Needham Public Library in Needham, Massachusetts, the New York Public Library, and the Schomburg Center for Research in Black Culture in New York.

This book might never have been written without the support of two people in Willie's life. Jeffrey L. Bleich, a partner at Munger, Tolles & Olson LLP in San Francisco, is Willie's lawyer, adviser, and friend. He helped convince Willie that an authorized biography was indeed in his best interests, and he smoothed out negotiations among all the parties. Even after Jeff accepted a temporary assignment at the White House, he was a reassuring presence in his informal capacity as a Friend of the Book.

Rene Anderson is Willie's personal assistant, but that understates her true role. She is Willie's organizer, scheduler, gatekeeper, traveling associate, protector, and guardian angel, and my own debt to her far exceeds anything I could ever pay.

This book needed a publishing house that placed great value on good baseball and good writing, and I found one in Scribner, starting with the publisher, Susan Moldow, and the editor in chief, Nan Graham. Scribner's entire team—Brian Belfiglio, Kate Bittman, Anna deVries, Roz Lippel, and Katie Rizzo—has been enthusiastic and supportive, and I owe a special thanks to Brant Rumble for his time, patience, and editing acumen.

Luise Erdmann has now been my copyeditor for all five of my books, at two different publishers. I'd have no objection if our burial plots were 60 feet, 6 inches apart.

My agent, Todd Shuster, didn't give up on Willie, and his faith in him, and me, made this book possible.

My thanks to my father, Ed Hirsch, and his partner, Dolly Newport, to my brother and sister, Irl Hirsch and Lynn Friedman, and their families, and to Aileen Phillips.

Finally, my family, as always, made the greatest sacrifice. At least in this case, Sheryl and I were able to take our children, Amanda and Garrett, to San Francisco so they could watch a game at AT&T Park with Willie Mays. It's a pretty good way to spend an afternoon.

NOTES

Prologue

2 *"Glad you could make it so soon"*: Willie Mays with Einstein, *Willie Mays*, 87–89.

3 *"He'd lay his hand on that rope"*: Einstein, *Willie's Time*, 12.

4 *"a contagious happiness that gets everybody on the club"*: *New York Post*, June 24, 1951.

4 *"the frivolity in his bloodstream"*: Rickey, *American Diamond*, 125.

6 *"I changed the hatred to laughter"*: *GQ*, April 1994.

7 *"The first thing to establish"*: *Los Angeles Times*, May 23, 1962.

Chapter One: Alabama Roots

9 *"the adventure of steel making"*: TCI President A.V. Wiebel, in an undated cover letter on a TCI brochure, Birmingham Public Library (Tutwiler Collection).

9 *"A spell had been laid over everything"*: Excerpted from *A Nigger: A Novel*, in Fullerton, *Striking Out Jim Crow*, 40.

10 *"I didn't have any heroes"*: Mays with Sahadi, *Say Hey*, 21.

10 *"It went from him"*: Einstein, *Willie's Time*, 13.

11 *"the most important ritual"*: Fullerton, *Striking Out Jim Crow*, 46.

12 *"I made it during the Depression"*: Einstein, *Willie's Time*, 12.

12 *"the type of young person you like to deal with"*: Ibid., 13.

12 *"My God, look at those hands!"*: Ibid., 23.

13 *"We didn't know what to do"*: *Born to Play Ball*, 2000.

13 *"See the ball! See the ball!"*: Mays with Sahadi, *Say Hey*, 7.

13 *"I knew he was gonna be special"*: Kahn, *The Era*, 246.

14 *"I was pretty good"*: *Sport*, May 1969.

14 *"By the time Willie was six"*: *Sports Illustrated*, April 13, 1969.

14 *"Pick it up!"*: Linge, *Willie Mays*, 5.

14 *"Cat was an indoctrinator"*: Author interview.

14 *"Stand up"*: Mays with Einstein, *Willie Mays*, 60.

15 *"When I try to remember events"*: Mays with Sahadi, *Say Hey*, 13.

15 *"simply extraordinary"*: From an unpublished chapter in McWhorter, *Carry Me Home*.

16 *"a mill town of perpetual promise"*: Ibid.

16 *"Our parents took us to church"*: Stokes, e-mail to author.

17 *"We were somewhat sheltered"*: Author interview.

18 *"because we got the better view"*: Author interview.

Chapter Two: Raised to Succeed

19 *"I told Willie, 'Just tell the truth'"*: Author interview with Judi Phillips.
19 *"I never saw Cat negative in any way"*: Author interview.
19 *"My father was much more private than me"*: Author interview.
20 *"I felt nothing bothered him"*: Author interview.
20 *"I played with him for two years"*: *Born to Play Ball*, 2000.
20 *"He was basically a quiet, happy-go-lucky kid"*: Author interviews.
20 *"My father gave me that one thing, positive thinking"*: Author interview.
20 *"You want to smoke?"*: Mays with Sahadi, *Say Hey*, 13.
20 *"Cat always told us"*: Author interview.
22 *"Willie's hands were quicker than your eyes"*: Author interview.
22 *"Willie got into minor things"*: Author interview.
22 *"confessed [to] Christ"* : From a tribute to Sarah May, distributed on her death, at Jones Chapel A.M.E. Church, July 22, 1954.
22 *"My mom talked about it all the time"*: Author interview.
23 *"She didn't whip me that much, because I didn't like it"*: Author interview.
23 *"It was just a happy place to be"*: Author interview.
23 *"Sarah fed us every day"*: Author interview.
23 *"a good woman who took care of Willie"*: Author interview.
23 *"She carried me to the hospital"*: Author interview.
23 *"We were worried to death"*: Author interview.
24 *"Willie, you're going to be a ballplayer"*: Author interview with Mays.
24 *"I didn't know life could be so cruel"*: Author interview.
25 *"That shook him up because Otis was like a brother"*: Author interview.
25 *"When you lose a friend like that"*: Author interview.
26 *"They would bite you"*: Author interview.
26 *"If you didn't bring it back clean"*: Author interview.
26 *"If I got put in jail and they got put in jail"*: Author interview.
27 *"We'd play in the street"*: *Sporting News*, February 17, 1960.
27 *"They were concerned about the quality of our lives"*: Author interview.

Chapter Three: Supernatural Gifts

28 *"high behind"*: *Born to Play Ball*, 2000.
28 *"I knew he was not an ordinary person"*: Author interview.
28 *"It was absolutely crazy"*: Author interview.
29 *"I don't like to say this too much"*: Author interview.
29 *"We'll call you Bing"*: Mays with Einstein, *Willie Mays*, 40.
29 *"Call me DiMag"*: Ibid., 59.
29 *"I had a hope then that I could be"*: Author interview.
29 *"He was always a great athlete"*: Author interview.
29 *"He was the greatest passer I've ever seen"*: Author interview.
30 *"heaved a seventy-yard pass which was caught, then he ran for the extra point"*: Oliver, *End of an Era*, 90.
30 *"We had a center"*: Author interview.
31 *"You were bearing down too hard out there"*: Mays with Einstein, *Willie Mays*, 64.
31 *"This was about survival"*: Author interview.
31 *"We thought he was going to throw the ball"*: Author interview.

32 *"In the South, you only had"*: Interview with the Academy of Achievement, A Museum of Living History, February 19, 1996.

32 *"I ain't going back for the money"*: Author interview.

32 *"Okay . . . you play baseball"*: Author interview with Mays.

33 *"I said to myself right then"*: Chattanooga Times, October, 15, 1954.

33 *"We learned it was a big world"*: Author interview.

33 *"We'd go out there early, look at the field"*: Author interview.

33 *"Willie and I would have finished the trip alone"*: Chattanooga Times, October 15, 1954.

33 *"We'd eat loaves of stale bread"*: Einstein, Willie's Time, 308.

34 *"You be back tomorrow?"*: Ibid.

34 *"My father had always been a symbol"*: Mays with Sahadi, Say Hey, 14; Mays with Einstein, Willie Mays, 70–71.

Chapter Four: A Mother's Love

35 *"Both my mother and my father had tempers"*: Author interview.

36 *"Willie never felt disconnected to her"*: Author interview.

36 *"My mom had a mouth"*: Author interview.

37 *"It don't pay to dig up the past"*: Sport, June 1960.

Chapter Five: The Black Barons

38 *"We want Piper!"*: Described in an obituary distributed at Davis's funeral on May 24, 1997.

38 *"If [Davis] had a chance"*: Tygiel, Baseball's Great Experiment, 261.

39 *"Boy, what are you doing here?"*: An interview of Piper Davis, on June 30, 1980, archived at the National Baseball Hall of Fame & Museum; Mays with Sahadi, Say Hey, 15; and author interview.

40 *"Well, I'm going to the ball game"*: Birmingham World, May 9, 1950.

42 *"If you was black"*: Tygiel, Baseball's Great Experiment, 19.

42 Mays's first game: Mays with Sahadi, Say Hey, 22. The Diamond: The Official Chronicle of Major League Baseball, July 1993.

42 *"I ain't never seen a ballplayer like that in my life"*: Born to Play Ball, 2000.

43 Davis's instructions to Willie: Mays with Sahadi, Say Hey; The Diamond, July 1993; recorded interview at the Hall of Fame.

46 *"they played baseball without the baseball"*: Author interview.

46 *"He was the most exciting young player you've ever seen"*: Author interview.

47 *"He did some impossible catches in the outfield"*: Born to Play Ball, 2000.

47 *"Nobody, and I mean nobody"*: Einstein, Willie's Time, 309.

47 *"That's it"*: Author interview with Mays.

49 *"It was an arduous existence"*: Irvin with Riley, Nice Guys Finish First, 67.

49 *"Rarely were we in the same city"*: Campanella, It's Good to Be Alive, 65.

49 *"He was just standing there on the highway"*: Born to Play Ball, 2000.

49 *"If we came to a right turn"*: Einstein, Willie's Time, 293.

50 *"Got to play a game, fellas"*: Mays with Sahadi, Say Hey, 34.

50 *"You can't leave me!"*: Ibid., 31.

50 *"She took off her apron"*: Ibid., 33.

51 *"was the greatest sleeper I ever saw"*: Sporting News, February 9, 1955.

51 *"It was a history lesson"*: Author interview.
51 *"We were one of the sharpest dressed teams in the league"*: Author interview.
52 *"We would laugh about that"*: Mays with Sahadi, *Say Hey,* 26.
52 *The man stepped off the bus*: Fullerton, *Striking Out Jim Crow,* 83.
53 *"dare not be seen"*: Rowan, *South of Freedom,* 161.
53 *"With all the rejection we had to suffer"*: Author interview.
53 *"Keep your mouth closed"*: Author interview.

Chapter Six: The Giants Call

55 *"He didn't receive accolades"*: *Born to Play Ball,* 2000.
57 *"Give us $2,000 and you can have that kid"*: Recorded interview at the National Baseball Hall of Fame & Museum.
57 *"Give it to me! Give it to me!"*: *Birmingham News,* July 9, 1965.
57 *"I'd stand on the roof at Rickwood and watch him"*: Ibid.
58 *"He was kind of skipping and dancing around"*: Author interview.
59 *"They moved slower back then"*: *Birmingham News,* July 9, 1965.
59 *"Listen, you forget about Perry"*: Ibid.
59 *"a young Negro ballplayer"*: *Look,* May 3, 1955.
59 *"I had no inkling of Willie Mays"*: Ibid.
60 *"He told me he had seen enough of Perry"*: *New York Journal American,* June 28, 1954.
60 *"Would you like to play professional baseball?"*: Mays with Sahadi, *Say Hey,* 39.
61 *"Why should Mr. Hayes get anything?"*: Einstein, *Willie's Time,* 303.
62 *"The kid can't hit a curveball"*: Campanella, *It's Good to Be Alive,* 144.
62 *"Ownership thought there was a surfeit"*: Tygiel, *Baseball's Great Experiment,* 306.
62 *"He was the greatest prospect I ever saw"*: *Boston Globe,* August 3, 1994.
62 *"has the attitudes"*: Kahn, *The Era,* 190.
63 *"When I finally get a nigger"*: Thorn, *Glory Days,* 30.
63 *"Of course we knew segregation was wrong"*: Kahn, *The Era,* 188.
64 *"I don't look at race that way"*: Author interview.

Chapter Seven: The Minors

66 *"History was made last night"*: *Philadelphia Daily News,* August 10, 2004.
66 *"Hey, man, I don't need no help here"*: Interview with the American Academy of Achievement, February 19, 1996.
67 *"Who's that nigger"*: *Philadelphia Daily News,* August 10, 2004.
67 *"I went 0-for-Maryland"*: Mays with Sahadi, *Say Hey,* 43.
68 *"I never knew a peg"*: Honig, *Mays, Mantle, Snider,* 103
68 *"They look like Popeye's"*: Mays with Sahadi, *Say Hey,* 43.
68 *"I just didn't hear it anymore"*: Ibid., 47.
69 *"One-and-two, hitter's weakness is high inside"*: Mays with Einstein, *Willie Mays,* 75–76.
69 *"He's a major league prospect"*: *Sport,* June 1956, 60.
70 *"He might be a little tight"*: Angell, *Five Seasons,* 275.
71 *"You had to be better than good"*: Mays with Sahadi, *Say Hey,* 50.
72 *"You've got a great chance"*: Ibid., 50.
72 *"Hey, kid, what are you going to show me today?"*: Ibid., 48.
72 *"I could tell you every move Mays"*: Durocher with Linn, *Nice Guys Finish Last,* 272.
73 *"When the game was over,"*: Mays with Sahadi, *Say Hey,* 49.

73   *"Willie, we're taking you with us to Minneapolis"*: Ibid., 51.
73   *"I have been toning it down"*: Ibid., 53.
73   *"Why aren't you here?"*: Ibid., 54.
74   *"literally climbed the right-center field wall"*: Hoffbeck, *Swinging for the Fences*, 134.
74   *"I just caught my spikes in the wall"*: Mays with Sahadi, *Say Hey*, 54.
74   *"That little son of a bitch"*: Ibid., 54.
74   *"Willie, you're losing your control"*: Ibid., 52.
75   *"He's as good, at this stage"*: Hoffbeck, *Swinging for the Fences*, 134.
75   *"Many veteran observers feel he may well become"*: Ibid., 135.
76   *"I like to think that before he died"*: Kahn, *The Era*, 249.
77   *"We pick up the papers one week and say"*: *New York Times*, June 29, 1952.
77   *"If Willie Mays is in the audience"*: Mays with Sahadi, *Say Hey*, 56–57.
77   *"You just broke my heart"*: *New York Times*, May 25, 1951.
78   Conversation between Mays and Durocher: Mays with Sahadi, *Say Hey;* Mays with Einstein, *Willie Mays*.
78   *"I didn't want to go because"*: Hano, *Willie Mays*, 17.
79   *"That Stoneham letter quite frankly"*: *Sporting News*, June 27, 1951.
80   *"I had to go pack his stuff"*: *Sports Illustrated*, July 6, 1987.
80   *"You know . . . I really don't like you"*: Interview with Monte Irvin.

Chapter Eight: The Savior Arrives

81   *"No minor league player in a generation"*: *New York Times*, May 25, 1951.
82   *"My big fellows! My giants!"*: *New Yorker*, May 1958.
83   *"Dad came home one night"*: *Sports Illustrated*, May 5, 1958.
84   *"I always liked it better up there"*: Ibid.
84   *"Horace Stoneham's bartender"*: Author interview.
84   *"Are they still in the league?"*: Rosenfeld, *Great Chase*, 4.
85   *"Stick it in his fucking ear!"*: Eig, *Opening Day*, 39.
85   *"Those were real nice home runs"*: Allen, *The Giants & The Dodgers*, 193.
86   *"Don't clutter your brain with ethics"*: *Sport*, August 1969.
86   *"Good sportsmanship is so much sheep dip"*: *Time*, July 26, 1954.
86   *"Figure, you and Durocher are shipwrecked"*: Kahn, *Memories of Summer*, 151.
86   *"If Durocher keeps them hustling"*: Prager, *Echoing Green*, 15.
86   *"public fornication"*: Kahn, *The Era*, 28.
87   *"Leo has an infinite capacity"*: Ibid., 22.
87   *"Carve it on my gravestone"*: Durocher with Linn, *Nice Guys Finish Last*, 13.
87   *"I happened to be one of the heretics"*: Day, *Day with the Giants*, 22.
87   *"undermining the moral training"*: Rosenfeld, *The Great Chase*, 5.
87   *"Boys, I hear some of you don't want to play"*: Kahn, *The Era*, 35–36.
88   *"an accumulation of unpleasant incidents"*: Hynd, *Giants of the Polo Grounds*, 350.
88   *"poison at the gate"*: Ibid.
88   *"My daughter"*: *Sports Illustrated*, May 5, 1958, 77.
88   *"Who did you have in mind?"*: Hynd, *Giants of the Polo Grounds*, 350.
89   *"Then why am I listening to this?"*: Kahn, *The Era*, 152.
89   *"Your future lies over the river, Leo"*: Day, *Day with the Giants*, 70.
89   *"Leo was on the horns of a dilemma"*: Thorn, *Glory Days*, 57.
90   *"If we don't win it next year, boys"*: Kiernan, *Miracle at Coogan's Bluff*, 57.
91   *"the Giants' outfield seemed like a trio of morticians"*: Ibid., 29.
91   *"he was so hot you could've fried eggs"*: Ibid., 66.

91 "I won't say that Leo was suicidal": Day, Day with the Giants, 19.

91 "Don't let the guys give up": Peary, We Played the Game, 152.

92 "My God": Mays with Einstein, Willie Mays, 87.

92 "Willie, they're going to try to find out about you": Sporting News, August 15, 1951.

93 Mays arrives in Philadelphia: Mays with Einstein, Willie Mays, 90–93; Mays with Sahadi, Say Hey, 64–66.

94 "He popped it up": Peary, We Played the Game, 152.

95 "I'm thinking, 'Wow' ": Philadelphia Inquirer, May 25, 2001.

95 "Hey, Leo, how do you like him?": Hodges with Hirshberg, My Giants, 96.

95 "Listen, man": Kiernan, Miracle at Coogan's Bluff, 78.

95 "because I'm not feeling easy up there": New York Post, May 28, 1951.

95 "Is everybody here crazy except me?": Mays with Einstein, Willie Mays, 93.

96 "For the first sixty feet": Einstein, Willie's Time, 42.

96 "I never saw a fucking ball leave": Honig, Mays, Mantle, Snider, 106.

Chapter Nine: Rookie of the Year

98 "This is only the beginning": Amsterdam News, May 26, 1951.

99 "slud into third": Herkowitz, Mickey Mantle, 69.

99 "new way of knowing": Tygiel, Past Time, 66.

100 "was perhaps the most one-dimensional": James, New Bill James Historical Baseball Abstract, 220.

101 "You came slowly down the John T. Brush": New Yorker, May 1958.

101 "the mightiest temple": Thornley, Land of the Giants, 66.

102 "To a batter standing at home plate": Prager, Echoing Green, 60.

102 "There were men faster than Willie Mays": Posnanski, Soul of Baseball, 33.

102 "Putting Mays in a small ballpark": Honig, Mays, Mantle, Snider, p. 95.

102 "It's only a slump": Sport, June 1956.

102 "If anything, he seemed even younger than twenty": Author interview.

103 Durocher and Mays in the clubhouse: Durocher with Linn, Nice Guys Finish Last, 273–74; Mays with Einstein, Willie Mays, 94–95; Mays with Sahadi, Say Hey, 69–71.

105 "With Willie . . . you have to just keep patting him": Durocher with Linn, Nice Guys Finish Last, 274.

105 "Mays was the only player": Hodges with Hirshberg, My Giants, 98.

105 "You play like my kid": Durocher with Linn, Nice Guys Finish Last, 274.

105 "All those nice things Leo says": Ebony, August 1955, 36.

105 "I know they expect much from me": Rosenfeld, Great Chase, 52.

106 "Aren't you guys playing today?": Irvin, Nice Guys Finish First, 132.

106 "Look, there's something about Willie Mays": Durocher with Linn, Nice Guys Finish Last, 276.

107 "Did you notice how the third baseman was": Mays with Sahadi, Say Hey, 75.

107 "can't run, can't hit, can't field": Ibid., 75.

107 "I would spike my mother": Kiernan, Miracle at Coogan's Bluff, 33.

108 "How should we pitch to this kid?": Gilbert, The Seasons, 103.

108 "He was all smiles": Author interview.

108 "Goddammit, can't someone tell that guy": Interview with Eddie Bressoud.

109 "had revolutionized outfield play": Hano, Willie Mays, 57.

109 "Hey, Leo, didn't you see what": Sport, August 1969; Honig, Mays, Mantle, Snider, 107.

110 "With the average player, you take for granted": Ibid., 111.

110 "I don't think any ballplayer ever related": Honig, Mays, Mantle, Snider, 106.

110 *"the kid everybody liked"*: Sporting News, August 15, 1951.

110 *"Shame on you for not catching that ball"*: Sport, June 1965.

112 *"the life of the party"*: Rosenfeld, Great Chase, 54.

112 *"He electrified the clubhouse"*: American Weekly, March 30, 1958.

112 *"Willie answers all your questions breathlessly"*: Meany, Incredible Giants, 54.

112 *"a ferryboat whistle tooting frantically in a fog"*: New York Journal-American, June 30, 1954.

112 *"You have to hand that thing over"*: Day, Day with the Giants, 202.

112 *"Race you the rest of the way for five dollars"*: Mays with Einstein, Willie Mays, 101–102.

113 *"Coke! . . . That's six you owe me"*: Sport, August 1959.

113 *"Naturally, you stay a little laid back"*: Thomson with Heiman and Gutman, "The Giants Win the Pennant! The Giants Win the Pennant!," 161.

114 *"as violently as anybody"*: Honig, Mays, Mantle, Snider, 116.

114 *"my pigeon"*: Campanella, It's Good to Be Alive, 163–64; Irvin, Nice Guys Finish First, 148; Hano, Willie Mays, 64.

114 *"You think he's a good pitcher, Willie?"*: Author interview.

114 *"When I was his age"*: Sporting News, September 5, 1951.

114 *"When I first met Willie"*: Time, July 26, 1954; Life, September 13, 1954.

115 *"maybe four or five would be after Willie"*: Ibid.

116 *"When she hit the floor"*: Ibid.

116 *"Willie takes that man's word"*: Time, July 26, 1954.

116 *"Okay, James, let's go!"*: Durocher with Linn, Nice Guys Finish Last, 278–79; Mays with Sahadi, Say Hey, 72–75.

117 *"I'm empty, man"*: Ibid.

117 *"How'd you like one of these?"*: Argosy, September 1964.

118 *"He's an athlete"*: Irvin with Riley, Nice Guys Finish First, 31.

118 *"He's the next DiMaggio"*: Posnanski, Soul of Baseball, 224.

119 *"a bear trying to open"*: Hodges with Hirshberg, My Giants, 94.

119 *"Tell him what to do and how to do it"*: Author interview.

119 *"Being an infant"*: Hano, Willie Mays, 63.

119 *"Coming from the South"*: Author interview.

120 *"innate gayety of soul"*: Osofsky, Harlem, 184.

120 *"Ah gives baserunners the heave ho!"*: Tygiel, Past Time, 160.

121 *"straw boss" and "plantation hand"*: Rosenfeld, Great Chase, 52.

121 *"It bothered me a little too"*: Author interview.

121 *"Black folks had their own language"*: Author interview.

122 *"When the newspapermen used to ask me questions"*: Saturday Evening Post, May 20, 1961.

122 *"I know you not hitting"*: Life, September 13, 1954.

122 *"Willie gave me a lift"*: Author interview.

122 *"The single greatest factor"*: Irvin with Riley, Nice Guys Finish First, 156.

123 *"Leo, Leo, you in there?"*: Kiernan, Miracle at Coogan's Bluff, 91; Rosenfeld, Great Chase, 36.

124 *"took off as though it had a will of its own"*: Kiernan, Miracle at Coogan's Bluff, 95.

124 *"Let it go!"*: Ibid., 95.

124 *"Willie Mays . . . is reaching up"*: Thrive: Boomers and Beyond, Volume 1, Issue 26, July/August 2007.

125 *"I'd like to see him do it again"*: Rosenfeld, Great Chase, 52.

125 *"That was the luckiest throw I ever saw in my life"*: Sporting News, February 24, 1954.

125 *"I have been in baseball for forty-five years"*: Ibid.
125 *"I was absolutely astounded"*: Kiernan, *Miracle at Coogan's Bluff*, 95.
126 *"We have to catch the Dodgers"*: Author interview.
127 *"Warren Spahn had the best move to first base"*: Durocher with Linn, *Nice Guys Finish Last*, 276.
128 *"They were having a hell of a time"*: Prager, *Echoing Green*, 112.
128 *"I don't think there's ever been a club"*: Kiernan, *Miracle at Coogan's Bluff*, 117.
129 *"Back in those days"*: Ibid., 245.
130 *"touched off the wildest set-buying spree"*: Einstein, *Willie's Time*, 48–49.
130 *"by more sets of eyes than had ever before"*: Prager, *Echoing Green*, 179.
131 *"Sal, you had a hell of a year"*: *Sports Illustrated*, April 22, 1968.
132 *"sitting there like a deer in the hunting season"*: Rosenfeld, *Great Chase*, 226.
132 *"Attention, press"*: Prager, *Echoing Green*, 209.
133 Please don't let it be me: Mays with Sahadi, *Say Hey*, 5.
133 *"Willie may not have had a great average last year"*: *Sporting News*, January 25, 1952.
133 *"Get [Thomson] out"*: Rosenfeld, *Great Chase*, 233.
133 *"It's true, that first pitch was a blur"*: Kiernan, *Miracle at Coogan's Bluff*, 144.
133 *"It was the biggest crowd noise I ever heard"*: Thomson, *"The Giants Win the Pennant! The Giants Win the Pennant!,"* 253.
134 *"He was acting like a condemned man who had just received"*: *Saturday Evening Review*, August 26, 1972.
134 *"he got excited and fell out"*: Irvin with Riley, *Nice Guys Finish First*, 161.
134 *"I'm glad they didn't"*: Mays with Sahadi, *Say Hey*, 89.
134 *"I want you to know one thing"*: Bitker, *Original San Francisco Giants*, 65.
134 *"It was likely the most dramatic and shocking event in American sports"*: Tygiel, *Past Time*, 144.
135 *"Bobby Thomson brought New York City"*: Kiernan, *Miracle at Coogan's Bluff*, 147.
136 *"Look how I hit"*: Author interview.
138 "Willie Mays is in a daze": Einstein, *Willie's Time*, 71
138 *"Why would he want to take a picture with me?"*: Mays with Sahadi, *Say Hey*, 90.
140 *"I had played like a twenty-year-old"*: Ibid., 96.

Chapter Ten: War Stories

142 *"He drove a car faster than anyone"*: Author interview.
142 *"He's o-u-u-t-t!"*: Nunnelley, *Bull Connor*, 12.
145 *"owes perhaps a greater obligation to"*: April 15, 1952 (Unidentified newspaper in San Francisco Public Library, Research Center, Willie Mays's archives).
146 *"Get up, nigger!"*: Irvin with Riley, *Nice Guys Finish First*, 128.
147 *"That's all right"*: Tygiel, *Baseball's Great Experiment*, 315.
147 *"There wasn't much you could do except ignore them"*: Author interview.
148 *"His spikes caught"*: Hano, *Willie Mays*, 76
148 *"On the bench . . . we could hear the ankle pop"*: *Sporting News*, April 9, 1952.
148 *"I couldn't stand to look at it"*: *Sporting News*, September 3, 1952.
149 *"They're carrying our pennant chances off the field"*: *Sporting News*, April 9, 1952.
149 *"that it was doubtful that anyone in the park"*: *Baltimore Afro-American*, April 22, 1952.
150 *"My heart was in my mouth"*: Author interview.
150 *"Jackie was coming out here to see if I was all right?"*: Mays with Sahadi, *Say Hey*, 82.
150 *"The greatest catch I ever saw in my life"*: *Baltimore Afro-American*, April 22, 1952.
150 Praise for Mays's catch: *Sporting News*, February 24, 1954.

150 *"Because I didn't have to"*: Author interview.

151 *"This was in Brooklyn"*: Reprinted in the *Philadelphia Inquirer,* June 29, 1952.

151 *"I sure am going to miss him"*: *New York Sun,* May 29, 1952.

151 *"It's undoubtedly for the best"*: *New York Journal-American,* May 28, 1952.

152 *"Just hold 'em until I come back, fellas"*: Author interview.

152 *"He was just having fun"*: Author interview.

153 *"Those young recruits would have just mobbed him"*: Author interview.

153 *"If you didn't feel like soldiering"*: Mays with Einstein, *Willie Mays,* 148

154 *"There would be four or five thousand people"*: *Army Times,* November 14, 1973.

154 *"You gotta be crazy"*: Mays with Einstein, *Willie Mays,* 150.

155 *"That gives it a sense of risk"*: Author interview.

155 *"The pocket, where the ball hits"*: Hano, *Willie Mays,* 80.

155 Mays's trip to North Carolina: From a letter to Mays and author interviews with Akers and Mays.

157 Mays's time with Poo Johnson: Author interviews.

158 *"Hey, Willie, where you been?"*: *Sport,* June 1961.

159 *"I did it"*: Author interview.

159 *"He was aware that he was helping the cause"*: Author interview.

159 *"You'd never have thought Willie had ever been away"*: *Sporting News,* November 19, 1952.

160 *"I always have believed"*: Mays with Sahadi, *Say Hey,* 102.

160 *"He just made such a difference out there"*: *Sporting News,* January 21, 1953.

161 *"Willie catches the triples"*: Ibid.

161 *"chamber of gloom"*: *Sporting News,* November 4, 1953.

162 Congressional hearing: *Baltimore Afro-American,* May 13, 1954, and July 24, 1954.

162 *"I have no pride in my Army career"*: Mays with Einstein, *Willie Mays,* 148.

Chapter Eleven: "I'd Play for Free"

164 Mays's return to the Giants and train ride with Kahn: Kahn, *Memories of Summer,* 161–64; *Sport,* August 1969; *Sport,* October 1954; *Sporting News,* March 10, 1954.

166 *"Willie must have been born under some kind of star"*: *Newsweek,* April 5, 1954.

167 *"Well, it wasn't that good a throw"*: *Sport,* October 1954.

168 Mays at casino: Kahn, *Memories of Summer,* 258–61; author interviews with Irvin, Kahn, and Mays.

170 Mays at the Biltmore: Author interviews with Irvin and Mays.

172 *"If there was a machine"*: Rickey with Rigor, *American Diamond,* 124

172 *"that it was still soaring when it crashed into the seats"*: *Sport,* October 1954.

173 *"I told ya"*: Mays with Sahadi, *Say Hey,* 111.

174 *"Dodger fans, we thought you would want to know"*: *Sporting News,* July 7, 1954.

175 *"Even the Yankees themselves spend half their time"*: Ibid.

175 *"Of course I know"*: *Sporting News,* July 21, 1954.

176 *"That's funny stuff"*: *Sport,* June 1965.

176 *"For the first time"*: Mays with Sahadi, *Say Hey,* 112.

176 *"When reporters started asking him"*: *Sport,* June 1956.

176 *"Willie Mays is the only ballplayer"*: *Collier's,* September 3, 1954.

176 *"Look, Mays just lost his halo"*: *Sport,* June 1961.

177 *"Willie is wonderful to me"*: *Sport,* June 1956.

177 *"He was a captive of his hometown admirers"*: *Life,* September 13, 1954.

178 *"Durocher divided his energy between"*: *Saturday Evening Post,* April 13, 1957.

178 *"The inevitable conclusion"*: Hano, *Willie Mays*, 96.
179 *"TV natural. He spoke his lines"*: Art Flynn's brochure promoting Mays.
179 *"I don't know. Just turn those cameras on"*: Peters, *Tales from the San Francisco Giants Dugout*, 158.
179 *"It has gotten to the point the last couple of weeks"*: *Newsweek*, July 19, 1954.
182 *"I want my boy well protected"*: *Sporting News*, September 29, 1954.

Chapter Twelve: The Catch

185 *"Willie, I want you to do something"*: Mays with Sahadi, *Say Hey*, 113.
186 *"All my life"*: *Amsterdam News*, August 1954.
187 *"I had a big lucky year"*: *Sporting News*, September 29, 1954.
187 *"He'd be miffed whenever a ball was just"*: Mays with Sahadi, *Say Hey*, 114.
188 *"Sure, Willie was a bouncing, bubbly boy"*: *Saturday Evening Post*, April 13, 1957.
188 *"there were resentments on the club"*: *Sport*, June 1956.
188 *"Once you got to know how good he was"*: Author interview.
189 *"I told you so"*: Mays with Sahadi, *Say Hey*, 114.
189 *"the man who lost the hitting title to Willie Mays"*: Einstein, *Willie's Time*, 90.
189 *"If I hadn't won it"*: Ibid., 116.
190 *"equal to the receptions for Eisenhower"*: *Sporting News*, October 6, 1954.
190 *"Willie Mays is the greatest player"*: Mays with Sahadi, *Say Hey*, 117.
192 *"My pelvis is tilted"*: *Sports Illustrated*, September 27, 1955.
193 *"muscular men not long in grace"*: James, *Historical Baseball Abstract*, 220.
194 *Ball game:* Author interview.
194 *two runs:* Author interview.
196 *"This has to be the best throw"*: Conlan and Creamer, *Jocko*, 131.
196 *"Normally, an outfielder has to make two"*: Author interview.
197 *"That was a helluva catch, roomie"*: Author interview.
197 *"Willie came running in and grabbed it off the grass"*: *Sporting News*, October 20, 1973.
198 *"He used to raise two hundred gallons"*: Hano, *Willie Mays*, 91.
198 *"Me and Willie play left field"*: Author interview.
198 *"It was the longest out"*: *Daily News*, September 30, 1954.
199 *"greater than Al Gionfriddo's in the 1947 Series"*: *Sporting News*, October 13, 1954.
199 *"What the fuck are you talking about?"*: Kahn, *Memories of Summer*, 194.
199 *"I've been playing ball since I was a kid"*: *Daily News*, September 30, 1954.
199 *"Nobody else could've made that play"*: *San Francisco Chronicle*, September 24, 2004.
199 *"We knew Willie had it"*: Burns, *Baseball*, 1994.
199 *"and without making it look so hard"*: *Sporting News*, April 13, 1955.
199 *"I had the ball all the way"*: *Sporting News*, October 13, 1954.
199 *"This was the most perfectly sculpted"*: Author interview.
200 *"I'm playing a shallow center field"*: Kahn, *Memories of Summer*, 255–56.
201 *"It was more than just a great catch"*: Burns, *Baseball*, 1994.
202 *"When Willie would wash dishes"*: Author interview.
203 *"Losing the first game hurt us the most"*: *Sporting News*, October 13, 1954.
203 *"We finally found his weakness"*: *Sporting News*, October 13, 1954.
203 *"If Cleveland had won Game One"*: Author interview.

Chapter Thirteen: "Ole Mira!"

206 *"into the game"*: Burns, *Baseball*, 1994.
206 *"magnificent throw"*: Hano, *"A Day in the Bleachers,"* 45.
207 *"I don't know about other players"*: *Sports Illustrated*, April 13, 1959.
209 *"We didn't want the Giants to have"*: Maraniss, *Clemente*, 37.
209 *"I always said that was the greatest"*: Ibid., 57.
209 *"Instructions? What could you tell Willie?"*: *Collier's*, January 7, 1955.
210 *"Look at that boy. He just can't wait to get things started"*: Ibid.
210 *"He had a real nice apartment"*: Ibid.
210 *"Perhaps to some people it seemed I had changed"*: Mays with Sahadi, *Say Hey*, 128.
211 *"Give me the ice pick"*: Bitker, *Original San Francisco Giants*, 54.
212 *"take it easy"*: *New York Times*, January 13, 1955.
212 *"remains one of the most dramatic clouts"*: Shannon, *Willie Mays*, 29.

Chapter Fourteen: A New Archetype

215 *"The emphasis shifted from maximum* advance*"*: Koppett, *Fan's Thinking Guide to Baseball*, 80.
217 *"that the ball sounded a little different"*: ESPN documentary, 1999.
217 *"If I knew I was near a record"*: *Sporting News*, May 16, 1956.
218 *"Willie runs too much"*: Campanella, *It's Good to Be Alive*, 270.
219 *"the geometric possibilities of the play"*: Author interview.
219 *"Zimmerman exploded upon contact"*: Einstein, *Willie's Time*, 155.
220 *"I was kind of using his head as a fulcrum"*: Mays with Einstein, *Willie Mays*, 102.
220 *"I've seen him go up in the air trying for a catch"*: *Sporting News*, June 5, 1957.
220 *"the only player I ever saw"*: Conlan and Creamer, *Jocko*, 131.
220 *"Those two rabbits started running"*: *San Francisco Examiner*, September 29, 1957.
221 *"Just safe!"*: *Sport*, 1962.
221 *"A line drive"*: Bitker, *Original San Francisco Giants*, 122.
221 *"I didn't play much those first couple of years"*: Author interview.
222 *"He was the game's premier warrior"*: Stanton, *Ty and the Babe*, 27.

Chapter Fifteen: Jackie, Willie, and All Deliberate Speed

223 *"the favorite of all is Willie Mays"*: Day, *Day with the Giants*, 201.
224 *"It wasn't until the letters came in"*: Author interview.
227 *"The Negro stars have certainly done something"*: *Look*, September 21, 1954.
227 *"A major league baseball player must have something besides"*: Tygiel, *Past Time*, 84.
227 *"smaller cranium, lighter brain, [and] cowardly and"*: Hirsch, *Two Souls Indivisible*, 90.
227 *"Don, you and Jackie and Roy"*: Aaron with Wheeler, *I Had a Hammer*, 297.
228 *"was the most difficult ballplayer"*: Conlan and Creamer, *Jocko*, 151.
229 *"anger as a confederate"*: Rampersad, *Jackie Robinson*, 306.
229 *"He was the kind of man who had"*: Tygiel, *Baseball's Great Experiment*, 62.
229 *"Robinson, by virtue of seething pride, unforgiving resentments"*: Honig, *Mays, Mantle, Snider*, 98.
229 Mays at the White House: *Sporting News*, July 20, 1955; *Chicago Defender*, July 23, 1955.
230 *"out run, out throw, and out field"*: *Sporting News*, January 26, 1955.
230 *"I appreciate the nice things Leo said about me"*: *Sporting News*, February 2, 1955.

230 *"Mays stole the show"*: *Sporting News,* February 9, 1955.
230 *"I'm for playing the game"*: Author interview with Mays.
231 *"They had a black maid"*: Author interview.
231 *"His achievement beyond excellence"*: From an NPR commentary.
232 *"I saw him his rookie year"*: Author interview.
232 *"Willie was the greatest player playing"*: Author interview.
235 *"never seen a body so badly deteriorated"*: Rampersad, *Jackie Robinson,* 320.

Chapter Sixteen: "Willie Mays Doesn't Need Help from Anyone"

236 *"Where can a guy take a piss?"*: Durocher with Linn, *Nice Guys Finish Last,* 287.
237 *"What do you mean, 'boss'?"*: Mays with Sahadi, *Say Hey,* 130.
237 *"Just send it, "Care of the skipper' "*: *Our World: A Picture Magazine for the Whole Family,* June 1955.
237 *"I remember Willie was always very friendly"*: Author interview.
238 *"Monte, you're not swinging the bat"*: Author interview.
238 *"I'll miss Monte"*: *St. Louis Post-Dispatch,* June 26, 1955.
239 *"If you hit the ball to right field"*: Mays with Sahadi, *Say Hey,* 132.
239 *"In our field, if you miss it in center, it's gone"*: *Sporting News,* August 31, 1955.
241 *"I played in a small town in Milwaukee"*: Author interview.
241 *"food outfit"*: *Sporting News,* April 6, 1960.
242 *"That's another twenty down the drain"*: *American Weekly,* September 19, 1954.
243 *"Everybody seems to be after him"*: *Our World,* June 1955.
243 *"Willie volunteers about as much information"*: *Sports Illustrated,* April 13, 1959.
243 *"They ain't kidding me"*: *Our World,* June 1955.
244 *"I want to tell you something"*: Mays with Sahadi, *Say Hey,* 133; Durocher with Linn, *Nice Guys Finish Last,* 280.
246 *"probably wouldn't have made it"*: Mays with Sahadi, *Say Hey,* 145.
246 *"To the extent that Leo Ernest Durocher"*: Author interview.
246 *"His departure . . . was a source"*: Mays with Sahadi, *Say Hey,* 145.
246 *"It was a big change"*: Kiernan, *Miracle at Coogan's Bluff,* 161.

Chapter Seventeen: The End of an Era

248 *"one of the hippest women I've ever met"*: Linge, *Willie Mays,* 77.
248 *"America's leading dusky playgirl"*: *Whisper,* June 1956.
248 *"He was Mr. Baseball to me"*: *Sporting News,* October 2, 1957.
248 *"He got to the point"*: Author interview.
248 *"I don't believe in that"*: Author interview.
249 *"Marghuerite came down and went out"*: Author interview.
249 *"Sometimes a country boy needs to be with"*: Author interview.
249 *"a beautiful woman . . . who stared hard and knowing when she said hello"*: *Sport,* June 1956; *Sport,* August 1969.
250 *"there was no security in the major leagues"*: Bitker, *Original San Francisco Giants,* 150.
251 *"Mrs. Marghuerite Mays seems to be a very charming"*: *Saturday Evening Post,* April 13, 1957.
251 *"It wasn't like that"*: Author interview.
251 *"He's the most wonderful human being"*: *Sporting News,* October 2, 1957.
252 *"Aside from center field, shortstop, and right field"*: Linge, *Willie Mays,* 78.
252 *"I don't think I could have made him"*: *Sporting News,* May 2, 1956.

253 *"Rigney was out to prove that Willie was just one of twenty-five guys"*: *Saturday Evening Post*, April 13, 1957.

253 *"There is some general truth to that"*: Mays with Einstein, *Willie Mays*, 187.

253 *"The one thing you must never do is holler at Willie"*: Durocher with Linn, *Nice Guys Finish Last*, 299.

253 *"You don't lose players that are part of a winning"*: Mays with Sahadi, *Say Hey*, 140.

255 *"in some ways, it was one of my most difficult seasons"*: Ibid., 142.

255 *"until it looked like a doll house"*: *Sporting News*, January 16, 1957.

255 Description of house: Hano, *Willie Mays*, 131.

256 *"The problem wasn't bad investments"*: Mays with Einstein, *Willie Mays*, 252.

256 *"When they hit it to him"*: Einstein, *Willie's Time*, 62.

256 *"He told me to go out"*: Mays with Sahadi, *Say Hey*, 145.

257 *"All I can say is"*: *Sports Illustrated*, April 13, 1959.

257 *"He thought I didn't care about him"*: Bitker, *Original San Francisco Giants*, 54.

257 *"the ballplayers dressed in silence or sat, heads down"*: Hano, *Willie Mays*, 118.

257 *"Playing before crowds of twelve hundred"*: *Sporting News*, March 5, 1958.

258 *"We thought from the bench"*: Author interview.

258 *"that expansive green grass field"*: Mandel, *San Francisco Giants*, 248.

260 *"Getting a major league team into San Francisco"*: Tygiel, *Past Time*, 179.

260 *"Do you want to move to California?"*: Hodges and Hirschberg, *My Giants*, 137.

261 *"There is no longer any chance to survive here"*: *Sporting News*, August 14, 1957.

262 *"Horace, one of New York's own"*: *Sporting News*, October 9, 1957.

262 *"Willie's lid flew off so easily because of his receding forehead"*: *Sporting News*, August 29, 1956.

263 *"I don't like him to do it"*: *Sporting News*, October 2, 1957.

263 *"I don't envy Willie"*: Associated Press, April 18, 1955.

263 *"I never saw the stickball-in-the-street phase"*: Unnamed magazine (from San Francisco Public Library), "Trials of a Negro Idol," June 22, 1963.

264 *"The 'Say Hey Kid' helped his image"*: Author interview.

264 The final game at the Polo Grounds: Hano, *Willie Mays*, 125–28; Mays with Sahadi, *Say Hey*, 146–49; *New Yorker*, May 1958; *Sporting News*, October 9, 1957; *Washington Times*, December 15, 2008.

Chapter Eighteen: Miraloma Drive

269 *"wistfully curling tendrils"*: *Saturday Evening Post*, January 4, 1958.

271 *"Some of us drink too much"*: *Sports Illustrated*, May 5, 1958.

272 *"When I'm in a slump, anybody can get me out"*: *Sporting News*, January 15, 1958.

275 Housing controversy on Miraloma Drive: "Housing a Giant, A Memorandum on the Willie Mays Incident," by Edward Howden, San Francisco Public Library; author interviews with Howden and Mays.

Chapter Nineteen: Welcome to San Francisco

283 *"When they first start out"*: *Sports Illustrated*, March 21, 1960.

284 *"You felt that no one could ever top New York"*: Bitker, *Original San Francisco Giants*, 185.

285 *"it was like you were sitting in the same kitchen together"*: Ibid., 110.

285 *"There is nothing quite like the smell of new beer"*: Ibid., 17.

286 *"It's like a World Series"*: Peters, *Tales from the San Francisco Giants Dugout*, 2.

286 *"It was such a thrill"*: Author interview.

287 *"Willie Mays is the world's greatest athlete"*: Peters, *Tales from the San Francisco Giants Dugout,* 155.

287 Near riot in Pittsburgh: Author interviews with Cepeda, Mays, and Lon Simmons; Bitker, *Original San Francisco Giants,* 104; Peters, *Tales from the San Francisco Giants Dugout,* 102; *San Francisco Examiner,* May 26, 1958; *Sporting News,* June 4, 1958.

290 *"How do you feel?"*: *Sporting News,* July 2, 1958.

290 *"They ask me, am I physically tired or mentally tired"*: *Sport,* May 1959.

291 *"Mays always looked out for us"*: Bitker, *Original San Francisco Giants,* 126.

292 *"He was a laid-back guy"*: Peary, *We Played the Game,* 468.

292 *"He didn't get up in the clubhouse"*: Bitker, *Original San Francisco Giants,* 224.

293 *"Do they want me to talk to them like I would to old friends?"*: *Sporting News,* April 2, 1958.

293 *"That irritated the rest of us"*: Unidentified newspaper from the San Francisco History Center at the San Francisco Public Library.

294 *"I got to learn to play center field all over again"*: *Sporting News,* November 13, 1957.

295 *"the Babe Cobb of Puerto Rico"*: Cepeda with Fagan, *Baby Bull,* 2.

295 *"a bronze statue standing at dress parade"*: Bitker, *Original San Francisco Giants,* 17.

295 *"It's too bad he's a year away"*: Ibid., 53.

295 *"I was in the right place at the right time"*: Ibid., 103.

296 *"They didn't expect Willie Mays to land there"*: *Los Angeles Times,* May 23, 1962.

296 *"I didn't have the disadvantage Willie Mays had"*: Bitker, *Original San Francisco Giants,* 25.

296 *"Willie is the one guy I felt a little sorry for"*: Author interview.

296 *"This was Joe DiMaggio's town"*: *Sporting News,* July 11, 1964.

297 *"I wish I could have it, it's so beautiful"*: *Ebony,* September 1954.

297 *"absolutely no basis for Willie Mays divorce rumors"*: *San Francisco Examiner,* September 20, 1958.

297 *"He hit her like he owned her"*: Mays with Einstein, *Willie Mays,* 187.

298 *"My wife slipped and fell down the stairs"*: *Sport,* April 1959.

299 *"Willie told both of us to guard the line"*: Peters, *Tales from the San Francisco Giants Dugout,* 156.

300 *"No, I'm not disappointed"*: *San Francisco Examiner,* September 29, 1958.

Chapter Twenty: Black Barnstormers

302 *"I don't think it would have mattered who we played"*: Aaron with Wheeler, *I Had a Hammer,* 146.

303 *"Willie was playing his usual reckless game"*: *Sporting News,* May 20, 1959.

304 *"Imagine that. People getting tired of baseball"*: *Sporting News,* November 21, 1956.

304 *"I think if you play 154 games in the majors"*: *Sporting News,* January 16, 1957.

304 *"They must have declared a holiday"*: *Sporting News,* October 30, 1957.

306 *"I'll try my best on the field"*: *Sporting News,* November 2, 1960.

306 *"I've disappointed the Japanese fans"*: *Sporting News,* November 9, 1960.

306 *"The only thing impressive . . . is Willie Mays's"*: *Sporting News,* November 9, 1960.

306 *"What am I going to do?"*: *Sporting News,* November 23, 1960.

306 *"We will not barnstorm this year"*: *Sporting News,* November 8, 1961.

Chapter Twenty-one: Cheers for Khrushchev

307 *"ragged, ugly wound"*: *San Francisco Chronicle*, March 13, 1959.

308 *"It wasn't his fault"*: *Sporting News*, June 17, 1959.

310 *"There goes an $80,000 pop-up"*: *Sport, Baseball's Best*, 1960.

310 *"How can they call that a double"*: Mandel, *San Francisco Giants*, 106.

310 *"The boner of the year!"*: *San Francisco Examiner*, May 8–9, 1959.

310 *"What can I say?"*: Ibid.

311 *"[The boos] were hard to understand, but I never let on that they hurt me"*: Mays with Sahadi, *Say Hey*, 161.

311 *"This is the damnedest city I ever saw"*: Einstein, *Flag for San Francisco*, 7.

313 *"It's a business, Vin"*: Hano, *Willie Mays*, 14.

313 *"Brandt was outspoken"*: Author interview.

315 *"I didn't know any of my neighbors"*: *Confidential*, April 1960.

315 *"They ran sightseeing buses to point out"*: *Saturday Evening Post*, June 22, 1963.

316 *"I don't pursue people"*: *Sport*, June 1961.

Chapter Twenty-two: Headwinds

317 *"Taking down a mountain to fill a sea"*: *Giants Yearbook*, 1960.

318 *"as long as the Coliseum in Rome"*: Ibid.

318 *"Willie should have his greatest year"*: *San Francisco Chronicle*, April 11, 1960.

318 *"Until I played at Candlestick"*: Peters, *Tales from the San Francisco Giants Dugout*, 100.

318 *"The area stinks, literally"*: Bitker, *Original San Francisco Giants*, 18.

318 *"Does the wind always blow like this?"*: Einstein, *Flag for San Francisco*, 14.

319 *"Would you please take care of our"*: Bitker, *Original San Francisco Giants*, 94.

319 *"You'd start the game and the wind would be in your face"*: Ibid., 95.

320 *"I thought I was going to die"*: Ibid., 110.

320 *"Well, the cleanup crew is gonna go out there"*: Ibid., 149.

320 *"Who's the stenographer?"*: Ibid., 156.

320 *"The wind blew me off the mound"*: *San Francisco Examiner*, June 12, 1961.

320 *"The wind, you have to feel it to believe it"*: Peters, *Tales from the San Francisco Giants Dugout*, 94.

320 *"We're not going to put Willie in the sheriff's warehouse"*: Unidentified newspaper clipping from San Francisco History Center, San Francisco Public Library.

321 *"after all, it was his first one"*: Einstein, *Flag for San Francisco*, 13.

321 *"The Candlestick weather leaves you depressed"*: Peters, *Tales from the San Francisco Giants Dugout*, 98–101.

322 *"It's not bad"*: Rosenbaum and Stevens, *Giants of San Francisco*, 70.

322 *"the howlingest winds in Candlestick history"*: *Sporting News*, July 19, 1961.

322 *"The people who built the ballpark just didn't know"*: *Saturday Evening Post*, May 20, 1961.

323 *"Willie was always swinging to hit the long ball"*: Author interview.

324 *"baseball's second dead-ball era"*: James, *Historical Baseball Abstract*, 249.

324 *"It looks like you've got something to tell me"*: *Sporting News*, June 29, 1960.

324 *"It was Rig's job to arouse the players"*: Ibid.

324 *"Horace felt pressured into making a decision that he"*: Mays with Sahadi, *Say Hey*, 166.

325 *"I think Omar the tentmaker had to make it"*: Bitker, *Original San Francisco Giants*, 156.

325 *"an engaging old windbag"*: Sports Illustrated, July 18, 1960.

325 *"He was in uniform in body only"*: Mays with Sahadi, Say Hey, 167.

325 *"If a guy can pitch, he can pitch anywhere"*: Saturday Evening Post, May 20, 1961.

325 *"I guess the old man"*: San Francisco Examiner, September 15, 1960.

326 *"I made up my mind if the throw went to second"*: San Francisco Examiner, May 31, 1960.

327 *"General Douglas MacArthur and me have something"*: Sporting News, November 16, 1960.

328 *"When baseball people were asked what was wrong with the Giants"*: Saturday Evening Post, May 20, 1961.

328 *"so short-legged that when he sits down"*: Einstein, Flag for San Francisco, 34.

329 *"I wasn't going to squeal"*: Leavy, Sandy Koufax, 128.

Chapter Twenty-three: There's a Feel in the Air

330 *"Any time I knock in a hundred runs"*: Sporting News, February 1, 1961.

331 *"He has had substantial raises in the past"*: Ibid.

332 *"I've already counted eight insults to our city"*: Einstein, Flag for San Francisco, 25.

333 *"The only hope now is if we crash"*: Ibid., 104.

333 *"They heard"*: Ibid., 82.

333 *"The only player on the team who doubted Willie Mays's"*: Dark and Underwood, When in Doubt, Fire the Manager, 76.

333 *"Without Willie, the Giants are just an ordinary team"*: Mays with Sahadi, Say Hey, 172.

333 *"I was trying to give him the credit he deserved"*: Dark and Underwood, When in Doubt, Fire the Manager, 77.

333 *"It's hard to say"*: Einstein, Flag for San Francisco, 38.

334 *"Dark knew that Bolin was fighting"*: Mays with Sahadi, Say Hey, 171.

335 *"I had the feeling that I was on one side"*: Ibid., 167.

335 *"frictions"*: Chicago Daily Defender, January 4, 1961.

335 Willie's separation and divorce: Los Angeles Examiner, July 18, 1961; San Francisco Examiner, July 13, July 18, August 10, September 15, and November 22, 1961, January 12, 1962; Sporting News, July 26 and November 29, 1961.

339 *"incompatibility of characters"*: San Francisco Examiner, January 18, 1962.

339 *"I don't blame anybody but ourselves for what went wrong"*: Mays with Einstein, Willie Mays, 187.

339 *"When I was first divorced"*: Saturday Evening Post, June 22, 1963.

339 *"When you trust someone and all of a sudden that someone"*: Author interview.

340 *"Once I find the right kind of girl"*: Saturday Evening Post, June 22, 1963.

340 *"Lots of times"*: San Francisco Examiner, February 19, 1962.

340 *"I was really scared"*: Author interview.

340 *"You going to play today?"*: Author interviews; Mays with Sahadi, Say Hey, 173; San Francisco Examiner, May 2, 1961.

342 *"I walked to the mound"*: Sport, June 1967.

342 *"Man, after you get two in a game"*: Milwaukee Journal, May 1, 1961.

343 *"I feel terrible about that bat"*: Author interview.

344 *"We'll never play tonight"*: Einstein, Flag for San Francisco, 225.

344 *"Ladies and gentlemen"*: Ibid.

345 *"New York . . . hadn't forgotten me"*: Mays with Sahadi, Say Hey, 175.

Chapter Twenty-four: Acceptance, at Last

346 *"The man who was in the dirt more than any other"*: *Sport,* August 1963.

347 *"You have to throw at him twice"*: Author interview with Robert Creamer.

347 *"I was just wild"*: *Sporting News,* May 4, 1960.

347 *"That's a damn lie"*: Associated Press, April 25, 1957.

347 *"Use Marichal"*: Einstein, *Willie's Time,* 246.

348 *"I'll wear it until it falls off"*: *San Francisco Examiner,* February 28, 1962.

348 *"Who wouldn't approve of a deal for Mays?"*: *Sporting News,* April 25, 1962.

349 *"I don't want to manage Dark's club for him"*: *Sport,* October 1962.

349 *"If he had known how upset"*: Ibid.

349 *"I have the shakes"*: Author interview.

350 *"I thought the pressure on Mays"*: Plaut, *Chasing October,* 132.

350 *"Win"*: Ibid., 98.

351 *"lacked the guts to be a manager"*: Einstein, *Flag for San Francisco,* 41.

351 *"Let's go, bussy"*: Plaut, *Chasing October,* 108.

351 *"The driver cranked up the motor"*: Ibid.

352 *"I've seen eight hundred guys with their shirts off"*: Author interview.

352 *"I used to have to ask Durocher"*: Plaut, *Chasing October,* 140.

352 *"The Big Man just discovered who the Big Man really is"*: *San Francisco Chronicle,* June 11, 1971.

353 *"The place is full of ghosts"*: *Sport,* October 1962.

353 *"Yeah, my first fight and I hope my last one"*: *Chicago Defender,* May 29, 1962.

354 *"Willie . . . is a lucky boy"*: *San Francisco Chronicle,* May 30, 1962.

355 *"It was getting hot in the pennant race"*: Mays with Sahadi, *Say Hey,* 178.

355 *"I've never been so tired"*: *San Francisco Chronicle,* September 17, 1962.

355 *"The trip from the West Coast"*: Plaut, *Chasing October,* 156.

355 Cincinnati collapse: Einstein, *Willie's Time,* 168; Mays with Sahadi, *Say Hey,* 179; Perry, *We Played the Game,* 540; Plaut, *Chasing October,* 157; *San Francisco Chronicle,* September 9, 1963; *San Francisco Examiner,* September 14, 1962; *Saturday Evening Post,* June 22, 1963; *Sport,* August 1963.

357 *"They just mobbed him"*: Author interview.

357 *"most African American players were jealous of Willie"*: Author interview.

360 *"Then when they saw my number"*: *Sporting News,* September 29, 1962.

360 *"Willie, the Dodgers could have taken charge"*: Mays with Sahadi, *Say Hey,* 182; Plaut, *Chasing October,* 164.

361 *"Can you guys score a run?"*: Mays with Sahadi, *Say Hey,* 183;

361 *"were staying out until three or four o'clock in the morning"*: Plaut, *Chasing October,* 166.

361 *"wrathful glances over at Dark and the coaching staff"*: Ibid., 167.

361 *"I just didn't realize how many outs there were"*: *San Francisco Examiner,* September 28, 1962.

363 *"We owe the Giants something"*: *Sports Illustrated,* October 8, 1962.

364 *"Maybe the ball got away"*: *San Francisco Examiner,* October 2, 1962.

364 *"I think it was the moment where San Francisco fans"*: Plaut, *Chasing October,* 175.

364 *"I let him know it was a bad call"*: *San Francisco Examiner,* October 3, 1962.

365 *"Only Willie Mays"*: Mays with Sahadi, *Say Hey,* 189.

365 *"Durocher got up laughing"*: Plaut, *Chasing October,* 182.

366 *"Even the most famous player of his day might top that sinker"*: *Sporting News,* January 17, 1979.

366 *"To be truthful"*: Plaut, *Chasing October*, 184.
367 *"Worst inning I ever saw in my life"*: Durocher with Linn, *Nice Guys Finish Last*, 11.
367 *"You crazy?"*: Einstein, *Willie's Time*, 172.
367 *"I don't like to be around drunks"*: Plaut, *Chasing October*, 189.
368 San Francisco airport scene: Author interviews; Einstein, *Willie's Time*, 172; Mays with Sahadi, *Say Hey*, 190; Plaut, *Chasing October*, 193; Rosenbaum and Stevens, *Giants of San Francisco*, 30; *Sporting News*, October 13, 1962.
369 *"Willie, are you as tense"*: Rosenbaum and Stevens, *Giants of San Francisco*, 182.
370 *"Well, naturally—they have men"*: Hano, *Fall Classics*, 178.
370 *"Even Candlestick Park"*: Caen, *Best of Herb Caen*, 30.
370 *"If we lose now"*: Hano, *Fall Classics*, 181.
371 *"It was the one ugly moment in the Series"*: Ibid., 180.
371 *"How do you feel about the nation's economy?"*: *TV Guide*, October 5, 1963.
371 *"I didn't eat breakfast this morning"*: *Sports Illustrated*, October 15, 1962.
372 *"Once he had gone into left center"*: Hano, *Willie Mays*, 188.
372 *"After that Mazeroski home run in 1960"*: Ibid., 182.
373 *"I was going for the bomb"*: Rosenbaum and Stevens, *Giants of San Francisco*, 190.
373 *"I felt I had real good stuff on it"*: Plaut, *Chasing October*, 197.
373 *"A man . . . rarely"*: Rosenbaum and Stevens, *Giants of San Francisco*, 192.
374 *"A few inches"*: Hano, *Fall Classics*, 175.
374 *"By the time they got the ball home"*: Mays with Einstein, *Willie Mays*, 247.
374 *"A man hits the ball as hard as he can"*: Hano, *Fall Classics*, 175.
374 *"Matty would have been out by a mile"*: Plaut, *Chasing October*, 197.
374 *"Elston Howard and I"*: Bob Costas interview, 1994.
376 *"I never set goals"*: *Birmingham News*, February 9, 1968.
376 *"I committed myself to make the trip"*: *Sporting News*, October 17, 1962.

Chapter Twenty-five: Youth Is Served

378 *"Get me talking about kids"*: *Coronet*, May 1955.
379 *"Hey, Willie"*: Described by Knox, and confirmed by Mays, in unpublished article.
380 *"You and I have to work together"*: Author interview with Simmons.
380 Mays's visit to the Western Pennsylvania School for the Blind: *Pittsburgh Press*, May 3, 1963; *Sporting News*, May 18, 1963; *San Francisco Examiner*, May 3, 1963.
381 *"Are you the batboy this year?"*: Author interview with McKercher.
382 Mays with O. J. Simpson: *Sports Illustrated*, May 11, 1987; author interview with Mays.
384 *"I know Willie has helped out a lot of people financially"*: Author interview with Johnson.

Chapter Twenty-six: A Man Named Mays

386 *"Dear Willie"*: All letters from the *Sporting News*, December 15, 1962.
386 *"They didn't come to see me"*: *Sporting News*, March 2, 1963.
387 Mays's house, description and quotes: *Ebony*, August 1963.
388 *"If I had a dollar for every time someone asked"*: Author interview.
389 *"Mays set a lifestyle standard"*: Author interview.
389 *"He treated me as if I was someone in the family"*: Author interview.
390 The Mendelson documentary: Author interviews with Mendelson and Mays.
391 *"No prepared documentary in the history of television"*: *San Francisco Examiner*, October 6, 1963.

392 *"Make sure you show me doing bad too"*: *TV Guide,* October 5, 1963.
394 *"no longer commanded the conscience of America"*: Einstein, *Willie's Time,* 176.
395 *"I can't explain exactly how I feel"*: McWhorter, *Carry Me Home,* 442.
395 *"What this country needs is a few first-class funerals"*: Ibid., 503.
396 *"unless immediate federal steps are taken"*: Ibid., 530.
396 *"What could I have done at that particular time to stop all that?"*: Author interview.

Chapter Twenty-seven: Befriended by a Banker

398 *"That's just the way Willie is"*: Author interview.
398 *"I've never had an argument with him"*: *Saturday Evening Post,* May 20, 1961.
399 *"When you hit over .300"*: *Sporting News,* November 5, 1966.
399 *"trying to destroy [me] emotionally"*: Cepeda, *Baby Bull,* 85.
400 *"The only guy who was nice to me in the clubhouse was Willie"*: Author interview.
401 *"From a business standpoint"*: Mays with Einstein, *Willie Mays,* 255.
401 Mays talking to Shemano about bankruptcy and finances: Ibid., 252–56.
401 *"the quick way to find your way to the soup kitchen"*: Mays with Sahadi, *Say Hey,* 211.
403 *"If I had met Jake ten years ago"*: *San Francisco Examiner,* April 22, 1964.
403 *"Hey, Gary!"*: Author interview with Shemano.
403 *"If Willie wasn't the greatest"*: Ibid.
404 *"In the twelfth or thirteenth"*: *New York Times,* July 2, 2008.
405 *"In the dugout, every time Willie comes up"*: *San Francisco Examiner,* June 3, 1963.
405 *"You could just mention it in passing"*: Einstein, *Willie's Time,* 175.
405 *"It is the closest I've seen a man come to being killed:"* Hano, *Willie Mays,* 192.
405 *"only way to get Willie out is to hit him in the back"*: *Argosy,* September 1964.
406 *"Here we go again"*: *Sporting News,* June 15, 1963.
406 *"The 32-year-old superstar is about as washed up as General Motors"*: Ibid.
406 *"We want to know, Mr. Stoneham"*: Mays with Sahadi, *Say Hey,* 213.
407 *"Willie: Sorry I didn't make the team"*: *Sporting News,* July 20, 1963.
407 *"I just play the game"*: *Chicago Tribune,* July 10, 1963.
408 *"take the boys to supper"*: Mays with Einstein, *Willie Mays,* 258.
408 *"Alvin managed percentages, not people"*: *Sporting News,* October 2, 1965.
408 *"He didn't convert anyone to his politics"*: Mays with Sahadi, *Say Hey,* 215.
408 *"You laid down on me"*: Einstein, *Willie's Time,* 199.
409 *"Could Felipe Alou have come across"*: *San Francisco Examiner,* September 8, 1963.
409 *"Very well built"*: *New York Times,* April 11, 1964.

Chapter Twenty-eight: Captain Mays

410 *"We came to a par-3 hole"*: *San Francisco Chronicle,* December 23, 2003.
411 *"A man doesn't have to move around"*: *San Francisco Chronicle,* May 2, 1964.
413 *"I knew what Dark was saying"*: Mays with Sahadi, *Say Hey,* 218.
413 *"Willie, I'm making you captain of the Giants"*: Mays with Einstein, *Willie Mays,* 259.
414 *"laughed at our jokes even when they weren't funny"*: Author interview.
414 *"Okay, twenty-four, let's go over the ground rules"*: Mays with Sahadi, *Say Hey,* 217.
415 *"I told you something like this might happen"*: Einstein, *Willie's Time,* 205.
415 *"It's too early to think about managing"*: *New York Journal-American,* 1964.
415 *"bigot, an advocate of white supremacy"*: Rampersad, *Jackie Robinson,* 386.
415 *"the last Negro in the Deep South has it made"*: Ibid., 390.
417 *"It hurt him a lot"*: Author interview.

417 *"Breast or bottle?"*: Leavy, *Sandy Koufax*, 127.
418 *"Those of us who were accustomed to the way Dark"*: Einstein, *Willie's Time*, 207.
419 *"Shut up!"*: Ibid., 210–11.
420 *"I was definitely misquoted on some"*: Dark and Underwood, *When in Doubt, Fire the Manager*, 96.
420 *"I thought I proved my feelings"*: Mays with Einstein, *Willie Mays*, 268.
420 *"I was actively sick"*: Ibid.
421 *"is the greatest player"*: Author interview.
421 *"It is my own opinion that you cannot"*: Hano, *Willie Mays*, 198.
421 *"I have a lot of tension"*: *New York Herald Examiner*, May 5, 1964.
422 *"I've spent a lot of time with Willie"*: *Sporting News*, November 28, 1964.
422 *"I love it"*: *New York Post*, June 1, 1964.

Chapter Twenty-nine: The Peacemaker

423 *"as a very mixed up little boy"*: *New York Daily News*, September 5, 1964.
423 *"I'm always more aggressive then"*: *Saturday Evening Post*, June 22, 1963.
423 *"a stand-up comic"*: Author interview.
423 *"Have you ever suffered from fainting spells?"*: *Sporting News*, March 19, 1966.
423 *"Home run in the Polo Grounds"*: Einstein, *Willie's Time*, 107.
424 Mays's testimonial dinner: *Sporting News*, January 30, 1965.
425 *"Suppose it had been Mays and McCovey"*: *Sport*, September 1966.
426 *"could cuss, chew tobacco, spit"*: Prager, *Echoing Green*, 49.
426 *"I'm scared to death of guns"*: *Sporting News*, January 30, 1965.
427 *"I think it makes any job easier"*: *Sporting News*, October 2, 1965.
427 *"When the Giants are on the road"*: *Sporting News*, January 30, 1965.
427 *"As for periodic rests"*: Ibid.
427 *"I'm going to put more responsibility"*: Ibid.
428 *"All the players were friendly toward us, but Willie exceptionally so"*: Author interview.
428 *"I watch [Mays] in the outfield"*: *New York Post*, September 13, 1965.
428 *"He was a like a second father"*: Author interview.
428 *"Given the amount of ground that Willie covered in the outfield"*: Author interview.
429 *"a nod a hello and a throaty chuckle"*: *Sporting News*, July 30, 1966.
429 Mays and Jim Ray Hart: Mays with Sahadi, *Say Hey*, 229; author interview with Mays.
430 *"Why all the fuss?"*: *Sporting News*, June 12, 1965.
430 *"If I'm in the park, I'm playing every play even if I'm not in the game"*: *Sport*, 1965.
430 *"as if his upper torso was chasing his legs"*: E-mail from David Rapaport.
432 *"Here comes the king!"*: *Sporting News*, July 24, 1965.
432 *"He's like Mantle"*: *St. Paul Dispatch*, July 13, 1965.
435 Roseboro-Marichal fight: Cepeda, *Baby Bull*, 98; Einstein, *Willie's Time*, 242–47; Roseboro, *Glory Days with the Dodgers*, 1–13; Leavy, *Sandy Koufax*, 180; Mandel, *San Franciso Giants*, 130–35; Mays with Einstein, *Willie Mays*, 279–83; Mays with Sahadi, *Say Hey*, 231–35; Peters, *Tales from the San Francisco Giant Dugout*, 76; Vrusho, *Benchclearing*, 63–68; *NINE: A Journal of Baseball History and Culture*, "Crime and Punishment: The Marichal-Roseboro Incident," Spring 2004; *New York Times*, August 23–24, 1965; *Sports Illustrated*, August 30, 1965; *Sporting News*, September 4, September 11, and November 27, 1965; author interviews.
442 *"I will always treasure"*: Mays with Einstein, *Willie Mays*, 287.
442 *"Are you sore?"*: *Sporting News*, September 11, 1965.

443 *"I threw you the first one":* Mays with Sahadi, *Say Hey,* 236.
443 *"She can have it":* Sporting News, October 2, 1965.
443 Home run off Claude Raymond: Angell, *Game Time,* 82–84; Einstein, *Willie's Time,* 226–28; Hano, *Willie Mays,* 206; Mays with Sahadi, *Say Hey,* 236; *Sporting News,* January 1, 1966.
446 *"Don't forget":* Sport, May 1968.

Chapter Thirty: A Piece of Willie's Heart

447 *"Willie, the kids will listen to you":* Mays with Sahadi, *Say Hey,* 239.
447 *"Cool it, baby":* Hearst Headline Service, November 24, 1965.
448 *"I know, but I've been going":* Sporting News, January 1966.
449 *"I don't think Shemano's doing a damn thing for you":* Author interview with Franks.
449 *"Sometimes when you have a friend":* Author interview.
450 *"I constantly told Willie":* Author interview.
450 *"My father ended up losing everything":* Author interview.
450 *"My dad's got a couple of days left":* Author interview.
450 *"I was a guy who couldn't handle that":* Author interview.
451 Mae Louise Allen: *San Francisco Chronicle,* December 15, 1971; *San Francisco Examiner,* February 1, 1976; *San Jose Mercury News,* February 17, 1995; author interviews.

Chapter Thirty-one: Milestones and Miseries

456 *"Willie surrounded that base":* Argosy, September 1964.
456 *"He would swing them from behind his right":* E-mail from Rapaport.
456 *"I know what you're doing":* Interview for HBO special, *Costas Now,* July 2008.
457 *"a mounting roar from the stands":* Sports Illustrated, April 10, 1961.
458 *"I know the way he runs":* Einstein, *Willie's Time,* 63.
458 *"Do you know you're only eleven behind":* Sporting News, September 25, 1965.
458 Breaking Mel Ott's record: Einstein, *Willie's Time,* 248; Mays with Sahadi, *Say Hey,* 243; *New York Sunday News,* June 26, 1966; *Saturday Evening Post,* July 30, 1966; *San Francisco Examiner,* May 5, 1966; *Sporting News,* May 21, 1966, and January 7, 1967; author interviews.
462 *"That one":* San Francisco Examiner, August 18, 1966.
462 *"We're supposed to be impartial":* Hano, *Willie Mays,* 216.
463 *"No, goddamn safe!":* Einstein, *Willie's Time,* 250–51.
465 *"I think that record is here to stay":* Sporting News, August 13, 1966.
466 *"Look, time marches on":* Sporting News, July 8, 1967.
466 *"He looked tired and weak and sick":* Sports Illustrated, August 7, 1967.
466 *"Some guys can go 0-for-4 the way I have and lose":* Ibid.
467 *"I can't think just of myself":* Ibid.
467 *"I could have got you, kid:":* ESPN documentary, 1999.
467 *"Willie Mays . . . is not Willie Mays":* Sports Illustrated, August 7, 1967.
467 *"I was furious and embarrassed":* Mays with Sahadi, *Say Hey,* 247.

Chapter Thirty-two: A Doctrine of Brotherhood

469 Robinson's comments on Mays, and Mays's response: *Chicago Daily Defender,* February 20, March 18, and April 6, 1968, August 20, 1966; *Pittsburgh Press,* April 15, 1968; *Sporting News,* March 30, 1968.

473 *"If any part of me was not satisfied with Willie"*: Author interview.
474 *"Sometimes people misunderstand the civil rights era"*: E-mail to author.
475 *"Willie, it wasn't me"*: Author interview.
475 *"What Willie appears to have forgotten . . . is that there have been MANY times"*: Baltimore Afro-American, April 2, 1968.
475 *"This award means a great deal to me"*: Einstein, *Willie's Time*, 73.
476 *"more time with hospital inmates than any other six athletes"*: Baltimore Afro-American, February 9, 1965.

Chapter Thirty-three: The Wisdom of the Years

477 *"No, that wasn't it"*: San Francisco Examiner, January 24, 1979.
477 *"next Willie Mays"*: Mandel, *San Francisco Giants*, 153.
478 *"He had to find ways to entertain himself"*: Author interview.
478 *"You had the greatest baserunner against the greatest fielder"*: Author interview.
478 Bobby Bonds: *Chicago Defender*, August 7, 1973; *Cleveland Plain Dealer*, September 20, 1979; *Sporting News*, July 3, 1965; *Sporting News*, March 19, 1966, October 19, 1968, June 26, 1971; author interviews with Mays, Barry Bonds, and Pat Bonds.
480 *"I was trying to be nice and warn Mays"*: Sporting News, June 29, 1968.
480 *"He didn't want to go to a team unless"*: Author interview.
481 *"Willie was always challenging me,"*: Linge, *Willie Mays*, 152; author interview.
484 *"Why do you want me to bat leadoff?"*: Mays with Sahadi, *Say Hey*, 251.
484 *"Look at him"*: Einstein, *Willie's Time*, 63.
484 *"Ordinarily, you don't mind needling from the fans"*: Sporting News, September 28, 1968.
485 Dugout incident with King: *San Francisco Examiner*, June 25, 26, 29, 1969; Einstein, *Willie's Time*, 315; Mays with Sahadi, *Say Hey*, 252.
485 *"People cringed in sympathy"*: Pro Sports Weekly, October 9, 1969.
486 Home run number 600: Associated Press, September 23, 1969; *Atlanta Journal*, September 16, 1969; *New York Times*, October 1, 1969; *Pro Sports Weekly*, October 9, 1969; *San Francisco Chronicle*, September 23, 1969; Mays with Sahadi, *Say Hey*, 253.

Chapter Thirty-four: Baseball Royalty

488 *"It's been written, Curt"*: Snyder, *Well-Paid Slave*, 104.
491 *"I believe I was crying"*: Author interview.
491 *"Friends came out to see how I was doing"*: Interview with Bob Costas, *Costas Coast to Coast*, 1994.
492 *"Is that Gibson?"*: Gibson on HBO special, *Costas Now*, July 2008.
493 *"I don't feel excitement about this now"*: Sporting News, August 1, 1970.
493 *"In twenty-two years . . . Willie has gained a pound and a half"*: Sporting News, August 28, 1971.
493 *"The pitcher, Don Sutton, looked"*: Sporting News, August 22, 1970.
496 *"I remember that very distinctly"*: Author interview.
496 Mays's birthday party: *San Francisco Chronicle*, May 7, 1971; *San Francisco Examiner*, April 20, 1971; *Sporting News*, May 7, May 22, July 17, 1971; author interviews.
496 *"Some people look at their fortieth"*: San Francisco Examiner, January 12, 1971.
499 *"He couldn't get out of the way"*: Author interview.
499 *"They kept saying we were a dead horse"*: Sporting News, October 16, 1971.
500 *"Let them celebrate"*: New York Post, October 1, 1971.

501 *"I felt one of them could get Tito home"*: *Chicago Daily Defender,* October 9, 1971.
502 *"I believe he was hurt and embarrassed"*: Author interview.

Chapter Thirty-five: New York, New York

503 *"I want to marry you"*: *Ebony,* February 1972.
503 *"Hi, little boy, you need anything?"*: Author interview.
504 Wedding and married life: Associated Press, February 26, 1974; *Ebony,* February 1972; *San Francisco Chronicle,* December 15, 1971; *San Francisco Examiner,* November 29, 1971; *San Jose Mercury News,* February 17, 1995; author interviews with Willie Mays, Jessie and Bud Goins, and Judi Phillips.
507 Mays's trade: Associated Press, May 6, 1972; *New York Daily News,* May 14, 1971, May 12, 1972; *New York Times,* May 10, May 12, 1972; *San Francisco Examiner,* May 12, 1971; *Sporting News,* May 20, 1972, September 8, 1973; author interviews; audio tape provided by Lon Simmons.
511 *"Willie gave me his glove right there:"* Author interview.
511 *"It's kinda hard to consider Buck the enemy"*: *Chicago Daily Defender,* May 16, 1972.
511 *"I felt something in my leg"*: *Born to Play Ball,* 2000.
511 *"Willie Mays ran the bases"*: *Sport,* October 1972.
512 *"When I went out in the outfield"*: *New York Times,* May 12, 1972.
512 *"Willie Mays had always been my hero"*: Golenbock, *Amazin',* 290
512 *"I looked at him and the top button of his uniform"*: Author interview.
514 *"I wanted to come and talk to you fellas"*: August 18, 1972, unidentified newspaper clip in Mays file in the San Francisco History Center of the San Francisco Public Library.
515 *"Mays knows that we New York fans"*: *Sport,* October 1972.

Chapter Thirty-six: The End of a Love Affair

516 *"I can't live on that"*: Author interview with Alden.
516 *"Christian, Jewish, Muslim"*: *Black Sports,* June 1973.
516 *"It's simple"*: Ibid.
517 *"I think I sacrificed only ten times in my career"*: Rosengren, *Hammerin' Hank, George Almighty & the Say Hey Kid,* 99.
517 *"It was not just one guy like Willie Mays"*: Barra, *Yogi Berra,* 357.
518 *"His failings are now so cruel"*: Einstein, *Willie's Time,* 334.
518 *"When he was batting, I felt I was up there"*: Associated Press, February 27, 1974.
519 *"unless public opinion demands it"*: Rosengren, *Hammerin' Hank, George Almighty & the Say Hey Kid,* 218.
519 *"I don't know what I'm going to do next"*: *San Francisco Examiner,* May 11, 1973; *New York Daily News,* May 16, 1973.
520 *"Willie was forty-two and he was hurt a lot"*: Golenbock, *Amazin',* 293.
520 *"There are individuals you know"*: Author interview.
520 *"Grant was derogatory against Willie"*: Author interview.
520 *"The Mets didn't want him"*: Author interview.
520 *"This is my personal gift to you"*: Author interview with Sirkis.
521 *"black power"*: Ibid.
521 Final press conference: *Long Island News,* September 21, 1973; *New York Daily News,* September 21, 1973; *New York Times,* September 21, 1973; *Sporting News,* October 6, 1973.
522 Farewell night: *Chicago Daily Defender,* September 29, 1973; *Long Island News,* Sep-

tember 26, 1973; *New York Daily News,* September 27, 1973; *New York Post,* September 26, 1973; *New York Times,* September 26, 1973; *San Francisco Chronicle,* September 26, 1973; Mays with Sahadi, *Say Hey,* 269; author interviews.

524 *"We began pouring it on":* Rosengren, *Hammerin' Hank, George Almighty & the Say Hey Kid,* 237.

525 *"Look at the scoreboard!":* Ibid., 247.

526 *"If those are Met fans":* Sporting News, October 1973.

526 *"I came in a winner, and I'm going to leave a winner":* Vintage World Series Films, DVD, Oakland Athletics.

527 *"The Mets . . . have no name players":* Rosengren, *Hammerin' Hank, George Almighty & the Say Hey Kid,* 313.

527 *"It's got so you pray they won't":* Einstein, *Willie's Time,* 338.

528 *"Here's the unusual thing":* Rosengren, *Hammerin' Hank, George Almighty & the Say Hey Kid,* 275.

529 *"No way! He didn't touch him!":* Vintage World Series Films, DVD, Oakland Athletics.

529 *"I can't see, man":* Born to Play Ball, 2000.

529 *"He had to get a hit":* Fall Classics, 202.

530 *"I think he had a good shot at it":* Born to Play Ball, 2000.

531 *"I don't care if he was in a body cast":* Rosengren, *Hammerin' Hank, George Almighty & the Say Hey Kid,* 296.

532 *"I don't feel nothin' yet, man":* Ibid, 297.

532 *"Mae could tell you":* Bob Costas interview, 1994.

Epilogue

533 *"For two years after I retired":* New York Times, July 14, 1979.

534 *"unanimity is a word some baseball writers can't spell":* New York Times, September 18, 1978.

534 *"It wouldn't be normal":* Associated Press, January 25, 1979.

535 Hall of Fame Speech: Associated Press; *Daily Press* (Utica), August 6, 1979; *Hershey Telegraph,* August 10, 1979; *Morning Union,* August 6, 1979; *New York Daily News,* August 6, 1979; *New York Post,* August 6, 1979; *New York Times,* August 6, 1979; *St. Louis Post-Dispatch,* August 6, 1979; *Sporting News,* August 18, 1979; United Press International.

537 Banned from baseball: *Akron Beacon Journal,* February 25, 1981; *New York Post,* October 27, October 30, 1979; *New York Times,* October 30, 1979; Snyder, *Well-Paid Slave,* 100; author interviews.

538 *"When you're the star of a ball club":* Mays with Sahadi, *Say Hey,* 276.

538 *"Jackie! There's twenty-two thousand people":* Author interview with Brandt.

539 *"When they didn't put him in the starting lineup":* New York Post, July 20, 1983.

539 Amphetamines controversy: *Times Union* (Albany), September 13, 1985; *Boston Globe,* April 19, 2002; *Kansas City Times,* September 11, 1985; *New York Daily News,* September 14, 1985; *New York Times,* March 3, 1986; *Pittsburgh Press,* March 31, 1986; *Costas Now,* on HBO, July 17, 2008; author interview with Mays.

541 *"I didn't like it when I started":* West, March 24, 1991.

541 *"It's killing me":* Author interview with Baer.

541 *"we are going to look for stronger, more clarified":* New York Times, March 19, 1985.

541 *"This is a happy occasion":* Ibid.

542 *"My wife knew that every day when I got up":* San Francisco Chronicle, February 13, 1986.

543 *"He's constantly on the road"*: Unidentified newspaper clip in the Mays file in the San Francisco History Center of the San Francisco Public Library.

543 *"It would be real hard to write a job description"*: West, March 24, 1991.

543 *"Who's going to tell this nigger"*: Author interview with Zeller.

544 *"He started out with pretty normal skin"*: Author interview.

544 *"You have to assume that everyone wants something"*: Interview with Judy Kaufman.

544 *"Well, it's good and bad"*: West, March 24, 1991.

545 *"This is the greatest moment of my entire life"*: Pearlman, Love Me, Hate Me, 142.

545 *"Willie said, 'I got the answer'"*: Author interview.

545 *"Can he hit?"*: Author interview.

546 *"He would always give me his blessing"*: Author interview.

546 *"I want him back on the field"*: San Francisco Chronicle, August 24, 2003.

546 *"Barry came in"*: Author interview.

546 *"I think it's appropriate"*: MLB.com, April 12, 2004.

547 *"Be nice to those guys"*: Author interview with Miller.

547 *"I've always told Barry"*: USA Today, April 14, 2004.

547 *"If not for my father or for Willie"*: Author interview.

547 *"If I get robbed"*: Author interview.

548 *"When Willie would come to visit"*: Author interview.

550 *"What's in here?"*: Author interview.

551 *"I think in these kids"*: Author interview.

552 *"This is Giant's house"*: Author interview.

552 *"always symbolized perfection"*: Einstein, Willie's Time, 35.

553 *"I did things that no one else did"*: Author interview.

555 *"It came from the heart of each and every one"*: E-mail to author.

556 *"It's important that the people of Fairfield"*: Author interview.

BIBLIOGRAPHY

Aaron, Henry, with Lonnie Wheeler. *I Had a Hammer: The Hank Aaron Story*. New York: Harper Perennial, 2007.

Allen, Lee. *The Giants and the Dodgers: The Fabulous Story of Baseball's Fiercest Feud*. New York: Putnam's, 1964.

Alou, Felipe, with Herm Weiskopf. *Felipe Alou . . . My Life and Baseball*. Waco, Tex.: Word Books, 1967.

Angell, Roger. *Five Seasons: A Baseball Companion*. Lincoln: University of Nebraska Press, 2004.

———. *Game Time: A Baseball Companion*. Orlando, Fla.: Harcourt, 2003.

Bak, Richard. *Joe Louis: The Great Black Hope*. Dallas: Da Capo Press, 1998.

Baldassaro, Lawrence, and Richard A. Johnson, eds. *The American Game: Baseball and Ethnicity*. Carbondale: Southern Illinois University Press, 2002.

Barra, Allen. *Clearing the Bases*. Lincoln: University of Nebraska Press, 2002.

———. *Yogi Berra: Eternal Yankee*. New York: Norton, 2009.

Barthel, Thomas. *Baseball Burnstorming and Exhibition Games, 1901–1962: A History of Off-season Major League Play*. Jefferson, N.C.: McFarland, 2007.

Biography of a Business: Tennessee Coal & Iron Division, United States Steel Corporation, Birmingham Public Library.

Bitker, Steve. *The Original San Francisco Giants: The Giants of '58*. Champaign, Ill.: Sports Publishing LLC, 2001.

Blackmon, Douglas A. *Slavery by Another Name: The Re-enslavement of Black Americans from the Civil War to World War II*. New York: Doubleday, 2008.

Bouton, Jim. *Ball Four*, Twentieth Edition. New York: Wiley, 1990.

Bowden, Mark. *The Best Game Ever: Giants vs. Colts, 1958, and the Birth of the Modern NFL*. New York: Atlantic Monthly Press, 2008.

Bunning, Jim, Whitey Ford, Mickey Mantle, and Willie Mays. *Grand Slam: The Secrets of Power Baseball*. New York: Viking Press, 1965.

Caen, Herb. *The Best of Herb Caen, 1960–1975*. San Francisco: Chronicle Books, 1991.

———. *One Man's San Francisco*. Sausalito, Calif.: Comstack Editions, 1976.

Campanella, Roy. *It's Good to Be Alive*. New York: Signet, 1974.

Castro, Tony. *Mickey Mantle: America's Prodigal Son*. Washington, D.C.: Potomac Books, 2002.

Cepeda, Orlando, with Herb Fagen. *Baby Bull: From Hardball to Hard Time and Back*. Dallas: Taylor, 1998.

Conlan, Jocko, and Robert W. Creamer. *Jocko*. Lincoln: University of Nebraska Press, 1997.

Conrad, Barnaby, ed. *The World of Herb Caen: San Francisco, 1938–1997*. San Francisco: Chronicle Books, 1997.

Cook, Ben. *Good Wood: A Fan's History of Rickwood Field.* Self-published, 2005.

Cramer, Richard Ben. *Joe DiMaggio: The Hero's Life.* New York: Touchstone, 2001.

Creamer, Robert W. *Babe: The Legend Comes to Life.* New York: Simon & Schuster Paper-backs, 1974.

D'Antonio, Michael. *Forever Blue: The True Story of Walter O'Malley, Baseball's Most Controversial Owner, and the Dodgers of Brooklyn and Los Angeles.* New York: Riverhead, 2009.

Dark, Alvin, and John Underwood. *When in Doubt, Fire the Manager: My Life and Times in Baseball.* New York: E. P. Dutton, 1980.

Day, Laraine. *Day with the Giants.* Garden City, N.Y.: Doubleday, 1952.

Decaneas, Anthony, ed., with photographs by Ernest C. Withers. *Negro League Baseball.* New York: Harry N. Abrams, 2004.

DeLillo, Don. *Underworld.* New York: Scribner's, 1997.

DeVito, Carlo. *Yogi: The Life and Times of an American Original.* Chicago: Triumph Books, 2008.

Dobbins, Dick, and Jon Twichell. *Nuggets on the Diamond: Professional Baseball in the Bay Area from the Gold Rush to the Present.* San Francisco: Woodford Press, 1994.

Durocher, Leo, with Ed Linn. *Nice Guys Finish Last.* Richmond Hill, Ont.: Pocket Books, 1976.

Early, Gerald. *Tuxedo Junction: Essays on American Culture.* Hopewell, N.J.: Ecco Press, 1989.

Edwards, Harry. *The Revolt of the Black Athlete.* New York: Free Press, 1969.

Eig, Jonathan. *Opening Day: The Story of Jackie Robinson's First Season.* New York: Simon & Schuster, 2007.

Einstein, Charles. *A Flag for San Francisco: The Stormy Honeymoon of a Proud City and Divorced Baseball Team.* New York: Simon & Schuster, 1962.

———. *Willie's Time: Baseball's Golden Age.* Carbondale: Southern Illinois University Press, 2004.

Fainaru-Wada, Mark, and Lance Williams. *Game of Shadows: Barry Bonds, BALCO, and the Steroids Scandal That Rocked Professional Sports.* New York: Gotham, 2006.

Fleder, Rob, ed. *Great Baseball Writing: Sports Illustrated, 1954–2004.* New York: Sports Illustrated Books, 2007.

Flood, Curt, with Richard Carter. *The Way It Is.* New York: Trident Press, 1970.

Franklin, Jimmie Lewis. *Back to Birmingham: Richard Arrington, Jr., and His Times.* Tuscaloosa: University of Alabama Press, 1989.

Fullerton, Christopher Dean. "Striking Out Jim Crow: The Birmingham Black Barons." A thesis. Birmingham Public Library, 1994.

Gilbert, Bill. *The Seasons: Ten Memorable Years in Baseball, and in America.* New York: Citadel Press, 2003.

Gittleman, Sol. *Reynolds, Raschi and Lopat: New York's Big Three and the Great Yankee Dynasty of 1949–1953.* Jefferson, N.C.: McFarland, 2007.

Golenbock, Peter. *Amazin': The Miraculous History of New York's Most Beloved Baseball Team.* New York: St. Martin's Griffin, 2002.

Greene, Lee. *The Baseball Life of Willie Mays.* New York: Scholastic Book Services, 1970.

Halberstam, David. *October 1964.* New York: Fawcett Books, 1994.

Hano, Arnold. *A Day in the Bleachers (The 50th Anniversary of "The Catch").* Cambridge, Mass.: Da Capo Press, 1995.

———. *Willie Mays.* New York: Grosset & Dunlap, 1966.

———. *Willie Mays: The Say Hey Kid.* New York: Bartholomew House, 1961.

Harris, Mark. *Pictures at a Revolution.* New York: Penguin Press, 2008.

Heidenry, John. *The Gashouse Gang: How Dizzy Dean, Leo Durocher, Branch Rickey, Pepper Martin, and Their Colorful, Come-from-Behind Ball Club Won the World Series—and America's Heart—During the Great Depression.* New York: Public Affairs, 2007.

Herskowitz, Mickey, with Danny and David Mantle. *Mickey Mantle: Stories & Memorabilia from a Lifetime with the Mick.* New York: Stewart, Tabori & Chang, 2006.

Hirsch, James S. *Riot and Remembrance: The Tulsa Race War and Its Legacy.* Boston: Houghton Mifflin, 2002.

Hodges, Russ, and Al Hirschberg. *My Giants.* Garden City, N.Y.: Doubleday, 1963.

Hogan, Lawrence. *Shades of Glory: The Negro League and the Story of African-American Baseball.* Washington, D.C.: National Geographic, 2006.

Honig, Donald. *Mays, Mantle, Snider: A Celebration.* New York: Macmillan, 1987.

Hynd, Noel. *The Giants of the Polo Grounds: The Glorious Times of Baseball's New York Giants.* Garden City, N.Y.: Doubleday, 1988.

Irvin, Monte, with James A. Riley. *Nice Guys Finish First: The Autobiography of Monte Irvin.* New York: Carroll & Graf, 1996.

James, Bill. *The New Bill James Historical Baseball Abstract.* New York: Free Press, 2001.

Jenkins, Mollie Beck. "The Social Work of the Tennessee Coal Iron and Railroad Company." A thesis. Birmingham Public Library, 1929.

Jennison, Christopher. *Wait 'Til Next Year: The Yankees, Dodgers, and Giants, 1947–1957.* New York: W. W. Norton, 1974.

Johanson, Matt, and Wylie Wong. *San Francisco Giants: Where Have You Gone?* Champaign, Ill.: Sports Publishing, 2005.

Kahn, Roger. *The Era: 1947–1957, When the Yankees, the Giants, and the Dodgers Ruled the World.* Lincoln: University of Nebraska Press, 1993.

———. *Into My Own: The Remarkable People and Events That Shape a Life.* New York: St. Martin's Griffin, 2007.

———. *Memories of Summer: When Baseball Was an Art, and Writing about It a Game.* Lincoln: University of Nebraska Press, 1997.

Keiter, Les, with Dennis Christianson. *Fifty Years Behind the Microphone: The Les Keiter Story.* Honolulu: University of Hawaii Press, 1991.

Kiernan, Thomas. *The Miracle at Coogan's Bluff.* New York: Thomas Y. Crowell, 1975.

King, Joe. *The San Francisco Giants.* Englewood Cliffs, N.J.: Prentice-Hall, 1958.

Koppett, Leonard. *The Thinking Fan's Guide to Baseball.* Wilmington, Del.: SPORTClassic Books, 2004.

Lacy, Sam, with Moses J. Newson. *Fighting for Fairness: The Story of Hall of Fame Sportswriter Sam Lacy.* Centreville, Md.: Tidewater, 1998.

Lamb, Chris. *Blackout: The Untold Story of Jackie Robinson's First Spring Training.* Lincoln: University of Nebraska Press, 2004.

Leavy, Jane. *Sandy Koufax: A Lefty's Legacy.* New York: HarperCollins, 2002.

Linge, Mary Kay. *Willie Mays: A Biography.* Westport, Conn.: Greenwood Press, 2005.

Liss, Howard. *The Willie Mays Album.* New York: Hawthorn, 1966.

Littlefield, Bill, and Richard A. Johnson, eds. *Fall Classics: The Best Writing About the World Series' First 100 Years.* New York: Crown, 2003.

Mandel, Mike. *San Francisco Giants: An Oral History.* Self-published, 1979.

Maraniss, David. *Clemente: The Passion and Grace of Baseball's Last Hero.* New York: Simon & Schuster Paperbacks, 2006.

Mays, Willie, with Charles Einstein. *Willie Mays: My Life In and Out of Baseball.* New York: Dutton, 1966.

———, with Lou Sahadi. *Say Hey: The Autobiography of Willie Mays.* New York: Pocket Books, 1988.

McLain, Denny, with Eli Zaret. *I Told You I Wasn't Perfect*. Chicago: Triumph Books, 2007.

McWhorter, Diane. *Carry Me Home: Birmingham, Alabama: The Climactic Battle of the Civil Rights Revolution*. New York: Touchstone, 2002.

Mead, William B. *The Explosive Sixties*. Alexandria, Va.: Redefinition, 1989.

Meany, Tom. *The Incredible Giants*. New York: Barnes, 1955.

Miller, Marvin. *A Whole Different Ball Game: The Inside Story of the Baseball Revolution*. Chicago: Ivan R. Dee, 2004.

Montville, Leigh. *The Big Bam: The Life and Times of Babe Ruth*. New York: Broadway, 2006.

———. *Ted Williams: The Biography of an American Hero*. New York: Broadway, 2004.

Moore, Joseph Thomas. *Pride Against Prejudice: The Biography of Larry Doby*. New York: Praeger, 1988.

Nan, Chuck. *Fifty Years by the Bay: The San Francisco Giants, 1958–2007*. Bloomington, Ind.: AuthorHouse, 2006.

Nunnelley, William A. *Bull Connor*. Tuscaloosa: University of Alabama Press, 1991.

Ogletree, Charles J. *All Deliberate Speed: Reflections on the First Half-Century of Brown v. Board of Education*. New York: Norton, 2005.

Oliver, Edmond Jefferson. *The End of an Era: 1924–1968, Fairfield Industrial High School*. Birmingham Public Library, 1975.

Osofsky, Gilbert. *Harlem: The Making of a Ghetto: Negro New York, 1890–1930*. Chicago: Elephant Paperbacks, 1996.

Pearlman, Jeff. *Love Me, Hate Me: Barry Bonds and the Making of an Antihero*. New York: HarperCollins, 2006.

Peary, Danny, ed. *We Played the Game: Memories of Baseball's Greatest Era*. New York: Black Dog & Leventhal, 1994.

Perlstein, Rick. *Nixonland: The Rise of a President and the Fracturing of America*. New York: Scribner, 2008.

Peters, Nick. *Tales from the San Francisco Giants Dugout*. Champaign, Ill.: Sports Publishing LLC, 2003.

Plaut, David. *Chasing October: The Dodgers-Giants Pennant Race of 1962*. South Bend, Ind.: Diamond Communications, 1994.

Pomerantz, Gary M. *Wilt, 1962: The Night of 100 Points and the Dawn of a New Era*. New York: Three Rivers Press, 2005.

Posnanski, Joe. *The Soul of Baseball: A Road Trip Through Buck O'Neil's America*. New York: Morrow, 2007.

Prager, Joshua. *The Echoing Green: The Untold Story of Bobby Thomson, Ralph Branca and the Shot Heard Round the World*. New York: Pantheon, 2006.

Rampersad, Arnold. *Jackie Robinson: A Biography*. New York: Ballantine, 1998.

Rhoden, William C. *Forty Million Dollar Slaves: The Rise, Fall, and Redemption of the Black Athlete*. New York: Crown, 2006.

Rickey, Branch, with Robert Riger. *The American Diamond: A Documentary of the Game of Baseball*. New York: Simon & Schuster, 1965.

Robinson, Jackie. *I Never Had It Made: An Autobiography*. New York: Ecco, 1995.

Robinson, Ray. *Iron Horse: Lou Gehrig in His Time*. New York: Norton, 1990.

Roseboro, John, with Bill Lilly. *Glory Days with the Dodgers and Other Days with Others*. New York: Atheneum, 1978.

Rosenbaum, Art, and Bob Stevens. *The Giants of San Francisco*. New York: Coward-McCann, 1963.

Rosenfeld, Harvey. *The Great Chase: The Dodgers-Giants Pennant Race of 1951*. Jefferson, N.C.: McFarland, 1992.

Rosengren, John. *Hammerin' Hank, George Almighty & the Say Hey Kid.* Naperville, Ill.: Sourcebooks, 2008.

Rowan, Carl T. *South of Freedom.* New York: Knopf, 1952.

Schott, Tom, and Nick Peters. *The Giants Encyclopedia.* Champaign, Ill.: Sports Publishing, 1999.

Shannon, Mike. *Willie Mays: Art in the Outfield.* Tuscaloosa: University of Alabama Press, 2007.

Smith, Curt. *Pull Up a Chair: The Vin Scully Story.* Washington, D.C.: Potomac Books, 2009.

Snyder, Brad. *A Well-Paid Slave: Curt Flood's Fight for Free Agency in Professional Sports.* New York: Plume, 2007.

Stanton, Tom. *Ty and the Babe: Baseball's Fiercest Rivals—A Surprising Friendship and the 1941 Has-Beens Golf Championship.* New York: St. Martin's Press, 2007.

Stein, Fred, and Nick Peters. *Giants Diary: A Century of Giants Baseball in New York and San Francisco.* Berkeley, Calif.: North Atlantic Books, 1987.

Stump, Al. *Cobb: A Biography.* Chapel Hill, N.C.: Algonquin Books, 1996.

Sweet, Ozzie. *Legends of the Field: The Classic Sports Photography of Ozzie Sweet.* New York: Viking Studio Books, 1993.

Thomson, Bobby, with Lee Heiman and Bill Gutman. *"The Giants Win the Pennant! The Giants Win the Pennant!": The Amazing 1951 National League Season and the Home Run That Won It All.* New York: Zebra Books, 1991.

Thorn, John, ed. *The Glory Days: New York Baseball, 1947–1957.* New York: Collins, 2007.

Thornley, Stew. *Land of the Giants: New York's Polo Grounds.* Philadelphia: Temple University Press, 2000.

Tye, Larry. *Rising from the Rails: Pullman Porters and the Making of the Black Middle Class.* New York: Owl Books, 2004.

Tygiel, Jules. *Baseball's Great Experiment: Jackie Robinson and His Legacy.* New York: Oxford University Press, 1997.

———. *Past Time: Baseball as History.* New York: Oxford University Press, 2000.

Vincent, Fay, ed. *We Would Have Played for Nothing: Baseball Stars of the 1950s and 1960s Talk About the Game They Loved.* New York: Simon & Schuster, 2008.

Vrusho, Spike. *Benchclearing: Baseball's Greatest Fights and Riots.* Guilford, Conn.: Lyons Press, 2008.

Welcome to TC: Fairfield Steel Works, Fairfield Tin Mill, Birmingham Public Library, 1939.

Whiting, Marvin Y. *Fairfield: Past, Present, Future, 1910–1985, In Celebration of the Seventy-fifth Anniversary of Fairfield, Alabama.* Birmingham Public Library.

Zimmermann, Karl R. *20th Century Limited.* St. Paul, Minn.: MBI, 2002.

INDEX

Bannister, Roger, 205
Barber, Red, 85
Barnhill, David, 71, 73, 283
barnstorming tours, 11–12, 42, 52, 62, 70,
   72, 93, 142, 143, 159, 242, 244, 274,
   282, 301–6, 376, 377, 522
   fan attendance in, 303, 304, 305, 306,
      377
   income earned in, 302, 303, 304, 377
Barthel, Thomas, 377
baseball:
   African Americans in, see African
      American ballplayers; Negro
      Leagues
   barnstorming and exhibition games in,
      5, 11–12, 42, 48, 70, 72–73, 77, 87,
      91, 93, 137, 142, 143, 146–47, 148,
      159, 166, 167, 191, 206, 207, 226,
      233, 238, 242, 244, 271, 273, 274,
      282, 301–6, 307, 310, 343–45, 352,
      405, 411, 423–24, 456–57, 479, 512
   beanballs in, 86, 113, 206, 211, 215,
      253, 287, 346, 347, 348, 428–29,
      433, 435–36
   bench-clearing brawls in, 287–89, 308,
      353–54, 436–42, 445, 525
   broadcasting innovations in, 99–100
   contract and labor disputes in, 250,
      291, 330, 351, 399, 425, 448,
      488–89, 506, 510
   "dead-ball" eras in, 108, 214–16,
      323–24, 411, 479, 482, 553
   integration of, see integration of
      baseball
   "live-ball" era in, 100, 214–16, 553
   Mays's great love for, 5, 6, 152, 167, 183,
      210, 229, 231, 378, 422, 441, 467,
      505, 519–20, 521, 533, 535–36, 537,
      544, 550–51
   New York's "golden age" in, 4, 97–98,
      100, 203, 377, 510
   night games in, 41, 90, 323, 411, 553
   in pre-expansion San Francisco,
      269–70, 273
   Puerto Rican winter leagues of,
      207–13, 236, 426, 559–60
   racial baiting from fans and opposing
      players in, 67, 68, 114, 123, 146–47
   racial discrimination countered in,
      226–27, 232–33, 412
   scouting of players in, 33, 38, 55,
      56–63, 64, 76, 77, 78, 91, 118,
      282–83, 286

segregated ballparks in, 40, 41, 53
segregation in, 11, 18, 40, 41, 42, 52, 63,
   137, 145, 180, 234; see also Negro
   Leagues
Southern semipro and industrial
   leagues in, 10–12, 15, 19, 30–34, 38,
   39, 40, 157, 159
team camaraderie in, 48, 49, 51–52,
   66, 67, 68–69, 75, 128–29, 407, 441,
   470, 490, 519, 535
television's role in transformation of, 5,
   90, 99, 171, 204, 259, 303, 377, 488
transition to "modern" era of, 204, 323,
   363, 377, 411, 506, 553
in U.S. military, 153–54, 155–56, 157,
   161, 162
Baseball (documentary), 204
*Baseball Barnstorming and Exhibition
   Games* (Barthel), 377
Baseball Has Done It (Robinson), 412, 413,
   416
Baseball Magazine, 101
Baseball Writers Association of America,
   147, 406, 534
basketball, 29, 30, 32, 35, 36, 38, 44, 45, 97,
   154, 166, 180, 423, 480, 556
"basket catches," 154–55, 383, 494
Bassett, Pepper, 50, 51
Battey, Earl, 432
batting helmets, 75, 346, 348
batting titles, 191, 192, 230, 328, 542
   1954 NL race for, 185, 186, 187–89
   1958 NL race for, 298–99, 300
Bauer, Hank, 139
Bavasi, Buzzie, 209
beanballs, 86, 113, 206, 211, 215, 253, 287,
   346, 347, 348, 428–29, 433, 435–36
Bearnarth, Larry, 405
Bell, Cool Papa, 4, 48
Belli, Melvin, 320
Berger, Sy, 450, 520, 557–59
Berra, Yogi, 138, 511, 512, 514, 515, 518,
   519, 521, 525, 526, 527, 529, 531
   Mays's tense relationship with, 512,
   517, 520
Bewitched, 179
Biederman, Les, 288, 380, 407
Birmingham, Ala., 6, 9–12, 15, 16, 32, 33,
   34, 35, 44, 57, 59, 60, 65, 70, 93, 144,
   242, 302, 335, 336, 396, 397, 416,
   535, 554, 555
   church bombing in, 52, 394, 395–96
   civil rights demonstrations in, 394–95

media (*cont.*)
   Candlestick Park criticized in, 317, 318,
     319, 321, 370
   condescending coverage of African
     American athletes by, 75–76,
     120–21, 181, 183–84, 205, 264, 328,
     414, 423
   Dark's controversial racial remarks in,
     412–15, 417–21, 423
   dwindling coverage of Negro Leagues
     by, 56
   Giants relocation to San Francisco and,
     262, 271, 286
   late-career tributes to Mays in, 493–95
   Mays criticized and scrutinized by, 6,
     155, 240, 248–49, 254–56, 274, 293,
     297–98, 300, 306, 309–11, 335–36,
     345, 356, 361–62, 376, 382, 411,
     414, 497, 498–99, 519
   Mays honored and awarded by, 205,
     487
   Mays in pre-MLB coverage by, 48, 55,
     60, 73, 74, 75–76
   Mays's accessibility and generosity to
     children in, 181–82, 294, 377, 378,
     380
   on Mays's arrival and first MLB games,
     81, 82, 94, 95, 96
   Mays's bouts of exhaustion and
     hospitalizations in, 290, 356,
     357–59, 371, 448
   Mays's decency and character praised
     in, 181, 184, 294, 347, 375–76, 380,
     440
   Mays's declining skills and impending
     retirement in, 406, 407, 408, 425,
     467–68, 500–501, 508, 518, 519, 528
   Mays's first marriage and divorce in,
     248–49, 250–51, 255–56, 297–98,
     300, 335–36, 337, 339, 345
   Mays's happy-go-lucky image in, 4, 55,
     120, 121, 161–62, 179, 180, 181,
     183–84, 229, 243, 263–64, 290,
     312–13, 467–68, 497
   Mays's loss of youth and innocence in,
     111, 205, 262–64, 312–13, 468, 508
   Mays's milestone and record chases in,
     175–76, 411, 443, 458–59, 460–61,
     462, 485, 492–93
   Mays's military service in, 144–45
   Mays's press conference on race rela-
     tions in, 469–72
   Mays's reluctance in speaking with, 19,

     120, 121–22, 177, 183–84, 243, 290,
     293, 294, 376, 460, 461, 467, 509,
     543, 547, 557, 558
   Mays's salaries scrutinized in, 166, 293,
     306, 309–10, 362–63, 425
   Mays's tense relations with, 6, 293,
     375–76, 460, 467, 494, 497, 498,
     543, 558
   Mays trade and return to New York in,
     508, 509–10, 513, 515
   MLB teams' cozy relationship with,
     329, 417
   MVP voting by, 375–76
   negative racial stereotypes perpetuated
     by, 42, 76, 120–21
   1951 Giants-Dodgers playoffs in, 128,
     130, 135
   racial controversies and issues in, 163,
     168–69, 224–25, 274, 277, 278–81,
     311–12, 315–16, 327–29, 394–96,
     418–20, 441, 469–73, 474, 475,
     517
   racist attitudes in members of, 120–21,
     138, 141, 327, 328
   San Francisco housing controversy in,
     277, 278–81, 311, 315–16
   Sports Illustrated's controversial cover
     photo and, 223–25, 230
   sportswriting revolution in, 417
   tributes to Mays written in, 272, 313
   World Series and playoff coverage in,
     128, 130, 135, 138, 192, 195–96,
     199–200, 366, 367, 371, 372, 417,
     500–501, 528, 529, 530, 531
   see also television; *specific newspapers
     and sportswriters*
Medtronics Associates, 320–21
Memorial Stadium, 66, 170
Memories of Summer (Kahn), 169
Memphis Red Sox, 45–46
Mendelson, Lee, 390–93, 396, 397, 405,
   446, 495–96
Merchant, Larry, 523
Merrill, Robert, 168
Metro, Charley, 357
Mexican League, 89, 118
Mexico, 5, 71, 87, 191, 304, 305, 339
   Mays's wedding in, 503–5
Milano, Clarissa, 555
Miles College, 23, 25, 523, 554, 556
military, U.S., 172, 252
   athletes given special treatment in,
     153–54, 162

301, 309, 321, 323, 324, 330, 370,
378, 442, 502, 515, 527, 530, 534,
546, 553–54, 560
Mays in challenge to HR records of,
175–76, 185, 186, 273–74, 289, 411,
421, 446, 458, 462, 554

Saddler, Phil, 455
Sadecki, Ray, 463, 529, 545
Sain, Johnny, 139, 140
St. James' Center (Pittsburgh), 384–85
St. Louis Browns, 39, 61, 137n, 170, 233
St. Louis Cardinals, 85, 89, 99, 104, 126,
145, 146, 161, 185, 217, 220, 234,
254, 257, 299, 361, 362, 363, 376,
420, 433, 448, 459, 460, 462, 463,
467, 478, 479, 481, 482, 492
Mays in proposed trade to, 260–61
St. Mary's Hospital (San Francisco), 466,
467
Salas, J. B., 240–41
Salsido, Ron, 494
San Diego Padres, 348, 482, 484, 486, 491,
499
Sanford, Jack, 314, 325, 360, 364, 369, 370,
372
San Francisco, Calif., 146, 269–70, 271,
273, 286, 325, 332, 335, 337, 355,
371, 382, 390, 400, 424, 453, 469,
476, 482, 495, 503, 509, 515, 539,
544, 547
Coke-bottle incident in, 311–12, 315,
316
fan celebrations and ticker-tape
parades in, 284, 367–69
fans eventual acceptance of Mays in,
364, 369, 461, 509
fans slow to accept Mays in, 294–97,
300, 309–11, 312, 314, 326, 333,
349, 362, 369, 393, 461, 535
Giants' relocation to, 5, 171, 260–62,
264, 269, 270, 271–74, 276, 283–84,
317
Mays as part of community in, 386–87,
400, 424, 448, 470–71, 504, 509
Mays in move from, 315–16
Mays's arrival and adjustment to,
271–81, 284, 292, 294–95, 315, 335,
378, 386, 424, 509, 535
Mays's Forest District home in, 386,
387–90, 396, 399, 401, 416
Mays's racial housing controversy in,
274–81, 311, 315–16, 469, 470, 560

Mays's tense relations with media in,
293, 497, 498
Mays's trade and departure from,
509–10, 535, 536
pre-expansion baseball in, 269–70, 273
race riots in, 464
San Francisco Call-Bulletin, 293, 299
San Francisco Chronicle, 274, 277, 279,
280–81, 284, 294, 312, 314, 318,
347, 356, 360, 362–63, 414–15, 453,
461, 497
San Francisco Examiner, 272, 288, 293,
294, 298, 299, 310, 312, 329, 337,
338, 339, 347, 355, 358, 361–62,
377, 407, 440, 471–72, 474, 477,
485, 492, 494, 496, 498
San Francisco 49ers, 270, 296, 363
San Francisco Giants, 31, 270, 276, 277,
280, 292, 294, 309, 336, 337, 346,
352, 380, 381, 382, 384, 386, 389,
391, 398, 400, 424, 470, 477, 482,
496, 498–99, 510, 516, 536, 541,
543, 544–47, 555, 557, 560
Barry Bonds as member of, 544–47
in brawls, 287–89, 308, 353–54,
436–42, 445
Cepeda as fan favorite on, 295, 298
city's 1962 pennant celebration in,
367–69
contracts and salaries offered by, 272,
283, 291, 330, 331, 337, 351, 402,
425, 448, 482–83, 489, 506
Dark as new manager of, 332–35, 340,
343, 345, 351
Dodgers' rivalry with, 354, 433, 434,
435–42
exhibition games played by, 305–6, 307,
310, 334, 343–45, 352, 405, 411,
423–24, 479, 512
farm system of, 269, 291, 328, 411, 480,
483, 545; *see also* Minneapolis Millers
financial woes of, 482–83, 507, 508, 544
first game of, 285–86
Franks as new manager of, 426–27
injuries of, 307, 308, 312, 314, 315, 322,
350, 354, 361, 365, 369–70, 411,
421, 430–31, 432, 463, 465, 466,
485, 497, 499–500, 501, 506
Japanese exhibition tour of, 305–6, 327,
332, 423–24
King as manager of, 483–85, 486, 491
Mays hyped by, 272–74, 296, 318